American Blacklist

American Blacklist
The Attorney General's List
of Subversive Organizations

Robert Justin Goldstein

 University Press of Kansas

Published by the University Press of Kansas (Lawrence,
Kansas 66045), which was organized by the Kansas
Board of Regents and is operated and funded by Emporia
State University, Fort Hays State University, Kansas State
University, Pittsburg State University, the University of
Kansas, and Wichita State University

Library of Congress Cataloging-in-Publication Data
Goldstein, Robert Justin.
    American blacklist : the attorney general's list of
subversive organizations / Robert Justin Goldstein.
        p.   cm.
    Includes bibliographical references and index.
    ISBN 978-0-7006-1604-6 (cloth : alk. paper)
    1. Civil rights—Government policy—United States—
History—20th century. 2. Civil rights—United States—
History—20th century. 3. Subversive activities—United
States—History—20th century. 4. Political persecution—
United States—History—20th century. 5. Internal
security—United States—History—20th century. I. Title.
    JC599.U5G57 2008
    322.4′20973—dc22   2008021324

British Library Cataloguing-in-Publication Data is
available.

Printed in the United States of America
10 9 8 7 6 5 4 3 2 1

The paper used in this publication is recycled and contains
30 percent postconsumer waste. It is acid free and meets
the minimum requirements of the American National
Standard for Permanence of Paper for Printed Library
Materials Z39.48-1992.

Contents

Abbreviations

ABA	American Bar Association
ACLU	American Civil Liberties Union
ACPFB	American Committee for the Protection of the Foreign Born
ADA	Americans for Democratic Action
AFL	American Federation of Labor
AGLOSO	Attorney General's List of Subversive Organizations
ALB	Abraham Lincoln Brigade
ALPD	American League for Peace and Democracy
ALW	Association of Lithuanian Workers
ALWF	American League against War and Fascism
ALWLA	American Lithuanian Workers Literary Association
ANP	American Nazi Party
APC	American Peace Crusade
APM	American Peace Mobilization/American People's Mobilization
ARI	American-Russian Institute
ASC	American Slav Congress
ASU	American Servicemen's Union
AYC	American Youth Congress
AYD	American Youth for Democracy
BPP	Black Panther Party
CAA	Council on African Affairs
CAW	Congress of American Women
CGS	Commission on Government Security
CIO	Congress of Industrial Organizations
CLP	Communist Labor Party
CLS	California Labor School
CP	Communist Party
CRC	Civil Rights Congress
CSC	Civic Service Commission
DAS	Dante Alighieri Society
DOD	Department of Defense
DOJ	Department of Justice
EPL	Elsinore Progressive League
FBI	Federal Bureau of Investigation
FCC	Federal Communications Commission

FISB	Federal Internal Security Board
HCSC	House Civil Service Committee
HISC	House Committee on Internal Security
HUAC	House Committee on Un-American Activities
ICEI	Interdepartmental Committee on Employee Investigations
ILD	International Labor Defense
INS	Immigration and Naturalization Service
IRS	Internal Revenue Service
ISA	Internal Security Act (1950)
ISD	Internal Security Division (DOJ)
ISL	Independent Socialist League
IWO	International Workers Order
IWW	Industrial Workers of the World
KKK	Ku Klux Klan
LAW	League of American Writers
LYL	Labor Youth League
LRB	Loyalty Review Board
JAFRC	Joint Anti-Fascist Refugee Committee
NAACP	National Association for the Advancement of Colored People
NACASD	North American Committee to Aid Spanish Democracy
NCASF	National Council on American-Soviet Friendship
NFCL	National Federation for Constitutional Liberties
NLG	National Lawyers Guild
NNC	National Negro Congress
NNLC	National Negro Labor Council
NOI	Nation of Islam (Black Muslims)
PHA	Public Housing Authority
PIC	Peace Information Center
OLC	Office of Legal Counsel (DOJ)
SACB	Subversive Activities Control Board
SISS	Senate Internal Security Subcommittee (of Senate Judiciary Committee)
SJC	Senate Judiciary Committee
SNYC	Southern Negro Youth Congress
SOS	Subversive Organizations Section (DOJ)
SP	Socialist Party
SWP	Socialist Workers Party
SWPU	Special War Policies Unit
SYL	Socialist Youth League
TCEL	Temporary Commission on Employee Loyalty
UPWA	United Public Workers Association
URW	Union of Russian Workers

VA	Veterans Administration
VALB	Veterans of the Abraham Lincoln Brigade
WA	Workers Alliance
WBA	Washington Bookshop Association
WCC	White Citizens Councils
WCDA	Washington Committee for Democratic Action
WCF	Washington Commonwealth Federation
WP	Workers Party
WPU	Washington Pension Union
YCL	Young Communist League

Preface

In his 1952 book *The Loyalty of Free Men*, Alan Barth, a *Washington Post* editorial writer, described the so-called Attorney General's List of Subversive Organizations (AGLOSO)—which the Truman administration began publishing in late 1947 as part of its wide-ranging federal employee loyalty screening program—as "perhaps the most arbitrary and far-reaching power ever exercised by a single public official" in American history, allowing the attorney general to "stigmatize" and "proscribe any organization of which he disapproves." This conclusion may have to be modified in the wake of post–September 11, 2001, developments, which led the George W. Bush administration not only to claim sweeping executive powers as part of the "war on terror"—including the right to establish secret prisons and hold detainees indefinitely without charges, trials, or the right to habeas corpus—but also to refuse to even submit such policies to court challenges on the grounds that such would involve the disclosure of "state secrets." Many "anti-terror" programs, including government compilation of lists of "suspect" organizations without any legal proceedings, so much resembled those of the post–World War II Red Scare that ACLU lawyer Jameel Jeffer declared in 2007 that sometimes it seemed that "what the government has done is taken the communist-era playbook and replaced every instance of the word communist with terrorist." Similarly, Georgetown University law professor David Cole declared that the 2001 so-called Patriot Act, the keystone of the government's "war on terror," "in effect resurrects the philosophy of McCarthyism, simply substituting 'terrorist' for 'communist.'" But although Barth's 1952 analysis may have to be reevaluated in the light of subsequent developments (and he may have overlooked some earlier events, such as President Abraham Lincoln's unilateral Civil War suspension of the writ of habeas corpus), the essence of his allegation is unquestionably accurate. Ultimately the justification for this book is that AGLOSO (whose origins can be traced back to 1903 but only became important when it was first widely publicized in late 1947) is, in my view, the single most important domestic factor that fostered and facilitated the Red Scare (which is popularly known as McCarthyism, but was well under way long before Sen. Joseph McCarthy appeared on the red-hunting political scene in February 1950). Moreover, perhaps because documentation about AGLOSO has generally been unavailable—I was able to obtain it through Freedom of Information Act requests to the FBI and the Department of Justice (DOJ), as well as via the requested declassification of massive National Archives material—it has attracted little scholarly attention.[1]

Until now, the only substantial general study of AGLOSO was a chapter in Eleanor Bontecou's important 1953 work, *The Federal Loyalty-Security Program*. A massive 2007 818-page online bibliography on "American Communism and Anti-Communism" compiled by John Earl Haynes, which lists thousands of books and articles, has exactly three articles on AGLOSO, all presented at a 2005 American Historical Association panel I organized in connection with research for this book. Perhaps the single most important book about the Red Scare, Ellen Schrecker's 1998 *Many Are the Crimes: McCarthyism in America*, never mentions AGLOSO. In addition, there is no entry or (according to the index) even any mention in the text of William Klingaman's 1996 *Encyclopedia of the McCarthy Era* (bizarrely, Klingaman prints an AGLOSO list as an appendix, without any explanation as to what it means or why it is important. In fairness to Schrecker, she also prints a list in her 1996 book *The Age of McCarthyism: A Brief History with Documents* (2nd ed., 2002), along with the accurate statements that AGLOSO designation was "usually a kiss of death to an organization" and that the "stigma associated" with AGLOSO "usually made it impossible" for listed groups to function. Of three massive encyclopedias on American civil liberties published in 2005–2006, two lack either entries or (at least judging by their indexes) *any* textual mention of AGLOSO. Moreover, there are no articles or index entries on AGLOSO in the *Encyclopedia of the American Left, The Harry S. Truman Encyclopedia,* or *The FBI Encyclopedia* (although the FBI played a key role in AGLOSO listings and used the "need" to investigate groups for possible designation as a leading justification for sweeping political surveillance during the 1947–1974 period). Even the popular online Wikipedia encyclopedia offers only a short entry consisting almost entirely of misinformation. One could cite numerous other sources relevant to the Red Scare that completely omit (or barely mention) AGLOSO, but the point has been made.[2]

The reader might well ask at this point if perhaps the reason AGLOSO has been so neglected is that it really wasn't very important. I believe and hope that this book will overwhelmingly establish that in fact AGLOSO was critically important to the entire Red Scare, far more than McCarthy. However, the reader need not take my word for it, for as is extensively documented here, this was the repeatedly expressed private view of top government officials in the FBI and DOJ, as well as that of numerous contemporary commentators. There is no point to repeating here at length what is reported in the text, but to give just a few examples of such statements, in November 1953, Oran Waterman, the head of the DOJ unit concerned with AGLOSO designation, wrote to his boss that "if the amount of mail received is any criterion, the public is probably more cognizant of the [AGLOSO] Designation Program than any other aspect of the Government's anti-subversive work," and that it had been "more effective in combating the

Communist front movement than any other program"; four years later, the same official noted, "when an organization was designated, it only became a question of time as to its final dissolution." Similarly, in a 1956 internal FBI memo, agent C. H. Stanley reported that the DOJ received 600 inquiries monthly about AGLOSO, that it had "proved to be the most effective weapon in combating the Communist menace," as evidenced by the "rapid demise" of cited organizations 'and, indeed, was "so effective a device" in causing listed groups to "rapidly disintegrate" that "it should not be lightly abandoned." In 1961, DOJ Internal Security Division head and assistant attorney general Y. Walter Yeagley similarly reported, in connection with a review of AGLOSO for Attorney General Robert Kennedy, that designations had the impact of "eventually destroying" listed groups. AGLOSO became so pervasive an aspect of the American political atmosphere between 1947 and about 1957 that during a 1948 congressional hearing, Rep. Karl Mundt (R-SD) cautioned Department officials that *failure* to place an organization on AGLOSO amounted in the public eye to putting a "Good Housekeeping seal of approval" on the group. Although AGLOSO affiliations officially provided only one "piece of evidence" in making federal loyalty determinations, in practice they became the dominant element in the loyalty program: as Seth Richardson, first chairman of the supervisory Loyalty Review Board (LRB), privately told the LRB in May 1948, "the overwhelming number of cases have to do with membership or affiliation or activity" of employees with AGLOSO-designated groups. In 1953, Richardson's successor, Hiram Bingham (who had become famous forty years earlier for "discovering" the "lost" Inca city of Machu Picchu), privately termed AGLOSO the key "to the intelligent and effective operation of the [loyalty] program" and the "heart and soul" of loyalty determinations, which in "99% of the cases" were based on "membership in, affiliation with or sympathetic association" with listed groups. In a September 1955 *Progressive* magazine article entitled "The Tyranny of Guilt by Association," Sen. Richard Neuberger (D-OR) wrote that "each week" his office received "many pitiful letters from men and women who have been summarily discharged from the civilian or military arms of the federal government because of suspected disloyalty—almost always stemming from some form of guilt by association."[3]

Although AGLOSO has, as pointed out above, not been studied in any depth since 1953, numerous contemporary observers and recent scholars have agreed with such assessments, writing that AGLOSO, which was massively publicized in the media, became what amounted to "an official black list," which came to have in the public mind "authority as *the* definitive report on subversive organizations" and was understood to be a "proscription of the treasonable activity of the listed organizations" and "the most widely used litmus for 'subversive tendencies.'" Historian Roger Keeran (correctly, in my view) terms AGLOSO "the cornerstone of the whole Cold War repression". An April 28, 1949, *New York Times* story about the listing of additional AGLOSO organizations was headlined

"Government *Proscribes* [emphasis added] 36 More Groups as Subversive," while AGLOSO-related files at the Eisenhower Presidential Library are marked "black-listed organizations." The November 1956 *Elks Magazine* began an article entitled "What the Attorney General's List Means" by accurately noting that "there are few Americans who have not heard of 'the Attorney General's subversive list'" and concluded by summarizing AGLOSO's clear message: "There is no excuse for any American citizen becoming affiliated with a group on the Attorney General's list today." More generally, the loyalty program, whose "heart and soul," as LRB chair Bingham noted, was AGLOSO, has been widely recognized as critical in fostering the Red Scare: thus Schrecker notes that "no other event, no political trial or Congressional hearing, was to shape the internal Cold War as decisively" as the loyalty program, and historian Peter Buckingham writes that the program and AGLOSO "can be said to have marked the beginning of a new red scare."[4]

Above all, what makes studying AGLOSO important is that, at least in my view, it played a central role in molding an entire cohort of Americans (known as the "silent generation" on college campuses) who feared to join organizations, sign petitions, or otherwise express their views, especially because organizations might be designated for AGLOSO at any time, without any indication of what they had done that was "subversive" and when they had done it. Although it is impossible to disentangle the impact of AGLOSO from that of other repressive governmental measures during the Red Scare, such as the numerous Congressional "red hunting" investigations, AGLOSO was such a pervasive presence in the political atmosphere at the height of the scare that is surely helps to explain statements such as those by University of Chicago president Robert Hutchins, a stalwart defender of academic freedom, who confessed that he was so intimidated by the suffering endured by those who were punished for their affiliations that he refused to join *any* organization, "even one whose sole objective is merely to preserve and perpetuate Mother's Day in America," and by actress Judy Holliday, who, when hauled before a 1952 Congressional committee due to her political activities, declared, "I don't say 'yes' to anything now except [organizations fighting] cancer, polio and cerebral palsy, and things like that." When 112 citizens of Madison, Wisconsin, were asked to sign a petition containing only quotations from the Declaration of Independence and the Bill of Rights on July 4 during the height of the Red Scare, all but one refused. Interviews with 70 federal employees in the Washington, D.C., area in the early 1950s led two researchers to conclude that the "security issue" had become so ingrained in the "prevalent climate of thought" that their subjects sought to avoid "anything that might conceivably arouse anyone's suspicion" since the risks of being investigated "even if one is subsequently cleared" were "so great." One government employee who had been investigated and cleared several times said, "If the communists like apple pie and I do, I see no reason why I should stop eating it, but I would."

In his November 1948 *Harpers* article "How Not to Get Investigated: Ten Commandments for Government Employees," published a year after the issuance of the first Truman AGLOSO, former federal appeals court judge and assistant attorney general Thurman Arnold listed the "pure conduct" lessons being taught by the loyalty program, based on his experiences as a Washington, D.C., lawyer advising government employees accused of "disloyalty." They included: avoid "any social gathering, no matter how large, at which a 'subversive' may also be present," including dances; "never talk, even to your neighbors or at social gatherings, about controversial issues" or subscribe to any "liberal publication" or read "any books about Russia"; cancel any gifts of such publications "at once, with an indignant letter" to avoid the conclusion that "you have communist friends"; avoid giving money "for the legal defense of some old acquaintance or college classmate charged with disloyalty"; do not "marry anyone who, however, many years before, had radical associations in college" or who "ever visited Russia, read Karl Marx or contributed to war relief drives for the Spanish [anti-Franco] loyalists"; and do not take a government post if "any relative of yours, no matter how distant and no matter how much you disagree with him, has ever been a 'radical.'" Ralph Brown, in his 1958 book *Loyalty and Security*, which fifty years later remains the leading study of Red Scare governmental and private loyalty programs, similarly concluded that alert citizens "noted that one enters the zone of suspicion as soon as one moves any distance from the most orthodox of political or civic involvement" and might "reasonably" conclude that "the safe course is to avoid any involvement." House Committee on Un-American Activities (HUAC) scholar Robert Carr concluded in 1952 that while HUAC had to assume a "large measure of responsibility," it "would be difficult to imagine any force better calculated" than the loyalty program to have taught federal employees that "it is wise to think no unusual thought, read no unusual books, join no unusual organization, and have no unusual friends." University of Michigan professor Robert Sklar wrote in 1972 that during the Red Scare, "Nearly everyone learned to be careful, to be anxious, to fear: not to sign a petition, not to join an organization, not to give money, not to be seen with certain books . . . Everyone knew that Siberia was the cold and barren place where the Russians sent their dissidents for punishment. Yet all too few Americans realized that they were generating their own Siberias in their own minds." Melville Jacobs, a professor at the University of Washington who was put on "probation" for two years following lengthy investigations (which led to the firing of two colleagues) after admitting past Communist Party membership, responded when asked if he might join the party again if there was a threatened "fascist resurgence," that he had "been through a lot, especially in recent months," and as a result, "Something would have to happen to some of the cells of my cerebrum before anybody could persuade me to ever touch politics with a ten-foot pole after what I have been through." The great physicist Albert Einstein, who had fled the tyranny of Nazi Germany for the United States (and who, as discussed below, became the subject of an 1,800-page FBI file that stressed his AGLOSO and other "suspect" political affiliations), lamented in 1954: "If I would be a young man again and I had to decide how to make my living, I would not try to become a scientist or scholar or teacher. I would rather choose to be a plumber or a peddler in the hope to find that modest degree of independence still available under present circumstances." An intriguing 1951 experiment lends some clear empirical support to the argument made above: 200 Americans, when presented with a mixture of actual and manufactured names of organizations and asked which they thought were on AGLOSO, revealed that what the authors termed "a relatively high percentage" of respondents identified "non-Communist" groups as "subversive" and that including words like "peace," "people's," and "world" in the titles of supposed organizations (i.e., "World Citizens' League" as opposed to "National Citizens' League") significantly increased the percentage of those who viewed them as "subversive."[5]

Aside from greatly adding to an atmosphere which stifled dissent, another pernicious result of AGLOSO was that it provided a continuing excuse for the FBI to carry on virtually unlimited political surveillance of American political organizations and activities, which often involved the massive use of undercover informants along with wiretaps and clearly illegal burglaries, on the grounds that it was simply implementing the need to determine whether groups might qualify for AGLOSO designation. Thus, a former top FBI domestic intelligence official told Congress in 1975 that, although no new AGLOSO listings occurred after 1955, the primary justification for continued FBI surveillance of organizations to detect possible Communist "infiltration" was so that it could advise the DOJ concerning possible AGLOSO designations; in 1966 another high Bureau domestic intelligence official noted in an internal FBI memo that although burglaries were "clearly illegal," they had been used because they "represent an invaluable technique in combating subversive activities" and had allowed the FBI to "on numerous occasions . . . obtain material held highly secret and closely guarded by subversive groups."[6]

This book is essentially a chronological account of AGLOSO and is therefore primarily organized by time period. The first chapter traces the origins of AGLOSO back to fears about anarchists in the wake of the 1901 McKinley assassination and discusses its first significant implementation during the 1919–1920 Red Scare, the immediate roots of the 1947 Truman AGLOSO in World War II–era security concerns, and the molding of the 1947 AGLOSO. Chapter 2 departs from a solely chronological approach to discuss the general impact, intent, and spread of AGLOSO. Chapter 3 discusses the first significant legal challenge to AGLOSO, which led to a 1951 Supreme Court ruling that forced the DOJ two years later to, for the first time, grant organizations slated for listing an opportunity to challenge their designation. Chapter 4 focuses on AGLOSO's decline after 1954 as the Red Scare gradually dissipated and congressional hearings and designated organizations increasingly challenged and criticized the list. During this period, the DOJ became increasingly paralyzed by the unworkability of its 1953 contestation procedures and by fears that further designations (the last group was listed in 1955) and/or defending AGLOSO in court would eventually lead to a Supreme Court ruling striking down the entire program. Chapter 5 discusses President Richard Nixon's failed 1971 attempt to "revive" AGLOSO and the successful congressional rebuff to his efforts, which, in retrospect, provided a precursor of Watergate, complete with hostile hearings chaired by Sen. Sam Ervin (D-NC) charging abuse of executive power.

As this introduction summarizes what I have tried to achieve in this book, I have not included a separate conclusion. Because AGLOSO listings are widely available elsewhere (as noted above) and also since, as this book explains, there were many different such lists, I have not included one in this book (although most designated organizations are mentioned in one place or another). To conserve space, when complete citation information is included in the text (i.e., newspaper and magazine dates and legal citations for court cases), it is not repeated in endnotes. For the same reason, many abbreviations are used in both the text and notes: abbreviations used in the text are listed in the front of the book; notes are consolidated at the end, with abbreviations used therein listed at the start of the notes. To help guide the reader through the many hundreds of sources cited in the notes, a short Bibliographic Essay at the end of the book highlights the most important sources that were used.

Acknowledgments

Anyone writing a book primarily based upon archival sources quickly runs up many debts that can never truly be repaid. As is suggested in the Bibliographical Essay, I was assisted by many archivists and librarians, too many to individually thank here. However, I am truly grateful to all of them, and especially to Leslie Farkas and Fred Romanski, who did yeoman work on my behalf, under severe time pressures, at the National Archives in College Park, Maryland. Yeshiva University Professor Ellen Schrecker kindly read this book in manuscript form and made numerous useful suggestions, for which I am much indebted to her. I am also deeply grateful to the University Press of Kansas for support, patience, and understanding during what has turned out to be a very long and winding road, above all to editor-in-chief Mike Briggs, the prototype of a gentleman and a scholar. Shelley and Cicero entered my life and provided much joy during the final stages of my research and writing, and Mlicko hung on. As usual, only I can be blamed for any errors, and no one would be more astonished than I if none had inadvertently crept into a work of this length and complexity.

American Blacklist

1

The Origins of AGLOSO, 1903–1947

Immigration Law and the First "Attorney General's List," 1903–1938

The so-called Attorney General's List of Subversive Organizations (AGLOSO)—that is, a list of groups in which membership was officially designated as grounds for possible exclusion from federal employment—entered the general American consciousness in December 1947, when it was first published in connection with President Harry Truman's March 1947 "loyalty program." However, AGLOSO's remote origins date back to 1903, and a secret, although nonetheless formalized, "subversive organizations" list was maintained continuously by the federal government after 1940.

In 1903, the principle of "guilt by association" in connection with perceived political beliefs, which was at AGLOSO's core, was first entrenched in federal law in response to President Theodore Roosevelt's request for a statute authorizing the "absolute" exclusion from the country of "all persons who are known to be believers in anarchistic principles or members of an anarchistic society." The 1903 immigration law was the first to impose any political test for entry into the United States; until then, the country had been regarded as an asylum for foreign political offenders. The new law barred so-called alien anarchists, defined as those believing in or advocating the "overthrow by force and violence" of the American government, all governments, or all forms of law, or the assassination of public officials, as well as those who "disbelieve[d] in" or opposed all organized government and those "affiliated with any organization entertaining and teaching such disbelief." Moreover, resident aliens fitting this description were barred from naturalization and subject to deportation for up to three years after entry, even if their "disbelief" in government was completely peaceful and their adherence to "anarchist" groups was passive or if they were ignorant of the organizations' alleged doctrines.[1]

The 1903 law (and similar laws passed by four states in 1902–1903) resulted from the "anarchist scare" touched off by the 1901 assassination of President William McKinley by a native-born American citizen with a foreign-sounding name who claimed to be an anarchist. While the 1903 federal law had little immediate impact—between 1903 and 1921 there were only thirty-eight exclusions under it and between 1908 and 1917 not a single deportation based upon it—it established a model eventually emulated by Truman's AGLOSO. During subsequent periods of fear, internal crisis, and/or panic, laws with similar "guilt by association" provisions, which typically extended to membership in, assembling with, or circulating the doctrines of targeted groups, were repeatedly passed to facilitate prosecutions, deportations, denaturalizations, and exclusions from government employment. Thus, many states passed "criminal syndicalism" and "sedition" laws between 1917 and 1920, aimed at the militant, radical Industrial Workers of the World (IWW) labor union, and again between 1947 and 1954, directed at the Communist Party (CP). Federal immigration laws passed in 1917, 1918, 1920, 1940, 1950, and 1952 were used to exclude and deport IWW and CP members and other political radicals, while the 1939 federal Hatch Act (which most directly led to Truman's AGLOSO) sought to exclude members of "subversive" organizations from federal employment, and the 1940 Smith Act aimed both to exclude Communists and other radicals from the United States and to facilitate prosecution of those already resident.[2]

Immigration laws passed in February 1917 (shortly before American entry into World War I) and October 1918 (the month preceding the end of the war) extended the concept of political guilt by association introduced by the 1903 law as fears of foreign-inspired espionage and sabotage increased. Thus, the 1918 law expanded the grounds for exclusion of alien radicals and completely eliminated all time limits for deportation of those in the defined categories. These included "aliens who are members of or affiliated with any organization that entertains a belief in, teaches, or advocates the overthrow by force or violence of the government of the U.S. or of all forms of law," the "disbelief in or opposition to all organized government," the "unlawful assaulting or killing" of government officials, or "the unlawful destruction of property" (the latter provision specifically aimed at the IWW). Altogether, deportation proceedings under the 1917–1918 laws were initiated against 697 people during World War I; by November 1, 1918, 60 of them had been deported and 88 were under deportation orders (162 of those targeted had by then succeeded in having deportation orders canceled; the remaining cases were still pending). Many of these cases involved membership in organizations allegedly advocating anarchy or revolution, including at least 150 IWW members (of whom about 25 were eventually deported).[3]

The federal government did not, during World War I, formally list the IWW as an *organization* falling within the immigration bans, as both Attorney General Thomas Gregory and Secretary of Labor William Wilson (whose department had ultimate jurisdiction over immigration matters until 1940) held that individual guilt always had to be established. However, in practice, IWW members were often targeted for deportation proceedings by federal officials, especially in the Pacific Northwest. In Seattle, for example, immigration officers considered that simply contributing to an IWW defense fund amounted to unlawful "advocacy" of property destruction. As historian William Preston writes, deportation was seen as "the most flexible and discretionary weapon available" for attacking labor radicals, because "proof of individual guilt was the great stumbling block in labor disturbances," while deportation could be based solely on organizational ties. Subversive aliens were not the only subjects of repression during World War I, but only they could be legally targeted by the federal government *solely* for their associations. Under the 1917 Espionage Act and the 1918 Sedition Act, virtually all criticism of the war, including by citizens, was banned, but at least in theory proof of individual activity was always required. Over 2,100 people were indicted and over 1,000 were convicted under these laws during the war, in every case solely for verbal or written opposition to it. Over 100 of those convicted were sentenced to jail terms of ten years or more, and on appeal the Supreme Court and other federal courts almost invariably upheld the convictions. The IWW and the Socialist Party (SP), both thriving and at least moderately influential organizations before 1917, were largely destroyed by such prosecutions.[4]

With the end of the war in November 1918, the Espionage and Sedition Acts could no longer be employed by the federal government, but immigration laws still authorized deporting and excluding aliens solely for their relationship to allegedly subversive organizations. Moreover, during the war and the subsequent intense "Red Scare" of 1919–1920, about half of the states passed criminal syndicalism laws, aimed primarily at the IWW, which outlawed virtually any association with organizations deemed to advocate the use of violence to foster social change. Between 1917 and 1920 at least 2,000 people were prosecuted, and at least 400 convicted, by state officials under these and similar laws, including "sedition" and "red flag" laws (which outlawed displays of such ensigns).[5]

In 1919, amid the rapid demobilization of thousands of soldiers and a massive influenza epidemic, the nation was caught up in a whirlwind of inflation and the largest strike outbreak in the country's history, all against the backdrop of growing fears of worldwide Communist revolutionary outbreaks following the 1917 Russian Revolution. Blame for the strikes and other unrest was increasingly placed by conservative politicians and newspapers on alien Communists. The distinct procedural advantages of implementing membership-based deportations quickly became apparent to A. Mitchell Palmer, newly appointed attorney general in March 1919, just as the Red Scare was significantly intensifying. This was especially so in the wake of a wave of unexplained bombings (one of which blew up part of the front porch of Palmer's Washington, D.C., home) in the spring and the emergence of the CP and the Communist Labor Party (CLP) as left-wing splits off the SP in September. A British journalist wrote later:

> No one who was in the U.S. as I chanced to be in the autumn of 1919 will forget the feverish condition of the public mind at that time. It was hag-ridden by the spectre of Bolshevism. It was like a sleeper in a nightmare, enveloped by a thousand phantoms of destruction. Property was in an agony

of fear, and the horrid name "Radical" covered the most innocent departure from conventional thought with a suspicion of desperate purpose. "America" as one wit of the time said, "is the land of liberty—liberty to keep in step."[6]

Clearly influenced by the bombing of his home and growing demands from politicians, the public, and the press for stern action against radicalism, in late 1919 Palmer settled upon the immigration laws as the solution to the perceived menace: not only could they be used against foreigners, who were largely blamed for all of America's ills, but they authorized wholesale deportations, without requiring demonstrated individual responsibility beyond membership, of aliens allegedly affiliated with groups determined to be advocating "the overthrow by force or violence of the government of the U.S." Moreover, since deportation orders were Labor Department *administrative* decisions (with limited appeal rights to the federal courts), affected aliens were not entitled to trials and lacked other protections associated with criminal proceedings. As Louis Post, acting secretary of labor in 1920, subsequently wrote, "the force of the delirium [of the 1919–1920 Red Scare] turned in the direction of a deportation crusade with the spontaneity of water flowing along the course of least resistance."[7]

However, before deportations solely based on organizational membership could be effected, a determination of organizations falling within the immigration laws was needed, a requirement that spawned the first governmental list of "subversive organizations" (although it was not then so labeled). Like subsequent AGLOSOs, the 1919–1920 version was determined secretly within the Department of Justice (DOJ), with no notice or opportunity for hearings or challenge by the listed groups. However, unlike subsequent versions, whose primary official purpose was to facilitate purging subversives from federal employment and that listed a wide variety of organizations, the 1919–1920 version, based solely on the immigration laws, targeted only groups viewed as predominantly composed of alien radicals. Also, unlike the Truman AGLOSO, which was massively publicized by the federal government, the 1919–1920 list became known only as it was implemented via mass raids aimed at members of the designated groups. Moreover, the 1919–1920 list was officially revealed only *subsequent* to the notorious "Palmer Raids," which rounded up thousands of allegedly subversive radical aliens, and played no significant role in *fostering* the Red Scare (which proved to be in its final stages). In contrast, the Truman AGLOSO played a major role in drastically strengthening and expanding a nascent Red Scare that would extend for almost a decade with extremely high intensity.

The attorney general first disclosed the existence of his subversive organizations list to the House of Representatives Rules Committee on June 1, 1920, five months after the November 1919–January 1920 "Palmer Raids." Palmer provided the committee with the names of six organizations that the DOJ's Bureau of Investigation (BI, renamed the FBI in 1935) had determined to be "of a revolutionary character." According to Palmer, the list had been created following several conferences with Labor Department officials to facilitate the "carrying out of the provisions of the [immigration] act of October 16, 1918, familiarly known as the 'deportation statute'" and reflected the BI's conclusion that "the predominating cause of the radical agitation in the U.S. was the alien population of this country." Palmer's list included two tiny anarchist groups, the El Ariete Society and L'Era Nuova, with estimated respective memberships of 12 and 25; the IWW, with a (probably overestimated) membership of 300,000; the Union of Russian Workers (URW), believed to include 4,000 members; and the CP and the CLP, with estimated respective memberships of 40,000 and 10,000.[8]

The primary target of the November 1919 Palmer Raids, involving about a dozen cities, was the URW, while the raids of January 2, 1920, encompassing about thirty cities, were aimed at alien CP and CLP members. During the November raids, perhaps 1,000 people were rounded up, with many of the hundreds detained in New York City suffering severe police beatings; during the January raids, between 5,000 and 10,000 were arrested, totally overwhelming many detention facilities, with the result that many detainees faced overcrowded and grossly unsanitary conditions. The January raids, supposedly designed to save the country from a looming Communist revolution, uncovered a total weapons arsenal of three pistols. During both raids, carefully supervised by an obscure young lawyer named J. Edgar Hoover, head of the BI's Radical Division, mass roundups and searches, generally without the use of arrest or search warrants, were conducted at gathering spots frequented by members of the targeted groups. Only aliens were supposed to be detained, but due to the raids' massive, indiscriminate nature, many of those arrested proved to be American citizens and/or to be engaged in completely innocent activities, such as attending night classes, a theater performance, or a concert. The raids' key goal was to facilitate wholesale deportations based on the DOJ's finding that membership alone in the targeted groups justified deportation, and although in theory final deportation decisions were to be made by the Labor Department, in practice the DOJ made the preliminary organizational determinations and dominated the raids' planning and execution. Thus, according to BI and Immigration Bureau instructions telegraphed to agents across the nation shortly before the January 1920 raids, "since the grounds for deportation in these cases will be based solely upon [CP or CLP] membership," it was of "prime" and "utmost" importance to obtain "proper and usable evidence" of membership in "one or the other of these organizations," and it would "not be necessary for you to go in detail in[to] the particular activities of the persons apprehended."[9]

According to Palmer's June 1920 congressional testimony and other DOJ submissions, deportation warrants were also obtained by the department against members of El Ariete, but the Labor Department had failed to enforce them after four months, and deportation warrants against at least eight members of L'Era

Nuova were canceled (presumably by the Labor Department) following a February 1920 raid on the latter group's New Jersey headquarters that led to twenty-nine arrests. DOJ officials had declared after the raid that L'Era Nuova consisted of "anarchists of the worst type," who preached the "use of bombs and other engines of destruction to create terror and fear," that "every one of the men arrested confessed after examination," and that their admissions were sufficient to send them "forever from America."[10]

In his June 1920 House Rules Committee testimony, Palmer declared that both the Justice and Labor Departments had found it "conclusive" that the URW fell under the terms of the 1918 immigration law, as it was deemed an organization of "anarchists" formed for the "sole purpose of destroying all institutions of government and society." No evidence of criminal activity was ever traced to the group, which in practice largely served as a social and educational center for Russian immigrants, many of whom lacked any knowledge of the organization's officially proclaimed revolutionary goals. Nonetheless, on December 21, 1919, as the result of the November raids, almost 200 URW members (along with about 50 alleged anarchists deported for their individual beliefs) were shipped from New York to Finland (to be sent on to Russia) on the army transport *Buford*, dubbed the "Soviet Ark" by the press. One of those deported, Joseph Polulech, who had entered the United States in 1912, had been arrested while taking a mathematics class in the URW building, with the only evidence against him the listing of his name in a URW membership book.[11]

The aftermath of the January 1920 raids against the CP and the CLP was far more prolonged and disorderly. Palmer, aided by supporting memoranda drawn up by Hoover (who sat beside him during the June 1920 hearing), told the Rules Committee that the two groups were ideologically indistinguishable (a position subsequently confirmed by their 1921 merger into what became the modern American Communist Party, in response to directives from Moscow) and that both were pro-Bolshevik groups committed to a revolutionary overthrow of American capitalism and democracy (which was true, but only in a purely theoretical sense). However, the Labor Department, clearly affected by a backlash against the Palmer Raids, which gradually developed into a major storm in early 1920, ultimately drew what it claimed was a distinction between a "violence-advocating" CP and an only theoretically revolutionary CLP, therefore holding that CP, but not CLP, membership required deportation under the 1918 immigration law. Thus, on January 23, 1920, in the so-called *Preis* ruling, Secretary of Labor Wilson declared that the CP was an organization "membership in which [alone] makes an alien liable to deportation" because it sought "to overthrow the government of the U.S. [by force or violence]," but on May 5, 1920, in the so-called *Miller* ruling, he held that the CLP was not such an organization because, while its program indicated "an extremely radical objective" that was likely "reprehensible" to many Americans, it had demonstrated no intentions "incompatible with the use of parliamentary machinery to attain the radical end it has in view." While the general backlash against the Red Scare and the Palmer Raids that emerged in the interim between the two rulings was probably far more important than any real difference between the two parties in explaining the disparate rulings, perhaps a more critical factor was that after Wilson became ill in March 1920, Assistant Secretary of Labor Post, a longtime sympathizer with the downtrodden in American society, became acting secretary. Working literally day and night, Post personally reviewed the pending cases and cancelled about 70 percent of the approximately 2,000 deportation warrants, due to their sole reliance on CLP membership, use of illegally seized evidence, denial of access to counsel, and/or lack of evidence that alleged CP members knew of the organization's goals. Only about 500 out of the thousands arrested during the January 1920 raids were ultimately deported. Even so, Post subsequently wrote in 1923, none of those deported "had been connected in any way with bomb-throwing or bomb-placing or bomb-making," but he had been forced by the immigration laws to punish "many aliens whom not even a lynching mob with the least remnant of righteous spirit would have deported from a frontier town."[12]

A further heavy blow against wielding the immigration laws as a meat-axe to decimate radical movements by wholesale deportations was delivered in June 1920 by federal district court judge George Anderson, in *Colyer v. Skeffington* (265 F. 17), a case involving pending deportation orders against thirteen aliens. Anderson struck down nine of the proposed deportations, which were based solely upon alleged CP membership, on grounds of lack of "due process," declaring that the BI investigations leading to the detentions were "wholly inadequate and unreliable" and that the subsequent deportation hearings denied the accused "a fair and impartial trial," leading to deportations orders grounded "upon records misrepresenting or omitting facts of controlling importance." Moreover, he held, the "great mass" of the plaintiffs had had SP memberships transferred to the CP without their knowledge or consent and therefore "had no real comprehension of any important or material change" in their affiliation or the "purposes sought to be achieved by their negligibly weak organizations." Anderson declared that the immigration laws "could not have intended to authorize the wholesale deportation of aliens who, accidentally, artificially, or unconsciously, in appearance only" were found to be "affiliated with an organization of whose platform and purposes they have no real knowledge." In the remaining four cases proposing CP membership deportations in which Judge Anderson found no "due process" violations, he held that Secretary Wilson had lacked sufficient evidence to properly classify the CP within the 1918 immigration act, because "not a scintilla of evidence" warranted the "finding that the Communists are committed to the 'overthrow of the government of the U.S.' by violence." He described most of the arrested aliens as "perfectly quiet and harmless working people, many of them not long ago Russian peasants."

Political deportations based on membership in allegedly "subversive" organizations decreased precipitously with the end of the Red Scare, reflecting not only opposition to the Palmer Raids, but also that World War I and the repressive acts of 1919–1920 had effectively destroyed the most important radical organizations in the United States, namely the SP, the IWW, the CP, and the CLP. While there were 760 political deportations in 1920–1921 (virtually all of which originated by early 1920), only 16 such expulsions occurred between 1926 and 1930. That *any* such deportations occurred after Judge Anderson's 1920 holding that the Labor Department had improperly designated the CP under the 1918 immigration law reflected that aliens could still be deported for *individual* political offenses (such as personally advocating the violent overthrow of the government or the assassination of political leaders); that in June 1920 Congress broadened the definition of organizations deemed "subversive" enough to warrant membership-based expulsions; and that Anderson's holding was subsequently overruled.[13]

The June 5, 1920, immigration law, the last institutionalized gasp of the Red Scare, expanded the "membership" basis for expulsion to include "giving, loaning or promising money or anything of value to be used for the advising, advocating or teaching" of doctrines that made individuals subject to deportation. Other added offenses were belonging to or being "affiliated" with groups that circulated seditious literature (such as material that advocated the "unlawful assaulting or killing" of governmental officials "or of any other organized government" or the "unlawful damage, injury or destruction of property") or simply possessing or distributing the literature of such groups. Judge Anderson's 1920 holding that the CP did not seek the violent overthrow of the government was overturned by a 1922 federal appeals court ruling (*Skeffington v. Katzeff*, 177 F. 129). *Skeffington* found that under legal precedents, since deportations resulted from administrative proceedings, absent violation of the Labor Department's own rules, they could be overturned by the courts only if there was "no substantial evidence which justified the order of deportation for the reason assigned," while the CP's program offered "substantial evidence" that it "teaches and advocates the overthrow of government by force and violence." In the aftermath of this ruling, as immigration historian Jane Perry Clark wrote in 1931, "the all-important question" in immigration proceedings became "that of proving membership" in the CP (or, occasionally, as pointed out below, other organizations, including the IWW).[14]

The federal courts almost invariably upheld such "membership" deportation proceedings during the 1922–1938 period. Thus, of about twenty-five published federal court rulings in such cases, the vast majority involving the CP, only a few overturned deportation orders, and then generally on procedural rather than substantive grounds. Typically these decisions held that the "subversive" nature of the CP was established beyond question, and repeatedly they interpreted immigration laws in an expansive way that gave the Labor Department close to carte blanche in deporting politically dubious aliens. Thus, in *Fortmueller v. Commissioner of Immigration* (14 F. Supp 484, 1936), a federal district court judge declared that the conclusion that the CP favored the violent overthrow of the government was "so nearly universal that I think it would be a waste of time to review the evidence introduced on the subject." In the 1932 case of *Wolck v. Weedin* (58 F. 2d 928), a federal appeals court upheld a deportation based on allegations of selling CP literature, contributing money to the CP, belonging to an organization "indirectly associated" with the CP, and expressing "sympathy" with the CP and the Russian government, holding that such conduct amounted to sufficient "affiliation" with the CP to legalize deportation. Use of the "membership" provisions of the immigration laws was also upheld in several federal court rulings to ban aliens from naturalization, as in *In Re Olson* (4 F. 2d 417), a 1925 IWW case, and to denaturalize aliens on the grounds that they had fraudulently obtained their citizenship by claiming to be "attached" to American constitutional principles in violation of a 1906 immigration law, as in *U.S. v. Tapolcsanyi* (40 F. 2d 155), a 1930 case involving alleged Communist sympathies.

The Growth of the Communist Party and "Communist Fronts," 1929–1939

Between 1938 and 1945 the federal courts, including the Supreme Court, showed considerably greater disinclination than before to blindly support "membership" deportation proceedings. Given the general tendency of the courts to be affected by changing currents of public opinion and American and world political developments, this changing legal orientation probably reflected drastic changes in the CP's public orientation in the mid-1930s and its increasing acceptance and significance in American society during most of the next decade (with the very great exception of the 1939–1941 period, when the CP supported Russia's short-lived alliance with Nazi Germany). Before about 1930, the CP, which had been driven underground and virtually decimated by the Red Scare, had basically been a tiny, insignificant sect, almost entirely divorced from American political realities. The massive discrediting of American capitalism during the Great Depression provided the CP with a modest amount of political legitimacy and facilitated a considerable increase in open CP activity, especially due to the party's often extremely courageous attempts to organize industrial workers, the unemployed, and southern blacks. However, CP influence was still severely limited, due partly to a new wave of repression directed against it—"political deportations" increased from one in 1930 to seventy-four in 1933 and local governmental responses to CP organizational efforts were often extremely brutal—and due also to its own extremely dogmatic and militant "line" during the 1928–1935 period. Before 1935, CP gains were substantial, but still extremely modest, with an estimated membership increase from 7,500 to over 33,000 between 1930 and 1934.[15]

In 1935, CP policy took a drastic turn, primarily in response to new directives from Moscow, when it adopted a "popular front" posture that preached political moderation and actively sought to join domestic coalitions with liberal, socialist, and other antifascist organizations, reflecting the new Soviet foreign policy of seeking wide-ranging anti-Nazi coalitions. Adopting the slogan "Communism Is Twentieth-Century Americanism," the CP began celebrating American patriotic heroes and effectively endorsed President Roosevelt's New Deal, which it had previously castigated as objectively "social fascist" in nature. The CP subsequently enjoyed a substantial increase in influence, legitimacy, and membership, with the latter tripling to about 100,000 by 1939. Relatively few people joined because they believed in the imminence, or even the desirability of, a Communist revolution, or because they were robots controlled by Stalinist Russia, which became the dominant image of American communism during the post–World War II Red Scare. Some members did fit such descriptions, including a few hundred who became Russian espionage agents during the 1930–1945 period, but the vast majority joined for other reasons, notably the CP's support for a broad antifascist alliance at a time when the CP and Russia were spearheading such efforts and the western democracies were pursuing a policy of appeasing Nazi Germany, especially in the aftermath of the July 1936 fascist-supported military uprising against the elected Spanish government. Others joined because they were lonely, because, ignorant of or uninterested in the massive, brutal repression occurring in Stalinist Russia, they viewed Russia as showing an economic path out of the Great Depression, and/or because the CP often displayed enormous courage and principle supporting the rights of workers and blacks.[16]

Whatever their motives for joining, static membership figures greatly understate the number of individuals—perhaps half a million—who joined the CP at one time or another during the 1930s. The falsity of the popular Cold War image of CP members as Russian robots is clearly demonstrated by the fact that the vast majority of them quickly departed, due to varying combinations of boredom, lack of time or energy to participate in the party's all-encompassing social and political activities, disgust with its authoritarian nature, outrage at the CP's support for the Nazi-Soviet Non-Aggression Pact of August 1939, and the (often ultimately correct) fear that membership might lead to future employment problems. The latter concern led most members to keep their CP affiliation secret, which subsequently fed both the Cold War image of the CP as a sinister underground conspiracy and the government's reliance on membership in alleged "Communist fronts" as an indicator of CP affiliation or sympathies. In fact, far more significant than formal membership in expanding the party's influence during the late 1930s was its role in such alleged "fronts," a term generally used to characterize organizations in which CP members played significant or dominant roles, often without the knowledge of most members. Including membership in organizations affiliated with such groups, CP "fronts" attracted probably well over 10 million Americans during the 1930s, at a time when the entire national population (including children) was about 130 million.[17]

In some cases, such as the International Labor Defense (ILD), which specialized in defending Communists and blacks who faced (often trumped-up) legal proceedings, and the International Workers Order (IWO), a ethnic-oriented fraternal benefit society that sold low-cost life insurance, alleged "fronts" were in fact unquestionably formed by individual Communists or by the CP and always under party control. In many other cases, as with the American Youth Congress (AYC), the National Lawyers Guild (NLG), the National Negro Congress (NNC), the Workers Alliance (WA), the League of American Writers (LAW), the American League against War and Fascism (ALWF)—and its successors, the American League for Peace and Democracy (ALPD) and the American Peace Mobilization (APM)—CP members or CP-dominated groups clearly exerted important influence during at least part of their organizational lives, but its extent either varied considerably over time or has been the subject of continuing controversy. Alleged membership in or affiliations with such "front" organizations were to play critical roles when AGLOSO was first constituted in connection with the screening of federal employees in 1940 and even more so after 1947 when the previously secret listings were first published by the Truman administration. Some organizations with significant Communist memberships during the 1930s that were subsequently placed on AGLOSO attained considerable size, influence, and respectability, including the AYC, NNC, WA, LAW, and ALWF (and its successors). In a few states, including Minnesota, California, and Washington, Communists gained substantial influence within the left wing of the Democratic Party during the 1930s. Moreover, primarily because Communists often were the most skilled and courageous labor organizers, they also played significant roles in the organization and subsequent leadership of almost half of Congress of Industrial Organization (CIO) unions following the 1935 CIO split from the American Federation of Labor (AFL). However, as was sometimes the case with other alleged "fronts," such influence often translated into little more than the frequent passage of relatively meaningless resolutions that supported the CP "line" or taking a broader interest in American society rather than the "dollars and hours" outlook of most unions.[18]

In most alleged "fronts," CP members were modest minorities, although frequently they exerted vastly disproportionate significant influence because they were more dedicated, better organized, and more ideologically focused than most other members. Thus, according to Harvey Klehr, a leading historian of the popular front CP, less than 10 percent of the estimated 8,000–9,000 active ALPD members were Communists, but with their extraordinary "energy and activity," they "dominated" this and other organizations in which their membership was similarly proportionately small (such as the IWO, with only 7 percent of 116,000 members in 1936). Reflecting a general scholarly consensus, Klehr writes, "There were never more than 100,000 American Communists at any one time, yet labor unions, youth groups, peace organizations, civil rights bodies, and a host of miscellaneous clubs, gatherings and assemblies faithfully followed the Party's direction."[19]

The AYC (first designated for the secret World War II AGLOSO in 1943) was a federation of youth groups founded in 1934. It soon became a leading popular front movement, assembling what historian Robert Cohen has termed "an amazingly broad group" of overwhelmingly non-Communist affiliates, ranging from the YWCA to the Young Communist League (YCL), with a claimed combined membership of 4.5 million in 1939, most of whom represented "underprivileged young Americans," including blacks, the jobless, poor students, and blue collar workers, who "traditionally had been ignored by the political process." The group became so influential in its lobbying for youth training and jobs programs that first lady Eleanor Roosevelt and other influential figures in the Roosevelt administration regularly consulted its leaders. The organization was effectively granted official recognition as the leading spokesman for American youth when it was given the only position accorded any such group on the National Youth Administration advisory committee. Eleanor Roosevelt (who later maintained that she was misled by AYC officers into believing that none had any Communist ties) supported the group in her newspaper column and spoke to AYC gatherings; when the red-hunting congressional Dies Committee held hearings into alleged Communist domination of the AYC in late 1939, she sat next to AYC leaders in the committee room, brought them to the White House for lunch and dinner and invited members to stay the night. Scores of other prominent Americans supported the AYC or AYC-sponsored programs, including Hollywood figures Mickey Rooney and Orson Welles, New York City mayor Fiorello La Guardia, and leading political figures such as James Farley, Henry Morgenthau, and Clare Booth Luce. In February 1940 President Roosevelt addressed 4,000 AYC members on the White House lawn, but effectively broke with the group, drawing boos when he denounced the AYC's New York chapter for endorsing the Soviet invasion of Finland and termed the Soviet Union a "dictatorship as absolute as any other" in the world. After Eleanor Roosevelt and other leading liberals also broke with the AYC as Communist domination of the group became increasingly apparent, its influence quickly deflated and the group ceased functioning in early 1942.[20]

The NNC (AGLOSO-designated in 1943) was founded at a 1936 Chicago conference that assembled the broadest coalition of black groups ever gathered, with 5,000 people attending the opening session, including 800 delegates representing over 500 labor, religious, cultural, and political groups with claimed combined memberships of over 30 million. Most of these organizations and most leading NNC participants were non-Communists, including its first president,

Brotherhood of Sleeping Car Porters leader A. Philip Randolph. Its membership encompassed liberals, clergymen (including future congressman the Rev. Adam Clayton Powell, Jr.) socialists (including Socialist Party President Norman Thomas), prominent leaders of the National Association for the Advancement of Colored People (NAACP, including Walter White and Roy Wilkins), and leading black academics (including Howard University political scientist and future American and UN diplomat Ralph Bunche). Only ten out of the seventy-five members of the first NNC national steering committee were Communists, although NNC executive secretary and prime mover John Davis was clearly, at the least, close to the CP, and the CP was both a key originating and driving force in the NNC. The NNC briefly became one of the most influential American black organizations, with a program of increasing black educational, employment, and cultural opportunities, fighting lynching, police brutality, and other forms of racial discrimination and opposing European fascism. It developed strong ties with the CIO and played a significant role in supporting the organization of black industrial workers, especially in steel and automobiles. Future Detroit mayor Coleman Young served as executive secretary of the Michigan NNC, and other NNC members also subsequently emerged as prominent postwar civil rights activists, including Walter Washington, James Farmer, Bayard Rustin, and Ella Baker. The NNC was severely weakened, as was the case with almost all other popular front groups, when splits between CP and non-CP elements widened in the wake of the 1939 Nazi-Soviet pact, a development that was exacerbated by growing attacks on the CP in the late 1930s by the Congressional Dies (HUAC) Committee and other governmental agencies. At the third national NNC convention in 1940, following a nationally broadcast address by isolationist CIO leader John W. Lewis, backers of the decidedly non-Communist Lewis and of the CP combined to adopt resolutions opposing American intervention in what was termed the "imperialist war" then raging in Europe, a development that led Randolph and others to resign, sometimes to the accompaniment of bitter attacks upon the CP and Russia. Randolph made clear that his departure partly reflected his fears that the NNC could not survive being branded as Communist-dominated: thus he wrote that "Our people cannot afford to add to the handicap of being black, the handicap of being red," and that "if we should ever be even suspected of abandoning this priceless jewel, our loyalty to our fatherland, God help us!" Although the NNC remained active during World War II, supporting the war effort after the CP "line" changed with the 1941 Nazi attack on Russia, and continuing to support civil rights programs, it never recovered from the aftermath of the 1940 convention. It showed considerable signs of revival in 1946, but was soon severely weakened by rising anti-Communist sentiment during the postwar Red Scare (especially by a substantial withdrawal of CIO support) and was dissolved in early 1947 and folded into the CRC (AGLOSO-designated in 1947, discussed in the following chapter). According to historian Mark Solomon's assessment, before its collapse the NNC registered "remarkable gains in consolidating the black-labor alliance, in cultivating a new generation of militant black youth, and in advancing the struggle for human rights."[21]

The WA (AGLOSO-designated in 1943) was formed in 1935 as a union for employees of the Federal Works Progress Administration; it was hailed by AFL president William Green as a "bona fide organization loyal to the [vehemently anti-Communist] AFL." In 1936 the WA merged with the Communist-controlled Unemployed Councils and thereafter grew to a peak of 250,000 members, with over 1,200 local branches in forty-six states. CP influence thereafter increased, as was reflected in a vigorous campaign of multiracial organizing in the South. At its peak in 1938 an alarmed *New York Times* warned that the WA was becoming "an enormous pressure group compared with which the American Legion and the farm lobbies may pale into insignificance"; two scholars writing in 1993 described the WA as "perhaps the most formidable organization of the able-bodied unemployed in American history." However, in 1938 and 1939 the WA came under congressional investigation, including by the fledgling Dies Committee on Un-American Activities, which sought to identify both the WA and the Works Progress Administration with subversion. In October 1938 chair Martin Dies (D-TX) boasted that his committee had "destroyed" the WA's "legislative influence," while in 1939 Congress banned Communists from federal relief programs and limited workers to eighteen months of consecutive work in such programs, provisions that the *New York Times* reported were "aimed directly at the Worker Alliance and its alleged parent, the Communist Party." Largely due to such external pressure, segments of the WA began to defect in 1938 and form competing organizations. Following the August 1939 Nazi-Soviet pact, WA internal divisions related to the role of CP became increasingly sharp, culminating in the 1940 resignation of founder David Lasser, who publicly denounced CP domination of the WA and announced the formation of a "new national unemployment movement which will be 100% American and free of isms." The WA thereafter dwindled away and collapsed completely by 1941.[22]

The LAW (designated in 1948) was clearly organized in 1935 under CP auspices, but before 1939, according to the scholarly consensus, it was not under Communist ideological domination, and it was never accused of doing anything more "subversive" than harboring highly unpopular views even thereafter (in particular by failing to condemn the 1939 Nazi-Soviet Non-Aggression Pact and thereafter clearly following CP guidelines). The leading historians of the LAW, Arthur Casciato and Judy Kutulas, have respectively described it, at its peak between 1937 and 1939, as the "largest and most influential cultural organization" of the popular front era and the "largest and most prestigious literary organization in America." The LAW's members or contributors (sometimes involving little more than signing petitions or sending greetings to LAW conferences) included numerous distinguished American writers and artists (in the words of an FBI report to Director Hoover, who kept the LAW under intense surveillance and obtained photographs of its confidential files, apparently resulting from an FBI break-in, "A good majority of the outstanding American writers at one time or another participated in the League's activities"). A small sample of them included Ernest Hemingway, William Carlos Williams, Granville Hicks, Max Lerner, Ralph Ellison, Richard Wright, Edna St. Vincent Millay, Upton Sinclair, Dashiell Hammett, William Faulkner, Thomas Mann, John Steinbeck, Theodore Dreiser, Lincoln Steffens, Malcolm Cowley, Archibald MacLeish, Robert Benchley, James Thurber, Carl van Doren, Erskine Caldwell, Katherine Anne Porter, John Dos Passos, Lewis Mumford, Langston Hughes, Lillian Hellman, Heywood Broun, Dorothy Parker, James Farrell, Nelson Algren, Clifton Fadiman, and William Saroyan. At its early 1939 peak, the LAW had 800 formal members (about 20 percent of whom were close to the CP or official members) and had become respectable enough that President Roosevelt expressed "hearty appreciation" in accepting an honorary membership and honorary vice presidency. Aside from holding annual national and regional conferences, the LAW organized lectures and writers' schools, produced radio broadcasts and issued a few publications, raised funds for and backed the Spanish loyalists and European literary exiles, supported civil liberties and opposed censorship, and, as in a 1937 meeting attended by 4,000 people in New York addressed by Mann and MacLeish, voiced opposition to Nazi Germany. Poet Ruth Lechlitner later wrote that the LAW provided a "genuine feeling of fellowship among both established and beginning writers" and its meetings were, especially for younger authors, "a source of hope and encouragement." The LAW formally dissolved only in 1946 but it was effectively moribund by late 1941, following attacks upon it by the Dies Committee, numerous prominent defections (including most of its elected officers, so many that the group had to reprint its letterhead—without any names on it) in the aftermath of the Nazi-Soviet pact, and its final national conference in early June 1941, at which resolutions were adopted that faithfully followed the CP line in opposing American support for Britain and terming the European war a purely imperialist struggle "for profits, territories and markets." After the Nazi invasion of Russia two weeks later, the LAW quickly changed lines to support American intervention against Germany (and tellingly abandoned the usual publication of its just-concluded but now-repudiated conference proceedings).[23]

The origins of the ALWF (designated in 1943) dated to a 1933 conference attended by over 2,000 delegates from a wide variety of organizations who declared their opposition to American "imperialist" policies in Latin America and elsewhere. Although Communists were active and influential in the organization from its origins, prominent socialist, liberal, religious, women's, labor, and farm leaders and organizations increasingly participated as the ALWF rapidly grew amid the fertile protest climate of the 1930s, and the organization backed a wide variety of social, labor, and antiracist programs, while increasingly emphasizing antifascist foreign policies rather than its earlier pacifist leanings. In 1936, the ALWF changed its name to the ALPD (AGLOSO-designated in 1948). At its early 1939 peak, the ALPD claimed 20,000 individual members, as well as affiliated organizations with combined claimed memberships of over 7 million. Secretary of the Interior Harold Ickes sent a letter of greeting to the ALPD's January 1939 conference. According to a hostile account by CP historians Irving Howe and Lewis Coser, the ALWF/ALPD became a "respectable agency through which to influence Congressmen, labor leaders and public figures who could not be reached by open Communists." Like many other popular fronts, the ALPD was torn apart by internal divisions in the wake of the 1939 Nazi-Soviet pact and collapsed shortly thereafter. The ALPD was effectively succeeded by the American People's Mobilization (APM, designated in 1943), which was organized at a 1940 conference that attracted about 10,000 people. The APM included non-Communists, but it always followed the post–popular front CP "line," including opposing American intervention in the European war before the 1941 German invasion of Russia. The APM thereafter reversed its position on American intervention in Europe and renamed itself the American Peace Mobilization before quickly fading into oblivion.[24]

The considerably enhanced legitimacy and significance of the CP in American society that developed during the popular front era was clearly reflected in 1938–1939 federal court rulings in the deportation case of Joseph Strecker, an Austrian-born restaurant keeper who had entered the United States in 1912, admittedly joined the CP in November 1932, and quit a few months later. In *Strecker v. Kessler* (95 F. 2d 976), a unanimous three-judge 1938 federal appeals court overturned a 1932 federal appeals court ruling in *Yokinen v. Commissioner of Immigration* (507 F. 2d 707), which had held that the 1918 immigration law, mandating deportations for aliens "who, at any time after entering the U.S." were members of various described groups, applied even to former members. However, the 1938 *Strecker* court held that changes in the nature of the world situation and the American CP since 1920 necessitated the finding that CP membership no longer required deportation. Noting that "much water, socially and politically, has gone under the bridge since 1920," the court declared that there was no recent evidence that either Strecker or the CP taught the forceful overthrow of the government and that "nothing in our Constitution or our laws" banned a party that peacefully sought to create a "government of the proletariat, by the proletariat and for the proletariat." On April 17, 1939, in *Kessler v. Strecker* (307 U.S. 22), the Supreme Court upheld this ruling, declaring that Strecker could not be legally deported, although it ruled on far narrower grounds, focusing only on whether past, as opposed to present, organizational memberships could justify deportation. Although the 1932 *Yokinen* federal appeals court had held this was "plain" in the language of the immigration laws, the *Strecker* Supreme Court termed such a linguistic construction "unnatural and strained" and struck down Strecker's deportation solely on this ground, thus finding no need to evaluate the nature of the CP.

The Supreme Court *Strecker* ruling attracted enormous media coverage, partly because by then congressional conservatives, led by Rep. Dies, head of the House Committee on Un-American Activities (popularly known as HUAC), were engaged in a growing assault on the Roosevelt administration for allegedly being "soft on communism," both as an alarmed response to the growing impact and legitimacy of the CP in American society and for blatant political reasons. HUAC had been created by the House of Representatives in 1938 primarily in response to the activities of several small but highly vocal and visible pro-Nazi groups, especially the German-American Bund, which claimed about 20,000 members at its height in 1938, and to growing fears and tensions in American society as Europe teetered on the brink of war. Many backers of the resolution creating HUAC, including some popular front organizations such as the ALPD, expected the committee to concentrate on the pro-Nazi groups. However, Dies, a rock-ribbed Texas conservative, quickly focused widely publicized hearings, including some convened on the eve of the 1938 congressional elections, on the CP and its alleged fronts and especially upon allegations of widespread CP infiltration of the federal government and the CIO. Thus, in October 1939, Dies referred to "thousands of members of communist-controlled organizations scattered throughout" the federal government, and his committee publicly released the names of over 500 federal employees allegedly found on an ALPD list (whether a membership or mailing list was unclear), which the committee had earlier labeled a "Communist Front." The Dies hearings and allegations were given enormous and often uncritical press attention, so much so that, according to one study of media coverage, during one four-month period in 1938, HUAC "received more newspaper space than any other single institution in the nation."[25]

The Red Scare of 1939–1941

By mid-1939, the growing storm over allegations of Communist (and, to a lesser extent, pro-Nazi) infiltration of the federal government led to congressional actions that were to lay the legal foundation for the modern AGLOSO, which originally emerged as a secretly created 1940–1941 government listing of organizations in which membership alone would raise doubts about suitability for federal employment. The first such legislative measure, included in a June 1939 relief appropriations act, was aimed at recipients of federal relief programs, such as the Works Progress Administration: it banned federal payments to "any person who advocates or who is a member of an organization that advocates the overthrow of the government of the U.S. through force or violence." This principle was generalized to all federal employees in the Hatch Act, signed by President Roosevelt in early August 1939, which banned from government employment anyone with "membership in any political party or organization which advocated the overthrow of our constitutional form of government." Similar provisions were thereafter regularly included in congressional appropriations acts.[26]

Behind the scenes, President Roosevelt had already, in 1934 and 1936, secretly asked FBI director J. Edgar Hoover (whose agency had been directed in 1924, when Hoover was appointed its new head, to cease engaging in general political intelligence gathering not connected to allegations of lawbreaking) to begin broad political surveillance of Nazi, fascist, and Communist groups. In late 1939, Hoover informed his field offices that the FBI was preparing a "list of individuals, both aliens and citizens," for emergency detention "in time of war or national emergency" if it was deemed their "presence at liberty" would be "dangerous to the public peace and the safety of the U.S. government." Candidacy for FBI inclusion on such lists was gradually expanded from persons with "strong" Communist or Nazi "tendencies" in 1939 to those with "Communistic, Fascist, Nazi or other nationalistic background" in 1940 and to members of any "Communistic" or "front" organizations by 1941. During this period, the FBI also began secretly wiretapping and burglarizing a wide variety of allegedly subversive individuals and organizations. Presumably both to facilitate the compilation of FBI detention lists and to aid the congressionally mandated exclusion from federal employment of persons belonging to organizations targeted by the 1939 Hatch Act, on December 17, 1940, in a memo captioned "communist fronts" (and in a similar January 22, 1941, memo), Hoover instructed FBI field offices to report on about thirty-five such groups, most of which would eventually be placed on AGLOSO. Field office responses make clear that the FBI had already begun surveillance of such organizations; thereafter they began regularly filing reports on "subversive" groups.[27]

The Nazi-Soviet Non-Aggression Pact of August 23, 1939, followed shortly by the German and Soviet invasions of Poland, the Soviet invasion of Finland, and the June 1940 Nazi overrunning of France and the Low Countries, transformed what had been a developing "red" and "brown" scare into full-fledged panic and repression. Thus, Rep. Thomas F. Ford (D-CA), noting the growing antialien feeling that accompanied this hysteria, declared that the mood in the House in June 1940 was "such that if you brought in the Ten Commandments today and asked for their repeal and attached to that request an [anti-]alien law, you could get it." On June 20, 1940, in explicit response to the Hatch Act, the Civil Service Commission (CSC) issued a formal circular (first reported in the *Washington Post* on May 30) that the "removal" from federal employment of any "member of a political party or organization which advocates the overthrow of our constitutional form of government in the U.S. is mandatory." In the first formal step toward creating the modern AGLOSO, the circular added that therefore, "as a matter of official policy," the CSC "will not certify to any department or agency the name of any person when it has been established he is a member of the Communist Party, the German Bund or any other Communist, Nazi or Fascist organization."[28]

The CSC action failed to stem the tide of congressional demands for a political cleansing of the federal government and the nation. Thus, the June 26, 1940, Emergency Relief Act declared that "no alien, no communist and no member of any Nazi bund organization" could be employed in any federal relief project (a proposal with this language, which had passed the House on May 23, was specifically cited by the June 20 CSC circular). On June 28, 1940, Congress enacted the Alien Registration (Smith) Act, which combined the first peacetime sedition law in American history since 1798 with a variety of antialien provisions. The sedition provisions outlawed advocacy of the forceful overthrow of the government, as well as membership in groups so advocating, thus including the first federal legislative "membership" provisions encompassing American citizens. The alien sections required all noncitizens to register annually with the federal government and expanded the grounds for deportation to cover past beliefs or activities, including membership in "subversive" organizations by aliens "at any time" after their entry into the country, thus expressly seeking to overturn the Supreme Court's 1939 *Strecker* ruling. The September 1940 Selective Service Act declared that "whenever a vacancy is caused in the employment rolls of any [even private] business or industry" due to conscription, such vacancies should not be filled "by any person who is a member of the Communist Party or the German-American Bund."[29]

In the June 28, 1941, Justice Department Appropriation Act, Congress directed that $100,000 be "exclusively" devoted by the FBI to investigate federal employees who were "members of subversive organizations or who advocate overthrow of the government" and that the bureau "report its findings to Congress." Responding to this directive, on June 30, 1941 (one week after the Nazi invasion of Russia totally transformed the stance of the CP, which suddenly abandoned its "neutral" posture of 1939–1941 for a position strongly backing American intervention against Hitler), Attorney General Francis Biddle effectively established the first formal modern AGLOSO (hereafter the Biddle AGLOSO). The list was compiled by the DOJ in accordance with the 1939 Hatch Act and the 1941 Appropriations Act for loyalty screenings of federal employees and applicants. On that date Biddle advised the FBI that the CP and the German-American Bund were "subversive organizations" under the congressional definition of advocating the violent overthrow of the government, as were several other organizations with Communist backgrounds or affiliations that Biddle noted were "popularly known as Communist 'front' organizations." Biddle also asked the FBI to submit information about additional organizations to determine if they fell within the congressional guidelines. According to Don Whitehead's authorized 1956 history of the FBI, the Biddle AGLOSO was forwarded to FBI field offices on September 15, 1941, and included, beyond the CP and the Bund, the APM, NNC, AYC, and the National Federation for Constitutional Liberties (NFCL, a predecessor of the post–World War II CRC, discussed below) and two of its local affiliates, the Michigan Federation for Constitutional Liberties and the Washington Committee for Democratic Action (WCDA).[30]

On November 5, 1941, FBI director Hoover informed Special Assistant to the Attorney General Alexander Holtzoff that he had forwarded summary memoranda on the APM, WCDA, NFCL, and AYC a week earlier to Executive Assistant to the Attorney General Ugo Carusi and that copies would be "prepared and forwarded to the interested Government agencies in the event such action met with his approval." According to a "strictly confidential" May 5, 1942, DOJ memorandum to Hoover, the department formally listed the CP and the Bund on June 30, 1941, the APM on July 24, the NFCL and its two affiliates on July 31, the AYC on August 6, the NNC on August 11, and the WA on September 18 (too late for the September 15 memo to FBI field offices). In the meantime, on March 16, 1942, the CSC established the standard that a federal applicant or employee could be denied a position if there was a "reasonable doubt as to his loyalty to the Government of the U.S." As with the subsequent Truman administration AGLOSO published beginning in late 1947, no notice, charges, or hearings were provided to the organizations secretly listed during World War II.[31]

While FBI surveillance activity and the AGLOSO listings were conducted in deep secrecy, in late 1939, in the aftermath of the Nazi-Soviet pact, the Roosevelt administration, clearly partly in response to congressional pressure, began a highly publicized crackdown on Communist activities that had been previously tolerated during the popular front period. Thus, several prominent Communists, including CP leader Earl Browder, were prosecuted for passport frauds allegedly committed years earlier, and California CP Secretary William Schneiderman, who had entered the United States as a small child thirty years before, was subjected to denaturalization proceedings in December 1939 for allegedly fraudulently obtaining his citizenship in 1927 by concealing his Communist affiliations. The changed political climate with regard to communism clearly affected the courts as well as the legislative and executive branches. Browder was convicted and sentenced to an astounding four-year prison term in January 1941 for passport fraud, based solely on the allegation that he had falsely denied in 1934, when applying for a passport, that he had previously owned one. In June 1940, in a ruling upheld a year later by a federal appeals court, a federal district court authorized Schneiderman's denaturalization, solely based on his Communist affiliations, on the grounds that he had falsely signed a 1927 citizenship oath disclaiming membership or affiliation "with any organization or body of persons teaching disbelief in organized government" and affirming his attachment to the principles of the Constitution.[32]

As the CP was coming under increasing external attack by the government, it was simultaneously shaken by an internal crisis that would prove highly relevant to subsequent AGLOSO developments. Until August 1939 the CP had spearheaded demands for the United States to actively join in a general antifascist alliance. However, after a brief period of stunned confusion following the Nazi-Soviet pact, the CP and Communists in popular fronts initiated a major campaign to keep the United States out of what was now termed the "imperialist war," complete with the slogan "The Yanks Aren't Coming," and denounced any criticisms of Russia for signing the pact and for its subsequent invasions of Poland and Finland. This sudden reversal severely discredited the CP, and, along with the party's consistent downplaying of ever-increasing reports of massive Stalinist repression and executions in Russia, enormously strengthened the long-standing view of many critics that the CP was more interested in obeying Russian orders than fostering the interests of American workers. The result was a sudden, drastic decline in CP membership and recruitment, and internal battles within many popular fronts that severely weakened or destroyed them. CP membership fell in half during the following two years from its estimated height of 100,000 in 1939, while popular front organizations were severely weakened by similar defections or sundered by debates over proposed resolutions denouncing the pact, the CP, and/or Russian foreign policy. Thus, the ALPD disbanded in early 1940 (to be replaced by the APM) after an estimated 1,000 members per month (of a total individual membership of about 20,000) resigned following the pact. Similar mass defections affected many other popular fronts, including the AYC, LAW, NNC, and WA, transforming some from highly diverse to clearly Communist-dominated groups, a development that later became significant after they were AGLOSO-designated. During this same period, many unions and liberal organizations, notably including the American Civil Liberties Union (ACLU), effectively adopted a "guilt by association" posture by formally barring all Communists and members of Nazi and fascist organizations from their ranks and/or leadership, regardless of their individual activities or viewpoints.[33]

The Nazi invasion of Russia on June 22, 1941, led to a drastic reversal both of CP policy and, especially after the late 1941 Japanese attack on Pearl Harbor brought the United States into the war as an ally of Russia against Hitler, of the CP's standing in the United States. The CP leapt to the forefront of the anti-Nazi resistance and soon began to bask in the glow of the Soviet Union's sudden positive new status as a wartime ally in American official and popular opinion. Thus, a March 1943 *Life* magazine special issue on the theme of American-Soviet cooperation informed its readers that Russians were "one hell of a people" who "look like Americans, dress like Americans and think like Americans," and that the Russian secret police were simply a "national police similar to the FBI." CP membership doubled within a year, and a variety of organizations sponsored by or close to the party also showed signs of considerable renewed health. Thus, IWO membership reached 185,000 by 1947, and tens of thousands enrolled during World War II in CP-sponsored educational institutions such as the Jefferson

School of Social Science in New York and the Abraham Lincoln School in Chicago. The CP's newly restored luster was soon reflected in a marked easing of repression directed against it, as the American government's "line" switched almost as dramatically and rapidly as did that of the CP. Thus, Browder's passport fraud sentence was commuted by President Roosevelt in May 1942 in order to "promote national unity," and during a December 1943 national radio address, Roosevelt declared that Soviet dictator Stalin represented the "heart and soul of Russia" and "I believe that we are going to get along very well with him and the Russian people—very well indeed." In seeming reciprocation, Browder dissolved the CP in 1944, replacing it with the Communist Political Association (CPA), a supposed interest group rather than a political party, while declaring that American Communists were "ready to cooperate in making capitalism work effectively in the post-war period."[34]

After the Supreme Court agreed in October 1941 to hear California CP secretary Schneiderman's appeal from his denaturalization order, Wendell Willkie, the defeated 1940 Republican presidential candidate, agreed to represent him without charge. In a June 21, 1943, decision, issued on the second anniversary of the Nazi invasion of Russia, the Supreme Court garnered nationwide front-page coverage by overturning the denaturalization (*Schneiderman v. U.S.*, 320 U.S. 118). Maintaining that its ruling "obviously" had nothing to do with American relations with Russia nor with "our views regarding [Russia's] government and the merits of communism," the 5–3 majority held that, in denaturalization cases in which citizenship already granted was in jeopardy, the government bore the burden of proving, by "clear, unequivocal and convincing evidence" that the CP advocated the violent overthrow of the government in 1927 and that it had failed to do so. Moreover, according to the Court majority, "under our traditions, beliefs are personal and not a matter of mere association," and therefore "men in adhering to a political party or other organization notoriously do not subscribe unqualifiedly to all of its platform or asserted principles." In the 1944 case of *Baumgartner v. U.S.* (322 U.S. 665), the Supreme Court applied similar logic to overturn the attempted denaturalization of a German-American who had begun espousing Nazi ideology a year after obtaining his citizenship in 1932, leading the government to abandon a massive campaign it had initiated in March 1940 to denaturalize Bund members and other alleged pro-Nazis. By then, however, the Bund, in the words of historian Leland Bell, had been "harassed out of existence" due to a wave of repression and public revulsion (over a score of Bundists indicted during World War II for violating the Espionage and Smith acts were freed when the cases collapsed). William Dudley Pelley, leader of the Silver Shirts (AGLOSO-designated in 1947), perhaps the most notorious pro-Nazi group besides the Bund, was sentenced to fifteen years for allegedly publishing seditious statements in his newspaper (which, along with about seventy other newspapers and publications, was banned from the mails during the first year of American entry into World War II alone).[35]

In its June 18, 1945, *Bridges v. Wixom* ruling (326 U.S. 135), the Supreme Court again made nationwide front-page news by following up *Schneiderman* with a sensational rebuff to the federal government's by then almost decade-long efforts (spurred on by strong congressional pressure) to deport maritime labor leader Harry Bridges for alleged Communist affiliations. The Labor Department had earlier been forced to drop deportation proceedings against Bridges begun in March 1938, due to the Supreme Court's 1939 *Strecker* ruling that *current* membership in proscribed organizations had to be demonstrated in deportation proceedings, coupled with the findings of a trial examiner that Bridges was not affiliated with the CP when the Labor Department had issued its deportation warrant. However, the DOJ, which was given jurisdiction in immigration matters in June 1940, reopened the proceedings after Congress, squarely aiming at Bridges, overrode the Court's *Strecker* ruling by rewriting the immigration laws in the 1940 Smith Act. A new trial examiner found in 1941 that Bridges was subject to deportation under the new law due to his past affiliations with the CP and the Marine Workers Industrial Union, and Attorney General Francis Biddle ordered him deported in May 1942, on the grounds that the two organizations advocated the forceful overthrow of the government. However, the Supreme Court's 1945 ruling held, 5–3, that the government had failed to prove that Bridges's ties with the two allegedly "subversive" groups had reflected anything "more than cooperative measures to obtain objectives which were wholly legitimate" and thus did not constitute grounds for expulsion. The Court held that the deportation proceedings had been based on a "misconstruction of the term 'affiliation' as used" in immigration law by giving it "a looser and more expansive meaning than the statute permits," as it required demonstrating an "adherence to or a furtherance of the purposes of the proscribed organization as distinguished from a mere cooperation with it in lawful activities." Justice William Douglas's majority opinion added that the Court "cannot believe that Congress intended to cast so wide a net as to reach those whose ideas and programs, though coinciding with the legitimate aims" of subversive groups, "nevertheless fall far short of overthrowing the government by force and violence."[36]

Although the federal courts and the public stance of the federal executive branch were clearly substantially affected by the glow of wartime goodwill surrounding the Soviet Union and the American CP, this was not true of congressional conservatives and secret executive branch activities. On October 19, 1941, a month after the FBI sent the first AGLOSO listing to its field offices, HUAC chair Dies set off a major public firestorm, trumpeted in front-page headlines across the country, by announcing that he had sent the DOJ the names of 1,124 federal employees, including "a large number" in "executive or policy-making positions," who were allegedly members of subversive organizations or advo- cated overthrowing the government. Four months earlier, the Dies Committee had subpoenaed a list of 1,200 members of the Washington Bookshop Associa- tion (WBA), in connection with an investigation that Dies promised would ex- pose "hundreds" of federal employees as active in seventeen "communist fronts operating" in Washington, D.C. By all accounts the WBA was a bookstore with somewhat vaguely leftist ties and an exceptionally good selection of books, which many people "joined" primarily to obtain a 10 percent discount on their purchases. Nonetheless, alleged WBA membership was to become one of the most frequent "charges" involving AGLOSO affiliations, especially during the post–World War II era. The release of FBI materials on the WBA in 2006 in re- sponse to a Freedom of Information Act (FOIA) request revealed that the bureau had over 4,500 pages of files on the organization dating from 1941–1946, of which almost 300 were deemed so sensitive that they were withheld sixty years later. Scores of "released" pages contained redactions, often of most or all of the page. The vast bulk of the released pages consisted of photocopies of printed material, including books by Lenin and Stalin, apparently purchased by FBI informants, much of which was widely available in bookstores and libraries (for which the FBI charged ten cents per page in its FOIA response). The files reveal that the WBA was viewed as so threatening that Attorney General Biddle personally au- thorized "technical surveillance" (either a wiretap or microphone "bug") of the store in April 1944 and that the surveillance continued until December 1945.[37]

DOJ officials told the press in October 1941 that the Dies list (which was not made public) would be sent to the FBI for investigation. However, Executive As- sistant to the Attorney General Ugo Carusi informed FBI director Hoover the fol- lowing month that the mere listing of an organization by Dies was "not by that fact alone to be considered subversive" as the "determination of subversiveness will be made in the same manner that governs organizations whose activities have come to our attention from other sources or through our own channels." Moreover, Carusi cautioned Hoover, even the "finding of a person's name on the 'active indices' of an alleged subversive organization does not necessarily deter- mine the advisability of further investigation," since such might include merely a "mailing list or even a list of persons who are periodically circulated to enlist their interest in particular programs or projects of the organization." Rather, Carusi added, each instance should be "taken on its own merits," with investiga- tions begun if "reasonable grounds" developed "to believe that the person may be a member of a subversive organization within the meaning of the [1941 Justice Department Appropriations] Act." Carusi also told Hoover that any complaint that did not "name a subversive organization to which the government employee belongs" but only made "general allegations that he belongs to a subversive or- ganization, or that he is a Red or a Communist, etc., is not sufficient basis for an investigation," although inquiries should be launched "following information that an employee has signed a petition" to place the CP on an election ballot or has "advocated the candidacy" of a CP member for public office.[38]

World War II and the Second AGLOSO, 1941–1945

On November 12, 1941, less than a month before Pearl Harbor, Attorney General Biddle announced that the government was drawing up plans to control aliens "in time of friction" with other countries, running from "the paroling of those not suspected of subversive activities to those whose actual detention would be necessary." On December 12, five days after Pearl Harbor, Biddle announced that 2,541 Japanese, German, and Italian aliens had been rounded up and detained as "dangerous to the peace and safety of the nation," all of whom had been "under investigation by the FBI for some time." As part of its attempts to classify and possibly intern and/or deport "enemy aliens" (or denaturalize citizens alleged to have ties with subversive organizations and thus to have falsely obtained their citizenship), the DOJ began, in early 1942, to compile a new AGLOSO, designed to facilitate such determinations by departmental Alien Enemy Hearing Boards (a purpose entirely separate from the Biddle AGLOSO, designed for screening federal employees under the Hatch and appropriations acts). In a February 2, 1942, memo sent to all U.S. attorneys, for the purpose of apprising "you and all Alien Enemy Hearings Boards of the significance" attached to "activity and membership by alien enemies in certain organizations," the department declared that the Bund, the Federation of Italian War Veterans, and two other named pro-Nazi groups were "under the direction" of the German or Italian governments and that "similar conclusions" had been reached with regard to seven additional German and Italian groups, although the evidence concerning these latter organizations was "not as conclusive." The memo reported the DOJ's "view" that any enemy alien who had been an officer of any of these organizations or participated in any of their *significant activities* for "any length of time" should be interned, absent "special countervailing factors," and that membership alone, without active participation, was deemed "sufficient to require surveillance through parole if the alien is released." Twelve additional organizations were characterized as under the "direct control of radical and nationalist elements in the Japanese army, navy or government" and therefore possessing a "high degree of dangerousness" that required the internment of all of their members, *even without active participation.* Another nine "Japanese organizations" were deemed under Japanese government "direction" and requiring the internment of officers and active members, absent countervailing factors, and the "surveillance through parole" of nonactive members "if the alien is released." The memo told U.S. attorneys that the information provided was "confidential" and should not be shared with anyone other than Alien Enemy Hearing Boards, as "public disclosure" of the lists "might lead to controversies which would be of no advantage at the present time and might also lead to the unwarranted inference that the organizations mentioned herein are the only dangerous ones." A March 10, 1942, DOJ memo to all U.S. attorneys added to the thirty-two groups earlier singled out for special attention the Nazi Party and the National Fascist Party, which were deemed organizations in which membership "for any length of time" required internment absent "special countervailing factors."[39]

In March 1942 the DOJ publicly announced its intention to denaturalize 1,000 American citizens believed to be active in the Bund and other pro-Axis organizations, on the grounds that their activities indicated that they had fraudulently obtained their citizenship by lacking the requisite attachment to the United States. In announcing the initiation of the first thirty such proceedings, Biddle declared on March 26 that those selected for immediate action had been engaged in propaganda, subversive organizations, and/or activities evidencing a disloyal attitude. Almost simultaneously with the DOJ announcement, Rep. Dies fired another blast at the Roosevelt administration by issuing a list of thirty-five employees of the Board of Economic Warfare, chaired by Vice President Henry Wallace, whom Dies claimed had Communist front affiliations. Three weeks later, apparently seeking to silence Dies, Biddle announced the creation of an interdepartmental committee to investigate alleged subversion within the federal government and to make advisory recommendations to federal agencies concerning 4,112 cases submitted by the FBI (including those forwarded by Dies in October 1941), in order to maintain a "uniformity of procedure and a fair and efficient discharge of the Congressional mandate" to investigate suspected subversive employees.[40]

On April 23, 1942, Special Assistant to the Attorney General Edwin Dickinson submitted a "confidential" memo to Biddle reporting that the new interdepartmental committee (hereafter the "Dickinson Committee") had "taken note" of the DOJ's 1941 determination that nine organizations were "within the congressional intent in directing investigations." Dickinson, the committee's executive secretary, who had previously served as law school dean at the universities of Michigan and California, reported that the committee understood this classification to mean that charges of participation in any such designated group would be "sufficient" to warrant "investigation" of a federal employee. However, he added, the committee understood that such charges would "in no circumstances be regarded as conclusive," because it was assumed that federal agencies would decide each case "on all the facts" presented by the FBI and that dismissals would be ordered only if hearings, providing for employee participation, were deemed necessary. Dickinson added that his committee had been "advised" that mere WA participation would be "excluded for purposes of administration," a decision "reported to have been taken" because the WA was "inactive at the present time and further because investigation has disclosed that most of its rank and file members were deluded into joining for legitimate and proper motives." Dickinson added that his committee recommended that six additional organizations be added to the Biddle AGLOSO "in conformity with the policy adopted" by the department concerning already-listed groups, based on FBI data, including two so-called "American Fascist" or "native rightist" groups (American Patriots and the Protestant War Veterans of the U.S.) and four "Communist fronts" (the ALWF/ALPD, the Congress of American Revolutionary Writers, the National Committee for the Defense of Political Prisoners, and the WBA). Dickinson declared that the WBA presented a "somewhat unique case," because there was "considerable evidence of Communist infiltration and 'Front' tactics," but it was "obviously likely" that a "great many innocent" people had joined the bookstore "without being aware of its sponsorship," and therefore the Committee found it inadvisable to "investigate [federal] employees charged with participation unless they are charged with more than mere patronage or subscription." Dickinson added that his committee had received material on thirty-one additional organizations and "further reports will be submitted as rapidly as studies may be brought to a satisfactory conclusion." This was apparently a slightly erroneous reference to the thirty-two organizations singled out for special attention by Alien Enemy Hearings Boards in the February 2, 1942, memo sent by the DOJ to all U.S. attorneys, all of which were added to the Biddle AGLOSO by the Dickinson Committee on May 13, 1942.[41]

In a May 5, 1942, "strictly confidential" memo to Hoover, Dickinson reported that on April 24 the DOJ had authorized "investigation on charges of participation by Federal employees," on the basis of FBI "factual memoranda" and his committee's recommendation, of the six organizations recommended for AGLOSO listing in his April 23 memo to Biddle (with the WBA proviso). He also told Hoover that the department had declined, on the basis of an FBI report, to authorize such investigations with regard to the NLG (which would eventually be proposed for AGLOSO designation in 1953) and that the department had referred to his committee seventeen additional specified organizations, which were "now being studied," including seven groups whose names indicated a primary interest in dance, photography, film, or theater.[42]

On May 22, 1942, Dickinson appeared before a closed House Judiciary Subcommittee for an unpublished hearing on a proposed bill demanding an "immediate report" from the FBI to Congress concerning its investigations under the June 1941 Justice Department Appropriation Act mandate. Dickinson reported that determining "the meaning of members of subversive organizations who advocate the overthrow of the government" had caused "difficulty" and "trials and tribulations" from the "onset," because Congress had not clearly defined the term "subversive" and it "would have been a very great help and would have saved a great deal of time and expedite[d] the investigation if Congress could have seen its way clear to do that." Although, Dickinson related, Biddle had informed

Hoover immediately after the mandate was enacted that the CP and the Bund "were organizations within the Congressional intent," the attorney general had thereafter "never said what organizations are subversive and what ones are not" before "asking for evidence, and upon the basis of evidence he has authorized or not authorized the FBI to embrace these organizations within its inquiries." Dickinson indicated that Biddle had relied upon "Mr. Hoover and a special defense unit [the Special War Policies Unit, or SWPU] to get special information on other organizations" and had quickly directed Hoover to "embrace within the scope of these inquiries" the "leaders who were participating in seven of the so-called front organizations" and that "other ones were added at a later date" in a process that had become "routine." He added that after FBI investigations were completed, the results were sent to government agencies for determinations, and they had been "disposing of the easy cases first," such as the infrequent cases in which there was "no trouble" about reaching a dismissal decision, as when "the employee makes an unqualified admission" of active CP membership, or the equally clear decision to retain "someone who bought a dictionary at the Washington Bookshop and at an indiscreet, uninformed moment" joined the ALPD.[43]

The DOJ and the Dickinson Committee, along with the Enemy Alien Hearing Boards and other federal departments and agencies, were at least partly guided in their determinations concerning subversive organizations by the SWPU, which Dickinson alluded to in his testimony. The SPWU included an "Organizations and Propaganda Analysis Section," which was further divided into "Nazi," "Communist," "Fascist [both Italian and Japanese]" and "Native Rightist" sections. Eleanor Bontecou, an attorney who served in the DOJ during World War II and clearly incorporated "inside information" concerning the Biddle AGLOSO determinations in her 1953 book, *The Federal Loyalty-Security Program*, apparently alludes to the SWPU in describing the listings as based on memoranda compiled by teams of lawyers and social scientists (led by Harold Lasswell, a leading political scientist and propaganda analyst). She writes that they developed an "elaborate scheme of analysis" based on FBI reports and many other sources, "including press reports, especially from the foreign language press, research monographs, legislative documents, private studies and other available relevant material." According to Bontecou, it quickly became apparent that the data provided by the investigative agencies, staffed by those "untrained in social history," was inadequate, originally resulting in "some embarrassing rule-of-thumb judgments."[44]

According to a lengthy, undated SWPU memorandum originating sometime before the summer of 1942, the SWPU had thus far made investigative reports on about 275 organizations, including newspapers, believed engaged in "subversive and propaganda activities," to more than a dozen government units, including, within the DOJ alone, the Alien Enemy Control Unit, the Dickinson Committee, the FBI, and the Immigration and Naturalization Service (INS), as well as to the State, Interior, Navy, and Treasury Departments and Vice President Henry Wallace. Among those organizations reported on to the Dickinson Committee were all fifteen groups AGLOSO-designated by the DOJ by April 1942, save for the CP and the Bund, which Biddle viewed as having been essentially specifically designated by Congress. According to the SWPU, its "most reliable source" of outside information came from FBI reports, but "a substantial part of the information concerning these organizations" was obtained by translating the foreign language press. The SWPU memo indicated that its recommendations had led the FBI to subpoena or obtain voluntarily the records of fifty-three organizations, and "it appears by this move alone, many of these organizations and their branches have collapsed or the membership has become so disintegrated that the group entity has substantially disappeared," with many members realizing that "their activities are under close scrutiny by the DOJ, with the result that any semblance of group movement has disappeared." The memo added that reports on another approximately fifty organizations were under way.[45]

While, behind the scenes, the DOJ was thus engaged in sweeping investigations of hundreds of organizations, Biddle made national front-page news on September 3, 1942, by publicly suggesting that such activities were largely a waste of time. In a published report to Congress on FBI investigations of allegedly subversive federal employees, Biddle declared that of 1,725 federal employees against whom charges of subversive activity had been made and about whom employing agencies had made final decisions following receipt of FBI reports, only 36 had been fired, with other disciplinary actions imposed in another 13 instances. While indicating that another 1,000 cases were still pending, Biddle declared that these figures demonstrated that "sweeping charges of disloyalty in the Federal service have not been substantiated" and that the government "is not 'infiltrated' with communists, bundists or fascists." He added that most of the allegations were "clearly unfounded" and "should never have been submitted for investigation in the first instance," a conclusion that he said was "conspicuously" true of the over 1,100 names submitted by Dies in October 1941. According to Biddle, it was "inevitable that such sweeping investigations should take on the appearance of an inquisitional action alien to our traditions," thus producing "disturbance and unrest" and a "feeling of uneasiness and insecurity" among federal employees, especially since the "occasional complaint" had "obviously been inspired by the jealousy or malice of a fellow-employee who knows that his identity as an informant will remain undisclosed." Moreover, Biddle declared, the investigations had made "clear that the objective test of membership in a 'front' organization is thoroughly unsatisfactory," as in such cases "the purposes of the organization are so stated as to make membership consistent with loyalty." In hundreds of cases, Biddle reported, employees had been alleged to be "subversive" solely because their names were on a particular organization's mailing lists and "a large number had not even heard of the organization."[46]

The Biddle AGLOSO was first publicly revealed in his September 1942 message to Congress, although most news accounts completely ignored or barely mentioned this revelation. After noting that Congress had "neither defined 'subversive organizations' nor indicated standards to be applied" to determine such classification, Biddle reported that the DOJ had found "ample authority" in previous judicial and administrative findings and legislative history to determine that the CP and its affiliates and the Bund fell "within the legislative intent." However, he added, the department had encountered "greater difficulties" determining whether "various 'front' organizations" should be similarly categorized, as most had been "founded for ostensibly patriotic purposes and their membership included many persons who were completely innocent of subversive advocacy or belief." However, first under his direction and subsequently under standards "laid down" by the Dickinson Committee, "the more important 'front' organizations were brought within the scope of the project." An accompanying August 22, 1941, FBI report added considerably more detail concerning AGLOSO, indicating that Biddle had advised the bureau on June 30, 1941, that "responsive to Congressional intent," the CP was "intended to be regarded a 'subversive' organization," as were "organizations having Communist backgrounds or Communist affiliations, thereby covering organizations which are popularly known as Communist 'front' organizations." To help Biddle determine which such groups fell within the congressional intent, the report stated, the FBI had thereafter sent him, at his request, "memoranda concerning various organizations," with the result that in addition to the CP and the German-American Bund, "seven groups were designated as coming within the purview of the congressional mandate [before October 1941]" and information on twenty-two additional groups was furnished to Biddle by mid-February 1942. On May 9, 1942, the FBI had requested the Dickinson Committee to "consider additional organizations within the purview" of the law, and on May 13 the committee had "ruled, with Biddle's approval, that thirty-two additional groups should be so considered." According to the report, that brought the AGLOSO total to forty-seven: "12 Communist or Communist 'front' organizations; 2 American Fascist organizations; 8 Nazi organizations; 4 Italian Fascist organizations; and 21 Japanese organizations" (the FBI did not explain a seeming discrepancy in the figures). According to FBI documents, the FBI had originally submitted a four-volume report to Biddle after obtaining "access to confidential records" of the forty-seven designated groups and had recommended that Biddle release its entire findings to Congress, but that President Roosevelt "was primarily interested" in discrediting the Dies Committee; as a result, after consulting with House Speaker Sam Rayburn (D-TX), Biddle had ordered a reluctant FBI to prepare for Congress only the twenty-page August 22 summary submitted in September. According to the FBI documents, the bureau had wanted to name every suspect federal employee and all forty-seven AGLOSO groups, but it was forced to supply Congress with a report that was "anonymous in nature both as to names of the persons investigated and the organizations which had been declared subversive." The documents add that Dies was aware that the original report "had been sent back to the FBI to be 'toned down'" and indicated that in several cases the FBI had burglarized targeted groups.[47]

The FBI report did not name any specific organizations beyond the CP and the Bund, but the thirty-two groups reported added by the Dickinson Committee on May 13 were the same organizations that had been singled out for special attention by the Enemy Alien Hearing Boards in the DOJ's February 2, 1942, memo to U.S. attorneys (bizarrely, the Nazi and Italian National Fascist Parties, which were added to the Enemy Alien Hearing Boards list in a March 10, 1942, DOJ memo, were never added to the Biddle AGLOSO). A January 29, 1947, internal FBI memo entitled "Tabulation of the 47 Organizations Declared Subversive by the Attorney General" gives estimated membership figures for thirty-four of the forty-seven Biddle AGLOSO groups, ranging from less than 1,000 for twelve organizations, to between 1,000 and 10,000 for fourteen groups, and over 10,000 in eight instances. The smallest organization, the Japanese Hokubei Zaigo Shoke Dan, had an estimated 12 members in 1941. The largest included the German-American Bund and the CP with estimated respective memberships of 20,000 and 74,000 in 1940; the American Patriots, with about 100,000 members in 1938; the WA, with about 160,000 members in 1940; and two Popular Front federations of organizations, the NNC, credited with 500,000 members in 1937, and the AYC, with 1.6 million in 1941.[48]

The vast majority of the thirty-five so-called native fascist (i.e., pro-Axis) organizations listed by Biddle (and again designated by the Truman administration in 1947) were totally insignificant; moreover virtually all of them still existent when the United States entered World War II quickly dissolved, collapsed, or were suppressed via deportation proceedings, exclusion of their newspapers from the mails and/or general federal and/or state harassment in the form of trumped-up charges, including sedition, espionage, draft evasion, and violation of the 1938 Foreign Agents Registration Act. Many of these cases were so flimsy that they collapsed in court, including notably a draft evasion conspiracy case and mass denaturalization campaign directed against the remnants of the Bund and a grotesque Espionage and Smith Acts conspiracy case against about thirty so-called native fascists, most of whom had nothing in common aside from their fascist inclinations and hatred for President Roosevelt, Jews, and Communists.[49]

Most of the Biddle AGLOSO groups have left no or few traces behind beyond what remains in FBI and DOJ files and, while unquestionably most were ideologically pro-fascist, there is little or no evidence that they posed even a minimal security threat or engaged in activities beyond speech and assembly. Moreover, while their leaders were generally hard-core fascists, many followers joined more for social and/or general ethnic-nationalistic than for ideological reasons. All of these characteristics of the World War II AGLOSO groups were especially true of the twenty-one "Japanese organizations." The January 1947 FBI memo gives membership figures for only nine of them, and only four had reported memberships exceeding 1,000. According to a July 17, 1956, internal DOJ memo sent to Subversive Organizations Section chief Joseph Alderman by subordinate Lee Michaloski, the designated Dai Nippon Botoku Kai, which reportedly had a membership of 500 in 1942, was formed to "train Japanese youth in the Japanese military arts, namely wrestling, fencing, spear and archery and at the same time [to] instill in them militaristic and pro-Japanese ideals and beliefs." Michaloski added that if the FBI could not furnish additional information "to show that this organization was devoted in whole or part to influencing the political activities, policies of Japan, a totalitarian government," the government could "not sustain its [AGLOSO] designation" if challenged under a hearing procedure that the department established in 1953 in the wake of a 1951 Supreme Court ruling (discussed in chapter 3), which ruled that organizations had to be given some opportunity to challenge their designations. What is apparently the only scholarly study with information about these groups, by Morris Schonbach, reports that the Botoku Kai "distributed materials some of which stressed racial differences and the inevitably of war" and notes that in general "little can be found concerning these groups." A 1947–1948 "Training Manual" prepared for the Loyalty Review Board (LRB), which administered the 1947 Truman AGLOSO (which, as discussed below, incorporated the Biddle AGLOSO wholesale), includes virtually no information on the Japanese organizations. Thus it says about the Hinode Kai only that it was "composed of enlisted and officer reservists" and about the Hinomaru Kai only that it was "composed of veterans of the Russo-Japanese War of 1904" (which suggests that many, if not most, of them were dead by World War II and certainly by 1947). The same largely applies to the four "Italian Fascist Organizations." The well-known Italian American political exile Gaetano Salvemini's encyclopedic 1977 study, *Italian Fascist Activities in the United States*, includes less than two pages on the designated "Mario Morgantini" Circle (for which the FBI provided no membership data), essentially limited to noting that the group pledged allegiance to Italian dictator Mussolini, gave fascist salutes, wore black shirts, and celebrated the 1936 Italian invasion of Ethiopia. Schonbach describes another listed group, the Dante Alighieri Society, as founded in 1890 to promote "Italian cultural relations abroad and numbering in its ranks many highly respected men," while Salvemini terms the group a fascist "transmission belt." The only even minimally significant of the four Italian groups appears to have been the Federation of Italian [World] War [I] Veterans in the U.S., which the FBI reported as having over 4,000 members in 1941 and which Salvemini describes in terms similar to the Morgantini group. According to a July 24, 1956, internal DOJ memo, the veterans and Alighieri groups were listed because "they were dominated and controlled by individuals sympathetic to the Fascist Government of Italy and served as media for the spread of fascist propaganda"; no allegations of illegal activities are mentioned. A DOJ memo dated October 26, 1955, suggested that perhaps the veterans group should be removed from AGLOSO as "it is extremely difficult to believe" that an "organization composed of veterans of the First World War" would include members who "would be applying for federal employment at this date." The 1947–1948 LRB "Training Manual" includes a substantial section about the veterans, declaring that they were "under the direct control of the Italian government," but says about the Morgantini Circle only that it had been "designated as subversive by the Attorney General." The fourth AGLOSO "Italian fascist" group, the Lictor Society, is described in the manual (which, bizarrely, describes numerous nondesignated Italian groups also) as the "Italian counterpart of the German-American Bund," with supposedly 10,000 members and engaging in "activist and propagandist" activities in close coordination with Italian consular officials, with a "main purpose" of organizing "pro-fascist" Italian Americans for "espionage and sabotage" and indoctrinating "Americans of Italian origin with fascist ideologies."[50]

Among the ten "Nazi" and "American fascist" groups that were designated, the German-American Bund and the Silver Shirts undoubtedly caused considerable public alarm with their frequent mass meetings, Nazi-style uniforms and salutes, quasi-military (but unarmed) parades and vicious anti-Semitism, but their only real threat was ideological (although fisticuffs often accompanied their appearances, they probably endured more violence inflicted upon them by their frequently vocal opponents than they initiated). According to the January 1947 FBI memo, in 1940 the Bund had 20,000 members and the Silver Shirts had 12,000, but their high visibility and levels of activity gave the impression that they were far larger organizations. Both groups were investigated by congressional committees before the United States entered World War II and were essentially battered into submission by federal and state prosecutions. Although the Bund formally dissolved the day after Pearl Harbor (earlier, it had been essentially outlawed in New York and New Jersey), federal agents effectively shut down its remnants by raiding its national headquarters on December 11, 1941, arresting its leaders, and impounding all of its records. Subsequently Bund leaders and members were subjected to a relentless campaign of harassment, including the denaturalization and deportation of Fritz Kuhn, its first leader, and a fifteen-year jail term for espionage and other offenses for his successor, Wilhelm Kunze. The Silver Shirts, which always revolved around their leader, William Dudley Pelley, who propounded a bizarre mixture of anti-Semitism, pro-Naziism, and mystical occultism, endured a similar fate. Although Pelley officially dissolved the group in 1940, he was sentenced to fifteen years' imprisonment in 1942 for sedition and indicted again that same year as part of the notorious "native fascist" conspiracy case that eventually collapsed; he was paroled in 1950, by which time nothing remained of the Silver Shirts. The 1947–1948 LRB "Training Manual" lists about forty groups under the "native fascist" and "Nazi" categories, although only ten such groups were designated by Biddle and redesignated in 1947. In some cases no information is provided about listed groups, while extensive write-ups are included for nondesignated organizations. For one of the AGLOSO groups, the Columbians, almost all of the half-page sketch consists of quotes from the organization's self-proclaimed purpose, namely, to preserve "race purity" as "part of the fundamental American doctrine on which our Nation was built, our God-given right to remain white."[51]

In his September 1942 letter to Congress, Biddle endorsed the conclusions of the Dickinson Committee, made to him in an enclosed report dated June 30, 1942. He specifically highlighted the committee's recommendation that any further federal loyalty investigations be made "without undue emphasis on the mere matter of [organizational] membership" and that procedures be developed that, had they been in force, would "have reduced the list of investigated cases during the past fiscal year approximately 90%." The report added that the result of investigations triggered by the Dies list had been "utterly disproportional to the resources expanded," that the "futility and harmful character of a broad personnel inquiry have been too amply demonstrated," and that federal employee investigations should be limited in the future to "matters clearly pertinent to the vital problems of national security" and to "instances in which there is substantial reason for suspecting that there has been a violation of law requiring prosecution or dismissal from Federal service." The committee added that the "overwhelming majority" of investigations proceeded because employees were allegedly listed on the "active indices" of one or more "Communist fronts," but that "in all but a small residuum of the cases, the lead provided by the 'active indices' of front organizations has proved to be utterly worthless," such as instances in which an individual had sponsored apparently "meritorious causes in no respect incompatible with his patriotic duties as a citizen, made nominal financial contributions, or attended occasional meetings" or had "knowingly permitted his enthusiasm" for such causes to "override any concern he may have felt about being" thus "associated with known Communists." The committee added that it had requested that federal agencies grant accused employees an opportunity to answer charges against them "in all doubtful and difficult cases," which the committee implied meant unless "the report or transcript recorded an admission" of CP or Bund membership.[52]

Biddle's message to Congress, reported under headlines such as "FBI Inquiry Brands Dies Charges as False," was hailed by a *Washington Post* columnist and a *New York Times* editorial, with the latter declaring that it had showed that the federal service was "not demonstrably 'infiltrated' with disloyalty" and that "perhaps this conclusion is worth the $100,000 the investigation cost." However, Dies immediately blasted it, declaring that "in plain English, Mr. Biddle's report means that he favors" the federal employment of members of organizations "which even Mr. Biddle has pronounced subversive [Dies named six groups, but since one of them, the ILD, was not then on AGLOSO, he apparently lacked access to the secret list]." Dies added that Biddle had "failed utterly to fulfill" his congressional mandate and only sought to "discredit" and "smear our committee," while effectively giving a "license to every Government employee to engage in any communistic subversive activity, so long as he does not go to the extent of actually carrying publicly a paid-up" CP membership card.[53]

On September 24, 1942, in a 90-minute House floor speech, Dies issued the names of nineteen federal employees whom he alleged had leadership roles in the NFCL and the WCDA. Dies accurately reported that Biddle had described the two groups as Communist-controlled in previously secret memoranda sent to federal agencies, adding that "on the basis of overwhelming evidence, we concur in the Attorney General's judgment." He also placed into the September 24 *Congressional Record* copies of what he described as "confidential memoranda" sent by Biddle to government agencies "branding 12 organizations as Communist-controlled," documents that clearly corresponded to materials described by the Dickinson Committee as being circulated to government agencies in its June 30, 1942, report to Biddle. They included the ALWF/ALPD, APM, AYC, LAW, NFCL, NNC, WBA, and WCDA. All of these organization had been listed by Biddle, but, with the exception of a fleeting reference in the September 4, 1942, *Chicago Tribune* (based on a letter from Dies to House Speaker Sam Rayburn criticizing Biddle's September 2 report to Congress), the national press did not report their names and the government's maintenance of an official, if secret, list of "subversive" organizations did not become widely known. Each memo provided a brief history of the organization, stressing its alleged control by CP members and/or the CP, but none alleged that the organizations had engaged in any illegal activities. For example, according to the LAW memo, the group was "founded under Communist auspices in 1935" during the popular front period and attracted "many of the most prominent American writers, Communist and non-Communist." Although supporting CP policy, such as interpreting the Spanish Civil War as "presenting an issue of communism versus fascism," CP control was at first "deliberately obscured," according to the memo, while following the 1939 Nazi-Soviet pact, the LAW began to "openly follow the Communist Party line as dictated by the foreign policy of the Soviet Union," and thereafter "most of the non-Communists disaffiliated themselves from it and declared their opposition to its policy." The WBA memo reflected the Dickinson Committee's recommendation in, uniquely, declaring that "in view of the nature of the enterprise," investigations "have been restricted to include only those fairly charged with participation in its administration," rather than encompassing ordinary members. The memo reported that the WBA was founded in 1938 "for the stated purpose of providing a meeting place for persons interested in literary and cultural activities, providing for the cooperative purchase and resale of literature and works of art," and "fostering other activities of a literary, educational and cultural nature." It added that "Communist penetration" of the WBA was evidenced by its "prominently" offering for sale CP and "front" literature and reports from "confidential sources" indicating "close contact" between WBA officers and employees with local Communists.[54]

The Dies list of nineteen individuals clearly indicates that he was "leaked" information on people as well as at least some of the Dickinson Committee's organizational memos. A brief examination of FBI reports on individuals under the June 1941 congressional mandate, comprising eighteen volumes of over 8,000 pages now maintained in the National Archives, indicates that most of those investigated allegedly had ties with the ALPD, the WBA, and the WCDA, with less frequent charges involving other alleged "front" groups such as the NNC and WA. Thus, in the case of an economist for the War Production Board, the FBI report indicates that he was listed by Dies in 1941 as a member of the WBA and the ALPD, both of which had been declared by the DOJ as "within the scope" of the 1941 Justice Department Appropriations Act on May 5, 1942, and that FBI information indicated that the employee's name "appeared on the active indices" of the WCDA and the APM, which were described as having been "declared subversive by the Department of Justice" in July 1941. The report added that, in a personal interview with an FBI agent, the employee denied any connection with the WCDA or the APM and had stated "that insofar as he knows, he has never been a member of any organization which he has reason to believe was dominated by the Communist Party." The FBI concluded by relating that the War Production Board had decided to retain the employee after being informed of the results of its investigation.[55]

Biddle announced six additional firings and one additional disciplinary action against federal employees on November 20, 1942, but Dies continued to suggest that the administration was deliberately coddling employees with subversive ties, and Congress demonstrated its support for him by appropriating another $200,000 to search out governmental subversives. In January 1943, the Dies Committee officially charged that the executive branch had failed to carry out the "mandate of Congress" to uncover subversion in the federal service, instead allowing "hundreds of employees" who were on its lists to keep their jobs "even though they belong to organizations which the Attorney General has held to be subversive." On February 1, 1943, Dies named almost forty alleged "subversive" employees in a two-hour House floor speech and demanded that the government fire such "irresponsible, unrepresentative, crackpot and radical bureaucrats." On February 5 the House voted 163–111, without any evidence beyond Dies's charges, to specifically ban federal payments to one of them, William Pickens, but rescinded its action a few days later after discovering that Pickens was one of the few blacks on the list. Clearly intending to be perceived as anti-red rather than anti-black, the House instead established on February 9 a special subcommittee chaired by Rep. John Kerr (D-NC) to determine if those accused by Dies were "unfit" to work in the federal service due to their present or past "association or membership in or with organizations whose aims or purposes are or have been subversive to the Government of the U.S." On that same day, presumably at least partly to mollify Dies, President Roosevelt publicly signed Executive Order 9300 (which had been recommended by the temporary Dickinson Committee and had been under consideration for several months). The order created a new permanent Interdepartmental Committee on Employee Investigations (ICEI) to "consider cases of subversive activity on the part of Federal employees" and serve as an "advisory and coordinating agency in all matters" concerning complaints alleging such conduct. The administration also briefly considered a suggestion by Secretary of the Interior Harold Ickes to additionally establish what he termed a presidential "committee of fair-minded Republicans to examine the general problem of employees accused by Congressman Dies ('reckless liar that he is') and others of being 'subversive.'" In a June 3, 1943, memo to Roosevelt, Ickes argued that establishing the ICEI had "mistaken the nature of the problem," which was "not a nice question of constitutional law" but a "vicious political campaign" designed to "smear and discredit the Administration" as well as "liberal or anti-fascist activities" generally, which could not be effectively answered by "carefully marshaled facts and closely reasoned arguments" but only by "fair-minded men who do *not* have implicit confidence in your department heads." The Ickes proposal was dropped after opposition to it was expressed by the CSC, which in a September 8, 1943, memo to the Budget Bureau expressed confidence in the ICEI and opposed "constantly jump[ing] from one proposed solution to another," thus throwing the ICEI's efforts "overboard" in order to establish another group to cover "identically the same ground."[56]

In response to a query from Rep. Kerr, Biddle wrote to inform him in early March 1943 that the DOJ regarded as "subversive," within the meaning of the 1941 Appropriations Act, the CP, the Bund, and the Silver Shirts, as well "certain organizations found to be dominated by enemy governments or organizations." With regard to the latter, Biddle enclosed a copy of the February 2, 1942, DOJ memorandum, intended for use by Alien Enemy Hearing Boards, listing thirty-two additional groups. He also provided a list of fifteen additional organizations, which he said were "generally described as Communist, Fascist or Nazi 'fronts,'" with sufficient "evidence of subversive infiltration or control" to clearly "require that they be brought within the scope of the investigation for administrative purposes," but which he confusingly added were "not regarded as subversive within the meaning of the legislative mandate." This list included, in addition to those clearly encompassed within the list of forty-seven organizations referred to by the FBI in its August 22, 1942, report to Congress, the All-American Imperialist League, the ILD, and the IWO. Adding to the confusion, Biddle said that the government also regarded the Socialist Workers Party (SWP) as "subversive" but had not officially listed it because "no Federal employees have been reported as involved at any time." This suggestion that only groups with then-serving federal employees had been officially placed on AGLOSO was clearly misleading, since the thirty-two allegedly "enemy-controlled" groups had been originally compiled for use in enemy alien internment determinations and not in connection with federal employment.[57]

The Kerr subcommittee held hearings in the spring of 1943, behind closed doors and without those accused allowed to have lawyers present, concerning nine of the federal employees accused by Dies on February 1, apparently relying primarily upon information from the FBI and Dies Committee. The Kerr subcommittee "cleared" six of those investigated, while recommending that three prominent officials be found unfit for federal employment due to their "membership and association" with organizations deemed "subversive" by the DOJ or the Dies Committee, as well as their "views and philosophies as expressed in various statements and writings." These individuals were former University of Chicago professor and author Robert Morss Lovett, then secretary of the Virgin Islands, and two high-ranking officials of the Federal Communication Commission (FCC), Goodwin Watson and FCC commissioner William E. Dodd, Jr. The House then voted 317–62 on May 18 to delete their salaries via a rider attached to a deficiency appropriations bill. Although the Senate rejected this provision five times, once by 69–0 (resulting in the delay of all government salaries for several weeks), it finally agreed to a compromise barring their salaries after November 15, 1943, unless their appointments had been submitted by President Roosevelt and confirmed by the Senate. Roosevelt signed the bill under protest and denounced the rider as unconstitutional, while Biddle refused to defend Congress when, after continuing to work without salaries for a short period to pave the way for a legal challenge, the trio went to court. In June 1946, the Supreme Court unanimously struck down the congressional action as a bill of attainder in *U.S. v. Lovett* (328 U.S. 303) and awarded the three a total combined back pay of $2,158.[58]

At about the same time that the Kerr subcommittee was beginning its hearings in early 1943, DOJ SWPU head Lawrence Smith recommended to Charles Fahy, director of the department's War Division, that membership in over 250 specified organizations, including about 180 "leftist" groups and about 75 "rightist" groups, should be "reason for careful examination of the applicant's political views and activities" when the INS made citizenship decisions. According to the SWPU, membership in the organizations was "not necessarily a basis for opposing admission to citizenship," but "may be indicative" of disloyalty, lack of attachment to American constitutional principles, a belief in violent overthrow of the government, or a "belief in the abolition of all forms of organized government." Subsequently, the SWPU's Organizations and Propaganda Analysis section prepared short descriptions of some of the listed organizations for the convenience of the INS. Thus, the Ukrainian-American League was described as a "federation of local Ukrainian pro-Communist organizations" and was characterized as having always "collaborated" with the CP and front organizations and having "consistently and unconditionally supported the policies of the USSR." The SWPU's suggested listing struck some INS officials as too sweeping in its inclusion of "leftish" groups. Thus, a handwritten note attached to SWPU chief Smith's letter to War Division director Fahy termed it "so indiscriminate on its face as to bring in thousands [of people] against whom charges or suspicions should not be made." Apparently due to such protests, on April 8, 1943, a pared-down list of about seventy-five "Communist" organizations, described as only including those "unquestionably bad and the more prominent 'front' groups as to which the available evidence is pretty clear," was subsequently submitted to SWPU Subversive Administration Section chief Ralph Boyd. Most of the alleged "front" groups on the original list, including several earlier placed on AGLOSO (including the ALPD, NNC, and NFCL), disappeared from the revised listing.[59]

DOJ Criminal Division official Raymond Whearty, the author of the memo submitting the revised listing to Boyd "in accordance with your phone request," expressed considerable unhappiness about eliminating some of the previously included groups. He lamented, "I don't see how we can conscientiously omit mentioning a 'front' organization as to which there is any *reasonable* basis for believing Communist or other subversive penetration to have existed, simply because we haven't sufficient information to *prove* that *all* of its members are 'black sheep'. . . . This isn't a public Dies list—it's a guide for inside government administration and it should include all possible leads, which is all these names are." Whearty added that the "170-odd [alleged "front"] organizations on my first list represented a culling down from a total of approximately 800 [originally considered for listing]." On April 29, 1943, SWPU chief Smith forwarded a final version of the "naturalization" list to the INS, with a cover letter that described the designated organizations as "carefully selected in accordance with an agreement" reached with INS officials. It included about seventy-five "front" organizations, almost, but not entirely identical with Whearty's April 8 list, plus the approximately seventy-five "rightist" groups that had appeared on the original March SWPU listing. According to an "explanatory note" accompanying the April 29 list, it included groups that "are or have been anti-Democratic, pro-Fascist, pro-Axis, Communist or Anarchist, or have been infiltrated or controlled, in varying degrees, by persons having such tendencies." The note added that in a "few" cases membership "alone should be sufficient to bar naturalization," but usually membership was "only a reason for careful examination" of the applicant's "political views and activities but, without more," not justification for instituting an "independent investigation." Along with the DOJ's February 1942 Alien Enemy Hearing Boards deportation/internment list and the Biddle employee loyalty AGLOSO (which itself seemingly assumed different forms depending upon the intended audience), the April 29 "naturalization" list constituted a third, distinct list of "subversive" organizations maintained by the government during World War II.[60]

On September 1, 1943, the new interdepartmental committee created by President Roosevelt on February 9, 1943, to coordinate governmental action against subversive infiltration (the ICEI, or the Gaston Committee, after its chair, Assistant Secretary of the Treasury Herbert Gaston) sent to all government agencies an "Outline of Policy and Procedures," which was published on September 11. No doubt reflecting recent House actions, the committee seemingly ignored Biddle's vigorous public rejection of relying solely upon membership in allegedly "subversive" organizations as a basis for investigation, instead urging the "dismissal or action looking toward dismissal" of federal employees on the basis of either "credible evidence of membership in an organization which has been authoritatively held to be subversive, i.e., one which advocates the overthrow of the Government of the U.S. by force or violence" or of similar personal advocacy. The guidelines added that even past "subversive" memberships or advocacy should not be disregarded absent "evidence satisfactorily showing complete severance of the membership or the discontinuance of the advocacy" long enough before "inception of the case" to render such activity "not repugnant to the pertinent statutes." However, the committee cautioned that employees should not be penalized due to "mere suspicion unauthenticated by credible evidence" and should be protected "against undue harassment, unwarranted dismissal and the unfounded stigma of disloyalty."[61]

The Gaston Committee's guidelines echoed Biddle's earlier letter to Rep. Kerr by maintaining that the DOJ had listed as "subversive" only the CP, Bund, and Silver Shirts, as well as "certain organizations found to be dominated by enemy governments or organizations," information concerning which would be "furnished to the employing agencies in connection with specific cases if it appears from the investigative reports or the records that the information would be pertinent." Clearly referring to alleged "Communist front" groups (which had in fact been secretly listed as "subversive" by the DOJ in 1942 and would be again so listed—publicly—in the Truman AGLOSO beginning in December 1947), the committee declared that membership in "certain other organizations whose history reveals participation in greater or lesser degree by subversive groups has been regarded as sufficient to warrant" FBI investigation and reports to employing agencies, but was "not to be regarded as determinative of subversive membership or advocacy" without evidence of personal advocacy of overthrow of the government or membership in one of the groups which the committee had just defined as "subversive." Endorsing a policy already in force, the committee recommended that all accused employees be given a hearing, but added that the DOJ had "taken the position that the [FBI] investigative reports should not be shown" to allegedly subversive employees, although "formal charges should be preferred in writing," giving reasons in "as particular detail as the circumstances admit," a restriction that severely limited or made it impossible for those accused to defend themselves. The committee offered to give advisory guidance to the employing agencies on "questions of subversive membership or advocacy," but made clear that final responsibility rested with them. In a February 12, 1944, report to Biddle, Gaston reported that thus far finality had been reached in 165 allegations involving "subversive" activity on the part of federal employees, with 141 individuals exonerated, 5 "discharged as subversive," and 3 subjected to "other disciplinary action." In 16 cases, proceedings were suspended because of "resignation or separation for reasons not within the purview" of the ICEI.[62]

What turned out to be the last major public World War II uproar related to allegations of subversive government infiltration erupted following publication in the December 2, 1943, *Congressional Record* of CSC guidelines for the interrogation of new applicants for federal employment. Two days earlier, Rep. Fred Busbey, a conservative Illinois Republican, had leaked them to the press, while demanding a House inquiry and declaring that if the guidelines were allowed to stand, "hundreds of known Communists" on the federal payroll would "rejoice" and "will never be eliminated," while the door would be opened to "let unlimited numbers of subversive elements in to join those already on the Federal payroll, to undermine and destroy the Government." The guidelines, which the CSC stated had been originally issued in August 1942 in almost identical form, instructed CSC staff that a government applicant should not be asked general questions concerning his "political philosophy, such as whether he believes in capitalism or what his opinion is regarding certain events of a current or historical nature," about anything involving "union membership, union associations or union activities" or about "any organization unless it has been authoritatively designated as subversive." CSC investigators were directed to "obtain all information" pertinent to establishing whether an applicant was a CP "line conformist," but were instructed not to ask about reading matter, "especially the [CP] *Daily Worker* and all radical and liberal publications," about social interaction with blacks, or about sympathies concerning the Spanish loyalists or "membership or interest in" the League of Women Shoppers, the SP, and the ACLU. They were also directed not to ask about several alleged "Communist fronts" that were either on Biddle's AGLOSO (i.e., the WBA) or would be placed on the Truman AGLOSO (i.e., the Abraham Lincoln Brigade [ALB] and the Harry Bridges Defense Committee). The guidelines vehemently stressed that "the whole matter" of the Spanish Civil War should be "scrupulously avoided" as "having any bearing on pro-communism," yet within five years numerous pro-Spanish loyalist relief groups would be listed on the Truman AGLOSO. The guidelines provided a short history of the CP "line" and declared that "a good definition of a Communist" was "one who has followed" it "through one or more changes."[63]

In December 1943, CSC Commissioner Arthur Flemming was subjected to hostile questioning from several congressmen about the CSC guidelines during an appearance before the House Committee on Appropriations. Thus, Rep. Joseph Starnes (D-AL) asked if the guidelines were "part and parcel of a policy that seemed to prevail" in the DOJ of "elaborate whitewash" to help retain government employees whose loyalty "to say the least, was seriously under question." However, Flemming flatly rejected this suggestion, declaring that the results of the department's 1942 inquiry had been "almost negligible," yet the CSC had "gone ahead vigorously pursuing the policy that has created all kinds of enemies for us," who assert that "we are in fact, persecuting genuine liberals and progressives," by "insisting that these [subversive] people should be kept out of the Government." In particular, Flemming declared, a CP member or follower of the "line" was classified as "potentially disloyal" and "has no place in the Government, in time of war or time of peace," but classifying persons as disloyal could not be "determined solely on the basis of the organizations to which he has belonged," because, concerning popular fronts, "it is still necessary to establish whether he is one of the genuine progressives or liberals within the organizations, or whether he is" a CP "liner."[64]

The controversy over the CSC guidelines died down almost immediately, a clear sign that by late 1943 the "subversives in government" issue had temporarily lost a considerable amount of its political élan, as the Russian-American alliance against Germany increasingly eclipsed memories of the Nazi-Soviet pact. Thus, there was no discernible aftermath to the public release of an "annual report" to Biddle by the Gaston Committee in February 1944, which concluded that federal workers were overwhelmingly "loyal" and that there was "no real basis for supposing that the Government harbors any significant number of persons who are members of organizations which advocate the overthrow of the government by force or violence or who personally so advocate." The committee reported that of 301 cases of incumbent employees investigated by federal agencies for alleged subversive affiliations or advocacy since its formation a year earlier, only five had led to dismissals and three to other forms of disciplinary action. However, it added that the entire problem was complicated because different agencies' approaches to the loyalty issue differed "more or less radically," accused employees could not see investigative reports that formed the basis of allegations against them, the names and background of informants was withheld from both the agencies and the employees, making it difficult to evaluate "information emanating from sources entirely anonymous," and there was frequently "uncertainty as to what are the real factual issues presented by the case." All of these problems would recur during the Truman loyalty program instituted three years later.[65]

In April 1944, the CSC, which investigated applicants for federal jobs (but not current employees), reported that out of 200,000 persons investigated during the previous four years, 1,011 were excluded due to doubts about their loyalty, including 563 found "ineligible because of their affiliations" with the CP or "adherence" to its "line" and 448 barred because they "belonged to or have followed policies sponsored" by pro-Axis organizations. According to CSC Commissioner

Flemming, the CSC had "resolved all reasonable doubts relative to loyalty in favor of the Government," using the CP "line test" to identify Communists and excluding as pro-Axis "those who, up to Pearl Harbor, were vigorously and openly espousing the Nazi and Fascist philosophy of life."[66]

From a political standpoint, perhaps the strongest evidence that the "reds in government" issue had by late 1944 lost a considerable amount of whatever potency it had gained in the late 1930s was delivered by the voters in that year's election campaign, during which Republican charges of alleged Communist domination of the Roosevelt administration were a major theme. Thus, Republican presidential candidate Thomas Dewey charged that the "communists are seizing control of the New Deal, through which they aim to control the government of the U.S." and that President Roosevelt had become a "political prisoner" of the Communists. Despite such allegations, Roosevelt was reelected to an unprecedented fourth term with over 53 percent of the vote (down only about 1 percent from 1940), while Democrats retained control of both houses of Congress by large margins, picking up twenty-four seats in the House and losing two Senate seats. Dies himself decided not to run for reelection and two Dies Committee members lost reelection bids.[67]

With the end of World War II and such seemingly clear signs of easing concern over alleged subversive infiltration of the government, the Gaston Committee recommended in October 1945 that it be abolished, with its functions of advising and coordinating government agencies handling "subversive" matters turned over to the CSC. On December 26, 1945, new attorney general Tom Clark sent Budget Bureau director Harold Smith a proposed executive order to implement the committee's recommendations. However, explosive events in 1946 soon drastically shook the view of both the public and governmental officials, as public opinion polls clearly recorded. Thus, while in 1940, during the Nazi-Soviet pact, 67 percent of Americans felt CP membership should be outlawed, only 44 percent held this view in 1946, but that percentage skyrocketed to 62 percent by 1947. Similarly, in 1940 only 32 percent felt CP members should be "allowed to speak on the radio," but this figure jumped to 49 percent in 1945, then plummeted to 36 percent in 1948.[68]

Eruption of a New Red Scare and the Making of the Truman AGLOSO, 1945–1947

A rapid, major deterioration in the civil liberties climate and the reemergence of the "subversives in government" issue between the end of World War II and early 1947 was largely attributable to four intertwined and reinforcing factors: (1) the drastic postwar deterioration of relations with Russia and the consequent eruption of the Cold War; (2) a growing obsession with perceived dangers posed by internal subversion in general and Soviet and CP espionage in particular, fueled by reports, some public and some held within the government, of Russian spy operations in North America, accompanied by a new CP "hard" line that echoed general Cold War tensions; (3) postwar economic tensions and frustrations in the United States, including massive inflation and a major strike wave in 1946, which fostered a general sense of anger and anxiety; and (4) perhaps most importantly, deliberate attempts by a powerful coalition of American conservatives, notably the FBI, significant elements in the business community, the Catholic Church, and, especially, an increasingly politically desperate Republican Party, to ignite a domestic Red Scare, motivated by a complex mixture of sincere belief, self-promotion, and a drive to discredit political enemies and gain political power.

The World War II American-Soviet alliance and the CP's fervent wartime support for American foreign policy fostered a general, although by no means universal, aura of goodwill toward Russia, which Americans were led to believe by their leaders would continue after the war. The rapid postwar deterioration of American-Soviet relations therefore came as a considerable shock to many Americans, especially as simultaneous revelations of apparently widespread Russian espionage activities suggested a serious domestic internal threat that revived fears of subversive infiltration of the government. Although the mid-1945 "*Amerasia* affair," involving massive leaking of classified government documents to a magazine focused on Far Eastern affairs, did not involve transmittal of information to foreign regimes, it suggested widespread espionage in the public mind, especially because Republicans and the conservative press repeatedly claimed that the Truman administration had engaged in a major cover-up. Fears of Russian espionage were far more realistically stoked with the early 1946 revelation of a Soviet spy ring in Canada, involving attempts to steal atomic secrets, which clearly had tentacles reaching into the United States. Privately, at about the same time, FBI director Hoover informed Truman about allegations of widespread Russian espionage in the United States made by two CP defectors, Elizabeth Bentley and Whittaker Chambers, during the previous fifteen years. The eruption of the Cold War and growing public alarm concerning Soviet espionage inevitably had a highly negative impact upon the CP's image in the United States, which was further reinforced when, under clear influence from Moscow, wartime CP leader Earl Browder was deposed and the party suddenly switched policies from what had amounted to an acceptance of capitalism and strong backing for an American-Soviet alliance to attacks on American "imperialism" and complete support for Russian foreign policy. Nonetheless, before the CP came under massive political and legal assaults, which markedly increased after early 1947, it retained about 75,000 members and considerable visibility, for example making 100 local radio broadcasts and two national network broadcasts in April 1947, alone. Another factor that exacerbated tensions after 1945 was the war's strained economic aftermath. In 1946, the largest strike wave in American history erupted, as workers who had overwhelmingly complied with no-strike pledges and engaged in wage restraint during the war erupted in anger as price levels jumped an estimated 33 percent above prewar levels. At least partly because business and Republican spokesmen stressed Communist activity among CIO unions, the strikes generated a wave of antiunion sentiment and led to both state and congressional passage of major antilabor legislation following Republican victories in the 1946 elections, during which many Republicans attacked Democratic opponents for being "soft" on communism.[69]

In fact, probably the single most important factor in explaining a sudden, intense deterioration in the civil liberties climate after early 1946, which increasingly featured allegations of Communist infiltration of the government, was the deliberate effort of a broad coalition of American conservatives, led by the Catholic Church, "big business," the FBI, and the Republican Party, to promote this issue. Although undoubtedly coalition members sincerely held intense anti-Communist beliefs, they also all had self-interested reasons to promote a Red Scare and did so extremely effectively. Thus, in October 1946, the U.S. Chamber of Commerce, representing "big business," published a widely circulated and publicized report (with the covert assistance of the FBI) that stressed subversive infiltration of labor and government, thus discrediting its trade union and political adversaries. The Catholic Church also utilized covert FBI assistance to initiate a similar crusade in 1946, partly to influence American foreign policy concerning Communist oppression of the Church in eastern Europe. The FBI simultaneously initiated its own major anti-Communist campaign, using leaks to cooperative journalists and congressmen to seek increasing public approval, congressional appropriations, and general power and influence by stressing its indispensability in fighting the red menace. Finally, the Republican Party, increasingly desperate due to its exclusion from the presidency and control of Congress for fifteen years, perceived a huge political benefit from tarring the Truman administration as "soft on communism" both in its foreign policy and by its alleged toleration of subversive infiltration of the government.[70]

In early 1945, the House of Representatives, under the effective control of a Republican–conservative Democratic coalition, for the first time made HUAC a standing rather than temporary committee and authorized its Civil Service Committee (HCSC) to study loyalty among government employees. These two committees both sprang into action amid the growing domestic and international anxieties of the 1946 congressional election year. Thus, HUAC investigated several alleged Communist "fronts" and an HCSC subcommittee concluded, after brief mid-1946 hearings, that American security was threatened by the federal employment of persons of "questioned loyalty" and that a government commission was immediately required to establish a "complete and uniform" program to protect the government against "individuals whose primary loyalty is to governments other than our own." During closed July 1946 hearings, CSC head Flemming told the subcommittee that, in the light of congressional passage of the 1939 Hatch Act and other legislation, the CSC had "no difficulty" in determining that CP members or followers of the CP "line," along with "persons actively associated with groups or organizations whose primary loyalty was to Nazi, Fascist or Japanese governments," should be barred from federal employment. He added that, so far as he knew, no CP members or followers of the CP "line" had been rated by the CSC as eligible for federal employment since 1939. Flemming indicated considerable confusion when asked about official governmental lists of "organizations regarded as subversive, or membership in which would show disloyalty." He accurately testified that the CSC had not itself "established formally such a list" but then incorrectly declared that it had "used a list provided by the FBI" (which in fact came from Biddle) and inaccurately stated that the list did "not brand the organizations" but only provided a "pretty clear idea so that you can determine that here is a front organization and here is one that is on the borderline, and here is one made up of both types of people." Flemming vigorously defended the CSC policy of not asking federal applicants about their association with certain organizations, including pro–Spanish loyalist groups and those opposing the deportation of Harry Bridges, since, along with "some Communist Party liners," those "whom you and I would never in the world classify as anything but very good progressives or liberals" had supported the loyalists, and asking about Bridges "was just a way of asking a fellow whether he belongs to the CIO," in violation of CSC policy of not asking about labor affiliations. Within two years, Bridges defense organizations and pro-loyalist groups would be publicly listed in the Truman AGLOSO.[71]

During his testimony, Flemming placed considerable emphasis on an April 1946 federal district court ruling, *Friedman v. Schwellenbach* (65 F. Supp. 254, upheld on appeal eight months later in *Friedman v. Schwellenbach*, 159 F. 2d 22, 1946), as supporting the CSC approach to loyalty cases, including its use of the CP "line" test as well as its reliance on membership in allegedly "subversive" organizations. The case involved the 1944 loyalty firing of Morton Friedman from a high-level War Manpower Commission post. According to the CSC dismissal letter, Friedman's firing was "mainly" based on his past active membership in the APM, a Biddle AGLOSO group, as well as his personal "shift in attitude and point of view" concerning American intervention in World War II after the June 1941 Nazi attack on Russia. The court held that the CSC determination posed "no unlawful infringement" of Friedman's constitutional liberties and that its administrative finding of "reasonable doubt" concerning his loyalty could not be overturned, because "there were reasonable enough grounds to believe that [the APM] was formed" under CP auspices and "it could hardly be said that there could be no reasonable doubt of the loyalty of a member of a communist organization" who changed his position and "became an advocate of war when this country became allied with Russia, a communistic and totalitarian state." In June 1947 Flemming told the House Post Office and Civil Service Committee that between July 1, 1940, and March 31, 1947, 7 million people had been placed in federal jobs, of whom 1,313 were later rated ineligible "on loyalty grounds," including 714 who were fired because "they were either Communists or followers" of the CP "line."[72]

In the interim between the two federal court rulings upholding Friedman's dismissal, Republican allegations of Communist infiltration of the federal government became a central theme during the 1946 congressional elections, bundled together with attacks upon the Truman administration's economic record under the slogans of "Had enough?" and "communism vs. republicanism." Thus, Republican National chair Carroll Reece referred to the "pink puppets in control of the federal bureaucracy," while House Republican leader Joe Martin pledged to prioritize "cleaning out the Communists, their fellow travelers and parlor pinks from high positions in our Government." Republicans won a major election victory, gaining over fifty House and about a dozen Senate seats and winning control of both houses of Congress for the first time since 1932. On November 25, 1946, two weeks after the election, President Truman suddenly announced the creation of the President's Temporary Commission on Employee Loyalty (TCEL), charged with determining loyalty standards and procedures to remove or disqualify "any disloyal or subversive person" from federal service (news reported on the *New York Times* front page under the heading, "President Orders Purge of Disloyal from U.S. Posts"). Truman's action implemented the earlier HCSC recommendation, on which he had failed to act for four months, despite its endorsement by CSC chair Flemming. The TCEL included representatives of six government departments and was chaired by Special Assistant to the Attorney General A. Devitt Vanech, an official close to the FBI, who, according to White House Counsel Clark Clifford's memoirs, served as Director Hoover's "stooge" on the TCEL. TCEL Treasury Department representative Steven Spingarn, later presidential special assistant for internal security affairs, characterized Vanech as "unbelievably stupid," "incompetent," and "ignorant, semi-illiterate."[73]

Truman's timing, along with his request that the TCEL submit a report within two months, left both contemporary observers and historians with the conviction that he acted primarily to preempt further moves on the loyalty issue by the incoming Republican Congress. That Truman's concern about "subversive" infiltration of the government was more political than substantive is supported by his own contemporary statements, by Clifford's subsequent comments, and by the conclusions of specialist historians. For example, on February 28, 1947, shortly before he instituted a sweeping new federal loyalty program based on the TCEL report, Truman wrote to Pennsylvania governor George Earle that "people are very much wrought up about the Communist 'bugaboo' but I am of the opinion that the country is perfectly safe so far as Communism is concerned—we have too many sane people." In his 1991 memoirs, Clifford declared that his "greatest regret" from his decades-long government service was his failure to "make more of an effort to kill the loyalty program at its inception, in 1946–47." Making clear that neither he nor Truman viewed Communist infiltration of the federal government as a serious problem, Clifford added that the 1946 elections "weakened" Truman but "emboldened [FBI director] Hoover and his allies," and the creation of the TCEL resulted from "pressure" from Hoover and Attorney General Clark, who "constantly urged the President to expand the investigative authority of the FBI." In an earlier 1978 interview, Clifford said "his own feeling was there was not a serious loyalty problem," that the "whole thing was being manufactured," and that Truman felt "it was a lot of baloney" but established the loyalty program in early 1947 because "we had a presidential campaign ahead of us and here was a great issue, a very damaging issue, so he set up this whole kind of machinery." Historian Francis Thompson terms "the most important factor" in the TCEL's creation Truman's concern "over the congressional trend toward the introduction of more and more restrictive legislation in the loyalty field," while Truman biographer David McCullough concludes that "by acting first on the loyalty issue" Truman hoped to head off HUAC and "also, importantly, he wanted no accusations of administration softness on communism at home just as he was calling for a new hard approach to communism abroad [in his "Truman Doctrine" speech to Congress on March 9, 1947]."[74]

The TCEL's investigation consisted of sending form letters to about fifty government agencies and hearing oral testimony from Clark, FBI assistant director D. Milton Ladd, Gaston Committee chair Herbert Gaston, and HCSC members Edward Rees (R-KS) and Jesse Combs (D-TX). The most important testimony appears to have come from Clark, who told the TCEL that while there were only two dozen Communists employed by the federal government, the "gravity of the problem" should be weighed "from the viewpoint of the serious threat which even one disloyal person constitutes to the security of the government." Clark prepared for his testimony with the aid of a lengthy memorandum from Hoover which stated that, under the Hatch Act, the FBI only investigated a federal employee if there were "definite and substantial indications that he is a member of one of the 47 organizations declared subversive by the Attorney General" or upon allegations that he "personally advocated the overthrow of the government or belonged to an organization advocating such." Hoover indicated that the FBI had thus far made 6,021 loyalty investigations of federal employees, leading to 101 dismissals.[75]

The TCEL's original February 1 deadline was extended until early March due to serious disagreements over Vanech's first draft, circulated on January 28. In a January 29 memo to Clark, Hoover asked for clarification of draft language proposing that the "Attorney General shall currently furnish information to the [CSC] on all organizations suspected of subversive activities" and that the CSC "will disseminate this information to all the employment departments." Hoover said that he interpreted this to mean that the attorney general would provide the CSC "an interpretation" concerning suspected subversive groups but would not disclose any FBI information that "would be detrimental to this Bureau in conducting further investigation," a qualification which, in practice, meant that those accused of subversive affiliations would, as before, generally not be furnished the sources relied upon for such accusations. Treasury representative Spingarn felt that Vanech's draft, based primarily on FBI information, considerably exaggerated the threat of subversive infiltration and warned Vanech that "the best way to start a witch hunt of the World War I variety is to overpaint the picture in terms of numbers" and to create a prohibition that would "include, for example, everyone who reads the [liberal] publications *PM* or the *New Republic*" via "appeals to emotion and hysteria," rather than "vigorous, effective counter-intelligence."[76]

The final TCEL report, submitted to Truman on March 2, was toned down from the first draft but still clearly bore the mark of Clark and the FBI in its core conclusion that the possibility of even *one* disloyal employee justified a comprehensive federal loyalty program. Declaring that past government efforts to ban "disloyal persons from government employment" had proved "ineffective in dealing with subversive activities which employ subterfuge, propaganda, infiltration and deception," the TCEL held that the governmental presence of "any disloyal or subversive persons, or the attempt by any such person to obtain employment, presents a problem of such importance that it must be dealt with vigorously and effectively." It therefore recommended that all 2 million federal employees and all future applicants be investigated, with the standard for "refusal of employment" to be that "on all evidence, reasonable grounds exist for believing that the person involved is disloyal" to the American government. The TCEL never defined the key terms "disloyal" or "reasonable grounds," but recommended that six types of activities be considered in loyalty determinations, using the exact language of the January 28 draft: (1) sabotage, espionage, and related activities; (2) treason or sedition; (3) advocacy of illegal overthrow of the government; (4) intentional and unauthorized disclosure of confidential information; (5) serving a foreign government in preference to the interests of the United States, and (6) "Membership in, affiliation with or sympathetic association with any foreign or domestic organization, association, movement, group or combination of persons designated by the Attorney General as totalitarian, fascist, Communist or subversive, or as having adopted a policy of advocating or approving the commission of acts of force or violence to deny other persons their rights under the Constitution of the U.S., or as seeking to alter the form of Government of the U.S. by unconstitutional means."[77]

Although the sixth, or AGLOSO, category, was clearly modeled on the Biddle AGLOSO, which in turn was predicated on the 1939 Hatch Act, the TCEL report, which was published along with Truman's subsequent executive order establishing a federal Loyalty Program on March 21, 1947, never explicitly referred to the Biddle listing, cited no legislative basis for AGLOSO, and provided no guidelines concerning how it should be compiled, what standards should be used to determine which of the six distinct categories of suspect groups (such as "fascist" or "totalitarian") an organization should be placed in, or whether the list should be published. The AGLOSO recommendation had been originally proposed January 9 by a TCEL subcommittee, which recommended that the attorney general keep the CSC apprised on subversive organizations to assist with loyalty determinations. In an earlier memo to the TCEL subcommittee, Treasury representative Spingarn had recommended legislative authorization to empower "some very high governmental authority," such as the president or the attorney general, to "designate specifically from time to time those organizations which are deemed to be organizations which advocate the overthrow of our Government, or which are otherwise subversive to such an extent that membership in them alone should preclude government employment." However, he urged that such designations be "exercised very sparingly and with great discretion," and specifically that organizations "infiltrated with Communists, for example, should certainly not be so designated if they contain known non-Communists elements of any consequence," as any wholesale ban on such groups would stifle "progressive thought and programs" and discourage anti-Communist liberals and progressives from fighting Communist attempts "to infiltrate and dominate liberal and progressive organizations." He added that it would be difficult to "frame particularized statutory criteria of loyalty which will not cover many patriotic and thoroughly loyal Americans, notably those progressive and liberal elements who favor, and belong to organizations which favor, many of the policies" of the Roosevelt and Truman administrations.[78]

Truman accepted the major recommendation of the TCEL in his March 21, 1947, Executive Order 9835, which established a loyalty program requiring the investigation of all existing and prospective federal employees, regardless of their responsibilities or ability to access sensitive information (during the World War II program, while all applicants were screened for loyalty, incumbent employees were investigated only if specific allegations against them surfaced). According to Clifford, Truman's executive order was "drafted by the FBI and the DOJ and passed through my office before it was approved by the President." One of the final barriers to Truman's issuance of his order was apparently eliminated by the Supreme Court's refusal on March 17 to hear an appeal in *Friedman*, in which the lower federal courts had seemingly given the government carte blanche to fire federal employees on wide-ranging loyalty grounds. Thus, a front-page *Washington Post* article reported that the Court's inaction had established the "government's right to fire Communist fellow travelers" and paved the way for issuance of a presidential order that federal officials had "been told for nearly a month" would be "issued momentarily" and would lay down a "clear-cut Administration policy to cleanse the Government of disloyal employees."[79]

Executive Order 9835 received nationwide front-page coverage on March 23, with screaming newspaper headlines such as "Purge of Disloyal on U.S. Pay Roll Ordered" and "Truman Orders Disloyal Employees Fired." While declaring that the loyalty of "the overwhelming majority of all Government employees is beyond question" and that "protection from unfounded accusations of disloyalty must be afforded" them, the executive order declared that the "presence within the Government service of any disloyal or subversive person constitutes a threat to our democratic processes" and required loyalty screenings of all present or prospective government employees, using the "reasonable grounds" standards and all of the specific loyalty criteria recommended by the TCEL, including the exact text of its suggested AGLOSO categories. The order also established a Loyalty Review Board (LRB), which would have the power to advise all federal agencies in making loyalty determinations, with the DOJ directed to furnish the LRB with a listing of all organizations "which the Attorney General, after appropriate investigation and determination," designated as belonging to one of the six AGLOSO categories; the LRB was charged with disseminating "such information to all departments and agencies." Each employee was granted the right to a hearing if "charged with being disloyal," as well as to written notice informing him "of the nature of the charges against him in sufficient detail, so that he will be enabled to prepare his defense." However, Truman's order added that the charges need only be "as complete as, in the discretion of the employing department or agency, security considerations permit" and that, in submitting information to government officials, investigative agencies such as the FBI could, at their discretion, "refuse to disclose the name of confidential informants" if they provided "sufficient information" so that government agencies could "adequate[ly]" evaluate the furnished information. In practice, because charges were usually based on FBI reports and the bureau was generally unwilling to divulge its sources and methods or make its agents or informants available for testimony, employees charged with disloyalty were usually provided only extremely vague charges, not told the sources of allegations against them, and denied the right to cross-examine their (unknown) accusers.[80]

Between the March 22, 1947, public announcement of the Truman loyalty program and the massively publicized December 1947 issuance of the "new" AGLOSO, the DOJ began compiling AGLOSO behind a thick curtain of secrecy that has still not yet been entirely lifted, as many relevant department documents have apparently been destroyed, were never transferred to the National Archives, or remain classified. Nonetheless, the process by which the Truman AGLOSO was compiled can be at least partly patched together from surviving FBI documents and statements made by DOJ officials after the list was published. These sources suggest that the FBI and the DOJ devoted massive resources to compiling AGLOSO under what was perceived as enormous political pressure, that both agencies felt overwhelmed by the task, and that, ultimately, decisions were made in a unclear and time-pressured manner that paved the way for years of subsequent chaotic confusion and contradiction. As the designation process for organizations got under way, a power struggle erupted between the FBI and the CSC over which agency would play the key role in investigating individual federal employees. Although originally Truman favored giving the CSC the primary role, FBI director Hoover, in memos sent to Clark in March 1947, threatened to "withdraw from this field of investigation rather than to engage in a tug of war" with the CSC. The DOJ and the FBI subsequently successfully lobbied Congress to give the bureau dominance over the opposition of Truman, who was characterized by a top aide in May 1947 as "very strongly anti-FBI" and fearing that the bureau might become a "Gestapo." On May 9, Truman marked on a memo to his aide Clark Clifford and that "J. Edgar will in all probability get this backward looking Congress to give him what he wants. It's dangerous." However, Truman ultimately acquiesced and in early November directed the FBI to make all loyalty investigations with "no exceptions."[81]

The authority granted the FBI by the loyalty program and, especially, AGLOSO, combined with a general lax supervision of the bureau by the DOJ, was used by the FBI during the next thirty years as key basis for its increasingly virtually unbounded investigation of individuals and groups throughout American society, including the widespread use of a variety of illegal burglaries, wiretaps, and other intrusive means. Thus, in a July 19, 1966, memo, FBI assistant director William Sullivan wrote to his fellow assistant director Cartha DeLoach that although burglaries were "clearly illegal," they had been used because they "represent an invaluable technique in combating subversive activities" and "through the use of this technique we have on numerous occasions been able to obtain material [such as mailing and membership lists] held highly secret and closely guarded by subversive groups and organizations." During 1975 testimony to a Senate Committee, FBI official F. J. Baumgardner, who headed the Internal Security Section of the bureau's Intelligence Division during the 1950s and early 1960s, reported that, although no AGLOSO listings were ever made after 1955, the primary justification for continued FBI investigations of Communist "infiltration" of groups was so that it could advise the DOJ about possible AGLOSO designations.[82]

FBI documents (obtained six decades later under the Freedom of Information Act) indicate that on or about April 3, 1947, the bureau, in response to a March 27 request from Assistant Attorney General Vanech for a compilation of "organizations thought to be subversive," provided a list, without any accompanying write-ups, of forty-one organizations "thought to be most dangerous within the purview of the recent Executive Order." According to a March 29 internal FBI document, these included the CP, thirty-eight alleged "front" groups, the Nazi Party, and the Ku Klux Klan (KKK). In an April 3 memo to Attorney General

Clark, the FBI reported that it had previously sent the DOJ "complete reports" on the CP and "all of the major communist fronts," totaling "some 50 organizations," a grouping that included the forty-one organizations listed in response to Vanech's request. The FBI subsequently apparently decided to submit new reports on the thirty-eight alleged "front" groups, with AGLOSO designations specifically in mind; an April 14 memo to Hoover from Assistant Director Edward Tamm reported that the bureau was submitting memoranda on two of the organizations "today" and thereafter "about 10 memoranda" weekly would "go through to the Attorney General until we have covered the list of some 38 organizations." Reflecting the dismissive attitude toward the department that the FBI often evinced, Tamm reported that although the bureau had already "submitted complete reports upon each of these organizations to the Department, it would be naïve of us to believe that the Department will do any research work on these files and we know that the decision as to the subversive nature of the organization will be predicated solely and exclusive upon what we include or exclude in our [new] memoranda." Therefore, Tamm told Hoover, "we have been trying to be extraordinarily thorough and exactly accurate in every statement, since the determination of an organization's future character will be solely dependent upon what we say or do not say about it" (to which Hoover responded in handwriting, "I most certainly agree with this").[83]

The FBI kept adding to its list of organizations for DOJ AGLOSO consideration during 1947, while increasingly groaning about the workload required for compiling the reports. A September 26 memo from FBI security division agent J. Patrick Coyne to Assistant Director Ladd reported that the bureau had already completed twenty-five organizational "summaries" for Clark, was completing eighteen more, and needed to consider sixty-six additional organizations (thus creating a list "considerably longer" than that originally submitted for consideration), but would not prepare summaries for the forty-seven Biddle AGLOSO organizations, making a total of "145 organizations being considered in connection with the Executive Order." Coyne indicated that twenty FBI agents had worked on AGLOSO designations between June 26 and September 24. On September 29, Tamm informed Hoover that the FBI had submitted to Clark the names of the sixty-six additional organizations referenced by Coyne, and, although the bureau had previously forwarded material on them to the department, the bureau was planning to submit new memoranda on forty-six of them, as well as on "certain additional organizations now dormant or relatively small and inactive but in which government employees might be members or active." However, Tamm suggested that the FBI consider halting any further such submissions, both because of the heavy workload they were imposing and because they would "appear to constitute a needless duplication of work" that he had just learned was also being performed by the DOJ. Tamm reported that Coyne and FBI official H. B. Fletcher had just been advised by DOJ Criminal Division official Raymond

Whearty that a "large staff" of department attorneys had compiled a list of "some 470-odd organizations upon which the Bureau had submitted material to the Department over a period of years" and was planning to submit to Clark by October 3 "memoranda and recommendations as to the subversive or non-subversive nature of some 200 organizations," including "all of the organizations upon which we have prepared or contemplate preparing memoranda." By halting its summaries, Tamm told Hoover, the FBI could "eliminate a great volume of work in the Bureau," which he described as reaching gargantuan proportions, involving "searches running into the thousands" and the "withdrawing of literally thousands of files." The "main" Joint Anti-Fascist Refugee Committee (JAFRC) file alone, Tamm reported, included "more than 70 volumes, with some 4,000 cross references to other files necessary for search and examination," and "the same approximate figures apply to the Bureau's" ALB search, with "3,000 or 4,000 additional searches and files" necessary for "the main officials of each file and the references to them." In response, Hoover marked on Tamm's memo, "I agree. Ok."[84]

On September 30, Tamm informed Hoover that he had just talked at "great length" with Assistant Attorney General and Criminal Division Head T. Vincent Quinn, who was supervising the DOJ's AGLOSO deliberations. According to Tamm, Quinn confirmed that the department had set a deadline for announcing "the subversive list," which could come at "any time from now on," and that "it would be unnecessary, in the light of the obvious duplication of the work being done simultaneously" by the FBI and a "staff of 30 lawyers" in the Criminal Division, for the bureau to prepare further organizations memoranda. Hoover thereupon wrote Quinn on September 30 to report that the bureau would discontinue preparing "summary memoranda" of organizations "of potential interest" for AGLOSO designation, since the department's "large staff of lawyers" had "undoubtedly reviewed all of the reports, memoranda and other material submitted to you over the past several years by the Bureau, which is identical with that" being relied upon for the FBI summaries.[85]

Only the sketchiest information on the DOJ's internal processes concerning AGLOSO determinations was made public when the first Truman list was published in early December 1947, but additional relevant information survives in archival material, subsequent oral histories and in congressional testimony by department officials. According to a November 24, 1947, letter from Clark to the LRB that was published on December 5 along with the Truman AGLOSO, the department had "compiled all available data" concerning organizations under review for AGLOSO, but the FBI was the only specific source of information mentioned. Testifying before a House Appropriations subcommittee on December 8, 1947, along with his top aides, Clark related that in carrying out his assigned responsibilities "to pick out organizations that I thought were subversive," department attorneys had considered "reports which would fill up this room" and that it had taken them "from 3 to 4 months to go through stacks of memoranda and consolidate this information." According to Criminal Division Head Quinn, ultimately 33 attorneys, borrowed from the Internal Security Section and other Criminal Division sections, of a total of 106 division lawyers, were detailed to work "full time and overtime" on the designations, with "perhaps another 100 or more organizations" yet to "go through the mill, and it is going to occupy a great deal of time by attorneys who are going to have to neglect some of their duties" to "get this list out." Similarly, a May 8, 1947, memo to Clark from Assistant Attorney General Theron Caudle reported that "a minimum of 34" Criminal Division lawyers were assigned to AGLOSO designations and "it will seriously affect the functions [of the Division] and many other important things will have to be neglected," so "if anybody criticizes us you will know the reason why." DOJ official Phillip Perlman stated in 1954 that James McInerney, head of the Criminal Division's Internal Security Section, coordinated the work of the lawyers.[86]

At the December 1947 House hearing, Criminal Division official Whearty reported that the thirty-three attorneys detailed to AGLOSO had worked "full time and including in some instances Saturdays and Sundays" between September 19 and October 31" and had thus far considered a total of 449 organizations for designation. He added that "if you took the number of organizations covered in that period of time and divided them by the number of people working on that, that it took close to a week for one man to process a little over, on an average, of two and a fraction organizations," not including "the stenographic personnel necessary to carry on the burden of the work, such as typing or so on." Whearty also reported that, while the department had already acted on all "those [organizations] which are the most important" and on "which we have the most information," it had "just scratched the surface" and there yet remained "probably 2,000 to 2,500 organizations which may have to be processed in the period of the next two years," a task that would take "one man a period of some 1,000 months." Clark told the hearing that once the thirty-three lawyers had studied FBI reports and written up each organization under consideration, "they were gone over" with Quinn and then with his first assistant, Peyton Ford, then with Ford and "the other five assistants [attorneys general] together with the Solicitor General and the Assistant Solicitor General." During testimony before a July 15, 1949, Senate Judiciary subcommittee hearing, Clark said that if his assistants "all agreed [about an organization] I went over them and I would place them on the list," but if not "we would have a meeting, usually at lunch, at which we would discuss each of the organizations that was not agreed upon" and then "might ask for more information from the FBI or whatever sources furnished the information." In 1975, Clark stated that if any of his top aides objected to designating an organization, it was not included on the list. According to an undated DOJ internal memo that apparently dates from early 1953, after the first two AGLOSO lists were issued in late 1947 and early 1948, "a simplified procedure was established whereby the initial review was made in the Internal Security Section of the Criminal Division with final determination still being made by the Attorney General."[87]

According to 1952 DOJ documents, in drawing up the first Truman AGLOSO, the department incorporated "in toto" the 1943 Biddle AGLOSO, without any review of Biddle's determinations and sometimes without any documentation about them. Thus, an October 1952 memo by Assistant Attorney General Charles Murray, head of the Criminal Division, declared that "no reexamination of [the Biddle] cases was made prior to their re-designation in 1947," and, with regard to many of the "Fascist" organizations, "incomplete or no files whatever have been located in the department and the basis upon which they were designated originally is unknown, save as summary memoranda prepared at the time may still be in existence." In a subsequent memo, Murray said that "organizations which had been previously designated" by Biddle were included in the 1947 AGLOSO "in accordance with recommendations which had been made to the Attorney General by someone other than the Criminal Division and I am not familiar nor does the file reflect the basis for the inclusion of these organizations." He added that not even "supporting memoranda" survived for "every one of these organizations."[88]

Touching on what would soon become one of the most controversial aspects of the "list," Clark related in his December 1947 congressional testimony that making AGLOSO designations was "a hard job and it is a trying job for the reason that we did not" grant organizations proposed for designation "any hearings," a procedure "a little bit contrary to our usual conception of democratic process so I wanted to be careful about it." The hearings issue, along with how to define criteria for designations and whether or not to publish AGLOSO, were all considered behind the scenes by the FBI and the DOJ during 1947, but available documentation on these subjects is extremely fragmentary. A March 31 internal FBI memo from Assistant Director Louis Nichols, reporting the views of the FBI "executive conference" (most top bureau officials aside from Hoover), reported a "unanimous" recommendation that the bureau take "no position" concerning whether hearings should be granted before declaring an organization "subversive or not subversive." However, an April 1, 1947, FBI memo from Nichols to top Hoover aide and FBI associate director Clyde Tolson reported that Hoover had "very grave doubts" about granting hearings and that Clark had been advised through a subordinate that he should give this matter "his most mature and considered reflection, bearing in mind that Attorney General Biddle did not give such hearings" and that, if hearings were granted, the attorney general "would be confronted with the possibility of facing court action, of having writs served upon him, of a constant round of bickering, vilification, pressure and abuse." In a 1961 speech, Clark, by then a Supreme Court Justice, declared that he had reached the same conclusion, namely, that if hearings were granted, organizations proposed for listing would (in the words of a reporter's summary of his presentation) "so contest and delay the list that it would never be gotten out." Clark added, "Perhaps we should, as I look back at it now, have given the parties an opportunity to be heard before we issued [AGLOSO]." (In a 1969 interview, Clark vehemently but incorrectly claimed that listed groups were given hearings and that he had personally attended two of them.)[89]

The fragmentary available evidence strongly suggests that Clark originally decided in the early spring of 1947 not to publish AGLOSO but subsequently changed his mind. In his April 1 memo to Tolson, Nichols reported that Hoover's view was "serious consideration would have to be given to the propriety of making such a list public," but that a top department official had told him, after talking to Clark, that the latter "was going to go very slow and doubted whether he would give out such a list." According to anonymous department officials quoted in late March and mid-April press reports, AGLOSO would probably or definitely not be published, as that would lead designated groups to go underground or change their names; Assistant Attorney General Vanech was quoted by name in late March as declaring that the list would probably "never" be officially released. Clark told reporters on May 10 that he was undecided whether or not to publish AGLOSO, but then announced on May 31 that it would be published, although "We don't want this to develop into a witch hunt." No public explanation was ever offered by the department for this decision, although Assistant to the Attorney General Ford, in a January 24, 1950, letter responding to the ACLU's request that the department denounce the utilization of AGLOSO by "non-governmental agencies and organizations having no relation" to the federal loyalty program, declared, "A great deal of consideration was given to the question of publication of this list at the outset, and it was finally decided that whether or not" the government published AGLOSO, the list "would gain just as widespread publication through other means." According to Ford, this was demonstrated by "experience with the original list published by Attorney General Biddle" (in fact, despite the unauthorized *Congressional Record* disclosure of information on a dozen Biddle AGLOSO organizations, the other three dozen Biddle listings were never disclosed until the Truman AGLOSO was issued in late 1947, and the existence of the Biddle AGLOSO was barely publicized). In an August 24, 1954, letter to a journalist, Assistant Attorney General and Internal Security Division (ISD) head William Tompkins offered the entirely different explanation that AGLOSO designations were "necessarily public information since Federal employees and applicants for Federal employment should know whether they will be questioned concerning" their affiliations.[90]

The available documentary record concerning the criteria used by the department to designate AGLOSO organizations is fragmentary, but the best evidence, above all the fact that department lawyers sporadically wrote lengthy memos on this subject for the next twenty-five years, is that no ultimate conclusion was ever reached. The earliest such example, a May 8, 1947, memo from Assistant Attorney General Caudle to Hoover, declared that while the department had "received voluminous reports from the [FBI] and I have many men assigned to study the various organizations" under AGLOSO consideration, the "only way to intelligently approach this subject" would be to establish "certain standards by which organizations can be adjudged subversive or not," and while the department had given "much thought to these standards," he wanted Hoover's views since he had been "unable to find any basis or yardstick" that Biddle had used to "determine what constituted a subversive organization." Two months later Caudle sent Assistant to the Attorney General Douglas McGregor what he termed the "latest" AGLOSO standards prepared by the Criminal Division to determine if organizations were "subversive." Consisting of two double-spaced pages, the "organizational standards" included some relatively specific criteria, such as advocating the overthrow of the government and approving the use of force to deny others their constitutional rights, along with some extremely vague ones, such as "consistently opposing the enactment of, or advocating the repeal of laws and measures designed to strengthen and improve the security of the U.S." and "closely cooperating with, supporting and furthering the aims of any subversive organization, association or combination of persons."[91]

On July 24, 1947, McGregor was sent another set of proposed standards in a nine-page memo from special assistants to the attorney general David Edelstein and Joseph Duggan, which included both "broad general criteria" for AGLOSO listing as well as "specific criteria" for categorizing designated organizations, as seemingly required by Truman's order, as "totalitarian," "fascist," "communist," or "subversive." Edelstein and Duggan began by noting the difficulty of seeking to establish adequate AGLOSO criteria, as apparently they were intended to "embrace the vast area of political, economic and social action which too often reside in the operation of the mind" and would therefore inherently be "particularly imperfect" and "unfortunately limited in scope by human frailty." Given this orientation, Edelstein and Duggan inevitably ended up with extraordinarily vague proposed standards. Thus, one of their suggested "broad general criteria" for designating organizations was an overall conclusion that the "actual principles" of an organization could be "deemed hostile or inimical to the American form of government, orderly democratic processes and the constitutional guarantee of individual liberty, so as to lead a person of reasonable prudence and discretion to conclude that such principles are opposed to or in contravention of the principles of the Constitution or laws or the U.S." Other suggested "broad" criteria were the overall conclusion that organizations lacked "bona-fide allegiance to the government of the U.S." or "attachment to the principles of the Constitution," or that they were "concerned with the success or failure of foreign political and economic experiments which would result in the destruction or abolition of the republican form of government guaranteed by the Constitution." The memo defined "subversive" as seeking to "undermine confidence in, pervert or corrupt the integrity of the operations of, overthrow, ruin, betray, cause the downfall of, change by revolution or force, or subordinate to a foreign power the government of the U.S.," regardless of the "means or methods adopted to effectuate such purposes." How to define the six specific Truman AGLOSO categories continued to be the subject of memos until the 1970s, while the first clear indication that even "broad" AGLOSO criteria were ever adopted dates only from 1952 (as discussed below).[92]

While the DOJ processed AGLOSO designations during the summer and fall of 1947, a public debate began as to whether the government should undertake to create an official list of "dubious" organizations at all and, if so, how this should be done. However, probably due to a combination of growing anti-Communist feelings and the largely abstract nature of the subject in the absence of a concrete listing, this discussion was oddly muted and limited. Most conservative voices remained silent in apparent tacit approval of the forthcoming AGLOSO list, while liberal organizations and leaders generally focused on details of how AGLOSO would be compiled and whether or not it would be published, without directly attacking its fundamental concept. The result was that, both before and after the first Truman AGLOSO was released, almost all of the frontal attacks on the basic concept that the government was entitled to issue lists of allegedly disloyal organizations came from targeted groups such as the CP, whose leaders denounced AGLOSO on December 7 as taking the country "a long way toward fascism and police state totalitarianism."[93]

The major arguments stressed by liberal groups both before and after the publication of the Truman AGLOSO were that designated organizations should be entitled to a hearing and/or review of some kind before being listed, that clear standards were required for designations, and that the listing should be published, so that present and prospective federal employees would know which affiliations might jeopardize their jobs. Such arguments may have convinced DOJ officials to discard their apparent original intention to keep AGLOSO secret (as had been the case, with considerable success, during World War II). If so, this was a highly ironic outcome: above all, it was the publication of the Truman AGLOSO that transformed a listing supposedly solely designed to help screen federal employees into what effectively became an official government blacklist, whose influence spread across American society, severely damaged or destroyed the listed organizations, and cast a general pall over freedom of association and speech. The ACLU, in a statement adopted by its board of directors in early April 1947, declared that the proposed AGLOSO posed the "greatest threat to civil liberties" because it appeared to be "without limit" and without "even any requirement that the list be made public so that an individual affected might not innocently join an organization already on the blacklist." Moreover, according to the ACLU, "suspect organizations should not be blacklisted" absent a "hearing which observes all of those safeguards commonly regarded" as necessary to insure due process of law, and the attorney general should "create an advisory panel of well known citizens outside Government service to act as hearing judges" to determine "whether an organization should be blacklisted" and "as far as feasible the list of proscribed organizations should be made public."[94]

Similar arguments were made by several other prominent "anti-Communist" liberal voices. Thus, former New York City mayor Fiorello La Guardia declared, in a lengthy newspaper column entitled, "Even a Dog Gets a Hearing," that "a decision of such far-reaching effect and susceptible of implicating a large number of innocent people should be based on ascertained facts, after a hearing and an opportunity for the organization to know the charges against it and a chance to present facts." Moreover, La Guardia maintained, "if mere membership, affiliation or 'sympathetic association' is sufficient to brand an individual for life, to hold him and his family to public scorn and disgrace, surely these organizations, associations, movements, groups or combinations of persons should be listed and publicized." Similarly, the *Washington Post* editorialized on March 29, 1947, that it would be a matter of "elementary justice" for the attorney general to make his "index expurgatorius" public, "so that the country as a whole may scrutinize it and judge its validity." (After the Truman AGLOSO was issued, the *Post* was far more critical in a December 9, 1947, editorial, although its primary anger was targeted at the very publication of the list it had earlier urged. The editorial maintained that the "only excuse for drawing up such a list" was the "legitimate business of determining whether individual employees are security risks" and that AGLOSO was actually "serving a very different purpose" as a "blacklist" that "stigmatized a great number of citizens who have no connection with the Government" and "openly invaded the rights of private citizens to think their own thoughts and choose their own associates without official molestation" in an "encroachment upon freedom" that could not be defended "in terms of American principles.") Historian Arthur Schlesinger, Jr., a founder of the liberal anti-Communist Americans for Democratic Action (ADA), declared in his 1949 book *The Vital Center* (which became a bible for the like-minded) that "whatever the merit of this type of list as a form of official procedure," AGLOSO "provides a convenient way of checking the more obvious Communist-controlled groups" like the CRC, but that the "inclusion of such anti-Communist revolutionary groups as the SWP" seemed "foolish and unwarranted." Schlesinger wrote in 1978 that the DOJ's relative tolerance during the Red Scare was indicated by the fact that "even the fellow-traveling Emergency Civil Liberties Committee was not" designated, a phraseology suggesting that his own rather accepting views of AGLOSO remained unchanged. During the 1948 elections, the ADA, which often seemed more interested in proving its anti-communism than its liberalism, bought advertisements in major newspapers seeking to undermine the Progressive Party candidacy of former Roosevelt vice president Henry Wallace by listing the names of leading Progressive contributors along with their alleged AGLOSO affiliations (at its 1950 convention, the Progressive Party, which was widely viewed as Communist-dominated, became one of the few nondesignated groups that denounced AGLOSO outright). Some liberal organizations, including the ACLU and the NAACP, were so frightened about being tainted with charges of Communist infiltration that some of their leaders, including NAACP legal director (and future first black Supreme Court justice) Thurgood Marshall, ACLU cofounder and general counsel Morris Ernst, and Irving Ferman, director of the ACLU's Washington, D.C., office, secretly sought FBI "clearance" of their personnel and shared other confidential information with the Bureau.[95]

2

The Spread and Impact of AGLOSO, 1947–1955

The Intent and Impact of AGLOSO Listings

Between the first Truman AGLOSO designations by Attorney General Tom Clark on November 24, 1947 (published on December 4, 1947) and the last AGLOSO additions by Eisenhower administration Attorney General Herbert Brownell on October 20, 1955, almost 300 organizations, most of them extremely obscure, were listed. During these eight years, and, in fact, until AGLOSO was formally abolished by President Richard Nixon on June 4, 1974 (two months before his resignation), virtually every aspect of the list was mired in confusion, including exactly how many organizations were designated, what AGLOSO's purpose and name was, what criteria were used to designate groups, and whether organizations were entitled to any means to challenge their listings. Perhaps the only clear things about AGLOSO were that designations were massively publicized and that listed groups (and their members) suffered serious and relentless penalties inflicted by many branches of the federal, state, and local governments, as well as by private organizations and employers, damage so severe that most still-functioning groups soon collapsed. Leading Red Scare historian Ellen Schrecker wrote in 2002 that AGLOSO designation was "usually a kiss of death to an organization," while forty years earlier a November 1956 *Elks Magazine* article entitled "What the Attorney General's List Means" noted that "few Americans" had not heard of AGLOSO and that the message it delivered was, "There is no excuse for any American citizen being affiliated with a group on the Attorney General's list today." Prominent University of Chicago chemist Harold Urey, who was criticized for his AGLOSO affiliations, accurately reflected the list's practical significance when he told an Illinois legislative investigating committee in 1949 that he objected to the attorney general's designations of groups as "subversive" being "accepted as though it were the Bible," thus effectively allowing that official to "think for us and make an ultimate, final decision as to what is good and what is bad." Distinguished historian Henry Steele Commager wrote in 1953 that the "crime of guilt by association," which he incorrectly asserted dated to the 1940 Smith Act, had, due to AGLOSO, grown from a "cloud no bigger than a man's hand" until "it fills the whole horizon."[1]

The Department of Justice (DOJ) generally publicly maintained that AGLOSO's sole purpose was to provide potentially useful information for federal personnel loyalty screening. Thus, in a 1954 letter to a journalist, Eisenhower Assistant Attorney General Warren Olney declared that "any reference to the list as a 'blacklist' would be without justification," since it imposed "no fines, penalties or sanctions of any kind" and, although the department could not control its usage following publication, its "single purpose" was to aid in federal loyalty determinations. Similarly, Internal Security Division (ISD) head William Tompkins told Assistant Attorney General and Office of Legal Counsel (OLC) head J. Lee Rankin in 1954 that AGLOSO was maintained "solely as an adjunct of the Federal employee loyalty security program." DOJ AGLOSO unit head Oran Waterman told his superiors in 1955 that because AGLOSO's "primary purpose" was in "connection with Federal employment," it was not even "appropriate for the Department to be circulating" AGLOSO lists. (However, in a 1956 memo, Waterman cautioned his superiors that claims that AGLOSO originated to facilitate federal loyalty screenings were "not true," as organizations were "first designated in connection with the [World War II] alien enemy hearing cases." In a 1961 memo Kennedy administration Assistant Attorney General J. Walter Yeagley similarly declared that "the original Attorney General's list" was compiled "for the use of the Alien Enemy Hearing Boards.")[2]

In practice, after the DOJ's first published 1947 AGLOSO lists, it quickly became a massively publicized, quasi-official blacklist that was utilized in an almost unlimited variety of punitive fashions by governments and private groups across the nation. Thus, a 1967 law journal declared that, beyond its function as an aid in federal loyalty screenings, the additional uses of AGLOSO "are almost innumerable." Similarly, in opening 1955 Senate hearings into the federal loyalty program, Sen. Thomas Hennings (D-MO) declared that his staff had "uncovered a far-flung use of the Attorney General's list and its spread into areas that do not have the remotest connection with national security," including its "extended use by States, cities and private organizations." AGLOSO designations had an especially devastating impact upon listed groups because they were accompanied by massive media publicity, which soon fostered a bewildering variety of federal, state, local, and private penalties and led members and supporters to quit designated groups and to cease providing financial or other assistance, almost inevitably thereby severely weakening or destroying listed organizations.[3]

There is no surviving "smoking gun" document establishing that the government consciously decided in 1947 to publish AGLOSO lists in order to damage or destroy then-existent designated organizations, which were generally critical, from the left, of President Harry Truman's foreign and domestic policies, rather than for the officially stated federal loyalty screening purpose (as well as bolstering Truman's anti-Communist credentials when he was under severe conservative attacks for being "soft" on communism). However, no explanation was ever given why AGLOSO publication was required, especially since the never-published Biddle listings apparently served its federal employee screening purpose satisfactorily. Moreover, many of the 1947–1955 listings were essentially useless for loyalty screening purposes, because a large percentage of the listed organizations were tiny and/or defunct. Thus, a 1954 memo by AGLOSO unit head Waterman reported that two groups listed in May 1948 were "non-membership and one-man paper outfits" that did not seem "of a type that was intended to be included."[4]

The Truman loyalty program early came under FBI domination, and a deliberate intent to damage designated groups was unquestionably the goal of the FBI's secret post–World War II program of leaking information to various media, organizations, and congressmen in order to destroy alleged left-wing subversion. Moreover, within two months of the first AGLOSO publication, Attorney General Clark, who was strongly influenced by the FBI, explicitly told Congress that AGLOSO's major goal was to render listed groups "impotent" by exposing their purposes to the "vaccine of public opinion," so that they could no longer "be used for subversive propaganda" or to promote "alien philosophies," which he repeatedly made clear was their perceived primary offense, as opposed to plotting to overthrow or infiltrate the government. Appearing before a HUAC subcommittee on February 5, 1948, Clark declared that the government's "strategic objective" was to "isolate subversive movements in this country from effective interference in the body politic," and he listed as two *separate ways* of accomplishing this the "continuous study and public listing" of AGLOSO and the "complete elimination of subversive persons from all Government positions." He added that the DOJ was preparing to list additional groups and sought "to continuously survey this field in order to prevent the listed organizations from using an alias, as well as additional organizations being used for subversive propaganda" and hailed HUAC's goal of "bringing into the spotlight of publicity the activities of individuals and groups," since there was "no more potent weapon" than "this weapon of publicity." Clark maintained that "victory" in the "fight against American communism" was "assured by continued vigorous prosecutions, by identifying and exposing subversive characters as well as their organizations," leading to the "vaccine of public opinion" rendering "these organizations and their members impotent" and the "cleans[ing]" of "our way of life" from those "who cling to alien philosophies." He assured the subcommittee that his department would provide Americans with "protection from those who try to force upon them a foreign ideology" (shortly before his HUAC testimony, Clark declared in a speech, "Those who do not believe in the ideology of the United States should not be allowed to stay in the United States," while in June 1947, he told a House committee that the massively publicized "Freedom Train," which traveled the United States during 1947–1949 with displays of historical documents, would help to "immunize the American body politic against the germs of subversive propaganda"). In a May 3, 1948, letter to J. Edgar Hoover, Clark stated that AGLOSO's purpose was "not alone, or even primarily" to facilitate federal loyalty screenings of *existing* affiliations, since "one of the important reasons" for AGLOSO was to "give employees warning regarding organizations to which a loyal employee should not belong." Years later, Clark complained that the widespread use of AGLOSO by governments and private groups was done "without our [i.e., DOJ] advice or approval."[5]

Throughout the 1950s, internal DOJ correspondence repeatedly noted that AGLOSO's impact had spread far beyond its official personnel screening function, enthusiastically hailed its growing use by governmental and private organizations, and pointed to its devastating impact on designated organizations as a prime reason to continue AGLOSO despite rising public, congressional, and judicial criticism of the list. Thus, in late 1953, David Irons, chief of the ISD's Subversive Organizations Unit, wrote that while AGLOSO's "official executive purpose" was for federal loyalty screening, "it is now being utilized by State and local government employee loyalty and security programs and an ever increasing number of private corporations, particularly those with government contracts. Moreover, public knowledge has reached the point that many individuals refuse to contribute funds or associate themselves in any manner with a designated organization." In an undated letter to Secretary of Defense Charles Wilson, Attorney General Brownell borrowed much of Irons's language, terming AGLOSO "an invaluable aid to our entire security program" and adding, "I cannot emphasize too strongly that the designation program has struck the Communists at the very heart of their most cherished conspiracy," in which "they seek to reach the mass of our population through establishing or infiltrating organizations that sponsor so-called popular causes."[6]

In a November 1953 memo to Irons, AGLOSO unit head Waterman maintained that terminating AGLOSO would "pull the props from under most state loyalty programs, denials of tax exemptions, passport and many other related uses to which this program has been diverted, legally or otherwise, but with tremendous and effective impact" upon Communist attempts to widen their influence. In a separate, simultaneous "personal & *confidential*" memo to Irons, Waterman noted that "if the amount of mail received is any criterion, the public is probably more cognizant of the Designation Program than any other aspect of the Government's anti-subversive work" and that AGLOSO had been "more effective in combating the Communist front movement than any other program in that it has crippled their 'united front' appeal which has been the major objective of the Communist Party for some time" and thus was "amply justified from the time and expense point of view." ISD "confidential assistant" John Doherty wrote in November 1954 that he had been informed that AGLOSO designations had "effectively broken the financial back of some organizations," while in early 1957 Waterman wrote ISD Subversive Organizations Section (SOS) chief Joseph Alderman that "when an organization was designated, it only became a question of time as to its final dissolution," even if "this is not the true purpose of the program." Similarly, in a 1961 memo to OLC head and Assistant Attorney General Nicholas Katzenbach, ISD head Yeagley wrote that AGLOSO listings resulted in "eventually destroying" the designated groups.[7]

FBI officials clearly agreed that AGLOSO had a devastating impact on listed groups. Thus, Hoover told the attorney general in 1952 that "the designation of organizations as subversive substantially impedes the effectiveness of those organizations." He referred to AGLOSO as the "proscribed" list of "subversive organizations" in an October 1953 memorandum to his top aides (a characterization used by Attorney General Clark in earlier correspondence with him). In a thirty-four-page, single-spaced 1956 internal FBI memo, agent C. H. Stanley wrote that "Communist front vehicles rapidly disintegrate once they are listed," that "this curtailment of the Communist Party's united front program is a significant accomplishment," and that AGLOSO was "so effective a device that it should not be lightly abandoned." He added that the DOJ received over 600 monthly inquiries about AGLOSO, which demonstrated that "the public has a vital interest in these designations." Stanley rejected claims that the list's widespread use for purposes "other than those initially contemplated" supported arguments for abolishing it, because "the menace of Communism" reached far beyond "the veil" of the Loyalty Program, and that to combat communism it was important that those outside the federal government "have available to them some definitive data for their guidance and use."[8]

While it is impossible to determine precisely how much damage AGLOSO inflicted, most listed groups clearly suffered significant damage and many were effectively destroyed, as private organizations and the media repeatedly reminded the public of their pariah status, memberships and contributions dried up, they were denied meeting places and tax-exempt status, and AGLOSO members and supporters faced threats of dismissals by governmental and private employers and investigations by federal and state authorities. According to DOJ information furnished in the 1970s to congressional committees and to the Subversive Activities Control Board (SACB), of the 260 AGLOSO organizations for which data was provided, slightly over half (132) were defunct even before their designations, 35 (14 percent) stopped functioning within a year (and often within a few months) of their listing, 27 (10 percent) collapsed between one and three years after designation, and another 30 (11 percent) ceased activities within three to five years. Another 24 groups (9 percent) reportedly continued to function for over five years after being listed, but were defunct by 1970, while only 13 (5 percent, including the CP, the Socialist Workers Party [SWP], the Industrial Workers of the World [IWW], and the Veterans of the Abraham Lincoln Brigade [VALB]) were reportedly still active in 1970. (According to 1965 congressional testimony by Assistant Attorney General Yeagley, by then only 20 of what he calculated as the total of 274 designated groups were still functioning.)[9]

In numerous instances, according to both contemporary published reports and DOJ submissions to Congress and the SACB decades later, designated groups quickly dissolved. Among the organizations that ceased functioning within a year of being designated were the Abraham Lincoln School of Chicago (listed November 1947, defunct by August 1948), American Poles for Peace (designated July 1953, defunct within two months), the American Committee for Yugoslav Relief (defunct within eight months after its May 1948 designation), the Benjamin Davis Freedom Committee (no longer functioning by May 1955, six months after being listed), the China Welfare Appeal (listed in January 1954 and nonexistent by June 1954), the Committee for the Negro in the Arts (dead three months after its January 1954 listing), Everybody's Committee to End War (no longer functioning ten months after its December 1954 designation), and the Maritime Committee to Defend Al Lannon (defunct by December 1953, five months following its listing). According to a 1954 report from the FBI's Denver office, an informant had advised that the National Association of Mexican Americans had "ceased to exist nationally" by the end of 1953 "because of the proposed" AGLOSO designation announced by Attorney General Brownell in April 1953.[10]

AGLOSO listings also clearly played a substantial role in the collapse of some larger and well-established groups that survived their listings by more than a year and that frequently endured a large variety of other forms of government harassment. Thus, according to a scholarly history of the Civil Rights Congress (CRC), "the listing by the Attorney General as a 'subversive' organization and the constant repetition of this charge in government reports and news media probably caused the most damage of all" the blows the group suffered, ensuring "that suppliers would be reluctant to handle their accounts, halls would be reluctant to rent to them" and "their contributors would be harassed." Enrollment at the New York City Jefferson School of Social Science (designated November 1947) declined from 14,000 in 1946–47 to 400 when it closed in 1956, due to what its board of trustees termed nine years of "unwarranted persecution." When the Joint Anti-Fascist Refugee Committee (JAFRC) announced its February 1955 dissolution, after six years of futile court challenges to its AGLOSO listing, its executive board attributed the decision to government "harassments, persecutions and prosecutions," which had made it "impossible" to pursue its stated purpose of providing Spanish loyalist refugee relief.[11]

Perhaps the clearest and most devastating impact of an AGLOSO designation upon a formerly robust and significant organization was the court-ordered dissolution of the International Workers Order (IWO), the largest still-functioning organization ever listed. The IWO was a fraternal benefit insurance organization chartered in New York state that enrolled over 1 million Americans between 1939 and 1950, most of whom belonged to about fifteen affiliated groups organized along ethnic lines. According to legal historian Arthur Sabin, the IWO was both "the most enduring, successful and stable Communist-affiliated organization" and the largest "left-wing, non-union organization" in American history. The IWO had almost 200,000 members holding premiums worth $122 million when it was designated in 1947, the overwhelming majority of whom joined because the IWO provided unusually comprehensive and inexpensive insurance policies at a time when government and private employers rarely provided such benefits and because it was extremely well run and provided extensive collateral social activities, including picnics, sports, music, dance, and film and theater programs, as well as about a hundred elementary schools, several secondary schools and separate summer camps for children and adults. It was the only American insurance company that covered workers in all professions and insured members of all races and ethnic groups at the same rates. It also pioneered the provision of preventive health and contraceptive services, all of which it declared formed an "integral part of the proletarian class-front against capitalism." As a 2007 scholarly study of the IWO notes, it was "perhaps the only organization in history that gave [female] members the opportunity to be fitted for a diaphragm and play in a mandolin orchestra." Famed painter Rockwell Kent, who was elected IWO president in 1944, responded to a query as to why he had joined the group by recalling, "I heard that it was not only an insurance order interested in paying premiums after the death of people, but was possibly the only so-called insurance organization in America that was primarily interested in keeping people alive." According to a scholarly study by Thomas Walker, the IWO was severely damaged by hostile headlines and news stories that continued "unabated" following its AGLOSO designation, depicting the group as "honeycombed by spies seeking to infiltrate and undermine American institutions" and representing an "urgency of a threat to American democracy" via "un-American and treasonous conspiratorial activity."[12]

Although the IWO clearly was a "Communist front," as traditionally defined, in that it was largely initiated (in 1930) and led by CP members and consistently supported CP policies, only about 5 percent of IWO policy holders belonged to the CP and no serious evidence ever emerged that it engaged in plotting or advocating the overthrow of the government or anything remotely similar. In various proceedings between 1938 and 1942, immigration officials and the Civil Service Commission (CSC) ruled that IWO membership alone was insufficient to bar aliens from citizenship or to require deportation or exclusion from federal employment. During World War II the IWO was praised by various public officials, including Secretary of the Interior Harold Ickes and Sen. Robert Wagner (D-NY) and was awarded a Treasury Department certificate of merit for selling almost $300,000 in war bonds. However, as historian David Caute has written, as "the most conspicuously successful Communist front in the U.S.," the IWO was "obviously a prime target for the authorities" during the Cold War, including, after its 1947 designation, special attention from the IRS, the INS, HUAC, and other government agencies.[13]

The IWO had repeatedly received high evaluations during regular reviews by both New York state and private insurance raters, had a substantial financial reserve, and had never been accused of violating state insurance regulations. However, New York insurance officials ordered another review of the IWO after its 1947 designation and subsequently brought legal action for its liquidation in 1949 on the grounds that its AGLOSO designation and political affiliations made it a "hazard" to its policy holders, because they might "be subjected likewise, to a charge of disloyalty" and because its assets allegedly might be diverted to Moscow if the Cold War worsened. The liquidation proceedings marked the first time in American history that an insurance company's political affiliations and views had triggered such action, but officials in at least four other states where the IWO operated soon imitated New York's action. James Haley, the lead New York state IWO investigator, charged that the IWO had repeatedly sought to "impugn the integrity of our country's President, his cabinet and the Congress, specifically in their conduct of foreign policy" but conceded that the organization had never committed a single "affirmative subversive act." However, liquidation proceedings were upheld by three New York state courts, primarily on the grounds that the IWO's very financial strength and liquidity posed an especial risk that its officers might convert its assets into revolutionary purposes. Ironically, although the IWO's AGLOSO designation triggered the events that destroyed it, the first New York court ruling upholding the group's liquidation declared, with regard to the state's stress upon the AGLOSO listing, it was "unthinkable and shocking to its conscience" to permit the attorney general to "condemn an organization without giving it notice of the action contemplated and a hearing on the charges." After the U.S. Supreme Court refused to review the New York court rulings, the IWO was ordered liquidated in August 1954. Within two years of its 1947 listing, the IWO lost almost 15 percent of its membership, while between 1949 and 1954 membership collapsed from 160,000 to 83,000. According to historian Sabin, the case remains the "only instance [in American history] of liquidation or destruction of an insurance company for reasons of its politics." In addition to liquidating the IWO, New York state officials also revoked the charter of the American Committee for the Protection of the Foreign Born (ACPFB) after it was AGLOSO-designated in 1948.[14]

As with the IWO and ACPFB, AGLOSO designations and alleged affiliations frequently were widely and massively used well beyond the federal civil service loyalty program and often became an absolute bar to government and private employment and benefits entitlements, rather than as only one possible indicator of "disloyalty" in federal loyalty determinations, supposedly AGLOSO's sole intended function. Thus in federal programs beyond the civil service, AGLOSO was utilized by the armed services to punish allegedly tainted draftees; by the Department of Defense (DOD), the Atomic Energy Commission, and the civilian merchant marine to screen private contract employees; by the Treasury Department to bar private organizations from tax-exempt status; by the State Department to withhold passports from American citizens and visas from foreign visitors; by the INS in deportation and exclusion decisions; and (under direct 1952 congressional mandates) by the Public Housing Administration (PHA) to ban AGLOSO members from subsidized housing and by the Veterans Administration (VA) to deny veterans' educational benefits to enrollees in AGLOSO schools. As historian Ellen Schrecker notes, AGLOSO leaders "when not fighting criminal charges or deportation proceedings, were on regular call before HUAC and other investigating committees," especially since information about AGLOSO designations and affiliations became staples of FBI reports and congressional and state investigative hearings into purported "subversive" activities, frequently emerged during judicial proceedings and were incorporated into many "loyalty" screening programs of state and local governments and private employers. AGLOSO's use even extended beyond official U.S. jurisdiction: in early 1953, the 1,700 American employees of the United Nations were required to state if they belonged to any listed groups.[15]

Under November 1950 regulations, civilian employers were authorized to deny employment to DOD contract employees involving access to classified military information, if "reasonable grounds" existed for belief they were or recently had been a "member of, or affiliated with, or sympathetically associated with" AGLOSO groups. According to 1953 DOD regulations, information that could be considered in making such clearance decisions included "membership, affiliation" or "sympathetic" interest or association with AGLOSO organizations, participation in "front" groups for such organizations if indicative of "personal views" that were "sympathetic" to their "subversive" purposes, and "sympathetic association" or current maintenance of "a close continuing association" with members of such groups (including living at the same address or "frequently" visiting them), even if such association was terminated by "distance," if "the circumstances indicate that renewal of the association is probable." To implement these guidelines, DOD civilian employees were required to report if they had "ever" had AGLOSO affiliations, including if they had ever "submitted for publication material" to such groups and if they were "now associating with" or had in the "past five (5) years associated with any individuals, including relatives, who you know, or have reason to believe, are or have been members" of any AGLOSO groups "within the past five (5) years." The highly conservative Senate Internal Security Subcommittee (SISS) concluded in 1955 that while theoretically AGLOSO affiliation was supposedly "only one factor" in defense contractors' employee decisions, the "practical effect" of such regulations was that "in most cases" applicants for positions requiring security clearances who disclosed

AGLOSO affiliations "cannot get a job." Thus, Harvard social relations professor Samuel Stouffer, who subsequently published a well-known book about the impact of the Red Scare on Americans' civil liberties views, was originally denied clearance in 1953 for employment on any classified military contracts because, according to the Eastern Industrial Personnel Security Board, he was a "close and sympathetic associate" of AGLOSO members and of "persons who have participated in the activities of such organizations and of organizations established" as fronts for "subversive organizations" (Stouffer regained his clearance after appealing the rulings). Testifying before a 1955 Senate subcommittee about DOD requirements that civilian job applicants report associations with others with AGLOSO affiliations, Congress of Industrial Organizations (CIO) associate general counsel Thomas Harris asked, "Is our government really in such grave danger of overthrow from within that we must become a nation of stool pigeons?" Soon afterwards, the DOD announced that it would cease requiring civilian employees to report their associations with others, while retaining questions about personal AGLOSO affiliations. Nonetheless, in June 1957 the government sought to deny security clearance to a Radio Corporation of America engineer because he "currently maintains a close, continuing association" with his mother, who allegedly had a "sympathetic interest in communism," associated with AGLOSO groups, "and has been or may still be" a CP member.[16]

The first indication that the federal government was using AGLOSO designations for reasons other than personnel screening came in a February 4, 1948, Treasury Department announcement that it was revoking tax-exempt status previously granted eight specific AGLOSO organizations, and that henceforth it would deny such status to "any organization where evidence demonstrates it to be subversive." The Treasury announcement came two days after FBI director Hoover wrote Attorney General Clark to "suggest" that Clark furnish the Treasury Department with AGLOSO listings, along with data reflecting that such groups "should not be considered as tax exempt organizations." In February 5 congressional testimony Clark stated that he had personally advised the Treasury Department that tax-exempt status should be denied to AGLOSO organizations, as they were "engaged in propaganda activity of a subversive nature." In 1952 congressional testimony, Assistant IRS Commissioner Norman Sugarman confirmed that it had been IRS policy since 1948 to "deny exemption to any" AGLOSO organization.[17]

That the State Department was using AGLOSO in making visa decisions was revealed in August 1948, when it announced a visa denial to the prominent Anglican clergyman Dr. Hewlett Johnson, widely known as the "Red Dean of Canterbury" for his political views, because his trip was being sponsored by the AGLOSO-listed National Committee for American-Soviet Friendship (NCASF). In what the August 25 Washington Post termed an "infantile" policy, press officer Michael McDermott declared that the department had no general objections to Dr. Johnson's planned lecture tour but "would regard a visit under the auspices of this organization as not in our national interest." Johnson was, in fact, permitted to enter the country two months later under the aegis of a group of religious and educational leaders. In other instances, AGLOSO affiliations provided the grounds for denying admission to the United States to professors and students who wished to teach, study, or lecture at American colleges. Thus, a planned 1949 Bryn Mawr College lecture series by University of Toronto professor Barker Fairley, vice president of the Canadian affiliate of the NCASF, had to be canceled.[18]

In 1952, Secretary of State Dean Acheson revealed that passports had been denied to ninety-five individuals "because of membership in subversive organizations" and withdrawn from another ninety-five persons per due to "indicated subversive affiliation or intent." Thus, after William Patterson, the executive secretary of the designated CRC went to Europe in 1951 to present a petition alleging that the U.S. government had engaged in "genocide" against American blacks, his passport was withdrawn, a fate also suffered by the black actor and singer Paul Robeson, who was active in the CRC and numerous other AGLOSO organizations. Nobel prize–winning California Institute of Technology chemist Linus Pauling was denied a passport in 1954, at least partly due to alleged AGLOSO affiliations. In a widely publicized ruling, the State Department was strongly rebuked in 1955 by a federal appeals court for apparently denying a passport to Independent Socialist League (ISL) chair Max Shachtman solely on the basis of the ISL's AGLOSO status, especially as the group had been repeatedly denied an opportunity to challenge its designation.[19]

Several court cases in the late 1940s and 1950s, as well as internal DOJ documents, revealed that the INS was using AGLOSO affiliations as at least a partial basis for deportation, naturalization, and exclusion proceedings. Attorney General Clark hinted at such uses in 1948 HUAC testimony in which he reported asking department attorneys for a list of "all the aliens who are active in subversive activities," because they had "no right to be in the U.S." During 1949 Senate testimony, Clark announced that 112 pending deportation orders had been issued on the basis of "subversive" activities and that another 833 such cases were "under investigation." The Eisenhower administration continued this policy: thus, Deputy Attorney General William Rogers announced in September 1953 that the new administration had deported 42 "subversives" during its first eight months in office, with another 142 such cases pending. Although neither Clark nor Eisenhower Attorney General Brownell specifically mentioned AGLOSO, several court proceedings demonstrated that the INS was utilizing AGLOSO designations in deportation and exclusion proceedings. Thus, in 1949 the INS Board of Immigration Appeals upheld the proposed deportation of a Greek merchant seaman named Kaloudis because he had belonged to the IWO, an organization "on the proscribed list issued by the Attorney General." A federal appeals court subsequently refused to block the deportation, ruling that, while the court could not know "whether the Attorney General had adequate grounds for 'proscribing'" the IWO and although Kaloudis had terminated his membership, it was within the attorney general's unreviewable discretion to find that "even past membership" in a "proscribed" organization made his continued residence "prejudicial to the public weal." Several other court and immigration proceedings also upheld such use of AGLOSO designations, but federal district court judge James Morris overruled a Board of Immigration Appeals deportation holding in 1955 and ordered reconsideration of a case that he characterized as involving the parents of three American children, "which also means in effect the deportation of such American children, upon the basis of 'confidential information' which may be no more than anonymous hearsay rumors, or even by unexplained membership in some organizations listed by the Attorney General as subversive."[20]

In *Hamasaki v. Brownell* (235 F. 2d 536), a federal appeals court in 1956 upheld a deportation proceeding that was partly based on past membership in the "Japan Fencing Association," which the court characterized as "a group contained in the Attorney General's list of totalitarian organizations." Although no group with this exact name appears on AGLOSO lists, DOJ files make clear that the case involved the Dai Nippon Butoku Kai (designated in 1943), which it translated as the "Military Virtue Society of Japan or Military Art Society of Japan." In an internal memorandum, AGLOSO section head Joseph Alderman reported that not only were "the files here incomplete" as was the case with "many old organizations," but it was a "real problem" that "Justice is using the list for reasons outside the scope" of the federal loyalty program, as had "outside government and private agencies," although "we have consistently taken the position that the list is for use solely in connection with Federal employment."[21]

The widespread use of AGLOSO in INS proceedings was confirmed in a March 18, 1957, memo from the INS commissioner to ISD head Tompkins, which stated that AGLOSO affiliations provided "the basis for inquiry" as to whether "an alien may be subject to Service proceedings." According to the memo, in naturalization cases, which were ultimately determined by the courts, the INS had concluded that since an alien with AGLOSO affiliations would presumably be "rejected from Government employment," to "bring him into the citizenry of the country would be an anomaly" and therefore the agency felt "duty bound" to "recommend denial of the petition," even absent any "admissible evidence to establish [the] proscribed nature" of the organizations. The memo stated that in deportation cases AGLOSO affiliations would normally be "irrelevant" to a hearing officer's determination, since such decisions had to be "based only on evidence of record," but that hearing officers were "authorized to rely upon and consider classified information, not contained in the record, when the [INS] Commissioner has personally determined that it is in the interest of national safety and security to do so," even without "independent evidence brought to the attention of the hearing officer" about the groups' aims and characters. In exclusion cases, according to the memo, no hearings were required and it was "conceivable" that aliens could be barred from entry to the U.S. partly due to "membership or affiliation with a listed organization," although the "applicant is not furnished with or advised of the facts constituting his exclusion." The INS conceded that its current procedures "appear[ed] to conflict" with announced DOJ policy concerning AGLOSO's purpose and use, but added that its procedures were "a matter of public record" only in connection with naturalization recommendations, while in exclusion and deportation cases "the conflict exists [only] in internal operations."[22]

In 1952, Congress mandated that VA educational benefits could not be used to provide tuition to AGLOSO-designated educational institutions and, in the so-called Gwinn Amendment, that AGLOSO members be barred from living in federally subsidized public housing. As will be discussed below, the courts almost uniformly struck down the Gwinn Amendment on constitutional or other grounds, and the DOJ abandoned attempts to enforce it in 1956. A variety of other miscellaneous uses of AGLOSO by federal agencies periodically surfaced. In December 1948, DOD officials revealed that membership in or close relationship or adherence to AGLOSO organizations would be grounds for barring news correspondents from accreditation for assignments to overseas areas controlled by American occupation forces, a rule that was officially confirmed in May 1949. At Harvard University, the Naval Reserve Officers Training Corps (ROTC) required in 1949 that its members pledge that they did not belong to any AGLOSO organizations and that they would report any fellow students observed at such groups, leading the Harvard faculty and Americans for Democratic Action (ADA) to formally protest what became known as the "stool pigeon" clause. According to 1955 ACLU Senate testimony, similar pledges were required of ROTC enrollees throughout the country. In 1956, it was disclosed that the Library of Congress had withdrawn an invitation to Albert Sprague Coolidge to serve as an adviser to a foundation established by a 1926 $600,000 donation from his mother, apparently because of his past membership in the listed North American Committee to Aid Spanish Democracy (NCASD). Proceedings during the 1950s revealed that the Federal Communications Commission (FCC) viewed alleged AGLOSO affiliations as grounds for potential denial of broadcast licenses.[23]

Allegations of AGLOSO affiliations were staples of FBI reports and numerous congressional committees that investigated "subversive" activities. As FBI director Hoover wrote to Assistant to the Attorney General Peyton Ford in late 1948, the FBI "consistently followed the practice of identifying [AGLOSO] organizations [whenever they were mentioned] in our reports as having been declared by the Attorney General to be within the purview" of Truman's loyalty order. Sometimes this policy reached absurd lengths, as in a 1956 memo from the Newark FBI office to Hoover, which identified the CP as an organization that "has been [AGLOSO] designated." The policy was followed in all FBI reports, extending far beyond those on federal employees and applicants to encompass also alleged AGLOSO ties of nondesignated organizations and of private individuals whose activities did not come under the loyalty program. Thus, a report on the Institute of Pacific Relations (IPR), a nondesignated group, which was transmitted to the Loyalty Review Board (LRB) by Ford in 1950, noted the AGLOSO affiliations of IPR officers and employees, including that the IPR secretary general's 1930s private secretary was listed in 1946 as a "consultant to the [designated] Committee for a Democratic Far Eastern Policy," on a "dinner program for a dinner sponsored by that organization."[24]

Although at least officially, FBI policy banned dissemination beyond the agency of information unless it had gathered the material itself and then only "within the Executive Branch," a June 1953 revision of the FBI Manual of Rules and Regulations exempted from these restrictions "information received from reliable sources which reflects membership in any group declared as subversive by the Attorney General," which could be shared with "responsible local authority such as a governor, mayor or chief of police" if it related to "subversive activities" in "public and semi-public organizations within a state." Such sharing could even involve information about people who were not AGLOSO members but were only on AGLOSO mailing lists and need not be restricted to listed groups but could also relate to affiliations with organizations "shown in Bureau files to be dominated or infiltrated by Communists." This revision apparently was connected with the FBI's so-called "responsibilities program," which clandestinely provided information to governors, local officials, and even some private corporations about approximately 800 "dubious" personnel, including college, high school, and elementary school teachers, between 1951 and 1955 (when the program was terminated due to news reports about it). AGLOSO affiliations were a regular focus of the "responsibilities program," as was also true of regular, massive leaks of supposedly confidential FBI material to at least ten congressional committees and selected, sympathetic congressmen (including Richard Nixon [R-CA] and Joseph McCarthy [R-WI]) and of FBI reports that were regularly sent directly to presidents Truman and Eisenhower. For example, a March 31, 1953, "responsibilities program" memo from Hoover to the FBI's Chicago office, referring to FBI dissemination of information "to appropriate authorities on a strictly confidential basis, concerning Communist or subversive elements in public utilities or public or semi-public organizations," recommended that certain information (which is blacked out in the released document) be provided about one or more individuals and that two organizations (also blacked out!) to which the individual(s) allegedly were affiliated "have been cited by the Attorney General" as "subversive organizations which 'seek to alter the form of government of the United States by unconstitutional means.'" A July 22, 1949, letter from Hoover to Truman military aide Harry Vaughan, marked "PERSONAL AND CONFIDENTIAL BY SPECIAL MESSENGER," reported that the FBI had "received information" that an appointment with the president might be sought by former Michigan state senator Stanley Novak and a delegation sponsored either by the Polish section of the IWO or the American Slav Congress (ASC) "which have been declared Communist organizations by the Attorney General." The letter added that Nowak had been past president of the ASC and a national vice president of the CRC, "also declared a Communist organization by the Attorney General." A May 10, 1955, three-page, single-spaced typed Hoover memo similarly dispatched to Eisenhower special assistant Dillon Anderson reported extensively on the political association of famed polio vaccine inventor Dr. Jonas Salk, including that he was affiliated with the American-Soviet Medical Society, which had allegedly helped organize a medical panel at the 1943 congress of the NCASF, an organization "designated by the Attorney General," and that his brother belonged to the CP and had been associated with an organization "closely affiliated" with the designated CRC.[25]

The FBI's 1,800-page file on scientist Albert Einstein, who never worked for any governmental agency, was filled with information on his alleged affiliations with at least a dozen AGLOSO organizations as well as many other supposedly suspect groups. Indeed, as journalist and scholar Fred Jerome notes in his book on the FBI's Einstein file, it "contains the most complete listing—the only listing—of the political causes Einstein supported," which, for example, occupy 90 of 143 pages in an August 1953 summary report on the world-famous physicist. According to Jerome, "most" FBI files on individuals "contain little or nothing else" beyond lists of their alleged affiliation with "subversive" organizations. Thus, the FBI maintained a large file with similar allegations of AGLOSO and other suspect affiliations on famed anthropologist Margaret Mead and numerous other prominent Americans who often had only peripheral—or no—relationships with the federal government. Thus, Mead, who held some federal contracts and served on a federal advisory committee, but whose main employment was as curator of ethnology at the American Museum of Natural History and professor at Columbia University, explained to the FBI that, although the bureau showed her as affiliated with the designated American-Russian Institute (ARI), she had only taken out a subscription for ARI publications as part of an Office of Naval Research contract at Columbia. The FBI's file on famed Harvard sociologist Talcott Parsons included allegations that in the mid-1930s he had worn a button of a Young Communist League (YCL)–sponsored group and that he belonged to a committee of the AGLOSO-designated American Committee for Spanish Freedom (also that he incurred five traffic tickets and that his son had supposedly once recited the *Communist Manifesto* from memory!). The FBI file on novelist John Steinbeck reported that the AGLOSO-designated American Youth for Democracy (AYD) had recommended and sold his book *The Moon Is Down*. Director Hoover was especially exercised that short story writer and wit Dorothy Parker, in her 500-page file, was reported to have had links with the designated JAFRC.[26]

When HUAC attacked the loyalty of eminent scientist Dr. Edward U. Condon, director of the Federal Bureau of Standards in 1948, a key allegation involved his reported past association with the NCASF. SISS investigator Benjamin Mandel cast doubt on the loyalty of an American UN employee by accusing her, in 1952, of having sponsored a 1947 dinner for the American-Russian Institute of New York City (listed in 1949), while, at a 1953 HUAC meeting, a California clergyman was attacked in an affidavit from two unidentified undercover FBI agents who charged him with ties to the designated American Peace Mobilization (APM). Sen. Joseph McCarthy regularly listed alleged AGLOSO ties of governmental officials and others whom he suggested were of dubious loyalty; when the transcripts of McCarthy's 1953–1954 closed-door hearings were released fifty years later, they revealed that he habitually asked each witness if he or she were "now" or had "ever been" a member of the CP or "any organization that is listed by the attorney general as subversive." During public hearings, McCarthy also leaned heavily upon AGLOSO. Thus, when a 1950 Senate committee investigated his allegations of widespread Communist infiltration of the federal government, his first target was Dorothy Kenyon, a former representative to a UN commission, whom he charged had been affiliated "with at least 28 communist fronts," including nine "cited as subversive by the Attorney General." McCarthy added that Secretary of State Acheson's wife was listed by HUAC as sponsoring the Washington branch of the listed Congress of American Women (CAW). Other prominent Americans who were charged with AGLOSO affiliations by congressmen or congressional committees included Truman's secretary of the interior, Oscar Chapman, Newbold Morris, nominated by Truman to head an administrative inquiry into governmental corruption, and G. Bromley Oxnam, the Methodist bishop of Washington, D.C.[27]

References to AGLOSO affiliations also frequently emerged during a wide variety of judicial proceedings, usually to discredit witnesses. Thus, when federal district judge Charles Wyzanski testified as a character witness for Alger Hiss during the latter's sensational 1949 federal perjury trial, prosecutors noted that a Boston newspaper had reported Wyzanski's opposition to the concept of guilt by association, in reference to the designated AYD, during a speech. Similarly, when U.S. Ambassador-at-Large Philip Jessup testified on Hiss's behalf, he was asked if he had belonged to two AGLOSO organizations. When Jessup was subjected to similar accusations from McCarthy in early 1950, he was reduced to defending himself by not only denying ever "knowingly" supporting Communist fronts, but adding that his English ancestors had come to North America in the seventeenth century, that his great grandfather had served as a delegate to the 1860 Republican convention, and that his wife's ancestors were of "English and Dutch pioneer stock." The first perjury conviction of William Remington, a federal employee prosecuted for denying CP affiliations on his job application form, was overturned in August 1951 by a federal appeals court partly on the grounds that the government had improperly made "numerous references" to his alleged AGLOSO affiliations when cross-examining him. The court held this was in error because the list was "purely hearsay declaration by the Attorney General," with no possible "probative value" in the trial," and thus demonstrated "no conceivable tendency to prove the defendant's alleged perjury even if it were shown" that Remington belonged "to some or all of the organizations listed." In 1951, a federal judge refused to accept bail for eleven leading Communists under Smith Act indictments because it had been posted by the CRC. The judge subsequently jailed four CRC officials, including Frederick Field, a scion of the Vanderbilt fortune, and famed mystery writer Dashiell Hammett, for refusing to reveal the sources of CRC funds. Attorney General J. Howard McGrath announced soon after that the government would refuse to accept CRC bail postings in any cases, and Assistant U.S. Attorney for New York William Sexon later declared that McGrath had "informally" told the INS that, in cases involving alien Communists, bail could not be furnished by any AGLOSO group.[28]

AGLOSO's impact was felt far beyond the precincts of the federal government, as it was also widely used as a loyalty standard by state and local governments and private organizations. In this wider arena, as Eleanor Bontecou notes in her 1953 study of the federal loyalty program, the formal cautions of federal officials that AGLOSO affiliations were only "one piece of evidence" to be considered in reaching conclusions were given virtually no significance, as the test "almost always" became "mechanical, working with automatic precision to exclude individuals from a variety of occupations or activities." According to numerous published accounts, including compilations of state and local "anti-subversive" laws and regulations issued in 1955 and 1965 by the Senate Judiciary Committee (SJC), about twenty states and territories and numerous cities imposed restrictions that clearly sought to incorporate AGLOSO (although sometimes with imprecise language) into their statutes and/or regulations; many more apparently informally invoked the list in administering hundreds of other laws that, without specifically referencing AGLOSO, imposed various sanctions on "subversive" organizations and/or their members.[29]

Among the state laws and regulations that incorporated AGLOSO-based restrictions, perhaps the most bizarre was a 1953 Alabama statute that required all publishers of "written instructional material" approved for use in the public schools to certify that neither any of their authors nor "the author of any book or any writings cited therein as parallel or additional reading" was a "known advocate of communism or Marxist socialism," a CP member or ex-member, or a "member or ex-member of a Communist-front organization (as designated by the U.S. Congress or any committee thereof, or the Attorney General of the U.S.)." This provision soon had the publishers of Alabama textbooks metaphorically tearing out their hair, if not the pages of their books, because they lacked access to AGLOSO membership lists to verify the required certifications. Acting Assistant Attorney General Yeagley provided them a 1954 affidavit that attested that the DOJ had never published a list of "known advocates of Communism or Marxist socialism, or who are members of the Communist Party or of so-called communist fronts." However, the American Textbook Publishers Institute apparently communicated with all AGLOSO groups that it could locate: residing in the (AGLOSO-designated) ISL files is a 1954 institute letter inquiring if the ISL could "assist us in complying" with the Alabama law with an "immediate reply" providing "a list of all your members, past and present." In response to an institute lawsuit, an Alabama court declared the law unconstitutional on May 10, 1954. A somewhat similar Texas law required that no textbook could be adopted for use in the public school unless the author swore an oath that he was not, and had not been for the preceding five years, a member of any AGLOSO organization (no explanation was given as to how deceased authors, like Shakespeare or Plato, could comply).[30]

At least seven states (and the territory of Hawaii) incorporated explicit AGLOSO references into laws concerning loyalty screenings of some or all public employees. Hawaii completely incorporated the 1947 Truman standards, including the use of AGLOSO affiliations, in making loyalty determinations concerning public employees, while Louisiana barred public employment of any person determined to be a "knowing member of a Communist front organization listed as such" by the DOJ. Washington State not only barred public employment of AGLOSO members, but completely outlawed AGLOSO organizations and membership, requiring that they dissolve and forfeit all of their property once found to have violated state law by a "court of competent jurisdiction." As a result, in 1956 the University of Washington banned all AGLOSO speakers from public campus gatherings, although this was modified in 1962 to ban only CP members. The provision of the 1955 Washington State law requiring that all public employees disavow AGLOSO membership was struck down by the state supreme court in 1959 on the grounds that the attorney general's AGLOSO designations were "unconstitutional" because they violated due process principles.[31]

Texas and Oklahoma both required all public employees to swear that they were not, and had not been, for the previous five years, AGLOSO members; Texas also denied tax-exempt status to listed groups. Arizona's 1952 public employee oath requirement retroactively covered three years of AGLOSO membership although it applied only to those working for state and county "boards of public welfare" (apparently "subversion" among other public employees was viewed as harmless). The 1951 Oklahoma law was struck down in 1952 by the U.S. Supreme Court in *Wieman v. Updegraff* (344 U.S. 183) because it did not require "knowing" membership in subversive organizations and thus was held to unconstitutionally group together "innocent with knowing activity" and thus "must fall as an assertion of arbitrary power," while the 1953 Texas law was struck down by a

1967 federal district court ruling, upheld the following year by the U.S. Supreme Court, on similar grounds (274 F. Supp. 75, 1967; 389 U.S. 572, 1968). Louisiana, Michigan, and Delaware compelled AGLOSO groups and/or members to register with the state. However, the Louisiana requirement was struck down by the Supreme Court in *Dombrowski v. Pfister* (380 U.S. 479, 1965) because the organizations involved had not been provided appropriate due process protections before being designated. Louisiana also directed all local sheriffs to remove any "propaganda" issued by AGLOSO organizations and to padlock any premises where such material was stored. According to Louisiana law, "Communist propaganda," which was defined to include the publications of all AGLOSO-designated "Communist" groups, posed a danger "even greater" than that from "narcotics, pornographic literature, switch blade knives, burglar tools or illicit alcohol in dry jurisdictions." Under Michigan's 1954 "Communist Control Act," "subversive" groups had to register with the state police, and Secretary of State Fred Alger banned the SWP from the state ballot due to its AGLOSO designation. Delaware required registration for all AGLOSO members "entering or residing" in the state, but 1955 congressional testimony revealed that no AGLOSO member had ever registered and that Delaware police were, in any case, utilizing a HUAC list (apparently supplied by the DOJ in response to a request for a copy of AGLOSO) with over 500 organizations on it, rather than the AGLOSO list then including less than 300 groups.[32]

Mississippi required the investigation of all organizations in the state with officers who were or had been AGLOSO officials, while applicants for the bar in Colorado, Georgia, Hawaii, Indiana, Idaho, and Oklahoma had to either swear they were not AGLOSO members or admit and/or explain if they were. Similar requirements applied to those seeking to serve as insurance brokers and agents in New York state and the District of Columbia and to potential lobbyists in Indiana. New York also required, for inclusion in its Commerce Department's annual children's camp directory, that camp owners or directors swear they did not advocate subversion or employ AGLOSO members. Alaska banned listed groups from either supporting or opposing any state legislative action. South Carolina banned state colleges from funding with public money "travel and/or any other expense items in connection with visits to these institutions by any person who is a member of an un-American organization" so branded by the attorney general. In addition to states that formally referenced AGLOSO in their statutes or regulations, by the mid-1950s virtually every state had adopted one or more provisions that incorporated vague references to "subversive" or "Communist-front" organizations, which, in practice, probably informally incorporated AGLOSO. In at least some such instances, it was the clear legislative intent that AGLOSO would be used to administer such provisions: thus, the commission that drafted Maryland's so-called "Ober Law" of 1949, which required candidates for appointive or elective office to swear if they belonged to any "subversive organizations," indicated in its report that it contemplated that AGLOSO would be used to police such oaths. Similarly, New York's 1949 Feinberg Law authorized the state Board of Regents to utilize AGLOSO in compiling its own list of subversive groups, after hearings, to screen public school teachers. State agencies clearly frequently informally invoked AGLOSO even without explicit legislative direction. Thus, a primary basis for the 1949 firing of Professor Ralph Grundlach from the University of Washington, according to university president Raymond Allen, was that Grundlach had neglected his duties by taking "an active part in many 'front' organizations, all of them [AGLOSO] listed as subversive." (Many colleges, both private and public, placed a wide variety of restrictions on speakers and organizations with AGLOSO designations or affiliations: thus all AGLOSO groups were banned from advertising in student newspapers at the University of California at Berkeley, at Queens College in New York City, and at Temple University in Philadelphia. CP and other AGLOSO-affiliated speakers were banned from talking at many colleges; and AYD and/or Labor Youth League [LYL] student groups were effectively banned at many colleges, including the University of Michigan and the University of Colorado, although the universities of Wisconsin and Chicago both resisted political pressure to ban the LYL.)[33]

Many city governments and agencies also explicitly or informally incorporated AGLOSO into a wide variety of loyalty screening and other programs. Perhaps the most extraordinary such instance was the District of Columbia Board of Public Welfare's attempt to block the adoption of a white child, born out of wedlock and abandoned by his father, by his natural mother and his black stepfather based on their interracial relationship and on their failure to sign a AGLOSO-membership disavowal required by public housing officials under the 1952 federal statute that had led to eviction proceedings against them. The adoption ban was rejected by a 1955 federal appeals court, which held that the couple had provided a stable and loving environment for the child, along with two children born out of their marriage, that neither proposed ground for blocking the adoption conformed to District of Columbia law, and specifically that their refusal to sign the AGLOSO disavowal established no "adverse reflection upon character." Detroit explicitly included AGLOSO membership as one basis for determining the "disloyalty of any municipal employee," following a 1949 popular referendum that approved such screening, while in 1955 Newark officials required all city employees to fill out a questionnaire asking, among other things, if they had ever belonged to any AGLOSO groups. In Indianapolis in 1950, the library began checking all periodicals to which it subscribed against AGLOSO, while two CRC members who worked for the state welfare department were fired shortly after the outbreak of the Korean War after they circulated the allegedly Russian-inspired Stockholm Peace Petition, on the grounds that they had aided a subversive organization and were causing "discord" and "public criticism" that had "destroyed confidence" in their effectiveness. The Philadelphia Board of Public Education suspended teacher Dorothy Albert in 1950 due to her alleged CRC membership, while Westchester County, New York, election officials refused to provide a list of voters to the CRC in 1951 due to its designation. It was disclosed in 1951 that prominent liberal columnist Marquis Childs and Pulitzer Prize–winning novelist Pearl Buck, among others accused of AGLOSO and other "subversive" affiliations, had been banned from speaking in the Washington, D.C., public schools. Superintendent Hobart Corning explained that he was submitting the names of all proposed speakers to HUAC for clearance, as "I wouldn't run the risk of employing anyone about whom there is any question at all." Mayor Stanley Church of New Rochelle, New York, told a 1955 Senate hearing that his thought was that "our police might check the various" AGLOSO organizations in order to implement a 1950 city ordinance which required all members of "Communist" organizations to register with the police. He reported that the provision had proved "meaningless because we had no machinery to enforce it" and that "not a one" Communist had ever registered with his town or been prosecuted for failing to register, although "we did think that perhaps some would come in." When asked if the ordinance was a response to "trouble" with "members of any Communist organizations," Crouch responded, "No, but we were worried about them" and "there were rumors that really disturbed me." The October 10, 1950, *Washington Post* reported the perhaps apocryphal story that a 60-year-old man had appeared at the New Rochelle police station to register under the ordinance, and when asked, "What subversive organizations are you a member of?" irately responded that he belonged to no such groups but "It said in the paper that all commuters have to register in New Rochelle, and I'm a commuter."[34]

New York City officials were especially prone to invoke AGLOSO for a wide variety of purposes. Thus, in 1949 they announced that AGLOSO groups would be banned from obtaining permits to solicit funds on public streets, in 1950 all city employees were required to disclose any AGLOSO affiliations, in 1951 public school facilities were barred to any organization or their affiliates if the DOJ found them to be "totalitarian, Fascist, Communist or subversive," and in 1953 employees working in eighteen designated city "security agencies" were required to answer questionnaires about their past or present AGLOSO affiliations. Sixteen city welfare department workers were fired for refusing to answer the questionnaire, but the requirement was later dropped and at least ten of them were reinstated after they convinced hearing boards of their loyalty. In 1954 the Queens College student council, with faculty support, voted to automatically suspend any campus newspaper that published advertisements by AGLOSO groups, while in 1957 New York City Police Lt. Jack Goloshin was subjected to a departmental trial for allegedly falsifying a questionnaire by failing to admit membership in the IWO and attendance at the Jefferson School of Social Science.[35]

Allegations of AGLOSO affiliation frequently arose in testimony heard by or in reports issued by state "un-American activities committees" modeled after HUAC, which proliferated after 1947. Thus, the Illinois Seditious Activities (Broyles) Committee reported in 1949 that it was appalled to discover that some college faculty "refused to accept the right of the Justice Department" to designate subversive organizations and declared that any AGLOSO member was "an undesirable person to teach our American school children of any age." It added that schools that employed such teachers should lose their tax exemptions and their governing officials should be removed from office. The Washington State (Canwell) committee recommended in 1949 that anyone with "proven affiliation with three or more known communist fronts which have been declared subversive by a qualified branch of the State or Federal government" be considered officially affiliated with the CP, while the Massachusetts Commission on Subversive Activities published in 1955 a list of eighty-five people charged with varying degrees of past or present subversive affiliations, including AGLOSO organizations.[36]

On several occasions, proposals to expand official use of AGLOSO proved too much for at least some DOJ and state and local officials. Thus, after the House of Representatives approved a 1950 bill requiring the National Science Foundation to refuse to employ or grant scholarships to anyone not cleared by the FBI for AGLOSO memberships, Assistant to the Attorney General Ford publicly condemned the proposal as potentially exposing the FBI to criticism as a "state police organization" and denying the foundation the services of "many Americans of unquestioned loyalty" who had "innocently joined a so-called 'front' organization with the highest motives and who withdrew upon their first suspicion of its subversive character." In early 1955, Assistant Attorney General Rogers opposed a proposal to ban the use of Department of Health, Education and Welfare funds for training at "any [AGLOSO] public or private facility," since AGLOSO designations were "solely for the purpose of guidance" to federal agencies in connection with federal loyalty screening. New York governor Thomas Dewey vetoed a 1949 state legislative bill that would have banned AGLOSO organizations from utilizing public buildings, and when Sen. William Jenner (R-IN) demanded the removal of several murals from the Indiana state senate chamber in 1953 because the artist was an AGLOSO member, a state senate committee unanimously rebuffed him, terming the choice of painter "unfortunate" but declaring that it would not "fall" for the "favorite trick of the Communists" by burning "great literature, music and art." Two trustees of the Burbank, California, public library unsuccessfully proposed in 1951 that all library books with AGLOSO authors be so identified with stickers, while a 1953 proposal overwhelmingly approved by the Texas House on the first two of three required readings (before being blocked by lack of the four-fifths majority required for immediate passage) would have required that any school or college library book with such authors be so branded on each volume with letters not less than one-quarter inch high. An internal 1957 DOJ memo includes the comment, "The Ubiquitous Attorney General's List!" attached to a California legislative proposal to ban tax exemptions from anyone who "willfully" allowed AGLOSO organizations to use their property. The "ubiquitous" nature of AGLOSO references during the 1947–1954 period was reflected in a sarcastic letter published in the Princeton University student newspaper in early 1950: reporting that "to our horror, copies of the works of Marx, Lenin and Stalin and other books propagating seditious red propaganda" had been sighted in the university bookstore, four students demanded that the store be placed on AGLOSO as a "Communist front," since "if we are to save Western civilization from the Marxist hordes, the serpent of Bolshevism must be extirpated wherever it rears its loathsome head." Along similar lines, *Washington Post* columnist George Dixon reported on July 29, 1955, that a professor had recently told him he was planning to resign from the 4-H Club (a group which promoted agriculture) "before it gets on the Attorney General's List" because "some 4-H members have been seen hanging around" a group of Russians who had been touring Iowa. After the Illinois American Legion passed a resolution questioning the Americanism of the Girl Scouts in 1959 (by which time AGLOSO had come under substantial attack and was largely moribund), a Washington, D.C., veterans' group voiced the opposite view, with their commander declaring that the Scouts "favor marshmallows and [actor] Gregory Peck" and opposed "homework and mosquito bites. None of these are on the Attorney General's list."[37]

Beyond official uses by federal, state, and local governmental agencies, private organizations and individuals frequently invoked AGLOSO to punish designated groups and their alleged members. In December 1949, the American Hotel Association sent copies of AGLOSO to its 6,000 members to alert them that listed groups "may seek to hold meetings in your hotel," and, according to vice president Charles Horrworth, hotels nationwide were beginning to use AGLOSO as a guide to future bookings. Conrad Hilton, head of the Hilton chain of thirteen hotels, was quoted at about the same time as declaring that he could not understand how the NCASF had successfully rented a New York City Waldorf-Astoria banquet room in November 1949, but that "we recently turned down this outfit at the Stevens Hotel in Chicago" and "neither this nor other subversive organizations are welcome in our hotels." (In March 1949, the Waldorf-Astoria had rented meeting rooms for a highly controversial Cultural Conference for World Peace; its resident manager explained that the sponsoring organization had been checked against AGLOSO and not found and therefore "certainly the hotel has no right to say that is a subversive organization.") Also in 1949, the American Jewish Congress expelled two of its affiliated organizations following their AGLOSO listing (the first expulsion in its thirty-year history), and the Los Angeles Country CIO voted to sever ties with any AGLOSO groups. In 1950, probate court reading of the will of Harvard professor Francis Matthieson revealed that he had recently cancelled previously planned bequests to two AGLOSO organizations, while New York's Madison Square Garden announced a ban on all AGLOSO meetings. The extent of AGLOSO use for employment screening by private businesses completely unconnected to the federal government is difficult to determine, but according to a 1967 law journal article, "appears to be widespread"; a 1956 law review article reported that courts had thus far invariably upheld the right of employers to question their workers about AGLOSO affiliations and that although "before 1950 most labor arbitration boards held that being a member" of an AGLOSO organization could not justify firing employees, after the 1950 outbreak of the Korean War the attitude of the National Labor Relations Board "and the courts towards discharges by the employer for 'disloyalty' changed." AGLOSO screening was apparently especially widespread in the entertainment industry: the Columbia Broadcasting System (CBS) revealed in 1950 that all regular radio and television employees were required to indicate any AGLOSO affiliations, while, behind the scenes, allegations of AGLOSO ties were published in private publications that became the informal "bibles" of the notorious "blacklist" of the broadcast and movie industries. Thus, upon being hauled before HUAC, prominent black folk singer Josh White repeatedly declared that he had ceased cooperating with AGLOSO groups after learning about their listings, in an apparent attempt to "cleanse" his name, maintaining that after coming "across a list of committees and organizations which the attorney general had just labeled 'subversive' [in 1947]," he was "horrified" to discover "I had been played for a sucker," as a "number of them were organizations for whom I had performed in the course of years without knowing their character." (If White's self-abasing response to questions about AGLOSO was perhaps extreme, probably rarer yet was that of noted artist Rockwell Kent, who, when asked by Sen. McCarthy if he had ever contributed to AGLOSO groups, replied, "The fact that they are listed by the Attorney General or by anyone else as subversive does not sway me to any degree. I am a man who makes up his own mind, and if I believe that they are serving a good cause . . . then I will join them. . . . What would America be without these so-called Communist fronts?")[38]

New York Times radio editor Jack Gould wrote in 1951 that there was a "new type of displaced person" in radio and television, consisting of artists, writers, announcers, and directors who were effectively "being deprived of their opportunity to make a living" because, once "listed" they became "controversial," and their "basic and fundamental rights have disappeared into thin air," as "innocence or guilt is now besides the point" for many prospective employers. Hollywood columnist John Crosby wrote in the *Washington Post* in 1952 that many movie stars "while still harboring the strongest possible convictions in private, are keeping their mouths shut in public," as actors had been "badly burned" during the previous four years after "many of the rallies they attended and helped promote in the past were found years later to be on" AGLOSO, and "the publicity has damaged and sometimes ruined careers." Until 1955, the American Bar Association (ABA) required prospective members to indicate if they had ever been AGLOSO members, but thereafter less specifically inquired if they had ever belonged to the CP or "any organization which to my knowledge is a subversive organization."[39]

During early 1950s congressional hearings concerning whether tax-exempt foundations were supporting "subversive" causes, spokesmen for the largest and most important American foundations repeatedly declared it their policy to never fund AGLOSO organizations. Thus, Rockefeller Foundation president Dean Rusk (later President Kennedy's secretary of state) declared, on behalf of both his foundation and the General Education Board, that "No grant has ever been made by either foundation to any [AGLOSO] organization." Fund for the Republic head and former University of Chicago president Robert Hutchins publicly denounced the congressional pressure on the foundations in a 1955 speech, in which he termed AGLOSO an "ex parte finding of guilt with no probative standing in law," while asking, "How many foundations would give money to an organization or even to an individual in an organization on the Attorney General's list, no matter how meritorious the project?" In June 1955, the fund awarded $5,000 to the Quakers of Plymouth Meeting, Pennsylvania, for hiring librarian Mary Knowles, who had been fired from her previous job after refusing to tell a Senate subcommittee her political views, while admitting outside the hearing room that she had been a secretary in the AGLOSO-designated Samuel Adams School. The Plymouth Quaker library, privately operated but open to the public, had lost its financial support from two local townships when the Quakers refused to fire Knowles, and the Plymouth Township school board officially barred teachers from taking children there.[40]

As with the broadcasting and movie blacklists, media and private allegations alleging AGLOSO affiliations against individuals frequently supplemented similar charges made by or before official bodies. Thus, in October 1954, the rabidly anti-Communist syndicated columnist George Sokolsky noted that Arkansas democratic gubernatorial candidate Orville Faubus (later famous for defying federal court orders to desegregate the Little Rock public schools in 1957) had been a student at Commonwealth College in the 1930s. During the 1954 Illinois senatorial contest, Republican candidate Joseph Meek's campaign distributed publications alleging that incumbent Democratic senator Paul Douglas (who won reelection) had been affiliated with many AGLOSO organizations; similar charges were influential in the 1950 primary defeats of North Carolina and Florida incumbent Democratic senators Frank Graham and Claude Pepper and Richard Nixon's 1950 triumph over incumbent Democratic California senator Helen Gahagan Douglas. Thus, Graham's opponent launched his campaign by declaring, "I do not now nor have I ever belonged to any subversive organizations" and that he would "never allow myself to be duped into the use of my name for propaganda or other purposes by those types of organizations." Pepper's successful primary opponent, George Smathers, circulated widely a booklet entitled "The Red Record of Senator Claude Pepper," which charged Pepper with belonging to more than a dozen Communist "fronts," while Nixon repeatedly charged that Douglas had a "pink" Senate voting record, and the head of the California Democrats for Nixon claimed that she had been associated with a dozen "Communist and subversive" organizations.[41]

Once organizations were AGLOSO-designated, news media, local and state governments, and private organizations repeatedly reminded the public about their status. Thus, a study of the impact of news coverage upon the IWO concludes that "with few exceptions, the media, rather than cry out against such a usurpation of power [as AGLOSO], relinquished its role as an ideological mediator and fell into line behind the Attorney General's" listings.[42] Newspapers routinely reminded their readers of the AGLOSO status of designated organizations when they mentioned such groups. Thus, the June 24, 1948, *New York Herald Tribune*, under the headline "Council Listed as Subversive Holds 2 Rallies," began its story with "The National Council of American-Soviet Friendship, one of the organizations listed as subversive by the Justice Department" and went on to say that the group was holding meetings to urge the peaceful settlement of American disputes with Russia. The February 11, 1948, *New York World-Telegram*, under the headline, "Communist Front Refugee Group Opens Fund Drive," began a story by reporting, "Within 24 hours after the Bureau of Internal Revenue revoked its tax-exempt privileges, the Joint Anti-Fascist Refugee Committee, classified as Communist and subversive by the Department of Justice, launched a new fund-raising drive, it was learned today." The April 26, 1948, *Newsweek* reported that the NCASF, "which recently was listed by Attorney General Tom C. Clark as subversive," was among the "front groups" that Communists had "started whipping up" to protest reported plans by Twentieth-Century Fox to make a film about Soviet espionage. The wire services routinely included information about AGLOSO designations in their stories: thus, on September 24, 1948, both the *Los Angeles Times* and the *Washington Post* printed an Associated Press (AP) story which, in reporting that ASC executive secretary George Pirinsky had been arrested for deportation proceedings, noted that the group had been AGLOSO-designated four months earlier. A two-sentence December 5, 1949, *Los Angeles Times* AP story reported that "Moscow" had sent "warmest greetings" to an NCASF meeting and that the organization "is on the Attorney General's list of subversive organizations." A January 10, 1951, *New York Times* AP dispatch similarly referred to the CRC in reporting that the organization's San Francisco executive secretary had been arrested for immigration violations. Even newspapers that frequently attacked AGLOSO as lacking in procedural fairness and/or First Amendment guarantee, such as the *New York Times*, the *Washington Post*, and the *Christian Science Monitor*, routinely included similar information when reporting on listed organizations. Thus, the first sentence in a February 19, 1949, *Times* story about the dissolution of AYD stated that the group was "listed as subversive by Attorney General Tom Clark." An April 12, 1949, *Monitor* story noted that a witness in the

Smith Act trial of top CP leaders had referred to the CRC, "which is on the attorney general's list," while on December 10, 1948, the *Post* inserted extremely unusual bracketed "editor's notes," into stories from the UP and a *Post* reporter stating that the CRC and the JAFRC were AGLOSO-designated.

Such constantly reiterated connections of AGLOSO organizations with "subversive" activities when they were mentioned in news accounts was accompanied by a tendency of mainstream newspapers to cease or drastically reduce reporting about their routine activities, with the result that after being designated, AGLOSO groups were often subsequently mentioned *only* in connection with various government allegations and/or proceedings against them. Thus, between the 1944 founding and the 1947 AGLOSO designation of the Jefferson School of Social Science, the *New York Times* frequently carried reports about mundane activities associated with the school, but thereafter largely ceased such coverage. For example, in a November 10, 1944, "Art Notes" column, the paper reported on a forthcoming "illustrated lecture on Picasso" at the School, while its January 6, 1947, "Books-Authors" column noted that "Dashiell Hammett, author of many mystery novels, will teach a course on 'Writing the Mystery Story' at the Jefferson School." After 1947, such stories virtually never appeared, although the *Times* frequently carried stories related to alleged subversive activities at the school. Similarly, according to scholarly studies of the Council on African Affairs (CAA) and the Photo League, soon after their November 1947 designations, the *Times* "virtually ceased to cover the activities of the Council," and "newspapers and magazines would no longer review the League's exhibitions or publicize its events." Frequent reiteration of AGLOSO designations by the media was complemented by the widespread circulation of AGLOSO listings by local and state governments and by private organizations. Thus, Detroit's superintendent of schools instructed that AGLOSO listings be sent to all 30,000 employees of the city's public and religious schools in 1948, while the New Hampshire state commission investigating "subversive" activities printed the entire list in its 1950 final report.[43]

When newspapers (or other sources) publicized AGLOSO designations, a punitive response was sometimes immediate, and, in at least one famous incident, extremely violent. Thus, immediately after the first Truman AGLOSO was published on December 5, 1947, a meeting room reservation for the newly listed Connecticut State Youth Conference at Hartford's Hotel Bond was suddenly canceled; the hotel manager declared, "the Hotel Bond is not open to them" and "the place for them to meet is in Russia." Similarly, within a few days of the 1947 listing of the Seattle Labor School, almost all area trade unions withdrew their previous financial support. The so-called Peekskill riots of mid-1949, one of the most notorious incidents of Cold War anti-Communist vigilante violence, were clearly at least partly instigated by intensive local newspaper publicity that focused on the AGLOSO designation of the CRC. An attempt by the CRC to organize an August 27 concert near Peekskill, New York, featuring the prominent black left-wing actor and singer Paul Robeson was prevented by severe rioting during which one man was stabbed and another suffered a brain concussion. Although Robeson was able to perform near Peekskill on September 4, the 20,000 concert-goers were attacked by a huge mob when they sought to depart, leaving 150 people injured and scores of cars and buses with their windows shattered and/or overturned and destroyed. The local newspaper, the *Peekskill Evening Star*, repeatedly drew attention to the CRC's AGLOSO designation immediately pre-ceding these events: thus, it featured an August 23 front-page headline reading, "Robeson Concert Here Aids 'Subversive Unit'" and subsequently reported that the "Russia-loving" Robeson was going to sing for a "Communist front organiza-tion" and that "every ticket purchased for the Peekskill concert will drop nickels and dimes into the till basket of an un-American political organization."[44]

The November 1947 designation of the NCASF and subsequent revelation that the group's chair was the Rev. William Howard Melish, associate reactor of Holy Trinity Episcopal Church in Brooklyn, led to a huge, nationally publicized row that bitterly divided the church, ending in lengthy court battles and the shut-tering of the church for twelve years. In March 1948, as the *New York Times* re-ported on its front page under the headline, "Red Row Stirred in Melish Church," the church's eleven-person lay governing body (the vestry) called for the ouster of Melish because his "outside activities" were deemed to threaten "the contin-ued successful progress of the church." The vestry subsequently also demanded the ouster of the church rector, the Rev. John Howard Melish, Melish's father and a nationally known liberal minister, due to his failure to curb his son's ac-tivities. Supervising Bishop James De Wolfe then ordered the elder Melish to step down, but he refused to do so after receiving a 261–27 vote of support from a general church membership meeting. Both sides went to court and the elder Melish stepped aside in 1949 after the U.S. Supreme Court refused to review a lower court injunction ordering him to obey De Wolfe's directive (the subject of a July 27, 1951, front-page *New York Times* story). The younger Melish, who suc-ceeded his father as church leader after a change in the vestry's composition, was similarly forced out in 1956, and De Wolfe, declaring that he could not "tolerate the church edifice being used as a battlefield," ordered the church closed and the parish abolished in 1957 as the controversy continued. The restored church, which was reopened under a modified name in 1969, honored the younger Mel-ish at a service celebrating the fiftieth anniversary of his ordination in June 1986, one month before his death, during which he declared, "It was a wild, hysterical period, when the cold war started. Now we've come full circle."[45]

The use of AGLOSO as a means of discrediting people and organizations became so widespread after 1947 that it became common for nonlisted groups to publicly suggest that lack of AGLOSO designation amounted to an official "clearance." During a 1948 HUAC hearing, conservative Rep. Karl Mundt (R-SD) cautioned DOJ officials that failure to place a group on AGLOSO "would put a Good Housekeeping label of approval on an organization," while a 1956 internal FBI memorandum declared that "in many instances the public has wrongly concluded that organizations not designated have received an indirect clearance from the Attorney General." In rejecting an INS recommendation that an alien be denied citizenship partly because he had belonged to the allegedly pro-Communist Chinese Hand Laundry Association, a federal judge noted in 1957 that the group had "never been placed" on AGLOSO. The first sentence of a 1951 *Los Angeles Times* article on the League of Women Voters quoted the group's president as declaring that it "has never been on any list of subversive organizations." In response to charges of subversive ties made against University of Chicago professors during 1949 state legislative hearings, the chair of the university's board of trustees responded that "only one instance" out of fifty such alleged affiliations involved "current membership in an organization listed by the Attorney General." Hawaii's attorney general rejected the veracity of 1953 congressional testimony alleging that Communists dominated the International Longshoremen's and Warehousemen's Union by asking, "If it were so steeped in communism, then why hasn't the Attorney General designated the ILWU as a subversive organization?" New York City officials rebuffed a 1953 request from a business group that sought to have striking workers banned from collecting funds on the public streets partly on the grounds that the union involved was not AGLOSO-listed. Similarly, newspapers often reported the "non-designation" of groups under attack for allegedly "subversive" activities. Thus, when the ACLU came under attack from the American Legion in 1952 as Communist, the *Washington Post* editorially declared that it had "never appeared" on AGLOSO. The *New York Times* repeatedly made similar statements in reporting attacks on the Emergency Civil Liberties Committee in early 1953, and both the *Post* and *Times*, in reporting 1950 FBI and HUAC attacks on the National Lawyers Guild (NLG), noted that the group was not AGLOSO-designated. However, after Attorney General Brownell announced in 1953 that he was seeking the NLG's designation (by then the DOJ had agreed to provide an AGLOSO hearing procedure, so organizations were first "proposed" for designation), newspaper references to the NLG regularly reported the *intended* listing (and some scholarly sources published decades later report that the NLG was listed, although, as is discussed in a later chapter, the DOJ in fact dropped attempts to designate the group after it went to court).[46]

Confusion over AGLOSO

Virtually every aspect of AGLOSO was clouded in confusion, including its very name and how many groups were included in it. Although internal FBI and DOJ memos routinely referred to it as the "Attorney General's List of Subversive Organizations" and the press adopted this appellation almost immediately after the first 1947 listings, the department sometimes insisted that this name was incorrect (in fact, as is explained below, only a handful of organizations were ever actually specifically designated as "subversive"). Thus, in a 1951 letter to U.S. Attorney George Garrity of Boston, who had written to inquire if he had the authority to disclose the names of "organizations on the Attorney General's subversive list" (which had been massively publicized for over three years!), Assistant Attorney General James McInerney declared that the "correct designation" for the list, to be "always used, is the list of organizations designated under the employee loyalty program." Similar appellations were used whenever official AGLOSO lists were published in the *Federal Register*. However, a 1954 memo from DOJ director of public information G. Frederick Mullen to Assistant Attorney General Tompkins stated that, although, when the list was begun, the department's Internal Security Section "felt that to use the word 'subversive' would hurt the program," the attorney general had subsequently "decided that for press releases and other purposes involving" public relations "we should say that the organizations have been 'designated subversive'" and "we will continue" that policy. Yet when Tompkins testified before Congress in 1955 and was asked if he used the term "subversive list," he responded, "I term it 'designated pursuant to [Eisenhower Executive Order] 10450.'"[47]

When AGLOSO was first published on December 5, 1947, screaming front-page headlines proclaimed, in the *Washington Post,* "91 Groups Branded as Subversive by Clark," in the *New York Herald Tribune*, "Clark Lists 80 Groups in U.S. as Subversive," and in the *Detroit Free Press*, "U.S. Calls 71 Groups, 11 Schools Disloyal." This numerical confusion continued throughout AGLOSO's life. Thus, the November 14, 1950, *Christian Science Monitor* referred to 186 AGLOSO groups, yet the next day's *New York Times* referred to "some 150 groups listed as subversive." On May 1, 1951, the *Washington Post* reported that AGLOSO then contained "nearly 200 names," but the *New York Herald Tribune* reported AGLOSO "now includes some 130 organizations." According to the *New York Times*, on December 3, 1950, and May 2, 1951, there were "130 organizations" on the list, "about 200" on July 29, 1951, "more than 100 so-called subversive organizations" on June 15, 1952, and 203 groups on July 19, 1951, yet no organizations were added or deleted between November 1950 and the latter date. The *New Dictionary of American History* states that by 1952 the number of designated organizations totaled 115. After Attorney General Brownell announced his final list of proposed designations on December 30, 1954, most newspapers, including the December 31 *New York Times* and *Washington Post*, agreed that the total of listed and proposed organizations was 282, which (or alternatively, 283) eventually became the overwhelming scholarly and popular "consensus" figure for total designations. Nonetheless, the *Times* reported on October 15, 1953, that AGLOSO had somehow previously drastically shrunk to 35, and on April 12, 1955, both the *Times* and the *New York Herald Tribune* printed an AP story that placed the total at 303, clearly because about 20 organizations had been double-counted (once when they were "proposed" for designation on December 30, 1954, and again when the DOJ announced that they were being formally designated for failing to contest their proposed listings). Perhaps due to this error, at least two scholarly studies state that eventually AGLOSO exceeded 300 organizations. Even more puzzling, leading Red Scare scholar Ellen Schrecker states in a 2002 book that by the mid-1950s AGLOSO "contained nearly 200 entries," and, in a December 1953 memo, department AGLOSO unit lawyer Oran Waterman, who had direct access to the relevant records, reported that AGLOSO "covers approximately 400 organizations," a figure corresponding to no other calculation.[48]

Further confusion about the number and names of AGLOSO organizations arose because entirely separate and disparate listings of "subversive" organizations were also issued during the Cold War by a wide variety of governmental agencies and private groups, leading Columbia University historian Henry Steele Commager to acidly write in 1953 that after 1947 "not only the Attorney General but almost everybody else was busy compiling lists—Congressional committees, state Attorneys General, state legislative committees, and scores of private organizations as well." Thus, in early 1948 the California Un-American Activities (Tenney) Committee characterized about 100 organizations as "Communist fronts," about twice as many as then on AGLOSO, while in late 1948 HUAC issued a 144-page listing of 562 "subversive" organizations, which encompassed those on AGLOSO as well as groups earlier "listed" by itself and state committees in California, Massachusetts, and New York. In March 1951, HUAC issued a new compilation of 624 groups. These different lists figured in a famous 1954 television dispute between CBS broadcaster Edward R. Murrow and Sen. McCarthy: in response to Murrow's declaration that McCarthy had engaged in deliberate falsification for terming the ACLU a "subversive" organization although it was not on the AGLOSO list, McCarthy responded that the ACLU had been cited by a California legislative committee and therefore "Mr. Murrow is not telling the truth." On August 19, 1955, the *New York Times* issued a correction that reflected similar confusion, stating that it had incorrectly listed the Institute of Pacific Relations as an AGLOSO group when "the story should have said that the institute had been cited as a Communist-front organization" by HUAC.[49]

While numerical uncertainty about AGLOSO may have partly resulted from sloppy journalism and confusion with other, similar lists, most such confusion undoubtedly was produced by the chaotic manner in which the DOJ published and categorized AGLOSO. Thus, a 1957 staff report for the Commission on Government Security, a congressionally created group authorized to study the federal loyalty program, essentially threw up its hands over the number of AGLOSO designations, noting that one listing (apparently from 1950) included "over 150 names" but "because of some duplications and additions, the exact number included is difficult to compute," and that the latest, November 1955 list had "287 names, some of which are simply different titles by which the same organizations have been called." As this report suggests, the department sometimes published entirely separate designations for the same "parent" organization under different names and/or affiliated groups, yet at other times published all such information as part of one designation. For example, when the department published a September 1948 "consolidated list" of previous designations, about ten groups that had earlier been separately listed, including four local CRC affiliates, no longer were mentioned by name in any manner (the CRC designation simply added "and its affiliates" afterwards). When the National Better Business Bureau wrote to Assistant Attorney General Alexander Campbell to inquire about this discrepancy, Campbell responded that various affiliated groups and organizational "aliases" that had previously been listed separately were "not used in the consolidated compilation but would naturally fall under the same category in the consolidated list as the organization itself" (subsequently the department listed the names of some, but not all CRC affiliates, as part of the CRC designation). However, although Attorney General McGrath informed the LRB in 1950 that the Pacific Northwest Labor School was "in effect but another name for the previously designated Seattle Labor School," the DOJ subsequently listed them as separate organizations, yet listed in another single designation the "People's Education Association (incorporated under the name Los Angeles Educational Association, Inc.) aka People's Educational Center, People's University, People's School." In the department's "consolidated" 1948 list, the SWP's "Communist" designation included the notation "including the American Committee for Workers' Relief," yet the committee was also separately designated as "Communist," while the SWP's additional designations as "subversive" and seeking to unconstitutionally alter the government entirely failed to mention the committee. In a late 1951 version of the "consolidated" list, the IWO was designated as including "its subdivisions, auxiliaries and affiliates," including fifteen specified groups, such as the Hungarian Brotherhood and the Polonia Society of the IWO, which were listed, indented, immediately below it so as to suggest one designation. Yet the subsequent consolidated list of April 29, 1953, separately listed each IWO affiliate, scattered in alphabetical order along with all other groups. Similarly, twelve CP "subdivisions, subsidiaries and affiliates," such as the Committee to Aid the Fighting South and the United May Day Committee, were listed under the "main" CP designation in the 1951 list (although only in the "Communist" designation, not in the two other classifications of the CP!), while they were separately listed in the 1953 AGLOSO.[50]

In apparent contrast to previous policy, in March 1956, Assistant Attorney General Tompkins, responding to a query from Sen. Hubert Humphrey (D-MN) at a time when AGLOSO was under broad and intense political attack, declared that the listing of the American Youth Congress (AYC) "was not intended to designate any of the so-called cooperating groups," because the AYC was a "loosely knit association of numerous youth organizations" and that most affiliated organizations, including "some of the most respected youth groups in the country," were "independent of control by the national organization." Yet eighteen months later Tompkins informed Assistant Attorney General George Doub that the Washington Youth Council was an AYC "branch," and that "membership in a branch of a designated organization is tantamount to membership in the parent organization," especially since the department "has not declared the Washington Youth Council free from communist domination" (the department, in fact, never formally "cleared" any organizations).[51]

Aside from the problem of duplications and inconsistencies with regard to listings of AGLOSO affiliates, another factor that complicated attempts to determine the number of designated groups was the repeated, chaotic changes in the manner in which organizations were categorized by the DOJ. When Clark published the first Truman AGLOSO in December 1947, none of the three subcategories he listed corresponded to the six categories that Truman's loyalty order seemingly required by directing the attorney general to designate groups as subversive, fascist, Communist, totalitarian "or" seeking to deprive other Americans of their constitutional rights "or" to unconstitutionally alter the government. Instead, his November 24, 1947, letter to the LRB, which was published two weeks later, listed: (1) the forty-seven Biddle groups, which he said had been labeled "subversive" by the department under Franklin Roosevelt's 1943 Executive Order 9300 (without clearly saying that he was endorsing that list under Truman's 1947 order); (2) thirty-three groups (including the CP and its "affiliated organizations," even though the CP also was on the Biddle list) that were "hereby designated," without any subcategories given, under Truman's order; and (3) a list of eleven schools, preceded by the statement that they were apparently CP adjuncts but that it was not Clark's view that "any institution devoted to the advancement of knowledge is subversive." (A December 1947 memo from FBI assistant director D. Milton Ladd to Director Hoover divided Clark's list into three categories—"Communist," "Fascist," and "Marxist or Trotskyist"—which corresponded neither to Clark's categorizations nor to Truman's order.)[52]

Clark's phraseology left in complete confusion whether the eleven schools were designated or not, as was reflected in the contradictory numbers cited in the December 5, 1947, newspaper headlines referenced above. Moreover, Clark's letter to the LRB ominously concluded that the enclosed list was not a "complete or final compilation," because "insufficient" information was available to make decisions about "many organizations not named"; because currently existing "presently innocuous" groups might "become the victims of dangerous infiltration forces and, as a consequence, become proper subjects for designation"; and because "new organizations may come into existence whose purpose and activities are in conflict with loyalty to the U.S." Clark first followed through with his concluding suggestion that the LRB would be furnished with lists of additional organizations "from to time" on May 28, 1948, when he designed another thirty-two organizations under Truman's executive order, but again without providing any subcategories. In response to complaints from the LRB, discussed further below, the DOJ, without any public explanation, published later in 1948 a consolidated list of all previously designated organizations (along with four newly listed groups), but now divided into the six subcategories of Truman's executive order, with the forty-seven Biddle listings and the eleven apparently nonsubversive schools listed earlier now simply categorized along with all other designated groups in the six Truman categories. Without providing any definitions or explanations, the consolidated list categorized twenty-two groups as "totalitarian," fifteen as "fascist," eighty-two as "Communist," six as "subversive," four as approving violence to deprive others of their constitutional rights, and five as seeking the unconstitutional overthrow of the government. In Clark's explanatory letter to the LRB, he stated that "under the elementary rule of statutory construction," each of the six categories "must be taken to be independent and mutually exclusive of the others," and therefore although a group "may fall within more than one of the specified classifications," a "reasonable interpretation of the Executive Order would seem to require that designation be predicated upon its dominant characters rather than extended to include all other classifications possible." While this statement clearly suggested that no group would be listed in multiple categories, in fact the CP, the SWP, and three other groups were all listed as "Communist," "subversive," *and* seeking the unconstitutional alteration of the government, while the Bund was termed both "subversive" and "fascist."[53]

Between September 1948 and early 1953, newly designated AGLOSO organizations were always subcategorized per the Truman order, as on April 27, 1949, when Clark listed thirty-six additional organizations and on September 5, 1950, when McGrath designated (depending upon how they were counted) between half-a-dozen and two dozen additional groups. However, when Attorney General Brownell, acting under President Eisenhower's Executive Order 10450 (which reauthorized the existing AGLOSO program, including the Truman subcategories), issued a consolidated list of (by most counts, 192) previously designated organizations on April 29, 1953, all of the Truman subcategories disappeared and all groups were simply listed as "previously designated" under Truman's order and now "redesignated" under Eisenhower's. No public explanation was given for this departure (and the news media barely mentioned it), but it may have simply reflected DOJ's inability to ever define such key terms as "subversive" and "fascist." Even FBI director Hoover was taken by surprise by the "declassifications," writing Deputy Attorney General Rogers in May 1953 to inquire whether "we should continue to afford these organizations the same descriptive data as they were formerly given" or "describe them merely" as AGLOSO-designated. In a 1956 internal DOJ memo, AGLOSO unit head Waterman related that he had informed an inquiring journalist that "publicly listing the organizations by category" had been discontinued because "considerable confusion has been created by the specific category of subversive" and by reference to the list as "AGLOSO," and, additionally, "for the purpose for which the list was promulgated, that is, in connection with the Federal employee security program, it was not deemed necessary" to include them, "particularly since the organizations often fell within two or more of these categories."[54]

Although the redesignated groups, along with sixty-two new organizations that Brownell proposed for future listing on April 29, 1953, were then, for the first time, offered an administrative hearings process for challenging their designations, in accordance with the 1951 Supreme Court *McGrath* ruling (discussed below), the pre-1953 listing was declared "in effect" in the "interim." Under Brownell's stewardship, a total of about ninety groups were added to AGLOSO, primarily the sixty-two groups proposed on April 29, 1953, and another twenty proposed on July 21, 1953. As will be discussed below, because the vast majority of the previously designated organizations were already defunct when the 1953 hearing regulations were announced and because the regulations were apparently (and successfully) designed to impose so many obstacles that groups effectively could not utilize them, only the ISL and two of its affiliated organizations ever were granted administrative hearings, as a result of which the three groups were officially "delisted" in 1958 when the department conceded that it could not prove its case. During the intervening years, as will be discussed below, the political and legal tide in the country decisively turned against the Red Scare, and the department effectively decided that the administrative hearing regulations, and AGLOSO in general, were so constitutionally and politically defective that the entire program would be struck down in the courts if the department continued to make designations. AGLOSO thereafter remained in administrative stasis for over twenty years, until President Nixon tried to revive it by transferring authority over AGLOSO to the SACB, created by the 1950 Internal Security Act (ISA, discussed below). Apparently primarily for political reasons, AGLOSO was not abolished in the interim, but no organizations were added after 1955.[55]

AGLOSO listings were marked by numerous anomalies in addition to those resulting from the appearance and disappearance of subcategories and the duplicative listings of the same organizations under different categories and names. Several listed groups were not organizations at all, at least in the normal sense of the word, but were one-time conferences. Thus, the "Japanese Overseas Convention, Tokyo, Japan, 1940" (first listed in February 1943), was described in a 1949 FBI "summary" memo as a meeting held in "commemoration of the 2600th anniversary of the founding of the Japanese Empire." Similarly, the "Emergency Conference to Save Spanish Refugees (founding body of the North American Spanish Aid Committee)" and the "National Conference on American Policy in China and the Far East (a conference called by the Committee for a Democratic

Far Eastern Policy)" were each designated in July 1949, yet their affiliated organizations had been listed three months earlier: in later lists the conferences and their affiliated organizations were designated separately. The "Congress of American Revolutionary Writers" (listed February 1943) was in fact the 1935 founding conference of the League of American Writers (LAW), which was separately designated in May 1948, after which both were listed independently. The California Labor School (CLS) was listed in May 1948 along with its street address, yet addresses were never provided for *any* other group (when the CLS moved, its new address was incorporated in later AGLOSO lists!).[56]

After the "American-Russian Institute" (ARI) was designated in May 1948 and a New York–based organization with that name protested bitterly, Attorney General Clark publicly announced a few months later that apparently "there are a number of organizations" with similar names and "in order to avoid any misunderstanding or inadvertent injustice," the words "of San Francisco" should be added to the ARI's previous listing to "more exactly designate the organization which has been found to be subversive" (although no organizations had yet been specifically categorized as "subversive"). Although this announcement was unquestionably intended to "clear" the New York ARI (and the organization issued a press release to that effect), in April 1949, without any explanation, Clark designated the "American Russian Institute of New York." Although the Biddle and 1947 AGLOSO listed "Shinto Temples," without any qualification, in September 1955 this designation was modified to read "Shinto Temples (limited to State Shinto abolished [by General Douglas MacArthur] in 1945)." A spring 1948 LRB training manual reported that whether the AGLOSO listing referred to "shrines (State Shintoism) or churches (Sectarian or religious Shintoism) is not clear," but "presumably the former is intended, since sectarian Shintoism was permitted in the war relocation centers [i.e., detention camps for Japanese-Americans] and still obtains in Japan under the [American military occupation] Supreme Command." However, the LRB manual reported, clearly based on FBI and DOJ information, that the distinction between the cult of state Shintoism, "which seeks to inculcate a belief that the [Japanese] emperor is of divine descent," and "Sectarian, or religious, Shintoism," was, in practice, "frequently slight" and that "it was difficult if not impossible, to determine where the line of demarcation, if any existed." The Shinto designation was qualified in 1955 after a department memo reported that Attorney General Brownell had adopted in April 1953 the policy that groups "organized solely for religious purposes" could not be designated and that the existing listing was "misleading and may be construed to apply to organizations which are a part of Sectarian Shinto, where such is not intended," although admittedly both types of Shinto "follow essentially the same doctrines and worship."[57]

After protests from the Blue Star Mothers of America and the Minute Women of the USA, AGLOSO listings of the National Blue Star Mothers of America (designated in 1949) and the Massachusetts Minutemen for Peace (designated in 1954) were modified to include parenthetical notations that the former two groups should not be confused with the latter two. However, responding to a 1955 letter from Rep. Clement Zablocki (D-WI) stating that the "Italian-American Mutual Aid Society, Giuseppe Garibaldi" wished the department to clarify that it had no connection with the designated "Garibaldi American Fraternal Society," Assistant Attorney General Tompkins declared that it was not "feasible" to compile a "definitive list" of nondesignated groups with "some similarity in name to groups which have been designated." In late 1957, Oran Waterman, then deputy chief of the department's Civil Section, recommended "clarifications" concerning three designated groups with names similar to other organizations, but no action was taken.[58]

In Clark's first AGLOSO list of late 1947, only one organization, the "Nature Friends of America (since 1935)," was listed with a qualifying date. Yet, most experts, including DOJ officials, agreed that many so-called "Communist front" organizations, especially those organized during the mid-1930s such as the National Negro Congress (NNC), AYC, and LAW, had come under obvious Communist domination only after the 1939 Nazi-Soviet Non-Aggression Pact, and that many non-Communists supported pro-Allied groups with Communist members after America entered the war, at a time when it was official American policy to support the Soviet Union. Thus, according to a DOJ report furnished to the LRB in 1948, the NACASD (listed in early 1949) included in its initial leadership and membership "many non-Communists" and "many reputable persons throughout the country who were sympathetic to the Loyalist cause in Spain" but that gradually many of the non-Communists left the organization "as communist domination became clearer." Department Assistant Solicitor General George Washington declared in a 1949 memo that since the American League for Peace and Democracy (ALPD, designated in May 1948) had as its announced objective the support of American foreign policy during its "popular front" heyday, "unless a member also joined a successor or predecessor organization with opposing objectives, the mere fact of membership does not appear to prove anything at all." Similarly, during 1950 congressional testimony, State Department loyalty board chair Gen. Conrad Snow declared, "It would be going pretty far to consider [suspect] someone who in 1941 sponsored a parade or the like" of a group "declared subversive in 1947."[59]

Nonetheless, the only organizations that succeeded in obtaining "time modifications" of their original designations were the depression-era Workers Alliance (WA, discussed earlier) and the Dante Alighieri Society (DAS), listed by Biddle in 1943. The DOJ changed the WA's AGLOSO affiliation in 1951, without any explanation, to include the parenthetical addition "since April, 1936," thereby changing its retroactively designated officially "subversive" character from since its 1935 founding (as of its November 1947 designation) to the new "cutoff" date.

In late 1948, Attorney General Clark changed the DAS listing to include the notation "between 1935 and 1940," on the grounds that the society had disbanded "approximately a year and a half prior" to America's 1941 entry into World War II and that Biddle's designation was only "intended to be effective" as of the listing date and "was not intended to apply to any period subsequent thereto." Clark's memo entirely failed to explain why similar time limitations did not apply to other AGLOSO organizations that became defunct before or after their designations, a circumstance true of at least half of AGLOSO by 1948.[60]

The Nature of AGLOSO Organizations

Although some AGLOSO-designated groups were fairly well known, the most striking fact about the vast majority of AGLOSO organizations is how completely obscure and insignificant they were. Computerized keyword searches performed in 2004–2007 for the entire press runs of the *New York Times*, the *Washington Post*, the *Los Angeles Times*, the *Christian Science Monitor*, the *Chicago Tribune*, and the *Wall Street Journal* revealed that about 70 percent (195) of the approximately 280 AGLOSO organizations were mentioned in *any* manner less than fifteen times in *all six newspapers combined*. Scores of these groups were never mentioned *except* in reports about their designations: among these were the American Christian Nationalist Party, American Poles for Peace, California Emergency Defense Committee, Cervantes Fraternal Society, Chopin Cultural Center, the Civil Liberties Sponsoring Committee of Pittsburgh, Connecticut Committee to Aid Victims of the Smith Act, Croatian Benevolent Fraternity, Freedom Stage, Harlem Trade Union Council, Hellenic-American Brotherhood, Japanese Overseas Central Society, Maritime Labor Committee to Defend Al Lannon, Michigan Council for Peace, National Association of Mexican-Americans, New Committee for Publications, Oklahoma Committee to Defend Political Prisoners, Palo Alto Peace Club, Philadelphia Labor Committee for Negro Rights, Provisional Committee on Latin American Affairs, the Romanian-American Fraternal Society, and the Union of New York Veterans.

Only thirty-one listed organizations (slightly over 10 percent of the total) were mentioned more than 100 times in all six newspapers combined, while the remaining fifty-five groups (about 20 percent) were mentioned between 15 and 100 times. The thirty-one organizations in the former group were generally fairly prominent and probably recognizable to a substantial percentage of Americans, including some organizations mentioned well over 500 times (often dating from well before 1947), such as the CP, Bund, SWP, CRC, WA, AYC, IWW, NCASF, International Labor Defense (ILD), and the Abraham Lincoln Brigade (ALB). However, most of them, including the IWO, LAW, ASC, AYD, CAW, ALPD/ALWF, NNC, VALB, and the Photo League, were mentioned at best a few hundred times. Most of the organizations mentioned between 15 and 100 times were very obscure, including the American Council for a Democratic Greece, American Patriots, American Polish League, Baltimore Forum, Council for Pan-American Democracy, Hollywood Writers Mobilization, and the National Negro Labor Council. Probably only a few of this group of organizations, including the JAFRC and American Committee for the Protection of the Foreign Born (ACPFB), were familiar to more than a tiny percentage of Americans, and even then most likely due to the groups' various legal encounters with the government.[61]

The prominence of AGLOSO-designated groups appears to have steadily declined between the first listing published in late 1947 and the last approximately ninety organizations proposed for designation in 1953–1954. While a fair number of the former were reasonably prominent national organizations, most of the latter were small, local groups: according to the computer search, almost all of them were mentioned fewer than ten times in all six newspapers combined, usually only in connection with their AGLOSO designations. Probably typical of such groups was the Elsinore Progressive League (EPL) of Elsinore, California, which was among the last twenty-seven organizations ever proposed for designation (on December 29, 1954) and one of the last four organizations actually designated (on October 20, 1955). The EPL is mentioned six times in the combined newspaper search, in every instance relating to its designation. The entire 110-page EPL FBI file, provided in response to a 2005 Freedom of Information Act request and seemingly complete save the redaction of names of FBI informants, reveals so little that even vaguely suggests "subversion" that the FBI placed its investigation on "inactive" status six weeks before the DOJ proposed to designate the EPL. According to a 1953 FBI summary, the EPL was organized in 1947 "as a social group for negroes and to contribute to the civic development of community" and included "numerous white members" and "some" members who "are known CP members." Most of the file relates to entirely routine activities, with the only other "subversive" information reported (which triggered FBI director Hoover's October 15, 1953, directive for a "thorough investigation" of the group) consisting of allegations that two EPL officers were or had been CP members, that Communists sometimes attended EPL functions, and that the organization occasionally rented its hall to allegedly Communist organizations and functions (including a wedding of two CP members). The file contains no allegations that the EPL ever passed "party line" resolutions or otherwise supported CP policy.[62]

The DOJ never included *any* information about the listed organizations when it announced AGLOSO designations, never provided any public explanation of either its general AGLOSO criteria or specific definitions for the six Truman subcategories, and, with the minor exceptions noted below, consistently rebuffed requests for such information from private individuals and even from government officials. Thus, in response to a 1951 inquiry from U.S. Attorney for Massachusetts Garrity, Assistant Attorney General James McInerney declared that while the department frequently received "inquiries as to the bases upon which the [AGLOSO] designations are made," in "each case [it] refuses to comply with such a request since the Executive Order contains no authority for disclosing the facts in any instance." Moreover, although alleged "membership in, affiliation with or sympathetic association with" AGLOSO organizations was deemed relevant in the Truman executive order for making loyalty determinations, the term "sympathetic association" was never defined. In response to a 1955 inquiry from Interior Department security director Frederick Schmidt as to what "sympathetic association" meant, DOJ ISD head Tompkins was informed by an underling, Benjamin Pollack, that the term had "never been defined by the Department" and "dictionary definitions are not helpful." Therefore, Tompkins responded to Schmidt by simply endorsing Schmidt's report that the Interior Department understood it to mean a "close association such as sharing, or affected by the feelings of another to a sufficient degree to maintain a congenial or harmonious relationship."[63]

During July 1949 Senate testimony Attorney General Clark described AGLOSO-designated organizations' purposes in a manner that clearly suggested generally entirely legal activities. He declared their scope was "generally indicated by the names of the organizations themselves," adding that some were clearly organized to foster "American policy favorable to the current policy of a foreign state" or to "teach Communist dogma and tactics," while others sought to serve "as legal defense or legal aid groups for Communists" or to aid "others whose cases can be rendered into cause célèbres to serve" Communist ends.[64] A categorization of AGLOSO organizations, based on their names and what is known of relatively prominent listed groups, indicates that the largest number consisted of civil liberties/civil rights defense organizations (fifty-two groups, or about 18 percent of the total), including the ILD, NNC, ACPFB, and CRC, as well smaller groups formed to defend specific individuals (i.e., CP officials prosecuted under the Smith Act). Other major categories were ethnic and fraternal groups (forty-one, or about 15 percent, many of which had an East European focus and/or were branches of the IWO, such as the Chopin Cultural Society, Hungarian Brotherhood and Croatian Benevolent Fraternity); self-described "peace" groups (fifteen, about 5 percent, such as the Peace Information Center, the East Bay Peace Committee, and Syracuse Women for peace); organizations focusing on foreign policy (twenty-one, about 7 percent, such as the Council on African Affairs and the China Welfare Appeal); groups concerned with the Spanish Civil War, including relief for war refugees (ten, about 3 percent, including the NACASD and JAFRC); those involved with education, religion, or the media (twenty-eight, about 10 percent, including Commonwealth College and the Jefferson School of Social Science); World War II–era alleged pro-Axis groups (thirty-five, or about 13 percent, such as the Bund, Lictor Society, and Japanese Protective Association); "native fascist" and racist groups (eleven, or about 4 percent, such as the KKK, the Silver Shirts, and the Columbians); youth organizations (eight, or about 3 percent, such as the AYD, YCL, AYC, and Socialist Youth League); and union-focused organizations and self-described political parties (seventeen, or about 6 percent, including the CP, the SWP, and the IWW). The remaining approximately fifty organizations (about 18 percent) typically had relatively unique concerns (such as the Photo League and the CAW), focused on general cultural or social policy/social justice issues, often with a local geographic focus (such as the Baltimore Forum, Washington Commonwealth Federation, Idaho Pension Union, and Citizens Committee of the Upper West Side, New York City), or were of an undetermined nature.

Almost twenty AGLOSO organizations were educational institutions. Commonwealth College of Arkansas, originally founded as part of an experimental utopian and vaguely "socialist" agricultural cooperative colony in 1923, never enrolled more than sixty students and closed in 1940, nine years before it was designated in April 1949. All Commonwealth students spent time both in class and working to keep the institution running, including growing, cooking, and serving the food and constructing housing and other buildings; the faculty served without salaries. The college was unquestionably always under "leftish" influences, but, except toward the very end of its existence, it was characterized more by general disorganization and ideological/personal factionalism than by any coherent dogma. The college received the endorsement or financial support of the Arkansas Federation of Labor, Supreme Court Justice Louis Brandeis, and many distinguished educators, including Alexander Meiklejohn and Roscoe Pound, and the New Deal Federal Emergency Relief Administration subsidized some of its educational programs. While pro-Communist faculty and students dominated its final years, the college never engaged in any activities more "subversive" than trying to help a floundering union seeking to organize brutally oppressed tenant farmers and sharecroppers. It was forced to close in 1940 after local officials, alienated by its growing "red" reputation, brought charges of anarchy and failing to display the American flag against it and seized its property for failure to pay resulting fines. Its most famous student was Orval Faubus, who as Arkansas governor refused to obey court orders to desegregate the Little Rock schools in 1957, leading President Eisenhower to send in troops. Faubus declared in a 1994 interview that he had "never been with a group of equal numbers" with "as many highly intelligent" people as at Commonwealth College."[65]

Virtually all of the other schools placed on AGLOSO were, sometimes quite openly, founded and supported by the CP, but they all focused on normal educational activities. The best-known institution, the Jefferson School of Social Science in New York City (designated November 1947), and the CLS in San Francisco (designated May 1948) were typical of the others—including the Abraham Lincoln School of Chicago, the Philadelphia School of Social Sciences and Art, the Samuel Adams School of Boston, the People's Educational Association of Los Angeles, and the Seattle Labor School (all designated in November 1947 and defunct by the end of 1949)—except that they were substantially larger and survived their AGLOSO designations considerably longer. The Jefferson School, founded in 1944, maintained a 30,000-volume library, offered over 300 courses, and enrolled over 5,000 individuals at its Manhattan campus alone during its 1946 peak (it also offered extension classes in Brooklyn, the Bronx, Harlem, and New Jersey). Many of its faculty (some of whom had been fired for their political beliefs from New York City municipal colleges at the beginning of the 1940s) had CP ties and, according to a 1949 *Saturday Evening Post* article, "everyone" attending classes "speaks and acts on the assumption that everyone else is already a communist or about to become one." A friendly scholarly account of the school terms it and similar institutions a "kind of Communist Chautauqua," noting that "Soviet-led Communism was portrayed as the sole exemplar of theoretical and practical rectitude." However, many courses apparently had little ideological content, including those on "The Music of Beethoven" and "Beauty and Fashion Clinic: Making the Most of Your Appearance." Leading black historian Herbert Aptheker offered a class on "Negro History," while pioneering feminist historian Eleanor Flexner taught women's history. The school's 1947 AGLOSO designation, along with the increasing Cold War climate, clearly wreaked havoc on the institution: by 1950, its class offerings had fallen to thirty-six, about half with explicit Marxist content, and the school began to cloak its students in anonymity, no longer taking attendance and or even asking for their names when they enrolled. By 1956, after further damaging publicity associated with the SACB's 1955 finding, in response to a 1953 petition from the attorney general, that the school was a "Communist front," fall enrollment slumped below 400, and the school announced that it would close due to "unwarranted persecution by the Federal government."[66]

The CLS (originally the Tom Mooney School) suffered a similar fate, including both AGLOSO designations and SACB proceedings, and closed its doors in 1957. In its early days, it was sponsored and financed by over 100 San Francisco Bay area AFL and CIO unions, as well as by the National Association for the Advancement of Colored People (NAACP), some local businesses, and even wealthy donors, such as prominent banker William Crocker and the Levi Strauss family. Many CLS faculty were affiliated with unions or also taught at nearby colleges, including Stanford, the California School of Fine Arts, and the University of California, while guest lecturers included architect Frank Lloyd Wright, film producer Orson Welles, and journalist Eric Severeid. The CLS originally offered hundreds of courses in a wide variety of fields at its San Francisco headquarters and widely scattered extension centers, including a course on painting by the well-known muralist Anton Refregier and classes on dance, ceramics, theater, and home decoration. A 1946 report on the CLS by the California state Department of Education reported that the Veterans Administration had concluded that the CLS was "clearly qualified to offer training to veterans" under the G.I. Bill of Rights. The State Department designated the school an official host for socialist and labor delegations attending the 1945 San Francisco UN founding conference, leading Secretary of State Edward Stettinius to write the CLS that "patriotic and public-spirited organizations such as you so ably represent have done much in making the conference a success, in helping to create a basis for a better understanding among the citizens of the United Nations." The president's Fair Employment Practices Commission honored the school's efforts to make America "a place where groups can live in harmony," while the 1946 California education report found that CLS course outlines compared "favorably as to objectives and content with schools accredited by state and higher educational agencies" and that the school maintained a "well-balanced library." In May 1946 the CLS cosponsored a conference with the University of California, and at its 1947–1948 height it enrolled about 5,000 students per semester. According to the most detailed study of the CLS, a 2005 dissertation by Jess Rigelhaupt, the school had by then become a "vibrant workers' education center that served as a vital nexus for building leftist social movements and creating a progressive culture in the Bay Area"; its "role in building social and cultural coalitions in the 1940s and 1950s" helped to shape the distinctive left-wing culture of the region and "had a lasting legacy into the 1960s." However, following attacks upon CLS by a California legislative (Tenney) committee in 1946–1947, but above all due to its mid-1948 AGLOSO listing and the consequent retroactive loss of its federal tax-exempt status (which encompassed a demand for $7,000 in back taxes), the school's enrollment, finances, and general fortunes quickly nosedived. Thus, the psychology department, which had offered six classes in 1946, could not offer a single class by 1949 and, according to the CLS, its total income fell from $150,000 to $25,000 between 1947 and 1950 (partly due to its decision to voluntarily surrender the right earlier accorded to it to accept student G.I. Bill tuition payments). Although the IRS had originally agreed to accept delayed payment of the back taxes, following the March 1957 SACB finding that the CLS was a "Communist front," the tax agency revoked the agreement and closed down the school by seizing its headquarters and padlocking the building on May 3, 1957. Until shortly before its closure, the CLS continued to maintain an active program of sponsoring folksongs, and in 1954 it published the first songbook by Malvina Reynolds, whose song "Little Boxes" would eventually become famous. According to a 1963 federal appeals court ruling that dismissed the school's attempt to overturn the SACB finding, the CLS, which educated an estimated 55,000 students during its fifteen-year lifetime, was already in the process of dissolution when the IRS acted.[67]

Among the ten AGLOSO groups primarily concerned with the Spanish Civil War, among the best known were the NACASD, ALB, VALB, and JACFRC (the latter three of which waged long legal struggles against their AGLOSO designations that are discussed below). The listing of the pro-loyalist Spanish Civil War organizations oddly contrasted with the earlier-discussed 1942 CSC directive that stressed that "the whole matter" of the Spanish Civil War should be "scrupulously avoided" as "having any bearing on pro-communism" in federal loyalty investigations. Although military recruitment and assistance to Spain violated American 1930s neutrality laws, most of the pro-loyalist groups were primarily concerned with humanitarian relief efforts and were never accused of any illegal activities. While Communists were clearly heavily involved in both military and financial assistance to the Spanish loyalists, many non-Communists also supported such efforts. Thus, according to scholar Eleanor Bontecou's 1953 assessment, most American supporters of the groups were primarily motivated by antifascist sentiments, and the percentage of Communists in them "varied markedly," with many non-Communists withdrawing when it "became evident that the Communists were taking over the Spanish-aid operations in this country." The 1949 NACASD designation drew unusual, bitter protests from the ACLU and the ADA, both strongly anti-Communist groups that had not expressed opposition to AGLOSO per se. The NACASD, created in 1936, was the largest of the pro-loyalist humanitarian organizations, with a list of sponsors, including Communists, socialists, and liberals, that one source characterizes as resembling a "Who's Who of the time." The group sent hundreds of tons of relief supplies to Spain, including almost 200 ambulances and eight hospitals staffed with over 100 American doctors and nurses. In a joint letter protesting the NACASD listing, ACLU head Roger Baldwin and ADA Executive Secretary James Loeb (both of whom had themselves served on the NACASD executive committee) denounced the listing as a "direct affront to thousands of Americans opposed to all forms of totalitarianism," especially since, they argued, after the group changed its name in 1939 to the Spanish Refugee Relief Campaign (AGLOSO-designated as an alternative name for the NACASD), with Secretary of the Interior Ickes as honorary chair, Communist elements were "forced to withdraw."[68]

Among the approximately twenty AGLOSO organizations primarily concerned with American foreign policy (aside from Spanish Civil War groups), only the NCASF (discussed in the next chapter) and the CAA were relatively prominent. Before its gradual disintegration following its late 1947 designation, the CAA was, in the words of a scholarly study, "the longest-lived and most influential American organization of its kind [i.e., focused on Africa]" and became the "major center in the country for regular formal and informal discussions on Africa." It was formed in 1941 to support education about Africa and African freedom from western colonialism. CAA members regularly communicated with the State Department and the organization maintained one of the country's finest libraries on Africa and published the leading periodical on Africa, with over 3,000 subscribers at its 1946 peak. Among its prominent members were Earl Dickerson, president of the black National Bar Association, distinguished Howard University sociologist E. Franklin Frazier, famed Columbia University anthropologist Franz Boaz, Howard University president Mordecai Johnson, at least two congressmen, and renowned singer and actor Paul Robeson (and others who, like Robeson, frequently supported the CP). Although the CAA never sought to become a mass organization and never claimed more a few score members, over 8,000 people attended its 1944 birthday celebration for Robeson, its longtime chair, at which greetings were received from such prominent Americans as Vice President Henry Wallace, CIO leader Sidney Hillman, and Rabbi Stephen Wise. Although the CAA unquestionably had what historian Hollis Lynch terms "a definite stamp of ideological radicalism," including policy positions generally parallel to the CP's, it was never charged with illegal activities. However, its 1947 designation triggered numerous defections and a bitter split over the role of CP influence, after which it steadily declined. By the time of its 1955 dissolution, after enduring investigations by the SACB, the IRS, and a New York state committee, the CAA had become, according to Lynch, "one more victim of McCarthyite repression."[69]

The vast majority of the over fifty AGLOSO groups that concentrated on civil liberties and civil rights defense issues were obscure organizations that focused on specific cases of governmental prosecution. Thus, according to a 1948 DOJ report provided to the LRB, one such group, the Dennis Defense Committee (designated November 1947), was formed to support CP secretary Eugene Dennis in connection with a contempt of Congress conviction, as "the most recent in a long line of organizations" created by the party for "the specific purpose of rallying support, issuing propaganda and collecting contributions in behalf of a convicted Party member." The only activities attributed to it were meetings and mailing appeals to public officials. Another defense group, the National Committee for the Defense of Political Prisoners (originally listed by Biddle in 1943), was a short-lived 1930s spin-off of the far more significant ILD (discussed immediately below). The committee was primarily known for its backing of strikers during the notorious 1931 "Bloody Harlan" coal strike in Kentucky, which was crushed by a general reign of terror by local officials and coal companies. The committee's leader, writer Theodore Dreiser, and many others were arrested for "criminal syndicalism" when they visited Harlan County to support the strike, and Dreiser was additionally arrested for adultery, leading him to ridicule the charge because, he declared, "Everyone knows I'm impotent."[70]

In contrast to most listed defense organizations, three such groups—the ILD, the CRC, and the ACPFB—were involved in numerous, often highly publicized, cases. While these three groups were undoubtedly close to the CP and often criticized for promoting CP interests ahead of their publicly avowed goals, their energies were concentrated on completely legitimate legal defense activities, often in highly controversial cases that "mainstream" lawyers shunned. The ILD (designated May 1948), founded in 1925 and folded into the CRC when the latter organized in 1946, focused on defending labor, political radicals, immigrants, and blacks. Although clearly dominated by CP members until 1937, when it became a "popular front" group, the ILD regularly offered its services to non-Communists and was supported by many liberals and radicals. According to historian Theodore Draper, by late 1926 the ILD claimed 156 branches with 20,000 individual and 75,000 collective memberships and outclassed virtually "all the other early fronts in staying power, widespread activity and far-reaching influence." It specialized in publicizing causes through demonstrations and publications (the so-called "mass protest" approach) and attracted general widespread attention to a number of notorious prosecutions, including the "Scottsboro" affair, involving the alleged 1931 rape of two white Alabama women by nine young blacks, and the case of Angelo Herndon, a black teenager who was sentenced to twenty years' imprisonment for "attempting to incite insurrection" due to his 1931 CP organizing efforts in Georgia. The ILD contributed substantially to the defense effort that saved the lives of the "Scottsboro boys," winning two landmark Supreme Court due process victories along the way, and played a critical role in a similarly important 1937 Supreme Court free speech ruling that gained Herndon's release. Even extremely hostile accounts concede that the ILD hired extremely competent defense attorneys in these and other cases, succeeded in gaining unparalleled national and international attention for their causes, and pioneered modern forms of mass mobilization, thereby creating a model for the post–World War II civil rights movement. According to a 1937 black newspaper editorial, absent the ILD, "Herndon would have been wearing a number instead of a respectable citizen's clothes." Rallies on behalf of the "Scottsboro boys" regularly attracted thousands of people in the United States and Europe; according to a perhaps apocryphal story, one New York City landlord, apparently tired of the constant agitation, told his complaining tenants, "All right, all right, I'll fix the plumbing and paint the halls, but I can't free the Scottsboro boys." The most detailed history of the ILD, a 2007 dissertation by Jennifer Uhlman, concludes that the ILD developed an "impressive arsenal of legal and public means to resist government clampdowns and support grassroots political activism," thus "reinforcing courtroom tactics with large-scale mobilization and protest" and obtaining "some impressive victories, most notably in the area of democratic and civil rights for communists, black Americans in the south and unions across the country." The author of a detailed study of the Herndon case similarly concluded in 1986 that the ILD contributed to a "growing awakening on the part of black America and its allies to the virtues of direct action and militant struggle."[71]

The CRC (designated November 1947) was founded in 1946 via a merger of the ILD, the NNC (discussed earlier), and the National Federation for Constitutional Liberties (designated in 1943). It was the most influential AGLOSO defense group still functioning when listed, with an estimated 10,000 peak membership. While Communists clearly played a leading role in the CRC, its causes were supported by many prominent Americans, including, in the artistic community, Arthur Miller, Leonard Bernstein, Gene Kelly, Edward G. Robinson, Elia Kazan, Gregory Peck, and Frank Sinatra. The CRC used the "mass protest" approach in its major cases, which frequently involved defending Communists and southern blacks, including those targeted in the Virginia rape prosecution of the "Martinsville Seven" (which ended with their executions—the largest number of executions in American history for a rape conviction). The CRC focused, especially in Los Angeles, on allegations of police brutality (a problem to become famous fifty years later during the 1992 Rodney King riots) and drew considerable international attention (and heightened American governmental anger) to American racial discrimination by petitioning the United Nations in 1951 to find the United States guilty of "genocide" directed against blacks, especially as reflected in the scores of post–World War II lynchings that marred the South. CRC lawyers (one of whom was Bella Abzug, who would emerge as a leading feminist and gain election to Congress in the 1970s) also succeeded in getting city ordinances in Jacksonville, Florida, and Birmingham, Alabama, which required the "registration" of Communists, struck down as unconstitutional. The CRC was relentlessly persecuted as the Cold War intensified, not only via AGLOSO, but also by repeated congressional investigations (resulting in the jailing of its leadership for refusing to disclose financial information), the courts, the SACB, and the IRS (which sued it in 1955 for $75,000 in back taxes and penalties, which the CRC claimed it was exempt from as a "civic league"). The CRC especially antagonized the government by bailing out Communists: when CRC bail fund trustee and millionaire Frederick Field was subjected to an anal search upon his 1951 imprisonment for refusing to turn over CRC records after several CRC-bonded Communists skipped bail, he declared, "You're not going to find four missing Communists up there." The constant persecution of the CRC and attacks upon it as Communist controlled frightened liberals into shunning the group, while the NAACP repeatedly attacked it, partly to establish its own non-Communist credentials, at the cost of trimming its sails, especially with regard to issues related to economic inequality. Thus, when the CRC asked to join the NAACP in legal defense of the "Martinsville Seven," the lead NAACP lawyer declared that neither his Richmond law firm nor the NAACP would be associated "with any organization which has been declared subversive by the U.S. attorney general," and NAACP official Roy Wilkins wrote later that "we were having enough trouble getting Congress to consider even the most elementary civil rights legislation; the last thing we needed was to give ammunition to red-baiting southern congressmen and senators, who would have loved nothing better than to paint us pink." The NAACP, which became a bitter rival to the CRC as it had been earlier to the ILD, constantly attacked the group for allegedly subordinating the interests of its clients to Communist dogma and recruitment needs, but as "Martinsville Seven" historian Eric Rise notes, "in reality both groups pursued cases that advanced their respective institutional goals." The CRC formally dissolved in 1956 due to what it termed "persistent persecution by reactionary forces in government," but it had been reduced to a skeleton long before that, with its few southern chapters in particular destroyed by what historian Sarah Brown has termed constant "harassment by conservative local civic organizations, terrorist groups, grand juries, police 'red squads,' state committees, HUAC and its corresponding Senate committee, and the FBI." By the early 1950s, according to the leading student of the CRC, historian Gerald Horne, the group seemed to largely remain "in business in order to defend itself." Historian Charles Martin concludes, however, that despite its collapse the CRC's militant tactics

> dramatized before a wide national audience the issue of racial discrimination and racial subordination in the South [and] helped fill the gap between the [ILD-type] black direct-action protests of the 1930s and the new wave of such activism that dates from the [1956 Rosa Parks] Montgomery bus boycott. . . . [The CRC] bequeathed to later civil rights activists the example of a militant, interracial movement committed to fighting racism through demonstrations and direct action protests as well as through legal action. Despite its strident rhetoric, the CRC also helped raise a question which could no longer be ignored: would a nation seeking to lead the democratic world against totalitarianism abroad commit itself to practicing democracy at home?[72]

The ACPFB (designated May 1948) was founded in 1933 to provide legal assistance for aliens seeking to obtain American citizenship and, especially, for labor and political radicals (and others) facing deportation and denaturalization proceedings. Even a generally hostile historian, who argues that the group was always clearly CP-dominated, concedes that it "exerted significant influence on the course of U.S. immigration and deportation activities from the mid-1930s into the 1950s" and that "hundreds, if not thousands, of foreign-born workers became American through its efforts, most of whom probably never realized that they were indebted to Communists." While clearly friendly to the CP, the ACPFB gained substantial support, especially in its early years, from many prominent non-Communists, including first lady Eleanor Roosevelt, ACLU head Baldwin, theologian Reinhold Niebuhr, educator John Dewey, and authors Ernest Hemingway, Archibald MacLeish, and Thomas Mann. Even during the period of the 1939–1941 Nazi-Soviet pact, when most alleged "Communist fronts" came under severe attack, the ACPFB was editorially hailed by the *New York Times*, and President Roosevelt messaged its 1940 conference that he was "glad" to greet the group, which had "undertaken the task of assuring fair play to the foreign born within the U.S." During the World War II Russo-American alliance, former Republican presidential candidate Wendell Willkie provided free legal services that helped the ACPFB win the 1943 Supreme Court *Schneiderman* denaturalization case, INS Commissioner Earl Harrison addressed the group, and it regularly co-operated with government agencies. As historian Ellen Schrecker has noted, after 1945 the ACPFB was inundated with deportation cases directed against those with alleged CP and other left-ties, "especially since mainstream civil liberties organizations refused to defend Communists." It soon became a major target of government harassment, including, aside from its AGLOSO designation, congressional, state legislative, and SACB hearings. By 1959 the organization had basically ceased functioning, its finances drained by legal struggles and massive liberal defections; it formally dissolved in 1982, merging with the National Emergency Civil Liberties Committee.[73]

Among the fifteen AGLOSO "peace groups," aside from the "popular front" movements discussed earlier (the ALPD, ALWF, and the APM), the most prominent organizations were the Peace Information Center (PIC) and the American Peace Crusade (APC), both of which were associated with the eminent black scholar W. E. B. Du Bois. The PIC, organized by Du Bois and a handful of other activists in early 1950 to support the Stockholm Peace Appeal, an international petition demanding outlawing of nuclear weapons, primarily came to public attention due to government attacks upon it. Shortly after the mid-1950 American entry into the Korean War, Secretary of State Acheson denounced the appeal, which had attracted the signatures of 1.5 million Americans, as a "propaganda trick in the spurious 'peace offensive' of the Soviet Union"; in February 1951 the PIC was indicted under an obscure 1938 law for failing to register with the federal government as the agent of a foreign power (although it had already dissolved in October 1950 precisely to avoid such action). The 1951 PIC trial proved a fiasco for the government, with the judge entering a judgment of acquittal for Du Bois and four other PIC members after clearly suggesting that the prosecution was a political assault upon the First Amendment and declaring that he could not allow a jury to "conjecture in the field of conjecture" over the PIC's alleged foreign links. In September 1953, the PIC was listed on AGLOSO, despite this legal rebuff and its defunct status. The PIC's successor, the APC, organized in 1951 with Du Bois as honorary chair, was designated in January 1954 and also subjected to SACB proceedings, which led to its 1955 dissolution, due to what it termed government "harassment" and a lack of resources to defend itself. Like the PIC, it unquestionably obtained CP support, but it engaged in entirely legal and peaceful activities, such as a 1951 "peace pilgrimage" to Washington, D.C. Despite its dissolution, the SACB formally declared the group a "Communist front" in 1957 following hearings, which, like all similar proceedings, primarily depended upon paid informants' testimony and revealed that Communists had deliberately avoided leadership positions in the APC, fearing, in the words of historian Robbie Lieberman, that "doing so would make it too easy for such organizations to be smeared and discredited." However, such efforts were largely in vain, because relentless government attempts to paint "peace" groups as Communist-inspired led most

Americans to conclude that, in Lieberman's words, "this sort of talk about 'peace' was subversive and un-American."[74]

Among the more than forty ethnic-oriented AGLOSO organizations, the most prominent were the IWO and its affiliates (discussed above), the ASC (designated in May 1948), the Southern Negro Youth Congress (SNYC, designated November 1947), and the National Negro Labor Council (NNLC, designated February 1954). When the ASC was organized in 1942 to support the war effort among ethnic Slavs, the conference call came from a Republican judge, its first president was a militant anti-Communist, and its inaugural meeting, attended by about 3,000 delegates and guests in Detroit, received greetings from President Roosevelt. Supportive messages were sent to the ASC during World War II by Secretary of State Cordell Hull, Secretary of the Interior Ickes, New York Governor Herbert Lehman, and New York City Mayor Fiorello La Guardia. Anti-Communist groups soon began to withdraw from the ASC, however, in a preview of Cold War struggles over the fate of Eastern Europe. Although most scholars agree that Communist domination of the ASC only became clear in 1945, an undercover FBI informant estimated that as late as 1944 fewer than 10 percent of ASC members were aware of Communist "infiltration" of the organization.[75]

The SNYC was organized as a youth spin-off of the NNC at a 1937 Virginia conference attended by over 500 delegates and about 2,000 observers, with the goal of advocating racial equality and social reforms. It was organized as a popular front group and cooperated with a wide range of organizations before and during World War II, including many church and fraternal groups. Its organizing conference was addressed by Howard University president Mordecai Johnson, and the group received the active support of many leading black educators, including the presidents of Fisk University and the Tuskegee Institute, and the endorsement of both the AFL and the CIO. After the war, the SNYC adopted an increasingly militant stance and lost much of its middle-class support as it faced an increasingly repressive atmosphere, especially after its AGLOSO designation. Attempts to hold its annual conference in Birmingham, Alabama, in 1948 encountered intense harassment from local authorities, who sought to prevent the group from obtaining a meeting place and arrested all whites who attempted to enter the church that was finally secured for violating local segregation laws. The Progressive Party vice presidential candidate, Idaho Sen. Glen Taylor, who was to be the main speaker at the conference, was knocked to the ground by police and arrested for disorderly conduct. The SNYC quickly faded away after 1948, but historian Robin Kelley terms the organization "one of the most significant precursors of the modern civil rights movement" and scholar C. Alvin Hughes similarly argues that the SNYC "kept alive the desire expressed in its motto, to achieve freedom, equality and opportunity for black youth in the South." Similarly, in her 1987 dissertation on the SNYC, Johnetta Richards concludes that the group gained "significant" influence "within southern black communities, and laid much of the foundation for the Civil Rights movement of the 1960s."[76]

The NNLC, organized in 1951, described its goals as seeking to end job discrimination against blacks and to "move the trade unions and our white allies" into "the liberation struggle for black people, with a primary concentration on economic issues as the key." It was immediately attacked, with United Auto Workers (UAW) and CIO leader Walter Reuther in the lead, as under Communist leadership and fostering "dual unionism." Despite some successes in making job gains for blacks, especially during major campaigns in Chicago and Louisville, and in combating hiring discrimination by the Sears, Roebuck department store chain, the NNLC was unable to overcome constant attacks from established unions and intense government hostility, which included HUAC hearings as well its 1954 AGLOSO designation. When the SACB scheduled 1956 hearings to designate the group as "Communist" under the 1950 Internal Security Act, the organization decided to disband rather than "dissipate the energies of our members attempting to raise the tremendous sums of money required to go through the SACB hearing, and at the same time, jeopardizing their personal well-being." The group's executive secretary and one of its main founders, Coleman Young, who had been purged from the UAW and blacklisted in the auto industry for his left-wing views, was elected the first black mayor of Detroit in 1973. After the NNLC was AGLOSO-designated, Young issued a protest letter to Attorney General Brownell, asking him "by what right" he had imposed his "secret concepts of subversion upon us," denouncing the FBI as a "political police" responsible for "increasing coercion, intimidation and persecution" of those seeking to utilize constitutionally protected rights, and declaring that the NNLC "openly" stood for the right of blacks "to choose their own organizations and leaders to win the status of first class citizenship which you have failed to provide with your authorized powers."[77]

Among the AGLOSO-designated youth groups (aside from the previously discussed SNYC), several were the official or unofficial youth wing of the CP, including the YCL, the AYD (designated December 1947), and the LYL (designated August 1950). Both the AYD and LYL were almost immediately crippled by widespread harassment by federal, state, and college officials soon after their listings. For example, after the CP dissolved the AYD and replaced it with the LYL in 1949, the latter group soon came under investigation by HUAC and state legislative committees, and its national administrative executive secretary, Roosevelt Ward, was indicted in May 1951, originally for draft evasion (a charge subsequently dropped). Ward was given an astounding three-year jail term in September 1951 by a federal district court judge for supposedly having failed to apprise his draft board of his new address after he had moved, a sentence upheld by a federal appeals court in April 1952 (*Ward v. U.S.,* 195 F. 2d 441) but overturned by the Supreme Court in February 1953 (*Ward v. U.S.,* 344 U.S. 924), because the record did "not support" the allegation that "there was deliberate purpose" by Ward to defy draft regulations. In April 1953 the Eisenhower administration asked the SACB to designate the LYL as a "Communist front" under the ISA, leading to such SACB action in February 1955. In February 1957 the LYL announced its dissolution, and subsequently a 1963 federal appeals court ruling (*LYL v. SACB*, 322 F. 2d 364) ordered the SACB ruling be placed in "indefinitely inactive status" since the LYL no longer existed and could not be legally viewed as continuing "to live as a disembodied spirit—a ghost without flesh, blood or bones—after its members and organs have all been removed."[78]

Among the approximately fifty AGLOSO organizations not previously discussed that were unique or otherwise difficult to classify, the Photo League (designated November 1947), Nature Friends of America (November 1947) CAW (May 1948), SWP (November 1947), Washington Commonwealth Federation (WCF, April 1949), and the Washington Pension Union (WPU, February 1954) were perhaps the most significant. The Photo League was among the most prominent American organizations devoted to photographic education and support for professional photographers, and, according to one scholarly account, was "at the heart of photographic life in New York City," its home base. The league's members and associates included virtually every then-prominent American photographer, including Ansel Adams, Margaret Bourke-White, Dorothea Lange, Richard Avedon, Lewis Hine, Henri Cartier-Bresson, Ben Shawn, and Paul Strand. Although the league originated in 1936 as an offshoot of a clearly Communist-led group, the Film and Photo League, and regularly sponsored photo exhibits highlighting American social problems, its members, who cumulatively totaled less than 400 during the group's fifteen-year existence, encompassed both Communists (some openly so) and non-Communists (including over twenty-five FBI informants, one of whom briefly served as its executive secretary). Many league members clearly had strong leftist sympathies and affiliations, but their photographs regularly appeared in such "mainstream" outlets as *Life*, *Look*, and *Fortune* magazines. The group's official activities rarely reflected any strong ideology or slant beyond a general concern with social issues and civil liberties and were primarily devoted to photography classes, lectures, symposia and exhibits, and the issuance of its newsletter, *Photo Notes*. Although the immediate impact of its 1947 AGLOSO designation was a sympathetic doubling in membership, especially after an FBI informant in early 1949 assailed the league as Communist-dominated at the sensational Smith Act trial of CP leaders, it became clear, as the group's historians have stated, that "careers could be destroyed and passports and citizenships revoked" for associating with it, and the league was forced to disband in 1951, as growing defections left it without the "membership dues to pay its rent or support its programs." Thus, in late 1949, league president Walter Rosenblum wrote to Paul Strand that registration in the organization's photography school had dropped from about seventy students to only thirty and no photojournalism class could be offered because "everyone is too afraid to teach it." In interviews given many years later, Rosenblum recalled, concerning the listing, that, "It's hard to understand the terror that existed at that time" and that "the pressure got worse and worse and people began to feel it more and more" and to "drop out." Scoffing at the AGLOSO listing, Rosenblum said, "We couldn't even afford to pay our rent, let alone buy bombs and bullets or whatever it is you're supposed to do when you're subversive." In announcing its dissolution, the league's Executive Committee termed the group's fate a "casualty" of the Cold War. According to a 1999 study by Lili Bezner, its demise was accompanied by a general decline in American documentary photography, as a "redbaiting, blacklisting climate forced many artists to retreat into safer, more private realms."[79]

The Nature Friends of America was the only AGLOSO group that was originally designated along with an indication of when it had been "subversive"; it was listed with the qualification "since 1935." The group was formed around 1910, as an American branch of a German organization dedicated to preserving wildlife and fostering affordable outdoor recreation. Its center was Camp Midvale near New York City, but affiliated camps in at least five other states were established by 1940. The Friends were primarily concerned with hiking and other outdoor activities, but it was clearly a left-wing group, with "fascists" barred from membership and fundraisers often held for overtly political causes sometimes linked to the CP. After its 1947 designation, members faced the usual harassment, and some of the affiliated camps withdrew from the Friends, which eventually turned over Camp Midvale to the Ethical Culture Society in 1968. Most FBI documents on the Nature Friends, which were "released" under the Freedom of Information Act in 1991, were apparently viewed as so sensitive forty years after they were compiled that they are almost entirely redacted—virtually all of the surviving legible text consists of references to various organizations, including the ASC, CRC, AYD, and IWO, which are characterized as "cited by the Attorney General of the United States as coming within the purview of [Truman's loyalty] Executive Order 9835."[80]

The CAW was organized in early 1946 as the American affiliate of the Women's International Democratic Federation, a group that claimed over 80 million members in about forty countries and that supported women's equality, peace, and children's rights, while following an antifascist, pro-Soviet foreign policy orientation. At its 1947–1948 peak, the CAW claimed about 250,000 members (although historian Kate Weigand concludes that its actual membership probably never "exceeded more than a few thousand"). The CAW was led by a broad interracial coalition of prominent liberal and Communist women, including Cornelia Pinchot, wife of a former Pennsylvania governor, actresses Florence Eldridge (Mrs. Frederick March), and Faye Emerson (daughter-in-law of President Roosevelt), American Jewish Congress vice president Anna Schneiderman, National Council of Negro Women's officer Charlotte Brown, and CP leaders Elizabeth Gurley Flynn and Claudia Jones. In foreign policy, the group urged friendship with the Soviet Union, while domestically it supported equality for blacks, national health insurance, and many programs that later became key aspects of post-1960 American feminism, including free public day care and an end to all forms of gender and racial discrimination, including equal pay for equal work. According to historian Amy Swerdlow, writing in 1995, the "CAW laid out a woman's agenda nearly fifty years ago that foreshadowed the contemporary feminist agenda," demonstrated "a much deeper awareness of class and race issues" than any predecessor women's rights or social reform organizations, and, in particular, "made racial equality a central plank in its platform and incorporated African American women in its leadership." According to Weigand, while the CP openly supported the CAW and supplied the organization with "leadership and direction" from its inception, the organization grew rapidly at first, "attracting attention from both progressive and more mainstream women," but its May 1948 AGLOSO designation "scared many of the group's supporters, drastically reduced the CAW's membership, and exacerbated the group's financial difficulties." The CAW disbanded in late 1950, following a 1949 HUAC report that termed it Communist-dominated, to avoid threatened federal prosecution for failing to register as a foreign agent. According to Swerdlow, while in its early years the CAW demonstrated a mobilizing potential for "peace and a progressive interracial feminist social agenda unlike that of any previous women's peace organization," it later came under increasing CP influence and lost many of its members, who were either "alarmed by Soviet policies or becoming politically cautious in response to government and media red baiting."[81]

Although the SWP was formally organized only in 1938, its roots dated to the expulsion of a group of CP members in 1928 for supporting Russian Bolshevik leader Leon Trotsky, notably his position that Soviet dictator Joseph Stalin had abandoned revolutionary internationalism in favor of consolidating a degenerate bureaucratic-personal regime in Russia. Although the "Trotskyists," especially in their early years, espoused considerable militant rhetoric, they never sought to implement any revolutionary plans. During the 1930s, Trotskyists gained significant influence in the industrial labor movement, especially among the teamsters, played a leading role in the victorious 1934 Minneapolis truckers' strike, and subsequently organized an estimated 250,000 teamsters in eleven states. However, their very success led to intense federal repression. In June 1941 the SWP's Minneapolis headquarters was raided and over two dozen top officials were indicted for alleged conspiracy to violently overthrow the government, based on an obscure Civil War–era antislaveholder statute, and for violating the 1940 Smith Act by allegedly conspiring to advocate the overthrow of the government. Historians generally agree that the real spur to the prosecution was that President Roosevelt sought to aid a rival teamsters' faction headed by Dan Tobin and Jimmy Hoffa, which was closely allied to his administration, and additionally was angered by repeated SWP attacks on his foreign policy. During the subsequent trial, the federal prosecutor conceded that the government could not establish any "overt act" in furtherance of the alleged conspiracies but argued that "though the defendants may never have done anything to bring about overthrowing the government, the defendants can be punished for advocating its overthrow."[82]

Although the judge directed a verdict of acquittal for five of the defendants and the jury acquitted all of the remaining defendants under the Civil War–era statute, the panel found eighteen SWP leaders, including national secretary James Cannon and national labor secretary Farrell Dobbs, guilty under the Smith Act. Despite a jury recommendation of leniency, the convicted defendants were sentenced to jail terms ranging from twelve to sixteen months. Due to the trial and sentences, which largely paralyzed the SWP for four years, the notoriously corrupt Tobin-Hoffa faction gained unchallenged control of the Teamsters' Union, while the SWP lost its Minneapolis bastion and never recovered its previous influence in the labor movement. The SWP was constantly plagued, both before and after the trial, by ideological splits, one of which led to the 1940 formation of the Workers Party (WP), which, renamed the Independent Socialist League (ISL), played a major role (discussed later) in challenging AGLOSO during the 1950s. The SWP's membership, which had never exceeded 2,000, fell to about 1,500 by 1945 and then collapsed to a few hundred by the late 1950s, due to a combination of its 1947 AGLOSO designation, popular anti-Communism, political splits, aging members, and postwar prosperity. The SWP experienced a modest revival during the Vietnam War era (regaining a membership of perhaps 2,000 by the mid-1970s), when it played a major role in organizing antiwar demonstrations. However, perhaps its most significant contribution was a 1973 lawsuit (discussed below) that laid bare three decades of harassment and sabotage, clearly constituting what one scholar has termed "severe and relentless repression," to which it had been subjected by the FBI and other government agencies.[83]

The WCF and WPU were left-wing groups that became extremely influential in Washington State between 1935 and 1955. The WCF was a broad-based coalition of socialists, reformers, and Communists that worked within the state Democratic Party to foster social reforms and civil rights legislation. Although, as was often the case with "popular front" groups, the WCF was severely damaged by internal dissension between 1938 and 1941, afterwards it gained substantial importance, winning many state legislative seats and electing U.S. Rep. Hugh DeLacy. By 1945 it had become a major influence within the state Democratic Party but dissolved itself as a contribution to party unity and on the grounds that it was no longer needed. However, the WPU, which the WCF had founded in 1937 as an adjunct, and which focused originally on pension rights and subsequently also on welfare, civil, and labor rights, in the meantime gained substantial influence, attracting 30,000 members by 1940 along with state CIO and AFL endorsements. When the state Democratic Party began to purge alleged Communists after Republicans successfully stressed anti-Communism during the 1946 state and congressional elections, the WPU leadership, which unquestionably always included a significant CP component, endorsed the Progressive Party of Henry Wallace in 1948. The WPU subsequently came under investigation by the state legislative "Canwell Committee" on "un-American activities" and suffered increasing harassment and allegations of CP domination from state and federal authorities, especially a 1952 federal Smith Act prosecution of leading WPU activists (including WPU president William Pennock, who died from a drug overdose during his trial), the 1954 AGLOSO designation, and a 1956 SACB finding that the group was a "communist front." Although in 1948 a major WPU social welfare ballot initiative won by a wide margin in a state referendum and as late as 1957 Governor Albert Rossellini met with WPU leaders, in 1961 the WPU formally dissolved, weakened by repression, defections, the deaths of many of its elderly members, and perhaps to some extent by its own success in winning social reforms.[84]

The Loyalty Review Board, AGLOSO, and the Federal Loyalty Program

Even the LRB, which was charged with supervising the implementation of the Truman loyalty program and thus, necessarily, with evaluating the ultimate significance of alleged AGLOSO affiliations, was originally not provided with any additional information beyond the bare fact of the designations and was therefore left in a state of considerable confusion concerning AGLOSO. The general impression left by reading LRB records, at least for the 1947–1950 period, is that the board was extremely skeptical about both the value and the validity of AGLOSO designations but was ultimately unwilling to challenge their formulation and use for fear of being labeled "soft on communism." During the period immediately preceding the publication of the first Truman AGLOSO list in December 1947, both President Truman and officials charged with administering the loyalty program repeatedly suggested that alleged AGLOSO associations were not viewed as terribly significant. Thus, on November 14, Truman, in remarks first made privately to the newly appointed LRB and then released by the White House, declared that the loyalty program would be free of "witch hunts," that AGLOSO membership would be "simply one piece of evidence which may or may not be helpful in arriving" at a loyalty determination, and that the interpretation by "some" that "any persons who at any time happened to belong to one of these organizations would be automatically dismissed" from federal employment was wrong. When Clark's November 24 letter to LRB chair Seth Richardson, containing the first Truman AGLOSO list, was released on December 4, it contained even more emphatic statements along the same lines. Thus, Clark reiterated Truman's "simply one piece of evidence" comment, while adding, "'guilt by association' has never been one of the principles of American jurisprudence" and "we must be satisfied that reasonable grounds exist for concluding that an individual is disloyal." On December 27, Richardson released a lengthy statement concerning LRB procedures (printed in full by the *Washington Post* and the *New York Times* the following day), which repeated Truman's promise that the loyalty program would not "degenerate into a witch hunt" and declared that the "probative evidence" of past or present AGLOSO affiliations could be "fairly evaluated only after determining, so far as possible, the character of the organization, the period, nature and duration of the association, whether the employee or applicant was aware of the subversive character of the organization at the time of the association, and the nature of his activities in connection with such organization." Moreover, according to the LRB, the "welfare of the Civil Service, upon the wisdom, independence and morale of which the security" of the nation was "heavily dependent," required that all federal employees and applicants "should not only be, but feel, free to join, affiliate or associate with, support or oppose any organization, liberal or conservative, which is not disloyal." The LRB specifically added that "advocacy of whatever change in the form of government or the economic system" of the nation did not constitute "disloyalty" unless it was coupled with the advocacy of "unconstitutional means to effect such change." At an accompanying press conference, Richardson declared that AGLOSO designations had given him a "great deal of anxiety," especially because he suspected that many had joined AGLOSO groups for nonpolitical reasons. He pledged, "We aren't going into any investigations hidebound by any list." An anonymous LRB member was quoted in early January 1948 as highly critical of Clark for failing to differentiate among AGLOSO groups, since a federal employee could have "joined the [Washington] Bookshop merely to buy books at a discount, but anyone who joins the Communist Party does so for an entirely different reason."[85]

By the time the LRB's December 27 statement was published in the *Federal Register* on January 20, 1948, Clark had explicitly refused to provide *any* information about AGLOSO organizations to the LRB and drastically modified his earlier evaluation of the significance of AGLOSO affiliations. These developments, along with Clark's December 4, 1947, issuance of three seemingly separate lists, none of which corresponded to the six AGLOSO subcategories in Truman's executive order, aroused considerable anger and dismay among LRB members, many of whom were already extremely dubious of the validity and significance of AGLOSO designations. Thus, at the first LRB meeting, on November 14–15, 1947, before the list was officially released, but during which the board was briefed by Clark on his forthcoming November 24 letter to them, New York lawyer George Alger declared, "We have no means of knowing whether this list has any justification" and asked, "What do I know that makes membership on that list indicate at all a man's character?" Chair Richardson, a prominent Republican Washington corporate lawyer and former Hoover administration assistant attorney general, declared that, based on press inquiries, AGLOSO was "evidently a very hot subject," that he felt "it would have been better if there had been no admonition [from Truman] that the Attorney General have any list at all," and that "since the list is so controversial and might be the source of a great deal of trouble, that the Board ought not to assume any responsibility with reference to it." Expressing similar sentiments during a discussion of the advisability of publishing AGLOSO, Washington attorney Wilbur LaRoe declared that "a very strong group in Congress" felt that the "public interest demands" publication and "if we take the burden on upon ourselves of suggesting that it should not be," he feared "some pretty heavy bricks will flow upon our defenseless heads" and "the whole committee that is after these reds will say that we are red, and what defense would we have for trying to squelch information?" LaRoe added, "we shall burn our fingers if we get into that list," and that "the responsibility is exclusively" on Clark for it, while all "we have to do is to follow the mandate of transmitting it to the heads of departments."[86]

When the LRB discussed Clark's plan to issue what appeared to be three separate lists, Richardson declared that the LRB "only wanted one list submitted by the Attorney General" and "that would be *the* list" and suggested that it would be "better if we eliminated the [Biddle] list of 1943, which is either part [of Clark's] list or none of our troubles [if not referenced under Truman's 1947 executive order]." Boston lawyer Garrett Hoag echoed Richardson, declaring, "we could forward [to federal agencies] only the list which [Clark himself] designated" and "if his language did not include Biddle's list, it would be out." He added, "I think we ought to simply say that we do not understand [Clark's draft] letter. We don't know whether both lists or only one list is being designated, and we want it made clear." Richardson responded that Clark apparently wanted to have "all of the organizations identified in Biddle's list" rest upon Biddle "as to the authority for their description so that much of [Clark's] trouble will be lifted from his shoulder." Ultimately, the LRB voted on November 15 to disseminate Clark's list and accompanying letter, as received, to federal agencies, with "suitable arrangements" to be made by Richardson with Clark to have both published.[87]

At the LRB's second meeting, on December 3–4, immediately before Clark's list was released for publication on December 4, Richardson reported that he had recently personally "suggested to the Attorney General that he forget any designation of what happened in 1943," but that Clark still intended to include the Biddle list, in an effort to "secure the support of what had gone before under another Attorney General as a moral support to him." Richardson added, "I spent a half hour with [Clark] and begged him to write a list without [three] separate identifications." When Columbia University professor and former State Department consultant Arthur Macmahon asked Richardson if the eleven allegedly CP "adjunct" schools were "included" in Clark's AGLOSO designations "as subversive" under Truman's order and if that meant "anyone on the faculty or anyone who ever attended," Richardson responded, "You know as much as I do," because Clark's "language is rather peculiar" in simultaneously indicating that the schools were not "subversive," yet were CP "adjuncts." Ultimately, the LRB voted on December 3 to forward Clark's list and cover letter to departmental agencies along with its own accompanying letter indicating that the LRB understood that the "three groups named" by Clark constituted the "list of subversive organizations which, under the President's Order, we are required to disseminate to all departments." According to LRB member and New York attorney John Clark, this phrasing would put the attorney general "right on the spot," and if Clark had "any doubt he can call it to our attention immediately" and "if he says nothing, we are in the clear." When University of Chicago professor and former Political Science Association president Charles Merriam asked how Clark had reached his determinations, Richardson responded that "under the Executive Order, he could make up the list out of his head," adding, "it would take quite an organization before any of us would be willing to certify that a man was disloyal because of membership unless it was supplemented by additional testimony to show what the character of his membership was." Richardson added his opposition to publishing AGLOSO, "because if you have an organization of 5,000 members on the list, you potentially make 5,000 enemies for the Board by making this list" and "it is a burden I hate to see the Board take on." He subsequently wrote to Clark on December 3 concerning the meaning of the tripartite listing, to which Clark responded on December 16, confirming the "correctness" of the LRB's "understanding that all of the organizations listed in my letter of November 24, including those formerly listed by my predecessor, and the schools mentioned therein, comprise the list to be disseminated by the Board as the organizations designated."[88]

At the LRB's third meeting, on December 16–17, Richardson complained that Clark's list didn't "differentiate" between the various groups "in point of timeliness or wickedness," and that he was "perfectly at a loss to know" how the board could make loyalty determinations concerning membership in groups such as the Washington Bookshop Association (WBA), since there were undoubtedly those who "patronize it as a bookshop" and "others who patronize it because it is holding up the Communist line." When Merriam asked if listing a school as "subversive" meant "if you went to school there or are a teacher there," Richardson responded, "That is the reason I think sometimes we ought to disregard the list entirely. I told Clark that the man who asked him to make this list was either crazy or wasn't his friend." When Boston lawyer Henry Shattuck declared that "there must be a large percentage" of members who joined AGLOSO organizations "because they think it is a progressive thing and something that youth might well affiliate itself with," Richardson responded, "Three-quarters of its principles are just the principles a youth should have." He urged having an "investigative agency like the FBI furnish us the digest" of government information about the organizations, since Clark "only knows what somebody has told him" and "the fact that it comes" from him "doesn't mean a thing to me."[89]

In response to the LRB discussion, Richardson telephoned FBI assistant director Edward Tamm on December 17 to request additional information on all listed groups, but, according to Tamm's subsequent memo, was told that the FBI "did not attempt to adjudicate the legal import of its information," and should not "even be in the position of determining what information should or should not be considered" by the LRB, since "departmental officials would make this evaluation." Richardson then wrote to Clark on December 18, stating that the LRB found it "essential" to "have available, from fact sources, some evidence relating to the character of activities of each" designated group, information that would be "entirely confidential" but would necessarily be made available to subordinate boards charged with making loyalty determinations. When Clark failed to quickly respond to Richardson's December 18 letter (the department's copy has "I don't think we should," scrawled on it in what appears to be Clark's handwriting), Richardson wrote again asking for Clark's answer "at the earliest possible moment." Clark responded with a sharp rebuke on January 7, 1948, which termed Richardson's request "incompatible" with Truman's executive order and declared that if the LRB felt the order "should be amended to place the responsibility for making determinations with respect to these organizations on some other agency, I suggest that you make such recommendation to the Director of the Bureau of the Budget" for Truman's consideration. He added, "I am convinced that the determinations once made should not be subject to continued controversy on the part of the various government departments and agencies, their review boards, and others to whom the evidence on which determinations were based would be made available under the plan you have in mind." Clark added that Richardson had apparently been "misled" in suggesting in his December 18 letter that Truman's and Clark's statements had indicated that AGLOSO membership was "simply evidential and not controlling" in loyalty determinations, as he had only sought to suggest that individuals "sometimes unwittingly become involved with these organizations" and the "question of intent, therefore, becomes of prime importance." Should investigation uncover "active and informed membership" in an AGLOSO group, Clark declared, this would be "sufficient" to justify "the separation of the individual" from employment.[90]

When the LRB next met in early March 1948, Richardson summarized Clark's response as declaring that additional information about AGLOSO organizations was "none of our business," that it was Clark's "duty and not our duty or that of anybody else to make the list and pass on the qualifications of the organizations," that if Clark provided the requested material it would "result in a lot of conflicting findings" by subordinate loyalty boards, and "if we don't like that, he says, go back to the President and get him to assign some different authority to make the finding." Richardson added that the latter's response reflected his feeling that "much" of the basis of AGLOSO was "confidential in nature" and that "dissemination of it among 150 [loyalty] boards would critically destroy all secrecy and all confidence with reference to it" but that, in any case, "I don't regard his summary as worth much more than his conclusion." On the other hand, Richardson suggested that perhaps it "might be wise for the Board to accept [Clark's] ruling because it relieves [the LRB] of all responsibility for characterization of those organizations he may add to the list." Many LRB members expressed bitter resentment over Clark's position, suggesting that he had misinterpreted the LRB's request for information and shifted his position concerning the significance of AGLOSO membership. Thus, Professor Macmahon declared that when Clark had briefed the LRB on November 24 he had never indicated that "active, informed membership" in AGLOSO groups was "automatically grounds" for dismissal and added, "I can't imagine anything worse than an automatic use of a list under which a man is beheaded if he is found to be a member of any one of these organizations," especially since it had been "one of the most preposterous bits of procedure that our Government has ever engaged in" to designate groups without ever giving them "a chance to offer their side of the story." New York lawyer Alger similarly declared, "As to dumping overboard all the constitutional principles of fair play I have ever heard of because the Attorney General gives us a list, I won't do it. I will get off the Board first. I will give his list just as much weight as it is entitled to, but there is no weight at all now." Boston lawyer Shattuck similarly declared that it would be impossible to make loyalty judgments on individuals "based on membership in one of those organizations without knowing something about them," as it was unlikely that any "member of this Board has any information whatever about the Nature Friends of America or the New Committee for Publications or the Photo League." Ohio lawyer (and former reform mayor of Cincinnati) Murray Seasongood added that "whether a man is a member of one of these subversive organizations just doesn't make sense unless you know what the organization is."[91]

As the result of its lengthy March 2 discussion, the LRB agreed that the Clark list should be considered "evidence" in loyalty hearings but also declared, in a formal resolution, that "without in any way impugning the Attorney General's list, but solely in order to properly evaluate evidence" concerning alleged AGLOSO membership by federal employees, the board "respectfully requests that the Attorney General furnish it with some information regarding these organizations, including, for example, a brief statement of their ostensible objects, total membership, the basis and types of membership, actual operations and activities, and any other matters" that he could provide "without detriment to the public interest." Lacking such information, the resolution added, "the Board believes it will be unable to decide what weight, if any, should be given to [AGLOSO] membership[s]." The LRB also requested an immediate meeting with Clark, but Richardson reported to the board on March 3 that the attorney general was "tied up" on Capitol Hill, so instead the LRB met that day with Assistant Attorney General Quinn and his assistant, Raymond Whearty, who supervised the Criminal Division's AGLOSO lawyers. Quinn indicated that the department would be willing to provide a "general statement of the organization and what it stands for," but that the "possibility that the information might get out" caused him to "hesitate," although Whearty conceded that when similar information about some of the Biddle AGLOSO listings had been published in the 1942 *Congressional Record*, it had caused no "great harm." An agreement appeared to be reached when Quinn declared that the department would make available to the LRB "the memorandum upon which these designations were made and then let you make it accessible to the boards under you," with the understanding that it would be kept confidential and that nothing would be included that would "give the lead to those who would be in a position to identify the confidential information" and that the sources of such information "would be of a character that you couldn't use as a witness." But this apparent agreement soon dissolved into confusion after FBI assistant directors Tamm and Ladd joined the discussion at Richardson's invitation. When they were asked by Richardson about the FBI's views "on disclosure of this information," they were noncommittal, with Tamm declaring, "I think it is a matter of policy to be passed on by the Attorney General." Quinn thereupon began to backpedal, declaring, "I can't see how any memoranda is going to help you any," since "you have still got to go along with what the Attorney General says." However, Quinn promised to provide a definitive answer to the LRB's request for AGLOSO summary memoranda within twenty-four hours.[92]

Aside from seeking to obtain additional basic information on AGLOSO groups, the March 2–3 LRB meeting included considerable discussion of the related and intertwined questions of exactly what significance should be attached to alleged individual AGLOSO associations in making loyalty determinations and of how precisely AGLOSO groups were categorized. These questions were interconnected because, while Truman and Clark had repeatedly suggested in late 1947 that AGLOSO associations were not to be considered conclusive in making loyalty determinations and that the program did not endorse the theory of "guilt by association," one of the Truman subcategories included organizations that sought to unconstitutionally alter the government, a seeming duplicate of the 1939 Hatch Act provision that barred outright federal employment of members of organizations "which advocated the overthrow of our constitutional form of government." Clark's failure to categorize the designated organizations in compliance with the Truman classifications thus made it impossible for the LRB to determine which groups, if any, occupied the forbidden Hatch Act terrain. Richardson asked, in the absence of such information, "how much we have to have beyond membership" to make individual loyalty determinations and suggested, "Don't we have to visualize in every one of these cases that arise under the Hatch Act or under the [similar congressional] appropriations acts requiring the Attorney General to furnish us enough evidence to support a finding in the matter?" He added that under the "old practice under Biddle's decision," CP membership required automatic dismissal, but the repeated declarations that AGLOSO membership could be construed as only one "piece of evidence" made it impossible to "take that position under the recent Executive Order." Richardson declared, "We have got to tell these [subordinate] boards that membership forecloses the thing or that it doesn't."[93]

Richardson's concerns were echoed by many other members of the LRB. Thus, Shattuck declared that the LRB could not act on "any of these organizations" under "the Hatch Act without certainly much further information from the Attorney General" and Boston lawyer Hoag declared that the LRB needed to "know how to differentiate between the weight" accorded to memberships in different AGLOSO groups, noting that Clark himself had seemingly indicated that "the mere fact that you are a student at the Samuel Adams School should not be given the same weight" as CP membership. According to Alger, while Clark "says it is bad" to belong to a designated organization, "What if the man didn't understand the organization? He may have just come into it because he had some interest but hadn't the remotest idea that there was any subversiveness." Therefore, he added, the LRB should tell Clark that "if you want us to give weight to that list," he would have "to show us something that justifies us in believing that membership in one of those organizations creates a presumption of disloyalty." Similarly, Kansas lawyer Harry Colmery declared that as people typically joined organizations "when they are tight [drunk] or when they have been wined and dined by somebody," there could be "many reasons why one might become involved" in "a subversive organization without having any intention to be really a party" to overthrowing the government.[94]

Based on Clark's January 7, 1948, letter and the LRB's subsequent March 2–3 discussions, the board concluded that it could not challenge Clark's AGLOSO determinations but that, to effectively supervise the loyalty program, it still required information about each designated group. Thus, Richardson wrote to Clark again on March 4 to this effect, while informing all federal agencies on March 9 that Clark's "determination as to the nature" of listed groups "must be accepted by all [subordinate loyalty] Boards" in order to make loyalty determinations and could not be subjected to "any evidential investigation" or "argument" for the "purpose of attacking, contradicting or modifying the controlling conclusion reached by the Attorney General." However, Richardson simultaneously informed the agencies, in a separate memo with a clearly different tone, of Clark's January 7 declaration that "active and informed" membership in any AGLOSO organization warranted dismissal from federal employment, while adding that membership in "any particular organization" should not be construed as "per se establishing disloyalty and that boards should "clearly understand" that their decisions were to "be based upon the entire record in the case." In a March 25,

1948, "handbook" provided to subordinate loyalty boards, the LRB stated that AGLOSO was to be considered the "final matter, which is not subject to attack by employees or groups, and as far as the Agencies are concerned is not to be questioned or allowed to be the subject of question by an employee or his counsel." The handbook also declared that AGLOSO membership "in and of itself" may not "be taken as conclusive proof of disloyalty" but was "only one piece of evidence, no matter how clear-cut and convincing it may be." However, in an echo of Clark's January 7 letter, the handbook added that subordinate boards should seek to determine whether an employee's "active participation is sufficient to establish clearly that his sympathies coincide" with the organization's and that his actions were "unmistakably taken in an effort to further" its purposes and that if evidence demonstrated knowing, active, and "definite" connection with a "subversive or un-American group," then "he should bear the consequence of his deliberate action."[95]

When Clark finally responded to the LRB's repeated requests for additional AGLOSO information on March 15, he had considerably changed his tune from two months earlier, assuring Richardson that the department had resolved the "difficulty" of "reconciling the requirements of security," including the "possible publication of any data released," with the "validity of the Board's basic position that information is essential to a proper evaluation of membership." He pledged to shortly forward to the LRB reports on the "various organizations designated" but asked the board to consider "in the interest of conserving personnel efforts, the preparation of memoranda only as to the more prominent organizations and those which are most likely to be involved in individual loyalty proceedings" (thereby suggesting that the department's frequent statements that AGLOSO was solely compiled to aid in federal loyalty determinations considerably stretched the truth). Summary memoranda concerning many AGLOSO groups were thereafter furnished to the LRB in March 1948. What these documents and other internal and confidential FBI AGLOSO summaries reveal is that, although groups were presumably designated for engaging in "subversive" activities, virtually none of them was ever characterized as actually doing anything more dangerous than expressing extremely unpopular opinions. As with the AGLOSO summaries placed in the 1942 *Congressional Record* by Rep. Martin Dies (discussed in chapter 1), Cold War–era FBI and DOJ AGLOSO summaries invariably focused (in the case of alleged CP fronts) on claims that group leaders had CP ties and/or that the organizations publicly supported the CP "line," activities that did not even verge on violating any laws. Similarly, in Clark's July 15, 1949, congressional testimony, referenced above, he never claimed listed groups had violated the law, instead summarizing their activities as engaging in fund raising meetings and gatherings "in local branches or lodges through schools" and engaging in "publicity campaigns, through the form of handbills, pamphlets and organization publications."[96]

The FBI's AGLOSO reports are filled with accounts of entirely routine, peaceful activities, often involving public meetings and publications. Thus, a typical thirteen-page, single-spaced September 10, 1953, memo from the FBI's St. Louis office on the local CRC branch noted that it had repeatedly published pamphlets and held meetings to support the defense of indicted Communist leaders and had issued leaflets between 1947 and 1953 to publicize such matters as Negro History Week and a "fried chicken dinner to be held at 818 N. Eighteenth St. on 1-13-51" in honor of "William Massingale, who, because he is a veteran civil rights fighter, is continually harassed by the courts." A 1955 FBI memo declared that the APC had formed in 1951 to coordinate and publicize "the Communist 'peace' offensive in the U.S." and engaged in sponsoring "rallies, expositions, meetings and other functions and affairs" and publishing and circulating "various literature for the purpose of carrying out its objectives." An FBI memo on the Families of the Smith Act Victims (designated January 1954) reported that its activities were "limited to raising funds for the assistance of the families of individuals prosecuted under the Smith Act" and that it had primarily obtained funds through "appeals made through the [CP newspaper] 'Daily Worker'; special holiday parties, for example, children's Christmas parties, socials, banquets, concerts; celebrations of special 'days,' for example, International Women's Day; fund campaigns conducted by other communist fronts; yearly national fund-raising campaigns conducted in 1953 and 1954, et cetera." A 1958 Chicago FBI SWP report related that the group's plans included "printing of election materials; election meetings held at SWP headquarters, solicitation of election petition signatures, and SWP members in attendance and speaking at election campaign meetings."[97]

The absence of illegalities similarly pervaded the brief organizational summaries prepared for internal FBI use when the bureau proposed groups for DOJ AGLOSO designation in early 1947. (Assistant Director Ladd told Director Hoover that the internal summaries were not being furnished to the department for fear that "such material will be used by the Attorney General as a basis for declaring some of the organizations subversive without an appropriate review of the material previously furnished.") The entirety of the bureau's summary of its CRC file stated that the organization's two "key officials" were "reported Communists," that its "program has closely paralleled that of the Communist movement for a considerable number of years," that its proclaimed purpose was to "provide assistance to aliens and foreign born citizens, as well as to propagandize in behalf of their rights," and that recently the organization had "interceded to fight Government deportation proceedings against 100 aliens who have had past or present" CP membership. The summary termed the group an amalgamation of "nationally known-communist fronts," whose 1946 formation was "propagated by Communist and Communist sympathizers" and which had "supported the Communist program, exploiting national and local conditions," especially on racial matters, with the "active support of the Communist press." The summary added that the CRC had "propagated the Communist program," such as calling for the abolition of HUAC and the passage of antilynching legislation, and was "one of the main organizations which has carried on smear tactics" against the DOJ and "this Bureau."[98]

In response to a September 1948 DOJ inquiry, the FBI provided similar summaries to the department on eleven organizations. Thus, the bureau's summary on the Council for Pan-American Democracy (which had already been designated in May 1948) stated only that it had been "controlled" from its inception until its demise in 1946 by CP members and sympathizers, that it had "particularly" propagandized the "Party line" on Latin America, and that it had been founded "for the stated purpose of promoting understanding, sympathetic cooperation and unity among the peoples of the Western Hemisphere." The FBI's memo on the American Ship Rescue Mission (which would be designated in July 1949) declared only that it "was reported" that the organization was a project of the United American Spanish Aid Committee (which would be separately designated in April 1949) for the purpose of providing aid to Spanish loyalist refugees and that the strongly pro-Franco *Brooklyn Tablet* had reported in 1940 that the committee and the mission were part of an interlocking combination that was "dominated completely by the Communist Party and its fellow travelers."[99]

DOJ summary memos included in a spring 1948 LRB "training manual" or subsequently drawn up were similar in character, neither alleging illegal activities nor providing any evidence to support the claims that they did contain. Thus, according to a *"strictly confidential"* memo on the AYD (designated in 1947), the organization was "to all intents and purposes a continuation of the Young Communist League," engaging in the "sponsorship of meetings, demonstrations and social events to publicize objectives which at the time represent the Communist program," including, especially among college groups, the issuance of "pamphlets, news sheets and periodicals which serve its immediate purpose." As was the "customary pattern," the memo added, the AYD's "nominal leadership" included "many persons who have no" CP affiliations. According to a mid-1955 department memorandum on the Idaho Pension Union (designated October 1955), the group was created and dominated by persons who were "members of or affiliated" with the CP and had engaged in activities consisting of publishing leaflets and booklets and supporting such CP policies as "condemnation of the U.S. in Korea, cease fire in Korea, withdrawal of all foreign troops from Korea, peace with Red China, stop defense spending, repeal of the [ISA, which established the SACB], repeal of the Smith Act and support of the [designated] American Peace Crusade."[100]

During 1953 legal proceedings brought by three organizations challenging AGLOSO's constitutionality (discussed in the following chapter) and in 1953 DOJ submissions to the SACB (which, completely separately from AGLOSO, as discussed below, was charged with ordering Communist "action" and "front" groups to register with the DOJ, but only after formal hearings and findings), the department made public summaries of its "subversive" claims concerning a dozen previously designated groups. The summaries also alleged entirely peaceful and lawful activities, typically consisting of openly propagandizing in support of CP policy, acting under CP direction and domination, and failing to ever contradict CP policies. Thus, in its SACB filing, the department charged that the Labor Youth League (LYL, designated in August 1950, whose executive secretary was prosecuted for draft evasion in 1951) had been under CP direction since its formation in 1949, that its officers had been continually "subject to Communist Party discipline," and that "its funds, resources and personnel have been used to further and promote" CP objectives, which included supporting CP policies on such topics as "production and control of atom and hydrogen bombs, opposing the policies and actions of the U.S. and the United Nations in defending South Korea" against North Korean and the Chinese Communists, and defending CP leaders prosecuted under the Smith Act. The department's SACB allegations against the CAA, the Committee for a Democratic Far Eastern Policy, and the ASC charged that the CP had dominated each of the organizations in their activities, such as, respectively, aiding Russian policy on "matters relating to Negroes and to the African colonies," publicizing the CP's position regarding affairs in the Far East by having its officers speak at public gatherings, and supporting the CP "through circulation of literature praising and supporting Communist leaders and governments and through other methods." The only specific activities attributed to the CAA were engaging in "propaganda among Negroes, meetings," and bringing "pressure on organizations and international gatherings."[101]

Ironically, despite its criticisms of AGLOSO's vagueness, the LRB relied on the DOJ for even vaguer characterizations of organizations to help it make appointments to subordinate regional loyalty boards. Undated LRB files that apparently were compiled in 1948 make clear that the board considered extremely general and completely unsourced departmental characterizations of various non-AGLOSO groups in screening nominees, some of them highly prominent, for such positions. Thus, according to an LRB document entitled "Proposed Members for Loyalty Board, Second Region," the LRB and the department agreed that a "brief informal statement from the Department as to whether their files raise any question of a particular organization would be acceptable as a characterization of the organization," and, "as a result, that Department has advised that various organizations are 'O.K.' or 'No good,'" meaning in the latter case that "the Department has unfavorable information on the organization." Thus, in connection with the proposed appointment of Ira Cross, a distinguished economics professor at the University of California, the LRB files relate that a "responsible official" from the department had characterized the Academic and Civil Rights Council and the Spanish Refugee Relief Campaign as "no good." LRB investigators recommended against further considering for regional board appointments two distinguished Harvard Law School professors, Zechariah Chafee and Roscoe Pound, partly because Chafee had affiliations with three AGLOSO organizations and three groups "characterized as Communist fronts" by HUAC, while two organizations Pound had reportedly associated with were characterized by a "responsible representative" of the department as "Communist infiltrated and considered bad." Well-known Columbia historian Allan Nevins was listed in the LRB files as affiliated with the AGLOSO-designated ILD and YCL, as well as with the American Committee for Democracy and Intellectual Freedom, which was reportedly characterized by the department as "defunct but bad," apparently since it had allegedly been cited as "Communist" or "un-American" by three congressional committees.[102]

The winter 1947–1948 flap between the LRB and Clark concerning the provision of additional information concerning AGLOSO organizations was quickly followed by a more intense flare-up, as Richardson continued to press the issue of whether the CP or other organizations were specifically considered to be seeking the unconstitutional alteration of the government (Truman's sixth category), thus seemingly automatically disqualifying *all* members for government employment under the 1939 Hatch Act. On April 21, 1948, Richardson had an explosive meeting with Clark and other top department officials on this topic: Assistant Attorney General Quinn reported in a summary memo that Richardson had maintained that it was "essential" to the LRB's "continued functioning" to secure a clear determination that the CP sought the unconstitutional alteration of the government, whether obtained by "designation, official opinion, officially certified statement of facts, legislative fiat or finding" by the LRB itself, thereby allegedly challenging Clark's authority to make AGLOSO designations at all. According to Quinn, the "clear and unequivocal intent" of Truman's order was that "fact-finding as to the character of the organizations" was the "sole responsibility and prerogative of the Attorney General" and the LRB had no province "to determine the validity" of his designation. Quinn declared that, because Clark's November 24, 1947, letter had "quoted in full" the listing of the six Truman categories, he had "in fact, include[d] a finding" that the CP sought to unconstitutionally alter the government, an interpretation which implied that all listed groups fell under all six Truman classifications. Quinn bitterly added that "no comment" was required by Richardson's position that because the categories were stated "in the alternative and not in the conjunctive [i.e., that Truman's order listed six categories connected by "or" rather than "and"]" they amounted to "no designation at all and the Board could not accept" it as finding that the CP "seeks the overthrow of the government by unconstitutional means."[103]

When the LRB met on May 4, 1948, Richardson described the April 21 meeting as a "battle royal over at the Attorney General's office," during which "we didn't see eye to eye" concerning the CP and the Hatch Act issue. However, he added that he was subsequently "startled" but "very much gratified personally last night" to hear by telephone from Clark "indicating that he had come over to my point of view" and would send President Truman a letter finding that the CP was an organization which, under the Hatch Act, justified a "judgment of dismissal based upon membership." Richardson reported he had told Clark on April 21 that, without clarification of the CP's Hatch Act status, "the Executive Order says that we can still refuse to discharge" individuals with "membership in a tabooed organization, whereas under the Hatch Act Congress has said if you are a member you are through." He added he had finally told Clark that, lacking "some authoritative statement from the Attorney General that we'd have to undertake it ourselves." Richardson declared that clarification of this issue was "the most important question" before the LRB, as the "overwhelming number of [loyalty] cases have to do with membership or affiliation or activity" of employees with AGLOSO groups that depended for their "wrong-doing" upon their CP "connection," yet, besides a "curbstone opinion from reading the [news]papers," there was no "sort of quasi-judicial basis" for determining the CP's "character." However, Richardson said, it "wasn't clear [from Clark] over the telephone whether in the broad sweeping determination [concerning the CP] he had made the [other AGLOSO] organizations" were "also contained," in which case, "if we were considering them under the Hatch Act we wouldn't go to the nature of the organization" but would simply authorize dismissals based on membership.[104]

When the LRB met with Assistant Solicitor General George T. Washington later on May 4, Washington reported that Biddle's 1940 determination that the CP was encompassed by the Hatch Act had guided the FBI ever since and that Clark "has no desire to revoke those instructions." Therefore, he declared, the CP "is an organization condemned by the Hatch Act," and the LRB need not "concern yourselves with the proof" of this held by the DOJ. Washington added that, concerning other AGLOSO designations, it was not "incumbent upon the [LRB] to undertake any hearings as to the justification for the Attorney General's designation of these organizations." When Richardson asked if there was any difference between a "front" organization "admittedly a part of the Communist picture" and CP membership itself, thus suggesting that the Hatch Act applied "to every single case we have," Washington ambiguously responded, "There is some action which is clearly in the white field and some action which is clearly in the black field, and I think that Congress has said that membership in the Communist Party is in the black field." He added that, to his best recollection, Clark had never "indicated that membership" in the "entire list" would require dismissal. Richardson and other LRB members made clear that Washington's account still left them extremely confused. Thus, Richardson said things were "still cloudy in my mind," because Clark's January 7 letter seemed to make "conscious, intentional membership" in all AGLOSO organizations a "Hatch Act case." When Richardson asked if any other AGLOSO organization was "sufficiently evil so that membership" violated the Hatch Act, Washington responded, "if there are others, it is our duty to tell you" but "what we are prepared to say now is that the Communist Party is a Hatch Act organization." Richardson lamented, "I still don't understand whether [Washington] understands it to be the position of the Attorney General that the only party fixed in the Hatch Act" was the CP, to which Washington replied, "At the moment" the CP is the Hatch Act organization, and the other organizations are "in a different category." After the May 4 LRB meeting, Richardson told reporters that the LRB had formally requested Clark to issue a directive clarifying the CP's Hatch Act AGLOSO status. On May 27 Clark sent to the LRB (and released at a news conference) a formal finding that the board, in light of past legislative and executive actions, should consider the CP and the by-then defunct Bund as organizations "within the scope" of the Hatch Act, therefore requiring the "mandatory" dismissal of affiliated employees. Clark added that in "all other cases" arising under AGLOSO "in which dismissals are predicated upon organizational memberships," the LRB was "invested with discretion to determine whether or not, upon all the evidence, reasonable grounds exists" for such action.[105]

On May 28, 1948, Clark made public thirty-two new AGLOSO designations, which were listed only as made "pursuant to Executive Order No. 9835," without any further classification or elaboration. Clark's twin announcements set off yet another row with Richardson, who wrote him on May 28 that the new listings and the original late 1947 designations left him "in doubt which of the alternative" six Truman AGLOSO categories was "applicable to a particular organization," because "there is apparently a difference between those various designations [such as fascist, totalitarian, and subversive]" and "at least one of them, number (5) [organizations which sought to deny others their constitutional rights] is not based upon a question of loyalty at all" and therefore not within the LRB's jurisdiction. Richardson added while Clark had "clarified" his CP designation," there was "no way of ascertaining" which classification the other listed organizations fell within and therefore they all might be assumed to come under the fifth category and not to "present any disloyalty aspects." Clark did not respond to Richardson's May 28 letter, with its implied threat that the LRB might entirely cease using AGLOSO absent further clarification of the classification issue, until September 17, when he provided what he termed a "consolidated" list of previously designated organizations, but now "segregated" according to the six Truman categories. Although Clark's cover letter clearly indicated that each organization would be placed in only one category based on its "dominant characteristics," as noted above the new listing (published September 25) put six groups in multiple categories. Altogether, Clark listed twenty-two groups as "totalitarian" (essentially Biddle's list of pro-Japanese organizations), fifteen as "fascist" (Biddle's pro-German and pro-Italian groups), eighty-two as "Communist" (about a dozen groups from the Biddle list plus about seventy Clark additions), four as advocating violence to deprive others of their constitutional rights (the KKK, the Silver

Shirts, and two other native "right wing" groups), five as seeking the unconstitutional alteration of the government (the CP, CPA, SWP, YCL, and WP, all of which were also listed as "Communist"), and six as "subversive" (the same five groups plus the Bund, which was also listed as "fascist").[106]

Although AGLOSO continued to be popularly known as a list of "subversive" organizations, only six designated groups were thus actually classified as "subversive." The vast majority of alleged "Communist front" groups were classified as "Communist" but not also as "subversive," an anomaly that would cause the DOJ considerable legal trouble in future years. Clark gave no explanations or definitions, either publicly or privately, either for his classifications or why they had not been previously made. However, in his September 17 letter, Clark rejected Richardson's conclusion that organizations categorized as supporting the violent denial of constitutional rights to others was "not based upon a question of loyalty" and therefore not within the LRB's jurisdiction and declared that it was "not open to the Board" or any executive branch agency to disregard "any" of the Truman categories. Moreover, without explicitly referencing the Hatch Act, Clark added that it would be "difficult to reconcile informed membership or activity" in any of the groups deemed to be seeking the unconstitutional alteration of the government as "consistent to loyalty" to the federal government, thus apparently modifying his January 7, 1948, letter, which suggested that only "*active* and informed" (emphasis added) membership in designated groups warranted adverse loyalty determinations. Clark concluded with the politely hostile expression that hopefully "this amplification of the designations previously made by me will serve to remove some of the difficulties which you state you have experienced."[107]

Subsequently, as the result of December 17, 1948, LRB executive committee action, the LRB declared in the *Federal Register* that Clark had determined that a finding of membership in organizations designated as seeking to unconstitutionally alter the government required the "mandatory" denial of government employment. Yet, in a 1951 address to the ABA, Hiram Bingham, Richardson's successor as LRB chair, declared that the board "has carefully followed the opinion of the Attorney General" that "only when membership in a questionable or subversive organization" was clearly" "informed" and "active" was such evidence "likely to be conclusive." Bingham, an archeologist who had become famous for discovering the "lost" Peruvian city of Machu Picchu in 1911 and later served as a U.S. senator from Connecticut, further confused the situation by immediately qualifying his statement as applying only to organizations affiliated with the CP among college graduates seeking government jobs, but not "young men who joined organizations in college" that "appeared to us to be more or less unpatriotic and tinged with disloyalty" but who, when a "little older and wiser," became "informed of the nature of the organization" and ceased taking "any active part or interest in it."[108]

The FBI frequently pressed for the broadest possible jurisdiction in making AGLOSO-related investigations and the DOJ generally acceded to its wishes. Thus, in an early 1948 memo, Hoover asked Clark whether federal employees and applicants who were not AGLOSO members but had "sympathetic" association with such persons should be "considered as properly" subject to FBI investigations, while making clear that he expected an affirmative response since "it is obvious where there is or has been substantial association" with "an individual upon whom we have information indicating disloyalty, such data should necessarily be reported." Clark's first assistant, Peyton Ford, responded by telling Hoover that "it is believed that it is necessary to report such information." In some cases, however, the department itself pushed the FBI to extend its investigations. Thus, according to a March 1948 internal FBI memo from R. W. Wall to assistant director Ladd, Assistant Attorney General Quinn directed the bureau on March 1 to initiate loyalty investigations of all federal employees and applicants belonging to or active in organizations, even if not AGLOSO-designated, "where there is any substantial evidence" that they might "fall within the purview of the Executive Order." Soon thereafter FBI offices began regularly submitting reports on "subversive groups" that the bureau reported "have not been cited by the Attorney General to date."[109]

However, in a mid-1948 memo to Assistant to the Attorney General Ford, Hoover sought to restrict the FBI's interpretation of Quinn's March 1 directive and a subsequent memo from Ford by reporting that frequently bureau files did not "show the extent or period of affiliations of members of suspect [non-AGLOSO] organizations, but, on the contrary, generally only show the fact that an individual is or was a member" and in such cases the FBI did not propose to "conduct any preliminary investigation or inquiry to ascertain whether that employee is active in that organization or otherwise engaged in activity as to provide reasonable ground to believe he may be disloyal." In response, Ford told Hoover that where federal employees or applicants were "shown to be a member of a designated organization, the Department sees no escape from the conclusion that such membership requires a full field loyalty investigation," although the FBI was not required to conduct "either a preliminary or full field investigation where nothing further is shown than mere membership" in "suspect but not designated organizations." Ford added that where "known activities are in themselves sufficient to raise a reasonable question as to loyalty, it obviously is immaterial whether he is a member or associate of any organization and in such cases an investigation should be initiated." On July 16 Ford informed Hoover that "activity in an organization as to which there is derogatory information may evidence disloyalty if it appears that the individual involved is one of the group whose activities within the group constitute the derogatory information concerning it," even if such activities had not "succeeded to the point" where AGLOSO designation was "required." Ford expanded the reach of this memo two months later by informing Hoover that membership alone in non-AGLOSO organizations that had been "the targets of Communist infiltrative efforts" constituted a "caveat or warning to inquire further into the facts," in order to determine, "in each case in which a Government employee or applicant has been a member of such a target organization," whether "his individual membership has been exercised *on behalf of* the infiltrating group."[110]

A full-scale bureaucratic skirmish erupted in 1948–1949 between the FBI and the LRB that apparently was provoked by FBI investigations of federal employee memberships in nondesignated groups. The quarrel originated with a June 1948 memo from Richardson to federal agencies instructing them that, "pending issuance" of further LRB guidance, they should "except in extraordinary instances" only consider "those organizations previously characterized by the Attorney General" under Truman's executive order. At the LRB's September 30, 1948, meeting, Richardson complained that the FBI was submitting to government agencies information about non-AGLOSO groups because they had been cited as "subversive" by congressional and state investigative committees such as HUAC, contradicting Clark's position that loyalty boards would "confine" their consideration only to AGLOSO affiliations. AGLOSO itself was a "slender reed you hang on to following the Attorney General's certification," he added, but "we at least have some sort of umbrella of fact over us" with AGLOSO, while the FBI had "no authority whatever to evaluate any information," and HUAC accusations provided "no evidence" and meant nothing "at all." Richardson added that the loyalty program should consider no activity or group unless it had "passed through the scrutiny of the Attorney General" and was certified "a bad organization." Richardson issued a follow-up memo to government agencies on November 2, 1948, which flatly declared that "insofar as an individual's connection with organizations is concerned, all Loyalty Boards shall confine their consideration" to designated organizations.[111]

Upon learning of this directive, Hoover fired off a series of increasingly insistent memos to Clark asking for "advice" regarding FBI policy concerning the LRB's "suggestion" and strongly urging that it be overturned so the bureau could continue to furnish loyalty boards information on non-AGLOSO organizations, such as reporting that they had been "cited" by HUAC and/or state investigating committees. In response to Hoover's first such memo, Assistant to the Attorney General Ford informed Hoover on December 14, 1948, that he had conferred with Richardson and LRB Executive Secretary L. V. Meloy and agreed with them that it was "entirely proper" for the LRB to ban subordinate boards from "preferring charges based purely on membership" in non-AGLOSO groups, although "disloyal activity as distinguished from membership" in such groups was "the proper subject" of "consideration and assessment" in loyalty cases. Therefore, Ford declared, it was agreed that the FBI should continue to investigate instances "where there is indication of activity of disloyal nature," whether involving AGLOSO groups, non-AGLOSO groups, or "entirely outside of any organizations" and "there needs to be no change in your present procedure." However, he added, the "suggestion arose" that "possibly it would be better" in the case of non-AGLOSO organizations for the FBI to "fail to characterize" them and specifically to make "no reference" to their citation by HUAC or state committees. Hoover responded to this bewildering memo a week later by declaring that if the FBI referred to non-AGLOSO organizations it would be "in the final analysis, placed in the position of arbitrarily deciding" which non-AGLOSO groups were "disloyal" enough to warrant investigation, and the "very inclusion" of such groups "in our reports without citation of authority" would leave the impression "created by innuendo that this Bureau has arbitrarily decided that the organization is disloyal." Therefore, he concluded, "it is felt that, for the protection of the Bureau," citations from "appropriate Federal or State" committees should continue to be included in FBI reports referencing non-AGLOSO groups and "pending receipt of further advice from you, we will continue to follow this procedure which we have followed since the inception of the Loyalty Program."[112]

Ford responded in late January 1949 that the LRB was concerned that FBI statements indicating that groups had been "characterized" by congressional or state investigating committees, "though having no legal effect whatever, gives the impression that the organization is actually subversive though not so declared by the Attorney General." Therefore, Ford stated, the FBI should "not imply" that a non-AGLOSO group was "subversive" by "indicating that a certain group has so stated," but still should not "hesitate to mention any organization, though not listed by the Attorney General, where such reference will assist in determining the circumstances under which certain alleged disloyal activity has been carried out by a particular individual." In a four-page, single-spaced response to Ford, Hoover complained that by not authorizing the FBI to note that "a certain group" had stated that non-AGLOSO organizations were "subversive," the FBI-LRB guidelines would "materially affect procedures being utilized by this Bureau," and therefore the "suggestion propounded by the Honorable Seth B. Richardson is worthy of further study and consideration" (a phrase repeated twice verbatim by Hoover, in a manner that suggested he viewed Richardson as less than "honorable"). Hoover maintained that by noting non-AGLOSO organizations had been cited by "an appropriate public Committee," the FBI was not "implying that such organizations are subversive," but only reporting a "material fact, upon which the adjudicating Loyalty Board can place whatever weight it deems appropriate." Especially since the DOJ had indicated that the FBI should not "hesitate" to mention non-AGLOSO groups "where such references will assist" in making loyalty determinations, Hoover declared, "if we are not permitted" to include such citations, "the impression might be created" that the FBI considered such organizations subversive but the department "does not." In what seemed to be a threatened FBI work strike, he added, "the question naturally also arises as to whether this Bureau should continue to conduct full field loyalty investigations" with regard to non-AGLOSO organizations if requested to "by the CSC and other agencies." Faced with an apparently unending stream of memos from Hoover, whose bulldog tenacity was legendary, and upon whose reports the DOJ was heavily dependent for AGLOSO determinations and all other aspects of the loyalty program, Ford completely capitulated in a February 14, 1949, memo that advised Hoover, "Your comments have been noted, and it is suggested that you continue the present practice with reference to characterization of organizations not on the Attorney General's list."[113]

In the meantime, the LRB had already rendered inoperative its November 2, 1948, memo to government agencies restricting loyalty consideration solely to AGLOSO organizations by dispatching, following a December 17, 1948, LRB executive committee meeting, a new directive that fully reflected the confusing nature of the intervening LRB-DOJ-FBI communications. On the one hand, the new memo directed the boards to "confine their considerations" to AGLOSO organizations "insofar as an individual's membership in, affiliation with or sympathetic associations with organizations is concerned," but, on the other, it added that "activity of alleged disloyal nature" with regard to non-AGLOSO groups could be the "proper subject of a charge or interrogatory," as could "alleged disloyal activity" not "connected with any organization," since "disloyal activities on the part of an individual are not privileged because they have occurred in connection with an organization not on the Attorney General's list." Insofar as this directive, which was incorporated into a lengthy LRB statement published in the *Federal Register,* could be translated into English, it suggested that, save for membership in organizations formally categorized as seeking the unconstitutional alteration of the government, in which membership had been previously determined to require automatic dismissal, henceforth little, if any difference, would exist concerning consideration allegations of AGLOSO associations and affiliations with non-AGLOSO groups.[114]

A similarly confusing "nondistinction" was made by the LRB Executive Committee with regard to publications in January 1949 when it voted, "with reference to the evidentiary value of a connection or affiliation with a circulated publication," that allegations concerning non-AGLOSO organizations "would not be given consideration, subject to the condition that anything said in the publication in question might be given evidentiary consideration in the usual way." Despite these rulings, which largely eliminated the distinction between AGLOSO and non-AGLOSO groups, in a public report issued in May 1950, the LRB stated flatly that "consideration by loyalty boards" was "confined" to organizations "listed by the Attorney General." In private, the LRB's standards with regard to non-AGLOSO groups were further loosened (or confused), when the board's executive committee agreed in October 1952 that such groups could be "properly referred to in notices or charges or interrogatories, or at any hearing, for the purpose of identifying, in detail, the informative facts relating to the time, the place, and in what connection the alleged activity of the individual occurred."[115]

While the DOJ, the FBI, and the LRB were trying to sort out the relevance of non-AGLOSO affiliations in federal loyalty determinations, another three-way conflict erupted concerning the desirability of the department's making additional AGLOSO designations after its initial late 1947 listing. Apparently for entirely bureaucratic reasons, the FBI repeatedly protested in 1948 that further listings would force it to expensively duplicate previously completed work. Thus, Hoover complained to Clark in April 1948 that there was no "practical way" that the bureau could determine if the 1.7 million federal employees who had already been investigated had participated in newly listed groups "except to recheck" all of the previously processed loyalty forms, which would require "a very substantial appropriation," and that "substantially all of the information upon all questionable organizations was transmitted to the Department prior to the time that your first list was compiled." Quite unusually, Clark, no doubt feeling political pressure to expand AGLOSO during an election year, rebuffed Hoover's demands to either cease adding new organizations to AGLOSO or to provide the FBI with additional funding, writing him in May 1948 that the FBI had already frequently and "necessarily" reported on employee memberships in organizations "not on the proscribed list," but in groups "under investigation by you" and "under consideration by me" for future designation and had "in many instances" requested "full field" investigations of such organizations. In an overt appeal to Hoover's vanity, Clark declared that this work "undoubtedly was done completely and competently in the first instance," so there "would appear to be no necessity for its repetition, irrespective of additional designations" and thus "no problem" of additional demands upon the bureau would arise. When Hoover protested to Clark in late May that the FBI had "no method whereby at this late date we can recheck any forms" for determining affiliations with "any newly designated organizations," Clark responded, "You should have devised different procedures, for the executive order itself provides for continual study and subsequent designations—Suppose a new organization was formed, what would you do?" When Hoover continued to protest, Clark responded by a written note to "Edgar" in early June that stated that "we should insist that an index be kept of government employees" so that when a new organization was listed "you could check its membership—if you do not have membership lists we could secure same through subpoena."[116]

At a mid-1949 LRB meeting, chair Richardson expressed concern similar to the FBI's regarding the impact of additional AGLOSO listings upon administration of the loyalty program, especially since, he said, Clark's recent designations did not indicate that newly listed groups had "suddenly become subversive" but rather that the DOJ had simply reached a conclusion during its "regular investigation" of organizations that had "undoubtedly been subversive," including in cases involving federal employees who had "already gone through our mill." He cautioned that "of course, in our proceedings, the legal principle of legal jeopardy doesn't apply because it isn't a court proceeding; but I think we ought to pay more than lip service to the question of double jeopardy because none of us, I am sure, wants to impose on an employee cruel and unusual punishment by a second hearing." Moreover, Richardson complained, Clark had suggested "to us that because it was becoming more difficult to get proof, we ought not to require so much proof," because, according to the FBI, "there has been a definite procedure by Communist organizations to eliminate all membership lists." He reported having written back "sharply" to Clark that, "I thought we'd gone as far as we could on finding disloyalty with reference to employees—we consider hearsay evidence; unsworn evidence that the employee never sees; we don't give him confrontation and cross-examination." Richardson reported that he had told Clark, "I don't think the Board will react favorably at all to the idea of reducing evidentiary standards."[117]

Several LRB members responded by reiterating their previous expressions of uneasiness with AGLOSO. Thus, Ohio lawyer Murray Seasongood declared that AGLOSO membership should not be "evidence against the person if he belonged to it before it was on the Attorney General's list," while New York lawyer John Clark complained that the "weakness of that list is that it doesn't have any dates as to when the organizations became subversive" and that the FBI appeared to be "utterly unaware" that there were "a whole lot of people who were in sympathy with Russia when Russia was fighting with us against Germany" and engaged in "communistic associations at a time when the Communists were supporting our program," because the bureau "makes no distinction whatever in its reports as to whether it was during that period or during a sensitive period since." Boston attorney Garrett Hoag added that it was "well known" that "many of these organizations started out as perfectly innocent and high-minded organizations" and therefore "membership may or may not have been significant, depending upon the date." Washington lawyer Wilbur LaRoe asked what the LRB should do if subordinate loyalty boards decided that an AGLOSO recommendation wasn't "any better than most of them that [Clark] makes" and "is hardly worth the paper it's written on," while New York attorney George Alger reported he and another LRB member had recently "spent an entire week wasting our time informing" Clark that on looking through one "entire record there wasn't anything to this miserable FBI stuff." When University of Chicago professor Harry Bigelow suggested that it would be "highly desirable if the Attorney General's office exercised a little more judgment in their scrutiny of the record before they remanded the cases to us," LaRoe responded, "Eliminate the word 'more.'"[118]

AGLOSO's Key Role in Federal Loyalty Determinations

As noted earlier, according to Truman's 1947 executive order and repeated, subsequent statements by him and other top officials, allegations of "membership in, affiliation with or sympathetic association" with AGLOSO organizations supposedly were only one "piece of evidence" that might or might not prove relevant in making loyalty decisions, especially as "guilt by association" was deemed outside the realm of American legal principles. While these statements clearly suggested that AGLOSO affiliations would be of relatively minor importance in administering the loyalty program, in practice allegations of AGLOSO connections quickly became the program's central focus. As historian Francis Thompson notes, "the attorney general's 'Black List'" quickly became the "heart of the loyalty program," and henceforth an employee's "acquaintance with the 'wrong people,' no matter how far in the past or what circumstances accompanied such acquaintances, became prima facie evidence of guilt, and guilt by association became the rule rather than the exception." Thus, during a May 4, 1948, LRB meeting, chair Richardson declared that "the overwhelming number of [loyalty] cases have to do with membership or affiliation or association or activity of a particular employee with a particular [AGLOSO] organization" that "depended for its wrongdoing upon its connection with the Communist Party." Similarly, in a 1951 letter to Attorney General Howard McGrath, new LRB chair Bingham declared that AGLOSO was "the heart and soul" of determinations concerning federal employee loyalty and "99% of the cases that are adjudicated" arose under the "membership in, affiliation with or sympathetic association" with AGLOSO organizations clause of Truman's executive order. Bingham added that, without AGLOSO, the over 150 federal loyalty boards would have to make individual determinations about the character of organizations, with a resulting "chaotic situation" and that AGLOSO therefore provided the "adjudicator with a uniform pattern and is an essential tool by which uniformity can be maintained." According to a 1955 analysis of 326 loyalty cases, Bingham's "99%" statement was only a slight exaggeration: 132 cases (40 percent) involved alleged affiliations with the CP or YCL, 119 (36 percent) involved claimed affiliations with other AGLOSO groups, and 63 cases included purported affiliations with non-AGLOSO organizations listed by HUAC or state committees. Fewer than 5 percent of cases involving AGLOSO affiliations included alleged leadership roles; instead the charges almost always involved ordinary membership (60 percent) or even more tenuous or unspecified connections, such as attending meetings or donating money to groups without joining them (38 percent). In 243 cases, charges included "associating" with other people, sometimes including spouses and parents, who allegedly had engaged in dubious activities; in 182 instances (56 percent), these allegations involved CP or YCL associations, while 67 (21 percent) involved associations with other AGLOSO groups. Of the total of 249 separate charges of association with those with alleged AGLOSO ties, only 24 claimed that the associates were AGLOSO leaders.[119]

In her 1953 book on the loyalty program, scholar Eleanor Bontecou, in the only previously published extensive examination of AGLOSO, concluded that in practice AGLOSO membership raised "a strong presumption of disloyalty, and created a prima-facie case upon which the [loyalty] boards" issued "charges which are equivalent to an indictment." Similarly, Yale University professor Ralph Brown, whose 1958 book *Loyalty and Security* remains the leading study of the post–World War II loyalty program, told Congress in 1955 that AGLOSO and "related lists," such as those of HUAC and state legislative committees, were the "foundation" of the program because the "two chief classes" of disloyalty charges were "organizational memberships and personal associations," and "the personal associations" usually involved alleged ties to another person who "is a member of such an organization or has a brother-in-law who is a member of such an organization, and so forth." The federal Commission on Government Security's mid-1957 report concluded that those making loyalty determinations apparently felt their mandate required "automatic dismissal of any person who claimed, or was found to have had, any affiliation with a named organization, or associated with a person so affiliated," although such measures "distort[ed]" AGLOSO's purpose from "merely supplying one factor to be investigated" to "that of an automatic disqualifier." As the result of the loyalty program's focus on AGLOSO affiliations, its real target effectively became "wrong thinking," as Attorney General Clark clearly suggested in his previously cited 1948 congressional testimony: while the non-AGLOSO criteria deemed relevant to loyalty screenings required evidence of some concrete "disloyal" action, such as engaging in espionage, charges related to AGLOSO affiliations (like earlier criminal syndicalism and immigration laws) required only allegations (that were often vague and almost always based upon confidential FBI sources and thus not subject to cross-examination) of often-loose ties to organizations (or to others with such affiliations) that lacked any claims of any illegal activities. By 1957, such instances had become so entrenched in the general political landscape that one movie included a vignette in which a man seeking a defense job, when asked about any AGLOSO affiliations, states, "Just because Dad happened to think back in the thirties that the Loyalists in Spain were on the right side, I'm not going to stop associating with him."[120]

Allegations concerning AGLOSO ties clearly became the central (although not the only) basis on which the FBI launched so-called "full field" investigations of federal employees and applicants and on which a large percentage of formal "loyalty" charges were lodged. Thus, in a 1948 memo to Clark, FBI director Hoover wrote that the "prima facie consideration in determining whether a full field investigation should be initiated as a result of the check of the loyalty form has been membership in or affiliation with those organizations and groups which have been declared subversive by you," although "other contemporary factors are considered." The desire to obtain information concerning AGLOSO associations was cited by the FBI as justifying continued extensive surveillance of targeted groups, which often involved break-ins and other illegal activities that had been common FBI tactics since before American entry into World War II. In an early 1948 internal memo, FBI assistant director Ladd wrote that, under Truman's order, "mere membership in or association with a Communist front organization, primarily those declared by the Attorney General to be within the scope of the Loyalty Order, constitutes sufficient grounds to institute a full field investigation," and therefore it was "advisable that the Bureau make every effort to obtain the individual membership lists, mailing lists or other lists maintained by these organizations showing the individuals affiliated with them." Hoover subsequently noted his personal approval on a 1948 memo from top FBI officials recommending that field offices throughout the country be directed to obtain "through informants and other investigative sources" the "membership and mailing lists showing individuals associated" with "any of the AGLOSO communist fronts." Revelations in the mid-1970s and afterwards make clear that FBI sources for such information included numerous secret informants and also non–judicially authorized electronic wiretaps and microphone implantations and clearly illegal burglaries, which were especially useful in obtaining secret membership, mailing, and funding lists. Thus, a March 1, 1948, memo from the FBI's New Orleans field office reported that local NCASF membership lists were maintained by an employee of Newcomb College at his office and that his "business files" had been "photographed but no membership list was found."[121]

The loyalty program's central focus on AGLOSO affiliations became especially pernicious because federal officials readily conceded that Communists were typically a minority in many listed "front" groups and that a large percentage of their membership was often unaware of the Communist role in them. Thus, according to an LRB "Training Manual" compiled in early 1948, hundreds of alleged "Communist fronts" had "gone out of existence when their true purposes have become known or exposed," and the CP had "never found it necessary to have a majority of the members of front organizations consciously on its side in order to exercise control," as "ordinarily an alert minority of Party members or sympathizers strategically placed" could "achieve the Party's objectives." According to an FBI report in the LRB files, the bureau had estimated that "about fourteen million persons [a clearly vast overestimate]" had been members or contributors of the APM alone, "the bulk of whom were undoubtedly unaware of the Communist control of the group." Similarly, Attorney General Clark wrote the ADA in 1949, in response to its protest of the NACASD's designation, that "there is no doubt that in connection with almost every [AGLOSO] organization," there "will be among the membership many persons, sometimes even a majority" unaware of "the true purposes and control of the group," and that loyalty boards would take this under consideration since "'guilt by association' is not and must never be a part of American jurisprudence."[122]

Although AGLOSO designations were supposedly made to guide federal employee loyalty determinations, a large percentage of them were extremely unlikely to significantly aid in such findings, because most of the listed groups were either completely insignificant or long defunct and few, if any, federal employees or applicants were likely to have belonged to them. An LRB spokesman reported in November 1949 that the great majority of the 123 federal employees fired during the first two and a half years of the loyalty program had been dismissed for alleged connections with "Communist fronts" and that "very few" had been fired for being fascists or members of the other AGLOSO categories. An analysis of 75 loyalty cases published in 1953 similarly indicated that allegations involving groups designated as fascist, totalitarian, or advocating the violent denial of constitutional rights to Americans were "negligible." According to this analysis, of the over 100 AGLOSO "Communist" groups, only 21 were ever mentioned in loyalty charges, and only 5 of those arose in more than 3 instances. By far the most common alleged AGLOSO affiliations in these cases, which included a total of 72 AGLOSO-linked charges, involved the WBA, mentioned in 16 cases, 3 of which claimed only "sympathetic association" (although under the Biddle AGLOSO, ordinary WBA membership did not even warrant further investigation). Four other groups (ALPD, APM, IWO, and Washington Committee for Democratic Action [WCDA]) accounted for another 25 of the AGLOSO charges.[123]

The verbatim charges involving AGLOSO (and other matters) lodged in 50 federal loyalty cases were published in an August 1955 book sponsored by the Fund for the Republic. Although loyalty hearings were conducted in private, this collection, compiled by scores of lawyers under the direction of Adam Yarmolinsky, was gathered from cooperating federal employees and their lawyers. AGLOSO charges published in the Yarmolinsky compilation and available from other sources included a wide variety of allegations, frequently involving charges of personal CP involvement, but just as frequently alleging associations with other AGLOSO groups or with other individuals alleged to have such affiliations. In most cases, both AGLOSO and non-AGLOSO allegations lacked specific evidence, sources, dates, or locations, presumably to protect the confidentiality of FBI material, thus making them extremely difficult to refute and cross-examination of the unknown accusers impossible. The entirety of the charges in one instance was that the employee had engaged in "continued sympathetic association with known Communists, read Communist literature and made pro-Communist statements." Every charge against another federal employee concerned her "close and continuing association" with her brother, who was alleged to have been a "close associate of reported Communist Party members and sympathizers," to have aided the CP by loaning his car for party work and via personal participation in "Communist sponsored activities," to have served as an officer of the AGLOSO-designated CAA, to have been "active" in the listed LYL, and to have "in 1951, pledged $10.00" to the CRC.[124]

Another employee was charged with otherwise unspecified past CP membership, membership in the AGLOSO-designated WCDA in "approximately 1941," and sharing living quarters in 1941 or 1942 with "a member of an [unspecified] organization designated by the Attorney General as subversive." In another case, the charges were that it was "reliably reported" that the employee had been a CP member in 1944 and had attended CP meetings in 1943 at specified locations, that in 1943 he had "resided and associated" with another man who was "reported" to have been an active CP member, and that in 1944 he listed as a reference a minister who, according to a newspaper article, had sponsored a 1945 dinner for Paul Robeson under the JAFRC "auspices." The wife of the employee in this case was also subjected to loyalty proceedings on the grounds that her husband had been a CP member, attended CP meetings, and had "closely associated" with a CP member, and that she had listed as a reference a woman whose husband was "registered as a member" of an AGLOSO CP school. Another employee was charged with having signed a 1940 nominating petition for the WP (a legal political party that was designated seven years later) and for listing as a reference a man whose name appeared on the mailing list of two AGLOSO-designated groups. Yet another employee was charged with serving as associate editor of a newspaper that had been "cited" as a member of the designated WBA and with having "closely associated" with a person "reliably reported" to have belonged to two AGLOSO groups and with "a known Communist" who worked for "official" publications associated with the AGLOSO-designated IWO; another charge against him was that it was "reliably reported" that the employee had been associated with and friendly" with a man "who held a meeting in his home for the benefit of the [designated] United American Spanish Aid Committee." Charges in another case included that the employee was "reported to have purchased books" from a store which was "a possible successor" to the WBA. Another included allegations that an accused employee had "received correspondence" from someone who "was listed as a member of several subversive organizations" and had "posted on a bulletin board" an appeal from the JAFRC. Charges in other cases included that an employee had been "closely associated with an individual" who belonged to the IWO and had maintained a "close and continuing association with [his] parents, with whom [he] resided until 1948"; and that an employee was "closely associated with [his] father, who reportedly" belonged to or was on the mailing list of four AGLOSO groups, including the CP.[125]

In a case that was publicly revealed in a 1955 Senate hearing, VA clerk Beatrice Murphy Campbell, a published black poet, editor, and book reviewer, was suspended in 1954, for allegedly holding WBA membership over a decade earlier, recruiting others to join the WBA, and falsely denying her past membership. She was reinstated four months later after proving that she had been bedridden during her alleged active WBA membership (as the VA knew, because it had insisted on repeated medical reports concerning her disability). In August 1955 Senate testimony and a lengthy article about her ordeal, published in the April 17, 1955, *Washington Post,* Murphy recounted that her only WBA contact had been attending public lectures there in 1940 by poet Langston Hughes and novelist Erskine Caldwell, which she said she was "thrilled" to attend, as there were "so very few places" offering such cultural opportunities to blacks in segregated World War II–era Washington. However, she added, most of her fellow workers were too scared to write letters supporting her denial that she had ever recruited others to join the WBA because, in the existing climate, there was a "real honest-to-God fear of one American to say a good word for another, a friend," out of concern of being branded subversive. She declared, "All the clearances in the world cannot wipe out the harm which has been done" and that her reinstatement (followed soon after by a merit award), came "too late to erase the corroding effect of the experience on my spirit," because "in order to save my sanity, I reached the point where one must shut off feeling or be lost. . . . I must keep praying over and over and over, 'Lord, keep me away from bitterness.'" When Charles Clift, a confidential assistant to FCC Commissioner Charles Durr, faced loyalty proceedings in late 1948, the allegations consisted of five charges alleging associations or affiliations from twelve years earlier, including "close" associations with members of the CP and the three other designated groups and supporting a CP member threatened with deportation, plus two charges of maintaining a relationship with his wife, who was allegedly a WBA member and "close associate" of six Communists.[126]

As anti-Communist hysteria increased after 1947, political pressure for the dismissal of federal employees allegedly involved in "subversive" activities mounted, while the standards for "loyalty" dismissals increasingly loosened. Thus, the *Washington Post* reported during the 1948 presidential election that one agency loyalty board member "confessed sheepishly," in a view "seconded by half a dozen others," that "employees have and will be rated disloyal and ineligible to hold their Federal jobs who would have been cleared for the lack of sufficient and convincing evidence a few months ago." When asked why, the board member stated that the "real and potential" political pressure had become "unbearable" and "too much for civil servants to take. We're now reluctant to clear a fellow who is charged with a few minor and perhaps unsubstantiated indiscretions for fear of being hauled up before a congressional committee at some future date and made to justify our decision because additional evidence and acts by the employee may make his disloyalty provable," with the result that "our own careers would be ruined." Similarly, a "top loyalty official" was quoted as declaring that "if this hadn't been a political year" every employee "would have been given a square deal," but "no one can tell now what will happen. I'm afraid to say what I really think." In a 1950 speech at Yale University Law School and during subsequent congressional testimony, LRB chair Richardson declared that Congress was pressing for a far stronger loyalty program, one with "spiked shoes on it," but denied that the existing program was akin to a "Gestapo" and maintained that federal employee morale was "higher than ever" and that "the only one who has anything to worry about is the one who has a dirty, smelly record." However, he admitted that among the 180 employees thus far fired for loyalty reasons "not one single case" involved either espionage or even evidence "directing towards espionage," which was presumably the basis for the entire loyalty program.[127]

Passage of the 1950 Internal Security Act

The postwar Red Scare and demands for stronger measures to find and discharge "subversives" from government employment intensified considerably after Sen. McCarthy emerged on the anti-Communist scene in February 1950 and, especially, after the outbreak of the Korean War five months later and a series of arrests involving alleged atomic espionage (the Rosenberg case) that both preceded and followed the dispatch of American troops to Korea. Thus, in April 1951, the Truman administration lowered the standards for making loyalty dismissals from a finding that "reasonable grounds" existed for belief that a person was "disloyal" to a finding of "reasonable doubt" concerning loyalty, and in May 1953, President Eisenhower, flanked at a White House ceremony by leading congressional red-hunters, including McCarthy, lowered the dismissal standard even further by requiring that federal hirings and retentions be found to be "clearly consistent with the interests of national security."[128]

Neither of these changes modified the key role that AGLOSO played within the federal loyalty system. But another result of the post-1949 deteriorating civil liberties climate would prove extremely important for the ultimate fate of AGLOSO twenty-five years later: the September 1950 congressional enactment, over President Truman's veto, of the Internal Security Act (ISA), sometimes known as the Subversive Activities Control Act or the McCarran Act (for Senate sponsor Sen. Pat McCarran [D-NV]). The ISA was largely modeled on the so-called Mundt-Nixon bill (cosponsored by a junior representative, Richard Nixon), which first passed the House of Representatives in 1948 but had been blocked in the Senate until after Korea. The heart of the ISA's numerous provisions was the establishment of a five-person Subversive Activities Control Board (SACB), empowered to designate "Communist action" and "Communist front" organizations upon petition from the attorney general, following hearings including the right to cross-examination of witnesses and subject to federal court appeals up to the Supreme Court. Unlike AGLOSO, which supposedly was compiled solely to facilitate federal personnel loyalty determinations and which, as an executive order, carried no criminal penalties (and, at least theoretically, no automatic penalties of any kind against either designated groups or their members), the explicit purpose of the ISA and the SACB was to "expose" Communist groups and its designations carried automatic and severe penalties that were clearly designed to cripple listed organizations. Designated groups had to file extensive reports about their operations with the attorney general, were denied tax exemptions, and had to label their publications, mail, and broadcasts as sponsored by a "Communist" organization; moreover, their members were denied passports, federal employment, or jobs with private defense contractors. Groups and individuals violating these provisions risked substantial penalties. Under the terms of the ISA, "Communist action" organizations effectively had to be found to be under Soviet control and only organizations found to be controlled by a "Communist action" organization could be determined to be "Communist fronts," provisions that would become highly significant during the 1960s, when AGLOSO proponents argued that AGLOSO, but not the ISA, provided the flexibility needed to list "subversive" groups that were not under direct or indirect Russian control.[129]

In a September 7, 1950, *Los Angeles Times* essay, Nixon claimed his law would solve the "whole problem" of AGLOSO's lack of due process (and those of federal and state legislative committees) by providing, via hearings, "needed protection to organizations charged with being Communist dominated." During 1948 House debate on the Mundt-Nixon bill, Nixon had similarly argued for it as a substitute for AGLOSO's "loose listing" of subversive groups, without hearings or "strict standards." Along the same lines, an October 1, 1950, *New York Times* news analysis said the SACB's task was to establish "a new and better blacklist of subversive organizations" than AGLOSO. Despite such attempts to draw distinctions between AGLOSO and the SACB, especially since AGLOSO was not discontinued with the enactment of the ISA, there was frequent subsequent confusion between them, since, in the end, both focused on the designation of "subversive" or "Communist" groups in proceedings initiated by the attorney general. (This confusion was probably increased when President Truman chose first LRB head Richardson to be the first SACB chair, an appointment that was blocked when SJC chair McCarran, who apparently viewed Richardson as "soft" on communism, refused to even hold confirmation hearings for him or the other four original Truman SACB appointees. Richardson, who had presided over a loyalty program in which individuals were charged without being able to know the evidence against them or to cross-examine their accusers, bitterly complained that "it makes me damned mad" that "decent Americans . . . can't have a hearing.") Despite the surface similarities between AGLOSO and SACB proceedings and listings, both in theory and reality the two were completely separate until (as discussed in chapter 5) President Nixon tried to combine them via a 1971 executive order that entrusted the SACB, rather than the attorney general, with AGLOSO designation power following a series of post-1965 Supreme Court rulings that essentially rendered the SACB toothless. Until then, the two "listings" operated simultaneously along parallel tracks; before 1960 SACB hearings usually involved groups that had already been AGLOSO-designated, although thereafter, by which time AGLOSO essentially was moribund, that was often not the case.[130]

Truman's ISA veto was overridden within an hour by a 286–48 House vote and within a day by a 57–10 Senate vote, with the vast majority of Democrats voting against him in both houses. Completely lost in the extensive nationwide front-page press coverage of the veto was that Truman's 5,500-word accompanying message (published in its entirety in the September 23, 1950, *New York Times* and often reprinted since, frequently as an example of Truman's courage in fighting Red Scare excesses) completely undermined the rationale of his own AGLOSO program. Thus, he complained at great length that the ISA provision authorizing SACB designation of "Communist front" groups would pose the "greatest danger to freedom of speech, press and assembly since the Alien and Sedition Laws of 1798" because it would allow "such a determination to be based solely upon the extent to which the positions taken or advanced by [groups] from time to time on matters of policy do not deviate from that of the Communist movement" (the same test apparently used to make AGLOSO "Communist" designations). According to Truman, this provision would "open a Pandora's box of opportunities for official condemnation of organizations and individuals for perfectly honest opinions which happen to be stated also by Communists," thus possibly leading to designating organizations advocating low-cost housing "for sincere humanitarian reasons" because "the communists regularly exploit slum conditions." The "basic error" involved, Truman added, was that such procedures moved in the "direction of suppression of opinion and belief," a "very dangerous" course because "any government stifling of the free expression of opinion is a long step towards totalitarianism," which would "delight the Communists" since it would

> make a mockery of the Bill of Rights and of our claims to stand for freedom
> in the world. . . . Obviously, if this law were on the statute books, the part
> of prudence would be to avoid saying anything that might be construed
> by someone as not deviating sufficiently from the current Communist
> propaganda line. And since no one could be sure in advance what views
> were safe to express, the inevitable tendency would be to express no views
> on controversial subjects. The result could only be to reduce the vigor and
> strength of our political life—an outcome that the Communists would
> happily welcome but that free men should abhor. . . . We will destroy all that
> we seek to preserve, if we sacrifice the liberties of our citizens in a misguided
> attempt to achieve national security.

A more accurate and eloquent description of the effect—and at least to some extent the apparent intent—of AGLOSO could hardly be written.

3

Challenges to AGLOSO, 1948–1955

The Supreme Court's Ruling in *Joint Anti-Fascist Refugee Committee v. McGrath*

In April 1951, front-page newspaper headlines across the country reported that the U.S. Supreme Court had struck the first major blow against AGLOSO in a complex and ambiguous decision, *Joint Anti-Fascist Refugee Committee v. McGrath*. The 5–3 ruling, overturning six lower court decisions by requiring that three AGLOSO organizations be allowed to contest their listings, was a consolidated case involving the Joint Anti-Fascist Refugee Committee (JAFRC), the National Council on American-Soviet Friendship (NCASF), and the International Workers Order (IWO). All three were left-wing groups that were among the largest and most prominent AGLOSO organizations. Each had been hailed during World War II by American officials but suffered serious damage and losses in the aftermath of their AGLOSO designations. As noted earlier, the IWO, an ethnic-fraternal insurance organization with almost 200,000 members when it was designated in 1947, quickly suffered a membership collapse and underwent prolonged New York state legal proceedings to liquidate it. JAFRC had been licensed in 1942 to provide medical aid for Spanish Civil War loyalist refugees in France by President Roosevelt's War Relief Control Board and, like the two other groups, had been granted tax-exempt status by the Treasury Department, which was withdrawn following its designation. JAFRC included Communists in its leadership, but, like the other two organizations, was never accused of illegal activities. However, it early attracted the attention of the House of Representatives Committee on Un-American Activities (HUAC), resulting in 1946 contempt of court sentences against its entire leadership for failing to supply HUAC with subpoenaed records. The NCASF was organized to promote Soviet-American friendship during World War II, when the U.S. was allied with Russia against Hitler. It was founded at a 1942 New York City mass meeting that received greetings from President Roosevelt and Vice President Henry Wallace and was sponsored by three cabinet members The founding meeting was attended by 20,000 people who heard speeches from New York governor Herbert Lehman, New York City mayor Fiorello La Guardia, and conservative AFL president William Green. A 1944 NCASF dinner held to celebrate the Soviet Army's twenty-sixth anniversary received congratulatory messages from five American generals, including

Dwight Eisenhower and Douglas MacArthur. Although during World War II its membership included at least three congressmen and Secretary of the Interior Harold Ickes, during the Cold War the NCASF became widely viewed as a Soviet propaganda outlet and its director was found in contempt of Congress in 1946 for failing to provide HUAC with subpoenaed records.[1]

Each of the three organizations had originally filed separate lawsuits against the attorney general and other federal officials in federal district courts in 1948–1949. They each maintained that their listing had unconstitutionally denied them free speech and due process rights by damaging their reputations and their ability to conduct legitimate and ordinary First Amendment–protected activities, fostering a wide variety of reprisals against them and depriving them of any opportunity to contest their designations. For example, the NCASF maintained that it and its affiliates had "lost numerous members, officers and sponsors; lost public support; lost contributions; lost attendance at meetings; lost circulation of their publications; lost acceptance by colleges, schools and organizations of their exhibits and other material; have been denied meeting places; have been denied radio time"; lost their federal tax exemption, costing "large sums of money which they would otherwise have received"; and lost the ability to "get members and support from federal employees," who feared that their "employment would be jeopardized." Beyond the alleged damage to their First Amendment rights, the organizations maintained that their Fifth Amendment due process rights had been violated because the government's designations were arbitrary, especially by denying them any opportunity to contest their listings. Thus, the IWO argued that its listing lacked "warrant in law" or "the slightest basis in truth or in fact and was made without notice or opportunity to be heard, without finding of fact or conclusions of law and without any prior or accompanying statement of explanation." The NCASF and the IWO explicitly denied that their activities provided any basis for their AGLOSO designations, while the JAFRC did so implicitly, by characterizing its activities as solely dedicated to aiding Spanish refugees.[2]

The Department of Justice (DOJ) filed two-sentence rejoinders to each of the three lawsuits, simply maintaining that "there is no present justiciable controversy" between the complaining organizations and the government, and that the complaints failed to "state a claim" against the government "upon which relief can be granted." In three separate federal district court rulings in 1948–1949, judges upheld the government. Thus, in a February 1949 ruling in the NCASF case, Judge Bennings Bailey declared that there could be no legal remedy for the "indirect effect" that might result from a governmental program whose sole purpose was to facilitate the administration of the federal loyalty program by providing "simply one piece of evidence, which may or may not be helpful" in reaching loyalty determinations. He added that he was satisfied that the attorney general, acting as a presidential agent, could not be restrained from providing "such information as he may have" to government agencies about groups "which, in his opinion are engaging in activities that operate against the maintenance of the Constitution and the welfare of the country," and that the "indirect" effects of AGLOSO described by the plaintiffs did not "constitute legal damage" or in any way subject them "to any civil or criminal liability."[3]

The three organizations each appealed to the federal court of appeals, essentially reiterating their previous arguments. The government's response was somewhat fuller than in the district courts, including sweeping claims that AGLOSO was based on executive powers that were not subject to judicial review and that, in any case, AGLOSO imposed no concrete damage to the complaining organizations that required a legal remedy. Thus, in the JAFRC appeal, the DOJ maintained that the AGLOSO designation imposed "no restrictions whatever" upon the organization and that its "sole interest" arose from the "damage to its public reputation" allegedly thereby caused, but that since AGLOSO did not "command the appellant to do or to refrain from doing anything" and the attorney general was constitutionally authorized to "designate appellant as a communist organization" as an agent of the president in carrying out his responsibilities to regulate admission to the civil service, "no justiciable controversy exists between the parties to this action." The department maintained that "certain executive powers" were not subject to court review, including the "right to speak forth freely to the nation and inform it of groups deemed to be operating against the best interests of our constitutional government itself," a power "necessarily inherent to preserve that government." According to the department, all of JAFRC's alleged injuries were "indirect and incidental" to AGLOSO, which had not "in any way altered the status or activities conducted by appellant," since JAFRC remained free to conduct its business, raise money, voice its views and publish its beliefs, and the listing issued "no directive to other federal, state or municipal officials." The department added while its allegedly nonreviewable AGLOSO power "might be subject to abuse," the only remedy was "the elective process" or presidential impeachment.

Federal appeals courts fully endorsed the government's position in three 1949–1950 rulings. Thus, in the JAFRC case, a three-judge appeals panel decided 2–1 on August 11, 1949, that the organization's complaint failed to "present a justiciable controversy" because the AGLOSO listing and Harry Truman's loyalty order "commands nothing of the Committee," denies it "no authority, privilege, immunity or license," and subjects it to "no liability, civil or criminal." The decision added that, in promulgating AGLOSO, the attorney general had merely complied with presidential directives in providing "information and advice" in pursuit of the government's legitimate interests in protecting the civil service from disloyal and "subversive elements," and that such communications could not be categorized as "laws or regulations within the meaning of constitutional prohibitions against abridgment of the rights of the people." The court added that the attorney general had only undertaken "that which the President could have done for himself," in which case "his action would have been within the realm of his executive power, not subject to judicial review," and thus AGLOSO's "essential character" was that of "acts of the President himself," which could not be "challenged legally." The court added that any resulting injury to JAFRC was "indirect" and "purely incidental" to the loyalty program's valid purpose. It further dismissed all challenges to procedural aspects of AGLOSO's promulgation and publication, for example, holding that lack of hearings implied no due process lapses because AGLOSO was a "necessary" step in implementing the loyalty program, thus affording "no ground for judicial review" if, as one of its "unavoidable consequences," it happened to "affect adversely" listed organizations. The court concluded that nothing in the loyalty program "deprives the Committee or its members of any property rights" or civil liberties since "freedom of speech and assembly is denied no one" and "no one has a constitutional right to be a government employee."[4]

The three organizations appealed the rulings to the Supreme Court, reiterating their previous arguments, adding that their cases were highly significant given the general context of increasing pressures on civil liberties and maintaining that the lower courts had erred in holding that the government bore no responsibility for the injuries resulting from their AGLOSO designations. For example, the NCASF urged the Court to intervene because the issues raised were of "great public importance," since its case presented "another application of the growing tendency of the making of administrative decisions," all "invariably justified by a claim of the needs of 'internal security,'" which "seriously impair individual liberties" without "procedural safeguards" and "on the basis of secret evidence locked in the bosom of the administrator and [therefore] never susceptible of rebuttal by those affected." It maintained that its injuries were caused by governmental officials "stimulating others to take action" and that the Constitution nullified "sophisticated as well as simple-minded encroachments on the freedoms of speech and assembly," and that therefore the contention that the Constitution distinguished between "indirect" and "direct" abridgement of guaranteed rights lacked any legal foundation. Moreover, it argued, the attorney general's "unfettered [AGLOSO] discretion" allowed him to "list any organization which incurs his displeasure" and "resist any inquiry into his illegal actions." The brief concluded by arguing that the Constitution gave "no power to any government official to list organizations as subversive or disloyal" and declared that AGLOSO empowered the attorney general "to make himself a judge of political orthodoxy and loyalty" and to "inform the public that certain ideas are officially discouraged and prohibited," thus violating "the most revered traditions of our Constitution."[5]

The DOJ responded to the briefs with short responses that urged denial of certiorari by reiterating its stance that no grounds existed to consider the lawsuit because "no justiciable controversy" was involved and the organizations had no legal standing because they had suffered no injury at the hands of the government. Thus, in its response to the JAFRC brief, the Department maintained that AGLOSO "in no way" changed JAFRC's "existing or legal status," imposed "no regulation or directive limiting the operation or conduct of petitioner's affairs," included "no directive to other federal, state or municipal officers which in any way subjects petitioner to the contingency of future administrative action," and subjected "neither petitioner nor its members to any criminal or civil penalties, either immediate or postponed." Moreover, the government maintained, any damage to JAFRC's "advantageous relationship with others" alleged to stem from its AGLOSO designation largely arose "from the force of public opinion and not from the direct action of respondents," and, in any case, it was legally "well settled that public officials are absolutely privileged to publish even false and defamatory matter in the exercise of official duties," and it was "plain that this alleged defamation was an official communication as to matters within the authority of respondents."[6]

The high Court agreed to hear each of the three cases during 1950, triggering another exchange of legal briefs, in which the organizations and the DOJ reiterated and elaborated upon their prior arguments, often in far sharper terms that reflected the growing Cold War tensions associated with the outbreak of the Korean War in June 1950 and Sen. Joseph McCarthy's appearance on the anti-Communist scene in February 1950. Thus, in its September 1950 brief, JAFRC rejected the claim that AGLOSO had inflicted no "direct" injury upon it, maintaining that it served as a "fixed, final and mandatory" loyalty program determination that put "civil service employees and applicants on notice that 'association' with the JAFRC will result in ineligibility," and that in the "political arena" the "intended and actual effect" of listing groups was to weaken or destroy "any efficacy among the electorate that such organizations might possess." The JAFRC brief ended by attacking AGLOSO's alleged "due process" deficiencies, declaring that even the "most elementary notions of fair play dictates that before a group of Americans may be officially stigmatized as 'disloyal' or 'subversive' they should be heard in their own defense."

While previous government briefs defending AGLOSO had generally been short and almost casual in tone, the Supreme Court's decision to hear the cases apparently came as a considerable shock to the DOJ, which responded to the JAFRC brief with a fifty-one-page reply (which it incorporated in briefer responses to the NCASF and IWO). The department stressed the blunt argument that AGLOSO was a "political" act promulgated by the president in pursuit of his constitutional powers to protect the nation and was therefore completely beyond review by the courts. Moreover, the brief maintained, AGLOSO had no "legally operative effect on First Amendment rights" and did not even require federal employees to "disassociate themselves from petitioner's activities" or "bar other federal employees from becoming members," as it simply designated JAFRC as an organization in which participation "may or may not be helpful in arriving at a conclusion based on all the evidence that reasonable grounds exist for belief that the employee involved is disloyal." In any case, the department said, well-settled law established that statements by public officials "are *absolutely* privileged" against legal assaults "irrespective even of a claim of malicious motivation," and since here the attorney general was acting "as the agent and *alter ego* of the President in the exercise of his primary executive power," his act was a political one "beyond the control of any other branch of the Government except in the mode prescribed by the Constitution through impeachment" or via "the elective process." This was especially so at present, the brief argued, since Cold War "tension and danger demands the utmost vigor and vigilance on the part of the President to take action which he deems required in the interest of national safety" and here he sought only to exercise his "constitutional and statutory authority" to regulate the "employment and discharge" of federal employees, which were "internal administrative matters concerning which the U.S. is free to act as it pleases without judicial compulsion or restraint at the insistence of an outsider such as petitioner." The department added that it was a "complete distortion of the intent and purpose" of AGLOSO to "conceive of it as a 'blacklist' calculated to injure petitioner by harassment and vilification" and that any "indirect consequences of public disclosure" were protected by the First Amendment, which banned interference with free expression but did not state that "Congress or the Executive may not inform the public" or seek to "protect persons against unfavorable public opinion, even though such opinion may be stimulated by disclosures made by or to an investigating body." Essentially, the department maintained, JAFRC sought to restrain the attorney general from complying with the president's directive to "determine and publish" AGLOSO (in fact Truman's order made no reference to publication), as was his "clear duty under the Constitution," and "determinations made by the heads of departments in the fulfillment of that duty are essentially political, not judicial, in nature" and thus "decisions of a kind for which the judiciary neither has the responsibility nor the facilities to review."[7]

The Supreme Court heard consolidated oral argument in the three challenges to AGLOSO's constitutionality on October 11, 1950, with both the *New York Times* and the *Washington Post*, quite unusually, reporting the developments in lengthy news stories the following day. Only eight justices appeared at the bench to hear the cases, as Tom Clark, the former attorney general who had overseen AGLOSO, abstained due to conflict of interest concerns. Former assistant attorney general O. John Rogge, representing JAFRC, denounced the list as a "star chamber" technique that made the attorney general's "whims final and correct," while NCASF attorney David Rein termed AGLOSO a "kind of censorship," currently "in its heyday as a technique for suppressing political dissent," which proclaimed that "certain persons, organizations, literature or doctrine are heretical, disloyal, subversive or otherwise officially obnoxious." When IWO attorney Allen

H. Rosenberg described the organization as the only American fraternal benefit society that banned segregation and welcomed blacks, Justice Robert Jackson asked who might be excluded from it; when Rosenberg responded, "perhaps professional strikebreakers," Jackson dryly retorted, "They might not be very good insurance risks anyway." Solicitor General Philip Perlman maintained for the government that careful investigation had preceded AGLOSO's promulgation and denied that any "wholesale blacklisting" of organizations had followed or that the organizations had suffered injuries real enough to provide them legal standing to challenge it. Perlman rejected Rogge's contention that AGLOSO's real purpose was to "regiment the American people," instead maintaining that its sole purpose was to "protect and safeguard our form of government" and that it served only as a "guide" and but "one element" in making federal loyalty determinations. When Justice Hugo Black asked Perlman if even the Catholic Church could be listed, the latter said it could, and, under questioning, Perlman conceded that since listed organizations had no right to a hearing or appeal, they had no remedy other than to have "the people elect another President who will appoint another Attorney General who will take it off." When Justice Felix Frankfurter said the "crux" of the cases was that listed groups were denied a hearing, Perlman responded that hearings would "ruin the whole loyalty program," since it would take "years and years" to settle the status of each organization. (Perlman later termed the Truman loyalty program "one of the blackest pages in American history.")[8]

The AGLOSO cases were clearly viewed by the Supreme Court justices and their clerks as simultaneously extremely divisive, important, and politically explosive from the very beginning, according to both the Court's public record and the files of justices that became available after their retirement and/or deaths. Two justices, Felix Frankfurter and Jackson, became so frustrated by the Court's handling of the cases that, as discussed below, they lashed out at their colleagues in extraordinarily harsh terms, while memos to the justices from their clerks reflect significant division among the clerks, between the clerks and the justices they served and, above all, an acute sensitivity to the political ramifications and importance of the issues involved. In two instances, justices rejected advice from their clerks that the Court use the recent passage of the 1950 Internal Security Act (ISA), which provided for hearings before the newly created Subversive Activities Control Board (SACB) and the right to seek subsequent judicial review before the government listed organizations (outside of specific consideration with regard to government employment) as communistic as an excuse for either indefinitely delaying any ruling on the cases or for backing the government (despite the clerks' conclusions that the AGLOSO organizations had valid cases). Thus, in an undated eight-page memo focused on the JAFRC case apparently written immediately before the Court heard oral argument on October 11, 1950, one of Justice Harold Burton's clerks concluded that there was "no doubt" the organization had raised a "justifiable" issue, since its AGLOSO listing was "just about to wreck" its mission, the attorney general's procedure "did not meet the procedural requirements" of Truman's order calling for "appropriate investigation and determination," and there was "no reason" why "relief cannot or should not be given." However, he urged the Court to seek to avoid the "unpleasant chore" of rebuking the executive by seeking governmental assurance at oral argument that, due to the ISA, it would either "rescind the old [AGLOSO] list" and thus moot the existing cases or else "promise" to utilize the act against the plaintiffs, in which case "these proceedings should be stayed pending" the completion of SACB hearings and the possible judicial review guaranteed under it. A fundamentally similar thirty-three-page October 9, 1950, memo from one of Frankfurter's clerks also invoked the ISA to urge the Court to avoid rejecting the government's arguments (advice that Frankfurter ultimately rejected, just as Burton rejected his clerk's recommendation).[9]

Justice Stanley Reed also ignored the advice of one of his clerks, although in the reverse direction. In a memo written when the court was considering whether to grant "cert" in the JAFRC case, Reed's clerk said that JAFRC had clearly "lost property" interests due to its AGLOSO listing and that the loyalty order had given the attorney general an "awful power," whose procedures were "squarely at odds with the most rudimentary notions of due process and fair play." Although, according to the clerk, JAFRC was a "genuinely Communist and 'subversive' outfit" and "there would be no doubt but that after [an administrative or judicial] hearing, its designation would remain as 'subversive,'" the "arbitrary power" granted the attorney general "to brand with this mark of the pariah is so dangerous" that it was in the "direct tradition of the medieval heresy court—and inconsonant utterly with [the] whole philosophy of Anglo-American law." (Reed voted not to grant certiorari and, later, against the organizations' claims.)

In other instances, the justices accepted impassioned recommendations from their clerks. Thus, Justice William Douglas was advised by a clerk, when the Court was considering hearing JAFRC's appeal in early 1950, that "it is not necessary to labor the point that this is one of the most important [cases] of the year," especially because "these days, there are few more serious charges than that an organization or person is Communist," while it appeared that the attorney general had abused his authority by ignoring "rudimentary fairness" in denying JAFRC "an opportunity to be heard before listing it as subversive or communist." One of Justice Jackson's clerks similarly advised him to grant "cert" in the JAFRC case, characterizing the existing AGLOSO procedure as a "method of prescribing orthodoxy in thought" and declaring that what made the attorney general's powers "so frightening" was the "complete lack of any of the usual trappings of due process." Clearly referring to Jackson's service as Nuremburg trial prosecutor of Nazi war criminals, during which hearings were held before organizations were labeled "Nazi," the clerk added, "I would find it embarrassing, to say the least, to try to explain why the German organizations were given a complete trial" while "American organizations are not entitled to one here."

The Court's records indicate extraordinary, intense, and prolonged divisions once the justices began to ponder the AGLOSO cases following October 11, 1950, oral argument. Notes taken by Justices Douglas and Reed at an October 14 conference indicate that the three ultimately dissenting justices, Reed, Chief Justice Fred Vinson, and Sherman Minton, agreed that the complaining organizations either had "no standing" to sue (Vinson's view), or, if they did, had "nothing to sue for" (in Minton's words) because (in Reed's words) there was no "actual controversy," and thus "none" of their constitutional rights had been violated. The opposite position was articulated by Douglas, Burton (who maintained that the attorney general "cannot without some hearing call them subversive"), and Black (who declared that "these organizations have been destroyed" and that no governmental officials could exercise the powers involved in the case "without hearings, evidence and the right to be heard," as such ran "counter to due process and our notion of fairness"). Jackson's comments were highly ambiguous, suggesting that an AGLOSO listing amounted to little more than "abuse piled on to the organization" and was "one of the risks" that organizations had to face; he indicated his primary concern was that individuals who faced loyalty dismissal proceedings due to AGLOSO ties have the right to "challenge the rating of the organization" and show it was not, in fact, "subversive," and therefore he intended to "wait on these three [organizational] cases until the Court votes on [the case of Dorothy] Bailey [a loyalty dismissal case in which the Court also heard oral argument on October 11, 1950]." Tally sheets maintained by several of the justices strongly suggest that Jackson first voted against granting relief to the organizations, creating a 4–4 deadlock that effectively would have upheld the lower court rulings, but subsequently joined Douglas, Black, Burton, and Frankfurter to create a 5–3 majority.

Burton was assigned on October 23 to write an opinion for the Court, which rejected the government's position on an extremely narrow basis by giving the complaining organizations the right to further legal proceedings to challenge their AGLOSO listings, while not accepting any general attack on the fundamental constitutionality of the concepts of AGLOSO or the loyalty program. Burton submitted a draft opinion on November 20, which Douglas joined on February 6 (Douglas also wrote a separate concurrence, which he circulated on April 11). Separate concurring opinions were circulated by Jackson on January 30, Frankfurter on December 21, and Black on February 9. Between Black's opinion, which created a definitive majority for overturning the lower court rulings, and Reed's April 6 draft dissent (joined by Vinson and Minton), Frankfurter and Jackson both exploded in rage over the Court's proceedings. Frankfurter's anger centered on what he viewed as the dissenters' unconscionable delay in circulating their views for weeks after the majority justices had submitted their opinions (perhaps fearing that Jackson might switch again or that some other development would affect the vote?), which he suggested violated norms of both the Court and of "decency." In a private March 19 letter to Reed, Frankfurter fumed that the dissenters' "holding up the judgment in the loyalty cases long after a majority has been ready" had "no equal since I have been on the court," and "I venture to believe nothing like it has happened for at least 50 years." He told Reed that among "the most unquestioned unwritten laws of the Court is that a man should put aside all to work on a dissent in a case that is ready to go down," and "in all decency" the ruling should be delayed no longer since the case involved "interests of great importance, both to the government and citizens." When Reed circulated revised versions of his dissent on April 12, 13, and 21, Frankfurter exploded again on April 27, writing to all of his colleagues to urge that "these cases come down without further ado," as "the lines have been drawn for more than six months, and the demands of public administration call for adjudication."

Jackson was similarly furious with his colleagues because he viewed the Court's impending decision, which mandated additional due process protections for the complaining organizations, as totally contradicting its pending *Bailey* decision to effectively uphold her federal loyalty firing without providing the right to learn of or cross-examine her accusers. While Jackson focused on the latter issue in his ultimately published, deeply angry concurring opinion, his fury also surfaced in his first draft concurrence, which was circulated in late January 1951, and, above all, in an amazingly angry uncirculated draft concurrence he placed in his files in mid-April, which especially reflected his bitter personal feelings about Douglas. Thus, in his January draft, Jackson termed the AGLOSO listings "administrative finding of a fact" made "without notice to anybody, opportunity for hearing, and standards" that could be "made without anything that a court would recognize as evidence, and so far as the record available to this court shows, it was so made." In a footnote, the draft pointed out that at Nuremberg, "every accused organization had opportunity to offer evidence in its defense" and "was confronted with and had a chance to cross-examine all prosecution witnesses" and declared that "lack of notice and lack of right to be heard I think preclude acceptance of the Attorney General's designation as final." In his never-circulated April 12 draft concurrence, Jackson essentially accused the Court of being "soft on communism" in its recent rulings, thereby blocking measures "which if taken in time might well have prevented much of the difficulty [in the loyalty area] that has ensued." Jackson thundered that attempts by the Roosevelt administration to take "'strong measures' against Communism to which the [Douglas draft] opinion pays lips service" had been "consistently defeated by this Court," with the result that "virtual assurance" had been given to "government employees and others that Communist organizations were quite proper for them to join or affiliate with." Rather than attributing the government's errors to a "good faith mistake in an unsettled and debatable field," Jackson charged the Court majority with joining the "Communist campaign to smear our own government."

On April 30, 1951, the Court finally announced its ruling, issuing what a United Press dispatch termed a "bombshell" decision. As the Associated Press lead summarized, the Court clearly "lashed out at the government for branding organizations as Communist without a hearing," yet simultaneously failed to give the plaintiffs anything even approaching a complete victory. Of the eight participating justices, six wrote separate, often heated, opinions that totaled 40,000 words, or seventy pages in print: as they announced the ruling by reading long excerpts from their written opinions, Jackson commented acidly that hearing them was "likely to make one delirious," while Clark, who had not participated in the case, sat by quietly. Five justices (Burton, in a controlling opinion joined only by Douglas, with separate concurring opinions by Douglas, Jackson, Frankfurter, and Black) agreed only that, based on the uncontested factual record before them (since the government had not contested any of the plaintiffs' factual assertions concerning their nature and post-AGLOSO damage to their ability to function), the complaining organizations had standing to sue, that the dispute was justiciable, and that the challenged AGLOSO determinations, in the absence of any process allowing contestation of disputed listings, were so "arbitrary" that their cases should be returned to a federal district court for "determination" as to whether the organizations "are in fact Communistic or whether the Attorney General possesses information from which he could reasonably find them to be so." The Court therefore ordered the cases remanded to district court "with instructions to deny the respondents' [government's] motion that the complaint can be dismissed for failure to state a claim upon which relief can be granted."[10]

In his controlling opinion, Burton held that, under legal precedent, by failing to contest the organizations' denials that they were "communistic," the government had "therefore admitted" the "facts alleged in the complaint," which must be "taken as true," and the Court therefore was compelled to find their AGLOSO listings "patently arbitrary," because Truman's order did not authorize the attorney general to list them "contrary to the alleged and uncontroversial facts constituting the entire record before us." Burton said the situation would be "comparable" if "the Attorney General, under like circumstances, were to designate the American National Red Cross as a communist organization" in the absence of "any contrary claim asserted against" its general reputation as a charitable and loyal organization. Burton's opinion flatly rejected the government's position on standing and justiciability, holding that "the touchstone to justiciability is injury to a legally protected right and the right of a bona fide charitable organization to carry on its work, free from defamatory statements of the kind discussed, is such a right." Brushing aside the government's claim that AGLOSO listings caused no direct harm, Burton held that the complainants had amply alleged "past and impending serious damages caused by their designations." He labeled the attorney general's actions "arbitrary and unauthorized," amounting to administrative discretion "run riot," because Truman's loyalty order had required that AGLOSO listings be preceded by "appropriate investigation and determination," yet the attorney general's actions had lacked "reliance upon either disclosed or undisclosed facts supplying a reasonable basis for the determination."

In the present case, Burton maintained, the challenged listings were "unauthorized publications of admittedly unfounded designations of the complaining organizations as 'Communist.'" Burton added that it would be "obviously" contrary to the intent of the Truman order to include designations that were "patently arbitrary and contrary to the uncontroversial material facts" and that an "appropriate" determination had to be "the result of a process of reasoning" and not "an arbitrary fiat contrary to the known facts." Declaring that AGLOSO listings resulted in crippling the functioning and damaging the reputation of designated groups, Burton concluded, "Whether the complaining organizations are in fact Communistic or whether the Attorney General possesses information from which he could reasonably find them to be so must await determination by the [federal] district court [which had earlier dismissed the lawsuits]." In a footnote, Burton noted that the Court specifically declined to rule on the validity of the government's "acts in furnishing and disseminating a comparable list in any instance where such acts are within the authority purportedly granted by the executive order." The ruling even failed to indicate whether the entire existing "list" (as opposed to the listing of the three challenging organizations) was invalid pending further proceedings, if the three complaining groups were to be "delisted" pending federal court determination, or even if all future AGLOSO designations had to be preceded by some kind of "administrative hearing" (as seemed to be suggested in a footnote) or if the sole future recourse of listed organizations was to challenge their designations in federal court, presumably after considerable damage to their reputations had already occurred. Thus, the immediate result of the ruling was, as the Associated Press reported, primarily to throw a "legal cloud" over AGLOSO, but it established little beyond that.

In their concurrences, Black and Douglas both suggested that the entire loyalty program was unconstitutional, and Black additionally thus characterized the entire concept of an official list of subversive organizations (with or without hearings). Douglas declared that the "paramount issue of the age" was the need to reconcile the need to provide both "security" and "freedom," but warned that when the country took "shortcuts by borrowing from the totalitarian techniques of our opponents" it opened the way to "a subversive influence of our own that destroys us from within," a trend illustrated by the AGLOSO and *Bailey* cases. Douglas declared that organizations branded "subversive" by the attorney general suffered the "real, immediate and incalculable" injury of being "maimed and crippled," and that, as currently administered, AGLOSO had "no place in our system of law" but only planted "within the body politic the virus of the totalitarian ideology which we oppose," and by avoiding due process consider- ations in branding groups as "subversive," it effectively started "down the totali- tarian path." Alone among the justices, Black's concurrence specifically declared that the government had no authority "with or without a hearing" to "determine, list and publicize individuals and groups as traitors and public enemies," a prac- tice he said was "tyrannical" and "smacks of a most evil type of censorship," and one that "effectively punished many organizations and their members merely because of their political beliefs and utterances." Black lamented that "in this day when prejudice, hate and fear are constantly invoked to justify irresponsible smears and persecutions of persons even faintly suspected of entertaining un- popular views," AGLOSO effectively found the three complaining organizations "guilty of harboring treasonable opinions and designs" and "officially branded them as communists," amounting, "regardless of their truth or falsity," to "the practical equivalents of confiscation and death sentences for any blacklisted or- ganization not possessing extraordinary financial, political or religious prestige and influence."

Frankfurter's concurrence, at twenty-five pages by far the longest of the six opinions, declared that the "heart of the matter" was that democratic principles implied "respect for the elementary rights of men, however suspect or unwor- thy," particularly the practice of "fairness," which could "rarely be obtained by secret, one-sided determination of facts decisive of rights" that served to "maim and decapitate" listed organizations "on the mere say-so of the Attorney Gen- eral." Jackson's concurrence, which often read like a dissent, complained about the "extravagance" and "intemperance" of some of his colleagues, terming it "un- fortunate that this Court should flounder in wordy disagreement over the valid- ity and effect of procedures which have already been pursued for several years" and declaring that the rulings "may create the impression that the decision of the case does not rise above the political controversy that engendered it." Jackson also blasted the Court for its same day 4–4 ruling that effectively upheld Dorothy Bailey's loyalty dismissal (in which she was denied the right to cross-examine, or even learn the identity of, her accusers). Jackson lamented, "this is the first time this court has held rights of individuals subordinate and inferior to those organized groups," terming it an "inverted view of the law" and "justice turned bottom-side up." Jackson suggested he was joining the majority only because of AGLOSO's impact upon federal employees accused of association with listed groups and their inability to challenge the designations in loyalty proceedings, because "unless a hearing is provided in which the organization can present evi- dence as to its character, a presumption of disloyalty is entered against its every member employee, and because of it, he may be branded disloyal, discharged and rendered ineligible for government service."

Reed's dissent (joined by Vinson and Minton) endorsed the government's key arguments, holding that listed organizations suffered no concrete damage from

AGLOSO, that AGLOSO's purpose of aiding government personnel loyalty investigations was valid, and that listed organizations had no "basis for any court action" because they were presumably designated after "appropriate investigation and determination." Reed's dissent also noted that "in investigations to determine the purposes of suspected organizations" in connection with personnel screening, "the Government should be free to proceed without notice or hearing" because loyalty programs did "not require 'proof' in the sense of a court proceeding" and "to allow petitioners entry into the investigation would amount to interference with the executive's discretion, contrary to the ordinary operations of government." According to Reed, although AGLOSO presumably could be "hurtful" to the "prestige, reputation and earning power," of listed groups, it threatened no First Amendment or property rights because the organizations were "not ordered to do anything and are not punished for doing anything" and were not deprived "of liberty of speech or other freedoms." Reed maintained the AGLOSO listings did not even constitute "guilt by association," because they had no "finality" in federal loyalty determinations, but only amounted to a "warning" to federal officials to "investigate the conduct of the employee and his opportunity for harm."

The Grapes of *McGrath*, 1951–1953

The *McGrath* ruling triggered immediate jubilation among the organizations that had challenged their ALGOSO listings, but their "triumph" soon proved to be, at least in the short run, a pyrrhic one. They were never "delisted," despite eight more years of litigation, during which IWO was dissolved by New York state officials, JAFRC disbanded due to what it termed relentless government harassment, and NCASF, the sole survivor, ultimately gave up legally. However, in 1963 NASCF was largely vindicated by a federal appeals court ruling that overturned a 1953 SACB determination that it was a "communist front," on the grounds that the SACB finding that the organization was "directed, dominated or controlled" by the CP was "not supported by a preponderance of probative evidence." Moreover, in the long run *McGrath* significantly, if not mortally, wounded AGLOSO. It led the DOJ to halt further listings until it instituted an administrative hearing process in 1953 that eventually proved so unworkable that, after a burst of new listings in 1953 and 1954, no additional groups were ever designated.

The instant reaction of the three litigating organizations to *McGrath* was to claim a major victory. Thus, the IWO's May 1951 *News Bulletin* carried a "Flash!" news account on its first page, which reported (incorrectly, as it turned out) that due to the Supreme Court ruling it was "off" AGLOSO and predicted (also incorrectly) that this development would have "profound bearing on the illegal liquidation proceedings" then occurring in New York, where state officials, inspired by AGLOSO, had brought action to dissolve it. Similarly, NCASF executive director Richard Morford told his national council in a May 2 letter that *McGrath* was a "significant victory" that "makes our long legal struggle worth its cost in money and effort." Leading liberal newspapers offered similar instant editorial reactions. Thus, the May 2 *Christian Science Monitor* hailed *McGrath* for "striking the names of three organizations" from AGLOSO and said it had "properly and healthily shifted the emphasis from government by decree to government by law." While the May 6 *New York Times* conceded that "with such a welter of judicial statements, it is impossible to determine precisely what the law is," its editorial, entitled, "Exit the Star Chamber," declared that "the Attorney General will now have to abandon his blacklist or prove through fair hearings that the organizations listed are subversive," adding that "government condemnation without a hearing is, as this newspaper has often pointed out, an inexcusable and un-American practice." News analyses of *McGrath* (as opposed to editorials) were somewhat more tempered: thus, the May 6, 1951, *Times* concluded that if President Truman "ignores the decision," any future loyalty screening use of AGLOSO "will certainly be challenged," but if he "responds to the court's finding, it means junking the list and depriving the loyalty boards of major evidence." A March 16, 1952, *Washington Post* story termed AGLOSO's legal status "rather cloudy today" (as remained the case until its 1974 abolition, as no definitive court ruling was ever issued on the fundamental question as to whether it was a proper governmental function to compile and publish an official list of "subversive" organizations, with or without hearings).[11]

Publicly and in the courts government officials indicated that their interpretation of *McGrath* was an extremely narrow one and that they had no intention of calling off various forms of legal harassment of the three *McGrath* organizations. Thus, immediately after the ruling, DOJ and Loyalty Review Board (LRB) lawyers told reporters that membership in the organizations would continue to be "weighed against Federal employees" in the loyalty program absent "some convincing explanation." Before, during, and after the *McGrath* litigation, the three organizations continued to face severe governmental harassment. On May 29, 1950, by refusing to grant JAFRC certiorari in a contempt of Congress case for refusing to hand over its files in 1947 to HUAC, the Supreme Court authorized jail terms for chair Dr. Edward Barsky and ten other members of the group's executive board. On November 6, 1950, the Court failed to intervene in a similar contempt of Congress case involving NCASF executive director Morford, resulting in a three-month jail term and a $300 fine. New York officials suspended Barsky from his right to practice medicine for six months because of his jail term, a decision upheld by the Supreme Court in *Barsky v. Board of Regents* (347 U.S. 442, 1954). Frankfurter, Black, and Douglas dissented partly on the grounds that references to Barsky's JAFRC affiliation during the suspension proceedings were illegal because AGLOSO was an unconstitutional bill of attainder and/or that reliance on it violated due process rights, as his affiliations were irrelevant to his medical qualifications. Douglas (joined by Black) acidly noted:

> So far as I know, nothing in a man's political beliefs disables him from setting broken bones or removing ruptured appendixes. A practicing surgeon is unlikely to uncover many state secrets in the course of his professional activities. When a doctor cannot save lives in America because he is opposed to Franco in Spain, it is time to call a halt and look critically at the neurosis that has possessed us.

However, the six-judge majority held that there was insufficient evidence to demonstrate that New York officials had relied upon AGLOSO in reaching their decision and that they had acted properly under valid state law. In October 1952, the Treasury Department demanded $307,000 in taxes allegedly owed by JAFRC on money raised between 1942 and 1949 for Spanish Republican refugee relief, while the New York state insurance department and three state court rulings between 1950 and 1953 ordered the dissolution of the IWO, an action clearly triggered by the organization's 1947 AGLOSO designation (the Supreme Court refused to hear the IWO's appeal in October 1953).[12]

Behind the scenes, DOJ and LRB officials furiously tried to determine what action to take post-*McGrath*. In a May 9, 1951, memorandum to Special Assistant to the Attorney General Clive Palmer, Assistant Attorney General Holmes Baldridge rejected either abolishing AGLOSO (because such action "might hurt our public relations" as it could be "interpreted as indicating that we had no real basis for making it in the first place") or holding departmental administrative hearings (which he deemed "obviously impractical," since "we would never complete them" and such were not "necessary to satisfy Justice Burton as I read his opinion"). He endorsed instead providing an "abbreviated" federal district court hearing to groups contesting their listings, as this would "meet the Court's requirement, save us public-relations-wise and require a minimum of effort," since the Criminal Division thought "probably no more than 35 organizations would eventually contest." Baldridge argued that the Supreme Court would uphold this approach by "a 4–4 split," since *McGrath* "did not strike down" AGLOSO but "only said that there must be some evidence to support" listings. He added that, to bolster AGLOSO and strengthen post-*McGrath* legal proceedings, the attorney general should promptly ask the SACB to have the three organizations designated as "Communist fronts" under the ISA (a suggestion adopted by the Eisenhower administration in 1953). However, another department official, J. Edward Williams, recommended to Palmer, also on May 9, that AGLOSO be abolished, because the Supreme Court ruling would make it "extremely difficult" to conduct administrative hearings, "which obviously would be greatly prolonged by the respondents" and because the loyalty program could still be "carried on effectively without the list," including via invoking the Hatch Act "in proper cases" and providing information about "*all*" organizations to loyalty boards, which could consider information about them "as evidentiary material in establishing guilt or innocence, rather than treating membership as establishing a prima-facie case of disloyalty." Williams maintained that abandoning AGLOSO would not be "embarrassing to the Department," as it "could be explained adequately in a press release," while continuing it "for the purpose of avoiding possible adverse criticism" was not justified.[13]

In an undated memo that he apparently wrote in May 1951 in response to the Baldridge and Williams submissions, Palmer supported "discontinuance" of AGLOSO, "at least in its present form," adding that the loyalty program could still effectively continue, especially since the LRB's interpretations concerning AGLOSO had "very often made it difficult to handle cases where questionable activities are involved, rather than membership in particular organizations," and loyalty screenings did "not depend upon any official lists" of allegedly subversive groups. Moreover, Palmer declared, it would be "an almost impossible task to go through [departmental] administrative hearings," and "more important," another agency, the SACB, had "now been established by law for the purpose of designating organizations." According to Palmer, "full information" concerning "various organizations believed to be subversive" could still be provided to the LRB, and the Hatch Act could still be "invoked in proper cases, as it was prior" to Truman's 1947 order, while uses of AGLOSO "separate and apart from the Employee Loyalty Program," which were "probably not contemplated in the beginning," would be destroyed.[14]

According to an early 1953 memo by Assistant Attorney General J. Lee Rankin, the department soon abandoned considering AGLOSO's abolition, "apparently" for reasons enunciated by Raymond Whearty, first assistant in the Criminal Division to Assistant Attorney General James McInerney, in yet another May 9, 1951, memo. Whearty had quoted LRB chair Bingham's letter of the previous day pleading that AGLOSO was the "heart and soul" of the loyalty program and an "essential tool by which uniformity" could be maintained between government loyalty boards, thus avoiding a "chaotic situation." Rankin further quoted Whearty as maintaining that AGLOSO "was essential to a number of agencies in connection with specialized situations," such as INS reliance on it for screening displaced persons seeking U.S. entry and its function of warning "prospective government employees of the requirements which they will have to meet and to discourage those who might be unqualified."[15]

On June 13, 1951, Solicitor General Perlman, the department's top legal representative in the federal courts, forwarded to Whearty a memo that had been prepared four days earlier by Perlman aide Robert Ginnane, in response to proposed draft regulations for AGLOSO administrative hearings. Ginnane objected to a variety of the regulations, which he declared "may fail to obtain judicial approval," including (1) proposals to notify organizations of intended AGLOSO designations solely through publication in the *Federal Register*, (2) informing groups that sought to contest their designations of the department's basis for action only "in the form of a *questionnaire*," (3) an "unreasonable" proposal that organizations' failure to answer any questions would be considered "an admission of the truth of the information in the Attorney General's possession upon which the information is based," (4) giving the attorney general sole discretion to determine if a hearing was "required for determination of the matter," and (5) holding all hearings in private. Ginnane made clear that he felt the proposed regulations failed to establish a procedure that would even "show on its face that an attempt is being made to accord as fair a hearing as is consistent with security considerations" and that such "departures or shortcuts merely to serve the government's convenience are unlikely to be approved" by the courts, especially since, in *McGrath*, the Supreme Court had already noted that in establishing the SACB, "Congress provided that identical determinations should be made in full and formal hearings." According to 1952 department memoranda, revised draft regulations for administrative hearings were submitted to Attorney General McGrath on June 28, 1951, and subsequently approved by him, but never finally approved because Perlman "decided it was preferable strategy in the [in post-*McGrath*] litigation to file an answer [in District Court]" that stated "so far as possible consistent with the national interests, the basis upon which the original designations were made and then move for summary judgment."[16]

The revised draft regulations, which eventually would be adopted almost verbatim by the Eisenhower administration DOJ two years later, declared that *McGrath* required granting each designated group "as desires it a notice of the grounds upon which it was or will be designated and an opportunity to contest such designations." The regulations suggested that organizations be required to respond to both a "statement of grounds" and "written interrogatories with respect thereto" within a set period, with failure to do so constituting "an acquiescence in designation" and failure to respond to "each interrogatory completely and with particularity" deemed an "admission of truth." Contesting groups were entitled to request a hearing (otherwise the attorney general was empowered to "determine the matter on the basis of the information available to him and the reply of such organization"), with the attorney general authorized to designate "such officer or board as he shall deem necessary" to conduct private hearings. The hearing officer or board was empowered to dispense with taking testimony if it was concluded that a determination could be "appropriately made" based on the statement of grounds, interrogatories, and replies and was additionally authorized to receive information from the attorney general "without requiring disclosure of classified information or the identity of confidential informants," matters which no governmental witness could be required to disclose during cross-examination. According to the draft regulations, the attorney general alone would make the final determination.

When the LRB met on May 17, 1951, its members were apparently so shell-shocked by *McGrath* that most discussion of it proceeded "off the record," even though the group always met in secret. During the brief "on the record" discussion, one member commented that without AGLOSO "we're at sea," to which LRB chair Bingham responded that he had already written to tell the attorney general that AGLOSO was key "to the intelligent and effective operation of the [loyalty] program." The LRB then voted, with only one dissent from the eighteen persons present of the total membership of twenty-four, to formally tell McGrath that it was the LRB's "hope" that "no change will be made in the list." According to a May 19 front-page *Washington Post* report, an LRB spokesman declared, "We have told [the DOJ] that we cannot operate the program without a list," and that the board would continue to use the existing list unless otherwise directed. At its mid-October 1951 meeting, the LRB's Executive Committee, perhaps accurately foreseeing that the DOJ would freeze AGLOSO until it could determine a *McGrath* response, approved a procedure to consider information about membership in "questionable" organizations that "have not been designated by the Attorney General," to be provided them in staff memoranda headed, "Membership in Organizations Not on Attorney General's List." Shortly thereafter, the LRB sent departmental loyalty boards two directives that effectively continued the board's past confusing ambiguity on this subject by declaring that "charges concerning activities which may create a reasonable doubt" about an employee's loyalty were "not privileged because they have occurred in connection with an organization not on the Attorney General's list," but such affiliations should by considered only "with the clear understanding" that such references were "solely for the purpose of identifying, in detail, the informative facts relating to the time, the place and in what connection the alleged activity of the individual occurred."[17]

These actions reflected the LRB's growing frustration with the DOJ's failure to designate any additional AGLOSO organizations post-*McGrath* or to often even respond to related LRB queries. Thus, Bingham complained about this to the department in an October 29, 1951, letter requesting rulings on six specific organizations, and at the December 13, 1951, LRB meeting he bitterly lamented that no allegedly "Communist" unions were AGLOSO-designated, even those that "surely" should be listed. Bingham added that the board had repeatedly asked the attorney general "to give consideration" to designating "quite a number of organizations" about which it had received FBI reports, but "in the last year, the Attorney General has been reluctant to place any organization on the list, and moreover, doesn't even answer our correspondence." LRB Executive Secretary L. V. Meloy added that, under past LRB directives, employees could not be charged with non-AGLOSO-designated affiliations, "no matter how bad [the organization] is, nor can you predicate your decision on it," and that he had had "no less than 15 conferences with the boys [at the DOJ] who do the [AGLOSO] work" but only got "very conflicting stories." In response to these remarks and Bingham's statement that he didn't want to further "bother" the attorney general, the LRB voted to appeal directly to President Truman to ask that AGLOSO be updated.[18]

While the DOJ pondered its response to *McGrath*, the ACLU lobbied the Truman administration to reform both AGLOSO and the entire loyalty program, but conspicuously without challenging the fundamental concept that the government had a right to determine and publish lists of "subversive" organizations. Thus, on May 29, 1951, ACLU attorney Herbert Levy met with department officials to urge that AGLOSO hearings be granted that would be "public or private at the option of the organization" and that designations include "more about the nature of the organization so as to be a bit more useful in evaluating an individual's connection therewith." On June 5, the ACLU wrote President Truman to urge him to reexamine and reform the loyalty program, which had "resulted in the creation of an atmosphere of repression, highly dangerous to democratic government" and had "envenomed and terrorized" government employees, who feared "to practice the good old American habits of speaking one's mind and joining organizations one believes in" or "to say or do anything unorthodox." The letter urged the AGLOSO reforms that Levy had earlier suggested to the department, including that public statements of when an organization became "subversive" be made following hearings resulting in designations, as "no distinction is [now] made between membership in an organization" when it was "subversive" and "when it was not."[19]

In a December 17, 1951, letter to Bingham, Assistant Attorney General McInerney revealed that the DOJ had decided not to make additional AGLOSO designations pending federal litigation resulting from *McGrath*. Noting that "the nature of the procedures to be followed prior to the designation have not been fixed with any precision by the Supreme Court and the matter is now before the district court to which the test cases were remanded," McInerney declared that the attorney general "does not desire to designate any additional organizations until the method previously employed has received the sanction of the courts" and that meanwhile "loyalty cases involving organizations not yet designated will have to be resolved without reference to the subversive character of the particular organizations involved." Despite this letter and continuing post-*McGrath* litigation, the LRB repeatedly continued to ask for departmental determinations of the AGLOSO status of various unlisted organizations. Thus, on March 12, 1952, Bingham pleaded with McGrath for him to reconsider, because the "various Loyalty Boards are prohibited from entertaining serious evidence of disloyalty" with regard to "Communist-dominated organizations" because of the "failure of your office to designate organizations which are part and parcel" of the CP. He added that the LRB felt constrained to "place itself on record" that this "failure" is "seriously jeopardizing the adjudication of individual cases" and if persons who "should not work" for the federal government were hired, the fault would lie with the department "and not with the Boards." Responding to a March 21 request from McInerney, ISD head William Foley reported on March 25 that previous department studies had concluded that six of the organizations Bingham had specifically inquired about "fell within" AGLOSO criteria and that one did not but was being restudied.[20]

Foley's March 25, 1952, memo for the first time (at least in department records deposited in the National Archives) mentioned specific AGLOSO "criteria," an apparent reference to an undated "confidential" document entitled "Criteria for Designating Organizations under 3 of Part III of Executive Order No. 9835," which appears in the 1952 department files. With a prefatory warning that use "is restricted to persons designated by the Attorney General, and are not for publication," the document listed nine criteria for "consideration" for designating organizations, membership in which "may be cause for refusal of, or removal from, government employment." It declared that "any organization may be declared totalitarian, fascist, communist or subversive" if it (1) advocated treason or sedition, (2) sought to promote foreign interests above those of the United States, (3) aided those serving "foreign governments or groups" seeking to perform acts "detrimental to the [nation's] security," (4) aided or supported espionage or sabotage against the country, (5) encouraged the unconstitutional overthrow of the government, (6) supported the denial of constitutional rights, (7) allowed or encouraged persons to obtain or transmit information to foreign countries "detrimental" to American security, (8) concealed or refused to "divulge its true purposes, membership or activities" to proper government authorities (if of "political or quasi-political character" and legally so required), or (9) "cooperates with or supports any subversive" group to advance goals which caused them to be declared "subversive" or aided in "recruiting, financing, building, or propagandizing, or otherwise increasing the size, strength, or influence" of such organizations "or combination of persons."

The DOJ's December 1951 decision to await further court developments before making additional AGLOSO designations did not gain a warm FBI reception. On March 10, 1952, following personal lobbying from an LRB representative who had complained that the board was frustrated by being unable to act against employees who belonged to "organizations which quite obviously were used as Communist fronts which had not been so listed by the Attorney General," FBI director Hoover wrote to Attorney General James McGranery to lament that "the effectiveness of the Loyalty and Internal Security programs is weakened by the Department's decision to refrain from adding" new names to AGLOSO. However, in a March 18, 1952, memo from FBI Intelligence Division official A. H. Belmont to Assistant Director D. Milton Ladd, the former conceded that due to *McGrath* "it is evident that the Attorney General" would have to allow future prospective AGLOSO groups to "defend or refuse any charges of subversiveness prior to being publicly designated" and therefore the department's inaction was "judicious and consistent" with *McGrath*. Belmont added that the FBI "has not limited the initiation of loyalty investigations solely to membership or activities in cited organizations," and although AGLOSO listings had "substantially impeded the effectiveness of the organization and continued membership of individuals more clearly evidences their Communist sympathies and permits a more accurate evaluation of their potential dangerousness." Upon reading Belmont's memo, FBI associate director Clyde Tolson wrote Hoover on March 18 that the FBI's "Security Division should have sensed the situation before preparing [Hoover's] March 10 memo" to McGrath, leading Hoover to append the handwritten comment, "I most certainly agree." (Subsequently someone placed a large "X" through the FBI's file copy of its March 10 memo.)[21]

While the DOJ continued to ponder AGLOSO's future, Assistant Attorney General McInerney wrote Bingham on April 8, 1952, and again a month later, that any decisions concerning additional designations would have to "necessarily await the attention of the new Attorney General." After U.S. District Court Judge James McGranery was confirmed as McGrath's replacement as attorney general in mid-1952, Bingham continued to repeatedly press the department regarding additional AGLOSO designations, complaining, for example in a September 18, 1952, letter to McGranery that it was "of the utmost importance, if the President's Loyalty Program is to succeed, that an immediate decision be reached" concerning the United Public Workers of America (UPWA). Bingham declared that there was "no doubt" that the UPWA, which had been expelled from the CIO three years earlier as Communist-dominated, "should be at once" listed and that the "matter is urgent" because the LRB "is under the necessity, at the present time, of deciding loyalty cases involving Government employees who are active members" of the group and "should be declared ineligible." Bingham also personally lobbied about the UPWA with FBI director Hoover in a meeting and a "confidential" September 23 letter. On September 19, Hoover wrote McGranery that Bingham was "quite concerned" about the department's failure to list additional groups as, especially in cases where employees had been fired for affiliations with unions expelled by the CIO for alleged Communist domination, their attorneys would "no doubt immediately go to the courts" seeking reinstatement on the grounds that "the organizations to which the employees belong and which are patently Communistic" had not been designated. Hoover concluded that it would be "most desirable" for the department to act "because there has been a delay of many months since any additional subversive organizations have been listed" and thus "the Loyalty Program is seriously impeded."[22]

During his May 1952 Senate confirmation hearings, McGranery, who had been an assistant to the attorney general before his 1946 appointment to the federal bench, seemed confused about both AGLOSO and the ISA. While conceding that he was "not too familiar" with the ISA, he said that he "most certainly would" carry out its mandates and generally suggested in response to questioning that he was against giving the power to determine which groups were "subversive" to any one person, while indicating that he would follow whatever guidance the FBI and/or Congress gave him on such matters. He testified that the World War II DOJ determination of subversive groups "did not meet with my approval," since he felt "rather strongly that you can get off into your own personal likes and dislikes" and it was a "pretty high-handed proposition" to leave it "to one man to classify a particular matter without a direction, as to what would be the standard." However, McGranery also said that he would "certainly go along" with "FBI findings and investigations," and when asked if he would continue to make AGLOSO designations, responded, "Based on the FBI reports, my answer to that would be 'Yes.'" He also said, "the Attorney General should follow the will of Congress in that direction," so that "if you gentlemen direct that they should be listed, they should be listed," since "I certainly would not want to set myself up as perhaps a czar."[23]

Further clarification of the department's position regarding AGLOSO did not emerge until Eisenhower became president in early 1953. In a lengthy July 11, 1952, memorandum composed by Assistant Attorney General McInerney for McGranery summarizing AGLOSO's history (but marked in hand "not sent" in the National Archives copy), the former reported that while *McGrath* "did not set any clear standard for the Department to follow in future designations," it presented the department "with the choice of either waiting for a determination by the District Court" as to whether the existing designation procedure "was adequate, or of establishing an administrative tribunal or some form of hearing process within the Department which would insure an organization the notice and hearing [it] so strongly suggested." He recommended regulations that had been drafted for a departmental administrative procedure, which McInerney reported had been approved by McGrath but "not promulgated" before his departure, while opposing providing evidence to the district court because of the likelihood that FBI classified information would be "ordered produced and the Department will be presented with the dilemma either of dismissing the procedures or complying with the court order," especially as "the designations have often been made upon evidence" adequate for an administrative hearing, but "frequently" insufficient to meet legal evidentiary requirements. McInerney also dismissed as "unsatisfactory" suggestions that the SACB be utilized for future AGLOSO designations, as this would "involve protracted hearings and fail to achieve the purpose for which the designations are made" in connection with the loyalty program, since defunct organizations "could not be probable subjects" of SACB petitions for registration with the government and because the SACB's legislatively mandated standards "relating to foreign determination and control" would "not be sufficiently broad" to serve the purposes of loyalty screening.[24]

An August 21, 1952, memo from ISD chief Foley to Charles Murray, Assistant Attorney General and head of the Criminal Division, urged that "regulations providing for some kind of [AGLOSO departmental] administrative hearing be issued in the near future," as pressure from the LRB and the "general public" made an early decision "highly important." This was especially so, Foley maintained, because the LRB viewed the department's failure to continue designating organizations "responsible for the slowing down of the Board's work and for its inability to adjudicate certain cases" and the federal district court might demand information about the existing designation process, which was based on evidence that "would more than not fail" to meet legal evidentiary requirements, such as relying on "reports of [unidentified] informants considered reliable by the FBI." According to a September 4 memo written to "the files" by Murray, a conference of five top DOJ officials had convened that day and agreed that in light of *McGrath*, "it would be necessary to set up a procedure for administrative hearings" to avoid the "necessity of the government presenting its evidence against these organizations in judicial proceedings." Murray attributed the failure to proceed with the regulations approved, but not promulgated, over a year earlier to Solicitor General Perlman's decision to proceed with the court cases.[25]

On October 10, 1952, Murray sent McGranery an eight-page, single-spaced memo that argued for administrative hearings and abandoning further court proceedings, essentially on the grounds that many AGLOSO designations could not withstand legal scrutiny, especially since the department did not want to reveal its sources of information, which often involved FBI informants, wiretaps, and burglaries. Murray told McGranery that, for "compelling reasons, an early decision" was "imperative" regarding setting up "appropriate procedures for future designations" and specifically whether the government should "defend on the merits in the pending [District Court] litigation or seek to substitute for judicial hearing such administrative procedures as may be adopted for designations." He declared that immediate action was needed because the LRB had complained that its work was "being substantially retarded, and the loyalty program correspondingly prejudiced" by the department's failure to make additional designations, because LRB chair Bingham had repeatedly sought to confer with the attorney general on this issue and as "several Congressional inquiries concerning further designations, as well as inquiries from affected organizations, remain unanswered pending decision by the Department as to the procedure it will follow." According to Murray, *McGrath* left "no doubt" that notice and hearings would be required for AGLOSO, but that the need for a "judicial hearing" was not clearly established, as "sufficient differences of views appear in the majority concurring opinions" to "warrant the belief that an administrative hearing, even at this stage as to organizations already designated" might meet legal requirements, and administrative hearings "clearly will suffice" with regard to future listings. Therefore, he added, the immediate question was if the government should seek to avoid a "full judicial hearing" in the pending litigation by "the substitution of an administrative procedure to accomplish the same result," a choice that would "establish the pattern conceivably to be followed with respect to all of the remaining 180-odd" AGLOSO organizations and thus assume "an importance transcending considerations in the particular case in suit which can easily be defended on the merits."[26]

According to Murray, future court challenges could pose far greater legal difficulties for the government than the current litigation because departmental files concerning many of the World War II AGLOSO listings were incomplete or could not be located "and the basis on which they were designated originally is unknown, save as summary memorandum prepared at the time" might still exist. Moreover, he added, the available evidence for many other AGLOSO groups lacked the same "quantitative quality as that available as to certain of the Communist organizations and in many other instances" designations were based on confidential sources, "which, although valid and sufficient for an administrative finding, cannot be made available for use in a judicial trial." In an oblique reference to the FBI's widespread, non–judicially authorized (or clearly illegal) use of wiretaps, bugs, and burglaries, Murray said "it is not presently known to what extent the use of confidential investigative techniques" might "complicate the Government's defense." Murray advised McGranery that "many of these potential difficulties" could be avoided if an administrative hearing process could be "successfully substituted" for judicial hearings, although the district court would have to approve such an outcome in the pending post-*McGrath* litigation. Murray submitted for McGranery's approval what he described as a "slightly" revised version of the regulations submitted in June 1951 to McGrath, which he described as an especially attractive alternative to judicial proceedings since "a high percentage" of previously designated groups were defunct, including over 80 percent of those classified as "Communist," and therefore they could not request hearings, and because the proposal required contesting groups to respond to a statement of grounds and interrogatories, a provision which "may result in eliminating any request for hearings." Murray noted that the regulations provided that failure to answer any interrogatory would be "deemed an admission of the truth of the facts to which such interrogatory refer," a requirement whose "potentialities" required "no amplification." Moreover, he added, the regulations authorized dispensing entirely with a hearing if the hearing officer or board determined that the statement of grounds, interrogatories, and responses made such unnecessary, and that if a hearing proceeded the organization had to make its presentation first, while the department could choose whether to make any presentation, a procedure whose "net result" was to "shift the entire burden of proof to the organization."

Since it was anticipated that the statement of grounds would "contain considerably detailed factual allegations," Murray continued, it was "felt that [the Attorney General] is not required to prove to the organization that basis for the designation exists" and that, under "certain of the [*McGrath*] concurring opinions" so long as the organization was informed about the nature of the department's case against it and allowed to contest its listing, Supreme Court "due process" concerns "will have been accomplished." As submitted to McGranery, the proposed regulations also declared that the hearings would be private, that the attorney general and testifying witnesses would not be required to disclose "classified security information or the identity of confidential informants," that existing AGLOSO designations would continue absent a "contrary determination" following a hearing, and that final determinations would be solely up to the attorney general. Murray concluded his lengthy memo by urging adoption of the regulations, whose "salient feature" and "distinct advantage" over "judicial hearings is that they permit the Department to retain control over the proceedings, in addition to which they promise substantial curtailment in the number of hearings necessary, and, by their interrogatory requirements, provide a powerful weapon for effective action." He also recommended that the department formally ask the district court to "defer judicial action pending completion of the administrative procedure," especially since "in a judicial forum, the more exacting requirements with regards to rules of evidence, production of records and inquiry as to investigative techniques forecast" potential difficulties.

McGranery failed to act on the AGLOSO issue before Dwight Eisenhower was elected president in November 1952, and therefore the "buck" was passed to the new administration. DOJ officials continued to write each other memos on the subject before Eisenhower was inaugurated in January 1953, however. Thus, on December 24, 1952, Acting Assistant Attorney General Ellis Lyons forwarded a twenty-page, single-spaced memo prepared in the department's Executive Adjudications Division to Deputy Attorney General Ross Malone that challenged the legal adequacy of Murray's October 10 proposed administrative hearing regulations. In essence, Lyons argued that the Murray proposals might well be rejected by the judiciary for failing to satisfy due process requirements. He suggested that many of the proposed regulations were legally dubious, including those for holding hearings in private, empowering the attorney general to appoint a hearing examiner or board (as opposed to utilizing independent examiners), authorizing the government to withhold classified information and the identity of confidential informants, and the "substantial difficulties" posed by seeking to "shortcut the hearings" and "shift the entire burden of proof to the organization." Lyons maintained that due process standards could only be met if a "reasonable amount of cross-examination" was allowed, the hearings were held in public (as was the case with SACB hearings), at least if the contesting organization requested this, and if the contesting organization were not required to "put in its evidence first."[27]

On February 13, 1953, the new head of the Criminal Division, Assistant Attorney General Warren Olney, wrote his deputy, William Rogers, that his division had reviewed the Murray and Lyons memos but was not "fully persuaded" that full due process protections would be required for future AGLOSO designations. However, he suggested several emendations to the Murray proposals "to enhance the probability of judicial acceptance," including making hearing officers "more independent" of the attorney general's authority, leaving the order of evidence submission up to hearing examiners, and slightly modifying Murray's proposed security limitations by granting a right to "cross examine concerning all information forming the basis of the decision," while still protecting the right of government witnesses to withhold "classified security information" or the "identity of confidential informants" that were not the source of their testimony. Olney accompanied his memo to Rogers with the notation, "I'm inclined to the view that this whole program has become obsolete." In a separate February 13 memo to Rogers, marked "CONFIDENTIAL," Olney indicated his doubts "as to the useful purpose" being then served by AGLOSO designations, adding that it was the unanimous view of those in the Criminal Division involved in the listings "that the designation of organizations could be abandoned under a loyalty-security program." Olney indicated that only 26 of the "139 Communist organizations" thus far designated were still active and that a hearing procedure for those still functioning or thereafter designated would duplicate SACB hearings, which the department had already initiated regarding the CP and was planning to request with regard to 23 additional "Communist-front" organizations. Olney added that while "no organizations have been designated in the past three years," it was "known that loyalty boards have considered in their deliberations organizations created since the last designations were made or which, for one reason or another, have not been designated by the Department" and that if "a substitute for any list, formal or informal," was needed, this could be provided by "preparing confidential factual summaries containing no conclusions to be furnished to the agencies upon request." Olney concluded, "Admittedly there will be some public opposition to abandon [sic] the list or organizations," but such "can be satisfactorily overcome." Rogers's only apparent response to Olney's "confidential memo" was the laconic handwritten note, "I don't think we should abandon the list. Let's just keep it inactive for the time being." Nonetheless, on February 25, 1953, according to an internal FBI memo that Director Hoover marked "Do Not File," a classification used only for the most sensitive FBI documents, DOJ ISD chief Foley called the bureau to report that Assistant Attorney General Olney had requested reports on each CP front organization "concerning which the

Department has information" and that he had been advised that the FBI currently had "approximately 187 known or suspected CP front organizations under active investigation" and had already submitted reports to the department if "substantiation of Communist front allegations" had been developed.[28]

In an undated twenty-six-page, double-spaced memo, apparently written in early March 1953, Assistant Attorney General Rankin, head of the Executive Adjudications Division, told new attorney general Herbert Brownell that "if affiliation with certain organizations is to continue to be considered relevant to security," maintaining AGLOSO was a "practical necessity" to "insure at least a minimum of uniformity" among federal agencies, especially since few of them had needed information or facilities to "make judgments as to the nature of the organizations involved." Rankin declared that the responsibility for AGLOSO "additions and deletions" should be retained by the Attorney General and that proposals to shift this function to the SACB were not "feasible," as the SACB had no investigative functions or facilities and its duties were limited by statute to determining, upon the attorney general's application, if organizations were "Communist-action" or "Communist-front" groups, a category that might exclude consideration of "Trotskyite" groups and "some fascist and totalitarian organizations, as well as some domestic organizations like the Ku Klux Klan." Rankin also rejected switching to a secret AGLOSO list because confidentiality would not be maintained "in practice" and the courts might view such action as an attempt to "prevent a judicial or administrative hearing on the propriety of listing the organizations." Rankin maintained that while only four *McGrath* justices had clearly indicated that hearings were required prior to even future designations, the department should offer hearings to both existing and prospective AGLOSO organizations to "indicate to the courts that, to the extent compatible with the maintenance of a security program, the Department is doing its utmost to be fair." He recommended that, pending hearings, already-designated groups be maintained on AGLOSO since "expunging" them in the interim "would immediately paralyze any security or loyalty program and inflict serious harm on the national interest," while it was "not clear" that granting prospective designees a hearing before their listings "would have the same effect." Rankin added that contesting groups would have to be "given a reasonable opportunity to cross-examine" and the "problem of protecting confidential information and informants" would therefore "inevitably be faced."[29]

Post-*McGrath* Litigation, 1951–1953

As the department continued pondering whether to implement a hearing procedure or respond in the courts to future AGLOSO challenges, JAFRC and NCASF returned to federal district court in mid-1951 to request the trial that *McGrath* had mandated (the IWO was apparently tied up in the New York litigation that led to its 1953 dissolution, but it later joined in the district court suit). Both sides maintained their original positions, with the organizations denying that they were "subversive" and declaring they should have been granted hearings before their listing, while the department argued that the attorney general, under presidential authority, could legally designate groups without hearings on the basis of confidential information (which department attorneys indicated they were unfamiliar with and so could not characterize the organizations' activities). JAFRC and NCASF responded in a December 1951 filing that the department's position amounted to "asking this court to disregard or overrule" the Supreme Court and "plaintiffs are accordingly entitled to summary judgment," but that even if the court determined there should be a trial it should first issue a preliminary injunction ordering their removal from AGLOSO. During March 17, 1952, oral argument, LRB chair Bingham told the court, via affidavit, that AGLOSO was "one of the standards" used to evaluate federal employee loyalty and that granting the plaintiffs' requests would "inflict great injury" upon the loyalty program, "thereby endangering national security," while DOJ attorney Edward Hickey asked for summary judgment, declaring that the *McGrath* requirement that the Court determine if there was sufficient "information" to list the organizations was met by an affidavit he submitted from Attorney General McGrath. McGrath's affidavit provided no information about the organizations but declared their designations had resulted from "careful investigation," based on materials including confidential investigative FBI reports, which could not be disclosed due to "public policy and national security" considerations. According to Hickey, the only issue was whether the attorney general had "any" information on which the listing was based, as opposed to acting in an "arbitrary and capricious manner," and no hearing was required in which the listed organizations could contest his finding. JAFRC lawyer Benedict Wolf responded by terming McGrath's affidavit "hearsay" and maintained "you cannot deprive anyone of rights on the basis of secret information."[30]

Subsequently, both sides filed affidavits further supporting their positions, with McGrath submitting summaries of "that part" of the basis of the three organizations' designation "which can be disclosed." However, McGrath declined to provide specific evidence or witnesses because "much of the evidence and information upon which this designation rests is derived from confidential" reports from the FBI and witnesses, none of which could be disclosed in order to avoid rendering "valueless for future use confidential sources of information essential to the preservation of our national security." The affidavit, as subsequently characterized by presiding Judge James Morris, alleged that the NCASF was organized under CP direction, had functioned with CP guidance, assistance, and CP-appointed leaders, and had never "knowingly deviated from the views and policies" of the CP "or the leaders of the world communist movement." On April

23, 1952, Morris declared that the department could not avoid disclosing the evidence supporting the AGLOSO designations and ordered a trial to determine the validity of the attorney general's findings, holding that the latter's bald assertion, "which in effect says that he had information which he believed to be true, and which convinced him that he did not act arbitrarily and capriciously," could not be accepted without further inquiry. Morris deferred ruling on whether adequate notice and hearing were required *before* organizations were listed, or if designations could only be subsequently challenged in court. Both sides' requests for summary judgment were denied, as was the organizations' request for a preliminary injunction, on the grounds that they could hardly claim "irreparable injury" if they continued to remain listed since, from their assertions, "they have already suffered substantially all of the injury" that might have resulted from their designations and because the government's procedures "ought not to be altered unless and until it is determined that the action in question is illegal and invalid."[31]

DOJ ISD head Foley quickly informed the FBI that Judge Morris was requiring the department to "present detailed evidence" concerning why the organizations had been listed and the department had not yet decided whether to "proceed in court or still attempt to operate through some administrative procedure." In a May 7, 1952, memo to Assistant Attorney General McInerney, Assistant Attorney General Baldridge urged a decision on this question "as promptly as possible." He supported offering an administrative hearing and then suggesting to the court "that further proceedings in the litigation should be stayed pending the outcome," as otherwise the government risked that the complaining organizations might seek pretrial discovery, which could force the government to reveal the basis of its designations. As with *McGrath*, Morris's procedural decision, while clearly a rebuff to the government, was far from a victory for the complainants. Thus, NCASF lawyer David Rein wrote NCASF executive director Morford on May 6, 1952, that Morris had "ducked the whole case" by refusing "to decide any of the issues." Rein recommended, after conferring with JAFRC and IWO attorneys, that Morris's refusal to grant a preliminary injunction be brought before a federal appeals court, but that the Supreme Court be asked to immediately intervene "to save time and money," since it was "conceivable that the [high] Court, in view of its past decision in the case, might consent to take the case at this point." This strategy was adopted, although Morford correctly told his fellow plaintiffs in a May 19 letter that this approach, while "proper, and perhaps necessary" had "little promise to it."[32]

On October 29, 1952, JAFRC and NCASF (the IWO having by then been dissolved by the New York courts) declared their intention to appeal the preliminary injunction request denial to the federal appeals court (which had been consistently hostile to attacks on AGLOSO), but before so doing petitioned the Supreme Court on January 23, 1953, to immediately intervene on the grounds that urgent action was required to protect their rights. JAFRC and NCASF argued that the district court had "refused to exercise its judicial function" by declining to issue a preliminary injunction and failing to "decide the issue as to whether the Attorney General's denial of notice and hearing invalidated the listing." They asked the Court to take the case immediately in order to decide if such inaction "violates the First and Fifth Amendments" and specifically whether the rejection of a preliminary injunction "was an abuse of discretion where on the admitted facts [alleging damage caused to the organizations by AGLOSO] the plaintiffs were entitled to relief." They added that the "climax of the trial court's errors was reached" in its holding that the alleged continuing damage they were suffering due to AGLOSO "should be discounted" because it had "already been incurred for a number of years," when that damage had only occurred because "of the originally erroneous action of the District Court in dismissing the petitioners' complaints, an action which was reversed by this [Supreme] Court [in *McGrath*]." The two plaintiffs urged the Court to immediately intervene since lengthy legal proceedings had already consumed four years, leading to "delay and continued frustration of the petitioners' rights"; because of the continuing harm caused by AGLOSO, as noted in *McGrath*; and because the high Court had already "determined that the issues posed by this case are important ones requiring consideration and adjudication by this Court" but that the notice and hearing issues had not been definitively settled and were now "ripe for adjudication." Moreover, they argued, there were "no issues" requiring a district court trial, as the government had indicated it "does not intend at any stage to introduce admissible evidence" to support the listings and Judge Morris, "in a mood of complete abdication of the judicial function," had declined to rule on "the only question to be determined," whether "the affidavits could justify judgment for the government." Pointing to AGLOSO's widening use as a "general blacklist," they added that until the Court ruled on the key issues, "harm to petitioners is continuing in an aggravated degree" and further delay in obtaining a final judicial resolution "would serve no purpose other than to continue the damage already done to the petitioners."[33]

In response, the DOJ, in a February 1953 brief cosigned by newly appointed Assistant Attorney General (and later Supreme Court Chief Justice) Warren Burger, maintained that the cases "do not present the exceptional and extraordinary circumstances" that would justify Supreme Court consideration before the appeals court acted and, because the district court had not yet inquired into the evidence supporting the AGLOSO determinations, "no useful purpose would be served by the granting of certiorari at this time." Moreover, the brief declared, the pending legal issue was not whether AGLOSO listing "without notice or hearing is unconstitutional, but whether the district court's denial of a preliminary injunction is an abuse of discretion," and "we think it is clear that the district court properly exercised its discretion," because *McGrath* had not required hearings prior to listings, but only that the lower courts determine whether designations were "reasonably" based on information in the attorney general's possession. The department declared, "in effect, petitioners are asking this Court to reconsider its prior decision and to pass upon constitutional questions which it declined to reach in advance of a determination of whether petitioners are in fact 'communist' organizations or whether the Attorney General possesses information from which he could reasonably find them so to be." The department denied that it would not introduce at trial evidence to sustain the listings, declaring that it was "prepared to prove" that "the information which can be disclosed" fully supported its action.[34]

Shortly before considering the JAFRC-NCASF petition for certiorari, the Supreme Court handed down a decision in another AGLOSO case that seemingly indicated its continuing hostility toward AGLOSO. Although, on March 3, 1952, in *Adler v. Board of Education* (342 U.S. 485) it had upheld the firing of New York state public school employees who were knowing members of organizations found, *after* hearings, to advocate the violent overthrow of the government because it was deemed proper to consider "the organizations and persons with whom [public employees] associate," on December 15, 1952, the Court unanimously struck down Oklahoma's requirement that public employees swear they had not, for the preceding five years, belonged to any group "officially determined by the U.S. Attorney General" or other "authorized" federal agency "to be a communist front or subversive organization." In *Wieman v. Updegraff* (344 U.S. 183), a ruling that received front-page coverage in the *New York Times,* the *Los Angeles Times*, and the *Washington Post*, the Court held that the Oklahoma law was an "assertion of arbitrary power" that unconstitutionally infringed due process protections because, as construed by the Oklahoma Supreme Court, it barred people from state employment solely on the basis of AGLOSO membership, even absent evidence that they knew the purpose and activities of such organizations. Although the Court had previously upheld seemingly similar oath requirements that did not specifically refer to AGLOSO, *Wieman*, ironically authored by former Attorney General Clark, held the Oklahoma requirement invalid as encompassing individuals who might "have joined a proscribed organization" unaware of its activities or goals, as well as those joining a group that had originally been "innocent, only later coming under the influence of those who would turn it towards illegitimate ends" or enlisting in a formerly "subversive" group that had "subsequently freed itself from the influences which originally led to its listing." Without noting that precisely such objections had been repeatedly lodged against AGLOSO usage for federal loyalty screening, Clark declared the Oklahoma law invalid because "the fact of association alone determines disloyalty and disqualification," regardless of "whether association existed innocently or knowingly," thereby inhibiting "the flow of democratic expression and controversy at one of its chief sources." Clark added that the Court felt no need to decide additional questions concerning the standards employed in AGLOSO determinations or the "limited evidentiary use" of AGLOSO in the federal loyalty program. This suggestion that the Court, if not exactly fond of AGLOSO, was not eager to revisit the issues raised in *McGrath,* was reflected in its March 9, 1953, refusal to grant certiorari in the JAFRC-NCASF case. NCASF executive director Morford told his fellow plaintiffs on June 25, 1953, that the organizations would return to the federal appeals court in hopes that "some day, nobody knows when" that court would uphold the district court, leaving the path "open properly for one more appeal to the U.S. Supreme Court."[35]

The Eisenhower Administration's AGLOSO Hearing Procedure, 1953–1955

Soon after the Supreme Court's refusal of certiorari in the *McGrath* follow-up cases, an April 25, 1953, internal FBI memo from Intelligence Division official F. J. Baumgardner to his colleague A. H. Belmont related that preliminary DOJ approval of its proposed administrative hearings regulations was reached at a March 25 evening meeting in the attorney general's office. The memo reported that the department's Criminal Division "alone will make recommendations to the Attorney General as to which organizations should go on the list and that in doing so, they will not be designated as to type, i.e., fascist, totalitarian, Communist, etc. It was also decided that the [SACB] will not be utilized to afford hearings to the new organizations to be listed." Baumgardner added that department ISD head Foley had called him on April 24 to request the "last known addresses of approximately 150 organizations which are going to be considered" for new "listing as subversive organizations," so that they could be notified "to advise them they are going to be listed" and that they were entitled to contest their designations. An unsigned March 25, 1953, DOJ memo headed "Agenda Relating to the Listing of Organizations in connection with the Employee Security Program" was apparently the basis of the AGLOSO discussions at the meeting held that day. The memo indicated considerable confusion as to whether the SACB would be asked to designate as "Communist fronts" groups that were also AGLOSO designated (as proved to be the case) or if the two lists would be entirely distinct. Thus, at one point the memo said that SACB hearings would "prevent duplication with respect to organizations which fall" within the 1950 ISA and that "such organizations comprise the large majority of Communist Front organizations now in existence," but elsewhere it indicated that departmental hearings "may duplicate" SACB hearings "for most Communist Front organizations but will be required in any event" for organizations not coming "within the [ISA] definitions."[36]

Bolstered by the Supreme Court's March 9 refusal to immediately consider the post-*McGrath* appeals, the new Eisenhower presidency, which had won the 1952 election partly by suggesting that Truman had been "soft" on communism, quickly announced a barrage of measures designed both to demonstrate its domestic anti-Communist credentials and to bring further pressure on the three *McGrath* organizations. Thus, on April 22, 1953, new attorney general Herbert Brownell petitioned the SACB to designate twelve AGLOSO organizations, including the three *McGrath* plaintiffs, as "communist fronts," following the SACB's finding two days earlier that the CP was a "communist action" organization. According to Brownell, the twelve groups were all CP "tools," operating under its "direction, domination and control." JAFRC termed Brownell's action a "fascist attack." At an April 29 news conference, Brownell announced that the department was effectively "reviving" AGLOSO and that he planned to add 62 new organizations to the list, while redesignating all 192 previously listed groups, under a new procedure in which both the newly designated and existing groups could contest their listings via an administrative hearing procedure (although redesignated groups would remain listed unless requesting a hearing and winning in resulting procedures). Brownell added that he expected AGLOSO "to play an important part" in President Eisenhower's newly toughened loyalty program, which substantially lowered the standards for loyalty dismissals and abolished the LRB, along with any appeal from departmental and agency loyalty dismissals. In an April 29 directive to federal agencies Brownell reiterated the department's official position that AGLOSO affiliations were to be "but one of the factors" in making decisions considering the new standard of employment or retention, namely, that such action was "clearly consistent with the interests of national security." Brownell's April 29 compilation no longer designated groups by categories (i.e., "Communist" or "subversive"), but rather listed them all under the heading "designation of organizations in connection with federal employee-security program." The decision not to classify organizations apparently was finalized at the very last minute, as department files include a categorized list dated April 27, 1953, attached to a memo prepared for distribution to agencies, which is crossed out and marked "not used."[37]

Bizarrely, although the April 29 regulations clearly allowed existing groups to request hearings, on May 1, ISD head William Tompkins, the top department official concerned with AGLOSO designations, suggested to Brownell that this was not the case by reporting that there was "nothing in the [April 29 press conference] transcript" so indicating. The new contestation process still authorized the attorney general to both propose and make a final determination on designations, as well as granting him the power to appoint "such officers or boards as he shall deem necessary" to respond to challenges to AGLOSO listings (with previously designated organizations given ten days to file a contestation request and newly listed groups generally given thirty days). Previously designated organizations that sought to contest their listing would not be deleted from AGLOSO until and unless a "contrary determination is made by the Attorney General."

The attorney general was required to send organizations, within sixty days of a written notice of contest, a statement of the grounds for their designation, along with written interrogatories. Organizations were required to "completely" respond within sixty days of receiving the interrogatories, with "a verified reply which shall be signed by the executive officers," and with failure to "answer any interrogatory or any part thereof . . . deemed an admission of the truth of the facts to which such interrogatory" refers and failure to respond in timely fashion to "constitute an acquiescence in designation." Contesting organizations could also (but were not required to) request a hearing. Hearing officials were authorized to refuse "irrelevant, immaterial, cumulative or repetitious testimony" and to make a recommendation to the attorney general "without the taking of evidence" at a hearing if they deemed the responses to interrogatories and other available information to constitute sufficient evidence. In providing evidence, the attorney general could submit "information or documentary material, in summary form or otherwise, without requiring disclosure of classified security information or the identity of confidential informants," and no government witness was required to disclose such information, while contesting organizations could be represented by counsel and cross-examine witnesses.[38]

Within a "reasonable time" following completion of such proceedings, the attorney general was empowered to "make a determination," while taking into "consideration any handicap imposed upon an organization by the non-disclosure to it of classified security information or the identity of confidential informants and by reason of the lack of opportunity to cross examine confidential informants." Shortly after this provision was reported to the FBI, Hoover, in a handwritten note to his colleagues on a May 14 memo, expressed concern that it "looks like a 'sleeper' to me," and on May 22 he wrote to the department to stress that "extreme care will be necessary to avoid the disclosure of our confidential informants" in any hearings and advised that utilization of bureau personnel in them would not be "desirable." However, Hoover effectively asked the department to grant the FBI secret special influence in its decision making, declaring that if the desire to protect confidential informants was a "determining factor" in the "Attorney General's decision that an organization would not be designated," it "would be appreciated if this Bureau were advised before such final decision is rendered" so "consideration may be given as to whether any additional steps may be taken by the Bureau to avoid the necessity for such a decision." On July 1, Assistant Attorney General Olney assured Hoover that he would consult the FBI prior to the release of any statements "in summary form" in connection with AGLOSO administrative hearings to ensure that "maximum protection" was "given to Bureau sources and to avoid the disclosure of confidential informants," and that if "in any case it appears essential" to call FBI personnel as witnesses "you will, of course, be consulted prior to [such] a determination."[39]

On July 6, 1953, Brownell asked Olney to determine if the new AGLOSO hearing regulations were adequate in view of a recent federal district court ruling (*Parker v. Lester,* 112 F. Supp. 433, 1953). The ruling struck down the government's heavily AGLOSO-based merchant marine screening program, on the grounds that four seaman denied employment for security reasons were provided only with vague allegations charging affiliations with unnamed "subversive" groups and were not allowed to cross-examine their accusers or otherwise examine the evidence against them. In a September 11, 1953, memo to Olney, ISD chief Foley assured him that the department's new AGLOSO hearings would be unaffected by the ruling "if the material contained in the statement of grounds and the interrogatories thereto are sufficient to advise the organization" of the reasons for its proposed designation, especially as this material appeared to afford organizations "sufficient opportunity to challenge the determinations of the Attorney General." Noting that the courts had "gone far in permitting limitations of the usual protections where national security is involved," Foley added that such rulings suggested that the attorney general did not have to divulge to organizations any material "which would adversely affect the government."[40]

On September 30, 1953, FBI assistant director Ladd informed Hoover of what clearly struck Ladd as an odd conversation initiated by Olney that morning. According to Ladd, "some of the attorneys in the Department" and "also various organizations" had the "misconception" that "they were entitled to a legal hearing before their name is to be placed" on AGLOSO which, in fact, was precisely what the April 29 regulations had provided, at least for newly designated (as opposed to "redesignated") groups. Ladd surmised that the department appeared to be "now concerned about having granted so much leeway to these organizations" in the new regulations and "is now frantically trying to find some way to get away from a legal hearing." According to Ladd, the department was especially concerned that "considerable trouble" would ensue if the hearing officers were inclined to "hold extensive hearings, which is not what the Department intended," as opposed to proceedings "merely for the purpose of reviewing the Bureau's and the Department's voluminous records, and accepting any information which the cited organizations desire to furnish, and then arriving at an administrative decision." Hoover wrote on Ladd's memo, "I think your surmise is correct."[41]

In fact, the DOJ struggled mightily after 1953 to avoid holding any AGLOSO hearings, primarily by delays and by requiring contesting organizations to respond to interrogatories that were so detailed that they were often either impossible to answer or essentially required the organizations to act as police informants on themselves. As a result, although numerous organizations informed the department that they wished to contest their designations, almost all of them either gave up rather than jump through such unpleasant high hurdles, or else their responses were found inadequate for various, often strained, reasons. Thus, the department announced on February 4, 1954, that nineteen organizations that had been newly proposed for designation nine months earlier had filed notices of contest but had since been AGLOSO-listed for failure to submit responses that answered "each interrogatory completely and with particularity," as required in the hearing regulations. Similarly, a June 28, 1956, letter from Acting Deputy Attorney General Olney to Loyd Wright, chair of a commission charged by Congress with investigating the federal loyalty program, reported that although fifteen organizations "redesignated" in April 1953, had originally sought hearings, almost all had "failed to comply with the applicable rules" and thus "did not proceed to hearings." According to a memo by FBI official C. H. Stanley, the department's "interrogatories are of such character that organizations are unwilling to submit to them since to do so will require exposure of the very Communist associations with which they are charged." Thus, he maintained, most designated groups had "acknowledged their subversive character through failure to contest" and "use of the interrogatory" had "proved effective."[42]

Internal files make it clear that the DOJ invoked every possible grounds to find the responses of contesting organizations inadequate. Thus, pursuant to a filing by Kurt Mertig on behalf of the Citizens Protective League and the German-American Republican League (according to DOJ records, Mertig was the *only* member of either group), Criminal Division head Olney responded on April 2, 1954, that Mertig had not only "obviously" failed to answer adequately the interrogatories, but that his communication was "unverified," whereas the hearing regulations required a "verified" reply. On May 21, 1954, Olney, in response to communications by lawyers for the Bridges-Robertson-Schmidt Defense Committee (proposed for designation in April 1953 and officially listed three months later) declared that the department had repeatedly rejected the organization's hearing requests because they were signed only by the committee's secretary, while the regulations required a response from the "executive officers." Although the lawyers had informed the department that the secretary was the only "executive officer," Olney responded that the department believed otherwise and that the organization had been "designated" as "the time for a hearing in this connection has long since expired." According to Olney's May 21 letter, the organization had sought redress in federal district court in January 1954, but the suit had been dismissed on March 15, 1954. A July 24, 1956, department memorandum reported that additional rejections based on findings of "improper" responses were made in "several" instances where the notice was "signed by only one officer," although contesting organizations were apparently not always specifically so informed. Thus, department files indicate that the World War II–era Dai Nippon Butoku Kai's attempt to contest its designation was rejected on such grounds, but the September 21, 1956, letter to the group simply stated that its "purported notice of contest" was "found not to be in accordance with the rules and regulations." As discussed below, the department eventually granted a hearing in only one instance, that of the Independent Socialist League (ISL) and two allied organizations, and then only after two years of delay, followed by a ruling issued another three years later, in which the DOJ conceded that it had failed to present sufficient evidence to support its case.[43]

Attorney General Brownell, meanwhile, began exploring further expansion of AGLOSO designations. Although, with a few exceptions, the department had previously adhered to a policy established in 1947 of not designating trade unions, in an October 21, 1953, memo to Hoover, Brownell declared that "those labor unions which are dominated and controlled by the Communist movement" had to be considered for both AGLOSO and SACB designation. Referring to a February 25, 1953, FBI memo, Brownell added that he was "concerned, as you are, that this supplementary investigation," while not directed against labor unions "as such, will undoubtedly be attacked by some labor groups as a 'union-busting' campaign" but maintained that the department had "no alternative" under its AGLOSO and SACB responsibilities. Brownell added that he was "anxious that insofar as possible this additional investigation avoid normal union activities and be directed at the leadership of Communist-dominated unions" rather than "against the large percentage of members of such unions who are undoubtedly loyal citizens forced to join such organizations" to keep their jobs. He expressed concern at an October 21, 1953, luncheon with Hoover that "certain Communist" unions in particular might engage in "twisting the facts to make it appear" that the department was engaged in a "labor union wrecking program." According to Hoover's October 21 memo to top FBI officials, he urged Brownell to move "swiftly" in designating AGLOSO unions. Also in late October, Brownell drafted a letter to Secretary of Defense Charles Wilson, which characterized AGLOSO as "an invaluable aid to our entire security program," which "not only must be continued but strengthened and maintained on as current a basis as possible."[44]

Despite Brownell's strongly voiced views, debate continued within the department concerning the advisability of continuing AGLOSO. In a November 20, 1953, twenty-page, single-spaced memo to Assistant Attorney General Olney, Criminal Division attorney William Nelson argued that AGLOSO should be abandoned because the loyalty program could be administered more effectively and with fewer constraints if the attorney general simply secretly informed governmental agencies about the character of dubious organizations, which need and should not be limited to previously AGLOSO-designated groups. According to Nelson, *McGrath* suggested that the publication of AGLOSO was the key factor that had "led to the hue and cry of so-called blacklisting" and was viewed by the Supreme Court as so damaging to the designated organizations as to require hearings, so that if confidential reports were substituted for AGLOSO, no group could seek legal redress "on the grounds that it had been publicly defamed and injured without a hearing." Nelson added that it was "naïve to presume that the organizations contesting proposed designations" would not seek to "delay and prolong [the administrative] hearings interminably," and it "would amount to a denial of a basic Communist tenet" if such organizations then did not thereafter "seek relief therefrom in the courts," possibly leading to legal rulings requiring the government to provide "that degree of proof and the administrative process required" in SACB proceedings. Moreover, Nelson argued, the loyalty program was "progressively moving towards" precluding consideration of associations with non-AGLOSO groups, yet the FBI and congressional and state legislative committees had reports about many such organizations that had a "significance to the employee security program" and "the problem arising in the great majority" of pending loyalty determinations was that "the only evidence available was evidence of membership only in non-designated but obviously significant organizations." While Nelson conceded that employees charged with disloyalty would still have to be provided with specific allegations concerning their organizational affiliations, and such charges would "no doubt" surface publicly, there was a "great difference between publicly characterizing certain organizations throughout the nation as Communist and so characterizing an organization" privately, a "difference that, if challenged, it is believed that the courts will recognize and uphold the power of the Executive so to act." He maintained that the government could execute a "gracious withdrawal from an increasingly untenable position" by asserting that while existing AGLOSO designations were unaffected, loyalty determinations were "within the absolute discretion of the Executive" and it was "no longer necessary to designate organizations," as administrative hearings would often duplicate SACB proceedings and "security considerations (protection of valuable informants implied) are also involved."[45]

Oran Waterman, a lawyer in the department's Subversive Organizations (AGLOSO) Unit within the SOS (which also handled SACB petitions and was part of the ISD), strongly rejected Nelson's position in two separate November 30 memos to his boss, David Irons. In one memo, marked "CONFIDENTIAL," Waterman, who presumably feared for his job, argued that Nelson's suggested changes could result in federal employees being charged with disloyalty based on alleged subversive organizational affiliations about which they had "no prior notice," thereby increasing the numbers of "innocent" members and the difficulty of identifying them. Waterman suggested that Nelson had failed to adequately consider that "front groups are, in most cases, not clearly identifiable as such until after a considerable pattern of conduct develops and that many of our outstanding citizens were taken in prior to such pattern," a position that was "used repeatedly in security hearings by the hearing officers but would be lost completely under the proposed changes." Additionally, Waterman maintained, Nelson's entire "thesis" was based on the argument that the courts would distinguish between public and confidential listings of "subversive" organizations, "even though both eventually receive wide publicity and the organization designated is harmed in both instances," a posture "difficult to reconcile" with *McGrath*, which found that "organizations suffer injury to their reputations when characterized publicly and should be afforded a hearing prior thereto." Waterman added that abandoning AGLOSO would shortsightedly give up a weapon "which has enabled us to take effective action against Communist fronts," a development that the CP "would welcome" and that would "pull the props from under most state loyalty programs, denials of tax exemptions, passports and many other related uses to which this program has been diverted, legally or otherwise, but with tremendous and effective impact upon the Communist 'United Front' Appeal." In a separate "PERSONAL & CONFIDENTIAL" November 30 memo to Irons, Waterman termed some of Nelson's facts and arguments "inaccurate" and "fallacious" and even more strongly reiterated his position. Waterman said that Nelson's suggestion that governmental loyalty boards are "currently unable to weigh membership in nondesignated organizations" was "not true," at least in sensitive agencies, such as the State Department and the military, while Nelson's argument that "absolute" executive discretion could be used to fire allegedly disloyal employees did not apply to nonsensitive agencies. He also maintained that Nelson was wrong in suggesting that the department could effect a "gracious withdrawal" from AGLOSO, as the amount of mail received concerning AGLOSO indicated that the public was "probably more cognizant of the Designation Program than any other aspect of the Government's antisubversive work" and would likely react with "alarm" over future dismissals based on membership in organizations "which [employees] had no reason to believe were subversive." Waterman added that AGLOSO had been "more effective in combating the Communist front movement than any other program" as "it crippled their 'united front' appeal," which had been the CP's "major objective," and moreover, it was the "foundation of a considerable number of state loyalty programs." Thus, AGLOSO appeared "amply justified," Waterman concluded, especially since hearings were anticipated in only a few instances.[46]

On December 30, 1953, Brownell sent Civic Service Commission (CSC) chair Philip Young a memo that amounted to a compromise between the seemingly incompatible positions of Nelson and Waterman. The attorney general effectively endorsed Nelson's views that governmental agencies should be able to fully consider non-AGLOSO associations but did so without taking any steps to abandon AGLOSO. Brownell informed Young that he had decided to override his own previous directive of April 29 that loyalty boards should not consider "relevant" information concerning non-AGLOSO organizations unless government agencies first "made available to the security hearing board the Attorney General's views as to the nature of the organization." Instead, he directed, the guidelines should state that "membership in, affiliation with or sympathetic association with, any organization, whether specifically designated" or not, was only one factor to be considered in making loyalty determinations, a guideline that seemed to entirely eliminate the difference between designated and nondesignated groups in making such decisions. Brownell said he had changed his posture because "ordinarily the Attorney General is not in a position to give his views as to the nature of organizations which have not been designated," and because loyalty determinations were the responsibility of agency heads "it does not seem appropriate to restrict their judgment." Brownell thereby ignored the explicit recommendations of Assistant Attorney General Rankin, now Office of Legal Counsel (OLC) head, who told him that his directive seemed to violate the intent of Eisenhower's Executive Order 10450, which had explicitly referred to AGLOSO, and, by removing the requirement that agency boards consult "some authoritative source concerning organizations without substituting any procedure in its place," could lead different agencies to reach "opposite results with respect to the same organization" and might put "within the discretion of numerous agencies and departments the authority to name" non-AGLOSO groups. Rankin added that it might also violate the *McGrath* requirement that hearings be held before organizations were categorized as relevant to employee loyalty "with the attendant publicity."[47]

In practice, Brownell's December 30 memo effectively shifted the power to determine whether nondesignated organizations were "subversive" enough for consideration in loyalty decisions to the FBI and to congressional investigating committees, since most agencies lacked the investigative resources to make their own determinations. Subsequently, when agencies or the CSC queried Brownell concerning specific nondesignated organizations, they were, in at least some cases, informed that it was "unnecessary for the Attorney General to furnish" such views and/or that agencies need not withhold their own determinations in such cases. However, according to a General Accounting Office policy statement issued on March 9, 1955, since the DOJ no longer maintained any "specific list of organizations" held to advocate overthrowing the government, the "Department should be consulted on an individual case basis whenever a question arises as to the subversive connection of any particular organization." Moreover, apparently because of the political sensitivity involved in determining if union membership was critical in loyalty determinations, several ranking department officials conferred on January 7, 1954, to discuss whether a Senate subcommittee's citation of the nondesignated UPWA as "communist dominated and controlled" was an adequate basis for loyalty charges. According to a March 19, 1954, memo reporting on this discussion from security officer Leonard Bienvenu to Deputy Attorney General Rogers, the former's office had concluded that "we may properly rely upon the finding of the Senate Subcommittee without further testimony," and that "in the instant cases, mere membership, standing alone, should not warrant a finding that the employee is a security risk," but that charges would be justified "where membership is coupled with activities on the part of the employee in behalf of the UPWA," including holding office or "passing out the handbills of the Union." Rogers subsequently forwarded the Bienvenu memo to Criminal

Division head Olney along with a "PERSONAL AND CONFIDENTIAL" inquiry as to whether "proceedings are contemplated" for designating the UPWA under AGLOSO. Although a July 23, 1954, letter from Rogers to top White House assistant Sherman Adams enclosed a list of "Communist-dominated unions" identified by the FBI, none of them were AGLOSO-designated before the department entirely stopped adding new listings after 1954.[48]

Even after adopting the new administrative hearing procedure in April 1953 and as the post-*McGrath* litigation continued in the federal courts, the DOJ conducted a parallel debate on AGLOSO's future. Thus, on October 14, 1954, SOS chief David Irons wrote OLC "confidential assistant" John Doherty that there were five alternatives the department could adopt: (1) eliminating AGLOSO entirely and henceforth relying on government loyalty boards to "decide each case on the basis of FBI reports on the organization," (2) publicly announcing the abandonment of all AGLOSO listings while secretly making confidential designations, (3) retaining the existing public list but making all future designations confidential, (4) continuing the existing program while making no further designations pending court rulings, and (5) continuing the existing program but initiating a "drive to designate all possible subversive organizations" prior to "possible adverse" court decisions. At least implicitly, Irons appeared to favor the fifth alternative. Thus, he quoted past arguments by Hoover and former LRB chair Bingham attesting to AGLOSO's importance, both in terms of federal loyalty screening and in impeding the effectiveness of listed groups. Irons warned that if individual loyalty boards were given no centralized guidance they would end up "establishing their own individual lists of proscribed organizations" but rejected the position that involvement in nondesignated groups could not be considered in personnel decisions, since evidence that a federal employee had "actively sponsored the subversive purposes" of a dubious organization or "engaged in any other activity such as association with the Communist members or officers" could be "charged and none of these charges need be based on *membership* in the particular organization." Irons also suggested that employees might be suspended (without specifying any distinction between membership and "active" involvement) even before formal AGLOSO designations, based on the attorney general's "prima facie determination that an organization should be cited."[49]

A November 12, 1954, memo to ISD official Yeagley from OLC "confidential assistant" Doherty clearly disagreed with Irons by maintaining that the AGLOSO process was "not essential" to the federal screening process and that the delays caused by providing administrative hearings created the prospect that "a truly subversive organization can come into existence for a specific purpose" and then disband upon accomplishing it while escaping AGLOSO designation. On November 15, OLC attorney Oran Waterman informed Irons that there was still no "policy decision as to the advisability of designating additional organizations."

Four days later, Assistant Attorney General and ISD head Tompkins advised top presidential aide Sherman Adams, in response to the "interest" that Adams had expressed in "these matters," that several right-wing "hate" organizations headed by the notoriously anti-Semitic Gerald L. K. Smith and Joseph Kamp had been considered for designation but had been determined to fall outside the guidelines because of "insufficient evidence" that they had advocated the forceful deprivation of others' constitutional rights and because they were "primarily one-man directorships under autocratic rule and without formal membership of any kind," thus "not of a type contemplated by the Executive Order." Tompkins added that the department would continue to study recommending "changes in our laws to encompass activities such as those of Smith and Kemp," but it appeared "extremely doubtful" that procedures could be amended to encompass such groups without violating "the rights guaranteed by the First Amendment." On December 15 Tompkins informed his superior, Deputy Attorney General Rogers, of the ISD's decision to not recommend "at this time any changes in the Internal Security Statutes or Executive Order No. 10450 to proscribe the activities of individuals such as Smith and Kemp or their organizations."[50]

On December 30, 1954, Brownell announced what would prove to be the final AGLOSO additions, proposing twenty-seven organizations for designation, while also declaring that all sixty-two organizations proposed for inclusion in April 1953 had subsequently been officially designated. In a typical example of the inconsistency that seemingly plagued virtually all AGLOSO-related activities, Brownell's December 30 press release, for the first time, listed the addresses of all of the newly proposed organizations and characterized them all as allegedly "communist-dominated" (although in 1953 such classifications had been abandoned and, in fact, they were never formally so listed). On April 11, 1955, the DOJ announced that twenty-one of the proposed new groups had not challenged the listings and were being formally added to AGLOSO, while the other six were declared to have filed "proper notices of contest," and that statements of grounds and interrogatories had either already been sent them or were being prepared by the department. Four of these six were designated on October 28, 1955, because, according to the department, they had subsequently failed to "file a verified reply answering each interrogatory completely and with particularity." They proved to be the last AGLOSO additions, as the two remaining groups (Californians for the Bill of Rights and the National Council for the Arts, Sciences and Professions) apparently ceased functioning and the department spent over three years trying to determine if their responses were adequate and then quietly dropped them from further AGLOSO consideration. That Brownell, along with Eisenhower, viewed the new designations as a political plus seems clear from the issuance of a joint statement by Brownell and OLC chief Tompkins on January 1, 1955, which hailed this action as one of a variety of administration initiatives to carry out anti-Communist initiatives at an "accelerated pace," in furtherance of the administration's goal to "destroy utterly the Communist conspiracy against this country." Although the DOJ never proposed any additional listings, the ISD regularly continued to ask the FBI for information in connection with possible AGLOSO designations, as in a January 19, 1955, memo from Tompkins to Hoover requesting reports about seven specific groups. According to a March 21, 1955, letter from CSC chair Philip Young to Brownell, on December 2, 1954, the Comptroller General of the United States had issued a finding, apparently resulting from the end of AGLOSO categorizations dating from April 1953, that "present membership" in *any* designated group required automatic termination of federal employment under the 1939 Hatch Act. However, Brownell apparently never responded to Young's request for clarification of this matter.[51]

Most critics of AGLOSO, unsurprisingly, reacted negatively to the announcement of the 1953 administrative hearing process. Thus, on May 8, 1953, the NCASF and JAFRC, which were still fighting their designations in court, informed the DOJ that they were explicitly rejecting the administrative hearing procedure. Their attorneys told Brownell that the new regulations would provide only a "sham hearing" designed to "obscure the issues presently in litigation before the courts without, in any legitimate fashion, complying with" *McGrath*'s "spirit and intent." They complained that the new procedures would "absurd[ly]" require their clients, who had been contesting their designation "for the past six years," to indicate their objections anew while remaining listed "without benefit of notice and hearing until you see fit to remove them, thus continuing the present illegal practice." Furthermore, they maintained, the new regulations made Brownell the "sole judge," acting "upon secret confidential information which will not be disclosed to the organizations," although "you cannot possibly act as an impartial judge" since "you have already indicated that these organizations should be designated" and were currently defending "in court the legality of the designation" as well as instituting SACB proceedings against the two organizations, "in which, as a prosecutor, you have the burden of proving the allegations which you would presumably set yourself up to pass upon in any hearing to be held before you." The lawyers declared that if Brownell "seriously" intended to conform with *McGrath*, he should immediately remove the groups from AGLOSO, discontinue the SACB proceedings, and "accord the fair and impartial hearing that is required by the Constitution," as the 1953 hearing procedures had been instituted "merely for the purpose of obfuscating the issues in an attempt to prevent a court decision with regard to the illegal acts which the Department of Justice has been engaged in for the past six years and which you in effect propose to continue."[52]

ACLU lawyer Herbert Levy told his organization's board of directors in a May 13, 1953, memo that the DOJ had improperly publicly announced the names of proposed new designees prior to hearings and that the new regulations were "not completely satisfactory" because they allowed determinations to be made "upon unverified statements submitted by the Attorney General, not subject to cross-examination or consultation" when allegedly sensitive material was involved. At a May 18 meeting, the ACLU directors tabled a motion to publicly criticize the prehearing announcement of the new designations, while simultaneously voting to condemn the department's practice of designating legal defense organizations for those accused of "subversive" activities. They maintained that "defense itself is never disloyal or subversive activity" and "contributions to legitimate defense are not of themselves evidence of disloyalty or subversion," and thus "no defense fund should be listed as disloyal or subversive" absent proof that it cloaked "disloyal or subversive activities," a task that could be facilitated by requiring defense funds to "make complete and public account" of their financial operations.[53]

In early May 1953, the Japanese-American Citizens League announced that it would protest the April 29 redesignation of twenty-one defunct pre–World War II Japanese organizations. National league president George Inagaki told reporters that the listings were being used to deny Japanese-Americans government employment, "to authorize the deportation of worthy aliens who are parents of American-born citizens, to prohibit the issuance of reentry for Issei [Japanese-born Americans] desiring to visit Japan, to deny visa applications to stranded Issei in Japan and to immigrants seeking to enter the U.S., and to cast suspicion on the otherwise generally favorable war records of the Issei and Nisei [American-born citizens with Japanese-born parents] in the U.S." On May 18, 1953, Washington league representative Mike Masaoka wrote to Brownell to additionally protest that the new contestation process provided no means by which defunct AGLOSO organizations could clear their names and to complain that the new list "makes no classification as to origin or motivation and lumps some 254 organizations together, implying to the public at large that all of these organizations are currently engaging in subversive activities," especially since, "in light of present public attitudes," most designated organizations were viewed as "Communistic." He declared, "we submit that such an impression does violence to the American concept of fair play and invites unwarranted and damaging suspicion against persons of Japanese ancestry in this country." Masaoka added that since "all of the prewar Japanese organizations are defunct, the public is given the erroneous impression that there are some 21 subversive Japanese organizations presently active." He appealed for a "reappraisal," which he said he was confident would lead to the elimination of the twenty-one groups from "any current list of proscribed organizations." In a May 25 letter to Brownell, league attorney Frank Chuman asked what procedure could be followed by "such defunct organizations" to get off AGLOSO, since "such organizations are not able to comply with filing a notice of protest" and such "failure to protest is deemed by the Attorney General to be an admission of such classification." On June 4, Assistant Attorney General Olney apparently closed off further discussion of this subject by wiring Chuman that, under the promulgated regulations, "notice of contest shall be signed by the executive officers" and therefore any protest "should be signed by such officers at time of dissolution," a clearly impossible requirement for groups defunct for almost twenty years.[54]

According to a March 10, 1954, memo from ACLU chair Baldwin to his staff counsel Herbert Monty, Baldwin received the same answer when he raised the issue of "defunct" organizations with DOJ ISD head Foley. Declaring Foley's suggestion that such organizations ask for a hearing was "impractical," Baldwin suggested trying to persuade the department to adopt a "statute of limitations" under which no federal employee would be investigated for associations dating back fifteen years or more, since if "his record were otherwise clear, no point would be served in going back beyond that time." Subsequently, the ACLU's National Security Committee, meeting on May 10, 1954, decided to take no position concerning Baldwin's suggestion or with regard to a proposal that the DOJ be requested to delete all Trotskyist, Nazi, and Japanese organizations from AGLOSO because past or "even present membership" in such groups "could hardly be considered harmful to our national security under today's circumstances." Perhaps in response, Baldwin sent staff counsel Levy a May 10 memo to inquire "what the official position" of the ACLU was on AGLOSO, specifically including whether the ACLU opposed the "government's listing publicly organizations, membership in which is held to be a disqualifying factor for government service." Baldwin additionally asked, if the ACLU did not oppose the principle of AGLOSO, "what limits do we advocate on listing outside of the requirement for a hearing upon request" and "can any steps be taken to prevent the abuse of this list, for purposes other than was intended both by government and private agencies?" In a June 4 memo, Levy told Baldwin that "in summary, we are not opposed to public listing, but we do oppose the [Attorney General's] lack of clear standards (which we have attacked in the past publicly), and we have also attacked his present method of conducting a hearing." Levy added that "we have always objected to listing without a hearing," but that the ACLU lacked any position concerning defunct organizations. He concluded, "I know of no steps that can be taken to prevent the abuse of the list" and that "neither I nor apparently any other lawyer concerned with the problem has been able to think of a good method."[55]

Because both AGLOSO and the SACB were both now simultaneously involved in holding hearings to designate "subversive" organizations—with AGLOSO designations supposedly only to aid federal personnel screening of individuals, unlike SACB designations, which directly imposed legal penalties on "Communist" groups and their members—the two procedures were frequently confused in the minds of the public, politicians, and the press. Thus, in mid-1953, when the SACB began hearings on 12 alleged "Communist front" organizations that Brownell had charged under the ISA, a May 14 *New York Times* article totally confused the two lists by reporting that the SACB would likely be busy "almost constantly for the next several years since there are 254 organizations now on" AGLOSO and each was "entitled to a hearing if it opposes the Attorney General's efforts to force it to register" (in fact until then Brownell had brought action before the SACB against only 13 AGLOSO organizations, including the CP).

In a November 4, 1953, memo to Brownell, President Eisenhower expressed concern over unwarranted and overly broad suspicions raised by the continued focus on the associations that individuals had joined many years earlier. Eisenhower told his attorney general that his concern had arisen due to a widely publicized recent speech by *New York Times* publisher Arthur Hays Sulzberger, who had proposed "the equivalent of a political amnesty" for those who had joined "Communist fronts" during the pre-Cold War era but had left them by 1948, when "postwar communism had plainly declared itself," because it was "high time" to distinguish between "the misled and the real Communist" and "get away from the destructive and dangerously distracting talk about which band leader and which movie actress belonged to what organization 10 or 15 years ago." Urging a Pennsylvania college audience to "condemn a new form of lynch law which has become too prevalent" and to "stand up and be counted, even when the crowd is hell-bent on burning a witch," Sulzberger had urged selecting "some arbitrary date, say the beginning of the Berlin airlift in 1948," and granting "amnesty," save for those in "particularly sensitive positions," for the individual who had joined "Communist fronts" before then, "provided he has clearly dissociated himself from any such group before the date set." However, Sulzberger added, "anyone who joined a Communist front organization thereafter must accept whatever consequences might befall him as a result of that association." Sulzberger declared that his proposal sought to change an atmosphere that had resulted in a "growing tendency to equate nonconformity with treason" and "disloyalty."

Eisenhower told Brownell in his memo that true Communists were "such liars and cheats" that "they are in a class set apart," but that he was concerned about "another individual entirely," namely, the "younger person who in the late thirties and early forties was inclined to leftish thinking" and "particularly towards giving expression to his sympathy for the Soviets" and "may have done this through joining organizations that later came to be classified as subversive." Noting that official American policy after Pearl Harbor was "to foster friendship with the Soviets," the president suggested that "the individual of whom I am speaking (who must have depended on people high in government for information and judgment) could very easily and very honestly have said many things that today would indicate or imply an unjustified support of Communism." Eisenhower added that while "anyone who, *after the [1948] the blockade of Berlin began,*" continued to support the Soviets or express "sympathy for them, is either very stupid or very dangerous," he assumed that "any American could have been excused for statements or actions favorable to the Soviets during the war and *even as late as 1948.*" Therefore, he suggested that "some formula" be developed that could apply to "individuals who have *never* been Communists, but who did in earlier years speak favorably of the Soviets, and who now, as teachers, preachers, professional people of all sorts, or workers in non-sensitive positions of government, may feel themselves under suspicion and are consequently living in doubt and fear." Eisenhower declared, "We must search out some positive way to put ourselves on the side of individual rights and liberties as well as on the side of fighting Communism to the death." He concluded by asking Brownell and FBI director Hoover to consider the subject, adding that if Brownell felt there was "*no value in this suggestion whatsoever*" he needn't "take up Mr. Hoover's time."[56]

At Brownell's request, Eisenhower's memo was pondered at some length by the DOJ. In response to a February 15, 1954, query from Assistant Attorney General Rankin in connection with a study that the OLC was making for Brownell concerning the potential impact of adopting the "Sulzberger rule," on March 3 Deputy Attorney General Rogers "strongly" advised against the proposal because promulgating it would "in a large measure thwart or tightly circumscribe" government security screenings. Rogers declared that the proposal would "negate or almost totally minimize obviously significant" "Communist front" associations from pre-1948, a period when such groups were "most numerous and active," and thus lead to retaining employees whose retention would "not be clearly consistent with the interests of the national security and the intent of the security program." Rogers added that the proposal would seriously impact the department's ability to consider each case on its merits, create "confusion and inconsistent adjudications" by conflicting with AGLOSO designations first made between 1947 and 1948, create an "unjustified but logically ensuing cloud of doubt" upon "adverse adjudications made prior to the adoption of such a rule," and lead the FBI and other agencies to cease reporting on pre-1948 organizational associations, which would "seriously affect" their investigations' quality.[57]

Brownell personally responded to Eisenhower's query, after almost six months, with a March 22, 1954, twenty-seven-page "confidential" memorandum that, without expressing a definite position on the Sulzberger proposal, apparently raised enough questions so that the entire idea was quietly dropped. Brownell said the proposal gave rise "to a number of interesting and difficult questions," including the meaning of "Communist front" connections, what the "proper cut-off date" should be, and whether those who joined many dubious groups before such date should be treated differently than those who only joined "a single organization and had no knowledge of its Communist nature." He added that mere past membership in a suspect organization, including even the CP, had not automatically led to exclusion from federal employment in the past, because the nature and length of associations were taken into account. Thus, according to Brownell, "remote" CP membership "did not result in an adverse loyalty finding" if agency loyalty boards were "satisfied that the individual himself had never been guilty of disloyal acts and had clearly" severed his CP ties, while those "with long histories of [CP] membership and those whose claims of having left the

Party were subject to doubt" were excluded from employment. Brownell added that there were "instances in which Communist front activities did result in adverse findings," but past participation in such groups was "obvious[ly]" seen as less significant by loyalty boards than CP affiliations, so that "only extremely aggravated circumstances of Communist front activity was considered a sufficient basis for an unfavorable loyalty determination" and "even existing participation in such organizations did not necessarily require a finding of disloyalty." Brownell subtly alluded to the possible adverse political risks of formally adopting an "amnesty" by reporting that the LRB had in 1949 rejected a proposal to flatly disregard CP memberships more than three years old after one member termed such "an arbitrary rule" both "unnecessary and, from the public relations standpoint, unwise," as "there are many in our populace who are so rabid on this subject that they would want to lynch us if we were to hold that a man who ever held a Communist ticket at any time should get by."[58]

According to Brownell, under the Eisenhower program, agency boards could take into account "the employee's statement of his reason for joining and his knowledge of the purposes of the organization," a standard that he conceded was narrower than the LRB's 1949 guidelines, which called for evaluating AGLOSO affiliations by "determining, so far as possible, the character of the organization, the period, nature and duration of the association, whether the employee or applicant was aware of the subversive character of the organization at the time of such association, and the nature of his activities in connection with such organization." Brownell concluded by telling Eisenhower that "the use of a uniform cutoff date" for loyalty determinations in cases involving past Communist affiliations "would not change the result in very many cases," but the "psychological effect on hearing boards, would, in all probability, result in a less stringent standard of the meaning of security risk, and almost surely the public would assume that the program was being 'liberalized' or 'softened.'" If Sulzberger's suggestion were adopted, he added, "practical methods for translating the proposal into action, without at the same time seriously weakening the security program" would be needed, but he noted that the proposal was restricted to Communist front, rather than CP membership, and that the risk to national security could be minimized by excluding positions "designated as sensitive" from the "amnesty." Moreover, he concluded, any such change should "make it abundantly plain that it would not serve ipso facto to clear every person who dropped out of Communist Front organizations prior to the cut-off date, regardless of the duration, nature and intensity of his organizational activity," although this limitation would admittedly "becloud the proposal in the public mind, and eliminate the 'certainty' which was one of the attractive aspects" of Sulzberger's plan.

That Brownell's suggestion that imposing a "statute of limitations" on AGLOSO affiliations might damage Eisenhower's repeated self-promotion as extremely "tough" on communism was probably a decisive factor in killing the entire issue is indicated by "Ike's" stress at a June 2, 1954, press conference on how many strong "anti-subversive" measures his DOJ had taken. He listed nine programs his administration had adopted to check subversive influences, including the "constant surveillance of Communists in this country" on a "twenty-four-hour, seven-days a week, fifty-two-weeks-a-year basis"; the arrest, indictment, and/or conviction of almost 70 alleged Communists; deportations, denaturalizations, or denials of entry of over 400 persons viewed as "subversive"; and the addition of 62 groups to AGLOSO, "making a total of 255." Eisenhower's June 2 statement was reissued and updated on December 7, shortly before Brownell proposed what proved to be the final 27 AGLOSO designations on December 30, in response to an attack by Sen. McCarthy criticizing the president as "soft" on communism.[59]

Brownell's stance could hardly have come as a surprise to Eisenhower, as the attorney general had especially identified himself with the anti-Communist crusade. Thus, in a September 4, 1953, *U.S. News & World Report* interview, Brownell had boasted about adding "60-some" organizations to AGLOSO and declared that the DOJ gets "them on the list as soon as we find out about them." In an April 25, 1955, interview with the same outlet, Brownell noted that no organization could be added to AGLOSO "without an opportunity for hearing" and declared that it was "quite significant" that "only 3 of the 192 organizations originally listed [by the Truman administration]" had utilized the procedure, without mentioning the steep barriers the government had erected to discourage such action. When asked why defunct organizations were still listed, Brownell said the government was entitled to know about its employees' past associations, that "it is a well-known Communist technique to create a front group and then let it become defunct as soon as it has been exposed," and that many organizations "found it more convenient to quietly go out of existence and seek to accomplish their ends under another 'cloak'" than challenge AGLOSO listings. "Because the essence of Communist tactics is deceit," he concluded, "to say that a one-time front organization now defunct should be forever removed from any future consideration of the security of present or future Government employers is the height of naïveté."

While the NCASF (and, until 1955, JAFRC) litigation proceeded slowly through the courts (as discussed below), AGLOSO's status remained uncertain within the DOJ. On January 19, 1955, ISD head Tompkins asked the FBI for additional information on seven organizations for possible AGLOSO designation, and an April 15, 1955, memo to SOS chief Oran Waterman from one of his underlings reported that the latter was preparing memoranda for the designation of nine organizations. In the meantime, in February 1955, Tompkins sent several colleagues a memo reporting that it had "been suggested" that the department seek legislation putting AGLOSO on a statutory basis by shifting the power to make designations to the SACB upon petition by the attorney general. The memo recommended emphasizing that such legislation's purpose was "solely and exclusively" in connection with federal loyalty screening, while associations with nondesignated groups might also be "considered as warranted in individual cases." Tompkins added that the legislation might also authorize the SACB to consider information that would not be disclosed to the affected organizations upon certification that "disclosure of the source would be against the interests of national security." The memo declared that such legislation would overcome four problems with "existing programs," by avoiding having the attorney general serve as both "prosecutor and judge" in making designations, providing "definitions and standards," granting the "subpoena power necessary to obtain witnesses for designation proceedings," and "most important," specifically authorizing the submission of secret information in designation hearings, which was required to "make designations in some cases," but which faced a doubtful future in the courts without a statutory basis, although it was "permitted under existing rules."[60]

In June 1955 Waterman informed his new boss, Joseph Alderman, that he supported Tompkins's call for legislation granting subpoena power in AGLOSO designation hearings, which he deemed "almost indispensable" on the basis of departmental preparations for the first such hearing, scheduled soon for the ISL. According to Waterman, at least nine people who had been identified as "available witnesses" for the government against the ISL had "for various reasons declined to testify" and if any request for individuals to testify was "placed solely on patriotic grounds, it falls short of the necessary persuasion to effect their appearance." Alderman endorsed Waterman's appeal in a September 1, 1955, memo to Harold Koffsky, chief of the department's Appeals and Legal Research, which declared that "recent attacks on Government witnesses have served to increase the natural hesitancy of prospective witnesses." Moreover, Alderman said, obtaining subpoena power from Congress could confer upon AGLOSO "certain inferences of possible legal significance" due to the consequent legislative "recognition" of it. In a January 27, 1956, memo to Waterman, Designations Unit attorney Francis Williamson argued that legal precedents suggested that withholding classified information in AGLOSO hearings would be upheld in the courts, so long as contesting organizations were provided with a "fair resumé" of such material. However, responding to SOS chief Alderman's request for comment on Williamson's memo, Waterman suggested on March 6, 1956, that a "summary of information by itself" would fail in the courts without "some independent method of determining that a 'fair resumé' of the classified information is, in fact, accurate and fair."[61]

Although AGLOSO-related work clearly continued within the department after Brownell's final proposed designations in late 1954, the unusual almost total lack of reference to AGLOSO during early 1955 congressional testimony by ISD head Tompkins provides considerable, if indirect, evidence, that its status was increasingly uncertain. Tompkins never mentioned AGLOSO during March

1 testimony before a House Appropriations subcommittee and, in a lengthy statement delivered a week later to a Senate subcommittee investigating the loyalty program, his only reference to AGLOSO was in a brief aside stating that the DOJ had "cited many communist-front organizations under Executive Order 10450." On March 5, 1956, Waterman responded with alarm to a prepared statement by Brownell for the Commission on Government Security (CGS), created in 1955 by Congress to investigate the federal loyalty program, because it failed to mention AGLOSO, declaring, "I may be aware of the reasons for de-emphasizing its coverage in this report, but I do not see how we can completely eliminate it." Apparently, Waterman was not aware that Brownell had originally discussed AGLOSO in a draft statement for delivery to the CGS, which was provided to Assistant Attorney General Warren Olney and to the FBI on January 10, 1956. It declared that although there was a need for "some one person or body" to designate organizations in order to standardize federal security screenings across the government, and that such listings were "competent evidence in an administrative proceeding against an employee" constituting "a hard, cold fact to be met," AGLOSO had been "abused and distorted beyond its intent and purpose" and should be abolished in favor of another method to list dubious groups, because "when significant numbers of our people evidence suspicion or disquiet over a particular process, whether resulting from misunderstanding or other cause, it is necessary to determine whether another method of dealing with the problem, equally protective but more generally acceptable is required." Brownell suggested that the listing power be conferred on the SACB if Congress "should so desire" to amend the 1950 ISA, which had empowered that agency, and that once such action was taken "the Attorney General's list should be contemporaneously eliminated." Brownell summarized his memo by declaring that while AGLOSO had "served a necessary and useful purpose, . . . another, equally effective method, but less subject to mis-use, is required for a long-term program." According to a thirty-four-page, single-spaced, March 9, 1956, internal FBI memo the FBI had responded by noting that it felt the list "had been a valuable aid in Government security programs and condemnation in such broad general terms was unwarranted" and that subsequently Deputy Attorney General Rogers had requested FBI assistant director Lewis Nicholas to return "all copies of the proposed statement and take no action." Although before 1956 the Eisenhower administration had repeatedly and proudly pointed to its additional designations as a clear indication of its strongly anti-Communist stance, an October 6, 1956, memo from Brownell to Eisenhower, while providing a long list of actions taken by the administration to combat subversion, including the filing of 23 petitions with the SACB and the deportation of 169 "aliens with subversive backgrounds," omitted any mention of AGLOSO.[62]

The uncertain status of AGLOSO may have led to a slacking off of related activity within the DOJ: on April 28, 1955, AGLOSO head Irons angrily complained to Waterman and other subordinates that he had been unable to locate any lawyers at "5:29 or 5:30" p.m., and that he had received reports of "whole suites of offices of this empty at 5:30" and of attorneys "observed leaving the building before or exactly at 5:30." Henceforth, Irons directed, "no attorney should depart from the office before 5:30 without cogent reasons properly communicated to his superiors," especially since "as a practical matter, with all of the work we have to do" it would seem that "a great many overtime hours would be experienced." Despite the evident uncertainty concerning AGLOSO's future, both the FBI and the department continued to keep close tabs on suspect organizations: thus, on April 14, 1955, Waterman, chief of the SOS Subversive Organizations Unit, reported to head Irons that 93 of the 282 designated AGLOSO groups consisted of "active Communist organizations." Similarly, in secret May 3, 1955, Senate testimony by ISD head Tompkins, he advised that there were "approximately 90 to 100 Communist organizations presently." Less than four months later, on August 31, 1955, Alderman, who replaced Irons as SOS chief on June 6, reported to department official A. di Girolamo that the FBI had recently advised that it was investigating "273 known or suspected Communist and Communist infiltrated organizations."[63]

Perhaps to demonstrate that he was truly "on the job," Waterman, now head of the renamed "Designations Unit," informed Irons on May 3, 1955, that his group had prepared "approximately 18 memoranda recommending designation of Communist front organizations" and that "based upon our past experience, it might be well to augment this number by an additional 20 prior to a review such as we had in December, 1954" (immediately preceding Brownell's announcement proposing the 27 ultimately final designations on December 30, 1954). Waterman added that, as his unit had only two attorneys, it was able to provide only "cursory treatment" to FBI reports on suspect organizations and, especially "in view of the potential number of hearings" contesting proposed designations, urgently pleaded for the assignment of additional personnel. In a June 2, 1955, report to department administrative officer Herbert Abell, Waterman reported that his unit now had three attorneys but pleaded for more resources, as among pending matters were the review of FBI reports on 238 organizations for possible AGLOSO listing, the upcoming administrative ISL hearing, possible AGLOSO challenges by other organizations, "preparation of a new type consolidated list to include organizations recently designated," and "research to provide definitions for the various categories under which organizations have been designated, i.e., Communist, Fascist, Totalitarian and Subversive." By August 3, Waterman was reporting to SOS chief Alderman that he expected to receive additional FBI reports on "approximately 100 new organization each month," until in six months "we will have received reports on all organizations being currently investigated, when it is estimated we will have a total of 600 to 700 organizations which should be reviewed for possible designation." He indicated that he expected that about "75 to 100 new organizations" would be proposed for designation within the next two years and asked that a total of six attorneys be allocated to his unit to handle the workload. Waterman's appeal apparently bore fruit, as a November 10, 1955, memo he wrote referred to nine attorneys working in the Designations Unit.[64]

An undated department memo apparently originating from the second half of 1955, entitled "possible queries from congressional committees regarding designation program," reflects the department's continuing sensitivity over AGLOSO's future. Among the suggested statements included in the six-page double-spaced document were that AGLOSO's "sole purpose" was for the "useful guidance" of federal agencies in loyalty determinations, but, in reference to its legal filings supporting the State Department's use of AGLOSO for passport determinations and enforcement of the 1952 Gwinn Act barring AGLOSO members from public housing, it added that the department had "an obligation to support legislation which is enacted by Congress" (although there was no statutory basis for AGLOSO usage in passport screenings). The memo also maintained that AGLOSO was needed despite the 1950 creation of the SACB, because the latter board could not act in cases involving fascist, Trotskyist, Nazi, or defunct organizations, as well as concerning Communist-dominated groups lacking "enough proof available of the direct domination" of the CP to "fall within the criteria" of the ISA. Other suggested replies stated that listed groups could "present evidence to the Attorney General indicating" that their character had changed if they wished to seek removal and that non-"membership-type" "hate mongers" such as organizations headed by Gerald L. K. Smith could not be designated unless they advocated the forceful denial of constitutional rights to others, because "expressions of prejudice are, of course, protected by the Constitution." The suggested replies also argued that past activities remained relevant in loyalty screening "whether the organization was designated two years ago, five years ago, or ten years ago," but that it "would not appear appropriate" to "dismiss an employee for membership alone" in a group that was "duly contesting the designation and concerning which no final determination has been reached by the Attorney General."[65]

The End of the Post-*McGrath* Litigation, 1953–1957

Speculation in the May 4, 1953, *Washington Post* that the new AGLOSO procedures (which reversed the DOJ's long-standing posture that no hearings were needed prior to designations) had been adopted as an alternative to continuing "a legal battle that looked like a lost cause" seemed borne out when the department moved for dismissal of the pending JAFRC-NCASF district court suit on the grounds that the entire controversy had been mooted. On July 2, 1953, however, the two organizations opposed the department's motion, maintaining that their original demand for deletion from AGLOSO remained a live issue, that their complaint "did not rest solely on the allegation that the organizations had been denied notice and hearing," and that the new procedure failed to "conform to the constitutional requirement" of due process, a claim that could be "decided only in the litigation." On April 6, 1954, Federal District Court Judge Edward Curran granted the government's motion to moot the JAFRC-NCASF case, leading to yet another request to the appeals court, which combined the "mootness" issue with the organizations' earlier appeal of the April 1952 district court denial of their request for an injunction to strike their designations. In two separate 1954 rulings, the appeals court upheld Morris's denial but conditionally reinstated the case by remanding it to Curran on the grounds that he had prematurely dismissed the case as moot although "the factual and constitutional grounds upon which appellants first sought relief have persisted throughout" and because of "the protracted litigation and the nature of the issues, the Supreme Court's action upon the substantial questions presented to it" and the "possibility that it might be urged that appellants' time to seek administrative review under the rules has expired." Therefore, in its August ruling, the appeals court gave the organizations an additional ten days (following a formal order from the district court on remand) "within which to avail themselves of the opportunity for administrative review," adding that if they failed to do so, the government could again ask the district court to moot the case.[66]

Reporting on these developments in an August 11 letter to his coplaintiffs, NCASF executive director Morford declared that the NCASF would not submit to the department regulations, which he termed a "phony procedure" and a "rigged business from the outset" in which the "Attorney General remains the final authority and bases his decision on the material gathered by his own DOJ, the FBI, etc." Therefore, Morford reported, "we are this week entering a Motion for a rehearing before the Court of Appeals" to declare that "the least we are entitled to is a decision, even if against us, so that we will have the basis for an appeal to the U.S. Supreme Court" in the hopes that the high Court would "face the constitutional issues in this whole controversy as they were unwilling to do in their first decision. We don't want any more playing around with this serious issue." On August 16, 1954, the two organizations asked the appeals court to reconsider its decision on the grounds that pursuing administrative review of their designation would be fruitless because the attorney general's earlier court affidavits terming them subversive and his request that the SACB designate them "Communist fronts" made it "inconceivable" that any administrative process leading to his determination could be anything but a "sham and that in fact no legitimate administrative review is provided in the rules issued by the Attorney General." They asked the court to rule on the merits of the case because it should be "unnecessary to go back to the District Court to obtain a determination on a legal issue which is ripe for decision by this Court," while remanding it for a determination "as to whether or not the appellants are required to apply for such a hearing will serve no purpose except further to prolong this litigation which is now more than six years old." The two groups urged the court to rule on the underlying constitutional issues so that "that review may be sought to the Supreme Court and the issues in this case finally determined" and "not kept open indefinitely."[67]

In February 1955, JAFRC disbanded, citing government "harassments, persecutions and prosecutions" making it "impossible to carry on the good and necessary work that we have carried on since our inception." As a result, in May the government dropped its SACB proceedings against JAFRC and in September, District Judge F. Dickinson Letts, acting with the concurrence of both the government and a JAFRC lawyer, dismissed the organization from its joint suit with NCASF. Before JAFRC was dismissed from the suit and after the appeals court refused to reconsider its August 1954 ruling, the case was remanded to the district court, which on March 7, 1955, gave NCASF ten days to request an administrative hearing. After NCASF failed to do so, on November 15, 1955, District Court Judge Luther Youngdahl granted the government's request for summary judgment because "under the Attorney General's rules such [in]action must be held to constitute an acquiescence in the designation" and because he declined to accept the plaintiff's assumption that "administrative hearings would be a sham" or would not comply with constitutional due process requirements. He added that he could not accept the plaintiff's apparent assumption that the "Attorney General would not alter his conclusion even if presented with facts to warrant such a change."[68]

On February 8, 1956, the NCASF sustained another blow when the SACB ruled it a "communist front" organization and ordered it to register with the attorney general under the ISA. The NCASF declared that it would appeal the SACB holding to the courts, while it meanwhile appealed Judge Youngdahl's AGLOSO ruling to the Federal Court of Appeals for the District of Columbia. The NCASF's attorney complained to the appeals court that in *McGrath* the Supreme Court had held "that the complaint states a valid cause of action" that "bristles with constitutional issues," but that the "appellants have not as yet obtained an adjudication one way or another on the substantial constitutional issues posed," which it termed the "least the appellants are entitled to." On February 28, 1957, the appeals court handed down what would be the final legal ruling in almost ten years of challenges by the NCASF to its AGLOSO listing. The court affirmed Youngdahl's ruling granting the government summary judgment due to NCASF's failure to utilize the DOJ's 1953 administrative hearing procedure, holding that the organization could not thus "default" yet still litigate in the courts absent a "showing of the inadequacy of the prescribed administrative relief" or "threatened or impending irreparable injury to flow from a possible delay incident" to pursuing "the authorized and prescribed procedure." The court concluded that it would continue to enforce "the long-settled rule of judicial administration that no one is entitled to judicial relief for a supposed or threatened injury until the prescribed administrative remedy has been exhausted. . . . The plight of the appellants is of their own choice and of their own making."[69]

In a March 18, 1957, letter to NCASF supporters, Executive Director Morford reported that the NCASF had for over ten years given the government "no quarter," but that "we know that our chances [of winning a Supreme Court appeal] are slim." On July 22, 1957, Morford reported that based on the feedback he had received, he "took the authority" to advise the NCASF attorney "that we would not try to go up to the U.S. Supreme Court" because the "chances of being granted a hearing were small" and the printing costs for an appeal were substantial. While promising that the NCASF would continue to legally fight the SACB's separate order that it register as a "Communist front," Morford concluded his final letter on the AGLOSO case by declaring,

> We kept the government in hot water on it a long, long time and at one point, as you remember, got a favorable decision from the U.S. Supreme Court [in *McGrath*] which caused the Attorney General to set up a new Presidential Order and make a gesture—it was a phony gesture—in the direction of due process. But then it is wise sometimes to withdraw on one front provided you are prepared to continue to fight on another.

After another six years of litigation on the SACB ruling, Morford's prediction that "some day we are going to win in the courts," made in a July 27, 1956, letter to supporters, came true. On May 16, 1963, the U.S. Court of Appeals for the District of Columbia held that the SACB's evidence suggesting substantial CP domination of the NCASF was "negligible" and thus its finding that the organization was "directed, dominated or controlled" by the CP was "not supported by a preponderance of probative evidence." None of the nation's major newspapers reported the court's ruling.[70]

4

AGLOSO under Attack and in Decline, 1955–1969

Congressional and Legal Attacks upon AGLOSO, 1955–1958

The general political tide with regard to AGLOSO clearly turned in 1955, when the loyalty program in general, and AGLOSO in particular, came under increasingly withering and sustained attack from broad sectors of American society, echoing a general sense that the post–World War II Red Scare had gone too far. Although this sense was perhaps most clearly reflected in the Senate's censure of Joseph McCarthy in December 1954, it was also greatly bolstered by the results of the November 1954 congressional elections, in which Democrats gained control of both House and Senate, and a diminution of Cold War tensions, as was especially reflected by the 1953 Korean War armistice and the first post-1945 Russian-American summit, held at Geneva with President Eisenhower in attendance in 1955. Perhaps the strongest single blow against AGLOSO was a series of 1955 verbal attacks on it by former Sen. Harry Cain (R-WA), a Subversive Activities Control Board (SACB) member and former McCarthy supporter, but it also came under attack in a series of congressional hearings and a variety of setbacks inflicted by the courts. After 1955, no additional designations were made and the significance and even public knowledge of AGLOSO very gradually faded until President Richard Nixon unsuccessfully attempted to "revive" it in 1971.

Sen. Cain, whose reputation was that of a hard-line anti-Communist, startled his backers—and virtually everyone else—when, starting in early 1955, he suddenly began publicly denouncing the federal loyalty program—especially AGLOSO—in a series of widely publicized and highly influential speeches that caused a sensation, often obtaining front-page coverage in leading newspapers such as the *New York Times* and the *Washington Post*. For example, on March 18, 1955, speaking to the National Civil Liberties Clearing House in Washington, D.C., Cain attacked AGLOSO as outdated and unfair, declaring that many listed organizations were defunct and that many accused of AGLOSO affiliations had joined the groups in question years before they were listed beginning in 1947. Noting that recently Attorney General Herbert Brownell had announced his intention to designate the National Lawyers Guild (NLG), Cain declared that "had I been an enterprising law school undergraduate or Negro lawyer in the late 1930s, I would probably have joined it," at a time when the American Bar Association (ABA) banned blacks and undergraduates. According to Cain, using AGLOSO concerning pre-1947 affiliations, save actual CP membership, was "causing an extravagant and futile waste of time and energy," especially since many of the listed groups "have been dead for years and in this sense they are defenseless," while many who joined them did so in complete innocence during the 1930s and World War II. According to Cain, "A person may have been a dupe in joining a listed organization which is thought now to have been subversive, but it does not follow that he necessarily was disloyal." Echoing Sulzberger's earlier proposal, he urged a "cutoff" in consideration of pre-1947 non-CP affiliations, along with prompt hearings to "liquidate" the list by clearing out "all of the dead wood" and adjudicating those proposed for listing "through procedures which our country supports." In any case, Cain maintained, "an examination of a person's record over an eight-year period from 1947 to 1955 is sufficient" to judge their usefulness and loyalty. In a May 1955 New York speech, Cain termed AGLOSO a "vastly mis-leading" and dangerous tool that was promoting a "contagion" of "distrust, sus-picion and misgivings" and being perverted by "busybodies, super patriots and vigilante groups" to stifle American freedoms and "to ostracize free citizens, to denounce and condemn them, to prohibit legitimate activities of individuals and to place other citizens outside the law." In a late 1955 Washington, D.C., speech to the National Conference on Citizenship, which had originally been sponsored by the Department of Justice (DOJ) and whose initial meeting had been inau-gurated by then–attorney general Clark, Cain received a standing ovation as he charged that, due to AGLOSO, Americans were "much less free to speak, to think, to join, to learn and to travel than we were 10 years ago," although its merits had "never been adjudicated by any judicial body" and therefore the attorney general "can list whatever organization he pleases."

While Cain's role has been ignored or seriously underplayed by most histori-ans of the post–World War II Red Scare, many contemporary observers agreed that he played a critical role in discrediting AGLOSO and helping to generally defuse anti-Communist hysteria. Thus, a June 15, 1956, *Christian Science Moni-tor* article termed Cain's "one-man crusade" responsible "for much" of a "sudden reassessment of federal security regulations," and a July 3 *New York Times* edi-torial declared that "the most telling protest against" AGLOSO had issued from Cain, "distinguished" for years by the "virulence of his anti-communist zeal." Rep. Stewart Udall (D-AZ) told the House in July 1956, "I think it is unanimously agreed by those who have followed our security program carefully that no one has contributed more during the last 18 months towards putting common sense and fair play into that system than has former Senator Harry P. Cain." At an Oc-tober 1956 testimonial dinner following Cain's resignation from the SACB, Thur-man Arnold, a former high official in the DOJ and former federal appeals court judge, declared that Cain had "woke the conscience of America" from the spread of "fear and suspicion," and as a result history "will give him pages" while "others will be lucky to get footnotes."[1]

Partly inspired by Cain's attacks, the newly Democratic-controlled Congress organized and conducted three separate hearings in 1955 that featured strong attacks on AGLOSO. In March, a Senate Government Operations Subcommittee held extensive hearings on Sen. Hubert Humphrey's (D-MN) proposal that a bipartisan commission be established to review all government security programs, an initiative that Congress eventually approved over the opposition of the Eisenhower administration. While the overall administration of the federal security program was the primary focus of the hearings, AGLOSO was singled out for attack by representatives of the CIO and ACLU. Thus, Ernest Angell, chairman of the ACLU's board of directors, testified that although there was a need for some "defined basis for judging an employee's associations," AGLOSO should be "re-evaluated" to exclude "dead horses" or organizations such as the Socialist Workers Party (SWP), membership in which would not be "really relevant in determining whether an individual's employment constituted a security risk." Angell also asserted that the names of organizations merely proposed for designation should not be publicized, that the administrative hearing regulations, "while not necessarily resulting in unfairness, do permit unfair methods to be used with impunity," and that the listing of "bona fide" defense committees, in particular, created an "additional evil" by interfering with legitimate "fund raising for proper defense purposes and thus constitutes a violation of the right to a fair trial."[2]

Hearings before a Senate Post Office and Civil Service subcommittee, chaired by Sen. Olin Johnston (D-SC), while also focusing generally on the federal loyalty program, heard considerable testimony alleging abuses of AGLOSO. Testifying on June 2, 1955, Cain urged a general reform of the security program but made AGLOSO his central focus, declaring that using past membership in organizations to determine current security risks was a "warped and wormy measuring rod" that might even place a dozen or so members of Congress who had been accused of sponsoring precursors of the AGLOSO-listed Civil Rights Congress (CRC) "under suspicion." Will Maslow, director of the Commission on Law and Social Action of the American Jewish Congress, termed the preparation of lists of "alleged subversive organizations" by government officials unconstitutional and urged at least implementing a "cutoff date" before which alleged affiliations with "Communist-front" organizations would not be considered "a danger to the U.S." Referring to revelations that federal employees and soldiers had been fired or disciplined for associations with relatives alleged to have AGLOSO connections, Irving Feldman, director of the ACLU's Washington, D.C., office, told the subcommittee, "Perhaps this is the first time in our history that having a family has become a dangerous thing," because although sometimes "sympathetic association through blood relationship or otherwise, of an individual in a sensitive position with those who have Communistic sympathies" might raise legitimate concerns, such considerations had been "too automatically and unrealistically applied," as in most such cases "no attempt was made to relate the significance of that relationship to the character of the individual concerned."[3]

Eleven days of massively publicized November 1955 hearings on the federal security program by the Senate Judiciary Committee (SJC) Subcommittee on Security and Constitutional Rights, chaired by Sen. Thomas Hennings (D-MO), included one six-hour session entirely devoted to evidence and testimony concerning the widespread use, and alleged abuse, of AGLOSO by federal, state, local, and private authorities. In announcing the hearings on November 12 and opening them two days later, Hennings reported that preliminary staff research had "uncovered a far-flung use" of AGLOSO, including "its spread into areas that do not have the remotest connection with the national security," while after the special AGLOSO session, chief counsel Len Hocker declared the testimony had demonstrated that AGLOSO and similar lists had been used "indiscriminately and carelessly, and perhaps ineffectively" throughout the United States. Testimony before Henning's subcommittee included Delaware state police criminal investigations chief Carl Lawrence's report that, in attempting to enforce a law requiring all AGLOSO members who resided in or passed through Delaware to register with state authorities, he had been unknowingly using the far larger House of Representatives Committee on Un-American Activities (HUAC) listing, which he testified he had gotten after writing to the DOJ for a copy of AGLOSO. Lawrence added that no one had either ever registered or been prosecuted for failing to register, because, with up to 75,000 automobiles passing through the state daily, enforcing the law was "pretty nearly impossible." District of Columbia Superintendent of Insurance Albert Jordan testified that in late 1953 he had begun inquiring of applicants for licenses to sell insurance if they had ever had AGLOSO affiliations, since those with such ties might be "an improper person" for such licensing, although he conceded having "had no trouble with Communists before that date, and as a matter of fact, we have had no trouble with them since that date."[4]

ABA president Smythe Gambrell defended his organization's policy of asking all applicants for membership to report past and present AGLOSO affiliations because, while such ties had not been an absolute bar to joining the association, they raised a "flag" that caused the ABA to take a "second look" at the applicant to check if "his attitude towards our country is not good" and ensure that all members were "good, loyal and true Americans." However, he announced at the hearing that while an admitted Communist would be "flatly turned down and we wouldn't even inquire about him," the ABA would henceforth ask if applicants were members of any "subversive" group rather than especially referencing AGLOSO. Herbert Gaston, chairman of the World War II Interdepartmental Committee on Employee Investigations (ICEI), which had circulated to government agencies the "Biddle" AGLOSO, testified that he regarded the entire procedure he had participated in as "improper," because no organization should be designated "subversive" unless so determined by a "court or by a board having quasi-judicial powers and following recognized judicial procedure." He added, "I do not think we need Russian or Fascist types of coercion to preserve confidence in the American system." Yale University law professor Ralph Brown referred to the DOJ hearing regulations, especially the authorized withholding of classified information, as amounting to "half a hearing," although he concluded that such "would probably be better than when there is no hearing." He added that AGLOSO was "often used as a substitute for intelligence" because "you have got a list and there it is; you do not go any further," yet it was "almost valueless" for the purpose of warning the general public about dubious groups, and "we should stop and ask ourselves whether it is the business of Government to draw up official lists of proscribed organizations."

Probably the most unexpected 1955 congressional blow to AGLOSO came from the SJC's Senate Internal Security Subcommittee (SISS), a group so widely known as staunchly anti-Communist that its June 28 report highly critical of AGLOSO's form and application garnered front-page headlines in the *Washington Post* and extensive publicity elsewhere. Thus, a July 3, 1955, *New York Times* article, headlined "Attorney General's List Comes under New Attack," declared that, coming from "such a pulpit for notorious crusaders against subversion" as SISS chairman Sen. William Jenner (R-OH) and Sen. Pat McCarran (D-NV), "it can be taken for granted that the people in charge have snapped to attention." The SISS report declared that AGLOSO had been "greatly and quite generally misconceived" as well as "widely misunderstood and misapplied," especially because it did not constitute an "adjudication" concerning organizations by the attorney general, but rather the listings were intended simply as advice to the president to be considered as "only one factor" in evaluating federal security cases. The report declared that while it was "technically true, in a legal sense, that no sanctions flow" from AGLOSO listing, "it is clear that, in a practical sense, there is a detriment, if not to the organization itself, certainly to members of the organization" and that applicants for nongovernment jobs that required security clearance "in most cases" could not obtain employment if they had belonged to an AGLOSO organization. SISS characterized this flawed situation as not arising directly from AGLOSO, but rather from a "system which, for the sake of expediency," had permitted AGLOSO to be "misconceived, and the list itself to be misused." It urged the attorney general to "as promptly as possible" publish a handbook with a "compilation of factual information with respect to the listed organizations" that would allow membership in them to be intelligently interpreted for security purposes, including their dates of formation and (if applicable) dissolution; their period under "subversive" domination, if such was "not coextensive with the existence of the organization cited"; the organizations' activities and geographical location; the nature of their principal connections with subversive groups; and their "principal subversive or subversive-seeking" goals. The report made clear that it was not calling for AGLOSO's demise; thus, it declared that the DOJ "urgently" needed more attorneys for its Subversive Organization Section (SOS).[5]

The SISS report revealed that the subcommittee had met in executive session on May 3, 1955, with DOJ officials William Tompkins and David Irons and SACB members Cain and Thomas Herbert to help prepare its recommendations. Internal DOJ documents generated immediately after the meeting reveal an unenthusiastic response to the suggestion that the attorney general publish an AGLOSO handbook. Thus, Internal Security Division (ISD) attorney Benjamin Pollack declared that the department lacked the manpower to compile such a guide, that there was no need for it for security screening purposes because the FBI had "always furnished such information" on request from security officers, and that it would not be useful to a general audience without including classified information that could not be made public. SOS head Irons declared that his impression was that the department's position was that "security officers do not need to know anything more about the character of organizations beyond the fact of designation" and that FBI reports he had seen "said nothing about the nature of the organizations beyond the flat statement" that they had been designated or the "organization was described as follows by the California Un-American Activities Committee or the like." By the second half of 1955, the department's response to the SISS suggestion apparently crystallized into flat rejection, as proposed responses to possible congressional queries concerning AGLOSO stated that a "handbook might, in some instances, assist security officers and on other occasions would lead to confusion and would result in the security officers reaching various designations with respect to the same organizations," and "in view of the careful [AGLOSO designation] procedure," "it would seem inappropriate to summarize this information and ask the security officer to oversee such evaluation."[6]

Aside from the intense 1955 congressional assault upon AGLOSO, the list also suffered a number of judicial rebuffs at about the same time. Many of them resulted from the 1952 congressional "Gwinn Amendment," which barred aiding local and state authorities in funding any federally subsidized public housing units occupied by any "member of an organization designated as subversive by the Attorney General." Passage of the amendment, which potentially affected about 800,000 people living in almost 200,000 public housing units, was apparently motivated by two perceptions: that governmentally funded housing was "socialized housing" that competed with the private real estate market and that the families who lived in public housing (by law limited to the very poor) included those most likely to be attracted to "subversive" doctrines. House enactment of the amendment was so unexpected that, according to a front-page United Press story in the April 20, 1952, *New York Times*, "federal housing officials almost fell off their swivel chairs" upon hearing the news. Following weeks of frantic efforts by the DOJ to determine exactly what was intended by the amendment, Deputy Attorney General Ross Malone wrote to House and Home Finance Agency administrator Raymond Foley on August 22, 1952, that the department had concluded that it encompassed "all organizations designated pursuant to the [AGLOSO] executive order whether or not they come under the subheading of 'subversive.'" Following additional communications between the housing agency, the DOJ, and the Budget Bureau, the Public Housing Authority (PHA) directed all federally subsidized local housing officials to adopt an affidavit incorporating the entire AGLOSO list of slightly over 200 organizations and to require a representative of all public housing families to certify that neither they nor, to their best "information, knowledge and belief," any other person within their domicile, belonged to "any such organization."[7]

Most editorial comments about the amendment and attempts to enforce it were extremely hostile. The April 22, 1952, *Washington Post* termed the amendment "absurd" and inquired, "Why not extend the loyalty oath to cover all applicants for books in the public library or to all those who benefit from publicly supported trash collection?" The June 3, 1955, *Commonweal* sarcastically maintained that "we should all sleep easier in our beds tonight" due to the amendment, and asked, "Exactly what are subversives supposed to subvert in housing projects?" The total number of "refuseniks" turned out to be extremely low, but many of them proved to be extremely tenacious, legally savvy, and ultimately successful in their defiance of and struggle against the Gwinn Amendment. According to a front-page April 23, 1953, *New York Times* United Press account, only 45 of the 61,000 family representatives thus far requested to sign the oath had refused, including some who objected on civil liberties grounds but were not necessarily AGLOSO-affiliated. Ultimately, according to court filings and press accounts, by mid-1955 almost twenty lawsuits were filed in at least eight states challenging the amendment's constitutionality or enforceability, and the government lost in every instance in which a "court of last resort," such as a state supreme court, had ruled. Newspaper accounts published in mid-1955 reported that attempts to enforce the amendment had cost hundreds of thousands of dollars, thousands of hours in legal work, and mountains of paper but led to the eviction of only one tenant, who had lost in a lower court and moved out (according to earlier published accounts, at least seven New York City and Newark tenants had left public housing following eviction orders for refusing to sign).[8]

In general, the government's defense of the Gwinn Amendment was soundly rejected by the courts, although with one major exception, such holdings were on limited or technical grounds that avoided frontal challenges to the fundamental constitutionality of banning members of subversive organizations from public housing. Thus, the Illinois Supreme Court, in *CHA v. Blackman* (122 N.E. 2d 522, 1954), rejected the constitutionality, not of the amendment itself, but of evicting tenants for refusing to sign the disclaimer without proof of individual knowledge that the organizations to which they belonged "in fact" advocated forceful overthrow of the government, a procedure voided for violating "due process of law." The court added that while the purpose of public housing was to "eradicate slums and provide housing for persons of low-income," the "exclusion of otherwise qualified persons" solely due to AGLOSO membership "has no tendency whatever to further such purpose." On July 20, 1955, the U.S. Court of Appeals for the District of Columbia, in a ruling (*Rudder v. U.S.*, 226 F. 2d 51) given front-page treatment in the *New York Times*, held that refusal to sign the AGLOSO disavowal could not sustain eviction from public housing because the Gwinn Amendment required ousting members of organizations designated as "subversive," yet the vast majority of AGLOSO groups had never specifically been deemed "subversive" but were on a consolidated list of groups labeled "totalitarian, fascist, communist or subversive," among other categories. The appeals court also held that refusal to sign the disavowal did not constitute proof of membership in any AGLOSO organization and therefore the government had acted "arbitrarily" in its eviction proceedings. It added that even proof of membership in an organization while "knowing nothing of its character, would be an arbitrary ground" for eviction; this was held especially so since neither the tenants involved in the case nor the listed organizations had been granted a hearing and, in any case, AGLOSO sought to measure federal employee loyalty, not to bar tenants from public housing, and "whatever validity the designation may have in connection" with its intended purpose, "in connection with other purposes it may not even be evidence." However, the court explicitly declined to rule on the constitutionality of the amendment, declaring there was no need to do so absent proof of AGLOSO membership. The New Jersey Supreme Court, in *Kutcher v. Housing Authority of Newark* (119 A. 2d 1, 1955), similarly held that the consolidated AGLOSO list contained many groups that had not specifically been designated as "subversive" and that therefore refusal to disavow membership in the entire list "was not proof that the tenant was a member of a subversive organization"; it added that even such proof, absent evidence of individual knowledge of a group's character, could "not sustain an administrative decision to evict a tenant from public housing."[9]

The most crushing blow to attempts by local housing authorities to enforce the Gwinn Amendment was delivered by the Supreme Court of Wisconsin on June 1, 1955, in *Lawson v. Housing Authority of the City of Milwaukee* (70 N.W. 605), which held the amendment violated the free speech provisions of the U.S. and Wisconsin constitutions. As Milwaukee housing authorities subsequently noted in an unsuccessful attempt to obtain U.S. Supreme Court review of the ruling, this was the first (and only) ruling "decided solely upon the grounds that enforcement of the Gwinn Amendment results in a violation of the First Amendment of the Federal Constitution." The Wisconsin Court declared that, in a case where one of the tenants who refused to sign was admittedly an AGLOSO member, housing officials had not shown how "the occupation of any units of a federally aided housing project by tenants who may be members of a subversive organization threatens the successful operation of such housing projects," and since free speech rights had been held inviolate by the courts absent the need to "prevent a substantial evil," the "possible harm which might result in suppressing freedoms of the First Amendment outweigh any threatened evil posed by the occupation of members of subversive organizations of units in federally aided housing projects." As in Milwaukee, Los Angeles authorities appealed to the Supreme Court for reconsideration of their 1955 loss in the appellate division of the Superior Court of Los Angeles (the highest court in California for appeals from municipal court rulings) in the case of *Housing Authority of the City of Los Angeles v. Cordova* (279 P. 2d 215). Backers of the Gwinn Amendment were dealt severe blows when the high Court refused to review either lower court decision, letting the Wisconsin *Lawson* ruling stand on November 7, 1955 (350 U.S. 882) and the California *Cordova* ruling on February 27, 1956 (350 U.S. 969).

Although, technically, Supreme Court refusal to hear a case makes no legal statement, the practical effect of the Court's inaction was to doom the Gwinn Amendment. In the immediate aftermath of *Lawson*, which was front-page news in the November 8, 1955, *Washington Post,* PHA officials maintained that they still planned to enforce Gwinn everywhere except in Wisconsin, adopting the technically accurate position that, lacking a definitive Supreme Court ruling, the Wisconsin Supreme Court decision had no legal significance elsewhere. However, after the Supreme Court's refusal to hear the *Lawson* appeal was quickly followed by 1955 New Jersey and New York rulings overturning Gwinn Amendment evictions and by the Supreme Court's refusal to hear *Cordova* in February 1956, PHA officials apparently decided to give up the ghost. The four-year-long saga of the Gwinn Amendment came to a truly bizarre and ignominious end in early August 1956, when PHA officials suddenly announced that in response to their request to the DOJ for "final" clarification of the amendment's status in early 1956, the latter had determined that the amendment had expired on June 30, 1954, as "temporary legislation" when Congress had not reenacted it after the 1954 fiscal year and that it had therefore informed all local public housing agencies on July 30 that the oath "cannot be enforced." PHA commissioner Charles Slusser nonetheless urged local authorities to still undertake to somehow "exercise administrative authority to prevent occupancy of any low-rent housing project by any person who is subversive." The PHA announcement failed to refer to either the agency's 1954 internal determination that the amendment was "permanent" legislation, or, as the *Washington Post* wryly reported, to the "legal beating" the government had been taking "in courts across the land." News coverage of the PHA's announcement included, on August 4, a front-page *New York Times* story and even a *London Times* dispatch. By then, according to press reports, about two dozen courts had struck down the Gwinn oath, and PHA officials complained that enforcing it had ensnared housing officials in a maze of administrative work, as well as sometimes leading to confrontations with tenants who took stands such as, "I'll sign your oath if you make sure I get hot water in this house." The August 11 *Washington Post* editorially greeted the news of the amendment's demise by terming it an "abomination which never was effective in combating subversion and which offended the sense of dignity of many Americans," while asking, "if, as the [Justice] Department now says, the oath requirement was in the form of an appropriations rider which expired on June 30, 1954, why is this just being discovered now? Where has the attention of the Department and of public housing officials been for the last two years?"[10]

The 1955 New Jersey Gwinn Amendment *Kutcher* case discussed above involved James Kutcher, who became perhaps the most famous individual victim of AGLOSO and whose case severely discredited the list. His story attracted massive, often front-page, press coverage for almost ten years, as he fought and won a series of court cases rebuffing governmental attempts to punish him for his SWP membership. Kutcher, who became widely known as the "legless veteran" (an appellation first used by journalist I. F. Stone), had fought during a series of World War II campaigns before both of his legs were blown off by a German mortar shell during the critical battle of San Pietro, Italy, in late 1943 (gaining him a Purple Heart). He had been an SWP member since 1936 and was still a member when he was hired as a VA file clerk in 1946. As discussed in chapter 2, the SWP, a socialist but bitterly anti-Stalinist and anti-Soviet group supporting the views of ex-Bolshevik leader Leon Trotsky, originated as a splinter group from the American CP in 1928 following Trotsky's falling out with Stalin. Although it was a political party that openly contested elections (obtaining 13,000 votes in the 1948 presidential election on a platform advocating socialization of all industry), it was included among the ninety organizations listed in the December 1947 first Truman AGLOSO. In the subsequent 1948 revision, the SWP was specifically characterized an organization seeking "to alter the form of government of the U.S. by unconstitutional means." In a December 17, 1948, ruling, the Loyalty Review Board (LRB) held that mere membership in the SWP and the four other groups so categorized, even absent evidence of individual illegal conduct, required "mandatory" dismissal under the 1939 Hatch Act, which banned federal employees from belonging to "any political party or organization which advocates the overthrow of our constitutional form of government." Subsequently, Kutcher was fired from his VA job, deprived of his VA pension, and subjected to attempts to oust him and his aged parents from public housing under the Gwinn Amendment (his salary and pension provided the sole support for his parents as well as himself), essentially purely due to his open SWP membership.[11]

Kutcher, who could walk only with the aid of two artificial limbs and two canes, consistently denied that he or the SWP advocated anything other than the peaceful introduction of socialism in the United States and repeatedly noted that he and the SWP detested the Soviet Union. Thus, he declared, "I do not advocate force and violence to achieve socialism; the only time in my life I ever practiced force and violence was under the orders given me in the Army by the U.S. Government." Kutcher added that he had not been asked about his political views when he was drafted, that "the German mortar crew did not ask me" when his legs were shot off during World War II, and the "army surgeons did not ask me" when "they amputated my legs." After an eight-year legal struggle, Kutcher was restored to his job by the courts—which issued a landmark blow against AGLOSO by holding that federal employees could not be fired for mere membership in AGLOSO organizations—but he had to file yet another lawsuit to regain his back pay (which he won in 1958, ten years after his original firing). In the meantime, Kutcher also won restoration of his VA pension and defeated the attempt to oust him from public housing. Kutcher's lengthy ordeal, featuring his low-key but extremely eloquent expressions of his plight, attracted widespread public attention and sympathy and severely discredited AGLOSO and, to some extent, the entire loyalty program. Thus, the December 24, 1955, *Washington Post* declared that few Americans could learn about the Kutcher case without weeping for their country and asked, "What has the majesty of the U.S. descended to when a crippled veteran can be so hounded and harassed in the name of national security! Perhaps the only words fit for this folly are words peculiarly appropriate to this season: 'Forgiven them, Father; for they know not what they do.'"[12]

On January 9, 1956, only three weeks after Kutcher's Gwinn Act victory in New Jersey, front-page stories in the *Washington Post* and the *New York Times* reported that, following a widely publicized hearing, the VA had decided to restore Kutcher's $329 monthly pension because it had "determined that all the available evidence does not measure up" to the "quantum of proof" required to establish that Kutcher had "beyond a reasonable doubt" acted to "knowingly and intentionally render assistance to an enemy of the U.S." When he won his VA job back in an April 20, 1956, federal appeals court ruling (*Kutcher v. Higley*, 235 F. 2d 505), the story was again front-page news in the *New York Times* and heavily covered elsewhere in the media. Although the VA restored his job with full seniority on June 20, 1956, and soon after even awarded him a ten-year length-of-service pin (although eight of those years had been spent on suspension while he challenged his firing), it refused to provide what Kutcher estimated was over $20,000 in back pay due him. Kutcher's ten-year ordeal finally came to an end on June 4, 1958, when the U.S. Court of Claims awarded him $13,589.94 in back pay, based on his $42 weekly salary when he was suspended in 1948 (the Court held that under the relevant statute it could not compensate Kutcher for automatic pay increases he would have received had he served continuously in his job). The Kutcher case probably attracted more public attention and sympathy than any other single development connected to AGLOSO, and thus the "legless veteran" contributed substantially to the gradual discrediting of the feared "list" that cast so long a shadow across the "land of the free" after 1947. (Ironically, Kutcher was expelled from the SWP in 1983 as a result of internal factionalism. When he died in 1989 he had become so forgotten that no major national newspaper, including the *Washington Post* and the *New York Times*, bothered to publish an obituary).[13]

Many of the repeated legal rebuffs dealt to AGLOSO in the Gwinn Amendment and Kutcher cases were handed down almost simultaneously with another harsh legal blow against AGLOSO issued on June 23, 1955, by the federal court of appeals for the District of Columbia in *Shachtman v. Dulles* (225 F. 2d 938). Overturning a lower court ruling, the court struck down the State Department's refusal of a passport to Independent Socialist League (ISL) national chairman Max Shachtman due to his organization's AGLOSO designation. As front-page coverage in both the *New York Times* and the *Washington Post* (the *Times* also published a full text) noted, the court delivered a stinging rebuff to the State Department's claim that there were "no judicially reviewable limitations" upon its "power to refuse to grant passports," including specifically for affiliation with "subversive organizations." Instead, it unanimously held that citizens had a "natural right" to travel abroad that could not be denied without "due process of law" and that AGLOSO membership was insufficient grounds for passport denial, "which the law cannot reconcile with due process," especially as the federal loyalty program did not consider affiliation with a listed group "alone" to warrant dismissal. The ruling specifically termed the government's action "arbitrary" since it had not denied Shachtman's allegation that the ISL had been designated "without notice or hearing or presentation of evidence or opportunity to answer" and that the group had attempted to gain a hearing "so that it could prove the injustice of the designation" for "nearly six years and on at least 15 separate occasions."

The Independent Socialist League (ISL) Hearing Case, 1955–1958

By the time the DOJ decided not to appeal *Shachtman*, the long-pending ISL AGLOSO delisting hearing under its 1953 administrative appeal procedures was finally under way. Departmental hearing officer Edward Morrissey opened the proceedings, which also involved two other AGLOSO groups, the ISL's predecessor organization, the Workers Party (WP), and its youth affiliate, the Socialist Youth League (SYL), on July 18, 1955. All three organizations had been included in the first AGLOSO list published in 1947 and were subsequently specifically categorized as "Communist" in 1948 and then redesignated without specific categorization in 1953. The ISL had disputed the listings of the three groups ever since 1947 but had to wait over two years for a hearing after immediately challenging the redesignations under the 1953 DOJ regulations. Another three years passed before the department suddenly ended the proceedings by dropping the listings of the three groups in July 1958.[14]

The ISL, WP, and SYL were small socialist groups that traced their origins to the ouster of "Trotskyists" from the American CP in 1928 following Soviet dictator Joseph Stalin's expulsion of rival Leon Trotsky from the Soviet Communist Party after a bitter dispute over politics, power, and personalities. American "Trotskyists" then formed the SWP, but in 1940 SWP dissidents, led by Shachtman, were expelled and subsequently formed the WP. The WP opposed all sides in World War II as imperialistic and actively opposed the "no strike" pledge adopted by most American unions and ultimately supported by the American CP. Informally known, along with its SYL youth group, as the "Shachtmanites," the WP supported "Communist" ideals of an end to private property, while advocating peaceful and democratic methods—including periodically contesting American elections and focusing on labor organizing. During the Cold War, the WP/ISL condemned the United States and the Soviet Union as both corrupt, imperialistic regimes that exploited ordinary workers under the slogans "Third Camp" and "Neither Washington nor Moscow." SYL member Michael Harrington later became famous for his 1962 book *The Other America*; its portrayal of American poverty jolted the nation's conscience and paved the way for President Lyndon Johnson's "War on Poverty."

The Shachtmanites always remained a tiny splinter group whose members, never exceeding 700, were mostly intellectuals who remained as isolated from American workers as from American elites. After rechristening themselves the ISL in 1949, the Shachtmanites largely abandoned electoral and labor activity and viewed themselves primarily as a propaganda organization, with most of their energies devoted to their newspaper, *Labor Action*, their magazine, *New International*, and fighting their AGLOSO listing. According to uncontested documentary material introduced at the 1955 hearing and other proceedings, on at least fifteen separate occasions between 1948 and 1955, the WP/ISL sought delisting subsequent to their 1947 AGLOSO designations. However, the DOJ repeatedly refused to grant a hearing, delist the groups, or explain the designations: for example, in response to one of Shachtman's many letters of complaint, Assistant Attorney General Alexander Campbell wrote on April 28, 1949, that President Harry Truman's executive order authorizing AGLOSO "contains no warrant or authority for disclosing the bases upon which the designations made pursuant thereto were formulated," and as the designations had been made "after careful consideration of the available information," the WP's request for delisting "must be denied." In the meantime, Shachtman and his organizations suffered the usual collateral AGLOSO damage: aside from the passport denial, in late 1951 Shachtman was barred from speaking at the University of California at Berkeley because, according to Dean of Students Hurford Stone, school policy banned "knowingly invit[ing] any officer of an organization declared to be subversive by official government sources to speak on the campus." By 1955, the ISL's membership had dwindled to less than 300.[15]

Following the DOJ's April 29, 1953, redesignation of AGLOSO organizations and its simultaneous announcement of post-*McGrath* administrative hearing procedures, in a telegram on May 4, 1953, the ISL requested a hearing at the "earliest possible date at which we may contest." In a special twelve-page issue published on September 28, 1953, which was entirely devoted to the AGLOSO controversy, *Labor Action* published the complete text of the department's July 9, 1953, "statement of grounds" for its proposed continued AGLOSO listing of the ISL, WP, and SYL, along with the text of thirty-eight interrogatories posed by the department and the ISL's responses. In essence, the "grounds" maintained that the three organizations supported principles of "revolutionary Marxism"; opposed American foreign policy in World War II, Korea, and the Cold War, as well as "the principles embodied in the Constitution"; likened the American government to Nazi Germany and Stalinist Russia, "which governments they advocated be overthrown by force and violence"; and sought to replace the American government by the "dictatorship of a privileged class," which would establish "an entirely new social philosophy and system of 'proletarian internationalism,'" to be accompanied by the "confiscation, without compensation" of "all privately owned means of production, with force if necessary." The "grounds" repeatedly strongly implied, yet never explicitly charged, the three organizations with supporting the violent and illegal overthrow of the American government, while explicitly and repeatedly charging them with harboring unpopular political opinions: thus, ground 25 maintained that they "regarded the existing form" of government "as oppressive in that they allege" it "is ruled by a minority which is exploiting the majority," and ground 23 declared that their policy included opposition to supporting "this country in any possible war between the U.S. and the Soviet Union since it would be a clash between two imperialistic powers." The accompanying thirty-eight "interrogatories" essentially requested a complete report on all ISL, WP, and SYL activities, including names and addresses of all members, officials, meeting places, printers, publication subscribers, financial contributors, associated or collaborating organizations (specifically including the CP); foreign connections of any kind; policies (including, specifically, views concerning American foreign policy, the Korean War, conscription, and the natures of capitalism and the American political and economic systems and whether and how they should be overthrown); and whether the organizations had "adopted any security measures designed to protect the identity of members or the content of intra-organization bulletins" and "if so, what are the measures?"

In their September 3, 1953, response to the department's allegations and questions, published in the September 28 *Labor Action*, the organizations, in a submission from Shachtman, refused to answer all questions requiring identifying information about members, officials, contributors, and subscribers on the grounds that such questions violated their First Amendment rights, were completely irrelevant to a determination of their AGLOSO status, and would open up such individuals to "harassment and abuse," as "all over the country" they had already endured FBI "abuse and harassment or both, either through loss of employment, through repeated visits and interrogations, or through coercive attempts to induce the individual to become an informer." The general thrust of the response concerning policies was that the three organizations favored a democratic and peaceful transition to a socialist state, that none of the allegations involved any violations of law, and that the entire AGLOSO process was part of a general "governmental persecution, prohibition or restriction of non-conformist ideas—'thought control'" that was "notoriously characteristic of Fascist, Stalinist and arch-military dictatorships" and "utterly inimical to the elementary principles of democracy." Shachtman described the ISL's "main objective" as the education and training of the "working classes of the country" by "open and democratic means, so that they may avail themselves of all their democratic and Constitutional rights to elect a Workers' Government, which will completely eliminate the present Government which, like its predecessors, we regard as capitalist," in order to "replace it with an infinitely more democratic governmental and state machinery, and then proceed gradually to reorganize the economic basis of the economy" along "socialist lines as the first great step" of a similar "reorganizing [of] the economy of the world." Shachtman said the only security measure taken by the ISL was to advise members against volunteering information, when not required by law, to anyone, including the FBI. *Labor Action* declared that the "grounds" made clear that ISL's "crime" was that "it opposes capitalism" and favored socialism, and "speaking in the frankest possible terms, the attorney general" terms "any organization which is opposed to this kind of society subversive." Shachtman's response was followed by repeated ISL requests for an immediate hearing. After two years of stalling, the DOJ finally scheduled a hearing for July 1955. Part of the delay apparently resulted from the department's difficulty in finding witnesses willing to testify that the ISL and its allied groups had, as Assistant Attorney General Tompkins wrote to FBI director Hoover on August 5, 1954, "attempted to conceal in recent years" their "basic adherence" to "the concepts of force and violence" through the use of "inconsistencies and Aesopian language," and that their real goal was to bring "about a Communist world state as envisioned by Leon Trotsky to be accomplished through the use of any means, including force, if feasible."

Shortly before the July 1955 ISL hearing began, the department suffered two closely related, widely publicized sharp rebuffs: the June 23, 1955, court decision striking down Shachtman's passport denial, discussed above, and a July 16 army announcement that, following consideration by the Army Discharge Review Board, it had granted a general discharge with "no stigma" to Barry Miller, twenty-four, who had earlier been given an "undesirable discharge" without a hearing due to his membership in the ISL and SYL while a University of Chicago student two years earlier. The *Shachtman* ruling and the delisting hearing sparked a new round of newspaper editorials denouncing AGLOSO and other aspects of the government's antisubversive campaign. Thus, the June 25, 1955, *Washington Post* termed the *Shachtman* holding a "rebuke to arbitrariness" that would "promote the recapture of civil liberties which Americans have too long allowed to fall into neglect," while the June 27 *Wall Street Journal* declared that it had "let some fresh air into the musty corridors of bureaucracy by opening this door for individual freedom." The June 25 *New York Times* hailed the decision as proving the devotion of the federal courts to constitutional liberties and expressed hope that it would help put AGLOSO "in its proper perspective" and prove "a major step toward restoration of a calm and sensible approach to the problem of internal security." A lengthy June 29 *Christian Science Monitor* analysis headed "List of 'Subversive Groups' Comes under Heavy Attack" lumped together the Shachtman ruling, Sen. Cain's attacks on AGLOSO, and the recent SISS report concluding that AGLOSO had been "widely misunderstood and misapplied" as reflecting a new climate in which AGLOSO was coming "under increasing attack."[16]

The ISL delisting hearing quickly descended into acrid disputes between the groups' attorneys, led by Americans for Democratic Action (ADA) President Joseph Rauh and hearing examiner Morrissey, with the latter repeatedly denying motions asking for clarification of both the hearing procedures he intended to use and the charges and standards utilized by the DOJ in its AGLOSO considerations. Much of the July 25, 1955, session was consumed by discussions of the difference between "capital C Communism" and "small c communism," with Rauh denying that the ISL had any connections with the CP, while avowing that it unquestionably believed in peaceful striving toward "a common ownership of the means of production and distribution," in keeping with democratic principles that could pose no "clear and present danger" of violence or possibly qualify as subversive. Department official Oran Waterman conceded that the organizations were viewed as "communist with a small 'c'" and were not charged with "being related to the Russian CP in any manner whatever," but he added that "we intend to prove force and violence" and even "small 'c' communism" entailed the use of "revolutionary means" and therefore justified the groups' AGLOSO designations. After Morrissey denied a formal motion by the ISL attorneys on July 26 that he disqualify himself as prejudiced, they announced a planned appeal to Attorney General Brownell, leading Morrissey to adjourn the hearing until Brownell ruled on the issue. On September 2, 1955, Brownell denied their petition, declaring that the ISL's allegation that Morrissey had a "fixed" determination to find against them was "not even remotely supported by the facts" they had submitted.[17]

Without any explanation from the department, the hearing did not reconvene until almost ten months later, on May 21, 1956. Thereupon, the government introduced two witnesses, one of whom had briefly been a WP member fifteen years earlier, who maintained the WP/ISL were oriented toward the advocacy and use of violence to bring about a socialist or Communist society. The government also read into the record over forty WP/ISL publications, including those opposing American participation in World War II and the Korean War, that it maintained demonstrated the organizations' support of the violent overthrow of the American government. In response, ISL attorneys, primarily via the introduction of their own witnesses, including Shachtman, Socialist Party (SP) leader Norman Thomas, former WP member and prominent intellectual Dwight MacDonald, and leading sociologist Daniel Bell, denied that the organization advocated violence. Thus, Shachtman declared it "not at all" the case that his organization's interpretation of Leninism required using violence, that it was "entirely possible and in many countries certain" that socialists could gain power by "normal, peaceful, democratic, constitutional means," and, quoting, from a 1950 article he had authored, that "without the realization of complete democracy all talk of the establishment of socialism is a mockery."

Following final testimony on July 11, 1956, the hearing recessed to allow the government and the ISL to submit "proposed findings." Both responded along expected lines, with the government maintaining it had proved the case outlined in its original "statement of grounds" and the ISL replying, as their attorneys summarized, that the DOJ was essentially stating that "mere disagreement with prevailing government policy or even lack of enthusiastic support therefore" was grounds for "placing organizations on the subversive list or permitting their names to remain on it." In December 1957, Morrissey, acting on a hearing record of over 3,000 pages, recommended to the new attorney general, William Rogers, that the ISL, WP, and SYL be retained on AGLOSO because they "were, and are, communistic, in the sense intended by the Executive Order [authorizing AGLOSO]," and "seek to alter the form of government of the U.S. by unconstitutional means." In appealing to Rogers on January 10, 1958, to overturn the recommendation, the ISL's lawyers told him that there "is no warrant in a free America for aggravating" the "past wrongs" inflicted on the organizations by continuing their AGLOSO listings and asked him, in "making his first civil liberties decision, to strike a blow for freedom." On July 16, 1958, the organizations' long ordeal ended when Acting Assistant Attorney General J. Walter Yeagley wrote Rauh to inform him that Rogers had issued a directive to remove the three groups from AGLOSO because he was "not satisfied that the evidence adduced at the hearings meet the strict standards of proof which should guide the determination of proceedings of this character" and that it was "impracticable due to the passage of time, the demise of possible witnesses and the unavailability of others in the absence of subpoena power," as well as the recent death of examiner Morrissey, to reopen "the proceedings for the presentation of additional evidence." Rogers's action followed an early July memo from Acting Assistant Attorney General and ISD head Yeagley to Executive Assistant to the Attorney General Harold Healey that warned that, absent a quick decisions on the ISL and other pending cases (such as that of the NLG, discussed below) the department was likely heading for imminent legal problems. Noting that no action had yet been taken, although the organizations had filed their response to Morrissey months earlier and that ISL attorney Rauh had indicated that he "intends to file suit unless the Attorney General reaches a decision in this matter in the near future," Yeagley dryly added, "This case was initiated [by the ISL's notice of contest] in May, 1953." Yeagley's memo apparently led directly to Rogers's decision to overturn the hearing examiner and delist the ISL and its two affiliates. As documented below, a year earlier the department had abandoned its cases against two designated Lithuanian organizations for fear that the Supreme Court might entirely strike down AGLOSO in those cases. A July 16, 1958, internal FBI memo reported that Rogers had decided to drop the ISL case, along with the pending NLG designation, for fear that otherwise "the cases would ultimately be carried to the U.S. Supreme Court and it was likely" that the Court would "throw out" AGLOSO entirely. Rogers "wanted to avoid this as he believed neither case" was "particular strong" and wished to avoid risking AGLOSO by "pressing" them. Hoover marked on an earlier July 11 memo from F. J. Baumgardner, head of the FBI's Internal Security Section, reporting that the FBI had learned that Rogers was contemplating dropping the ISL case, "I think we should leave it up to Dept." Baumgardner, however, had urged the bureau to argue, as it had in the Lithuanian cases, that the department had "apparently felt it had a good case" when it designated the ISL; that delisting would be a "temporizing" or "retreating" position that other listed groups would seize upon "as an opening wedge" to further attack AGLOSO and to use "for propaganda purposes; and that while the Bureau is not taking a position," its observations were "being furnished for Attorney General's assistance in arriving at a decision."[18]

ISL chairman Shachtman told the press that Rogers's action was a "historic milestone in the struggle for civil liberties" and demonstrated that AGLOSO had been "built without care or hearings." In the July 28 issue of *Labor Action*, he denounced the DOJ for taking "ten years in which to grant an elementary requirement of justice," which he said had only been reached for fear of the consequences of an adverse federal court ruling "if administrative satisfaction was not obtained." He added that since it was "surely safe to assume that the evidence (if that is what it can be called) submitted at the hearing" was the "very most that the attorney general ever had at his disposal," clearly the department "had, from the very beginning, no evidence to justify the listing of our organization," and therefore "for more than ten years it was guilty of a gross and flagrant injustice to a political organization, its member and friends, who were subjected to the sufferings, harassment, discriminations and disabilities notoriously associated" with AGLOSO. He denounced AGLOSO as being based upon the supposition that "the practice of politics requires a governmental license" and demanded its termination "along with all other forms of witch-hunting, thought-control and persecutions for democratic opinions which eat away the foundations of democratic rights." The ISL's ten-year struggle for delisting had an ironic denouement: in September 1958, less than two months after the DOJ's ruling, the ISL and the SYL merged into the SP and its youth group, the Young Peoples Socialist League, and thus disappeared. In the meantime, a DOJ official told reporters that the delisting wouldn't matter in any case, because federal loyalty boards could continue to consider ISL affiliations as grounds for firing or refusing to hire workers.[19]

A Changed Political Atmosphere, 1955–1957

Although the ISL delisting was not effected until 1958, by the second half of 1955 the combined effect of Cain's attack on AGLOSO, along with the previously recounted congressional hearings and reports and the adverse court rulings on AGLOSO in the *Shachtman* and Gwinn Act cases increasingly made clear that the temper of the country with regard to loyalty issues in general and AGLOSO in particular had significantly eased. Thus, a June 20, 1955, *Christian Science Monitor* article by highly regarded reporter Richard Strout began by declaring that "one of the biggest news stories of 1955 is the profound change of American thinking in loyalty-security cases." The August 14, 1955, *New York Times Sunday Magazine* published a lengthy article entitled, "The Security Issue: A Changing Atmosphere," by *Times* editorial board member John B. Oakes, which ratified and summarized a growing general political and journalistic consensus. He wrote that "people are breathing more easily," promising a "more rational and temperate discussion of the internal security problem" than had been "possible for several years," during which the "emphasis on loyalty oaths and forms, political and artistic blacklists based on associations torn totally out of the context of the times" and similar developments had reflected "the great failure during the last few years of national self-confidence." The *Washington Post* published a similar, lengthy article on February 12, 1956, under the headline "U.S. Has Moved Far from Loyalty Hysteria of '54," which declared that "within less than two years there has been a major shift" in American attitudes on loyalty-security issues. In an unusual article published in the November 1955 *Fortune* magazine, Supreme Court Justice Earl Warren signaled what turned out to be an imminent change in the high Court's orientation on security issues by warning that the nation must resist "day by day" the "temptation to imitate totalitarian security methods" and to require its citizens to "sacrifice" their "ancient liberties." By then, the chorus of anti-AGLOSO criticism had grown so loud that Deputy Attorney General Rogers declared on network television that the DOJ had repeatedly warned against "misuse" of the list.[20]

By late 1955 and early 1956, the changing political atmosphere was reflected in a lessened reliance upon AGLOSO by some federal agencies (and, as discussed below, in a freezing of further DOJ AGLOSO designations). Thus, on May 10, 1956, the Atomic Energy Commission announced that it would henceforth disregard past AGLOSO affiliations of its personnel if the individual withdrew from designated groups upon their listing, provided he had had no knowledge of or could subsequently establish his rejection of their "subversive aims." Two weeks earlier, the Army had announced that in a policy dated October 17, 1955, it had abandoned its earlier consideration of the affiliations and associations of soldiers unless it could be "logically inferred that the individual is motivated or influenced by or is sympathetic to, subversive aims and ideologies." The newly announced policy specifically banned reliance on the activities of "an individual's relatives or associates" unless information suggested that the person was "sympathetically influenced in thought or action by the subversive activities or ideologies" involved. In mid-1955, the Defense Department had announced it was no longer asking civilian contract employees about their associations with other individuals with alleged AGLOSO affiliations, while still requiring reports about their own AGLOSO connections. In a March 1958 ruling (*Harmon v. Brucker*, 55 U.S. 579), which was featured on the front page of the *New York Times*, the Supreme Court ordered an end to the military's practice of giving soldiers with satisfactory service records less-than-honorable discharges based solely on their preservice activities and associations, which had often been based on their AGLOSO affiliations or on the AGLOSO affiliations of their associates or relatives. The court's ruling overturned two lower federal court decisions (137 F. Supp. 475, 1956; 343 F. 2d 613, 1957), which had upheld less-than-honorable discharges of two soldiers based entirely on their preservice activities (and, in one case, the soldier's refusal to respond to questions about the political activities of his father and stepmother). The *Harmon* ruling confirmed evidence presented to Sen. Henning's November 1955 SJC hearings by Workers Defense League national secretary Rowland Watts, who testified that he had examined over 200 cases in which draftees were denied honorable discharges due to their alleged "subversive" affiliations and/or personal associations predating their military service. Bizarrely, despite the *Harmon* ruling, several months later an army reservist was given an undesirable discharge for activities undertaken after he had been transferred from active to reserve status in 1954, including his alleged membership in the AGLOSO-designated Labor Youth League and his reported 1955 attendance at the listed Jefferson School of Social Science (shortly before that institution closed its doors). The army maintained that reservists were subject to the same controls over their activities as were active-duty soldiers, a position upheld in May 1959 by federal district judge John Sirica (of subsequent Watergate fame), who ruled that "since the reserve forces are geared toward the possibility of active military duty, the required qualifications of a soldier are the same whether he be on active duty or in the reserves" (*Olenick v. Brucker*, 273 F. 2d 819). However, in December 1959 a federal appeals court ordered the case remanded back to district court for reconsideration, in a clear signal to Sirica to reverse his earlier holding.[21]

Critical evaluations concerning AGLOSO and its alleged misuse continued to be widely publicized in 1956 and 1957. Thus, at a special June 22–23, 1956, Senate Subcommittee on Constitutional Rights hearing, at which Cain alone testified (filling up over eighty pages of small type in the printed transcript), he declared that the "totalitarian practices" and use of "fascist tools" that characterized the loyalty program had turned the federal job application process into a "terrifying and inhumane trap," with the result that "scientists, universities, the foreign service, our governmental career service and research are being choked and stagnated in a mass of investigations, hearings, boards, statistics and court actions which hamper, rather than assist, our proper national purpose." Referring specifically to AGLOSO, Cain said that to list organizations "as bad without those in authority bothering to define why the organizations are bad, is to employ a weapon from the arsenal of the tyrant" and that he had "the most serious doubts about the need for a published proscription list of so-called subversive organizations in a free society." Noting that some AGLOSO groups that were subsequently controlled by Communists had originally attracted thousands of citizens who "willingly joined with anybody else" who shared their opposition to fascism before and during World War II, Cain declared, "That we continue to hold suspect the prewar and early-war membership in these endeavors, without providing an adequate opportunity to explain those memberships while relating them to how, when and where, is a premeditated insult to our intelligence and reputation for fair play." According to Cain, "The Communist has bedeviled us, but in ways which has done little to hurt us in these past ten years. Actions resulting from our fears of what we think he might do have hurt us much more deeply."[22]

Three different "mainstream" bar association organizations—which, especially in the case of the ABA, had typically been associated with support of "hardline" anti-Communist positions during the height of the Red Scare—issued reports in 1956 that strongly criticized AGLOSO's implementation. In February, the ABA's Special Committee on Communist Tactics, Strategy and Objectives found that while AGLOSO "should be an excellent public service as a source of information," its "misuse" could cause "serious injury to loyal citizens." The committee warned that the "deprivation of individual rights should be based upon the facts concerning each individual"; that the "activities and time of association of a person in such named organizations are far more important than the mere fact of membership"; and that "caution and care are of vital importance in separating the innocent, the fools and the knaves." In May, the Civil Rights Committee of the District of Columbia Bar Association asked its parent group to investigate the "establishment and utilization" of AGLOSO in view of its "apparently widespread misuse," especially as recent court decisions had strongly suggested that present or past AGLOSO membership by itself was an "incompetent and arbitrary basis for denial by a State or Federal Government agency of any right or privilege."[23]

In July 1956 a special committee of the Bar Association of the City of New York, basing its work on a fourteen-month study funded by a $100,000 grant from the Fund for the Republic, issued a report that urged wide-sweeping reforms in the federal loyalty program, including the complete abolition of AGLOSO unless substantial changes were implemented to overcome its "grave weaknesses." The report found that AGLOSO was being "misapplied" by federal, state, and local governments and private employers and concluded that its abolition would "not weaken in the slightest" the assistance which the DOJ could legitimately supply in support of federal loyalty determinations. The committee especially attacked "the fact that the list is public and bears the imprimatur of the highest law officer of the government," declaring that its publication was above all responsible for its "indiscriminate" use, yet was "in no way essential to its original purpose of giving information" to federal security personnel. According to the report, while the list was intended to be "used with care and discrimination" by the federal government, there was "strong reason to believe" federal security personnel had applied it so that mere AGLOSO membership was "taken as ground of disqualification for employment without any evidence as to the employee's knowledge of the nature of the organizations or as to the extent of his participation in its activities," an inquiry which was especially important where there was reason to believe that organizations "innocent in purpose" when formed were "later taken over" by Communists. Absent the abolition of AGLOSO, the committee recommended that all groups that had been defunct for ten years or that had "freed themselves from Communist domination" be deleted, that the list be kept current by including "new subversive organizations," but only after organizations were provided notice and hearings "in conformity with the requirements of due process of law," that information be provided about the "period and general nature of the subversive activity" of all listed groups, and that AGLOSO clearly state that membership alone did not establish "the subversive character of a member" unless this had been "made illegal by statutes."[24]

On July 21, 1956, two weeks after the publication of the latter report, the Senate Post Office and Civil Service subcommittee, one of the congressional groups that had investigated the loyalty program in 1955, characterized it as marked by "endless confusion," "positive injustice" to civil servants, and "dishonest" and "political" mudslinging by the Eisenhower administration. Among the subcommittee's numerous specific recommendations was that "clear and precise" legislation should clarify the "makeup and use" of AGLOSO. The last of the numerous major mid-1950s appraisals of AGLOSO and the federal loyalty program, an 800-page massively publicized report issued by the congressionally mandated Committee on Government Security (CGS) in late June 1957, called for sweeping changes in the overall loyalty program, which it declared had "sorely tried" public confidence and spread fear and unrest in the civil service but urged the maintenance of AGLOSO, declaring that AGLOSO or "something similar to it," was "essential" for uniformity in administering federal employee screening and that making loyalty determinations absent the list would "be more prejudicial to national security and freedom of association than the present system." Although the report recommended what it termed "major changes" to "minimize possible [AGLOSO] abuses," the net effect of the proposed reforms would have left the list substantially unchanged. According to the CGS, AGLOSO should be legislatively authorized and, with regard to "future listings only," the attorney general should be authorized to designate an organization only after a hearing before an examiner appointed by a newly created Central Security Office, with the right of appeal to a review board. However, the findings of both the hearing examiner and the appeal board would be advisory only to the attorney general and his decision would be final and not subject to further review. The proposed CGS hearing regulations were virtually identical to those in place, but the committee urged that AGLOSO affiliations not be taken as "conclusive evidence" of "unfitness for office," since such ties should be "viewed in the light of the member's knowledge of the purposes of the organizations or the extent to which such purposes had been "publicized at the time the individual," belonged and "the character and history of an organization must be closely examined, with the realization that loyal persons, ignorant of its true purpose, may have been persuaded to join for innocent reasons." The report also proposed a series of specific criteria for AGLOSO listings, most of which were extremely vague, such as that an organization sought to advance "the aims and objectives of the Communist movement" or to establish "any form of dictatorship in the U.S.," or was "affiliated with, or acts in concert with, or is dominated or controlled by" such groups.[25]

By March 2, 1956, the drumbeat of criticism directed against AGLOSO and the level of internal concern within the DOJ that the administrative hearing regulations could not survive legal scrutiny had grown so great that Assistant Attorney General and ISD head Tompkins formally recommended to Attorney General Brownell that the list be entirely abolished. He argued that AGLOSO was no longer useful because the "vast majority" of designated groups were defunct and government agencies therefore reported relying upon it "from very little to rarely," yet it was difficult to list additional groups that qualified for designation and the existing list was being misused and misinterpreted. Tompkins reported that about 230 of the 279 then-designated groups were defunct (a calculation reached by counting only once organizations listed under multiple names, while counting affiliates of organizations that were separately listed, except for the CRC, "because of their close ties to the parent organization"). He added that a total of about 300 "known or suspected Communist" organizations were "now in existence," yet only 38 were presently listed, but many nondesignated groups could not be added due to the department's "belief that factors of proof necessary in designation procedures must satisfy constitutional requirement of due process" and because "current Communist policies of [creating] short-lived organizations render it very difficult and often impossible to designate organizations until long after they become established or defunct." Tompkins added that the department felt the "presence of [both] designated and undesignated organizations [was] undesirable" because security officials were "prone to give insufficient weight to activities in undesignated organizations due primarily to fact that they have not be designated" and "many times [the] public wrongly concludes undesignated organizations have received indirectly [official] clearance."

Therefore, he continued, AGLOSO's "very existence" may have led some government agencies to "refrain from giving appropriate emphasis to membership in Communist-infiltrated organizations not listed," especially as some agency heads had the "idea that organizations not listed are not as bad as those of the list" and thus continued reliance on AGLOSO "could adversely affect" security concerns. He added that since current investigative reports included "information pertaining to undesignated organizations which are reported to be Communist-infiltrated or otherwise of questionable character," abolishing AGLOSO "could in no way impair" loyalty screenings as "organizations currently on the list could be handled in the same manner." Moreover, Tompkins said, the department had concluded that AGLOSO's widespread use by state and local governments and private organizations had led to "mishandling and misinterpretations . . . outside its intended scope," while abolishing AGLOSO would restrict the "significance of such membership" to its "originally intended area" and "no one then could then claim a classified or confidential black list was being maintained." He concluded that abolishing AGLOSO "would strengthen the [loyalty] program and prevent the abuses attendant to the publication of a list and would eradicate the idea that if an organization is not on the list it is legitimate."[26]

Upon receiving Tompkins's March 2 memo, Brownell asked that FBI director Hoover attend what proved a contentious March 12 conference, also attended by Tompkins and Deputy Attorney General Rogers, to discuss the FBI's response. According to subsequent internal FBI memos, Hoover declared that he "definitely opposed" Tompkins's proposal, as it would "seem to reduce rather than improve security," result in "greater lack of uniformity in application of security program," and lead the federal government to depend upon FBI reports "solely which would take the Bureau out of its traditional position of not evaluating information obtained by it." According to the memos, Brownell thereupon directed Tompkins to further study the issue in order to "meet, if he could" the FBI's objections to terminating AGLOSO, and the bureau subsequently "heard nothing more concerning this particular proposal." Hoover was presumably fortified at the March 12 conference by a thirty-four-page, single-spaced March 9 memorandum on AGLOSO prepared by bureau official C. H. Stanley, which included a full-scale defense of AGLOSO, essentially on the grounds that it had caused enormous damage to the Communists. Stanley declared that AGLOSO had "proved to be the most effective weapon in combating the Communist menace," as was evidenced from the "rapid demise" of organizations that are cited, "their prompt abandonment by the Communists when their effectiveness is curtailed," and the fact that they "rapidly disintegrate" upon listing. According to Stanley, AGLOSO's "effectiveness" was evidenced by the fact that, with "few exceptions," organizations proposed for designation had "defaulted rather than contest the proceedings," that government security officials felt "more confident" in making decisions when "their determinations are supported" by the list, and that the Communists had moved toward "utilizing smaller short-lived" and local organizations that "do not serve the Party's purpose nearly so effectively as organizations of long standing which are national in scope," due to AGLOSO's "deterrent" impact. AGLOSO, he maintained, "serves to eliminate the variable quality of personal evaluation by numerous individuals and provides a uniform standard," while the solution to the problem of nondesignated but dubious groups was not the "drastic step" of abolishing AGLOSO but to press for their "promptest possible designation."[27]

Stanley rejected the argument that the widespread use of AGLOSO beyond the federal employee security program posed a problem, as "to combat Communism" it was vital that "agencies, organizations and individuals other than the Federal Government have available to them some definitive data for their guidance and use in connection with their own operations." Stanley agreed with Tompkins that about 230 of the "279 organizations currently designated" were defunct but placed the number of "known or suspected Communist front organizations" in a "current active status being actively investigated" at 273. Much of his memo focused on the threat the proposed AGLOSO abolition might pose to the FBI's workload and reputation (echoing Hoover's well-known obsession with avoiding "embarrassment" to the bureau). Such a decision might dump in the FBI's lap the responsibility of answering the 650 letters and phone calls that Tompkins indicated the DOJ received monthly concerning AGLOSO, Stanley said. He also asserted that the proposed use of FBI reports "in lieu of AGLOSO" would lead to the "most undesirable" result that "criticism now directed against the list would be focused on the FBI" and "place the FBI in a position where it may be accused of evaluating organization activities and thus assuming responsibilities intended for the AG." Stanley argued that such reports "might well" be characterized as a "secret black-list," resulting in "considerable criticism" of the FBI and "jeopardizing" its "traditional position as a fact finding organization" in the "eyes of the public." Even in AGLOSO's absence there would be a need for "prepared authoritative characterizations of the subversive organizations" for use in federal employee screening, Stanley added, but to preserve the bureau's "position as a fact finding agency," such characterizations "should not be the responsibility of the FBI."

Following the March 12 meeting, the DOJ proceeded on two parallel but contradictory tracks, on the one hand considering abolishing AGLOSO (apparently without informing the FBI) and on the other hand gearing up to designate scores of additional organizations. On April 5, 1956, Designations Unit head Waterman, responding to what he described as a request from SOS chief Alderman to comment on a draft of a "letter to the White House recommending the elimination" of AGLOSO, indicated that he objected to the suggestion in the draft that the department had "insufficient evidence" to designate the "great majority" of the 273 existing non-AGLOSO organizations referred to as "known or suspected Communist influenced organizations," as this wording suggested that it was "a question of the Department" not "keeping up with these cases" when the problem was the FBI's failure to furnish the "necessary information to reflect that they should be designated." The draft's "intimation" that "all of the '273' organizations should be designated is therefore highly misleading," Waterman added, and a "guess might be that only 25 of those not designated should even be considered for designation." However, in an April 23 memo to Alderman, Waterman stated that even organizations not controlled by the CP could be designated upon showing that "individuals identified as Communists are directing, dominating and controlling the activities of the organization," even "where there is only one officer and he is identified as a Communist," or if it could be shown that a group's purposes served the CP "generally rather than a specific program sponsored by the Communist Party. It would appear sufficient for our purposes, for example, if the objective is to stir up racial agitation generally or to spread distrust of Government authority, 'peace,' etc., assuming other necessary factors are present." In a November 6, 1956, memo to ISD head Tompkins, ISD "confidential assistant" John Doherty recommended that AGLOSO be "revoked" and that "we should be prepared to advise" government agencies "on operation without a list." In a lengthy November 15, 1956, memo, deputy SOS chief James Devine told Alderman, his supervisor, that a proposal to shift "fact finding" power to the SACB to aid the Attorney General in making AGLOSO designations was fraught with "serious problems," which made it not "feasible under present statutory authority," although he recommended that "consideration be given to the possibility of legislative enactment in this field." According to Devine, because Congress had established the SACB, the executive branch could not enlarge its jurisdiction absent legislative action and it was doubtful if the SACB could legally accept such additional responsibilities for several reasons, including that a "conflict of interest" might be created if an organization was AGLOSO designated based on SACB fact finding and then subjected to a petition for SACB consideration under the Internal Security Act (ISA).[28]

On November 16, 1956, Alderman sent ISD head Tompkins two separate memos endorsing Doherty's November 6 call for AGLOSO's abolition, or, "if it is determined that the existing list cannot be revoked unless an alternative procedure for designation is instituted," proposed that congressional legislation be drafted to overcome "problems in the existing program," such as the prolonged ongoing contests involving the ISL, the NLG, and the Lithuanian organizations [discussed below]" and the "definitions question." As an alternative, he suggested requesting legislation establishing an "independent agency with subpoena power," namely, the SACB, to review "suspect organizations" upon the attorney general's petition, in order to call attention to the importance of affiliations by federal employees or applicants with organizations "with interests inimical to the country." Alderman added that the legislation "would include carefully defined categories of organizations which should be designated," would authorize the SACB to consider secret evidence provided by the attorney general if the latter "certifies the disclosure of the sources would be against the interests of national security," and would provide for automatic designation of any organization previously "ordered by the SACB to register under the ISA." According to Alderman, such legislation would remove the "numerous and difficult problems stemming from previous designations"; these included (1) correcting the "situation where the Attorney General is both prosecutor and judge," (2) providing definitions and standards "not spelled out in the present designations program," (3) solving the "extreme difficulty of obtaining the services of competent hearing officers" to preside over administrative challenges, (4) furnishing the subpoena power needed for designation proceedings, (5) greatly strengthening the "possibility of judicial approval of the use of classified information in such cases," (6) facilitating keeping the listings "on a somewhat current basis which is not possible in present circumstances," (7) providing an important new function for the SACB, and (8) meeting the "change in [Communist] Party policy" that sought to "overcome the effective enforcement of the ISA" by substituting attempted "infiltration of legitimate organizations" and "concentrating on small and local committees" rather than forming "front" groups and focusing on "larger Communist controlled membership" groups.[29]

While the department was thus clearly considering terminating AGLOSO in its internal 1956 deliberations, at the same time it was gearing up to make additional designations. Thus, on March 13, 1956, an SOS internal memo indicated that section attorneys had been instructed to submit their recommendations concerning the designation of at least ninety-five organizations "immediately." Although, reflecting typical confusion, the memo added that the "figures include organizations which may already have been designated," SOS chief Alderman jotted down the handwritten notation "Very good!" On April 13, Alderman wrote

Designations Unit head Waterman that he was "most anxious that we pick up the slack in review for designations before the end of the fiscal year." This message apparently led Waterman to lament to Alderman three days later that "it is most important that we immediately secure outside stenographic help" as "we only have one girl for nine attorneys." Although his unit thus was apparently already overloaded, Waterman repeatedly wrote to SOS attorney Troy Conner in April 1956 to complain that he had not yet received recommendations concerning scores of organizations being considered for AGLOSO designation. In the meantime, the ISD returned to the problem of defining the terms "Communist," "fascist," "totalitarian," and "subversive," an issue which, by early 1956, had dogged the department for nine years. According to a March 28 internal FBI memo, DOJ ISD executive assistant William Foley advised a bureau official that "the Department feels now that there is danger of attack by the courts since no clear guides as to the categories were set forth" and felt it was "highly desirable that reasonably clear-cut definitions be agreed upon" and therefore the ISD was undertaking the "project of defining those categories."[30]

Although department files are filled with numerous additional related memos, including many pages discussing various dictionary definitions of "subversive," it is unclear if any agreement was ever reached on this subject (although since no additional AGLOSO designations were ever proposed after late 1954, the matter remained entirely academic). In the meantime, on March 16, 1956, Assistant Attorney General Tompkins rebuffed CSC chairman Philip Young's request that the department include in its published AGLOSO lists the dates when groups were "originally designated," information long in the public domain, which had been provided to the Hennings subcommittee (and subsequently published) just six months before. Tompkins told Young that the designation date "is often misleading" because a "considerable gap" frequently developed, due to the investigative time needed between "the date when the organization's activities and membership" brought it within AGLOSO's "purview" and the date it was officially designated. "The most important consideration," Tompkins continued, was that including such dates in the lists "might give it greater importance than it deserves" and lead the period of employee membership to be "overemphasized" and suggest that organizational membership "prior to the date of designation is irrelevant," while postdesignation membership might unfairly suggest "an inference adverse to the individual involved."[31]

By late November 1956, the department had clearly decided to freeze further AGLOSO designation proceedings, at least in the short term. In a November 30, 1956, memo to SOS chief Alderman, Designations Unit head Waterman declared that the department was under "obligation to propose for designation any organization which falls within the criteria," and "our present policy of not proposing these organizations" might be "understandable for a short period of time, but if there might be considerable lapse of time, I believe we are in an untenable position." Waterman expressed particular concern that Attorney General Brownell had recently petitioned the SACB to act on several organizations that had never been proposed for AGLOSO, warning that, as a result, their members could be hired for federal employment "although, in effect, we have stated that the evidence [that they are "subversive"] is present by filing the [SACB] petition" and "we would be hard-pressed to explain why we did not propose the organizations under the Federal employee security program." On December 17, 1956, Alderman sent ISD head Tompkins a memo that discussed a number of AGLOSO cases involving existing or potential administrative or court challenges to proposed designations (all of which, he said in a handwritten note, had "plenty of room for the Dept. to get hurt in"). Alderman's memo said in the past year the number of no longer functioning AGLOSO groups had reached "close to 85 or 90%," but that the list was "anything but current," because the "practical necessity of public disclosure [in administrative hearings or legal challenges] has made it impossible to propose any organizations for designation in nearly two years" and because a "substantial amount of information in the files cannot be used for various reasons, such as confidential investigative technique, unsubstantiated opinion information, death of informant, refusal of informant to cooperate, and source currently furnishing information valuable to national security [and therefore unavailable for public testimony]." Nonetheless, Alderman maintained, the department had files on about thirty organizations that "may have sufficient evidence to propose for designation and proceed to hearing if necessary," although all were "small localized groups and most are inactive" and in each case "the release of current informants would probably be required."[32]

The department essentially remained paralyzed concerning AGLOSO throughout most of 1957, neither willing to propose additional organizations for designation, change the administrative hearing regulations, abolish the list, or ask Congress for legislation to solve AGLOSO's perceived ills. In a January 14, 1957, memo from Designations Unit head Waterman to SOS chief Alderman, the former strongly objected to language advocating the termination of AGLOSO in a draft letter prepared by Attorney General Brownell for President Eisenhower proposing a new executive order concerning federal employee security screening. He complained that while the draft stated AGLOSO was becoming "useless" because the CP was concentrating on "infiltrating legitimate organizations and organizing groups of a temporary and local nature," an approach that made it "difficult" to maintain a current list, that such tactics were largely "responsible for the AGLOSO's promulgation in the first place," and that currently nondesignated groups, which were "very small and local in nature," could easily be "immediately processed and if past experience is any criteria, less than 5% would properly contest their designation." According to Alderman, additional reasons to maintain AGLOSO were that the ISA might prove ineffective should the CP "disband and form a new organization" and that southern organizations of the

"Klan type" that advocated violence were difficult to prosecute under criminal statutes and "the only basis for investigating these organizations, as such" was via AGLOSO. Alderman concluded that the "most important" reason for Brownell "not to commit himself" to abolish AGLOSO was that pending cases "would be materially affected by any statements of the nature contained in the proposed draft," yet Brownell had previously stated that he "wishes these cases to proceed in an appropriate manner."[33]

Although it is unclear if Brownell eventually sent his letter to Eisenhower, by late January he clearly had communicated similar views to the CGS, as a January 24, 1957, CGS memo refers to the "Attorney General's statement that the list has outlived its usefulness." (In an interview broadcast on November 1, 1998, on the cable television network CNN as part of a series on the history of the Cold War, Brownell termed AGLOSO "rather misguided, because who's going to decide that question [of designations] and there was a danger, which proved to be true, that amateurs [presumably a reference to the FBI and DOJ attorneys] would be the judges and that perfectly harmless organizations that were, I guess you might say, in the ultra-liberal camp, and they had nothing to with Communism, would be included." Although, as noted above, Brownell had repeatedly hailed AGLOSO designations as a leading indicator of the Eisenhower administration's toughness in fighting communism between 1953 and 1955, he added in the 1998 interview that AGLOSO was not "very effective" and although the "purpose of it, I'm sure, was to alert people" that "some rather high-sounding high titles and innocuous-sounding organizations" were "operated and influenced by Communists and were used by them to subvert the public opinion, . . . in practice, it was almost impossible to develop a list that was meaningful and I don't believe that [AGLOSO] in itself did a great deal to further the fighting of the Cold War," while in "many cases" it "resulted in the stifling of free speech, unnecessarily and I always felt that the proper approach was to concentrate on the detection of actual spying activities.") Despite Brownell's conversion to opposing AGLOSO by early 1957, apparently due to severe opposition to the prospect of abolishing the list expressed by federal agencies in response to CGS queries, by mid-1957 the DOJ abandoned further consideration of formally abolishing the list. CGS records indicate that many federal agencies opposed terminating AGLOSO, generally on the grounds of inadequate resources to make their own determinations concerning allegedly "subversive" organizations and the consequent need for a reliable, centralized source of such information. Thus, security officials from the Government Printing Office, the Department of Health, Education and Welfare, and the Atomic Energy Commission, respectively, reported that "to prefer [security] charges practically necessitates such a list," that "each agency does not have the facilities to check the various organizations," and that, absent AGLOSO, "there might be a variety of interpretations as to what organizations were considered subversive and what were not."[34]

In mid-1957, ISD head Tompkins returned to exploring how to remedy AGLO-SO's continuing problems. On May 9, 1957, he wrote to Assistant Attorney General Wilson White, head of the DOJ's Office of Legal Counsel (OLC), to ask him to review the existing hearing regulations. According to Tompkins, their "most serious" problem was the lack of subpoena power, which had made it "almost impossible to secure witnesses," yet which would require legislative authority to remedy, thereby possibly subjecting the "entire program" to congressional review. On June 26, 1957, Waterman, now deputy chief of the DOJ's Civil Section, reported to section chief James Devine that there remained "no substantial national organizations that should be designated," with one exception, and therefore "no new designations should be proposed until new legislation has been approved," although he simultaneously noted that "should we decide to go ahead now with the designation of local organizations," there were "approximately 20 which could be proposed" and "only one or two notices of contest should result therefrom." Three months later, Devine told Tompkins that there was "sufficient evidence" to propose for designation about a dozen groups, and, in a lengthy September 30 memo in response to the CGS report, Devine told Tompkins that he questioned "whether the Legislative Branch should enact into laws matters wholly within the purview of the Executive Department." Devine also suggested that hearing examiners be granted subpoena power, which he termed "almost indispensable to the successful presentation of these cases," but maintained that if such powers were used to compel the government to produce evidence, "the Attorney General or his representatives can refuse to do so on the ground that it is privileged, if in the Attorney General's judgment its revelation would be prejudicial to the public interest." In a follow-up memo to Tompkins on October 30, Devine, referring to "a number of problems" connected with AGLOSO, reported that the department had "gone along" with the CGS recommendation that AGLOSO be given statutory authority "in view of the desire of the great majority of other agencies for the list and in the absence of any concrete and workable substitute." He also reported that the department had indicated that "if this program is enacted into legislation, all organizations which have been out of existence for 15 years will be removed from the list" and designation proceedings would be instituted against "certain groups presently not proposed for designation because of the necessity of maintaining confidential information, since the new legislation permits the submission of summaries of classified information." Devine added that since the department had just delisted two designated Lithuanian organizations (discussed immediately below) even though they had refused to respond to interrogatories, a decision was required as to "whether we are going to insist upon answers to interrogatories as a requirement" for hearings in future AGLOSO contestations, including the pending NLG challenge (discussed below). On November 21, Tompkins, while reiterating his March 2, 1956, recommendation that AGLOSO be abolished, recommended to Brownell that he respond to the CGS report by stating that the department intended to submit "specific recommendations" to Congress on the CGS which would provide legislative authority for "most of the rules and regulations" promulgated for AGLOSO hearings and also provide "standards and criteria for designation which are more explicit, and accordingly more workable" than provided under the existing executive orders.[35]

In a September 10, 1957, internal FBI memo that clearly reflected severe tension between the bureau and the department in the wake of the department's continued consideration of abandoning AGLOSO, FBI Intelligence Division official F. J. Baumgardner informed division head A. H. Belmont that department attorney Troy Conner had telephoned the previous day in order to ask when, during "the preparation of a case [under AGLOSO or SACB proceedings] the Bureau desired to be furnished the required list" of proposed witnesses and documents to be utilized and was "advised in a business like manner" that an August 23 FBI memo on the subject was "quite clear" and "that any further questions regarding this matter should brought to the Bureau's attention by memorandum." On his copy of the memo, Hoover scrawled, "Very properly handled. We give no 'guide' to that outfit."[36]

The Lithuanian Cases, 1953–1957

Shortly after Hoover indicated his disgust with "that outfit," the DOJ deleted two organizations from AGLOSO, in the first and what would ultimately prove to be the *only* instance in which an *already* listed organization was removed without *either* a DOJ hearing (as would be the case with the ISL and its two associated groups in 1958, the same year attempts to list the NLG were abandoned after they were challenged in court) or a court order (as with two Spanish Civil War veterans groups in 1973). The October 4, 1957, action, announced by Attorney General Brownell three weeks before his unexpected resignation, involved two obscure Lithuanian fraternal-cultural groups first designated only three years earlier, the Association of Lithuanian Workers (ALW) and the American Lithuanian Workers Literary Association (ALWLA). Although they had legally challenged Brownell's action, they had lost their cases in federal district and appeals courts and their request for Supreme Court consideration on appeal was still pending when Brownell reversed course. The delisting of the Lithuanian groups was little noticed at the time—it was not reported in any major newspaper—and has never been publicly explained. However, FBI documents released in response to a 2003 Freedom of Information Request reveal that the department's action, taken much to Hoover's disgust, reflected its fears that the Supreme Court might use the case to not only order the groups deleted from AGLOSO but also to find unconstitutional the entire concept that the government could properly promulgate lists of officially designated "subversive" groups. Brownell's decision clearly expressed the government's fear that the Court had unalterably turned against it in "antisubversive" cases, especially following its notorious June 17, 1957, so-called Red Monday rulings, in which it had significantly limited the powers of red-hunting Congressmen (in *Watkins v. U.S.*, 354 U.S, 178) and essentially made it impossible for the government to continue prosecuting CP officials under the 1940 Smith Act (in *Yates v. U.S.*, 354 U.S. 298).[37]

The ALW and the ALWLA were among the 62 organizations that Brownell announced, on April 29, 1953, he sought to add to the 192 AGLOSO groups previously designated by the Truman administration. The ALW and the ALWLA both informed the DOJ in May 1953 that they wished to contest their designations. Subsequently, the department sent the organizations a statement of grounds for designation, accompanied by numerous detailed interrogatories concerning all aspects of their membership and activities. According to the department's Supreme Court brief, its essential claim was that both organizations were "formed by and operated under the leadership" of CP members and had "constituted a vehicle to further the aims, policies and objectives" of the CP and "never knowingly" deviated from the CP's "program and objectives." Both groups denied that they were CP "fronts," while maintaining that the interrogatories were impossible to answer and/or unconstitutionally infringed on their First Amendment freedoms. Thus, in its September 8, 1953, reply to the department's interrogatories and statement of grounds, the ALW declared that its activities were "confined strictly to those of a fraternal insurance beneficial society," that it was "not a political organization," and that it was "not carrying out the policies" of the CP or "any other party." The ALW added that many of the interrogatories were "impossible" to answer, such as requiring information about the political beliefs and associations of all of its approximately 7,000 members, since "we do not have any records of any political affiliations of our members" and thus could not "supply you with this information, even if the officers of the Association" were prepared to violate its own rules and "the non-political principles upon which it is founded." The ALW additionally protested that the department's rules effectively barred it from a hearing because although it could seek to comply with the "unconstitutional and impossible" requirements imposed by the interrogatories, since the attorney general would be allowed to make a "determination solely on the basis of secret and confidential information which will not be disclosed to us" such a proceeding would not be "a hearing in any real or legal sense of the word." The department responded in November 1953 that, by failing to answer the interrogatories within the required time, the ALW had acquiesced in the proposed designation. The ALWLA's response to the department's statement of grounds and interrogatories was similar to that of the ALW, with the result that the two organizations were formally AGLOSO-designated by Brownell on January 22, 1954 (along with seventeen other organizations that had indicated intent to contest their proposed 1953 listings, also on the grounds that the organizations had failed to adequately answer their interrogatories).[38]

The two Lithuanian groups then filed suit in federal district court, asking that Brownell be enjoined to withdraw their designations as inaccurate and arbitrary and because the listings violated their First Amendment freedoms and Fifth Amendment due process protections. The organizations also claimed that their designations violated the terms of the authorizing executive orders because they had been made without appropriate investigation, notice, or hearings. Brownell responded by asserting that the groups were Communist fronts and that judicial relief was precluded by their failure to avail themselves of the administrative hearing procedure. The district court supported the government, without written opinion, on August 11, 1955, whereupon the two groups appealed to the federal court of appeals for the District of Columbia, which ruled against them on May 9, 1957 (*ALW v. Brownell*, 247 F. 2d 64), finding that they had improperly failed to exhaust existing administrative appeal procedures and therefore "cannot obtain judicial relief." On July 19, 1957, the two organizations asked the Supreme Court to hear an appeal and to rule, in particular, on whether the executive orders and procedures that authorized and governed AGLOSO were constitutional. Additionally, they asked the high Court to determine if the lower courts had properly precluded them from obtaining judicial review of their designations because they had failed to exhaust their "administrative remedies" when, in fact, they maintained, they had only failed to reply to interrogatories that "were irrelevant, burdensome, invasive of privacy and impossible to answer." According to their joint brief, the lower courts had effectively negated the 1951 Supreme Court *McGrath* ruling granting judicial review to AGLOSO-designated organizations, because they had conditioned that right "upon compliance with impossible and illegal conditions of the Attorney General." The brief termed the statement of grounds against them "vague, inconclusive and unparticularized charges" of Communist front activities, while the interrogatories were characterized as requiring the furnishing of "an immense mass of detailed information and data, much of it obscurely defined, much of it patently unavailable," and "virtually all of it of no possible relevance," together designed to "make it impossible for plaintiff to answer" and thus "to lay an artificial foundation for the defendant to hold plaintiff in default and deny it the hearing which the defendant's regulations purport to make available." Noting that seventeen other organizations that had sought to contest the attorney general's April 29, 1953, proposed designations had also later been formally listed for failing to respond "completely and with particularity" to the department's interrogatories, the Lithuanian groups declared, "this case explains the absence of hearings" in the other instances. They asked the Court to hear the case to "determine whether the petitioners were denied procedural due process, whether accused organizations are entitled to a hearing, whether the Attorney General may condition the right to a hearing on an organization's submission to an unlimited inquisition, and whether the Attorney General's hearing regulations violate the Constitution." The two groups urged the Court to defer "no longer" a ruling on the fundamental constitutionality of AGLOSO, which they termed a "blacklist of organizations which displease the government" and an invalid "governmental coercion of orthodoxy" that "condemn[s] organizations by designating them." They declared that a final determination of AGLOSO's legality was critical for "the preservation of constitutional liberties" and that their case presented "the important question, not yet resolved by this Court," namely, could the attorney general legally "destroy organizations by defamatory designations."[39]

The government's August 1957 reply brief maintained that the lower courts had properly rejected the organizations' claims because they had not exhausted their administrative remedies under the department's regulations. Noting that the appeals court had held that the "basic authority of the Attorney General to designate subversive organizations was not properly before it" but that "in any event it would uphold the validity" of AGLOSO, the department declared that, since in *McGrath* "only one of the majority Justices [Black] agreed that the listings were invalid for total lack of power" in the executive branch, it was clear that "the power exists," although "that issue is not properly in this case and need not be reached." However, as previously noted, on October 4 Brownell notified federal agencies that he had decided to rescind the AGLOSO designations of the two groups and therefore "you are requested to remove these organizations from your list in connection with the Federal employee security program." This action was published, without any explanation and virtually without any press coverage, in the October 10 *Federal Register*. On October 28 the Supreme Court accepted Solicitor General J. Lee Rankin's request that the case be dismissed as moot, although Rankin stressed that by rescinding the designations the government had "voluntarily acceded to petitioners all of the relief sought by them," save a "judgment that the regulatory procedures are illegal and unconstitutional," and that this latter issue, under federal precedents, should not be decided absent "a concrete, present, actual, and existing controversy in which a party's rights are really at stake."[40]

FBI and DOJ memos released in 2003 reveal that behind the department's sudden reversal concerning the Lithuanian groups was the fear that, especially in light of the Supreme Court's recent inclination to favor civil liberties claims in cases involving alleged "subversive activities," the Court might abolish AGLOSO entirely if it took the case. According to an October 4, 1957, memo from FBI Internal Security Section head Alan Belmont to Director Hoover, at a meeting that afternoon with Brownell and other top-ranking department officials, Brownell had indicated a need to make a decision "today," apparently because the Court would inaugurate its 1957–1958 term in two days. Belmont stated that department attorneys reported that "regardless of the action taken by the Government," including

offering the organizations a hearing or the opportunity to answer further interrogatories, the Court would hear the cases on appeal and it was "highly probable" that the Court would address the attorney general's fundamental authority
to "maintain a list of cited organizations" and "the Government would lose as to
these two cases and, further, stood a good chance to lose on the over-all question
of the AG's list." In response to Brownell's query whether the department "could
prove cases against these two organizations if hearings were held," the memo
continued, the attorneys advised that "witnesses had been lost due to the passage of time and there was not a good case against either organization." Belmont
added that he had responded to Brownell's request for his views that he "hated to
see the Department join the retreat too prevalent today before subversive forces"
and that the Lithuanian groups "had followed the CP line" and had apparently
been cited originally because "the Department felt it had sound cases." Belmont
added that he had told Brownell that "there were about 7,000 members in each"
of the two groups and that they were "not among the foremost communist front
groups in the country," but the "question involved was not so much these two
organizations as the results which might flow from the Department's action."
According to Belmont, Brownell then declared that he had decided to "delete
these organizations from the AG's list" and would immediately sign the "necessary documents," and, if asked why, would state that witnesses had been "lost"
with the passage of time "and the case is insufficient to move against the organizations." However, Brownell reportedly added that his real concern was fear
that "if the Supreme Court acted on these cases they would go into the over-all
problem and would attack the Department's procedures such as the nature of
the interrogatories submitted, et cetera," basing his conclusion on the attacks on
the department by the Court during its last session. The Belmont memo is confirmed by an October 4 department memo by Executive Assistant to the Attorney
General Harold Healy, which declares that Brownell "stated that he was satisfied
a failure to delist the two organizations at this time would run the substantial
risk of having the Supreme Court invalidate the Department's listing procedure
and that the enforcement problems and the public outcry which would follow
were too serious to risk on top of those following in the wake of recent Supreme
Court decisions adversely affecting the Department." Although Belmont's memo
clearly suggested that he had expressed FBI opposition to delisting the two Lithuanian groups, Healy's memo said that Belmont "took no position" concerning
the "advisability of delisting to avoid an adverse Supreme Court decision or as
to the adequacy of proof available to substantiate a listing." When Belmont sent
his memo to Hoover, the latter scrawled on it, with obvious disgust, "They are
running like scared rabbits."[41]

The sudden late 1957 delisting of the Lithuanian groups had a bizarre denouement. In a November 28, 1958 memo to a top assistant to Attorney General Rogers, Assistant Attorney General Yeagley reported that as an "economy measure"

in response to continuing "numerous requests for copies of the list" from the public and federal, state and local officials the department had continued to circulate already-printed but now outdated 1955 AGLOSO lists, which included the two delisted organizations with a line drawn through their names and a footnoted reference to their new status. Following the July 1958 ISL delistings (discussed above), CSC official David Williams, whose office had the formal responsibility for keeping the published AGLOSO lists current, angrily complained to Yeagley in an August 8, 1958, letter that the DOJ's actions had "again caused embarrassment" to the CSC by violating a December 15, 1955, pledge from Assistant Attorney General Tompkins that the CSC would be given "advance notification of changes in the list." According to Williams, news of the ISL delistings had reached the CSC after it had already approved the printing of 120,000 copies of AGLOSO, although "fortunately, through the cooperative efforts of both the General Services Administration and the Government Printing Office, we were able to stop the presses and delete the three organizations from the form." Yeagley responded to Williams on August 19 that it was "not feasible to give any substantial advance notice" concerning AGLOSO changes, because "prior to the Attorney General's decision, we cannot notify anyone." Despite the CSC memo just referenced, until already-printed AGLOSO lists were exhausted they were circulated, apparently for at least two years, with all *five* of the delisted groups appearing with lines drawn through their names (but easily readable), with asterisks tied to footnoted references to their removal.

Shortly after the DOJ's decision to drop the Lithuanian cases, it apparently quietly dropped the only other two pending instances in which organizations had sought hearings in response to their proposed 1954 designations, namely, Californians for the Bill of Rights and the National Council of the Arts, Sciences and Professions. Although the surviving archival record for the former group is sparse, that for the council indicates considerable internal conflict with the DOJ before the proceedings were apparently dropped. In an April 15, 1955, memo to SOS chief Irons, subordinate attorney Waterman complained that the "grounds and interrogatories" submitted to the Council had been drafted with "great haste" and that only one or two of them displayed "any effort to direct them to the particular organization involved, all others are merely questions copied from previously composed interrogatories [sent to other groups]." In an October 26, 1955, memo to SOS chief Alderman, Waterman declared that there was "still a considerable difference of opinion between my views" and that of another department attorney "who keeps repeating that he is not aware of what it takes to make a designation case." Matters were further complicated when the council reported its dissolution to the department, leading Alderman to ask ISD executive assistant William Foley in another October 26, 1955, memo "how a defunct organization can properly contest its designation," which he termed "one of the difficult problems inherent in the present program." Although subsequently the department received from the Council (and from Californians for the Bill of Rights) responses to its interrogatories and grounds, which Assistant Attorney General William Tompkins characterized as failing to "comply" in a March 2, 1956, memo to Assistant Attorney General (and future Supreme Court justice) Warren Burger, the Council case was referred to a departmental hearing officer in May 1956. Although the latter recommended in mid-1957 that the organization be designated as its responses to the sixty-seven interrogatories posed to it were "not made in good faith," the proposed council designation was apparently dropped in light of the department's decision in the Lithuanian cases. This decision may have been made partly in response to a memo from OLC lawyer W. Wilson White, who said the council had "done more to comply" with the interrogatories than had the Lithuanian groups, and that the department had acted in the latter instance because it was evidently "not too sanguine about ultimately being able to sustain" designations where organizations had failed to fully respond to interrogatories. White suggested this was especially so as "there would seem to be considerable doubt as to the fundamental fairness of an administrative process" in which the government could list organizations "without opportunity for them to be heard if they do not answer interrogatories put to them" particularly because the "unfairness of the interrogatory procedure" was "highlighted by its one-sidedness," as the "government grants itself the right to obtain evidence from the organization through interrogatories" but "does not extend a similar right to the organization," although court rulings had established that "the heart of [legal] discovery provisions is their mutuality."[42]

AGLOSO and the National Lawyers Guild, 1953–1958

As with the Lithuanian and ISL cases, the DOJ also retreated during the late 1950s from its attempt to list the NLG, probably the single most widely publicized AGLOSO designation controversy ever—again fearing that AGLOSO might otherwise suffer a fatal legal rebuke. The NLG was formed in 1937 as a popular front group, including radicals and liberals, that sought to provide, both in its orientation and its constituency, an alternative to the dominant, highly conservative ABA, which was primarily controlled by corporate lawyers working for large firms that focused on threats to private property while evincing little interest in civil liberties and excluding blacks from membership. The NLG proclaimed in its constitution that "human rights shall be regarded as more sacred than property rights," was open to all lawyers, and focused on the practical problems that many lawyers faced in making a living and on the daily legal needs of groups that traditionally had found it difficult to obtain legal services, including the poor, blacks, trade unions, and leftist organizations. The NLG's founders and members came from a typically broad popular front spectrum, including four subsequent Supreme Court justices (Abe Fortas, Arthur Goldberg, Robert Jackson, and Thurgood Marshall), numerous government officials (including two governors, three congressmen, and many highly placed New Deal attorneys), and many distinguished law professors (including Edward Levi, later University of Chicago president and Ford administration attorney general), federal and state judges, and the general counsels of the AFL, the CIO, and the NAACP. President Franklin Roosevelt sent greetings to the guild's 1937 founding conference and consulted with an NLG delegation at the White House in 1938, while Secretary of the Interior Harold Ickes's 1939 address to the organization's annual convention was broadcast over network radio and reprinted in full in the *New York Times*.[43]

While a key part of the organizational impetus for the NLG came from lawyers with CP affiliations, the vast majority of members were not Communists. Most of its early resolutions supported New Deal social programs and civil liberties and civil rights protections for trade unions, political minorities, and blacks. However, like many popular front groups, the guild was rent by internal divisions in the late 1930s, especially in the aftermath of the August 1939 Nazi-Soviet Non-Aggression Pact and a growing wave of popular anti-Communism. Although in early 1939 the guild condemned all forms of totalitarianism, including communism and fascism, and later that year the NLG executive board supported Finnish resistance to Russia's invasion, hundreds of members, who perceived growing signs of Communist domination or feared being associated with a group increasingly so viewed, departed, including many highly prominent members (among them then-attorney general Robert Jackson), resulting in a membership collapse from almost 4,500 to only 1,100 between early 1939 and mid-1940. However, at least half of the guild's non-Communist membership remained and the long-serving NLG president chosen in 1940, Robert Kenny, was a former California Superior Court justice who led the California delegation to the 1944 Democratic convention that renominated President Roosevelt.[44]

After Pearl Harbor, when the NLG strongly supported the American war effort, the organization regained some of its lost reputation and picked up new members. Its representatives regularly met with top government officials, including Attorney General Biddle, and the group received letters of commendation from Vice President Henry Wallace and Secretary of State Edward Stettinius. The guild was officially designated a "consultant" organization to the American delegation to the 1945 San Francisco United Nations founding conference, and President Kenny and another prominent NLG official served as consultants at the Nuremberg war crimes trials. Nonetheless, the earlier damage to the NLG's reputation was exacerbated during the early years of the Cold War when guild lawyers frequently represented radicals before congressional committees, courts, and other government agencies; increasingly criticized the Truman administration's foreign and internal security policies; and repeatedly and publicly clashed with the FBI (as early as 1941 the NLG had denounced the FBI for "Gestapo" activities and demanded the resignation of Director Hoover). In contrast to the ABA (and the ACLU), the NLG harshly denounced Truman's 1947 loyalty order, partly on the grounds that there was no constitutional authority to designate organizations as "subversive" and that to "impute the doctrines of an organization, so illegally determined, to its members, with a resultant dismissal from employment, is heresy hunting of the worst kind." After the Truman AGLOSO was first published in late 1947, the guild declared that the "power to wreck or greatly weaken organizations by government denunciation" was a "menace to the most fundamental freedoms of all the people." In 1950 the NLG supported UN intervention against North Korean "aggression" but opposed the prior unilateral American sending of troops to Korea and termed the conflict a result of "blind opposition to Communism" by the United States, "which ignores the economic, social and political problems of the ordinary people of the world who are struggling to obtain a better life."[45]

Attacks on the NLG reached new levels after it published in 1949 detailed evidence from DOJ files (released during the 1949 espionage trial of department employee Judith Coplon) that documented massive FBI surveillance of organizations and citizens, including numerous illegal wiretaps, break-ins, and mail openings, an account largely ignored or dismissed in the rapidly deteriorating Cold War climate, but officially documented twenty-five years later by post-Watergate congressional investigations. The NLG report concluded, "On a strictly numerical basis, the FBI may commit more federal crimes than it ever detects." The report indicated (and a 1989 lawsuit, discussed below, largely confirmed) that the FBI had burglarized NLG headquarters; tapped its phones; regularly leaked derogatory accounts about the group to friendly reporters, rival ABA officials, and conservative congressmen (such as Rep. Richard Nixon [R-CA]); scoured its trash; and surreptitiously obtained an advance copy of its 1949 report, which FBI memos attributed to a "highly confidential informant" (presumably an FBI break-in). Hoover and FBI assistant director Louis Nichols publicly branded the NGL as Communist-infiltrated in mid-1950, while a massively publicized September 1950 HUAC report (given front-page treatment in the September 17 *Los Angeles Times*), issued without prior hearings or notice and largely based on a leaked FBI memo, charged that the guild had become the "legal bulwark" of the CP and called for its AGLOSO designation. In August 1950, a month before the HUAC report was issued, Hoover instructed Nichols to "call the Attorney General's attention to it and to our previous memos" upon its release and to "suggest consideration again for designating [the NLG] subversive."[46]

Until 1953, the DOJ repeatedly resisted intense FBI pressure to designate the NLG. Thus, in a mid-1948 handwritten note to Hoover responding to persistent FBI inquiries, Attorney General Clark related, "Lawyers Guild not included on list—I have many friends on it and would give them a hearing before doing so." A few months later, the department informed the LRB that while "in many instances the Communists or fellow-travelers have been able to achieve positions of direction and control" in the guild, many members were "not only non-Communists but anti-Communists." In December 1949, Hoover presented Attorney General McGrath with a 300-page "summary memorandum" on the NLG, clearly intended to elicit AGLOSO designation, which, along with allegations of widespread CP membership and/or sympathies among NLG members, also reported that some, including then-NAACP counsel Thurgood Marshall, had been "particularly critical" of the FBI and that the guild had "consistently favored measures beneficial to labor." In March 1950, after the department informed FBI assistant director D. Milton Ladd that the NLG had "just barely missed" AGLOSO designation, partly because there was "some feeling, apparently in the Department" and on Capitol Hill that "many innocent people" had been "taken in by the organization," Hoover penciled on his copy that such people "should resign" and it was "all the worse to allow it to continue unbranded and serve as a trap for the gullible." A subsequent FBI random check of the NLG membership list led bureau investigators to conclude that only 6.6 percent of NLG members were CP members, although another 25 percent allegedly had affiliations or associations with groups that were Communist infiltrated or dominated, with CP members, or with those "sympathetic towards Communism." The NLG's "unlisted" status provided some protection for the group: in March 1951 Harvard Law School dean Erwin Griswold rebuffed demands that a planned talk by an NLG officer be banned and the student chapter disbanded, as the "Attorney General, with the resources of the FBI at his disposal, has not seen fit" to place the NLG on AGLOSO.[47]

On August 26, 1953, when the new Eisenhower administration was especially eager to demonstrate its anti-Communist credentials, Attorney General Brownell announced he planned to designate the NLG, due to its role as the CP's "legal mouthpiece," in a speech (reported on the front pages of the *New York Times, Washington Post*, and *Christian Science Monitor*), which, astonishingly, was delivered at the annual conference of the ABA, the NLG's leading rival. Aside from its extraordinary setting, Brownell's declaration was extremely unusual because all prior AGLOSO designations had been provided in large batches via press releases or conferences. Moreover, in his speech, Brownell virtually conceded that his case was somewhat lacking, by claiming that the NLG had consistently followed the CP "line" on every major issue, except those "so notorious that their espousal would too clearly demonstrate Communist control." Brownell subsequently alleged in a Veterans of Foreign Wars speech that the NLG had been "initiated, proposed and organized" under "direct [CP] supervision," but failed to explain why it had taken the department until 1953 to list the group or why, in an earlier speech, he had claimed only that the NLG had been under Communist leadership "at least since 1946." On June 9, 1954, NLG affiliation became the central issue in the most famous incident of the famous Senate "Army-McCarthy hearings," when, before a national television audience, McCarthy attacked lead army lawyer Joseph Welch for allegedly trying to "force" on the Senate Committee staff an associate in Welch's Boston law firm with past NLG membership (whom McCarthy named). This fact had been well publicized weeks earlier (including a screaming front-page headline in the April 15, 1954, *Boston Post* and April 16 stories in both the *Washington Post* and the *New York Times*) and had led Welch to decide *not* to have the associate serve on the committee staff. However, McCarthy was severely damaged when an outraged Welch declared that he had previously "never really gauged your cruelty or your recklessness," rebuked McCarthy for "assassinat[ing] this lad," and encapsulated the increasingly common view of McCarthy by asking, "Have you no sense of decency, sir? At long last, have you left no sense of decency?"[48]

After the NLG decided to fight the proposed designation in court rather than via the department's administrative hearings, FBI informants spied on the organization's legal defense planning, a development that so alarmed the department that the FBI was cautioned, apparently to no avail, about the "dangers attendant" to having informants participate in legal discussions concerning matters that were pending in the courts and the "reporting of information which may be privileged." When the NLG filed suit in November 1953 for a federal district court injunction to bar the department from further designation proceedings until the court could rule on AGLOSO's fundamental constitutionality, the department responded by asking the guild to answer sixty-six interrogatories, similar to those posed to organizations that had sought administrative hearings; they asked for masses of information concerning NLG officers, members, positions, and communications, especially material which might support allegations of CP domination. As Percival Bailey has noted in a 1979 dissertation, FBI files probably "contained more answers" to these questions than the guild could access, but since the bureau had obtained them through illegal burglaries "it could hardly acknowledge" this. The NLG told the district court that AGLOSO was an unconstitutional infringement on freedom of association and that Brownell's speeches attacking it and the nature of the interrogatories demonstrated that it could not gain a fair hearing from the department and thus was forced to resort to the courts, since designation would cause the group "irreparable harm." However, federal judge Richmond Keech denied the NLG's request for an injunction in December 1953 and ordered the guild to utilize the administrative hearing procedure before raising constitutional questions in the courts.[49]

Five months later, a federal appeals court (*NLG v. Brownell*, 215 F. 2d 485, 194) ordered the district court to reconsider the constitutional issues and granted the NLG a temporary injunction against further department proceedings in the interim. However, after the appeals court ruled in August 1954, in the case of the Lithuanian organizations, that they had to first exhaust their administrative remedies before the courts would rule on constitutional issues, the district court reaffirmed its earlier ruling in November 1954, a ruling upheld in October 1955 by the appeals court (*NLG v. Brownell*, 126 F. Supp. 730, 1954; *NLG v. Brownell*, 225 F. 2d 552, 1955). Although on May 7, 1956, the Supreme Court refused to hear a further NLG appeal (351 U.S. 927), leaving the guild with only the alternative of an administrative hearing, the DOJ stalled for two years and then finally abandoned the NLG designation attempt. On July 16, 1958, Hoover informed FBI subordinates that Attorney General Rogers had decided, in both the NLG and ISL cases, that designating the organizations would "ultimately" lead to Supreme Court consideration, in which it was "likely the Supreme Court would throw out" AGLOSO entirely, and that Brownell "wanted to avoid this as he believed neither of the two cases was particularly strong" and did not want AGLOSO to "be risked by pressing the two cases in question." Shortly before, Acting Assistant Attorney General and ISD head Yeagley had sent Executive Assistant to the Attorney General Harold Healey an urgent warning that, absent quick decisions on the NLG and other pending cases, the department was likely heading for imminent legal problems. Yeagley noted that on July 1, 1958, the NLG had filed a lawsuit requesting an injunction against further AGLOSO proceedings against it because the government had "no legal power to proceed" due to its "failure to diligently prosecute the proposal for designation." Yeagley predicted that the lawsuit would present "an opportunity for an unsympathetic court to be highly critical of the Department's handling of this case" and suggested that the department meet with the NLG so that "arrangements could possibly be made for the dropping of both the designations proceedings and the Guild's court action." In September 1958, Rogers wrote to the NLG to report that "without in any manner endorsing" the group, the department "hereby rescinded" the proposed designation, having concluded that, partly due to the death or unavailability of witnesses, "the evidence available for a hearing on the merits of this matter fails to meet the strict standards of proof which guide the determination of matters of this character."[50]

In the five years during which the NLG fought the proposed designation, newspapers regularly reminded their readers that the department was seeking its listing, and on several occasions, mistakenly indicated that the organization had already been placed on AGLOSO, an error also made by ABA president Loyd Wright, in ACLU publications, and even in some recent scholarly books. NLG membership, which had recovered to almost 2,600 members in early 1947, soon thereafter began plunging, falling to less than 1,500 by May 1950, shortly before the HUAC report, down further to about 770 in 1952, and subsequently to fewer than 575 in the aftermath of Brownell's 1953 AGLOSO announcement. So many federal lawyers departed that the Washington, D.C., chapter almost ceased functioning. Some of the losses clearly occurred well before either the HUAC report or the proposed AGLOSO designation, and the former accusation apparently caused more damage than the latter: Detroit chapter membership fell from 347 to 47 between 1947 and 1952, while San Francisco membership plunged from

129 members to less than 50 between 1947 and 1949, with those resigning including California attorney general and future governor Edmund Brown, the University of California Law School dean, and the state supreme court's chief justice. AGLOSO designation proved a near-mortal blow to an organization that was already in severe trouble: as a city judge declared in September 1950, shortly after the HUAC report, "If the Guild goes on the subversive list then I go off the Guild's list. I'll have nothing to do with any Communistic or any other subversive organization." One of the guild's most prominent non-Communists, Yale University law professor Thomas Emerson, declared in 1955 that if the NLG were ultimately designated, "there can be little doubt that the Guild will have to dissolve." Following the 1958 abandonment of the government's designation effort, the NLG enjoyed a renaissance, reaching a record membership of 10,000 by the 1990s.[51]

A $56 million damage suit filed by the guild in 1977 against the FBI and other government agencies forced the release of about 400,000 pages of NLG files the FBI had compiled between 1940 and 1975 (although determinations were made in both 1958 and 1974 that the organization was not subversive). The suit was finally settled in 1989, when the FBI publicly acknowledged that it had engaged in a broad effort to investigate and disrupt the NLG, including warrantless wiretapping of its national headquarters between 1947 and 1951, about seven burglaries, examination of the organization's garbage, using informers within law firm staffs, and providing information about members to groups which passed on lawyers' bar applications. U.S. Attorney Benito Romano told reporters that "obviously, under today's standards, a lot" of the government's activity against the NLG "would be illegal," but in the settlement the government did not admit any wrongdoing or agree to pay any damages, although it promised not to use any of the information that it had gathered (under the agreement, it was placed in the National Archives under seal until 2025). At a 1982 Senate hearing, Sen. Jeremiah Denton (R-AL) charged the NLG sought "to exploit the law in order to bring about revolutionary change," while FBI director William Webster said that groups that provided "legal assistance" could be "even more dangerous than those who actually throw the bombs." In 1987, as the July 30 *New York Times* reported on its front page, the Republican Senate Campaign Committee attacked Sen. Howard Metzenbaum (D-OH) for his alleged affiliations "with several Communist causes in the 1940's," including the NLG and the AGLOSO-listed Ohio School of Social Sciences, and charged that, via Metzenbaum, "Communist sympathies have found their way onto the Senate floor."[52]

AGLOSO in Paralysis, 1958–1961

As was recognized at the time, the DOJ's 1958 abandonment of the NLG case essentially publicly signaled the end of AGLOSO designations. Thus, the September 13, 1958, *New York Times* noted that the department's action in the NLG case "followed little publicized actions during the last years that dropped five other organizations [the ISL and related groups and the two Lithuanian groups]" from AGLOSO and left the "impression" that the "department had lost most of its enthusiasm for the list." The department essentially remained paralyzed concerning AGLOSO during the final three years (1958–1961) of the Eisenhower administration and the following presidencies of John Kennedy (1961–1963) and Lyndon Johnson (1963–1969). Thus, ISD head Tompkins began a February 18, 1958, memo to Attorney General Rogers by stating, "As you know, we are not taking any steps to propose any organizations for designations" or to make any decisions in the still pending challenges to AGLOSO listings in the ISL, NLG, and National Council on American-Soviet Friendship (NCASF) cases. According to Tompkins, governmental agencies were attempting to coordinate their responses to the CGS report and also needed to answer "certain questions" concerning AGLOSO, especially whether, by "mooting" the Lithuanian cases, if the department "has indicated that it will not in the future require answers to interrogatories as a prerequisite to hearing." He added that the ISD and the OLC "have always had serious doubts as to the legality of a procedure which requires interrogatories from organizations without permitting the organizations to file interrogatories upon the Government," especially since this contradicted guidelines in the Federal Rules for Civil Procedure, in which the "basis for interrogatories is, of course, their mutuality." Tompkins suggested that the most "prudent" course would be to await congressional action rather than proceed with the pending cases and "test the present procedure calling for unilateral interrogatories." He added that the ISD also hesitated to propose new listings because virtually all potential cases involved small, local, non-"significant" groups, about which the department could probably not "secure even a substantial number of the witnesses who are purportedly available" absent subpoena power. He concluded that if AGLOSO was "to be maintained, Congressional approval will have to be given for subpoena power and accordingly no action should be undertaken at this time with the prospects of success so meager."[53]

In a February 26, 1959, memo to ISD Appeals and Research Section chief Kevin Maroney, responding to Maroney's request for comments on pending congressional legislation concerning AGLOSO, Designations Unit head Waterman indicated that the department was unable to make any recommendations at all, because while all AGLOSO-related issues had been "under consideration by the Department for some time," thus far "no policy decision has been reached" and therefore it "appears premature to submit our views" since the proposed legislation was "hinged to a large extent" on the continuing existence of AGLOSO. He added that the department had designated no organizations since October 20, 1955, that action against groups about which "sufficient evidence" for designation existed "remains suspended," and that since the department had in

1957 endorsed legislation that "envisioned a continuance of the designations program," there had been "no indication" that it would be "resumed," although "there is no decision on this point." Nonetheless, in a December 30, 1959, memo for the files, Waterman wrote that he had just informed HUAC counsel Richard Arens that "organizations are designated" for AGLOSO "when an organization meets the criteria and the evidence is available."[54]

By the late 1950s, as Cold War tensions continued to ease, domestic anti-Communist hysteria concomitantly waned, and the government stopped adding names to AGLOSO, the "list" gradually faded from the media spotlight and public attention. Thus, although AGLOSO-related stories flooded the media in 1955–1956, during 1959 no substantive stories about AGLOSO appeared in the *New York Times*, *Washington Post*, *Los Angeles Times*, *Christian Science Monitor*, or the *Wall Street Journal*. Perhaps the clearest sign of the greatly lessened interest in AGLOSO and a growing consensus that it was either no longer needed or had been marred from its origins was an extraordinary confession given by Supreme Court Justice Tom Clark, who had published the first Truman AGLOSO list in late 1947, to a group of Columbia Law School students on March 8, 1961. Clark declared, "Perhaps we should, as I look at it now, have given the parties an opportunity to be heard before we issued [AGLOSO]." According to Clark, the decision to not allow organizations to contest their listings was made for fear that challenges would so delay creation of the list that it would never be issued.

AGLOSO did not disappear entirely from the news or from public consciousness after 1956. For example, when listed organizations were mentioned in the media (which was increasingly infrequent, no doubt partly because few of them had survived and partly because the mainstream press rarely covered the routine activities of such organizations), stories sometimes continued to remind readers of their listings, often, although not always, in the context of the organizations' feebleness or of penalties or proceedings against them which were often related to their alleged "subversive" status. For example, the *New York Times* reminded its readers of the AGLOSO status of the American Committee for the Protection of the Foreign Born (ACPFB) in reporting on a June 1957 New York state administrative and court order banning it from fund-raising on the grounds that its activities were "almost entirely directed towards the assistance of Communists or persons accused of being Communists or former Communists." The May 16, 1960, *Times* reported that an SWP vice presidential candidate claimed she had been banned from speaking at the State University of New York due to her group's designation; on October 7, 1963, the *Times* reported that the "tacit policy" at Indiana University was to refuse the use of school facilities *only* to listed groups. A 1961 U.S. Court of Claims ruling foreshadowed a series of subsequent court rulings during the later 1960s, which suggested that the federal courts were increasingly adopting a highly skeptical view of AGLOSO. In a May 3 ruling in the truly bizarre case of *Thomas v. U.S.* (289 F. 2d 948), Chief Judge Marilyn Jones directed that back pay be tendered to former army secretary Roberta Thomas, who had been suspended in 1954 for almost a year for failing to note on her security forms attendance at two 45-minute night classes in 1946 at two AGLOSO-designated schools. Thomas had reported the matter on other forms and discussed it with a government official, but said she did not consider 90 minutes' attendance as constituting "association, membership in or affiliation" with the schools, which had not yet been listed in 1946. Judge Jones compared the government's action to the infamous pursuit of Jean Valjean for stealing a loaf of bread to feed his family in Victor Hugo's famous novel *Les Misérables*, declared Thomas had not displayed "any effort at concealment," termed the charges against her "so much tweedledee," and accused the government of attempting to "kick an employee all over the lot as if she had no rights whatever."[55]

Periodically, proposals emerged or were implemented after 1957 to use AGLOSO to discriminate in government-related programs. Thus, in the early 1960s, Rep. Overton Brooks (D-LA), chairman of the House of Representatives Science Committee, introduced a bill requiring all applicants for National Science Foundation grants to sign non-AGLOSO disclaimers, an action that apparently immediately led the foundation to revoke an award it had granted to University of Illinois graduate engineering student Edward Yellin, on the grounds that his contempt of Congress conviction for refusing to answer questions posed by HUAC, then on appeal, might interrupt his studies. In 1963, it was revealed that the Coast Guard was requiring would-be seamen and dock workers, who needed "security" screening even if employed in the private sector, to report if they had ever been "associated with [AGLOSO organizations] in any way," ever "submitted material for publication" to such groups, or ever subscribed to any "matter, prepared, reproduced, published, or distributed by" any listed groups or "by any of their members, affiliates, associates or agents." Following protests by the ACLU, the latter question was deleted, but the other questions were retained. In April 1966, the Office of Economic Opportunity, the administrative mechanism for President Johnson's "War on Poverty," reported that members of AGLOSO-designated groups were barred from employment in the agency. In early 1967, army officials revealed that Reserve Officer Training Corps cadets in eight western states were being warned that they might be refused commissions as officers if they joined designated organizations and that they were required to state whether or not they had any affiliations with such groups.[56]

AGLOSO also surfaced in the news periodically after 1956 when alleged affiliations with "subversive" organizations were invoked in proceedings against individuals or used to attack public figures and when politicians and others demanded that nondesignated groups be added to AGLOSO. Such proceedings often had outcomes after 1956 that reflected the substantially changed general political atmosphere from the high tide of anti-Communist hysteria of the early 1950s. For example, in June 1957 the Federal Communications Commission announced that it was granting a license renewal to Edward Lamb, the owner of a Pennsylvania television station, after four years of investigation triggered by allegations that Lamb had supported the CP and belonged to eleven AGLOSO groups in the late 1940s. In July 1957, New York state unemployment insurance referee Philip Wexner upheld a ruling by state industrial commissioner Isador Lubin that CP employees were not entitled to state unemployment benefits; however, in a ruling involving the same individual, CP functionary William Albertson, Wexner overruled Lubin and found Albertson was entitled to such benefits in connection with his former employment by the AGLOSO-designated CRC, holding that the CRC was not a declared arm of the party (ironically, on the same day that Wexner's ruling was made public, the SACB formally declared the by-then defunct CRC a "Communist front"). In his ruling, Wexner declared that the authority to withhold unemployment benefits from CP members was based on the 1954 Federal Communist Control Act, which had stripped the CP of its legal rights and privileges, but that the CRC's AGLOSO status could not justify similar action because the 1954 law had not referenced the CRC. In August 1957, the Washington, D.C., commissioners voted to drop, on constitutional grounds, a decade-old requirement that applicants for insurance brokers' licenses report if they were Communists, members of any AGLOSO organizations, or had ever refused to testify before a court or any other "duly constituted tribunal."[57]

The outcome was quite different for Warrin Austin, an English professor at the City College of New York, who was fired in 1957 for conduct unbecoming his position for allegedly falsely denying CP membership, with evidence that he had attended the defunct AGLOSO-designated Jefferson School of Social Science cited as partial grounds for holding that he had lied. In late November 1957, the Supreme Court agreed to hear the appeal from a State Department passport denial from Rockwell Kent, a prominent artist with alleged AGLOSO affiliations, and in April 1958, the Court agreed to review a New Hampshire state contempt conviction of Dr. Willard Uphaus for refusing to provide state officials with a list of guests at his New Hampshire World Fellowship Center, a request made partly because of their alleged AGLOSO affiliations. The Supreme Court subsequently upheld Uphaus's contempt conviction but overturned the denial of Kent's passport. In early 1960, the U.S. Air Force withdrew a training manual and security guide that linked American churches to communism, including claims that thirty out of ninety-five members of a National Council of Churches of Christ committee that had prepared a bible version "have been affiliated with Communist fronts" and with ninety "Communist and pro-communist projects," including seventeen AGLOSO-designated groups. These allegations were based on a pamphlet originally published by a private organization.[58]

Periodically during the 1957–1967 period, attacks/revelations were made concerning public figures involving alleged past affiliations with AGLOSO organizations, and demands were made that unlisted groups be added to the "list." Thus, on October 5, 1957, conservative *Washington Post* columnist George Sokolsky published evidence that Arkansas governor Orval Faubus, then engaged in a massively publicized attempt to resist court-ordered desegregation of the Little Rock public schools, had attended AGLOSO-designated Commonwealth College and even served as student body president there. A candidate for the Montgomery County, Maryland, county council, Charles Horsky, was attacked in May 1958 for having served as a lawyer for two AGLOSO-designated groups and thus, according to his opponent, having built his professional reputation "in the employ of, and by gaining the confidence of, the subversive elements of our population." Allegations of past or present affiliations with AGLOSO organizations were also leveled at, among others, Coleman Young (later the elected mayor of Detroit) in connection with his nomination as a Democratic Party delegate to a Michigan state constitutional convention in 1961; Constance Baker Motley, a black nominee for federal district court judge in 1966, in connection with her alleged membership in the 1930s with the AGLOSO-designated Connecticut State Youth Conference; and Algernon Black, chairman of New York City's civilian police review board in 1966, concerning his alleged membership in, among other organizations, the ACPFB.[59]

Probably the best-publicized assault on a public figure for alleged past AGLOSO connections during the 1956–1967 period erupted in February 1961, when President John Kennedy's nomination of Robert C. Weaver as Federal Housing Administrator—a subcabinet post that would make Weaver the first black ever to hold such a high-level federal office—led to charges from southern senators that Weaver had subversive affiliations. In what a *Washington Post* headline termed a "revival of McCarthyism," Weaver, a Harvard PhD, chairman of the NAACP, and vice chairman of the New York City Housing and Redevelopment Board, was specifically charged with having had ties with three AGLOSO groups, the National Negro Congress (NNC), the Washington Bookshop Association (WBA), and Council on African Affairs (CAA). He testified before a packed Senate Banking Committee hearing that he had never knowingly been connected with any subversive organizations and had not been active in the three groups. Weaver said he had served as a panelist at a 1937 NNC conference that had received greetings from President Roosevelt and the republican mayor of Philadelphia, had joined the WBA only because "I buy books quite frequently and they offered a 20% discount" and had endorsed a CAA program for Africa because he had agreed with it, but had "no knowledge of any Communist infiltration" of the organization and had failed to subsequently disavow his endorsement after learning of the CAA's Communist leanings only because "nobody wants to volunteer he was a dupe."

Weaver's nomination was approved 11–4 by the Banking Committee and by a voice vote in the full Senate. He was sworn in on February 11, 1961, as President Kennedy looked on and declared, "I have the highest confidence in Mr. Weaver's loyalty, integrity and ability."[60]

Just as allegations of past AGLOSO affiliations were still periodically lodged against prominent individuals during the post-1955 era, demands were sometimes made that allegedly subversive groups be added to the "list." Thus, the NAACP and others urged that the segregationist White Citizens Councils (WCC), formed in the aftermath of Supreme Court desegregation rulings, be added to AGLOSO, while the South Carolina and Mississippi legislatures, the WCC, and other segregationists conversely demanded that the NAACP be listed (even though the NAACP, fearing the impact of such accusations, had attempted to avoid contact with alleged "front" groups and to otherwise avoid any taint of "communism"). In response to such repeated charges of subversion, NAACP executive secretary Roy Wilkins denied his organization was "Communist" or a "Communist front," adding that "neither the attorney general of the United States, the House Un-American Committee, nor any other official federal body" had so "branded the NAACP." Nonetheless southern states harassed the NAACP and other civil rights groups with techniques of investigations, disruption, arrests, and placement on their own subversive "lists" modeled on the federal campaign against "subversive organizations." The result, as historian George Lewis has noted, is that civil rights groups were forced to "expend large amounts of time and energy to make themselves appear free of any communist taint." In *NAACP v. Alabama* (357 U.S. 449, 1958), the U.S. Supreme Court overturned the Alabama law that—like that in at least five other southern states—required the NAACP and other allegedly "subversive" groups to provide members' names and addresses to state officials. The Court ruled that the law violated the right of NAACP members to "pursue their lawful private interest privately and to associate freely with others." In 1961, the Supreme Court ruled similarly in *Louisiana v. NAACP* (366 U.S. 293), but after 1952 it repeatedly declined opportunities to hear cases that might lead to similar rulings about AGLOSO's fundamental constitutionality (although Justice Felix Frankfurter wrote his colleague William Brennan in 1959 that no Court member "personally disapproves more than I do of the activities of all the un-American committees, of all the Smith [Act] prosecutions, of the Attorney General's list, etc").[61]

The DOJ repeatedly asked the FBI to investigate the WCC beginning in 1954 for possible AGLOSO designation, but concluded that evidence was lacking to prove that the WCC, as an organization (as opposed to individual members) directly used or advocated force to deny others their constitutional rights, partly because the term "force" was not construed to "include acts or threats of economic force or pressure." Moreover, according to a February 26, 1957, eleven-page, single-spaced memorandum sent to Attorney General Brownell by OLC acting assistant attorney general Nathan Siegel, AGLOSO had always been viewed in connection with "disloyalty," especially with regard to groups under the influence of "unfriendly foreign powers," so even if the WCC were determined to advocate the forceful denial of constitutional rights to others, "there is a real question as to whether it may be considered disloyal" since they were "wholly domestic" and their members' "loyalty to the United States, in the terms in which loyalty is ordinarily understood is not questioned." Rather, Siegel maintained, they differed "from other loyal citizens" only in their "deep and aggressive hostility" to desegregation and "labeling as subversive, and classing with Communist and Fascists, so large and otherwise loyal a group of individuals as compose the membership of the Citizens Councils would seem to be of questionable utility as a device for reducing opposition to the recognition of Negro rights." On March 21, 1957, Assistant Attorney General Warren Olney advised FBI director Hoover that in light of such conclusions by the OLC and the ISD, "no further investigation" of WCC groups should be undertaken in connection with possible AGLOSO designation. However, in a May 15, 1957, memo to Hoover, Assistant Attorney General Tompkins advised the FBI to continue to investigating "Klan-type organizations," which, according to an October 14, 1957, internal DOJ memo, reflected the fact that the KKK had previously been designated, as well as "the explosive nature of the Designation problem."[62]

The Los Angeles District Attorney suggested in May 1962 that both the WCC and the Nation of Islam (NOI, generally known as the Black Muslims) be designated, and Los Angeles Mayor Sam Yorty added that he would personally ask Attorney General Robert Kennedy to list the Black Muslims because designation would allow the police to close their meeting places and seize their literature. Behind the scenes, the FBI had been unsuccessfully pressing the DOJ to designate or prosecute the NOI for years; although the department repeatedly rebuffed such requests beginning in 1952, it also repeatedly asked the bureau to keep investigating the organization, partly on the grounds that AGLOSO designation was under consideration. Such responses increasingly angered FBI director Hoover, who wrote on an FBI document in August 1960, "Has the Department ruled on the NOI or are they still 'considering' it?" When Hoover sent Attorney General Rogers another memo on the subject in September 1960, he wrote "Just stalling!" on the department reply, which asked the FBI to continue its investigations but declared that there was insufficient evidence to designate the NOI under the AGLOSO criteria calling for the listing of groups that advocated or approved of violence to "deny others their constitutional rights." Similar exchanges occurred between the FBI and the department in 1962, 1963, 1964, and 1966, with the DOJ specifically requesting continued bureau investigation of the NOI in 1966 with possible AGLOSO designation in mind, even though no new listings had been made in over a decade and the department again noted that "insufficient evidence" existed for either designation or prosecution and added that there had been "no significant changes as to the character and tactics" of the NOI during the previous two years.[63]

The American Nazi Party Case, 1961

Numerous calls were issued in the early 1960s to have the tiny, publicity-hungry American Nazi Party (ANP) headed by George Lincoln Rockwell AGLOSO-listed. Partly in response to the call for listing the ANP and NOI, in early 1961 the DOJ began its first serious examination of AGLOSO in about three years, shortly before new attorney general Robert Kennedy told an April 6 press conference that no decision had been made about reviving the list. The ANP had received enormous media publicity—about fifty articles in the *Washington Post* during 1960 alone—which its handful of members clearly reveled in, as they appeared in public wearing Nazi storm trooper outfits, complete with swastikas and jackboots, sometimes attracting attacks from hostile crowds and/or local government bans on their demonstrations. On February 3, 1961, ISD head Yeagley wrote Attorney General Kennedy pointing out that "no organization has been added" to AGLOSO since 1955 and urging that it be "updated in the interest of the federal employee security program," with the ANP offering an "excellent vehicle as a means of reactivating the list and also as the best case for a test in the courts." Yeagley said that Kennedy's predecessor, Attorney General Rogers, had had "serious doubts" concerning AGLOSO's constitutionality, as Attorney General Brownell's 1953 hearing regulations had provided for the "submission of interrogatories [to organizations proposed for designation] without the same right of discovery being granted to the respondent" and because of the "lack of any provision for confrontation or cross-examination when confidential or classified information is used." However, Yeagley continued, the ISD did not view these and other problems as "insurmountable" but felt that the program's constitutionality would "depend more on the type of hearing actually afforded the organization than upon the regulations themselves." He added that proceedings against the ANP need not require the use of confidential information and thus "could grant complete confrontation and cross-examination" and not require "resort to the use of unilateral interrogatories." Characterizing AGLOSO as performing a "useful service" in alerting government officials and the public to the "nature" of such groups and proving "most helpful in providing an official finding" that federal agencies could use in loyalty cases, Yeagley requested authorization to designate the ANP. He conceded that it had "few members" and that a lengthy hearing procedure "might give it the opportunity for badly needed and extensive publicity" but argued that if AGLOSO was "to be retained the nature of this organization makes it the best vehicle" for a court test and that it was a group about which "we have had a great number of inquiries from the public and members of Congress."[64]

Assistant Attorney General and OLC head Nicholas Katzenbach responded to Yeagley on February 15, 1961, by reporting that he had been requested to advise Attorney General Kennedy on ANP designation and wanted detailed information concerning the group, a history of AGLOSO, "including a resumé of serious challenges to its validity which the Department may have received," an indication of which organizations "have been considered for listing since 1955 or may now be considered as possible candidates for listing in the future," and a statement of "uses of the list in the Government" beyond the federal loyalty program. Katzenbach added that he would appreciate Yeagley's views "as to the present usefulness of the list" and, the ANP aside, his recommendations on "the Attorney General's choice of three alternatives: a) take no present or future action with regard to the list and merely maintain it in its present status indefinitely, b) to add to it from time to time as the occasion may arise or c) to terminate it."[65]

Yeagley responded with a fifteen-page, single-spaced February 20, 1961, memorandum which, not surprisingly, reiterated his position that AGLOSO served a "worthwhile function," especially by disclosing "publicly to employees and prospective employees of the Government, the identity of organizations" in which membership might be considered inconsistent with national security and also by providing a uniform guide to federal officials in loyalty cases, as government agencies would otherwise have to individually characterize groups, leading to possible challenges from organizations "that they had been damaged by such characterization without a hearing." Yeagley added that while the ISA authorized separate proceedings before the SACB against "Communist-action, Communist-front and Communist-infiltrated organizations," it did not "authorize proceedings against organizations not under the domination and control of the Communist movement controlled by the Soviet Union, such as anti-Soviet communist organizations, fascist and other types of totalitarian and hate organizations." Noting that the government had recently dropped proceedings against the ISL, the NLG, and the Lithuanian organizations, Yeagley declared that, while no court "has, as yet, overturned the present procedures," the administrative hearing regulations permitting "unilateral interrogatories by the Government would probably not be sustained," and the "provision for the use of classified information without the right of cross-examination would, if utilized, probably be held unconstitutional, unless its use is limited." While conceding that the Supreme Court would probably not "uphold designation proceedings in which classified information was utilized as the rules now permit," Yeagley argued that it would accede to the "limited use of this information when an otherwise full hearing is accorded and if the organization is informed of the nature of the charges against it." He added that if the Government was forbidden to use "some information without confrontation" in contested designations, "valuable confidential informants would have to be released in order to make the case" and under such circumstances "it might not be worthwhile to maintain the list." However, Yeagley maintained, AGLOSO should "not be abolished" pending a final ruling on the ISA's constitutionality, litigation about which had been pending in the courts for a decade, as AGLOSO might prove to be "the only remaining weapon against so-called subversive organizations." Yeagley declared that AGLOSO's importance had been clearly demonstrated, as past listings had the impact of "eventually destroying" designated groups, and as a result it was "estimated that of the 274 organizations presently on the list less than 40 are still active." Therefore, he concluded, the attorney general should maintain the list and "add to it from time to time," realizing that "probably the first case will result in a court test" of AGLOSO's constitutionality. He added that if proceedings were begun against the ANP "we would grant full confrontation."[66]

In response to Katzenbach's specific queries, Yeagley appended to his memo two separate three-page listings, one summarizing the well-known uses of AGLOSO beyond the federal loyalty program and the other listing organizations under consideration for AGLOSO designation, which indicated that the ISD had reviewed reports on 490 organizations, of which, aside from the ANP, 24 groups, including four bookstores and three defense committees, were considered "possible" candidates for designation. However, he added, in each case the prospective witnesses against the organizations were "current confidential informants" and, following a 1957 agreement with the FBI, designation "proceedings were not instituted" against them while awaiting a still pending Supreme Court ruling involving SACB proceedings against the CP. However, Yeagley added, with regard to the ANP there was "no need to protect confidential sources and accordingly this matter was referred to Attorney General Rogers to proceed." He added that Rogers felt designating the ANP would "not serve the purpose for which the list was intended since the name itself was a clear warning," while the "added publicity of a hearing might serve to strengthen" the group and the "more effective method" of dealing with the ANP was via "action by local law-enforcement officials in instances where members violated laws involving disturbing the peace, incitement to riot, unlawful picketing, etc."

On June 26, 1961, Katzenbach weighed in on the ANP issue with a memo to Deputy Attorney General Byron White. Katzenbach argued against either seeking to designate the ANP or to "reactivate" AGLOSO. He termed the ANP "only a petty nuisance at most," as it had "only a few members (estimated at about 55)" and had failed to generate "any substantial sympathetic interest or popular support." Katzenbach added that recent court cases suggested that administrative hearing rules providing for "unilateral interrogatories by the Government organizations and their officers probably would not be sustained," but that the government was still entitled to ask prospective employees about organizational memberships, and anyone indicating ANP affiliation would "unlikely" be employed and obviously would not be "considered sufficiently trustworthy" to gain access to classified information. Moreover, Katzenbach maintained, designating the ANP would "almost assuredly" foster demands for similar actions concerning the right-wing John Birch Society, the WCC, and other groups, producing "much agitation and litigation" but doing "little to strengthen the security of the country," while providing "invaluable publicity" to the organizations involved if attempts to designate them failed.

Katzenbach also expressed the hope that the SACB's authority to compel organizations to register would be upheld and declared that, if necessary, the SACB's jurisdiction could be expanded to include "non-Communist subversive or totalitarian organizations," which, under existing laws and regulations could be AGLOSO-designated but not brought before the SACB. He concluded that if the "responsibility for characterizing organizations is restricted to the [SACB] and the Attorney General's list is allowed to remain dormant, the Attorney General will be relieved of the unfortunate dual role of serving as prosecutor and judge as he is now required to do under the existing designation procedures." In a separate June 26 memo to White, Katzenbach urged Attorney General Kennedy to simply "take no action" concerning AGLOSO, neither "to abolish the list" nor add to it. Although, according to Katzenbach, FBI director Hoover as well as Yeagley had "advised that [AGLOSO] still serves a useful purpose" in federal employee screening, "without regard to the usefulness of the existing list, I feel that little would be gained by attempting to add new organizations" as the Supreme Court might uphold the SACB's attempt to force Communist groups to register under the ISA and "other types of subversive or totalitarian organizations" such as the ANP "can hardly be deemed a threat to the national security at this time." Moreover, he argued, attempts to list them would only give such groups the "publicity and martyrdom they constantly seek and exploit" and, should they fail, raise the ANP's "prestige and position among lunatic-fringe elements" and provide it "a certain aura of respectability." He added that the "considerable expense" to the government of successfully obtaining designations "against those inconsequential organizations would far outweigh any benefit which might be derived" and the "litigation risks" thereby raised "would be considerable and the outcome thereof would by no means be assured."[67]

On August 4, 1961, Yeagley informed Hoover that Katzenbach had told him that Deputy Attorney White had approved Katzenbach's recommendations and that Katzenbach had specifically related that "these matters were the subject of discussion at the White House at a meeting at which he was present" and that "apparently no objections were voiced to proceeding along those lines." Commenting on Yeagley's memo, FBI domestic intelligence chief F. J. Baumgardner declared in an August 7 internal FBI memo that nothing related by Yeagley "in any way affects the Bureau's operations or responsibilities." The results of the

White House meeting referred to by Katzenbach were apparently reflected in a letter from Attorney General Kennedy to Sen. Kenneth Keating (R-NY) released by Keating on August 9, in which Kennedy rejected Keating's request for ANP designation on the grounds that such action would only give the group "a public forum for the further dissemination of its obnoxious doctrines" and that the best way to deal with the group was for local authorities to prosecute them if they violated the law.[68]

AGLOSO in Obscurity, 1961–1969

In late 1961, a committee of representatives from the DOJ, the Budget Bureau, and the CSC met for an overall review of federal loyalty programs, resulting in a December 18, 1961, report to President Kennedy from CSC head John Macy and Budget Bureau director Lee White recommending against discontinuing AGLOSO, as it was "operating effectively" and no need existed for "major program changes which might create uncertainty" among the "more than two million employees affected by the program and possible public relations and agency operating problems." The report termed AGLOSO "now a common denominator in security determinations," leaned upon "heavily" by government security officials, so if it were "discontinued, the stability and uniformity of the security program would probably be adversely affected" and the "courts might reverse adverse loyalty and security determinations based on" AGLOSO membership. The report added that the CSC's general counsel felt that "we could not do without the list," as the government would then have to "to be prepared to prove in court the subversive character of each organization individually." A cover note attached to the December 18, 1961, memorandum indicates President Kennedy subsequently approved it.[69]

Following the August 1961 public announcement of the DOJ's decision not to list the ANP and President Kennedy's approval of the 1961 security program review, AGLOSO largely dropped from the attention of both the news media and the federal government for about ten years. By early 1962, according to a *Washington Post* story, "persons familiar with the result" of recent congressional staff questioning of military personnel concerning their knowledge of communism reported that "only one out of 26 serviceman questioned at one Washington military installation" even "knew what" AGLOSO was. A June 7, 1962, Peter Edison column in the *Washington Daily News*, noting that AGLOSO had not been revised since 1955 except to delete several organizations, termed it "obsolete and almost meaningless," and reported that "the most authoritative sources [clearly in the FBI or the DOJ]" had revealed that "only 11 of the communist-front organizations are active today." Nonetheless, AGLOSO still retained a powerful symbolic importance to the politically sensitive: the 1962 "Port Huron statement," a manifesto issued by the then-fledgling Students for a Democratic Society that is generally viewed as the key inaugural statement of the "new left" movement that shook American society during the following ten years, specifically called for the abolition of AGLOSO, along with HUAC and other "anti-subversive" laws and institutions, in order to "eliminate the fears and apathy from national life." AGLOSO received fleeting attention during the Johnson administration, but ultimately no action was taken that affected it, thus effectively continuing the practice of "letting sleeping lists lie" that had been policy since 1955. In response to Johnson's February 24, 1965, request for an examination of federal security practices concerning executive branch civil employees, a committee consisting of CSC chairman John Macy, Assistant Attorney General Yeagley, and representatives of the Budget Bureau and the Department of Defense recommended on November 1, 1965, that the existing AGLOSO list "not be discarded because it serves an important function in preventing the relitigation of the character" of designated groups but added that "despite the desirability of bringing the list up to date, it is not practical to do so." The committee explained that the DOJ viewed the existing AGLOSO administrative hearing procedures as "of doubtful validity" since they afforded organizations "less than a full confrontation" and the Supreme Court would likely require such under the "Fifth Amendment requirements of procedural due process"; in any case, the committee added, if organizations proposed for designation "demanded a hearing, it would take so long to complete the proceedings that the organization could dissolve its membership and reorganize under another name before the designation became operative" and the hearing process would "require uncovering FBI informants to be used as witnesses." Earlier, on March 2, 1965, Yeagley had told a House appropriations subcommittee (in testimony made public in May 1965) that no groups had been listed since 1955 because the government would "gain little and lose quite a bit" by conducting AGLOSO hearings and thus giving free publicity to groups like the ANP. He added that only 20 of the total of 274 AGLOSO groups were still viewed as active by the DOJ, of which at most only the CP, ACPFB, Industrial Workers of the World (IWW), Ku Klux Klan, NCASF, SWP, and Veterans of the Abraham Lincoln Brigade (VALB) had any name recognition. United Press International summarized Yeagley's account by reporting that the department had revealed that it had "all but abandoned efforts to maintain an official public roster of subversive organizations."[70]

Suggestions that "unlisted" but allegedly "subversive" organizations be placed on AGLOSO no doubt reflected concerns that groups that were not AGLOSO-designated were somehow "approved" by government officials. In fact, not surprisingly, the non-designated status of groups whose loyalty had been attacked was often pointed to as evidence that they were not "subversive." Thus, in July 1962, when controversy arose in Arcadia, California, over the use of a public library meeting room by the ACLU, library board president James Young declared that the library had "checked with the U.S. attorney general and learned that the ACLU is not on the subversive list." In 1963, a federal CSC official disclosed that a dozen Black Muslims had been fired from federal jobs on the grounds that they had taken their oaths of office with "mental reservations," while adding that the CSC could not fire them solely for their affiliation because the Black Muslims were not on AGLOSO and "we doubt if it will be placed on it." Lee Harvey Oswald, who would be accused of assassinating President John F. Kennedy in November 1963, declared during a 1962 radio program concerning his handing out of pamphlets in New Orleans on behalf of the Free Play for Cuba Committee that the organization "is not now on the Attorney General's Subversive List" and therefore any allegations that it was a dubious group were irrelevant; according to a Web page entitled "The Last Words of Lee Harvey Oswald," he repeated this statement while in Dallas police custody in connection with the Kennedy murder less than thirty-six hours before he was shot to death by Jack Ruby. In 1964, while successfully seeking the Republican presidential nomination, Sen. Barry Goldwater (R-AZ) told reporters that he did not list the John Birch Society among various extremist groups that he explicitly repudiated, such as the CP and Klan, because "they're not on the Attorney General's list," while a 1965 *Christian Science Monitor* report on allegations of Communist influence in California, especially in connection with activities of the W. E. B. Du Bois Clubs, noted that "it is pointed out that the clubs are not" AGLOSO-listed.[71]

The IWW and VALB Cases, 1965–1973

Although public—and governmental—interest in AGLOSO reached a nadir by the mid-1960s, two designated organizations, the IWW and VALB, chose then to bring the first legal challenges to the list since the lawsuits initiated ten years earlier by the NLG and the two Lithuanian workers groups. After four years of litigation, VALB (and its predecessor organization, the Abraham Lincoln Brigade [ALB], which it also represented) obtained a court order requiring their delisting (on narrow, rather than fundamental constitutional grounds). However, the IWW remained listed until President Nixon was effectively forced by Congress to abolish AGLOSO in June 1974. The organizations' claims that AGLOSO was fundamentally unconstitutional were never decided by the courts.

VALB/ALB were designated in the first published Truman AGLOSO listing of late 1947. ALB consisted of Americans who fought, as part of the famous International Brigades, for the democratically elected government of republican Spain (the "loyalists") during the 1936–1939 civil war. After ALB formally disbanded in 1938, VALB was formed from ALB survivors (about half of the original 3,000 ALB fighters) to provide support services for them and to express their continued opposition to the forces of Spanish dictator General Francisco Franco, who, backed by Nazi Germany and fascist Italy, triumphed in early 1939. The American CP organized the recruitment of ALB fighters and many or most, if by no means all, of them were CP members or sympathizers. Although an estimated 600 ALB veterans were deemed "loyal" enough to fight in the American military during World War II, the ALB/VALB were not only AGLOSO designated in 1947, but in April 1953 Attorney General Brownell initiated proceedings to have the SACB force the VALB (the ALB being defunct) to register as a "Communist front" under the ISA. Lincoln veterans were increasingly portrayed as "subversive" by the American government and many lost jobs and passports due to FBI interventions and State Department political restrictions. Such pressures did not always work, however: according to ALB veteran Louis Gordon, interviewed in 1998, "I was a carpenter and one time an FBI agent came around and said to my employer, 'Do you know this man is a communist?' And my boss, to his ever living credit, tells the agent, 'Hey, do you know where I can find any more of them? This guy does great work.'"[72]

VALB did not file a notice of contest following its 1953 AGLOSO redesignation but did vigorously challenge the SACB proceedings simultaneously initiated against it. On December 21, 1955, the SACB designated the VALB a Communist front, following the recommendation of its hearing examiner, who declared that the "overwhelming weight of the evidence" indicated that the organization was "directed, dominated and controlled" by the CP. Acting under ISA provisions, which allowed court review of final SACB determinations, the VALB filed suit challenging the determination. Although a federal appeals court upheld the SACB in 1963, on April 26, 1965, the Supreme Court required it to reconsider on the grounds that the board had acted on the basis of stale information (*VALB v. SACB*, 380 U.S. 513). On April 20, 1966, the attorney general's petition to the SACB to force the VALB to register as a Communist front was vacated by joint agreement by VALB and the DOJ. A month later, VALB requested that the attorney general also remove its AGLOSO designation (as well as that of the ALB). When this request was denied, on March 23, 1967, VALB, acting also on behalf of the defunct ALB, filed a federal lawsuit to seek AGLOSO delisting, essentially on the same grounds brought by the NLG and other organizations that had legally challenged their designations in the mid-1950s, namely, that they were not "subversive" organizations, that their listing had seriously damaged their ability to function, and that AGLOSO violated their First Amendment free speech and Fifth Amendment due process rights.[73]

On November 14, 1967, federal district court Judge Sirica granted the government's request for summary judgment and dismissed VALB's complaint, citing a ruling two months earlier by the Federal Appeals Court for the District of Columbia in a similar case initiated by the IWW, which held that organizations that had failed to timely utilize the administrative procedures of the 1953 DOJ rules could not subsequently legally challenge their designations. The IWW, a once-flourishing, openly anticapitalist but also anti-CP industrial labor union, had been largely destroyed during World War I–era repression. It was targeted then by the federal government (as well as by state and local governments) for its perceived opposition to the war, its radical rhetoric, and its leadership of several wartime strikes in critical industries, which were portrayed by the press and the DOJ as designed to sabotage the war effort, although they largely resulted from abominable labor conditions. Primarily due to the World War I jailing of over 100 of its leaders and the incessant persecution of its surviving remnants, the IWW was reduced from a pre–World War I height of 100,000 members to an estimated 7,000 when on May 7, 1949, it became the first (and last) labor union to be AGLOSO-designated. By 1970, the IWW had been reduced to about 1,000 members. The IWW initiated its legal challenge to AGLOSO in federal district court on May 4, 1965, based on the same grounds advanced by VALB. In its August 27, 1965, response, the government likewise essentially repeated arguments presented in response to past legal challenges to AGLOSO: that the IWW had been properly designated, that it had failed to "state a claim upon which relief can be granted," that AGLOSO and its governing procedures were constitutional and not arbitrary, and that the IWW was barred from pursuing any legal remedy because it had failed to challenge its redesignation under the 1953 contestation regulations. On August 29, 1966, the district court, echoing the government, held that the IWW had failed to utilize its "administrative remedy" in timely fashion and had therefore "precluded itself from pursuing a judicial remedy." Although it lost again in the 1967 federal courts of appeals ruling (*IWW v. Clark*, 385 F. 2d 687) cited by Judge Sirica in the VALB/ALB case, the appeals court cracked open a door to continued administrative proceedings concerning the IWW demand for "delisting," which the IWW, ironically, was never able to take advantage of, but which soon proved critical for the VALB's ultimately successful court fight to achieve that goal.[74]

The IWW court declined to consider First and Fifth Amendment issues and held that the IWW had waived any legal opportunity to challenge its 1953 redesignation by failing to request a hearing within the allotted time. However, it added that, in post-1953 correspondence with the IWW, the attorney general had effectively "informally" added a process for delisting even after the expiration of the formal period to challenge the 1953 redesignation but had "articulated no standards" to determine what evidence would be considered adequate in such and had thus provided "something less than a wholly satisfactory administrative remedy." Therefore, the court concluded, the IWW had "timely raised a justifiable objection that the Attorney General's denial of relief [to its attempted later use of an administrative remedy] was arbitrary" and that the organization had adequately raised "an issue that the District Court had ignored" in simply relying on the group's failure to timely contest its 1953 redesignation. Therefore, the court remanded the case for district court reconsideration, pointedly noting that "since 1953, when the last deliberate decision to list the IWW as a subversive group was made, there has been a considerable development [toward an easing of] public and judicial attitudes towards control of subversives" and recent cases "may have some relevance in determining whether the Attorney General's conduct must be held arbitrary and capricious." The IWW subsequently appealed to the Supreme Court, which declined to accept the case (390 U.S. 948, 1968), and no further developments ensued.

However, when the ALB/VALB case came before the federal appeals court, although the court refused to strike the groups from AGLOSO or to declare AGLOSO unconstitutional, it remanded the case back to federal district court, citing the "same reasoning" it had invoked in its 1967 IWW ruling (*VALB v. Attorney General*, 409 F. 2d 1139, 1969). After a failed attempt by ALB/VALB to gain immediate Supreme Court intervention (*VALB v. Attorney General*, 396 U.S. 844, 1969), they obtained a November 20, 1969, order from Judge Sirica directing Nixon administration attorney general John Mitchell to conduct "further [administrative] proceedings in accordance" with the appeals court ruling. Mitchell then asked Sirica on April 13, 1970, to drop his order because he had (unilaterally) reviewed the existing designations and signed an order to amend them by adding the words "prior to April 20, 1966" (the date of the dismissal of SACB proceedings against VALB), thus suggesting that they had been "subversive" before then. FBI director Hoover responded to this news by ordering FBI agents to submit "pertinent information showing subversive aspects [of the two groups] since 4/20/66," while VALB asked Sirica to enforce his earlier directive to Mitchell. When Sirica denied this motion, VALB appealed Sirica's ruling to a federal appeals court, declaring that Mitchell had violated his order by acting without notice or hearing and requesting the immediate delisting of ALB/VALB along with the total abolition of AGLOSO on constitutional grounds. In an October 24, 1972, ruling (*VALB v. Attorney General*, 470 F. 2d 441), the appeals court declined to confront the constitutional issues but ordered the delisting of ALB/VALB, marking the first and only time in AGLOSO's history that a court so acted. The appeals court unanimously held that Mitchell, by continuing the AGLOSO designations while adding "prior to April 20, 1966," "*without* affording any opportunity for hearing and *without* any notice to plaintiffs," had flouted its 1969 ruling, which it declared had been issued "to afford the plaintiff herein an opportunity for a hearing." The court declared that the "burdens of unjustified listing" discussed in *McGrath* had not been "lessened by the inclusion of [Mitchell's] or similar words," but, to the contrary, "those words violate the spirit of, and effectively drive a horse and wagon through this Court's February 14, 1969 remand order." Further, given Mitchell's failure to either comply with the order or appeal it to the Supreme Court, the "continued listing of [ALB and VALB] cannot be tolerated." On February 15, 1973, new attorney general Richard Kleindienst issued Order 507–73, delisting ALB/VALB from AGLOSO.[75]

The December 12, 1972, VALB newsletter, "The Volunteer," termed the ruling an "important victory" that "brings to a halt 24 years of harassment of VALB and its members, but not without its heavy toll in lost jobs, interrupted careers, academic hardship and mental anguish. The tenacity with which the leadership and membership of VALB carried on guaranteed that it is still here today carrying out the pledge to the Spanish people not to rest until they have regained their freedom." Following Franco's 1975 death, Spain returned to democracy with startling speed, while in the aftermath of the Watergate scandal and growing revelations of FBI abuses in the early 1970s, the American political climate with regard to the "Lincolns" changed dramatically. Thus, a 1974 documentary movie, "The Good Fight," which lionized the role of the Lincoln Brigade in fighting for Spanish democracy, was widely hailed, and in early 1975 the *New York Times* published a long article by VALB national commander Steve Nelson (a former CP leader who had been prosecuted during the McCarthy period under the 1940 Smith Act) urging an end to American military support for Franco, so that "we who have fought a lifetime for Spanish democracy will feel that we haven't spent these years in vain." At the 1986 fiftieth anniversary of the Lincoln Brigade's formation, veteran William Susman was invited to speak about his experiences at over thirty colleges, including Yale, Harvard, Dartmouth, and Cornell. After Franco's death, ALB veterans began returning to Spain, as if in response to a famous 1938 speech by Spanish Communist leader Delores Ibarruri ("La Pasionaria") upon their withdrawal: "You can go proudly. You are history, you are legend. . . . and when the olive tree of peace puts forth its leaves again, mingled with the laurels of the Spanish Republic's victory, come back." Brigade members were increasingly treated as heroes in Spain and were made honorary citizens by the Spanish parliament. Charles Nusser, a vehemently non-CP veteran, told a reporter during celebrations of the ALB's fiftieth anniversary, "If the same conditions prevailed today, I would do it all again. It is the one thing in my life that I'm proud of." By 2001, ALB memorials had been placed in Seattle and Madison and were planned for San Francisco, although a memorial plaque that had been installed in the New Hampshire statehouse was taken down before its formal unveiling after the *Manchester Union Leader* attacked it as honoring those who had gone to Spain to "fight alongside communists."[76]

5

The Nixon Administration's Abortive Attempt
to Revive AGLOSO, 1969–1974

The Legal Evolution of the SACB and AGLOSO, 1965–1971

By the time Richard M. Nixon became president in January 1969, AGLOSO, while still in existence, had become essentially moribund, antiquated, and insignificant. The government had not added any new organizations for fifteen years and was afraid to defend AGLOSO in the courts for fear that it would be found unconstitutional. While theoretically the "list" was still officially in use for such purposes as screening federal employees and potential draftees (the present author was asked if he had AGLOSO affiliations during a 1969 draft physical), it was increasingly a fading memory to the general public. Furthermore, by the time Nixon took office, the Subversive Activities Control Board (SACB), whose somewhat parallel job, under the 1950 Internal Security Act (ISA), was to order official "registration" with the government of Communists and Communist fronts, with a series of automatic penalties following, had effectively been rendered toothless by a series of court rulings. For example, in two 1965 cases involving the AGLOSO-designated ACPFB and the VALB, the Supreme Court overruled SACB "Communist front" registration orders on the grounds that they were based on "stale" evidence submitted by dubious sources (*ACPFB v. SACB*, 380 U.S. 503, *VALB v. SACB*, 380 U.S. 513). Although the Court had upheld the SACB-ordered registration of the CP itself in 1961 (*CP v. SACB*, 367 U.S. 90), this ruling was largely undermined several years later in *Albertson v. SACB* (382 U.S. 70, 1965), which held that individuals could not be forced to register without violating their Fifth Amendment protections against self-incrimination, and in *U.S. v. Robel* (389 U.S. 258, 1967), which struck down the ISA's ban on any member of a "Communist action" organization (i.e., the CP) from employment in "any defense facility." In words pregnant with implications for any subsequent constitutional test of AGLOSO, *Robel* held that the ISA's language swept "indiscriminately across all types of associations with Communist-action groups, without regard" to the nature of the affiliation, and established "guilt by association alone, without any need to establish that an individual's association poses the threat feared by the Government in proscribing it."

Numerous other legal rulings during the mid and late 1960s and early 1970s further emasculated the remnants of both the SACB and AGLOSO and suggested an increasing reluctance of the federal government to defend them in court. For example, in January 1967, the government announced it would not appeal a recent federal court ruling striking down the requirement in the 1965 federal Medicare act that applicants for benefits sign disclaimers of belonging to any organizations ordered to register by the SACB. The government's decision was partly based on the Supreme Court's 1966 *Elfbrandt v. Russell* (384 U.S. 11) holding that an Arizona law requiring public employees to disavow membership in the CP, its "successors," any of its "subordinate organizations," or "any other organization" seeking to overthrow the government was too vague and broad because it did not require "specific intent" to further the groups' unlawful purposes and therefore rested "on the doctrine of 'guilt by association' which has no place" in the American constitutional scheme. In *Keyishian v. Board of Regents* (385 U.S. 589, 1967) the Court overturned its own 1952 *Adler v. Board of Education* ruling upholding New York's so-called Feinberg Law, which banned public school teachers from membership in "subversive organizations" designated by the New York Board of Regents. *Keyishian* also struck down other New York laws that required firing teachers who engaged in "treasonable or seditious" utterances or acts, holding that they were unconstitutionally vague and limited free association without permitting rebuttal via proof of nonactive membership or absence of intent to further unlawful goals, especially given *Elfbrandt's* holding that "mere knowing membership without specific intent to further the unlawful aims of an organization is not a constitutionally adequate basis for exclusion" from publicly funded teaching positions. In two 1971 cases, *Baird v. State Bar of Arizona* (401 U.S. 1) and *In Re Stolar* (401 U.S. 23), the Supreme Court banned Arizona and Ohio from inquiring whether prospective lawyers had ever belonged to organizations that advocated the forceful overthrow of the government, declaring in the former case that the First Amendment banned punishments solely because individuals belonged to "particular political organization[s]" or held "certain beliefs."[1]

While none of these Supreme Court rulings directly involved AGLOSO, the basic principles they established were applied to the list in a series of lower federal court rulings that threatened to emasculate AGLOSO's original supposed purpose of screening government employees. In August 1967, a federal district court, in *Gilmore v. James* (274 F. Supp. 75), struck down a loyalty oath required of all Texas state employees that required disavowal of CP membership throughout their lives, as well as, for the previous five years, membership in any organization designated either by AGLOSO or the SACB, unless they swore that when they "joined and throughout the period" during which they were members of such organizations, they were unaware of their proscribed subversive purposes. Citing *Elfbrandt* and *Keyishian*, the court ruled that the Texas oath mandated a forced "fettering of the exploration in the realm of ideas" that violated the First Amendment, by disqualifying persons for state employment "solely on the grounds of present or past" organizational memberships. The court maintained that "an individual is entitled to be judged by his own conduct, not that of his associates," and that to the extent the Texas law disqualified "passive or dissenting members" of putatively subversive organizations, "it is too broadly drawn." In *Soltar v. Postmaster General* (277 F. Supp. 579, 1967), another federal district court similarly ruled out the Post Office's practice of asking applicants for employment if they had ever been members of the CP, "any Communist organization" or (without specifically referencing AGLOSO), any organization exactly fitting AGLOSO's "mandate" (i.e., "totalitarian, fascist, Communist, or subversive" or seeking unconstitutional overthrow of the government or to deprive others of their constitutional rights). Citing precedents such as *Elfbrandt*, the court held that such inquiries violated First Amendment rights by "probing into protected" areas involving speech and association, with a resultant "chilling effect," so that those seeking federal employment would "'think first' before joining any political organization." In *Haskett v. Washington* (294 F. Supp. 912, 1968), *Stewart v. Washington* (301 F. Supp. 601, 1969), and *Cummings et al. v. Hampton et al.* (C-70 2130 RFP, 1971), federal district courts struck down federal loyalty oath statutes that sought to implement the 1939 Hatch Act provision that had undergirded the initiation of the World War II Biddle AGLOSO. Thus, *Stewart* held unconstitutional banning employment to applicants who failed to swear that they did not advocate, and were not members of groups they knew advocated, the "overthrow of our constitutional form of government," because the personal advocacy oath was not limited to those who sought the government's overthrow by force or violence, while the organizational membership oath, in violation of such precedents as *Elfbrandt* and *Keyishian,* applied even to those holding "passive and inert membership and even to members who may not share the views of the group on this advocacy." Two federal courts during the 1968–1970 period overturned less than "honorable" military discharges based solely on AGLOSO affiliations. In June 1968, a federal appeals court (401 F. 2d 1990) struck down an "other than honorable" 1952 discharge of an inactive naval reservist based solely on his allegedly "undesirable" CP associations, although no allegation was made that they had "any discernible impact" upon the "quality of his service." Similarly, in May 1970 a federal district court (314 F. Supp. 475) ordered the army to change to "honorable" from "undesirable" the 1968 discharge it had given to a soldier (who had received high conduct and efficiency ratings) solely for alleged "close, continuing and sympathetic association" with (1) the CP and other AGLOSO groups; and (2) with his girlfriend, who allegedly also had such ties with AGLOSO-linked organizations. Judge Charles Tenney held that there was no basis for the undesirable discharge because it was "impermissible for the army to punish an admittedly competent soldier merely because it disapproves of the company he keeps" and the record disclosed "not a scintilla of evidence connecting these allegedly guilty associations" with the soldier's military performance since he was charged only "with associations and beliefs, and not with military misconduct or matters affecting his military record."

The SACB and the Concept of Reviving AGLOSO, 1968–1971

Probably the most important factor in an ultimately abortive 1971 effort by President Nixon to revive both the SACB and AGLOSO was that sitting SACB members expressed the fear that without some new tasks to perform the board would go out of business and they would lose their jobs. Such fears were repeatedly expressed, especially by SACB chair John Mahan, during the years leading up to Nixon's 1971 executive order seeking to resurrect AGLOSO by effectively transferring its administration from the attorney general to the SACB; moreover, Mahan furnished both the idea and the original draft that led to Nixon's 1971 action. Thus, in an August 29, 1968, letter to President Lyndon Johnson's special assistant Joseph Califano, Mahan strongly urged the SACB's continued existence, as it had been a "significant deterrent" to the goals of the "world Communist movement," especially as many organizations that the SACB had determined to be Communist "fronts" were "eliminated because the organizations dissolved" when facing the potential resulting sanctions. Mahan conceded that SACB proceedings had largely halted due to recent court rulings, but argued that "protection against Communist efforts to subvert our way of life is of prime importance." In a February 11, 1969, letter to Nixon assistant Robert Ellsworth, Mahan first raised the idea that AGLOSO also required a "review and updating," terming such action "mandatory." He added that legislation was needed to further the SACB's "great and continuing interest in protecting the nation from those subversive groups and individuals who seek by unlawful means to destroy our form of government," including, in a clear reference to the increasingly strong anti-Vietnam War movement, "the so-called militant New-Left."[2]

The drive to resurrect the SACB, which ultimately led to Nixon's attempt to also revive AGLOSO, received a considerable boost in a highly irregular directive issued by Nixon assistant John Ehrlichman to his fellow presidential assistant Egil "Bud" Krogh on March 25, 1969, which declared that "the President would like the SACB to do an investigation of [black militants] Stokely Carmichael and H. Rap Brown," then much in the news due to their inflammatory rhetoric. In handwritten notes deposited in Krogh's file apparently shortly thereafter, the note taker, presumably Krogh himself, stated that under the existing SACB statute, the government would have to "*allege*" that Brown and Carmichael were associated with the Communist movement, but that this problem would be solved if the SACB's charge were amended so that it could "find a guy is a member of a 'violent action group'" devoted to the forceful overthrow of the United States. Apparently reflecting Krogh's perception that Ehrlichman's March 25 note required urgent action, Krogh wrote in a March 27 file memorandum, following a meeting with Mahan, that the SACB could, under the ISA, only proceed against persons "who can be labeled" CP members and that for it to proceed against Carmichael and Brown it would be "necessary to expand the grounds over which the Board could have public investigatory control. Mahan suggests expanding the groups to include 'violent action groups devoted to the overthrow of the U.S. government by force and violence.'"[3]

On April 30, 1969, Mahan sent Krogh a hand-delivered memo with a nine-page draft executive order that he "highly" recommended for Nixon's consideration, adding that it represented the "composite views" of SACB and Department of Justice (DOJ) Internal Security Division (ISD) attorneys. The memo set the basic parameters for numerous subsequent drafts and Nixon's ultimate June 1971 executive order, which attempted to resurrect both AGLOSO and the SACB by transferring jurisdiction over the former from the attorney general to the latter. In connection with considering association with suspect groups for governmental security screenings, the draft proposed that "membership in, or activity in behalf of" such groups (the term "sympathetic association" included in earlier loyalty orders was deleted) be defined by the attorney general as involving "knowing" affiliation, an apparent, if somewhat ambiguous, response to the recent court decisions discussed above (the draft was ambiguous because it only clearly required that the *affiliation* itself be "knowing," without specifying that the person must have knowledge about the suspect activities of the organization). Secondly, the draft greatly expanded the scope of groups to be considered for AGLOSO listing beyond that of "Communist" organizations by defining "organization" to include virtually any group that was "permanently or temporarily associated together for joint action on any subject." Such organizations were explicitly expanded beyond the "Communistic" and "totalitarian" groups originally targeted by the 1947 Truman executive order to include also, for the first time, "anarchistic" and "violent-action" organizations, with each such type of group defined in a broadly expansive manner. Thus, "anarchistic" groups included not only those engaged in violence but also those that advocated or had "among its purposes or objectives, the abolition, by force and violence, of organized government in the U. S." "Communistic" organizations encompassed any group adopting Marxist interpretations of history that advocated the "establishment of a single authoritarian party by means including force and violence with the ultimate objective of achieving a classless society," a formulation that seemingly also included organizations that sought such objectives via the ballot box. "Violent-action" AGLOSO organizations were defined as any group that advocated, sought, or adopted "as a means of obtaining any of its purposes" the "overthrow, destruction or substantial interference" with governmental operations "by coercion, force or violence, or any other unlawful act" or the "promotion of or participation in riots, civil disorders, or any other unlawful act" that sought to or in fact interfered with the "free exercise of any citizen" of any guaranteed rights "by coercion, force or violence or any other unlawful act."[4]

Thirdly, and most important (at least from the SACB's standpoint), the draft order gave the SACB the right to list and delete from AGLOSO such organizations, based on hearings following submissions from the attorney general requesting such action. The draft specified that in the case of "previously designated" AGLOSO groups, the attorney general was to furnish the SACB with "available information concerning the date of the last known activities of such organizations." The draft concluded that upon reaching its determinations, following notification to the affected organizations and hearings conducted "under and pursuant to such rules and regulations as the Board may prescribe," the SACB would furnish the attorney general with its findings for use "in maintaining a currently revised list of designated organizations." No reference was made to whether or not the list was to be published, but the overall context makes clear that publication was not only assumed but was a primary purpose of seeking to revive AGLOSO.

In response to a series of follow-up questions from Nixon assistant Peter Flanigan, on June 23, 1969, Mahan informed the former, via a memo sent by messenger, that the "major 'problems' which the Board faces in the next few years" involved the need to expand its authority, above all the power to "disclose the true nature of all organizations that teach or advocate violence or disorders," as "a number of non-Communist organizations" existed that "pose a threat to the national security and should be disclosed as a means of curbing their effectiveness." Mahan indicated he had personally discussed with Attorney General John Mitchell a draft executive order (apparently much like that furnished to Krogh on April 30) to give the SACB jurisdiction over AGLOSO, which would eliminate due process "problems" with the list by providing "pre-designation hearings by our Board on petition of the Attorney General" and would "significantly" improve "existing limitations as to the scope or coverage" by expanding the kinds of organizations that could be designated. Mahan added, "We are awaiting further word from the Attorney General."[5]

By Thanksgiving 1969, the continued failure of the White House to issue Mahan's proposed order was apparently driving him into at least a minor frenzy, largely propelled by fears of growing congressional criticism that the SACB was a "do nothing" body. Thus, on November 21, Krogh, now deputy presidential assistant for domestic affairs, wrote Mitchell that Mahan "has been calling me repeatedly about expanding the franchise of the SACB," accompanied by the notation that then-candidate Nixon was quoted during the 1968 election as promising to let the SACB lapse if elected unless the DOJ could demonstrate "what, if any, useful purposes the Board can serve" in the department's "anti-subversive activities" and that he would not allow the SACB to "remain a lucrative sinecure for friends of the Presidential family," a clear reference to President Johnson's appointment to the SACB of the husband of one of his secretaries. Continued inaction from the White House led Mahan to write Nixon directly on December 22, 1969, expressing the hope that "the proposed executive order now in the hands of Attorney General John Mitchell meets with your approval so our Board can finally start controlling subversives in the U.S." Mahan's ever-increasing anxiety about the SACB's fate may have partly reflected the impact of a December 12 ruling by the U.S. Court of Appeals for the District of Columbia in *Boorda v. SACB* (421 F. 2d 1142), which further rendered the SACB toothless by declaring unconstitutional a series of January 1968 congressional amendments to the ISA that had sought to at least partly revive the board by giving it additional duties. *Boorda* held the amendments violated the First Amendment, which banned the government "from claiming an interest in public disclosure of associations of innocent members of Communist-action organizations." Soon after Mahan's letter, White House aide Lamar Alexander wrote Krogh on February 16, 1970, to report that SACB counsel Bernard Waters had warned that the upcoming reappointment of Mahan (or a successor) as SACB chair "will probably be enough of an event to remind a number of people" to inquire if "the SACB is now doing anything," and that "Waters suggests it would be better to make sure that there is a good answer for this."[6]

Meanwhile, within the DOJ, on February 18, 1970, Assistant Attorney General (and future Supreme Court Justice) William Rehnquist wrote Mitchell, representing the Office of Legal Counsel (OLC), in response to a request from Mitchell and ISD head J. Walter Yeagley for recommendations concerning a "proposed transfer from the Attorney General to the SACB of the authority to designate subversive organizations." While conceding that precedents were "hazy and inconclusive" as to whether the president could change the functions of a congressionally created "traditionally independent" regulatory agency by executive order rather than via legislative authorization, Rehnquist concluded that such an order "may be legally accomplished." He recommended issuing an executive order based on an OLC draft that maintained the SACB's proposal requiring "knowing" affiliation with subversive organizations for penalties to ensue for individuals, transferred AGLOSO listing authority to the SACB (upon petition of the attorney general or, in the case of delisting, upon petition by listed group), created a new category of broadly defined "violent-action oriented" groups, and provided broad definitions of existing categories such as "totalitarian," "fascist," and "Communist." However, the OLC draft dropped the SACB's proposed new inclusion of "anarchistic" organizations. Rehnquist's memo clearly suggested that the OLC largely regarded the entire issue as more political than substantive. Referring to a July 23, 1969, memo to Mitchell, Rehnquist declared that AGLOSO was "not of great legal significance" and that it was "difficult to establish" that the failure to update it had "hurt government security" (although earlier listings "may have some value" in "causing these organizations to become defunct"), especially since government hiring agencies were "generally aware of all organizations" to which government applicants belonged and considered them "on a case-by-case basis," regardless of whether or not the organizations were AGLOSO-designated. Referring specifically to a black militant organization that would likely be targeted under a revived AGLOSO, Rehnquist commented dryly, "one would suspect that very few members of the Black Panthers are hired" by the government. He added that AGLOSO was of "no demonstrable help in dismissing employees," since court rulings had established that they must have been "knowing and active members" of suspect groups who had sought to "further the organization's unlawful activities." Rehnquist concluded that a presidential decision on issuance of the proposed order was "basically a non-legal one," but recommended action since a revived AGLOSO "may be necessary in order to give the SACB some responsibilities in order to get an appropriation" and, whatever the truth, "there are substantial elements who are convinced" that the SACB played or "at least should play, an important role in the internal security program." The increasing interest in the role of the SACB apparently triggered a bizarre February 19 memo from top presidential aide Bob Haldeman that suggests that he (and possibly President Nixon, who had largely authored the 1950 ISA that created the SACB) had no idea what the board was or what it did: Haldeman told his deputy Lawrence Higby to "find out quickly for me from someone" what the SACB "does," including "whether they are involved in subversive activities" and "what their funding sources are" as well as "who controls and directs" its activities (its members, of course, were presidentially appointed and legislatively funded), since "I've got to get a report to the President on it."[7]

On February 20, two days after Rehnquist's February 18 memo to Mitchell (a copy of which reached Krogh in the White House) and one day after Haldeman's panicked memo to Higby, Krogh was sent another memo touching on the SACB, this one from Tom Charles Huston, who was engaged in a general review of Nixon administration internal security policy, one that would eventually lead to a variety of illegal political surveillance operations, including the notorious "Huston Plan," the "White House plumbers" operation, and, eventually, to Watergate and Nixon's impeachment and resignation. Huston's memo made clear that he did not view the SACB as having any significant role to play in his plans, but nonetheless suggested giving the board "something worthwhile to do," although of "sufficiently low-profile nature as to avoid controversy," such as charging it with "conducting a government-wide review of personnel security procedures." Huston followed up with another memo to Krogh on March 20, in which he proposed a "four-phased program designed to increase the Government's capability to cope with the escalating threat to the internal security," which further downplayed the SACB's role. Huston "strongly" recommended against issuing the proposed executive order "until such time as we have had the opportunity to review the entire internal security problem and determine exactly how a revitalized SACB would fit into the picture." Although, apparently referring to right-wing pressure to support the SACB, he noted "there are political implications which restrict our maneuverability in this area," but declared, "I don't think we need to rush into something here which we may later regret."[8]

Mahan again wrote Krogh on February 20, claiming that recent talks "with persons in the White House and Department of Justice" suggested agreement that Nixon should issue an executive order "such as that proposed by the Board a few months ago," and that the "only question appears to be that of timing." Mahan made clear that it was a completely political issue as to whether the order should be "published immediately or in the very near future, or delayed until after the fall elections." He conceded that there was "merit in the position that it would be wiser to wait until after the elections," since "issues of domestic subversion and the SACB are quiet now and there is no use complicating things by stirring them up," but quickly added that "unfortunately, for the Administration," there were "factors beyond its control" that would make those issues of "great public interest in the near future" in "such a way as to place the Administration on the defensive if the Executive Order has not been issued." Among the factors that Mahan then listed were the scheduled appearance of himself or another SACB member before a congressional appropriations committee "within the next month or so," which would create the "embarrassing position of having to admit" that the SACB "has no work to do right now," leading to the "usual attacks" on the SACB for wasting money. Unless the order was issued quickly or could be promised "in the very near future," Mahan warned, both the SACB and the Nixon administration "will be in a very bad position." He urged quick action also because of forthcoming "planned subversive activities" to protest the Vietnam War, on the heels of massive late 1969 antiwar protests, which he termed the "largest Communist-manipulated" demonstrations in American history and "their most successful united-front operation in decades." Mahan added that even if "certain minority elements will criticize the order," the "'silent majority' which elected and supports the President, will react in an entirely different manner."[9]

Mahan followed up with a similar letter to White House assistant Flanigan on February 27, urging that the executive order be issued "as soon as possible," both because it was "highly desirable" to provide a "solid legal basis" for considering individuals' associations with "revolutionary and violent-action groups in determining their fitness for Government employment" and because otherwise "the opposition" would be able to "blast me or my successor, the Administration and the Board (as has been done in the past) on the grounds" that it "is a do-nothing agency." Noting that the 1969 *Boorda* ruling (which the government was then appealing) had left the SACB essentially paralyzed, Mahan pressed upon Flanigan the urgent need to establish "some way" to "get work to the Board" and concluded that nothing but the issuance of the proposed order could prevent attacks "which would harm both the Board and the Administration." On March 2, President Nixon, his knowledge of the SACB apparently now refreshed, wrote Haldeman to suggest that the SACB "now dormant, could make itself useful by investigating some of the sources of funds" of antiwar organizations and that congressional committees could also "take this problem on," since the nation was "ready for some outspoken confrontation on this issue, even though the witnesses will come in and raise hell and cause disturbances in the committee rooms. This in itself will help our cause."[10]

On April 13, 1970, when Mahan requested a 1971 budget of slightly over $400,000 at a House appropriations subcommittee hearing, his trepidations about a political assault on the SACB proved vastly exaggerated, as he was not asked a single hostile question and the SACB was not even once accused of "doing nothing." However, the SACB's legal and political position was considerably weakened when the Supreme Court refused on April 20 to hear the *Boorda* appeal. In the meantime, consideration of the proposed executive order continued to lumber on at the White House and the DOJ. A memo from White House aide Larry Higby to Krogh on April 10 suggested for the first time that Nixon had taken a personal interest in getting the order issued quickly: he asked if the administration was "ready to go" with it and declared that, "As you know, the President is anxious to get some activities underway there." On April 16, DOJ ISD head Yeagley sent to Krogh a proposed bill prepared "on the assumption that the Ex. Order will have been issued," which declared that the president had issued an executive order directing the SACB to conduct hearings, upon the petition of the attorney general, to "determine whether certain organizations come within the terms of the Executive Order," labeling such procedures "essential to the protection of the national welfare" and, without explaining why a law was needed if the president could act by executive order, empowering the SACB, renamed the Federal Internal Security Board (FISB), to "conduct hearings and make determinations" relating to "security requirements for government employment." SACB chair Mahan also sent Krogh a memo on April 16, essentially backing up Yeagley's communication and noting that the proposed executive order would give the FISB jurisdiction to "hold hearings on a new type organization—'violent-action' groups," and that this argued for changing the SACB's name since the word "subversive" was "now associated in the public mind with Communists, and some of the groups in the violent-action category (such as the KKK or Black Panthers)" did not "fit" this concept as "they are neither Communist nor foreign-controlled." In a truly bizarre twist, Mahan urged that the order be signed on April 22, because that was Earth Resources Day and in addition was "the 100th anniversary of Lenin's birth."[11]

Also on April 16, 1970, according to a memo from Krogh to top Nixon aides Ehrlichman and Haldeman, the proposed "executive order and legislation" concerning the "future mission" of the SACB was taken up at a White House meeting on internal security. The meeting was apparently attended by Huston, among others, and on May 6 he sent Krogh a memo endorsing the version of the proposed order that Assistant Attorney General Rehnquist had recommended to Attorney General Mitchell on February 18 (by May there were at least four different drafts circulating at the White House). Huston endorsed Mahan's warning that, without the order, board critics "can be expected to charge that the SACB is a waste of the taxpayers [sic] money since the members have nothing to do." He also forecast a "serious challenge" to its continued existence during the appropriation process and the renomination of existing SACB members or their replacements. Huston noted that "any attempt to revitalize the Board will arouse the opposition of the civil libertarians, the ACLU lobby and the more vocal portion of the Liberal community" but added that "the hard-core anti-communist community and a perhaps significant portion of the middle class concerned about subversion and domestic violence may be expected to express considerable alarm" if the SACB were "allowed to die." Huston summed up the basic purposes of the proposed executive order, "recommended by the SACB and the Justice Department," as transferring AGLOSO determinations to the SACB and redirecting the focus of "collecting information about groups and organizations whose leaders and sympathetic members may be unsuitable for federal employment" away from the "problem organizations of the 1950s and toward those of the 1970s—the so-called 'violent-action oriented' organizations," since the SACB believed that being able to add to AGLOSO groups "such as SDS [Students for a Democratic Society], BPP [Black Panther Party], etc." would "strengthen the federal security program and would also serve an important public information function."[12]

On May 25, Krogh sent yet another memo on the proposed order to White House official John Brown that reported "we are presently preparing a paper for the President" on whether the SACB should be "given an extended franchise to go after violent action groups," which he indicated was especially needed to target SDS. However, a May 28 memo to Krogh from Budget Bureau official Carl Schwartz indicated (correctly) that further delays with regard to the order could be expected from the DOJ. Apparently alarmed by this word from Schwartz, Krogh wrote to top Nixon aide Ehrlichman a June 1 memo which, very unusually, had "ACTION" typed above its text. Noting that *Boorda* made the SACB's future "uncertain," Krogh predicted that "unless a workload for the SACB is created by a new Executive Order, the Senate will probably" kill the board by refusing to appropriate further expenditures. Krogh's memo indicated considerable internal White House division about proceeding with the order: he stated that White House speechwriter Ray Price "has written his views as to how repressive this would make us appear" and White House lawyer Len Garment had "expressed his strong aversion to our exhuming the SACB," while Huston and Nixon adviser

Clark Mollenhoff "are quite anxious that the Order be signed to permit the Board to do some useful work." Krogh warned, "We are now faced with a day of reckoning," since inaction would "in all probability" lead to the Senate's "termination" of the SACB "by a refusal to appropriate funds," while giving the board "new life" via the order would "in all probability" lead to "brickbats" from longtime opponents of the SACB such as "the liberal media." Krogh ended his memo by suggesting that whatever decision was taken would have far more political than practical significance, since ultimately the SACB had become "a body which is vitally important as a *symbol*,—to both liberals and conservatives," with liberals greeting a renewal of the board "as a reactionary, somewhat clumsy effort to get at groups which are politically distasteful to us, such as the Black Panthers," while conservatives viewed the SACB as "an important symbol for protecting the government from infiltration by people, [who] while not Communist," nevertheless sought the violent overthrow of the government. He concluded, "it strikes me that it would be better to let the SACB dwindle away by taking no action," because "there is little effective work which the SACB can perform even if the order is signed," especially as public hearings could become the "arena for mock trials starring" militants such as the Black Panthers and prominent "Yippie" leaders Abbie Hoffman and Jerry Rubin, thus risking the creation of a "forum with high visibility leading to a constant celebration of the radical fringe." Krogh closed by asking Ehrlichman for his views and a determination as to "whether I should prepare a decision memorandum for the President on this issue."[13]

While the White House continued to ponder the executive order, on June 2, 1970, Rep. Richard Ichord (R-MO), chair of the recently renamed House Committee on Internal Security (HISC, formerly House Committee on Un-American Activities [HUAC]), announced that HISC had initiated a "broad inquiry" into the federal employee security program that would "inquire particularly into the present status" of the SACB, a clear sign that conservatives were rallying to keep it alive (meanwhile, the House approved the SACB's entire requested $400,000 appropriation soon after Mahan's April testimony). Citing *Boorda* and other court decisions that had gradually deprived the SACB of its mandate and the DOJ's failure to update AGLOSO since 1955, Ichord declared that a pressing need existed for a "comprehensive study" of the government's antisubversion programs and argued that since both the SACB and AGLOSO had been "brought virtually to a halt," it was time to decide whether "either or both should be maintained." In a June 12 memo to Ehrlichman, Krogh reported that Mahan had again contacted him to request that the White House "indicate our position" with regard to the executive order before his upcoming Senate appropriations subcommittee testimony; however, Krogh recommended that Mahan be simply told that "it is still under advisement" with "no elaboration. Hopefully, the issue of the Board's future and funding will be resolved solely in Congress." On

June 19, Mahan wrote to top White House legal aide Bryce Harlow, maintaining that there was a need for AGLOSO to incorporate "emerging organizations" that posed a "threat to the internal security of our nation." He urged Nixon to act, arguing that "people throughout the country" were looking to him "for leadership in characterizing emerging violent-action organizations. No other board or agency now is equipped to undertake this mission as is the [SACB], which could proceed immediately to its implementation."[14]

When Mahan appeared before the Senate appropriations subcommittee on June 24, 1970, he conceded that *Boorda* had made it impossible for the SACB to proceed further with regard to individuals but argued that the board still had jurisdiction to register various types of Communist organizations and maintained that past SACB proceedings had been highly effective against such groups, leading to the "dissolution or collapse of the great majority of those groups. It finished them." But he bitterly complained that the DOJ had almost entirely failed to make organizational referrals to the SACB for fourteen years, despite congressional, DOJ, and FBI evidence of "much Communist activity," including recent testimony by ISD head Yeagley that the department was investigating about "200 Communist front or infiltrated cases per year." According to Mahan, this activity should have kept the board "overworked instead of under worked," but only one organizational referral, the W. E. B. Du Bois Clubs, and two alleged "Communist front cases" had been referred during his five years on the SACB, a figure he termed "beyond my comprehension" in light of "so much evidence of Communist activity during this period." Without ever mentioning the pending executive order, Mahan declared that the American people "are entitled to a solid return on the money invested in the Board" and warned that if Congress failed to act, that the public would be "likely to decide they will have to do something themselves" and if "the destruction and violence taking place in this country today are not ended," they "may well," albeit reluctantly, "adopt a repressive form of government." After Mahan's testimony the subcommittee heard from Sen. William Proxmire (D-WI), a liberal, longtime SACB critic, and from Sen. Strom Thurmond (R-SC), a longtime conservative SACB backer. Proxmire urged that the SACB be completely defunded, declared that "in the last 20 years that is has been in existence, the SACB had never controlled a single subversive, not one" and maintained that *Boorda* had left it with "absolutely nothing to do." Proxmire termed the SACB possibly the "highest paid group of benchwarmers in the history of the Federal government" and urged that "this anachronism" be "relegated to the history books, where it belongs." Thurmond, however, argued that the need for the SACB was "as great as it has been any time in the past 20 years" and that, despite *Boorda*, the board maintained "intact" the ability to "undercut Communist operations effectively" by exposing Communist groups. Thurmond, who had close ties to the Nixon administration, also made the first statement on the public record indicating that the executive branch intended to revitalize the SACB, declaring that he had been informed by Mitchell that the latter planned "shortly" to "give the Board new and expanded duties."[15]

In the interval between Mahan's June 24 Senate testimony and HISC hearings into administration of the federal loyalty program in late September, there were a number of SACB-related developments: Congress approved SACB's budgetary request with minimal controversy, Mitchell made the first two "organizational" referrals to the SACB in five years, and Huston, then busily pursuing what would eventually become the notorious "Huston Plan," replaced Krogh as the White House "point man" dealing with the SACB/AGLOSO issue. Thus, on July 14, apparently as a stop-gap measure to keep SACB alive while the administration continued to ponder the executive order, Mitchell asked it to list as "Communist fronts" two extremely obscure groups, the Young Workers Liberation League (which the government maintained had been formed by the CP to replace the Du Bois Clubs as its youth organization) and the Center for Marxist Education. On July 29, 1970, Huston sent Haldeman a memo headlined "CONFIDENTIAL" referencing his May 6 memo to Krogh endorsing the proposed executive order, which stated that since the ISA only authorized the SACB to proceed against "Communist" organizations, it could only pursue "New Left and black extremist" groups via the executive order or legislation, but he deemed the latter option "not realistic given the present ideological composition of the Senate." Huston maintained that Nixon could transfer AGLOSO authority to the SACB via executive order, since the president's "authority to establish security standards for government employment is inherent," and, although the board could at "most" only place such organizations on AGLOSO without any additional "control" authority, which could only be provided by legislation, such listings would both "identify and publicize those groups and their activities" and at least "provide some basis" for officially and publicly dealing with the "membership, objectives and methods of operations of 'violent-action' organizations." However, he reported that Krogh had indicated to him that "Ehrlichman, the Attorney General and the President believe that it would not be politically prudent to issue such an Executive Order at this time because of the tension generated by [Nixon's April 30, 1970, invasion of] Cambodia and [the subsequent] Kent State ["massacre" of antiwar demonstrators by Ohio national guards on May 4]." On August 13, Ehrlichman aide Gregg Petersmeyer notified Huston that Ehrlichman had approved of "your taking responsibility for the SACB so you may want to go ahead and call in John Mahan and get started on a review of their problems."[16]

On September 15, Huston sent Haldeman a memo strongly urging issuance of the executive order. Huston said he understood "some people" felt it would not be "good politics" to take such action before the November congressional elections, apparently fearing "that it would foster an image of 'repression,'" but he rejected this position because "I think the repression issue is phony, while the violence issue is real." Huston declared that the "true value" of transferring AGLOSO authority to the SACB was "the publicity it focuses on violent-action organizations and the impression it gives that the Executive Branch is doing something about the spread of violence," and thus the "practical scope" of the order was "broader than suggested on its face," since it did not include any "control" features beyond listing organizations to aid federal personnel screening decisions. Huston argued that broad congressional support existed for the order and there would "obviously" be a "favorable" voter reaction, with the "secondary" benefit of giving "us an occasion to attack those Senators" who had voted to kill the SACB, including such Democratic nemeses as George McGovern (D-SD, soon Nixon's 1972 presidential opponent) and Edmund Muskie (D-ME, a leading 1972 presidential contender). Huston concluded that it was "imperative" to "regain the initiative" on student violence, as while "no doubt it was prudent to adopt a low profile in May [following Kent State]," since then "things have changed (including public opinion) and we should now take the offensive."[17]

In September 30, 1970, HISC testimony, Mahan declared that "in the view of Congress and many citizens, the Board in recent years has not been kept as busy as it should have been" but maintained that the SACB had been highly effective when asked to intervene. Thus, he declared that in response to a recent query from him the DOJ had reported that only three of the twenty-three alleged "Communist fronts" against which it had initiated proceedings upon departmental referral were still "functioning today" and even they were "mere shadows" of themselves. Mahan urged Congress to expand the SACB's authority, lamenting that there was a "glaring" need "today to control subversive activities," but that SACB was hamstrung in acting against organizations that were "preaching and organizing violence, killing and destruction and tearing down the Government" because it could only act against Communist, and specifically "Moscow-controlled," organizations. Moreover, he added, AGLOSO was in need of "updating and modernizing," as it played an "important part in the Government personnel security program, yet no groups have been added to it for 15 years." Since, Mahan maintained, the "major problem here has been a court decision [i.e., *McGrath*] that the Attorney General must grant an organization a hearing before placing it on the list," the SACB could step in "if legislation could be enacted that would bring about the reactivation of the list," since the board functioned as "a quasi-judicial hearing agency in this area" and therefore could "very easily . . . redo the list" and include "some of the new organizations," thus "doing a great service to the country." While Mahan did not mention the proposed executive order in his prepared statement, when chair Ichord referred to HISC having heard from "time to time about a proposed executive order that would expand" SACB activities, Mahan said that he had seen such a proposal "several months ago," but "I don't know where it is at the present time or the final form." In seeming contradiction to his secret White House communications, Mahan suggested that any executive order would need a "companion" law to be implemented, particularly to "give us the power of subpoena in this field." According to a letter subsequently submitted to HISC by DOJ ISD head Robert Mardian, only 13 of the almost 300 AGLOSO organizations were "currently active," including three that had "shown very little activity in the past few years."[18]

Following the HISC hearings, the White House continued to ponder the future of the SACB (which obtained its 1971 congressional appropriation with no significant debate), initiating yet another review of the executive order option. In an October 1 memo to White House counsel John Dean, Huston recommended that the DOJ be requested to refer to the SACB two minuscule labor organizations that FBI director Hoover viewed as Communist-controlled, a decision that Huston maintained "could serve a multitude of purposes," including giving the SACB "some important work to do." The following day Dean sent a flurry of "CONFIDENTIAL" memos (drafted by Huston) to the FBI and the DOJ, asking that the FBI and the ISD continue to keep track of the two organizations and that Mitchell refer them to the SACB. On October 2, Dean aide Tom Pauken, whom Dean had asked on September 29 to prepare a summary memo on the SACB's status, wrote Dean to take issue with what he termed the "underlying assumption" of Huston's September 15 memo urging issuance of the executive order because it would "provide a significant boost to the Administration public position on the subject of violence." Pauken maintained that Huston had offered "no evidence" that the SACB was "the best or one of the best modes of action in this area" and that the "attack" upon Senate SACB opponents that Huston had suggested could follow issuance of the order would "have to include" a number of conservative Republican senators "who have voted along with Senate liberals to abolish the Board." Moreover, Pauken added, expanding SACB authority to encompass "violent-action" organizations was a "highly questionable goal at best and a potentially self-destructive goal at worst," because radicals such as Jerry Rubin, who had "used the publicity afforded by HUAC" hearings to "first attract national attention," were experts at using the media for their purposes and "there is a good possibility that the radicals could turn the added publicity on their activities by the SACB to their advantage."[19]

While Dean thereafter initiated yet another review of the SACB/executive order issue, Mahan's patience was once again reaching its limits. In an October 27, 1970, letter to Nixon, Mahan asked for a personal meeting to discuss how the "Board can serve this country well." However, Dean urged that Mahan be temporarily rebuffed since the "entire area of the internal security laws and policies is under review" due to Mardian's recent appointment as DOJ ISD head, and it would only be appropriate for Mahan to meet with Nixon after Mardian had "a chance to develop appropriate recommendations," whereupon "Mahan, Mardian and the Attorney General should collectively reflect" on the SACB's future. Mahan was subsequently put off by a November 12 letter from Presidential

Assistant Hugh Sloan, using the standard excuse that "as much as the President would like to meet with you, it is impossible for him to do so at this time" due to his "unusually heavy schedule." In the meantime, the DOJ began yet another reexamination of the executive order issue. OLC lawyer Jack Goldklang, in two memos sent to Assistant Attorney General and OLC head William Rehnquist in late November, concluded that Nixon could legally transfer AGLOSO designations to the SACB and that the 1971 congressional SACB appropriation could be used to implement such an order, since it specifically authorized the SACB to use its budget for "necessary expenses," a term Goldklang deemed to include "any expenses necessary for executing tasks legally assigned to the agency." Goldklang maintained that "no rule" banned "traditionally independent regulatory agencies" established by Congress such as the SACB from "accepting [new] functions" assigned by executive order. While conceding that there was "much uncertainty" in this area, he argued that at least "some" precedents had established "certain tentative conclusions," namely, that an independent regulatory agency "may acquiesce in an order from the Executive to perform a new function if (a) it is otherwise authorized by law, (b) it does not interfere with other agency functions, (c) it is closely compatible with the agency's other activities."[20]

On November 30, Rehnquist forwarded the Goldklang memos to Mardian, who forwarded them to Mitchell on December 4 with a cover letter that Mardian said was based on the "assumption that a policy decision has been made" to confer additional functions on the SACB, either via legislation that would grant the SACB power to designate the new category of "violent-action oriented" organizations or by an executive order transferring AGLOSO-listing authority to the SACB and adding "violent-action oriented" groups to the types of organizations that could be listed. Mardian recommended the executive order approach, which he declared would solve many of the constitutional problems under current AGLOSO procedures, because the attorney general continued to act under them "as both prosecutor and judge" (although Mardian said that even with the SACB transfer the board would only "make a recommendation" and the attorney general "would still have to make a final determination as to the listing"). He added that the executive order would allow AGLOSO to be updated to "deal with the problems of the 1970s rather than those of the 1950s" to aid federal loyalty screening, and, referring to the Goldklang memos, noted that the OLC "has concurred in the view" that the president could act legally via executive action and thus "obviate the necessity of securing amendatory legislation to accomplish this purpose." Mardian's explanation of why the legislative route should be rejected was extremely cursory and primarily political in nature, namely, that "any hope" of gaining congressional approval would require an "aggressive effort," which "could well result in an adverse media reaction that would reduce many of the benefits to be gained" and might lead to "eventual defeat," which "would prove to be even more embarrassing for the Administration." He added that the benefits of a legislative approach were "minimal," because court rulings meant that the "sole practical result" of SACB listings would be to inform the public about particular organizations, and as such legislation could not thus be defended "solely" in terms of the personnel security program, "very serious doubts exist as to its constitutionality." Mardian failed to explain why legislation would not have the same benefits as an executive order (for example, dividing functions between the attorney general and the SACB, updating AGLOSO, and providing personnel security guidance), thus implicitly suggesting that the legislature was viewed as a hindrance rather than a vital source of legitimate governmental authority.[21]

The continued lack of a White House decision led to further anxiety at the SACB, which could only have been greatly intensified when, according to a January 29, 1971, memo from Huston to Dean, the SACB legal counsel called him that day and reported that Mardian had told SACB chair Mahan that the ISD "does not intend to forward any cases for board action in the next year." According to Huston, this "obviously" meant that the SACB would have to appear before an upcoming House budgetary hearing "with no justification for its continued existence—and under the circumstances it is more than likely that the Board will be abolished." In a February 8 memo, Dean wrote that he was still waiting for a DOJ decision, although his understanding was that Mardian had spoken to Mitchell and that Mitchell agreed that a decision on the executive order "is necessary in the immediate future if the SACB is going to survive the appropriations process for another year." Dean also reported that he had met that day with Mahan, who, unsurprisingly, had urged "immediate" issuance of the order and argued that if it was issued later "the climate might be so changed that a charge of repression could be made," which Mahan said "cannot be made" at present.[22]

On March 1, 1971, Mardian sent Mitchell a follow-up to his December memo, characterizing his latest message as "also submitted on the assumption that a policy decision" had been made to expand the SACB's power and that "the legislative approach would involve too many risks, be too time consuming and the same purpose can be served by an Executive Order." According to Mardian, the fundamental problem requiring a solution was that "the SACB is out of work" and "must be given additional responsibilities if it is to exist." Referring to the possibility of keeping SACB going via future DOJ referrals, Mardian lamented that the "only two cases in which the evidence is available concerned publishing firms," namely, the "well known Communist periodicals" *Daily World* and *People's World*, and thus would "involve serious First Amendment problems," which politically translated into fear of a considerable media and public outcry, yet without further referrals the SACB was "dead." Mardian identified the proposed executive order transferring AGLOSO authority to the SACB as the solution to this problem and submitted with his memo two drafts of the proposed order: (1) the draft recommended by OLC head Rehnquist to Mitchell in February 1970, which included and defined a new category of "violent-action" organizations (along with previously undefined categories in the existing AGLOSO, namely, "totalitarian," "fascist," "communist," and "subversive"), which Mardian said had been "forwarded to the White House in May 1970, and returned without specific comment about two months ago"; and (2) a new three-page version that defined only "violent-action organizations" and deleted reference to all other categories. Mardian indicated preference for the latter, which focused on "objectives and conduct, rather than doctrine" and thus might "appeal to those who might see little merit" in the entire idea, especially as it "abolished" categories that were "never defined and may be incapable of such definition that would be upheld by the Courts," yet was flexible enough to encompass groups "that fall within" the abolished categories, like the "Communist PLP [the Trotskyist-oriented Progressive Labor Party] or the Ku Klux Klan, which advocate violence" and could be targeted as "violent-action oriented" with "considerably less proof required." Mardian conceded that opposition "would come from liberal groups" but argued that the proposed order would benefit the administration by appealing to "large segments of our population who are genuinely concerned with the recent activities of violence-prone organizations," who felt that "something must be done" and "cannot understand" why AGLOSO "is not updated or why the SACB is dormant."[23]

Mardian sent another, separate, memo to Mitchell, also on March 1, which especially stressed that the proposed order would provide numerous improvements in the AGLOSO designation procedure. These he listed as including, for the first time, definitions of the categories of targeted groups, providing an independent hearing for them by the SACB instead of "placing the Attorney General in the posture of prosecutor, judge and jury in determining whether any organizations should be listed," allowing listed organizations to petition the SACB to be deleted if they had changed their "character," and requiring that "knowing" membership in AGLOSO organizations be demonstrated in connection with federal employment screening. He concluded that the order would facilitate federal employment screening, "guarantee the continued validity of the program in light of current circumstances," and "provide additional procedural safeguards."[24]

The 1971 Nixon AGLOSO Executive Order

Attorney General Mitchell finally approved the proposed order shortly after receiving Mardian's March 1 memos, according to an "ADMINISTRATIVELY CONFIDENTIAL" March 5 memo from White House counsel Dean to his assistant David Parker, which stated that the order was "about to be sent from Justice to the White House for our final approval." Dean told Parker that Mahan had been "deeply involved in the development of this order and is aware of its current status" but cautioned DOJ approval "is not public knowledge and should not be leaked before the appropriate approach and time is set for the release of the Executive Order after it has been fully reviewed here." Dean subsequently handwrote on the memo that he had "advised Mahan" on March 9; the latter apparently quickly passed on the word at the SACB's March 11 meeting, as that day's minutes report that the board decided that Mahan should ask Congress for "three more secretaries and two additional lawyers" to allow it "to carry out the duties that would be assigned to it in the very near future by executive order."[25]

While the White House contemplated final action, AGLOSO came up at several congressional hearings during the spring and early summer of 1971. At HISC subcommittee hearings, representatives of a variety of federal agencies suggested that AGLOSO was of little use because it had not been updated since 1955 and most of the few surviving listed organizations were insignificant. Thus, National Labor Relations Board lawyer Eugene Goslee termed AGLOSO of "little benefit," as current applicants "were not even born when" most AGLOSO groups "ceased existing entirely," adding that with 300 or more annual applicants for employment, "no one has ever" admitted to affiliations with any listed groups. HISC chair Ichord declared that it would be "rather ridiculous to even use" AGLOSO "if the Attorney General is not making any additions or deletions" to it, a state of affairs requiring the DOJ to "fish or cut bait." HISC subcommittee chair Rep. Richardson Preyer (R-AR) declared that using such an outdated list "actually demeans" the employee screening program and was "counterproductive, downright harmful," as it could "lead agencies sometimes into thinking that they have done a screening job, when they have done nothing" and because the average person, if asked to certify that he did not belong to over 200 "strange little esoteric groups" such as the Yiddisher Kultur Farbund and the Washington Pension Union would "say, 'Sir your law is an ass and an idiot.' If this isn't going to be updated, it ought to be thrown away." Some agency representatives indicated moderate to strong support for updating AGLOSO during the hearings. Thus National Aeronautics and Space Administration security director Batley Fugler termed AGLOSO currently "of not much use" but urged that it be updated since "it is an important part of our security processing" and Federal Communications Commission security officer Fred Goldsmith told HISC that AGLOSO was currently of "very little value" but that a revised list originating from the attorney general would "give us an up-to-date" starting point to inquire into employee membership in organizations. A few agencies reported that they had uncovered tiny scatterings of employees with past or present affiliations with the CP, the Socialist Workers Party (SWP), the BPP, SDS, or other suspect groups, but that (as in the case of the Post Office) "investigations failed to disclose grounds that could form the basis for administrative action" based "upon the employee's individual conduct and performance on the job." According to Preyer, the testimony indicated that "no department or agency has dismissed one single employee on [explicit] loyalty or security grounds during the past five years." Several agency representatives appeared less enthusiastic about reviving AGLOSO, in some cases because they felt comfortable in relying upon informal guidance from the DOJ concerning suspect nonlisted groups. Thus, Interstate Commerce Commission personnel director Curtis Adams related that his agency "periodically" received "most helpful" department information that was "obviously" not in AGLOSO, and that if such information was formalized through updating AGLOSO it might make it "less useful than leaving it to operate within an informal channel," since listed organizations might dissolve and then reappear under a different name, making it "more difficult to identify them."[26]

Appearing before the House appropriations subcommittee handling the annual SACB budget request on May 5, Mahan's testimony and subsequent committee questioning proved extraordinarily brief and perfunctory. The only reference to the swirling allegations that the SACB was a "do nothing" agency was one question from chair John Rooney (D-NY), who, referring to the board's request for an increased budget to buy publications, asked, "Is that because you expect to have more time on your hands, to try to catch up on your reading?" Mahan's July 6 appearance before a Senate appropriations subcommittee proved far more tempestuous, and, by attracting considerable press coverage, may have finally pushed President Nixon into issuing the proposed executive order, by then pending for over eighteen months. Appropriations committee chair Sen. John McClellan (D-AR) began the hearing by declaring, "We do not want to keep the Board and have people sit there and do nothing" and closed it by declaring "these Board members are being paid $36,000 a year to warm seats only." Mahan described the basic job of the SACB as to "expose," declaring that once the attorney general referred an organization to SACB "it is a deterrence to these groups," since "once he files on them they usually go out of existence." However, while noting that the SACB was currently processing three organizational cases, Mahan conceded that the agency had heard only three witnesses and spent ten days in hearings thus far in 1971 and pleaded for the attorney general to "send us more cases," since "disclosure to the American people of these dissident groups is healthy for the country and necessary." While indicating sympathy for Mahan's position, McClellan, a longtime SACB supporter, declared that "what is going to determine whether this agency survives or not is whether the DOJ is going to give it the work to do," and "if they are not going to give you any work, there is no use keeping the Board." Subcommittee chair Allen Ellender (D-LA) was far harsher in his comments, stating that "if you are not occupied it is just a waste of money and time" and suggesting that the SACB members appeared to primarily "sit around" and "kill time." At one point, Ellender forced Mahan to concede, "We do not have enough to fill our time," a comment which was widely reported in the media. In immediately subsequent July 6 testimony, Mardian reported (probably incorrectly, as noted below) that Nixon had already signed an executive order that would create "a great deal more work" for the SACB. (Moments earlier, Mahan, who had been frenetic about obtaining the order for months, had never mentioned it, while Mardian, who apologized at the beginning of his testimony for "lack of preparedness," said it had been signed "within the past two days," but could not say exactly when and although he produced a typewritten copy of the order with the notation that it had been signed, it lacked an actual signature or a date, unlike subsequent published copies that were signed and dated—almost certainly falsely—July 2). Mardian maintained, concerning an issue that was about to create a firestorm, that even without the legislation that he reported Nixon was concurrently sending to Congress to facilitate executing the order by granting the SACB subpoena and contempt powers, the president could unilaterally assign AGLOSO functions to the SACB, based on what he termed the president's "constitutional statutory powers." McClellan seemed dumbfounded by this stance, telling Mardian, "I do not see how the President, by Executive Order, can give to a Board created for one purpose by the Congress, with its powers and limitations prescribed, give it a function which the Congress did not authorize." Mardian maintained (clearly wrongly) that the order did not give the SACB "any additional powers" and included nothing that "purports to expand the authority of the SACB," because it currently had "the power to conduct identically this type of investigation." However, McClellan continued to express skepticism, vowing that "if you go beyond the act creating" the SACB "you will be in trouble."[27]

Meanwhile, although Mitchell had approved the executive order informally in early March, the DOJ did not formally notify the White House of this until May 6. Writing that day to Dean, ISD head Mardian implicitly noted that, while still shifting AGLOSO jurisdiction to the SACB, the approved draft completely eliminated the long-discussed proposed inclusion of a new category of "violent-action" organizations, instead using criteria "substantially the same" as in existing AGLOSO executive orders. Mardian added that he had been instructed by Mitchell to "seek your cooperation in having this Order signed as soon as possible." On May 11 Dean wrote to Budget Bureau director George Schultz and top White House domestic aide Ehrlichman asking for their approval of the proposed order. Dean added that the proposal had been "the subject of extensive discussion for more than a year" and "reflects the best judgment of the Department of Justice and is strongly recommended by the Attorney General"; thereafter he largely repeated Mardian's December 4 memo to Mitchell. These included the claims that under the order the SACB would designate AGLOSO organizations "in connection with the Federal Employee Security Program" (which, of course, was supposedly always AGLOSO's purpose) and therefore somehow "remove many of the constitutional difficulties that are created by listing such organizations solely for the purpose of informing the public, as the court will probably allow the government more latitude" when listing was done "to strengthen employment security programs," and that transferring AGLOSO to the SACB would "remove many of the constitutional problems that may be raised with respect to current procedures" in which the attorney general "acts as both prosecutor and judge" and thus be "more consistent than the requirements of procedural due process" (although Dean noted the final draft retained the attorney general's power to make a "final determination"). Dean also listed as advantages the updating of AGLOSO to "deal with the problems of the 1970s rather than those of the 1950s" (which had not been done before, he maintained, at least partly due to "doubts as to the ability of the designation procedure to withstand constitutional attack") and "vastly" enlarging AGLOSO's alleged secondary purpose of providing "some measure of public information" about the listed groups. Dean added that the OLC had "concurred in the view" that President Nixon had "the power to confer additional functions on the Board" and concluded that "the Attorney General has requested that action on this Order be expedited."[28]

On May 28, OLC acting assistant attorney general Thomas Kauper wrote Dean that the ISD had concluded that inclusion of a "violent-action" category for AGLOSO listings "might be highlighted for critical comment and misinterpreted by the press," although the OLC itself had "no particular view" on the subject. Kauper added that the OCL "believes that the scope of the SACB's inquiry would not be significantly narrowed by the proposed change," since "the distinction may mean little at the hearing stage" and that the "groups which are slated for hearings have actually engaged in illegal acts to the point where evidence of abstract advocacy would not be crucial in making final determinations." In a June 21, 1971, memo to Nixon, Dean urged that the president sign the proposed order, noting that the OLC, Mitchell, and Ehrlichman had all approved it. "By delegating this new responsibility to the SACB," Dean stated, Nixon would honor his "campaign pledge to give the SACB meaningful work and will make clear your determination to take every prudent, constitutional step necessary to safeguard the integrity of the federal service," as well as establishing a means to "provide credible information to the public" concerning organizations "which represent a pressing threat to the internal security." Dean added that if Nixon approved of the order, Mitchell would submit to Congress draft legislation giving SACB subpoena and contempt powers, as well as establishing a "number of 'due process' requirements" for board hearings, thereby answering "many of the procedural objections often raised" against the SACB.[29]

According to official records, President Nixon signed the proposal, Executive Order 11605, on July 2, 1971, although there is considerable suggestive evidence that in fact it was signed July 6 or July 7, in response to the widely publicized July 6 Senate appropriations subcommittee hearing, and then falsely backdated. The White House failed to announced Nixon's action until July 8, one day after the DOJ issued a press release stating that the order had been "sent to the *Federal Register* today" (and, as discussed below, with so many errors in its characterization of the order that it seems likely that the department's public relations officials had not yet seen it). Moreover, a White House memorandum dated July

7 and written by White House employee Ron Geisler "for the record" states that Dean had called that morning to direct White House clerical officials that the executive order "should be dated *July 2, 1971* [emphasis in original] and forwarded to the Archives immediately," a rather peculiar request to make if it actually had been signed on that date. The previous day, Dean had informed White House Press Secretary Ron Ziegler that Mardian had "informed" a Senate appropriations committee that Nixon had "signed an executive order" on AGLOSO/SACB and enclosed a copy of the DOJ press release on the subject dated July 7, wording that carefully avoided saying that Nixon had in fact actually signed it. The final text of Executive Order 11605 kept the categories of suspect organizations essentially unchanged from President Truman's 1947 order, but for the first time both required "knowing" affiliation with them in connection with federal employment screening and included definitions of the categories, with an extremely broad definition of organizations adopting a "policy of unlawfully advocating the commission of acts of force or violence to deny others their rights" or seeking to unlawfully "overthrow" the government, along the lines first suggested in SACB chair Mahan's April 30, 1969, memo to White House aide Krogh, which was clearly designed to specifically encompass militant "New Left" organizations and tactics such as draft board "sit-ins" that they frequently engaged in. Thus, the definition included any group that "engages in, unlawfully advocates, or has among its purposes or objectives, or adopts as a means of obtaining" such, the commission of "unlawful acts to deny others" their guaranteed "rights or benefits," the "unlawful damage or destruction of property or injury to persons," or the violation of laws "pertaining to treason, rebellion or insurrection, riots or civil disorders, seditious conspiracy, sabotage, trading with the enemy, obstruction of the recruiting and enlistment service of the U.S., impeding officers of the U.S. or related crimes or offenses." The order included the long-pending transfer of AGLOSO hearing functions to the SACB but, unlike earlier draft proposals, stated that while the initiation of such hearings depended upon the SACB receiving a "petition" for such action from the attorney general, the board had the power of final determination and could also, upon petitions initiated by either the attorney general or a listed organization, declare that an organization "does not currently meet the standards for definition." In its July 7 press release, the DOJ, while correctly reporting that Mitchell was sending Congress legislation to amend the ISA to grant subpoena and contempt authority, hopelessly confused the proposed legislation with the executive order. The press release said that the "new order" assured "certain rights to participants, including public hearings, an accurate stenographic record, the right to counsel, and the right to cross examination," as well as the right to appeal an AGLOSO determination to the courts, but these provisions were all contained in the legislation submitted to Congress on July 7 rather than in the order itself.[30]

On July 8, Mardian sent McClellan a letter, largely a rewrite of OLC lawyer Jack Goldklang's November 1970 memo, asserting that "there is no rule which forbids" the "traditionally independent regulatory agencies" like the SACB from "accepting functions assigned by Executive Order." The memo clearly contradicted Mardian's July 6 claim that the SACB had been given no "additional powers" by declaring that there had been "no relationship" between the board's duties and AGLOSO "until the recent" order, which had "given an important function" to the SACB, "i.e., the hearing function in connection with designations" for AGLOSO. The memo also revealed that the DOJ was "presently processing a large number of cases" to send the SACB for deletion from AGLOSO, since "of the 283 organizations now designated, not more than 20 are still in existence or have been active in the last several years." Mardian added that the department "currently has under consideration approximately 25 potential cases" for new AGLOSO designations, principally involving "violent-action organizations" that "have recently become part of our history" and were encompassed by the new order's criteria. The memo also claimed that while AGLOSO was "maintained for Federal personnel security purposes only, the thousands of requests received annually" by the department for copies of AGLOSO "demonstrate the urgent need for updating it."[31]

Political Assaults on Nixon's AGLOSO Executive Order 11605, 1971

The announcement of the executive order led to widespread news coverage and quickly caused a congressional firestorm, led in the Senate by Sam Ervin (D-NC) and in the House by Rep. Don Edwards (D-CA). Both argued that Nixon's order was an executive usurpation of congressional authority and that AGLOSO was, in any case, a completely unnecessary invasion of basic constitutional rights with echoes of "McCarthyism," especially since lawbreakers could and should be prosecuted in the courts. Similar positions were voiced by liberal and civil liberties organizations. Thus, the ACLU said Nixon had "seriously trespassed on the domain of Congress" and sought to give the SACB powers that raised "grave issues of personal liberty," and ADA vice chair Joseph Rauh termed it a "dangerous threat to civil liberties" with definitions "so broad and so vague that no activist political organization" would be "wholly safe." However, in a May 24, 1972, letter to Rep. Rooney, SACB chair Mahan declared in response that the CP, having opposed the SACB since its 1950 inception, was simply trying to "accomplish through the Congress" what they "have been unable to achieve in the courts." An important background presence in the anti-SACB/AGLOSO position was the suggestion that Nixon's order was another instance of abuse of his authority, as earlier allegedly reflected in such foreign policies as the 1970 American invasion of Cambodia and in a series of domestic actions viewed as repressive. The latter included the attempt, rejected in a 1971 Supreme Court ruling, to legally bar American newspapers from publishing the "Pentagon Papers," a secret Department of Defense study that revealed decades of official prevarication about the Vietnam War; the administration's claim that the president could order warrantless wiretaps in domestic "national security" cases (rejected in April 1971 by a federal appeals court ruling subsequently upheld by a unanimous 1972 Supreme Court); and growing indications of domestic intelligence abuses, especially involving widespread military and FBI spying on the antiwar movement. In response, Nixon's defenders argued that the proposed order simply assigned to SACB duties like those it had long carried out, responded to critics who claimed SACB members were freeloading on the government payroll, provided an effective means to both update AGLOSO and fight newly emerging revolutionary movements, and included far greater procedural protections for designated organizations than they had previously enjoyed. Moreover, they argued, the proper venue for settling constitutional arguments about the proposed order was the courts and that the Senate's July 19 action (discussed immediately below) to bar SACB jurisdiction over AGLOSO would have the ironic result of funding SACB while preventing it from conducting any significant work.[32]

Although the House of Representatives, with relatively little controversy, approved a $450,000 fiscal 1972 SACB appropriation, on June 28, shortly before the early July announcement of the new executive order, Nixon's action triggered an enormous storm during a bitter July 19 Senate debate. The Senate barely rejected, 47–41, a proposal to defund the SACB completely but immediately thereafter approved, 51–37, Sen. Ervin's amendment to ban the board from spending any funds to implement the order (with 36 of the 54 Democrats voting for it, along with an independent senator and 14 of 45 Republicans). On July 27, the House rejected by 246–141 an effort led by Rep. Edwards to accept the Senate amendment and on August 3 the Senate acquiesced by a threadbare 46–44 vote (eleven senators who had supported the Ervin amendment either abstained or voted for the conference report). Perhaps the clearest indication of the deep anger that the Nixon order aroused in the Senate was a harshly worded July 29 letter signed by 28 senators, including most Democratic liberals and several moderate Republicans, which termed it "an outrageous assertion of unauthorized executive power" that Congress "must not let pass," especially as recent years had witnessed "the tragic results of unchecked Presidential power in foreign affairs" and "this is merely another example on a domestic issue." Terming the SACB a "do nothing" group, the letter denounced the "specter of a group of five men determining what is 'American' and 'un-American' and creating an official blacklist which slanders those who hold unpopular or even outrageous views. The cost in personal suffering to thousands of citizens who may have what the Board regards as 'sympathetic association' with fringe political groups is too high for a nation which prides itself on freedom of thought, association and expression."[33]

The attack upon the executive order during extensive late July floor Senate debate was led by Ervin, who concentrated upon the "executive usurpation" argument, including ISD head Mardian's July 6 claim before the Senate appropriations subcommittee that the president's action was based upon his "constitutional statutory powers." Ervin termed Nixon's order an attempt to "write" laws "himself that he thinks he might have trouble getting through Congress" and maintained that "if Congress authorizes this appropriation, it is ratifying a usurpation of the power of Congress by the President." Ervin declared, "I have never heard of the President's 'constitutional statutory powers.' It is not in my copy of the Constitution." Ervin termed Mardian's claims yet another contention that the president had "inherent powers," claims that Ervin acidly maintained seemed to be cited "every time the Justice Department wants to do something that affronts the constitutional rights of Americans" and that were "just another name for a claim to eventual total unrestrained powers by one man," the "modern equivalent of the sovereignty of kings." Ervin maintained that there was "no need" for AGLOSO or the SACB because "if a person violates the law, let him be prosecuted according to the law," and therefore the real target could only be those viewed as "not physically but intellectually dangerous to the Government." According to Ervin, "America can well survive without" what he termed a "list of those citizens whom the Justice Department—or now the SACB—has decided are disloyal and traitorous to the country. It is an official blacklist—a notice to the entire country that these citizens are pariahs, that they should be shunned" as "un-American." Ervin added that the SACB would be empowered by the order "to do one of the things which the Board is set up to keep other people from doing, that is, denying people their rights under our Constitution." He termed it "alien to the American system of government" and reflecting the "spirit of McCarthyism" and, noting recent revelations of widespread military spying on dissidents, suggested that the government would likely define "disloyal" to include all "who disagreed with the administration on the great issues of the war in Vietnam, on the draft, on military defense and all those who were active in any way—and on either side—of the civil rights issue." In fact, Ervin suggested, given "how vague the [order's] definitions" were, the Nixon administration might itself qualify for AGLOSO listing for committing "unlawful" acts seeking to "deny others their rights or benefits guaranteed by the Constitution or laws," such as using wiretaps "in domestic security cases without statutory authorization" and "attempting to halt the publication of a newspaper despite the first amendment guarantees of freedom of the press." He declared that the order would allow the SACB to "blacklist" those who "merely advocate" extreme ideas and to "pry into every demonstration and into every group of people whose views the board considers to be intellectually disturbing to the Government," because, even if "a group or organization abhors violence," if at a demonstration even "one of the members on the spur of the moment commits an act of violence, then all associated with him, no matter how peaceful they may be, are subject to the scrutiny of the Board." Ervin added that the order would allow "a few men to define what they think is un-American" and "then designate those who disagree as subversive," and that "eventually, everybody but those making the lists comes under suspicion. And then they begin look at each other."[34]

Ervin's basic arguments were vocally supported by about ten other senators and representatives, mostly, although not entirely, Democrats. Thus, Sen. John Tunney (D-CA) lamented that "at a time when our citizens are deeply concerned about the nature and extent of their individual freedoms, the President proposed an incredible extension" of the powers of the SACB, "the very agency that threatens those freedoms most," creating the "specter of five men determining what is 'American' and what is 'un-American' and creating an official blacklist which slanders those who hold unpopular or even outrageous views." Sen. Ted Kennedy (D-MA) termed the order "unparalleled in scope, unprecedented in power and dangerous in purpose," one that established a "McCarthy Committee" by "Executive fiat," as President Nixon had "proposed, enacted, and signed into law, his own personal legislation" and "decided that Congress should no longer legislate." Sen. Edward Brooke (R-MA) declared that "although individuals properly should be punished when their dissent grows into criminal conduct, there can be no legal justification of their 'blacklisting'" as would be provided under Nixon's attempt to rejuvenate a "relic of the 'Cold War' years" by authorizing the publishing of lists of organizations that met "arbitrary criteria allegedly denoting subversive tendencies" in "violation of all the constitutional rights which this Nation was established to preserve."[35]

The lead—in fact virtually only vocal—Senate defender of the order during extended floor debates in late July, which filled over fifty three-column *Congressional Record* pages in tiny type, was Sen. Roman Hruska (R-NE), who declared that it provided the SACB "a great deal of activity with which to remain occupied" and sought to "breathe some life into our moribund employee-security program," while including "all of the customary due process procedures" in future AGLOSO determinations. Somewhat contradictorily, Hruska conceded that "there is much" to Ervin's constitutional arguments but declared that Nixon had not sought to "usurp legislative authority" but only to "use existing [SACB] resources and machinery" to update AGLOSO and therefore he was willing to "support the President's reasoning and await a final judgment in the courts." He maintained that the order provided badly needed machinery to update and circulate AGLOSO to "all Federal Government agencies and to the public" and especially hailed the provision for deleting the vast majority of the currently listed 283 organizations, since the DOJ "has information that 263 are no longer active."

In the House, Rep. Rooney provided rather tepid support for Nixon, as did HISC chair Ichord, who said he could not "see why the executive chose to proceed as it did" and reported "serious" doubt of the legality of an "obviously hastily drawn and patchwork" decree.[36]

The uproar on Capitol Hill and the unexpected Senate rebuff of the executive order, all of which received substantial press coverage, including front-page treatment on July 20 in both the *New York Times* and the *Washington Post*, stirred up substantial backbiting within the White House, which followed the Congressional debates extremely closely. Krogh wrote Dean on July 20 relating that Ehrlichman had, "in light of the successful [Senate] vote on the Ervin amendment," asked him to "determine exactly what steps were taken to result in the promulgation" of the order, including specifically "what consideration was given to alternative methods of accomplishing the revitalization of the SACB other than by Executive Order, such as by legislation." Dean fired back with an "ADMINISTRATIVELY CONFIDENTIAL" memo to Krogh the same day, relating his understanding that the order had been recommended by Attorney General Mitchell after "extensive discussions" between the DOJ and Congress as to whether to proceed by executive order or legislation and that he "assumed that you had reviewed this with John" before Ehrlichman had approved the order. Dean added, "As you know, I personally had reservations about this matter, but upon the Attorney General's request [for expedited approval, conveyed by Mardian on May 6] I felt it was incumbent to forward it to the senior staff members for their approval." Dean added (correctly, it turned out) that there was a "good (to excellent) chance" that Congress would ultimately "restore the full use" of SACB funds and reported that the White House would work to accomplish this in a "very quiet and without fanfare" manner, and thus the "ball game is far from over." He concluded by declaring that he could not "say that the decision to issue the Executive Order was wrong. If we lose, I still feel that the President has not been hurt and to the contrary, he has won the appreciation of many 'conservatives' for this effort. But I am making every effort to win!"[37]

As the Congressional battle proceeded, White House, DOJ, and SACB officials prepared talking points and memoranda that were furnished to sympathetic congressmen. Thus, Sen. Hruska and Rep. Gerald Ford (R-MI) each placed into the *Congressional Record* unidentified legal memoranda supporting the constitutionality of the executive order, which had in fact been drafted by the DOJ's OLC. The OLC memo, which Acting Assistant Attorney General Thomas Kauper sent to Dean on July 26, maintained that the Ervin amendment continued the board's appropriations "only on the condition that it remain essentially inactive" and declared that the order simply exercised presidential authority "specifically conferred by Congress" in earlier legislation to "prescribe regulations for the employment of individuals as will best promote the efficiency of the Civil Service." Acting far more openly, Rooney placed into the *Record* an SACB-attributed memo (which Rep. John Ashbrook [R-OH] also had printed in the *Record*, without attribution) that argued that if Ervin's amendment prevailed it would subject to "charges of illegality" a "substantial part of the Government's operations conducted under similar Executive Orders," while defending Nixon's order as remedying criticisms that the SACB had nothing to do by allowing it to "materially assist the national security" and providing "much stronger constitutional guarantees and due process procedures" for targeted groups.[38]

As the Congressional debate continued, ISD director Mardian appeared before a HISC subcommittee on July 29 and on August 3 as part of its continuing inquiry into administration of the federal employee personnel security program. The hearings took place in an explosive atmosphere: as they opened, HISC chair Ichord said he had had "considerable difficulty" in determining whether to "proceed with those hearings today in view of the fact that feelings do run pretty high on the issue." Mardian stressed that Nixon's order would provide greater "due process" protections than previously for AGLOSO determinations, but he repeatedly came under attack from the right by HISC members who accused the DOJ of having failed to keep SACB busy with referrals or found his answers nonresponsive or unacceptable. Thus, while longtime SACB supporter Rep. Preyer applauded much of Nixon's order, he condemned the administration for "doing by Executive order" what "can really only properly be done by legislation" and suggested that creating an entirely new agency would be preferable, due to the "baggage of the past" and "clouds of incredibility" that the SACB had accumulated over time. Rep. John Schmitz (R-CA) declared it was "no wonder" the department had not updated AGLOSO since 1955 "if the type of fuzz that has been going on for the last five minutes with regard to a simple question is an example of the type of fuzz that goes on over in the Department."[39]

The July–August 1971 events related to the SACB and AGLOSO attracted very considerable press attention and large numbers of editorials, over 80 percent of which (judging from those collected and published in the July 16–31 nonpartisan *Editorials on File*), were deeply hostile to the administration's position. Thus, the *Washington Post* (July 17, 19) termed Nixon's executive order a "ukase" which combined the "worst features" of the SACB and AGLOSO, "two malevolent hangovers from the era of McCarthyism," which had failed to render the "slightest service to national security." *Newsday* (July 19) termed Nixon's order an attempt to "pump new life" into the SACB, "an overstaffed, under worked vestige of McCarthyism," while the *Roanoke Times* (July 26) declared "there is no justice in blacklisting groups, a method that imputes guilt by association and discourages dissent of any kind." The *Charleston Gazette* (July 21) declared that the Senate had declined to completely abolish the "useless" SACB only because "the tenacious influence of McCarthyism" made them afraid to "abolish an agency that purports to combat communism," although it was a "wasteful fake." The *New York Times* (July 26) termed Nixon's order a "crafty" attempt to give the SACB "some new and probably unconstitutional tasks" and lamented that the Senate had voted to continue the "fraud" and "standing joke" of the SACB. Only a handful of hard-line conservative papers supported the Nixon order and the SACB's continuance. The *New York Daily News* (July 21) termed the Senate's July 19 votes an example of "two-ply Senate idiocy" and demanded that the House-Senate differences "damn well better be settled in favor of giving the SACB the powers Mr. Nixon thinks it should have," while the *St. Louis Globe-Democrat* (July 19) declared that "exposing the activities of subversive groups is the best way to nullify their efforts" and lamented that "subversives in the country have been having a field day" due to judicial restraints on the SACB.

A week after the Senate's August 4 acquiescence to the House approval of granting the SACB AGLOSO jurisdiction, White House counsel Dean wrote ISD head Mardian and correctly predicted that it "looks like we are going to hear more from Sen. Ervin," who was "now pushing legislation to take away from the SACB their newly granted powers" but incorrectly suggested that Ervin would not "be able to generate the same steam for his legislative proposal that he did for his recently ill-fated amendment." SACB chair Mahan reported to Dean on August 12 that the board had discussed the causes of its "public image problem" and concluded that "a significant improvement" would result if the board greatly increased its activity levels and obtained the "beneficial" effects of televised coverage of SACB hearings. The board specifically requested that Attorney General Mitchell forward the "names of at least 150 organizations" for possible delisting, with hearings held around the country, as "odds are that little national news coverage will follow if hearings are held only in Washington," and that he also submit "fifteen to 25 new cases for addition" to AGLOSO by "January 1972, before the Chairman appears before the House appropriations Committee," thus convincing Congress that the board has "a task of national importance to perform and that the Administration will live by its promise to give the Board a full workload." Mahan stressed that the solution to the "image problem is public exposure *as a working agency*, one that is continually holding hearings, issuing reports, etc.," but this required cases to be "continually" referred to it by the attorney general. Dean's files include several unattributed memos apparently reflecting his musings and/or those of other officials in response to Mahan's memo. One of them termed it "essential" that the SACB's new function "be pounded into the public as being important and absolutely necessary," including by "continuously and constantly" characterizing "the emergence of violent-action groups previously unknown" as a danger to all Americans' "personal and collective security," so as to "absolutely and positively" convince the public "that these groups have no good at all in them and possess the means and capacity for death and destruction." It concluded, "Unless the public is thoroughly frightened, we are not likely to get the support necessary from either the public or Congress to do this job properly."[40]

While the SACB began implementing its new duties, Sen. Ervin convened hearings in early October 1971 (which in retrospect provided a preview of Ervin's famous 1973 Watergate hearings) before his Senate Judiciary Subcommittee on the Separation of Powers to consider two of his own proposals. The first banned any DOJ or SACB employee from carrying "out any of the additional functions" conferred by the Nixon order and denied the two agencies funds to implement it, while the second declared it the sense of the Senate that the order sought to "usurp" congressional power and constituted an "infringement of the first amendment rights of all Americans." In a lengthy opening statement, Ervin declared that Nixon's action, granting the SACB "vast power to harass and stigmatize Americans," was clearly "inspired by a lack of faith" in First Amendment freedoms and fear of their exercise by persons "whose thoughts and words are understandably offensive to the establishment," but that "the first amendment is based upon an abiding faith that our country has nothing to fear from the exercise of freedom so long as it leaves truth free to combat error." Ervin declared that it was "not the function of government in a free society to protect its citizens against thoughts and associations it deems dangerous, or to stigmatize its citizens for thoughts or associations it thinks hazardous," but the Nixon order sought to empower the SACB to do "exactly" that, such as stigmatizing all AGLOSO members, including those who were inactive, unaware of, or in disagreement with any "unlawful aims" of such organizations. He maintained, "If America is to be free, her Government must permit her people to think their own thoughts and determine their own associations without official instructions or intimidation; and if America is to be secure, her Government must punish her people for the crimes they commit, not for the thoughts they think or the associations they choose." However, Sen. Edward Gurney (R-AK) defended the order as providing greater "due process" than in previous AGLOSO proceedings, facilitating the deletion of defunct groups and generally protecting the country's right "to prevent its destruction," as American freedoms "are in no way synonymous with subversion" and it was "absurd" to claim "society must permit those actively engaged in its destruction free rein."[41]

During two days of subsequent testimony, Assistant Attorney General and OLC head Rehnquist and SACB head Mahan defended Nixon's order, while George Washington University law professor Arthur Miller backed Ervin. Additionally, ACLU legal director Melvin Wolf submitted a written statement that attacked Nixon's order as "the perfect embodiment of the McCarthy era, when the government made the fatal mistake of trying to stamp out intellectual freedom by thoughtless fiat" and sought to drive ideas "distasteful" to the administration "out of existence by threatening whoever holds such ideas with public blacklisting." Rehnquist maintained that the order was a "valid exercise of the powers that Congress has specifically conferred upon the President" to make civil service regulations and delegate functions vested in him elsewhere in the executive branch. He argued that Nixon had simply "decided that instead of the Attorney General" the SACB would help determine federal employee loyalty, a decision with a "complete and adequate legal basis" that was "completely compatible with the basic assignment given [the SACB] by Congress." Using folksy phraseology that would become famous two years later, Ervin denounced Rehnquist's citing of past executive orders as validating Nixon's action, "because that way Presidents could lift themselves up by their own bootstraps," and protested that because "murder and larceny have been committed in every generation," that "has not made murder meritorious nor larceny legal." Ervin termed investigating entire groups because some members might apply for federal jobs "like sailing clear across the Atlantic" when "your objective is to get across the creek," adding that it was "as plain as the noonday sun in a cloudless sky that the President cannot delegate anything to anybody" unless it had been specifically "vested in him by law," as "otherwise, he would be making legislation." Rehnquist denied that the order would let the SACB brand groups as "politically or intellectually dangerous," since it was "drafted in terms of acts of violence" and "conduct, not political views."[42]

Mahan fully endorsed Rehnquist's position on the legality and wisdom of Nixon's order, declaring that "it is not only the President's right but, more importantly, his inescapable duty to take steps which, in his judgment and in conformity with the Constitution, are required to protect the Government service from infiltration and subversion." Mahan argued the new order improved existing AGLOSO procedures as it gave "much greater protection against false, mistaken or unjustified listings," especially by providing definitions of the classifications of organizations and by terminating the attorney general's authority to make final determinations. Ervin, however, declared that the "vagueness of the past does not justify the vagueness of the present" and termed the definitions broad enough to encompass any grouping of even "two people in the U.S. who fall into any of these various categories" or "who on the spur of the moment engage in a riot," regardless of whether they were federal employees or applicants. Asked by Ervin if he was not concerned that the attorney general did not "have to make an allegation that even a single member" of a targeted organization was a government employee or applicant in his AGLOSO petitions, Mahan accurately responded, "He has never had to do so under the Truman and Eisenhower orders either." Responding to a question about the SACB's workload, Mahan reported that "on Friday [four days previously, and, perhaps not coincidentally, three days after Ervin announced his hearings] the Attorney General sent over 25 cases of [previously listed] organizations" to determine "whether they are defunct or should be taken off."[43]

Miller termed Nixon's order "faulty" both in substance and promulgation through its invalid and "bald assertion of raw Executive power," which sought to "add new responsibilities to administrative agencies beyond those" authorized by Congress, a claimed authority lacking "either in the Constitution or in any statute." Referring to other alleged Nixon abuses of authority, including the refusal to spend over $12 billion of congressionally appropriated funds, judicially rejected attempts to authorize warrantless domestic security wiretaps and prevent publication of the Pentagon Papers, assertions of "executive privilege" to withhold information from Congress, and assertions that the president could commit over 500,000 troops to Vietnam "without express congressional authorization," Miller declared that it was "past time" for legislators to halt an "exponential jump" in the "gradual aggrandizement" of executive power. He attacked Nixon's order as threatening a "chilling effect" on First Amendment freedoms and allowing "punishment without the procedural safeguards of the Bill of Rights," including deprivation of governmental jobs, simply due to "the actions of the group" an individual belonged to, in violation of American principles requiring demonstrated "personal" guilt and allowing punishment only after individual hearings. Miller argued that the order empowered the SACB to investigate all American organizations, "the Boy Scouts included," although "less than one-hundredth of 1 percent of them probably have anything to do with this." Ervin closed the hearing by echoing Miller, declaring that the order was "saturated with a lack of first amendment rights and their exercise by people who have violated no law," even affecting Boy Scouts, who if, "instead of helping an old lady across the street," obstructed the "old ladies" in violation of the "ordinance of some village."[44]

Even as Ervin held his early October 1971, hearings, the SACB began to implement its new authority. On September 10, it published "rules of procedure" in the *Federal Register*, which required of the attorney general, in seeking to list new organizations or delist old ones, or of listed organizations that sought to be delisted, to file petitions with "concise" statements stating why the groups did or did not "meet the standards for designation." Organizations and the attorney general could respond to each other's petitions, and determinations were to be "based on oral testimony taken under oath or affirmation and documentary evidence adduced at open, public hearings" at which each party was entitled to the rights to counsel, to present evidence, and to engage in cross-examination. Unlike previous AGLOSO determinations, in which the names of designated organizations were published without any explanation, the new rules required SACB AGLOSO listings to include "a description of the origin, history, aims and purposes of the organization; leadership of the organization; the geographical area or areas in which the organization has operated; and any other facts of a specialized nature respecting the organization." If defunct organizations were delisted, the "date when an organization ceased to be of the type involved" was to be published.[45]

Following publication of the rules, between October 1, 1971, and October 17, 1972, the DOJ referred to the board, in nine separate batches, 257 AGLOSO groups (out of the 283 total) for delisting as defunct. Following completely uncontested public hearings that typically lasted less than one minute each, the SACB delisted 233 organizations between November 22, 1971, and October 13, 1972. In its twenty-second and final annual report, published in 1973, the SACB plaintively noted that it had been unable to complete delisting action on the final group of twenty-four petitions because Congress had (as discussed below) defunded the board "effective October 25, 1972." In each instance, the sole information the department provided the SACB about delisting candidates was the group's last known address and the statement that the organization had "ceased to exist more than ten years prior to the filing of this petition," along with a specified date when it had "ceased to exist." No information about why the organization had originally been listed was transmitted, and the department informed the board that, absent a "specific request" at least ten days prior to scheduled hearing dates, it planned no "further factual showing." The department also furnished the board with evidence that, on about the same day it petitioned the SACB, it had attempted to notify the affected group via registered mail at its last known address. The letters could not be delivered in 90 percent of the cases, while in the others they were delivered but no one representing the group asked to appear at a hearing. Since the SACB never asked the department to furnish testimony or any additional information about the organizations, the hearings were completely *pro forma*. Thus, the SACB formally delisted fifteen groups on December 14, 1971, following November 22 "hearings" that lasted a total of twenty minutes—less than fifty seconds per organization.[46]

The Final Legal Assault on AGLOSO, 1971–1973

While the congressional debate over the future of the SACB/AGLOSO continued, AGLOSO was further undermined by new court rulings that chipped away at the list without challenging its fundamental constitutionality. The SWP was involved in the two most important such cases, *Socialist Workers Party v. Klassen*, which originated in the 1969 firing of postal carrier Duncan Gordon solely due to his SWP membership and sought to have AGLOSO declared unconstitutional, and *American Servicemen's Union* [ASU] *v. Mitchell*, in which nine organizations urged a similar holding, maintaining that, among their other baneful results, the 1971 Nixon order and AGLOSO "chills and deters the free exercise of the right of speech and association by the plaintiffs, their members and prospective members." In the former case, Gordon was reinstated to his position with full pay after filing what was originally an individual lawsuit, *Gordon v. Blount*. Although a federal district court dismissed Gordon's challenge to AGLOSO's constitutionality in a late 1971 ruling (336 F. Supp. 1271), it held that the Civic Service Commission (CSC) had utilized the list in what the government had already "conceded as an unlawful manner" by rehiring Gordon, thus making clear that organizational membership alone, even in a group that the DOJ had categorized as seeking the violent overthrow of the government, could not be the basis for firing federal employees. The SWP joined Gordon in appealing the part of the district court's ruling that upheld AGLOSO's constitutionality, but a March 3, 1973, federal appeals court reaffirmed the ruling and the Supreme Court refused to grant a further appeal on October 9, 1973 (*SWP v. Klassen*, 414 U.S. 879). That same day, the two-year-old ASU lawsuit was dismissed by joint agreement of the government and parties as moot due to what by then appeared (correctly) to be the imminent demise of AGLOSO. The ASU suit, filed on September 1, 1971, sought to enjoin implementation of the Nixon order on the grounds that the order and/or AGLOSO infringed on congressional powers, constituted an unconstitutional Bill of Attainder, violated First Amendment free speech guarantees, invaded Fourth and Ninth amendment privacy rights, violated Fifth and Sixth amendment due process protections, and infringed the Eighth Amendment's ban on cruel and unusual punishments. Three of the nine plaintiff organizations, the CP, SWP, and the Industrial Workers of the World (IWW), were AGLOSO-designated, while the other six included several anti-Vietnam war groups and two organizations then under consideration by the SACB under the ISA. Most of the nine groups openly described their ideologies as Marxist and/or aimed at the abolition of capitalism and/or the immediate removal of American troops from Vietnam, views that they maintained were constitutionally protected, even if calling for "radical changes" in the American economic and political system. However, they argued that such views might subject them to AGLOSO proceedings, with the result, as with the three already listed groups, that their members would be "punished, penalized, burdened, deprived of government employment," and subject to "irreparable injury solely because of their political beliefs and associations." In response, the DOJ asked that the suit be dismissed on a wide variety of grounds, including that the federal courts lacked jurisdiction to hear an attempt to "subject to judicial review executive action which is committed by law to the discretion of the executive"; that the case was not ripe for adjudication because the three listed organizations had failed to utilize the 1953 administrative remedies; and that the organizations' professed fears were "unjustified" and "illusory" as none of them, according to their self-descriptions, would come under the Nixon order since they had not "suggested that they seek to accomplish their purposes by illegal or unlawful means." The plaintiffs' suit was characterized as a "premature attempt to construct a legally cognizable controversy," because the nondesignated organizations had "never been aggrieved or designated in any manner" and thus "allege nothing but an imagined injury," while the listed groups had "alleged no new injury" and were required to first utilize the new "administrative [delisting] remedy" under Nixon's order. The department denied that the order threatened to either "chill" First Amendment rights (because the plaintiffs' contentions were "abstract, vague, remote and patently not judicially recognizable as a sufficient basis for [legal] standing") or to infringe upon congressional authority (since Congress had allegedly "ratified" the order by approving the requested 1972 SACB appropriation after debating this question "at great length").[47]

On January 10, 1972, federal district court Judge Gerhard Gesell dismissed the ASU lawsuit on the grounds that it was "premature" and not yet "ripe for [judicial] determination," although he strongly suggested that eventually Nixon's order and the AGLOSO/SACB would be declared unconstitutional as posing significant threats to First Amendment liberties (*ASU v. Mitchell*, Civil Action No. 1776-71). Gesell said the order contained "numerous broad, imprecise definitions of terms," which "appear on their face to raise constitutional problems" due to "their vagueness and overbreadth and the resulting effect on the rights of many government workers," especially since they tended to "expand and becloud meaning to a point where it is fairly obvious" that AGLOSO proceedings could be brought against almost any group engaged in mass demonstrations, including "so-called 'non-violent' techniques associated with many antiwar organizations." He termed the attempt to "revitalize a loyalty program that has found little favor" one with "disturbing implications," raising extremely serious issues that "must eventually be resolved," including the complete lack of "precedent for a President delegating to an independent, quasi-judicial body far-reaching responsibilities different in form and effect" from those originally authorized and not subsequently approved by Congress. Nonetheless, Gesell added, no groups or individuals had yet suffered under the new order, so professed fears of a "chilling effect" were "premised more on political intuition than on legal developments of which the Court can take cognizance." Therefore, he reasoned, the substantive issues should not be decided until the litigants' rights were "immediately threatened by an actual and ascertainable controversy," because sound judicial principles required that a "latent controversy" be allowed to mature so that a legal "decision can be made in the context of established fact" rather than having the courts act as the "immediate arbitrators of every potential conflict." Gesell concluded that the three listed groups had not demonstrated how they would be "irreparably injured" by the order's new delisting procedures, and, in any case, if they wished to challenge them, "they must first exhaust their administrative remedies" by invoking them. But he added that an "informative petition" of the attorney general seeking to list an organization would provide the basis to "test the delegation and the alleged overbreadth of the Order before [SACB] hearings are held," thus suggesting that he would strike the Nixon order as unconstitutional as soon as an attempt was made to implement it. (During the next few years, Gesell would preside over the trial of the so-called White House "plumbers" and jail Ehrlichman for his role in the notorious burglary of the psychiatrist of Daniel Ellsberg [of "Pentagon Papers" fame]. During the plumbers' trial, Gesell rejected White House claims that it could order burglaries on national security grounds, just as the Supreme Court, in a ruling handed down shortly after the mid-June 1972 Watergate burglary arrests, rejected Nixon's assertions that he could order warrantless wiretaps in domestic security cases.)

Following the Gesell ruling, the ACLU-backed plaintiffs appealed to the U.S. Court of Appeals. They especially focused on Gesell's contention that they could not obtain judicial remedy without showing a present injury, and, with regard to the three listed groups, must first utilize the new delisting procedure. They argued that this finding was erroneous because AGLOSO's creation exceeded the president's constitutional powers, as the order allegedly violated constitutional guarantees, was "vague and undefined in the extreme," invalidly gave SACB the "power to list and delist," and because they were "being compelled to initiate proceedings for delisting before an administrative body that does not have the power to conduct such proceedings," which in "any case would be conducted under unconstitutional standards." The organizations added that they were suffering the "present injury" of "deterrence" from First Amendment–protected political activity. The DOJ/SACB response endorsed Gesell's basic holding while stressing the failure of the three listed groups to utilize their "administrative remedies" and maintaining that there was "no rational basis" to conclude that the new order would affect the complaining groups. The response brief concluded that the new tasks delegated to the SACB by Nixon were "completely compatible with the basic assignment given it by Congress and therefore entirely justified from the point of law and public administration." Before the appeals court could rule, 1972 congressional developments discussed below led to the abolition of the SACB in June 1973 and the likely imminent demise of AGLOSO; therefore the lawsuit was dismissed as moot by joint stipulation of the parties on October 9, 1973.

Shortly before this termination of the ASU suit and the simultaneous failure of the Supreme Court to hear the SWP appeal in *Klassen*, in 1973 the SWP filed another lawsuit, this one requesting $40 million in damages from the FBI and other federal intelligence agencies due to decades of alleged illegal spying and disruptions of constitutionally protected activities. Soon after the suit was filed, the government revealed that FBI director Hoover had initiated a formal sabotage program against the SWP in 1961 on the grounds that it had recently been "openly espousing its line on a local and national basis through running candidates for public office and strongly directing and/or supporting such causes as Castro's Cuba and integration problems arising in the south." After fourteen years of litigation (during which Attorney General Griffin Bell was briefly held in contempt of court for refusing to release FBI files), Federal Judge Thomas Griesa awarded the SWP $264,000 in 1986, finding, in a 210-page opinion (*SWP v. Attorney General*, 642 F. Supp. 1357) that between 1940 and 1976 the FBI had infiltrated and disrupted the party while failing to uncover any instances of "planned or actual espionage, violence, terrorism or efforts to subvert the governmental structure" or evidence leading to even "a single arrest for any Federal law violation." Griesa reported that the FBI had instead directed all of its actions against "entirely lawful and peaceful political activities," that its investigation had revealed that the SWP expelled members who advocated "violence or disorder," and that the 8 million FBI file entries reported on the "marital or cohabitation status, marital strife, health, travel plans and personal habits" of party members. Griesa declared that FBI files revealed "little or no information bearing on national security and no information about actual or planned violence against public officials, but rather a mass of information about peaceful political activities and the private lives of individuals." Griesa added that during its "patently unconstitutional" campaign against the SWP, conducted without any "legal authority or justification," the FBI had committed almost 200 burglaries and 46 acts of "disruption" designed to create internal party turmoil, tapped SWP telephones for at least 20,000 days, and paid almost $2 million to 1,300 informers who infiltrated the organization and its youth group, the Young Socialist Alliance (YSA) (whose combined estimated membership never exceeded 3,000). FBI documents released during the trial revealed that over 300 of the informers had become members of the two groups, including 40 who held SWP office and several who ran for election as SWP candidates. The FBI originally defended its actions because members of "subversive groups" were "presumed" to view the "use of violence as a political tool" as "inevitable" and because SWP members might "gain responsible positions not only in government but also in industry and education." However, after Attorney General Edward Levi ordered the bureau to stop spying on the SWP in 1976 following revelations of massive FBI surveillance abuses and illegal actions against numerous dissident groups and individuals (FBI documents revealed it was still then using over 60 SWP informants), FBI director Clarence Kelley conceded, "We agree it is now necessary to discontinue such investigations." As late as 1981, however, the government maintained that it could "legally investigate individuals or organizations regardless of their nature" and that the issue was not whether SWP or YSA were "guilty of a crime beyond a reasonable doubt," but whether the government could investigate the "groups that openly advocate revolutionary change" even if "such advocacy might be within the letter of the law." Even after losing the case, the government argued that it had "important legitimate needs" for continuing to use the fruits of its SWP surveillance, especially with regard to "security clearance" for government employees and contractors; however, it finally decided not to appeal Judge Griesa's injunction banning such action.[48]

The Final Congressional AGLOSO Debate, 1972

While the ASU and Klassen lawsuits made their way through the courts, in late January 1992 the HISC Subcommittee on Loyalty and Security reconvened its long-running hearings into the administration of the federal loyalty program. Among the legislation under consideration was the Nixon administration's proposal to bolster the revived SACB by granting it contempt and subpoena powers and providing listed AGLOSO groups with a right to judicial appeal. Appearing on January 27, Kevin Maroney, deputy assistant attorney general in the DOJ's ISD, urged adoption of the administration bill so that the SACB's new functions "could be better accomplished," helping to make AGLOSO "current and more significant than it is today, than it has been in recent years," especially because its new definitions "relating to violent action organizations" would foster the "designation of some of the new revolutionary terrorist organizations." Maroney, like Mardian before him at the subcommittee's July 29, 1971, hearing, mostly seemed to elicit irritation from HISC members, both from the conservative majority and from the lone HISC liberal, Rep. Robert Drinan (D-MA). When Rep. Preyer told Maroney that Judge Gesell's January 10 ASU ruling had clearly suggested "he is going to enjoin you" with the "first organization you cite" if "you insist on enforcing" the Nixon order, Maroney responded, "there is a lot of handwriting on the wall to that result, but we feel that the Executive Order is legally defensible." When Maroney seemed uncertain concerning whether or not any "loyalty firings" had occurred during the previous five years, HISC counsel Alfred Nittle declared acidly, "You would know the answer to [the question] if you had read the committee's investigation," and a moment later Nittle termed one of Maroney's remarks "nonsense." Asked by Preyer what the supposedly reinvigorated SACB was doing in the "six months since this new order has been in existence," Maroney pointed to the SACB's delistings, but conceded that no DOJ requests for listing new organizations had been made. He first declared that "we probably would not file any [new] cases" while the ASU ruling was on appeal, but then said that new cases would soon be referred. Drinan, referring to the SACB's recent request for a massive budgetary increase, questioned how the administration could fail to initiate "any single proceeding against those alleged terrorist organizations that are so terrible that the President wants to double the appropriation to catch them."[49]

Not surprisingly, Maroney's position in support of the administration's legislation was strongly backed in a written statement submitted by the SACB, which termed passage of the administration bill "essential if the Board is to effectively and expeditiously carry out its duties in relation to the personnel security program." The SACB especially stressed the need to obtain contempt powers "in view of the nationwide publicity given in the last few years to the efforts of various elements to disrupt court proceedings and all inquiries related to subversion." It also maintained that AGLOSO, although "incomplete and outdated," had historically played a "key role" as the "principal yardstick" used by Government officials to determine the loyalty of Government employees and applicants, and that without it "federal security officials would have no guide for determining the significance of a person's organizational activities."[50]

In contrast to the views of the SACB and the DOJ, Yale University law professor Thomas Emerson, a leading First Amendment authority, told the subcommittee that any government loyalty program "designed to probe widely and deeply into the area of political thought and expression" was likely to be "manned by petty and fearful bureaucrats" and would inevitably require an "elaborate apparatus of investigations, professional informers, amateur informers, blacklists, files of citizens' activities" and other intrusive measures, all undertaken in "almost total secrecy, with no opportunity for the press, the public or the academic scholar to know and appraise what is going on." Similarly, Washington, D.C., attorney Lawrence Spieser warned that a "broad scale investigation into the background and the attitudes of all Government employees" would have the "great disadvantage of affecting freedom of belief and the willingness of Government employees or potential Government employees to experiment, to engage in intellectual jousting, to go to organizations, to hear speakers, to read books, to engage in the kind of experimentation" that "should be part of college life and not fear the consequences in the future." However, Notre Dame law professor Charles Rice maintained that "a man's associations are relevant in determining what sort of a man he is" and that the government should be able to exclude those who belonged "with specific intent, to organizations which have as their purpose the overthrow of the Government." New York attorney Kieran O'Doherty took a similar posture, arguing that the SACB, HISC, and (by implication) AGLOSO had "already protected thousands of innocent, unknowing people who might have" otherwise "joined subversive organizations and indeed have been prevented thereby from obtaining federal employment."[51]

In late February 1972, the annual round of congressional appropriations hearings led to additional testimony concerning the attempted SACB/AGLOSO revival; anticipating "appreciably expanded" activities due to the new "requirement to update" AGLOSO, the Nixon administration asked for $706,000 for the SACB for the 1973 fiscal year, almost 60 percent higher than 1972's $450,000 appropriation, with a proposed staff increase from 15 to 26. On February 29 and March 1, DOJ ISD head Mardian, appearing before a House appropriations subcommittee, reported that the ISD was concentrating on referring defunct AGLOSO groups to the SACB for delisting in order to "clean out the deadwood" on the list, since the current AGLOSO "represented something other than reality." He added that the department was also "preparing cases for presentation" to the SACB for new listings that would encompass the "new situation" of groups whose members constituted "a new brand of radical in this country." Appearing before the same subcommittee on April 10, SACB head Mahan faced skeptical questioning from Rep. Rooney, which was primarily provoked by the increased budgetary request. Mahan responded by pointing to an anticipated "substantially increased caseload" and maintained that Judge Gesell's January 10 ruling meant "there is no legal bar to going ahead with proceedings." Mahan reported that the SACB had already delisted 82 organizations, while anticipating additional petitions for an estimated 150 delistings and 30 new listings, as well as 6 anticipated organizational delisting petitions.[52]

By then, however, the department had not requested any new listings (and never did before AGLOSO was terminated), leading Mahan to earlier send a February 22 letter to White House assistant Pete Kinsey pleading for "some cases involving groups to be added to the list" in the hopes of redeeming the SACB's "public image," especially since, although its press releases reporting delistings had "been picked up by the press" the board was concerned about "how long the press will continue to pick up the releases—because they are all basically the same old thing." In a January 17 memo to the SACB, Executive Secretary Francis McNamara had claimed that "there are about 475 officially cited [by federal and state agencies other than the DOJ] Communist organizations" that had never been AGLOSO-designated. Although the delisting requests invariably specified that the organizations had been defunct for at least ten years and the SACB had always approved them, McNamara suggested that, as many older federal employees might have been involved with subversive organizations decades earlier, only groups defunct for at least twenty years should be delisted. However, he conceded that "once you get beyond the 20-year period, it would be possible to argue endlessly about the precise cut-off year" and that "the list can be made to look ridiculous" and "laughable" if "defunct groups are kept on it too long."[53]

On April 26 Mahan faced brief, mild questioning from a Senate appropriations subcommittee. Trying to put the best face on the SACB's activities and prospects, he largely repeated his earlier House testimony; HISC had since favorably recommended a bill to "give congressional approval to the authority the President gave us," Mahan reported, thus allegedly remedying "any problem" concerning the constitutionality of the Nixon order, as well as granting the board subpoena and contempt powers. Mahan maintained that the nation "needs an organization such as ours more now than ever before" and rejected the allegations of "critics who say we are witch hunters," because "the FBI does the investigating and the Attorney General has to file the petition," while the SACB simply listened as a "judicial body." As Mahan reported to the Senate subcommittee, on April 25 HISC had recommended, 5–1, that the House endorse a (significantly amended) version of the Nixon administration proposal to give the revitalized SACB (to be renamed the FISB) subpoena and contempt powers. HISC embellished the Nixon bill with a last-minute amendment sponsored by HISC chair Ichord that seemingly completely abandoned any restrictions on the types of organizations to be considered for AGLOSO by authorizing the president to delegate to the FISB, "under such regulations as he may prescribe," the function of "conducting hearings and making findings" with "respect to the character of relevant organizations to be designated in furtherance of programs" related to federal loyalty screenings. The dissenting HISC vote was cast by Rep. Drinan, who termed the amended bill unconstitutional, especially due to its "total abdication to the President" of power over the SACB via the "last minute afterthought" of the Ichord amendment, with its "wholly unspecified, undefined and unlimited transfer of legislative authority." He termed the bill too vague and overbroad, thus undermining "our most precious freedoms—the freedom to assemble and speak our beliefs without fear of punishment by the Government," because it would grant "any president" the power to "create new zones of impermissible associations" unrestrained or guided by Congress, with the result that "no citizen would have any guide as to what groups he could join without placing his reputation and livelihood in jeopardy."[54]

The HISC majority report, published on May 9, endorsed the Ichord amendment as resolving "any controversy as to the propriety" and constitutionality of the Nixon order, which it declared was "not authorized" by the ISA (which had established the SACB), by "expressly authorizing" the president to delegate additional functions to the SACB. HISC maintained that the amended bill would bolster the original purposes of the administration's bill, which it declared were to provide both an "additional function" for the board in view of its "present light workload" and a "sounder basis for updating" AGLOSO than the previous procedure, by dividing the "prosecutor and fact-finder" functions previously both implemented by the attorney general between him and the board, granting designated organizations the right to judicial review, giving the FISB contempt and subpoena powers, and, for the first time, defining the categories of designated organizations. HISC declared that the "maintenance of a current and reasonably comprehensive" AGLOSO was "indispensable to the efficient operation of" federal employee screening programs. According to the report, all cabinet departments and twelve major independent agencies had been queried and virtually all had "supported the concept" of AGLOSO, viewed it as "helpful in the execution of the loyalty-security programs," and deemed the "formal determination of the character" of organizations of "great importance." In several cases, the report added, agencies had stressed that "they have neither the expertise nor the facilities for independently" assessing such matters and "have urged that the determination of such questions be centralized." HISC added that virtually all government units found the current state of AGLOSO unsatisfactory because it had not been updated since 1955 "and of the approximately 283 organizations now listed, all are defunct with the exception of 13," although the "evidence indicates that there are probably more than 100 [Communist] front (and action) groups currently operating."[55]

In May and June debate over the fate of the SACB/AGLOSO shifted to the floors of Congress—for what turned out to be the last time. Although the House twice delivered substantial victories to the revived SACB/AGLOSO in May, in June the Senate issued a death blow. On May 18, after a brief and cursory debate, the House rejected by 206–106 a proposal to defund the SACB, although the approved 1973 appropriation was for $450,000, the same amount granted in 1972, rather than the $706,000 requested by the board. The House floor proposal to completely defund the SACB was sponsored by Rep. Sidney Yates (D-IL), who termed it a "dead agency which should have been buried" years earlier but was "still being kept alive in the hope that perhaps some day a law will be written [to give it work] that will be found constitutional." Yates said the board had "nothing to do" except for deleting defunct AGLOSO groups, "which a high school student can do in 2 weeks," at far less cost than the annual $36,000 salaries paid to SACB members. In response, HISC chair Ichord declared that the committee's proposal would respond to his concerns about the "severely circumscribed" role of the SACB and added, "The real question here involved is, do we want the U.S. Government to operate a program designed to weed out persons who are disloyal?" Rep. Drinan replied that no Representative opposed to "wasting money" by an agency whose "only accomplishments" had been to "clog the courts and waste the time and money of the DOJ in expensive and protracted constitutional litigation" should be "intimidated by the discredited and shameful ploy that he is 'soft on communism.'"[56]

On May 30, the House passed, 226–205, the HISC bill to grant the president broad powers to delegate AGLOSO functions to the SACB, to give the board subpoena and contempt powers, and to authorize AGLOSO designees to appeal SACB findings to the federal courts, after a prolonged, bitter, and widely reported debate that filled twenty-five *Congressional Record* pages. Aside from ground well trodden previously, debate centered especially on whether or not federal agencies had expressed a serious need for a continuation of SACB/AGLOSO during HISC's recent hearings and about the wisdom of the broad discretion the proposal granted the president, particularly by authorizing him to delegate to the newly named FISB AGLOSO designation power with respect to otherwise-undefined "relevant organizations" under "such regulations as he may prescribe." According to HISC chair Ichord, such broad discretion was needed both to settle constitutional questions arising from Nixon's 1971 executive order and to avoid basing the revived AGLOSO on its language, which he termed "very rigid," "inartistic," and "not too well framed," especially in its definitions of categories of organizations, which he deemed "extremely tautological, to say the least." Supporting Ichord, Rep. Ashbrook said that "all of the executive agencies as well as national patriotic agencies" backed revitalizing AGLOSO, and, as evidence of its past effectiveness in carrying out the "primary obligation of any government" to "defend itself against those who would destroy it," declared that over 90 percent of listed groups "are now defunct in a substantial part, due to the fact that their designation" had cost them membership and financial support.[57]

In opposition, Rep. Edwards maintained that "a careful reading" of the HISC hearings indicated a "real lack of enthusiasm" for updating AGLOSO and attacked the proposal as abdicating congressional legislative authority by granting the president "total, unfettered and absolute power to write the loyalty-security laws," enabling the executive branch to "create any criteria they want" with respect to organizations referred to the FISB, thus creating a situation in which "no citizen would have a guide as to what he could say or what group he could join without placing his job and future in jeopardy. This 'chilling effect' on freedom of association and of speech is more than a chill, it is a deep freeze." Edwards added that while a "legitimate program" was needed to insure employee loyalty, the DOJ, the FBI, and other agencies could perform such tasks, so there was no need to "return to the dark days of guilt by association, witch hunting and burning books" that indicated "a particular individual 25 or 30 years ago joined an organization which, within the past few days, the SACB has declared questionable." Rep. Emmanuel Celler (D-NY) agreed, arguing that the delegation of "totally unlimited authority" to the president to "prescribe political associations" of employees "boggles the mind." He added, "We cannot rely on the executive branch to narrow its use of the unfettered power which this bill would give it."[58]

What was to be the last significant congressional floor discussion concerning SACB/AGLOSO occurred in the Senate on June 15, 1972, where after an impassioned debate that occupied twenty-five *Congressional Record* pages, the Senate voted 42–25 to totally defund the SACB (a decision reported on the front page of the *Washington Post*), which ultimately sealed the fate of both the board and AGLOSO. Twenty-nine of thirty-four voting Democrats supported the measure, as did thirteen of thirty-three Republicans. Senate SACB opponents, again led by Proxmire and Ervin, entered the debate with victory already largely won, because the Senate appropriations committee, in reporting the bill to the floor, approved $450,000 to fund the SACB but incorporated Ervin's amendment to ban it from implementing Nixon's executive order. Since, unlike the House, the Senate had neither taken up nor accepted the HISC bill to authorize the SACB to administer AGLOSO, even acceptance of the committee proposal meant paralyzing both programs. Proxmire and Ervin both stressed their earlier arguments that the SACB had only wasted money and violated First Amendment rights for years and that both Nixon's order and AGLOSO in general were unconstitutional and could therefore never be successfully implemented, as Judge Gesell had suggested five months earlier. Proxmire declared that "this revised edition of SACB will do no more and cost no less than its expensive and impotent predecessors. How many times do we have to find this well dry before we conclude there is no water in it?" He said Nixon's order suffered from a "double case of unconstitutionality," since the president could not decree "an entirely new set of functions for an agency established by an act of Congress" and, in any case, "an official blacklist in the hands of five men is inconsistent with our democratic society."

Ervin declaimed that the pending proposal should be entitled "a bill to give un-employment benefits to five bureaucrats," since the board had done nothing for a year but delist "111 organizations that no one had heard anything about for 20-odd years," in "nonsense" hearings lasting "28 seconds to hear each case," which were likely "the most expensive in the history of the American bureau-cracy" and "a travesty of bureaucracy in inaction."

Ervin termed the House bill the "biggest fool legislation ever passed by ei-ther House" and termed complete SACB defunding an unusual opportunity to simultaneously "vote for freedom under the Constitution and for economy in government," since the American political system "contemplated that no man shall be punished" except for a crime in which "he has been convicted according to constitutional standards in a court of justice." He added that a board dating from an era "when Communists were being discovered under every rosebush" and which told "people what thought they can think and what associations they shall choose" made him "fear for the continuance of my country as a free so-ciety." In a hilarious satirical peroration, Ervin declared that the only difficult problem that SACB had to ponder was the "profound" question of "determining whether an unincorporated association has died and, if so, the exact moment of its passing," a question he termed "more elusive and difficult" than the "meaning and definition of human death." He asked, "What if the only members actually present at such a meeting were FBI agents? Would they be considered bona fide members?" Ervin concluded:

> If we invest another half-million dollars in the Board we will eventually get this classic statement on this most important problem—associational suicide. We will have a classic essay on one of the issues of great moment to the future of western civilization. An issue which can only be compared to such fundamental questions as: How many angels do stand on a pin? Does a tree make a sound if it falls with no one to hear it? Where does the flame go when a candle is blown out? Does a pond ever stop rippling when a stone is dropped in it? Who killed cock robin?[59]

In response to Ervin and Proxmire, several leading conservatives, including senators Ernest Hollings (D-SC), Thurmond, and Gurney, maintained that the SACB and AGLOSO carried out vital national security functions. Thus, Hollings declared "there is a continuing necessity to keep close tabs on what the Commu-nists are doing" and to have an "authoritative source" to designate "communist" or "subversive" organizations. Responding to complaints about recent SACB in-activity, he argued, "One cannot say that a policeman in front of the Capitol is useless because he has not arrested anybody in the last year." Similarly, Thur-mond argued that the SACB had "played a vital role in the protection of national security," something that "can be done through the mere process of exposure" and that was feared by "Communist front organizations" beyond "anything else." Gurney argued that "in view of the proliferation of subversive groups of all types in the nation today, there seems to be more, rather than less, reason for continuing" the SACB. Hollings said the appropriations committee had incorporated the Ervin amendment only because it felt that Nixon's order had gone "beyond the purview of the executive" but argued that Congress, rather than acting "precipitately" to abolish the SACB, should "make it a more effective vehicle for the exposure of the Communist menace," since "to lower our guard now, at this critical time in history, would be the ultimate folly" that could "be the lull that destroys our society."[60]

The Final Death Agony of AGLOSO, 1972–1974

The 42–25 June 15, 1972, Senate vote to defund the SACB (two days before a group of Republican Party operatives were arrested while burglarizing Democratic Party headquarters in the Watergate complex in Washington, D.C.) proved a mortal wound to AGLOSO. However, like an actor in a bad melodrama (and some good operas), the "list" lingered on for another two years in a prolonged death agony. It was finally formally abolished by President Nixon in early June 1974, two months before the equally mortally wounded president resigned after an similarly long death agony, due to the Watergate affair and other related scandals, in which, in essence, illegal activities that had long been tolerated or winked at when directed against fringe groups caused a huge political uproar when directed against the Democratic Party. Nixon was famously (or infamously) pardoned by his appointed successor, Gerald Ford, while many of those who had worked with him to revive AGLOSO, including Mitchell, Dean, Krogh, Ehrlichman, and Haldeman, were jailed in connection with Watergate and related crimes (Mardian won an appeal on procedural grounds from his conviction and was never retried, while Kleindienst, Mitchell's replacement as attorney general, who presided over AGLOSO's final days, received a suspended jail term).

Right-wing politicians, newspapers, and groups frequently suggested that Communists and other subversives were behind and/or would be the prime beneficiaries of SACB defunding. Thus, Rep. Ashbrook told the House on June 8, a week before the critical Senate debate, that vocal support for the proposal by the CP's *Daily World* newspaper illustrated "who would gain from the elimination of the SACB." The American Legion declared on June 13 that such action would only encourage groups that sought to "change our democratic form of government to a totalitarian state." The *New York Daily News* wrote on June 17 that killing the SACB would "give aid and comfort to a hatful of our most dangerous enemies"; the notoriously right-wing New Hampshire *Manchester Union-Leader* declared on June 19 that the CP would be "guilty of gross ingratitude" if it failed to "formally thank" the Senate; and the July 16 *Christian Crusade Weekly* declared that the Senate action had sparked "great rejoicing among the Communist conspirators and their allies." Conversely, liberal newspapers and spokespersons hailed the Ervin proposal and the Senate action: thus, the June 10 *Washington Post* termed the upcoming vote a "great opportunity to finally lay this offense to the Constitution and to budget-conscious government watchers to rest, once and for all," combining "pollution control and budget trimming all in one fell swoop." The June 27 *New York Times* termed the SACB a "useless left-over" and "shoddy relic" of McCarthyism, whose actions had been reduced to "near-zero" by court rulings and which would be acting with "probable illegality" if the Nixon order took effect. NBC anchor David Brinkley termed the SACB "an agency that does nothing" and "has no reason to exist" in his July 21 evening news commentary.[61]

At a brief June 29 Senate Internal Security Subcommittee hearing on the House-approved HISC bill, SACB chair Mahan pleaded for Congress to allow the board to close the "gaps in the present program by updating" AGLOSO and "making it a meaningful and useful yardstick instead of a considerably outdated instrument." However, the Nixon administration, apparently resigned to the ab-olition of the SACB and AGLOSO following the Senate vote, declined to send a representative (claiming late notification) and submitted only, via Deputy At-torney General Ralph Erickson, a written statement that it had "no objection" to the HISC bill. An October 10, 1972, congressional conference committee, appar-ently seeking to achieve the impossible by reconciling the drastically different House and Senate SACB provisions, approved $350,000 board funding (as part of a much larger appropriations bill), but also approved Ervin's proposal ban-ning the board from carrying out any of the new duties assigned it by Nixon's order. On October 13, Congress approved this "compromise," which, in Ervin's words during a brief Senate debate that day, left SACB members with nothing to do but "draw their breath and their salaries" and amounted to "little more than unemployment benefits for five bureaucrats" and "their secretaries, who will as-sist them in doing nothing." Proxmire echoed Ervin's characterization, declaring that the bill would do nothing but provide funds for SACB members to "draw their salaries and maybe play bridge with each other," while ensuring that they "do not have to go out and hunt for new jobs." On October 24, AGLOSO sus-tained another blow when, as discussed earlier, a federal appeals court ordered the DOJ to delete the ALB/VALB, the first (and last) such court-ordered delist-ing in AGLOSO's history; the next day, the appropriations bill with the Ervin rider became law and the SACB and AGLOSO were effectively left in suspended animation.[62]

By then, the Nixon administration (increasingly preoccupied by Watergate) and the SACB were apparently resigned to the death of the SACB and the conse-quent continued paralysis of AGLOSO. Although before mid-1972, White House and SACB files are filled with memos focused on strategies to revive the board and AGLOSO, the only relevant surviving archival materials thereafter are a December 7, 1972, memo from White House counsel Dean to Ehrlichman recommending that President Nixon ask for the resignations of SACB members (a suggestion rejected by Ehrlichman), followed by a January 26, 1973, letter from Budget Bureau deputy director John Carlucci informing SACB chair Mahan that Nixon had decided to propose no 1974 SACB funding, thus contemplating that board activities would "be terminated and all of its financial obligations satisfied with the resources appropriated for 1973." Clearly seeking to head off any further SACB maneuvering, Carlucci instructed Mahan that "the full support of this decision" by all SACB members is "expected by the President" and "should be given in testimony before congressional committees, in informal contact with members of Congress and their staffs, and in speeches and meetings with outside groups."[63]

Nixon's budget proposal was published in late January 1973 (shortly after the trial of the Watergate burglars began) with the laconic explanation, entirely lacking any reference either to his 1971 executive order or recent congressional action, that no SACB funding was being requested because "as a result of a series of court decisions, the board's workload has diminished in recent years." A lengthy January 29 *Washington Star* report concluded that the "beleaguered and often controversial" board had "lost the support of one of its few remaining friends in the federal government—President Nixon." Bizarrely, on February 1, 1973, presidential consultant Leonard Garment wrote SACB chair Mahan to request the participation of SACB officials in a planned April "Annual Design Assembly," which would focus on how the government could "most vigorously assist the arts and artists and how arts and artists can be of help" to government agencies; in a February 2 telephone response, according to a handwritten note in the SACB files, chief counsel Bernard Waters informed the White House "that the Board would be closing down." On the same day, Mahan wrote Democratic Senate majority leader Mike Mansfield (D-MT) that he was notifying SACB employees of their impending layoffs and was closing down his agency "in an orderly fashion by June 30, when our current appropriation expires." In its final official action, the SACB issued a report on March 22 which, under its ISA authority, labeled the Center for Marxist Education a "communist front." On June 27 (two months after Nixon announced the forced Watergate-related resignations of Haldeman, Ehrlichman, Dean, and Attorney General Kleindienst and a month after Sen. Ervin's nationally televised Watergate hearings began), Budget Bureau director Roy Ash wrote to Mahan, praising him for the "efficient and effective manner, with a minimum of fanfare and publicity" in which he had "deactivated" the SACB and commending him for "accepting the President's decision to terminate the Board's activities and unselfishly implementing that decision in the spirit in which it was made."[64]

The board's impending dissolution was accompanied by a modest final spate of news stories, editorials, and commentaries, including a lengthy March 3 *Christian Science Monitor* report, which declared that the SACB was winding up "with hardly a whisper," having been "abandoned" by Nixon, and a late March Copley News Service article, which quoted Mahan as declaring, "It's never pleasant to close down an operation, but this is particularly hard. We all have the feeling that we're leaving behind so much unfinished business." In a long March 28 House speech, HISC chair Ichord called for the creation of a new "Federal Employee Security and Appeals Commission" empowered, upon petition by the attorney general, to make "determinations of [subversive] organizations" following "due process hearings." Otherwise, conservative voices remained largely silent, while liberals welcomed the SACB's demise: the March 1973 *Progressive* magazine sarcastically declared that it could "hardly hold back our tears," the March 29 *New York Times* editorially declared "good riddance" to the board, and *Washington Post* columnist Clayton Fritchey wrote on March 24 that Nixon had "strangled" it, while Congress had sensed that the "anti-Communist frenzy which gripped the American public for so long is not what it used to be" and had "quickly noted that there was no public reaction" against the SACB's impending demise. The July 1, 1973, *Washington Post* marked the end of the board with a front-page account that noted that the board's liquidation "ironically" came at the hands of Nixon, who "as a young California congressman initiated the bill that set up the SACB to expose Soviet undercover operations, but who as President publicly embraced Soviet leader Leonid Brezhnev last week in a continuing search for global détente." SACB executive secretary Francis McNamara was quoted as being not "bitter" but "disappointed," since "someone has to determine what groups are subversive." Mahan was quoted as urging Congress to "hold hearings to decide whether a disclosure-type committee like this is still needed. Personally, I've always believed in a personnel security program."[65]

The SACB's demise left both AGLOSO and Nixon's 1971 executive order still technically in effect, yet in a bizarre state of limbo, since AGLOSO was theoretically under the tutelage of an agency that no longer existed. Thus, in an August 1973 legal brief in the *Klassen* Supreme Court appeal (discussed above) that challenged AGLOSO's constitutionality, Solicitor General Robert Bork (soon to become acting attorney general after Elliot Richardson resigned that post during the October 1973 so-called Watergate Saturday night massacre) conceded that "there is presently no method available by which a designated organization may challenge its listing," although he stated that the DOJ is "presently considering new regulations to remedy this situation." In fact, as the result of a review initiated in June 1973 by Attorney General Richardson, the department, with the passive consent of the FBI, recommended that AGLOSO be terminated. The first post-SACB department document concerning AGLOSO's future, a twelve-page, single spaced June 5 memo from Assistant Attorney General Henry Peterson to

Richardson, declared that the key issue was to "provide adequate due process procedures," which he suggested could be "accomplished, at least as an interim measure, by revoking" Nixon's order and "re-establishing the program as previously carried out" under the 1953 Eisenhower administrative hearing procedures. However, Peterson concluded, his opinion was "that the list should be abolished" as AGLOSO was of only "slight value" in connection with federal loyalty screenings, because many "federal agencies have long since ceased to use" it due to "its not being up to date" and "because of the substantial constitutional problems which surround [its] maintenance."[66]

The department's OLC, in an almost equally lengthy August 6, 1973, memo from Assistant Attorney General Robert Dixon, endorsed Peterson's recommendation, especially because of "our understanding" that the FBI included in its personnel "background investigations" information about "the affiliations of [federal job] applicants with organizations that it believes significant from a national security standpoint whether or not the organization" was on AGLOSO. Dixon concluded that it had therefore been "a long time since the list has been considered a useful or necessary tool in judging the security aspects involved in employment" and, in any case, recent court rulings (as discussed above) had seemingly established that employees "could not be discharged based on membership alone" absent a showing that the employee was a "knowing and active member who intended to further the organization's unlawful activities," and AGLOSO was not "of great help in such situations." Moreover, Dixon noted, while Peterson's memo had termed the "due process" concern with regard to AGLOSO's continued use the central outstanding issue, "no complaints" had arisen during the nine months since there had been "no agency legally authorized to hold [AGLOSO] designation hearings" and "if the list is no longer important it can be abolished and the due process problem" would "disappear." Dixon added that AGLOSO had become "to a large extent" a "political football," with "internal indications" that some of its past advocates viewed it as appealing "to a large segment of the public concerned with extremist organizations," while evidently a "substantial body in Congress" viewed AGLOSO as "an unfortunate memento of the McCarthy era" and (in an oblique reference to the burgeoning Watergate scandal) "recent Executive Branch revelations may well strengthen those feelings," so "considerable caution should be exercised to avoid antagonizing these members of Congress and the public they represent" absent "some clear offsetting balance to be gained."[67]

In a September 28, 1973, memo to Dixon, FBI director Kelley (who, following the 1972 death of J. Edgar Hoover, had succeeded Director Patrick Gray when the latter resigned in disgrace in April 1973 after confessing to have destroyed documents related to the metastasizing Watergate scandal), raised several questions about the concept of abolishing AGLOSO without flatly opposing such action. Kelley termed AGLOSO an "important element as a guide in Federal personnel matters for many years" and warned that its abolition would leave security officials "without official guidance of any kind." However, his main expressed concern (strikingly similar to Hoover's repeatedly expressed concern that, above all, "embarrassment" to the FBI was to be avoided) was that, since federal officials would largely be reliant upon FBI reports if AGLOSO were ended, if federal agencies were forced to "exclusive[ly]" rely upon bureau characterizations of organizations, the result might be "allegations that the FBI is actually evaluating organizational activity and thus assuming responsibilities originally intended for the Attorney General." Kelley asked that if it was "decided to abolish the list" that guidance be furnished the FBI concerning "our policies in regard to the investigation" of formerly designated groups and those under investigation for possible designation. In an October 12, 1973, memo, Dixon characterized the FBI's posture as one of "not affirmatively support[ing] abolition of the list but not . . . strongly opposed to that course." He conceded that terminating AGLOSO might "from a public relations posture" somewhat "highlight" the FBI's role in loyalty screening, but "the fact that the FBI characterizes groups is not secret" and the department had to assume that the "present situation is not secret to anyone who has taken the time to think about it" since "we could hardly take the position" that for loyalty screening purposes "sole reliance is placed on the present list which was essentially put together in the 40s." He added that in "fairness" to presently designated groups, "some solution" that allowed them to challenge their listings "should be proposed within a reasonable length of time."[68]

In mid-January 1974, Dixon reported the above views of the DOJ and the FBI to Attorney General William Saxbe (Richardson's replacement) and asked for his "guidance" as to which of three alternatives to recommend to President Nixon: abolishing the list, taking no action and thus preserving the "status quo," or giving the DOJ or "some other body power to make listing decisions." In response, according to an undated memo to Saxbe from Dixon that appears to have been written in early April 1974, Saxbe approved of the "abolition" option and decided to brief the press on his decision. In the memo, Dixon reported that the FBI had "no objection" to an executive order to abolish AGLOSO and bar "use of the existing list for any purpose," which had been drafted by the OLC in consultation with an FBI representative and officials from various department divisions. The department's consideration of abolishing AGLOSO was first made public in late August 1973, when a spokesman confirmed an Associated Press story that the issue was under advisement. The story quoted an anonymous department official as declaring that "they're tending now toward abolishing it. This list is of dubious value. Why have something that's absolutely worthless?" On April 3, 1974, Saxbe told reporters that a decision to "revise or get rid of" AGLOSO was "on the front burner" after having "kind of went into limbo" following Richardson's October 20, 1973, resignation. (During this six-month interim, the House Judiciary Committee had begun impeachment proceedings against President Nixon, while seven top White House aides, including Mitchell, Haldeman, Ehrlichman, and Mardian, were indicted in connection with the Watergate cover-up; six Watergate burglars were convicted and jailed; and a series of stunning public revelations of FBI abuses during the post-1945 period emerged, notably the bureau's so-called COINTELPRO sabotage program directed against such organizations as the CP, the SWP, and anti-Vietnam War "New Left" groups). Saxbe told reporters on April 3 that AGLOSO had become obsolete due to a relaxation in attitudes toward international communism, because "world wide trends" made "terrorism" rather than communism the key subversive threat and because "the Jewish intellectual" was no longer "very enamored" with communism (thus triggering intense criticism, including calls for his resignation from Jewish organizations and others). Bizarrely, on the same day Saxbe was telling reporters that AGLOSO's fate was uncertain, FBI director Kelley publicly said it had already "been abolished, of course."[69]

On April 18, Saxbe sent Budget Bureau director Ash a draft executive order designed to "terminate the Attorney General's function of maintaining and disseminating a list of subversive organizations for personnel purposes" and to "prohibit the use of the existing list for any purpose." On May 3, Budget Bureau general counsel Stanley Ebner forwarded the draft, with his office's endorsement, to presidential aide Robert Linder. According to Ebner, abolishing AGLOSO would simply recognize that it was an outdated instrument no longer "viable" in personnel security cases because many listed groups were "defunct and many that are now considered to be subversive are not listed." Relying on AGLOSO, he warned, could result in disregarding affiliations with "potentially dangerous" nonlisted groups. He added that top presidential legal and political advisers, including Leonard Garment, David Gergen, and Fred Buzhardt, had no objections to the draft and suggested that the press be briefed when Nixon signed the order "to avoid any possible misunderstanding concerning the reasons for abolishing the list."[70]

Nixon's subsequent final decision to abolish AGLOSO was leaked to the press on June 1, 1974. According to one anonymous official, the list's termination "is more important symbolically than in fact," because although "absolutely worthless, it has a ring to it of enemies of the government" (an allusion to the Nixon administration's by-then notorious "enemies list" of those targeted for actions such as the Watergate burglary). On June 4, Nixon formally signed Executive Order 11785, which revoked his 1971 order, declared AGLOSO was "hereby abolished and shall not be used for any purpose," and banned all government agencies from making AGLOSO designations or publishing or circulating AGLOSO lists. No doubt because his action had been so widely forecast, it generally attracted relatively modest press attention (thus, the June 5 *New York Times* published only a short wire service story on page 46). However, the *Washington Post* carried a lengthy front-page story, whose lead declared that Nixon had acted "with little fanfare and no evidence of nostalgia" to abolish AGLOSO, which it declared, dating it from Truman's 1947 order, was twenty-seven years old (although, since the government had continually maintained AGLOSO since Biddle's World War II list, thirty-four years old was a more accurate calculation). According to press accounts, Saxbe termed the list a "vestigial tail" of government security programs that "serves no useful purpose" and whose "most serious failing" perhaps was its failure to provide designated groups with due process protections. If AGLOSO "serves no other purpose now," Saxbe added, it should be a reminder that "whatever we do must be fair and in full accord with the law and the protections it affords to all." "Naturally," according to Saxbe, the government would continue to administer personnel security programs, while Deputy Assistant Attorney General Kevin Maroney was quoted as reporting that the FBI would continue to actively investigate fifty-two organizations that it was then monitoring. The *Post* reported that only the DOD had recently been using AGLOSO and that DOJ officials stated that existing copies of the list would be destroyed.[71]

The end of AGLOSO was widely hailed, even by the notoriously conservative *Wall Street Journal*, which declared on June 6 that the list had long "outlived any usefulness it might have had" as it was "outmoded," "few Americans anymore look to Moscow for guidance," and Russia "no longer seems quite as belligerent or reckless as it once did." Furthermore, the *Journal* added, recently emerging "terrorist" groups were "largely refuges for criminal and disordered minds" and the "way to deal with them is not through subversive lists but through just application of the criminal law." Among liberal outlets, the June 8 *New York Times* termed AGLOSO the "ghastly relic of an era to be remembered only in national shame and embarrassment," which had served as an "ill-conceived directory for witch hunters" and "symbolized the vicious doctrine of guilt by association," with the resultant "persecution-by-list" ruining "many careers and reputations." In an editorial entitled "They Had a Little List," the June 7 *Washington Post* hailed the consignment to the "junk heap" of a relic of the "clanking, rusty machinery of the post-war 'anti-subversive' drive," but, referring to the ongoing trial of the Nixon administration "plumbers," declared that recent revelations had "demonstrated for all who care to see that government is ever capable of devising new and different means for encroaching on the rights of individuals— just listen to the testimony in Judge Gerhard Gesell's courtroom." But not all reactions were so positive: a "news story" in the June 15 conservative weekly *Human Events* reported that "security specialists in Washington are still reeling from the shock" of Nixon's action, which "flies in the face of all serious studies of the list and the government's personnel loyalty-security program." White House files contain a June 17 telegram from the national chair of the American Legion Auxiliary that declared, "Never have been so shocked as we were this morning to read where you have abolished the red list of traitors in our country. What goes?"[72]

Two months after the abolition of AGLOSO, on August 8, 1974, Richard M. Nixon, facing certain congressional impeachment and conviction, resigned as president of the United States. Perhaps fittingly, and certainly ironically, Nixon, who had first gained attention as one of the earliest and fiercest post–World War II anti-Communists, and who served as vice president in an administration that repeatedly boasted of its anti-Communist prowess, including making numerous additions to AGLOSO, was forced to resign essentially for using against "mainstream" political opponents the same kinds of repeated illegal and repressive measures that had long been accepted when targeted against "fringe" groups such as those listed on AGLOSO.

Although AGLOSO was dead, its effects and, in some cases, its ghost, lingered on: the Pentagon revealed in November 1974 that it was still using AGLOSO to blacklist military personnel, and in 1980 the INS was revealed to be maintaining a list of almost 700 "questionable" groups to help screen and deport immigrants and aliens. In fact, it is not clear whether the abolition of AGLOSO substantially reduced FBI investigations of "subversive" groups or not, since Nixon's June 4, 1974, executive order authorized continued screening to determine if federal personnel maintained "knowing membership with the specific intent of furthering the aims of, or adherence to and active participation in, any foreign or domestic organization" or "combination of persons" seeking to unlawfully overthrow the government or deny others their constitutional rights. November 11, 1974, DOJ instructions to the FBI directed it to continue to investigate organizations "with a potential" for falling within these standards although such investigations were to terminate upon reaching a "stage that offers a basis for determining that the activities are legal in nature," and FBI director Kelley was specifically advised two days later that AGLOSO groups would "still come within the criteria" if engaging in "activities" proscribed in the June 4 order. Due to a series of 1976 federal district court rulings, the CSC announced in September of that year that it was removing from job application forms a variety of loyalty oaths, including those disavowing membership in organizations advocating the illegal overthrow of the government, but a CSC spokesman told reporters that this did "not mean that in making a background investigation an investigator cannot ask those questions if loyalty were a factor in selection." Two 1983 books published by conservative groups argued that as a result of such restrictions, the federal loyalty program needed to be tightened up again.[73]

Twenty years after the formal demise of AGLOSO, during the William Clinton administration, one of the first tools endorsed by Congress as part of the "war on terror" was to give the government the right to compile and publish lists of "terrorist" groups, without any hearings, charges, or evidence. Although, unlike the Truman AGLOSO, the vast majority of the hundreds of groups that were listed during the Clinton and subsequent George W. Bush administrations under this and later legislation were foreign rather than domestic, and the listings seemingly were not intended to suppress domestic dissent, these due process breaches helped pave the way for further abuses that drastically multiplied after the horrendous September 11, 2001, attacks on the United States. Many such abuses were so deeply encased in unprecedented levels of government secrecy that many details remained unknown, but as of early 2008 they included, with regard to aliens, and in some cases American citizens also, secret prisons, indefinite detention without trials, elimination of the right to *habeas corpus* proceedings, warrantless wiretaps, and other forms of electronic snooping, and the use of interrogatory techniques widely viewed as constituting torture.

But these developments are the subject of many other books.

Notes

Abbreviations Used in Endnotes

ACLU	American Civil Liberties Union
AGLOSO	Attorney General's List of Subversive Organizations
CGS	Commission on Government Security, NA, Record Group 220
CR	*Congressional Record*
CSC	Civil Service Commission Papers, NA, Record Group 146
CSM	*Christian Science Monitor*
CT	*Chicago Tribune*
DDE	Eisenhower Presidential Library, Abilene, Kansas
DLP	David Lasser Papers, University of California at San Diego Library
DOJ	Department of Justice
DOJA	DOJ Papers, NA, Record Group 60, File 146-200-2-012
DOJB	DOJ Papers, NA, Record Group 60, File 146-200-2
DOJC	DOJ Papers, NA, Record Group 60, File 146-200-2–04
DOJD	DOJ Papers, NA, Record Group 60, File 146-06
DVP	Devitt Vanech Papers, HST
EAL	*Encyclopedia of the American Left* (Urbana: University of Illinois Press, 1990)
EBP	Eleanor Bontecou Papers, HST
EKP	Egil "Bud" Krogh Papers, RMN
FBI	Federal Bureau of Investigation
FMP	Francis McNamara Papers, George Mason University Library, Fairfax, Virginia
FOIA	Freedom of Information Act request
FR	*Federal Register*
HAC	House Appropriations Committee
HCR	House Committee on Rules
HCSC	House Civil Service Committee
HISC	House Internal Security Committee
HST	Truman Presidential Library, Independence, Missouri
HUAC	House Committee on Un-American Activities
IWO	International Workers Order
JAFRC	Joint Anti-Fascist Refugee Committee
JDP	John Dean Papers, RMN
LAT	*Los Angeles Times*
LBJ	Lyndon Johnson Presidential Library, Austin, Texas
LRB	Loyalty Review Board Papers, NA, Record Group 146
NA	National Archives
NCASF	National Council on American-Soviet Friendship
NYHT	*New York Herald Tribune*
NYT	*New York Times*
OF	Office File
PACLU	ACLU archives, Princeton University Library, Princeton, New Jersey

RMN   Richard M. Nixon presidential papers, housed in NA during period of
             book research, since scheduled for transfer to Nixon Presidential Library,
             Yorba Linda, California
SAC   Senate Appropriations Committee
SACB   Subversive Activities Control Board Papers, Record Group 220, NA
SCL   Supreme Court Library, Washington, D.C.
SCSC   Senate Civil Service Committee
SGOC   Senate Committee on Government Operations Subcommittee on
             Reorganization
SISS   Senate Internal Security Subcommittee of SJC
SJC   Senate Judiciary Committee
SJS   Stephen J. Spingarn Papers, HST
TECL   Temporary Commission on Employee Loyalty
TL   Tamiment Library, New York University
UM   Special Collections, University of Michigan at Ann Arbor library
WHCF   White House Central Files
WP   *Washington Post*
WS   *Washington Star*

Preface

1. Alan Barth, *The Loyalty of Free Men* (New York: Pocket Books, 1952), 110; *NYT*, September 26, 2007; David Cole, "The National Security State," *The Nation*, December 17, 2001. See also Cole, "The New McCarthyism: Repeating History in the War on Terrorism," *Harvard Civil Rights—Civil Liberties Law Review* 38 (2003), 1–30.

2. Eleanor Bontecou, *The Federal Loyalty-Security Program* (Ithaca, NY: Cornell University Press, 1953), 157–204; John Earl Haynes, compiler, "American Communism and Anti-Communism: A Historian's Bibliography and Guide to the Literature" (April 2007), http://www.johnearlhaynes.org/page94.html, accessed November 2007; Ellen Schrecker, *Many Are the Crimes: McCarthyism in America* (Boston: Little, Brown, 1998); William Klingaman, *Encyclopedia of the McCarthy Era* (New York: Facts on File, 1996), 442–45; Ellen Schrecker, *The Age of McCarthyism* (Boston: Bedford, 2002, 2d.), 47, 190. Otis H. Stephens, John M. Scheb, and Kara E. Stooksbury, eds., *Encyclopedia of American Civil Rights and Liberties* (Westport, CT: Greenwood, 2006), and Paul Finkelman, ed., *Encyclopedia of American Civil Liberties* (London: Routledge, 2006), lack entries or (apparently) any references to AGLOSO, while there is a short entry in David Schultz and John R. Vile, eds., *The Encyclopedia of Civil Liberties in America* (Armonk, NY: Sharpe, 2005). There are no articles (or index entries) on AGLOSO in Mari Jo Buhle, Paul Buhle, and Dan Georgakas, eds., *Encyclopedia of the American Left* (Urbana: University of Illinois Press, 1992); Richard S. Kirkendall, ed., *The Harry S. Truman Encyclopedia* (Boston: G. K. Hall, 1989), or Michael Newton, *The FBI Encyclopedia* (Jefferson, NC: McFarland, 2003) For the Wikipedia entry, see http://en.wikipedia.org/wiki/Attorney_General's_List_of_Subversive_Organizations (accessed April 2008).

3. NA DOJA: Waterman to Irons, November 30, 1953; Waterman to Alderman, January 14, 1957; FBI FOIA, Stanley to Rosen, March 9, 1956; FBI FOIA, Yeagley to Katzenbach, February 20, 1961; "Hearings on Proposed Legislation to Curb or Control the Communist Party," HUAC, 80th Cong., 2d Sess., February 5, 1948, 30; NA LRB, Minutes of May 4, 1948, meeting, 66–73, Minutes of May 17, 1951, meeting, 101–2; NA DOJC, Bingham quoted in DOJ memo for the attorney general by J. Lee Rankin (undated, but early 1953); Richard Neuberger, "The Tyranny of Guilt by Association," Sidney Hillman Foundation, 11 (reprinted from article in September 1955 *Progressive Magazine*).

4. Barth, *Loyalty of Free Men*, III; Athan Theoharis, *Seeds of Repression: Harry S. Truman and the Origins of McCarthyism* (Chicago: Quadrangle, 1971), 106–7; Athan Theoharis, "The Escalation of the Loyalty Program," in Barton J. Bernstein, ed., *Politics and Policies of the Truman Administration* (Chicago: Quadrangle, 1970), 264, Robert Griffith, *The Politics of Fear: Joseph R. McCarthy and the Senate* (Amherst: University of Massachusetts Press, 1987), xii; DDE, Central Files, Office File, 133-E-10, Box 662, Book 2, for examples of Eisenhower Library documents marked "blacklisted organizations"; Ellen Schrecker, *No Ivory Tower: McCarthyism and the Universities* (New York: Oxford University Press, 1986), 5; Peter Buckingham, *America Sees Red: Anticommunism in America* (Claremont, CA: Regina, 1988), 59; Roger Keeran, "The Italian Section of the International Workers Orders," *Italian-American Review* 7 (1999), 7.

5. Haynes Johnson, *The Age of Anxiety: McCarthyism to Terrorism* (Orlando, FL: Harcourt, 2005), 232; Robert Justin Goldstein, *Political Repression in Modern America* (Urbana: University of Illinois Press, 2001), 377–79; Marie Jahoda and Stuart Cook, "Security Measure and Freedom of Thought," *Yale Law Journal* 61 (1952), 303–18; Ralph Brown, *Loyalty and Security: Employment Tests in the United States* (New Haven, CT: Yale University Press, 1958), 190; Robert Carr, *The House Committee on Un-American Activities* (Ithaca, NY: Cornell University Press, 1952), 456–57; Robert Sklar, "Introduction," in I. F. Stone, *The Truman Era* (New York: Vintage, 1972), ix; Lawrence Wittner, *The American Peace Movement, 1941–1960* (New York: Columbia University Press, 1969), 221; Nell Elfin and Leonard Zweig, "The Battle of Political Symbols," *Public Opinion Quarterly* 54 (1954), 205–10.

6. "Intelligence Activities and the Rights of Americans," Book II, Senate Select Committee to Study Governmental Operations with Respect to Intelligence Activities, 94th Cong., 2d Sess., "Intelligence Activities and the Rights of Americans," 43; Athan Theoharis, ed., *From the Secret Files of J. Edgar Hoover* (Chicago: Ivan Dee, 1991), 129.

Chapter 1. The Origins of AGLOSO, 1903–1947

1. Paul Avrich, *Sacco and Vanzetti: The Anarchist Background* (Princeton, NJ: Princeton University Press, 1991), 130; Jane Clark, *Deportation of Aliens from the United States to Europe* (New York: Arno, 1969), 215.

2. See Sidney Fine, "Anarchism and the Assassination of McKinley," *American Historical Review* 9 (1955), 777–99; William Preston, *Aliens and Dissenters: Federal Suppression of Radicals, 1903–33* (New York: Harper & Row, 1963), 33; Eldridge Dowell, *A History of Criminal Syndicalism Legislation in the United States* (New York: Da Capo, 1969); Zechariah Chafee, *Free Speech in the United States* (New York: Atheneum, 1969). Fear of anarchism dated back at least to the so-called Haymarket bomb incident in 1886 and recurred periodically thereafter. See, for example, James Green, *Death in the Haymarket* (New York: Pantheon, 2006); Robert Justin Goldstein, "The Anarchist Scare of 1908," *American Studies* 12 (1974), 55–78; Mitchell Tilner, "Ideological Exclusion of Aliens: The Evolution of a Policy," *Georgetown Immigration Law Journal* 2 (1987), 15–37.

3. Preston, *Aliens and Dissenters*, 188–90, 200–207; Donald Johnson, *The Challenge to American Freedoms: World War I and the Rise of the American Civil Liberties Union* (Lexington: University of Kentucky Press, 1963), 125; David Cole, *Enemy Aliens: Double Standards and Constitutional Freedoms in the War on Terrorism* (New York: New Press, 2003), 105–15.

4. Preston, *Aliens and Dissenters*, 100, 173; Eleanor Bontecou, *The Federal Loyalty-Security Program* (Ithaca, NY: Cornell University Press, 1953), 59; Cole, *Enemy Aliens*, 110; H. C. Peterson and Gilbert Fite, *Opponents of War, 1917–1918* (Seattle: University of Washington Press, 1968); Robert Justin Goldstein, *Political Repression in Modern America* (Urbana: University of Illinois Press, 2001), 103–136.

5. Robert Murray, *Red Scare: A Study in National Hysteria, 1919–1920* (New York: McGraw-Hill, 1964); Goldstein, *Political Repression in Modern America*, 137–64.

6. Avrich, *Sacco and Vanzetti*, 34, 174; Charles McCormick, *Hopeless Cases: The Hunt for the Red Scare Terrorist Bombers* (Lanham, MD: University Press of America, 2005), 33; Murray, *Red Scare*, 17.

7. Preston, *Aliens and Dissenters*, 83; Cole, *Enemy Aliens*, 119.

8. "Attorney General A. Mitchell Palmer on Charges Made against the Department of Justice," Hearings, HCR, 66th Cong., 3rd Sess. (1920), 166.

9. *Colyer v. Skeffington*, 265 F. 17 (1920), 8–10, 12, 13. For detailed accounts of the Palmer Raids, see Murray, *Red Scare*, 190–222; Kenneth Ackerman, *Young J. Edgar: Hoover, the Red Scare and the Assault on Civil Liberties* (New York: Carroll & Graf, 2007), 93–187; Regin Schmidt, *Red Scare: The FBI and the Origins of Anticommunism in the United States* (Copenhagen: Museum Tusculanum, 2000), 236–99; and Julian Jaffe, *Crusade against Radicalism: New York during the Red Scare, 1914–1924* (Port Washington, NY: Kennikat, 1972), 169–97.

10. "Charges," 168, 541–42.

11. Ibid., 168; Constantine Panunzio, *The Deportation Cases of 1919–1920* (New York: Da Capo, 1970), 61.

12. "Investigation of Administration of Louis F. Post, Assistant Secretary of Labor, in the Matter of Deportation of Aliens," Hearings, HCR, 66th Cong., 2d Sess. (1920), 150–55; Cole, *Enemy Aliens*, 123; Schmidt, *Red Scare*, 303.

13. Goldstein, *Political Repression in Modern America*, 173, 197. On the impact of World War I repression of these organizations, see James Weinstein, *The Decline of Socialism in America, 1912–1925* (New York: Vintage, 1969); Melvin Dubofsky, *We Shall Be All: A History of the Industrial Workers of the World* (Chicago: Quadrangle, 1969); and Theodore Draper, *The Roots of American Communism* (New York: Viking, 1963).

14. Murray, *Red Scare*, 250; Preston, *Aliens and Dissenters*, 228; Clark, *Deportation of Aliens*, 222–23.

15. Goldstein, *Political Repression in Modern America*, 196–97; Theodore Draper, *American Communism and Soviet Russia* (New York: Viking, 1960); Harvey Klehr, *The Heyday of American Communism: The Depression Decade* (New York: Basic Books, 1984); Irving Howe and Lewis Coser, *The American Communist Party: A Critical History* (New York: Praeger, 1962), 144–387; Harvey Klehr and John Haynes, *The American Communist Movement* (New York: Twayne, 1992), 8–95.

16. Ronald Radosh and Allis Radosh, *Red Star over Hollywood: The Film Colony's Long Romance with the Left* (San Francisco: Encounter, 2005), 38–39.

17. William Goldsmith, "The Theory and the Practice of the Communist Front" (Ph.D. diss., Columbia University, 1971).

18. See, generally, Klehr, *Heyday*; Fraser Ottanelli, *The Communist Party of the United States: From the Depression to World War II* (New Brunswick, NJ: Rutgers University Press, 1991); Richard Vallely, *Radicalism in the States: The Minnesota Farmer-Labor Party and the American Political Economy* (Chicago: University of Chicago Press, 1989); and Harvey Levenstein, *Communism, Anticommunism and the CIO* (Westport, CT: Greenwood, 1981).

19. Klehr, *Heyday*, 371–74, 385.

20. Robert Cohen, *When the Old Left Was Young: Student Radicals and America's First Mass Student Movement, 1929–1941* (New York: Oxford University Press, 1993), 188–95, 234–47, 298–307; Klehr, *Heyday*, 319–23; Walter Goodman, *The Committee* (Baltimore: Penguin, 1969), 77–80; Howe and Coser, *American Communist Party*, 359–61; Michael Ybarra, *Washington Gone Crazy: Senator Pat McCarran and the Great American Communist Hunt* (Hanover, NH: Steerforth, 2004), 237–40.

21. Mark Naison, *Communists in Harlem during the Depression* (New York: Grove, 1984), 169–203; Klehr, *Heyday*, 345–47, 402–3; Howe and Coser, *American Communist Party*, 355–58;

John Streater, "The National Negro Congress, 1936–1947" (Ph.D. diss., University of Cincinnati, 1981); Erick Gellman, "'Death Blow to Jim Crow'" The National Negro Congress (Ph.D. diss., Northwestern University, 2006); Mark Solomon, *The Cry Was Unity: Communists and African-Americans, 1917–1936* (Jackson: University Press of Mississippi, 1998), 303.

22. On the WA, see Klehr, *Heyday*, 294–98, 402; Bontecou, *Federal Loyalty-Security Program*, 194–98; James Lorence, *Organizing the Unemployed: Community and Union Activists in the Industrial Heartland* (Albany: State University of New York Press, 1996); Chad Goldberg, "Haunted by the Specter of Communism: Collective Identity and Resource Mobilization in the Demise of the Workers Alliance of America," *Theory and Society* 32 (2003), 725–73 (quotes from 730, 741, 743, 752–53).

23. On the LAW, see Arthur Casciato, "Citizens Writers: A History of the League of American Writers, 1935–1942" (Ph.D. diss., University of Virginia, 1986); Michael Denning, *The Cultural Front* (London: Verso, 1997), 224–25; Klehr, *Heyday*, 353–56; Franklin Folsom, "Notes on Writergate," *Monthly Review*, May 1995, 25–26; Judy Kutulas, "Becoming 'More Liberal': The League of American Writers, the Communist Party and the Literary People's Front," *Journal of American Culture* 13 (1990), 71–80.

24. Bontecou, *Federal Loyalty-Security Program*, 18–84; Klehr, *Heyday*, 107–112, 116–17; Howe and Coser, *American Communist Party*, 348–55, 394–95; Doug Rossinow, "'The Model of a Model Fellow Traveler': Harry F. Ward, the American League for Peace and Democracy and the 'Russian Question' in American Politics, 1933–1956," *Peace and Change*, 29 (2004), 177–220.

25. Goldstein, *Political Repression in Modern America*, 241–44; Goodman, *Committee*, 3–89; August Ogden, *The Dies Committee* (Washington, DC: Catholic University Press, 1944); *LAT*, *WP*, *NYT*, October 26, 1939.

26. Bontecou, *Federal Loyalty-Security Program*, 10–12, 164–65.

27. Goldstein, *Political Repression in Modern America*, 215–16, 247–48, 272–73; Athan Theoharis, *Spying on Americans: Political Surveillance from Hoover to the Huston Plan* (Philadelphia: Temple University Press, 1978), 40–42, 66–75, 97–100; Athan Theoharis, *The FBI and American Democracy: A Brief Critical History* (Lawrence: University Press of Kansas, 2004), 44–64; FBI FOIA, Albany FBI Office to Hoover, January 23, 1941; Washington, DC, FBI Office to Hoover, January 23, 1941; New Orleans FBI Office to Hoover, May 31, 1941.

28. Chafee, *Free Speech in the United States*, 446; Bontecou, *Federal Loyalty-Security Program*, 285–86 (text of June 20, 1940, Civil Service Commission directive).

29. Chafee, *Free Speech in the United States*, 446–90; Goldstein, *Political Repression in Modern America*, 244–46.

30. *WP*, April 4, October 21, 1941; *CR*, April 3, 1941, 3626; "Report of the FBI," 77th Cong., 2d Sess., House of Representatives Document 833, 12, 19; Don Whitehead, *The FBI Story* (New York: Pocket, 1956), 434.

31. NA DOJA, Hoover to Holtzoff, November 5, 1941; Justice to Hoover, May 5, 1942; DDE, Contor to Edwards, Louis Rothschild papers, January 18, 1957.

32. Maurice Isserman, *Which Side Were You On? The American Communist Party during the Second World War* (Middletown, CT: Wesleyan University Press, 1982), 67–73; George Sirgiovanni, *An Undercurrent of Suspicion: Anti-Communism in America during World War II* (New Brunswick, NJ: Transaction, 1990), 33–37; Ottanelli, *Communist Party of the United States*, 191–205; *LAT*, January 12, 1940; February 18, 1941, June 23, 1940; *NYT*, January 23, 1940, November 29, 1941.

33. Radosh and Radosh, *Red Star over Hollywood*, 64; Isserman, *Which Side Were You On?* 38, 71; Ottanelli, *Communist Party of the United States*, 198–204; Klehr and Haynes, *American Communist Movement*, 93–94. On the ACLU, see Samuel Walker, *In Defense of American Liberties: A History of the ACLU* (New York: Oxford University Press, 1990), 127–33.

34. Goldstein, *Political Repression in Modern America*, 288; Klehr and Haynes, *American Communist Movement*, 100–101; Ottanelli, *Communist Party of the United States*, 206.

35. *NYT*, November 30, 1941;Goldstein, *Political Repression in Modern America*, 259, 268–71; Leland Bell, *In Hitler's Shadow: The Anatomy of American Nazism* (Port Washington, NY: Kennikat, 1973), 104.

36. *NYT*, February 9, 1943; Milton Konvitz, *Civil Rights in Immigration* (Ithaca, NY: Cornell University Press, 1953), 114–22. In general on Bridges, see Charles Larrowe, *Harry Bridges* (New York: Lawrence Hill, 1972).

37. *CSM, LAT, NYT*, October 20, 1941; *WP*, May 17, 18, 20, October 20, 21, 1941; Bontecou, *Federal Loyalty-Security Program*, 175, 200; FBI FOIA, Washington Book Shop Association File, Hoover to Biddle (date obscured, but April 1944, with handwritten note by Biddle indicating "authorized," dated April 10, 1944); "Recommendation for Installation of Technical or Microphone Surveillance," October 2, 1946.

38. NA DOJB, Carusi to Hoover, November 8, 1941.

39. NA DOJC, DOJ to all U.S. attorneys, February 2, 1942, March 10, 1942.

40. *NYT*, March 30, 31, April 23, 1942; *WP*, March 30, April 23, 1942; NA DOJC, Spingarn to Secretary of the Treasury, February 2, 1942.

41. DLP, Dickinson to Biddle, April 23, 1942; *WP*, March 28, 1943.

42. DLP, Dickinson to Hoover, May 5, 1942.

43. "To Provide for an Immediate Report to Congress by the FBI with Respect to Investigations Heretofore Made by It of Certain Employees of the Federal Government," House Judiciary Committee (unpublished), 77th Cong., 2d Sess., 46–52.

44. Bontecou, *Federal Loyalty-Security Program*, 165.

45. NA DOJD, "Memorandum for Mr. L.M.C. Smith, chief, Special War Policies Unit" (undated, but c. May, 1942).

46. *CSM*, September 2, 1942; *NYT*, September 3, 1942; "Report of the Federal Bureau of Investigation," 77th Cong., 2 Sess., House of Representatives Document 833, 3–4.

47. "Report of the FBI," 2, 12–14; Kenneth O'Reilly, *Hoover and the Un-Americans: The FBI, HUAC and the Red Menace* (Philadelphia: Temple University Press, 1983), 65–66.

48. FBI FOIA, Hoover to Clark, January 29, 1947.

49. On World War II repression of pro-fascists, see, generally, Richard Steele, *Free Speech in the Good War* (New York: St. Martin's, 1999), and Goldstein, *Political Repression in Modern America*, 262–84.

50. NA DOJC, Michaloski to Alderman, July 17, 1956; Waterman to Alderman, July 24, 1956. Morris Schonbach, *Native American Fascism during the 1930s and 1940s* (New York: Garland, 1985), 83, 204–7; Gaetano Salvemini, *Italian Fascist Activities in the United States* (New York: Center for Migration Studies, 1977), 77–88, 107–23, 237–38; NA DOJA, Waterman to Alderman, October 26, 1955; NA CSC, Box 14, "Training Manual Prepared by the LRB Staff."

51. On the Bund, see Bell, *In Hitler's Shadow*; Sander Diamond, *The Nazi Movement in the United States, 1924–41* (Ithaca, NY: Cornell University Press, 1974); and Susan Canedy, *America's Nazis: A Democratic Dilemma. A History of the German-American Bund* (Menlo Park, CA: Markgraf, 1990). On the Silver Shirts, see Scott Beekman, *William Dudley Pelley* (Syracuse, NY: Syracuse University Press, 2005); NA DOJA, Waterman to Alderman, October 26, 1955; NA CSC, "Training Manual Prepared by the LRB Staff."

52. "Report of the FBI," 4, 23–28.

53. *CSM*, September 2, 4, 1942; *NYT*, September 3, 4, 1942; *WP, LAT*, September 4, 1942.

54. *NYT, LAT, WP*, September 25, 1942; *CR*, September 24, 1942, 7441–49. M. Stanton Evans, *Blacklisted by History: The Untold Story of Sen. Joe McCarthy* (New York: Crown Forum, 2007), prints a photocopy of one of the organizational memos on p. 56.

55. NA DOJB, "FBI Report Prepared Pursuant to Public Law No. 135, 77th Congress," 1373–75.

56. *WP*, November 21, 1942, February 3, 7, 1943; *NYT*, November 21, 1942, February 2, 7, 1943; *LAT*, January 4, February 7, 1943; NA DOJC, Ickes to Roosevelt, June 3, 1943; CSC acting president McMillin to Bailey, September 8, 1943. Executive Order 9300 is published in Bontecou, *Federal Loyalty-Security Program*, 272–73.

57. DLP, Biddle to Kerr, March 8, 1943; "Report of the Federal Bureau of Investigation," 14.

58. *WP*, April 8, May 14, 15, December 14, 1943; Frederick Schuman, "'Bill of Attainder' in the Seventy-Eighth Congress," *American Political Science Review* 37 (1943), 819–29.

59. NA DOJD, Smith to Fahy, March 13, 1943; Whearty to Boyd, April 8, 1943.

60. NA DOJD, Smith to Harrison, April 29, 1943.

61. EBP, Internal Security File, "Interdepartmental Committee on Employee Investigations: Outline of Policy and Procedure;" *WP*, September 12, 1943.

62. NA DOJC, Gaston to Biddle, February 12, 1944.

63. *CSM*, November 30, 1943; *WP*, December 3, 1943; *CR*, December 2, 1943, 10253–57; Bontecou, *Federal Loyalty-Security Program*, 310–12.

64. "Independent Offices Appropriations Bill for 1945," House Committee on Appropriations, 78th Cong., 2d Sess., 1080–87.

65. *WP*, February 24, 1944; NA DOJC, Gaston to Biddle, February 12, 1944.

66. *CSM*, *WP*, April 25, 1944.

67. *NYT*, October 31, 1944; Goldstein, *Political Repression in Modern America*, 289; Richard Fried, "Voting against the Hammer and Sickle: Communism as an Issue in American Politics," in William Chafe, ed., *The Achievement of American Liberalism* (New York: Columbia University Press, 2003), 105–6; Goodman, *Committee*, 161.

68. NA DOJC, Washington to Cook, December 17, 1945; Clark to Smith, December 26, 1945; Jonathan Casper, *The Politics of Civil Liberties* (New York: Harper & Row, 1972), 47.

69. On the *Amerasia* affair, see Harvey Klehr, *The Amerasia Spy Case: Prelude to McCarthyism* (Chapel Hill: University of North Carolina Press, 1996). On the general issue of Soviet espionage, see John Earl Haynes and Harvey Klehr, *Early Cold War Spies: The Espionage Trials That Shaped American Politics* (Cambridge: Cambridge University Press, 2006). On the impact of the rise of the Cold War on the fortunes of the CP, see Goldstein, *Political Repression in Modern America*, 293–97, David Shannon, *The Decline of the American Communist Party* (New York: Harcourt, Brace, 1959), 13–110; Joseph Starobin, *American Communism in Crisis, 1943–1957* (Berkeley: University of California Press, 1972), 51–152.

70. See Athan Theoharis, *Seeds of Repression: Harry S. Truman and the Origins of McCarthyism* (Chicago: Quadrangle, 1971); Theoharis, *FBI and American Democracy*; and many of the essays in *The Specter: Original Essays on the Cold War and the Origins of McCarthyism* (New York: New Viewpoints, 1974).

71. Goodman, *Committee*, 178; *NYT*, July 3, 21, 1946; *WP*, July 21, 1946; "Report on Investigation with Respect to Employee Loyalty and Employment Practices in the Government of the United States," HCSC, 79th Cong., 2d Sess. (1946), 3, 6–7; "Personnel Practices Concerning Loyalty of Government Employees," HCSC, 79th Cong., 2d Sess. (unpublished, 1946), 239, 264, 441, 456, 478–79, 487–490.

72. "Personnel Practices," 266–69; "Federal Employees' Loyalty Act," Hearings before the House Committee on Post Office and Civil Service, 80th Cong., 1st. Sess., June 1947, 54.

73. Fried, "Voting against the Hammer and Sickle," 107; Michael Bowen, "Communism v. Republicanism: B. Carroll Reece and the Congressional Elections of 1946," *Journal of East Tennessee History* 73 (2001), 4; *NYT*, November 26, 1946; HST, OF: "President's TCEL," Flemming to Attorney General, July 22, 1946, Elsey to Clifford, August 1, 1946; Clark Clifford, *Counsel to*

the *President: A Memoir* (New York: Random House, 1991), 176; Ybarra, *Washington Gone Crazy*, 404.

74. *NYT*, December 1, 1946; Francis Thompson, *The Frustration of Politics: Truman, Congress and the Loyalty Issue, 1945–1953* (Rutherford, NJ: Fairleigh Dickinson University Press, 1979), 27; Clifford, *Counsel to the President*, 175, 177–78; Carl Bernstein, *Loyalties: A Son's Memoir* (New York: Simon & Schuster, 1989), 197–200; David McCullough, *Truman* (New York: Simon & Schuster, 1992), 551.

75. HST, OF, "Report of the President's TCEL;" Ybarra, *Washington Gone Crazy*, 403; NA DOJC, Hoover to Clark, January 22, 1947.

76. Alan Harper, *The Politics of Loyalty: The White House and the Communist Issue, 1946–1952* (Westport, CT: Greenwood, 1969), 31–33; DVP, Hoover to Clark, January 29, 1947; Ybarra, *Washington Gone Crazy*, 404.

77. HST, OF, "Report of the President's TCEL."

78. Harper, *The Politics of Loyalty*, 41–42; SJS, "Miscellaneous Documents," Spingarn to TCEL Subcommittee, December 31, 1946.

79. Clifford, *Counsel to the President*, 178; *NYT*, March 18, 1947; *WP*, March 18, 19, 1947.

80. *LAT*, *WP*, March 23, 1947. The text of Truman's March 21, 1947, Executive Order 9835 is published, among many other places, in Bontecou, *Federal Loyalty-Security Program*, 275–81.

81. Peter Steinberg, *The Great "Red Menace": United States Prosecution of American Communists, 1947–52* (Westport, CT: Greenwood, 1984), 27–28; "Intelligence Activities and the Rights of Americans," Book II, Senate Select Committee to Study Governmental Operations with Respect to Intelligence Activities, 94th Cong., 2d Sess., 44.

82. Athan Theoharis, ed., *From the Secret Files of J. Edgar Hoover* (Chicago: Ivan Dee, 1991), 129; "Intelligence Activities and the Rights of Americans," 43.

83. FBI FOIA, Tamm to Hoover, March 29, 1947; Ladd to Hoover, March 29, 1947; Hoover to Clark, April 3, 1947; Tamm to Hoover, April 14, 1947.

84. FBI FOIA, Ladd to Coyne, September 26, 1947; Tamm to Hoover, September 29, 1947.

85. FBI FOIA, Tamm to Hoover, September 30, 1947, Hoover to Quinn, September 30, 1947.

86. *NYHT*, December 5, 1947; "Department of Justice Appropriations Bill for 1949," HAC, 80th Cong., 2d Sess. (1948), 12–13, 67; DVP, Caudle to Clark, May 8, 1947; Steinberg, *Great "Red Menace,"* 29.

87. "Department of Justice Appropriations Bill for 1949," 12–13, 71–72; "Communist Activities among Aliens and National Groups," SJC, 81st Cong., 1st Sess. (1950), 322; Steinberg, *Great "Red Menace,"* 30; NA DOJA, undated (but apparently early 1953), unsigned memorandum.

88. NA DOJA, Murray to Attorney General, October 10, 1952; Murray to Malone, November 14, 1952.

89. "Department of Justice Appropriations Bill for 1949," 13; FBI FOIA, Nichols to Tolson, March 31, 1947; Nichols to Tolson, April 1, 1947; *NYT*, March 9, 1961; Thompson, *Frustration of Politics*, 57.

90. FBI FOIA, Nichols to Tolson, March 31, 1947; Nichols to Tolson, April 1, 1947. *WS*, March 24, 1947; *NYT*, April 13, 1947; *New Republic*, March 31, 1947, 10.

91. *NYT*, May 11, June 1, 1947; NA DOJA, Ford to Forster, January 24, 1950; Tompkins to Overstreet, August 24, 1954.

92. DVP, Caudle to Hoover, May 8, 1947; Edelstein and Duggan to McGregor, July 24, 1947. NA DOJA, Caudle to McGregor, July 21, 1947.

93. Steinberg, *Great "Red Menace,"* 81.

94. ACLU records, microfilm reel 242, 5–6.

95. La Guardia column in ACLU records, microfilm reel 240, undated column from *PM*; *NYT*, March 26, 1947, March 19, 1978; *WP*, March 29, 1947; Arthur Schlesinger, Jr., *The Vital Center*

(Boston: Houghton-Mifflin, 1962 reprint of 1949 edition), 121; Athan Theoharis, "The Rhetoric of Politics: Foreign Policy, Internal Security and Domestic Politics in the Truman Era," in Barton Bernstein, ed., *Politics and Policies of the Truman Administration* (Chicago: Quadrangle, 1970), 221; *CT*, February 26, 1950; Derek Leebaert, *The Fifty-Year Wound: The True Price of America's Cold War Victory* (Boston: Little Brown, 2002), 119; Walker, *In Defense of American Liberties*, 333–34; Harrison Salisbury, "The Strange Correspondence of Morris Ernst and J. Edgar Hoover," *Nation* (December 1, 1984).

Chapter 2. The Spread and Impact of AGLOSO, 1947–1955

1. Ellen Schrecker, *The Age of McCarthyism* (Boston: Bedford, 2002), 47; Francis McNamara, "What the Attorney General's List Means," *Elks Magazine*, November 1956; E. Houston Harsha, "Illinois," in Walter Gellhorn, ed., *The States and Subversion* (Ithaca, NY: Cornell University Press, 1952), 124–25; Henry Commager, "Guilt—and Innocence—by Association," *NYT Sunday Magazine*, November 8, 1953.

2. NA DOJC, Tompkins to Attorney General, March 28, 1947; Waterman to Alderman, November 16, 1955; Waterman to Alderman, April 5, 1956. NA DOJD, Tompkins to Rankin, September 9, 1954. FBI FOIA, Yeagley to Katzenbach, February 20, 1961.

3. "The Bill of Attainder Clauses and Legislative and Administrative Suppression of 'Subversives,'" *Columbia Law Review* 67 (1967), 1505; "Security and Constitutional Rights," Hearings before the Subcommittee on Constitutional Rights of the SJC, 84th Cong., 2d Sess. (1956), 3.

4. NA DOJC, Waterman to Irons, March 25, 1954; Olney to Mertig, April 2, 1954; Wendy Wall, *Inventing the "American Way": The Politics of Consensus from the New Deal to the Civil Rights Movement* (Oxford: Oxford University Press, 2008), 217.

5. On the FBI's role, see Athan Theoharis, *The FBI and American Democracy: A Brief Critical History* (Lawrence: University Press of Kansas, 2004), 65–105; Kenneth O'Reilly, *Hoover and the Un-Americans: The FBI, HUAC and the Red Menace* (Philadelphia: Temple University Press, 1983). "Hearings on Proposed Legislation to Curb or Control the Communist Party of the United States," HUAC, 80th Cong., 2d Sess. (1948), 16–18, 22–23, 31; NA DOJC, Clark to Hoover, May 3, 1948; Haynes Johnson, *The Age of Anxiety: McCarthyism to Terrorism* (Orlando, FL: Harcourt, 2005), 128; Peter Steinberg, *The Great "Red Menace": United States Prosecution of American Communists, 1947–52* (Westport, CT: Greenwood, 1984), 31.

6. NA DOJC, Irons to Foley, October 27, 1953; Brownell to Wilson, undated (but approximately October, 1953).

7. NA DOJC, Waterman to Irons, November 30, 1953 (two separate memos); Doherty to Yeagley, November 12, 1954; Waterman to Alderman, January 14, 1957. FBI FOIA, Yeagley to Katzenbach, February 20, 1961.

8. Hoover quoted in NA DOJC, Irons to Doherty, October 14, 1954. FBI FOIA, Hoover to Ladd and others, October 21, 1953; Stanley to Rosen, March 9, 1956.

9. A comprehensive listing of the dates that AGLOSO organizations were first designated can be found in "Administration of the Federal Employees' Security Program," Hearings of the Senate Post Office and Civil Service Committee, 84th Cong., 1st Sess. (1956), 889–93. DOJ findings as to when AGLOSO organizations ceased functioning can be found in NA SACB, Box 8. Yeagley's testimony is reported in *LAT*, May 18, 1965.

10. FBI FOIA, Denver FBI Office to Hoover, June 2, 1954; *NYHT*, December 19, 1950.

11. Gerald Horne, *Communist Front? The Civil Rights Congress, 1946–1956* (Rutherford, NJ: Fairleigh Dickinson University Press, 1988), 49, 68; *NYT*, February 16, 1955, January 10, 1956, November 28, 1956.

12. On the IWO generally, see Arthur Sabin, *Red Scare in Court: New York versus the International Workers Order* (Philadelphia: University of Pennsylvania Press, 1993) (quotes from

xiv, 12); and Thomas Walker, "Tainted Sources: Government/Media Misrepresentation in the Case of the International Workers Order," in Thomas Walker, ed., *Illusive Identity: The Blurring of Working-Class Consciousness in Modern Workers Culture* (Lanham, MD: Lexington, 2002), 145–86 (quotes from 154, 158); Elizabeth Temkin, "Contraceptive Equity: The Birth Control Center of the International Workers Order," *American Journal of Public Health* 97 (2007), 1737–1745; Roger Keeran, "The Italian Section of the International Workers Order," *Italian-American Review* 7 (1989), 63–82; Michael Deming, *The Cultural Front* (London: Verso, 1997), 94–97.

13. Eleanor Bontecou, *The Federal Loyalty-Security Program* (Ithaca, NY: Cornell University Press, 1953), 187; Walker, "Tainted Sources," 183; Thomas Walker, *Pluralistic Fraternity: The History of the International Worker's Order* (New York: Garland, 1991), 35, 90; David Caute, *The Great Fear: The Anti-Communist Purge under Truman and Eisenhower* (New York: Simon & Schuster, 1978), 173.

14. Sabin, *Red Scare in Court*, 51, 53, 54, 62, 210, 243; Walker, "Tainted Sources," 50; Walker, *Pluralistic Fraternity*, 25; *Application of Bollinger*, 106 NYS 2d 953 (1951); Schrecker, *Age of McCarthyism*, 58.

15. *Digest of the Public Record of Communism in the United States* (New York: Fund for the Republic, 1955), 77–78; FBI FOIA, Katzenbach to Yeagley, February 15, 1961; Schrecker, *Age of McCarthyism*, 58.

16. "Commission on Government Security," Hearings of the SGOC, 84th Cong., 1st Sess. (1955), 205, 592, 959–60, 969–70; Sigmund Diamond, *Compromised Campus: The Collaboration of Universities with the Intelligence Community, 1945–1955* (New York: Oxford University Press, 1992), 134–35; "Subversive Activities Control Act of 1950," SISS Report, 84th Cong., 1st Sess. (1955), 5; *CSM, NYT*, March 18, 1955; *NYT, WP*, April 21, 1955; *CT*, June 6, 1957.

17. *NYT, WP*, January 30, 1948; *NYT*, February 3, 5, 1948; "Hearings on Proposed Legislation," 32, 35; *WP*, November 20, 1952; NA DOJD, Hoover to Clark, February 2, 1948.

18. *LAT*, August 24, 1948; *NYT*, March 19, October 30, 1948, October 3, 1949; *WP*, March 20, 1948; Bontecou, *Federal Loyalty-Security Program*, 177.

19. *WP*, June 12, 1955; "Security and Constitutional Rights," 131–33, 208; *Shachtman v. Dulles*, 225 F.2d 938 (1955).

20. "Hearings on Proposed Legislation," 33; "Communist Activities among Aliens and National Groups," Hearings by SJC Subcommittee on Immigration and Naturalization, 81st Cong., 1st Sess. (1950), 323, 325; *NYT*, September 30, 1953, May 21, 1958; *U.S. ex rel Kaloudis v. Shaughnessy*, 180 F. 2d 489 (1950); *WP*, July 23, 1955.

21. NA DOJC, Tompkins to Swing, November 1, 1956; Alderman to Tompkins, December 17, 1956.

22. NA DOJC, Immigration and Naturalization Service Commissioner to Tompkins, March 18, 1957; Tompkins to Attorney General, March 28, 1947.

23. *Digest of the Public Record of Communism*, 77; *NYT*, December 15, 1948, December 2, 1949, May 6, 1954, February 1, 1956; *WP*, February 9, 11, 1950, May 6, 1954, January 19, 1956; *CSM*, February 11, 1950; "Commission on Government Security," 489.

24. NA DOJC, Hoover to Ford, December 21, 1948. FBI FOIA, Ladd to Hoover, February 15, 1950; Newark FBI Office to Hoover, June 21, 1956. DOJ FOIA, Ford to Richardson, May 15, 1950.

25. Diamond, *Compromised Campus*, 273; Steven Laffoley, "The Techniques of Freedom: The FBI's Responsibilities Program and the Rise of Liberal Anti-Communism in the United States, 1951–52" (M.A. thesis, St. Mary's University, Halifax); Kenneth O'Reilley, ed., *McCarthy-Era Blacklisting of School Teachers, College Professors and Other Public Employees: The FBI Responsibilities Program* (Bethesda, MD: University Publications of America, 1990; microfiche, includes March 31, 1953, memo from Hoover to Chicago FBI office); HST, WHCF, Hoover to Vaughan, July 22, 1949; DDE, White House OF, Hoover to Anderson, May 10, 1955.

26. Fred Jerome, *The Einstein File: J. Edgar Hoover's Secret War against the World's Most Famous Scientist* (New York: St. Martin's, 2002), 121–23, 171–75; David Price, *Threatening Anthropology: McCarthyism and the FBI's Surveillance of Activist Anthropologists* (Durham, NC: Duke University Press, 2004), 25; Mike Keen, *Stalking the Sociological Imagination: J. Edgar Hoover's FBI Surveillance of American Sociology* (Westport, CT: Greenwood, 1999), 126–34; Herbert Mitgang, *Dangerous Dossiers* (New York: Donald Fine, 1988), 67–68; Natalie Robins, *Alien Ink: The FBI's War on Freedom of Expression* (New York: William Morrow, 1992), 251. In some cases, as with Einstein, Steinbeck, Paul Robeson, and W. E. B. Du Bois, FBI files filled with such information are available on the FBI's public website: foia.fbi.gov/famous.htm. Masses of FBI memos sent to congressional committees including such information can be found in the NA, DOJ Record Group 60, file 146-100-5.

27. *WP*, March 25, 1948, February 4, 1952, April 5, 1953, July 15, 1955; *CR*, April 26, 1948, 4849–51; *CSM*, July 30, 1953; *WS*, March 9, 1950, February 4, 1952; *NYT*, March 9, 1950, February 4, 1952; *CT*, September 6, 1950; Johnson, *Age of Anxiety*, 291; Stephen Whitfield, *The Culture of the Cold War* (Baltimore: Johns Hopkins University Press, 1991), 180.

28. *CSM*, June 25, 1949, July 28, 1951; *WP*, June 21, 1949, July 17, 1951, August 3, 1951; *NYT*, March 21, 1950, July 12, 1951, August 16, 1951; *U.S. v. Remington*, 191 F. 2d 246 (1951).

29. Bontecou, *Federal Loyalty-Security Program*, 178. Unless otherwise specified, this and the following paragraphs are based on the compilation of state and local statutes included in *Internal Security and Subversion: Principal State Laws and Cases*, SJC, 89th Cong., 1st Sess. (1965), and "Security and Constitutional Rights," 249–96, both of which list "anti-subversive" laws classified by state and/or locality.

30. *NYT*, January 31, 1954; NA DOJD, Yeagley affidavit, March 18, 1954; TL, Max Shachtman Papers, American Textbook Publishers Institute to Independent Socialist League, April 6, 1954; "Security and Constitutional Rights," 252; *WP*, July 19, 1953; Jay Murphy, "Book Labeling—An Ominous Venture in Censorship," *Alabama Law Review* 6 (1953–1954), 186–234.

31. Jane Sanders, *Cold War on the Campus: Academic Freedom at the University of Washington, 1946–64* (Seattle: University of Washington Press, 1979), 91; *Nostrand v. Balmer*, 335 2d 10 (1959).

32. *Internal Security and Subversion*, 398; *NYT*, August 27, 1954, October 15, 1953; *CSM*, April 19, 1952, January 13, 1956; *WP*, November 26, 1956.

33. "Security and Constitutional Rights," 294; *NYT*, March 3, 1954; Vern Countryman, *Un-American Activities in the State of Washington* (Ithaca, NY: Cornell University Press, 1951), 214, 248, 259; www.ulwaf.com.Daily-Bruin-History/14C_Death.html; Albert Glotzer papers, Hoover Institution, Stanford University, Whittaker to Davison, April 21, 1955; *NYT*, December 6, 1950, March 2, 1954; *CT*, February 16, 1952, March 15, 1953, May 13, 1956; James Selcraig, *The Red Scare in the Midwest, 1945–1955* (Ann Arbor, MI: UMI Research Press, 1982), 101–15; Ellen Schrecker, *No Ivory Tower: McCarthyism and the Universities* (New York: Oxford University Press, 1986), 85–93.

34. *Re Adoption of a Minor*, 228 F. 2d 446 (1955); *NYHT*, September 19, 1950; Selcraig, *Red Scare in the Midwest*, 39, 83; *NYT*, May 23, 1951, May 25, 1955; *WP*, January 25, 28, 1951; "Security and Constitutional Rights," 255, 322–25.

35. *NYT*, January 25, 1949, August 8, November 3, 1950, January 3, 17, 27, July 20, 1951, December 11, 15, 1953, April 23, 1954, March 29, 1957; *New York Journal-American*, January 21, 1949; *New York Sun*, February 23, 1949.

36. *NYT*, April 24, 1949; Edward Barrett, *The Tenney Committee* (Ithaca, NY: Cornell University Press, 1951), 142, 219; Countryman, *Un-American Activities in the State of Washington*, 65, 123–25, 180; Harsha, "Illinois," 128–31; *CSM*, June 9, 1955.

37. *LAT*, October 7, 1951; *WP*, March 14, August 5, 1950, July 17, 1951, July 19, 1953; August 13, 1959; *NYT*, January 18, 1951, May 8, 1954; *CT*, March 18, 1950; NA DOJD, Tompkins to Stephens,

September 28, 1953; NA DOJC, Tompkins to Rogers, April 11, 1955, memo to Olney, April 16, 1957; Lawrence Chamberlain, *Loyalty and Legislative Action: A Survey of Activity by the New York State Legislature, 1919–1949* (Ithaca, NY: Cornell University Press, 1951), 190; Selcraig, *Red Scare in the Midwest*, 41; www.tigernet.princeton.edu/~class51jan50.html (accessed November 27, 2007).

38. *New York World-Telegram*, December 13, 1949; *NYT*, June 8, 1949, April 8, 1950; *LAT*, April 24, 1949; *CSM*, September 9, December 22, 1950, February 26, 1951; *CT*, March 6, 1949, September 2, 1950; "Bill of Attainder Clauses," 1508; Donald King, "The Legal Status of the Attorney General's 'List,'" *California Law Review* 44 (1956), 756–57.

39. *NYT*, April 22, 1951; *WP*, October 27, 1952, October 12, 1955; "Security and Constitutional Rights," 332.

40. *NYT*, December 10, 11, 1952, July 12, 1954, January 27, June 20, 1955; *CSM*, December 10, 1952, August 5, 1954; *WP*, July 25, 1954.

41. *WP*, October 19, 1954; *CT*, September 21, 1948; *NYT*, June 2, 1952, October 24, 1954; Michael Ybarra, *Washington Gone Crazy: Senator Pat McCarran and the Great American Communist Hunt* (Hanover, NH: Steerforth, 2004), 498; Julian Pleasants and Augustus Burns, *Frank Porter Graham and the 1950s Senate Race in North Carolina* (Chapel Hill: University of North Carolina Press, 1990); Greg Mitchell, *Tricky Dick and the Pink Lady: Richard Nixon v. Helen Gahagan Douglas—Sexual Politics and the Red Scare, 1950* (New York: Random House, 1998); Jonathan Bell, *The Liberal State on Trial: The Cold War and American Politics in the Truman Years* (New York: Columbia University Press, 1994), 204, 227, 331.

42. Walker, "Tainted Sources," 156.

43. Hollis Lynch, *Black American Radicals and the Liberation of Africa: The Council on African Affairs, 1937–1955* (Ithaca, NY: Cornell University Africana Studies and Research Center, 1978), 65; Anne Tucker, *This Was the Photo League* (Chicago: Stephen Daller Gallery, 2001), 18.

44. *CT*, December 6, 1947; Countryman, *Un-American Activities in the State of Washington*, 32–33; Joseph Walwik, *The Peekskill, New York, Anti-Communist Riots of 1949* (Lewiston, NY: Mellen, 2002), 15, 55, 60, 61, 64; Roger Williams, "A Rough Sunday at Peekskill," *American Heritage* 27 (1976), 75.

45. *NYT*, April 2, 1948, January 1, 1949, February 27, 1951, July 22, 1957, May 26, June 16, 1986; *CSM*, March 8, 1949.

46. "Hearings on Proposed Legislation," 30; FBI FOIA, Stanley to Rosen, March 9, 1956; NA DOJD, Tompkins to Overstreet, August 24, 1954; *Petition for Naturalization of Yee Wing Toon*, 148 F. Supp. 657 (1957); *LAT*, September 22, 1951; *NYT*, April 30, 1949, September 17, 1950, January 20, 31, February 1, July 4, August 14, 1953; *WP*, February 4, September 18, 1950, August 30, 1952; *CT*, April 30, 1949; Jeff Woods, *Black Struggle, Red Scare: Segregation and Anti-Communism in the South, 1948–1968* (Baton Rouge: Louisiana State University Press, 2004), 136, 205.

47. NA DOJD: McInerney to Garrity, Febuary 8, 1951, 146–6, Mullen to Tompkins, October 14, 1954; *FR*, December 4, 1951, 12214; "Administration of the Federal Employees' Security Program," 887.

48. Michael Martin and Leonard Gelber, eds., *The New Dictionary of American History* (New York: Philosophical Library, 1952), 35; Patricia Sexton, *The War on Labor and the Left* (Boulder, CO: Westview, 1991), 151; William Spinrad, *Civil Liberties* (Chicago: Quadrangle, 1970), 134; Schrecker, *Age of McCarthyism*, 46; NA DOJC, Waterman to Irons, November 30, 1953; FBI FOIA, Stanley to Rosen, March 9, 1956.

49. Gellhorn, *States and Subversion*, 17; *NYT*, December 22, 1948, November 8, 1953; March 11, 13, 1954; *WP*, March 8, 1951; *CSM*, March 15, 1954.

50. DDE, Records of Louis Rothschild, "Correspondence, February 1957," Contor to Edwards, January 18, 1957; *FR*, December 31, 1948, 9366–69, September 21, 1950, 6307, December

4, 1951, 12215–16, May 12, 1953, 2741–42; NA DOJD, National Better Business Bureau to Campbell, October 13, 1948; Campbell to Burke, October 20, 1948.

51. NA DOJC, Tompkins to Humphrey, March 5, 1956; Tompkins to Doub, August 7, 1957.

52. *CSM*, December 5, 1947; FBI FOIA, Ladd to Hoover, December 8, 1947.

53. *CSM*, December 5, 1947; *NYT*, May 29, 1948; *FR*, December 31, 1948, 9368–69.

54. *NYT*, April 28, 1949, April 30, 1953; *WP*, September 16, 1950; *FR*, May 7, 1949, 2371; November 29, 1950, 8145–48, May 12, 1952, 2741–42; NA DOJC, Hoover to Rogers, May 21, 1953; Waterman to file, June 7, 1956.

55. *NYT*, *WP*, July 22, 1953.

56. FBI FOIA, "Japanese Overseas Convention, Tokyo, Japan, 1940," November 18, 1949; NA DOJC, Attorney General to Heads of Departments, January 22, 1954.

57. *NYT*, August 13, 1948, April 28, 1949; ACLU microfilm 252, ARI press release, August 9, 1948; FBI FOIA, Memo re: American Russian Institute, March 19, 1948; *FR*, September 27, 1955, 7201; NA CSC, Box 14, "Training Manual Prepared by the LRB Staff"; NA DOJC, Waterman to Alderman, August 31, 1955; Alderman to Tompkins, September 21, 1955.

58. EBP, McGrath to Bingham, April 25, 1951; NA DOJC, Alderman to Tompkins, September 21, 1955; Waterman to Devine, October 9, 1957. NA DOJD, Tompkins to Zablocki, February 17, 1955; Tompkins to Closton, June 15, 1956.

59. NA LRB, "Reports of Investigators," Box 5; *NYT*, May 6, 1950.

60. Bontecou, *Federal Loyalty-Security Program*, 194–98; NA DOJA, Attorney General to Bingham, August 31, 1951; ACLU microfilm reel 253; NA CSC, "Training Manual Prepared by the LRB Staff."

61. Computerized searches were performed using the Proquest Historical Newspapers database.

62. FBI FOIA, Reports by San Diego office, August 31, 1953, November 18, 1954; Hoover to San Diego Office, October 15, 1953; Hoover to Olney, October 15, 1953.

63. NA DOJD, McInerney to Garrity, February 8, 1951. NA DOJC, Schmidt to Tompkins, January 25, 1955; Pollack to Tompkins, February 4, 1955; Tompkins to Schmidt, April 11, 1955.

64. "Communist Activities among Aliens and National Groups," 321–22.

65. William Cobb, *Radical Education in the Rural South: Commonwealth College, 1922–1940* (Detroit: Wayne State University Press, 2000) (quotes from 9, 37); Bontecou, *Federal Loyalty-Security Program*, 191–94 (quote from 193).

66. Marvin Gettleman, "'No Varsity Teams': New York's Jefferson School of Social Science, 1943–1956," *Science & Society* 66 (2002), 336–359 (quotes from 339, 342, 346); Marvin Gettleman, "The Lost World of United States Labor Education: Curricula at East and West Coast Schools, 1944–1957," in Robert Cherny, ed., *American Labor and the Cold War* (New Brunswick, NJ: Rutgers University Press, 2004), 205–15; *NYT*, July 8, 1946, October 3, 1950, July 2, 1955, November 28, 1956; *LAT*, November 29, 1956.

67. Gettleman, "Lost World"; Marvin Gettleman, "'Education for Victory and Action': The California Labor School in the Popular Front Era," paper presented to the History of Education Society's annual meeting, 1990; UM, California Labor School Collection, "Report on California Labor School," California Department of Education, October 15, 1946, letter appealing for funds, March 4, 1949; *CLS v. SACB*, 322 F. 2d 393 (1963); *EAL*, 122–23; Jess Rigelhaupt, "'Education for Action'": The California Labor School, Radical Unionism, Civil Rights, and Progressive Coalition Building in the San Francisco Bay Area, 1934–1970" (Ph.D. diss., University of Michigan, 2005), quotes from 84, 106, 180.

68. Bontecou, *Federal Loyalty-Security Program*, 180–81; Harsha, "Illinois," 118; *EAL*, 537; *WP*, April 30, 1949; *CIO News*, May 23, 1949; ACLU press release, May 9, 1949, in ACLU microfilm reel 262. For general information about Spanish loyalist relief organizations, see Eric Smith,

"Anti-Fascism, the United Front, and Spanish Republican Aid in the United States, 1936–40" (Ph.D. diss., University of Illinois at Chicago, 2007), and Peter Carroll and James Fernandez, eds., *Facing Fascism: New York and the Spanish Civil War* (New York: Museum of the City of New York, 2007).

69. Lynch, *Black American Radicals* (quotes from 17, 22–24, 52); and Clarence Contee, "Black American 'Reds' and African Liberation: A Case Study of the Council on African Affairs," in *Proceedings of the Conference on Afro-Americans and Africans* (Washington, D.C.: Howard University Graduate School, 1975); FBI FOIA, Belmont to Boardman, June 2, 1955; *NYHT*, February 2, 1948.

70. NA LRB, "Attorney General's List of Subversive Organizations," Box 17; Tony Bubka, "The Harlan County Coal Strike of 1931," *Labor History* 11 (1970), 41–57; Lawrence Grauman, "That Little Ugly Running Sore: Some Observations on the Participation of American Writers in the Investigation of Conditions in the Harlan and Bill County, Kentucky Coal Fields in 1931–1932," *Filson Club Historical Quarterly* 36 (1962), 340–54; *WP*, March 18, 1974.

71. Theodore Draper, *American Communism and Soviet Russia* (New York: Vintage, 1986), 180; Charles Martin, "Communists and Blacks: The ILD and the Angelo Herndon Case," *Journal of Negro History* 58 (1986), 138, 139; Charles Martin, *The Angelo Herndon Case and Southern Justice* (Baton Rouge: Louisiana State University Press, 1976); Dan Carter, *Scottsboro* (Oxford: Oxford University Press, 1971); *EAL*, 366–67; Mark Solomon, *The Cry Was Unity: Communists and African-Americans, 1917–1936* (Jackson: University Press of Mississippi, 1998), 197; Jennifer Uhlmann, "The Communist Civil Rights Movement: Legal Activism in the United States, 1919–1946" (Ph.D. diss., University of California, Los Angeles, 2006), 3.

72. Horne, *Communist Front?* 156; *EAL*, 134–35; Caute, *Great Fear*, 178–80 (quote from 179); *CT*, September 29, 1955; *NYT*, January 9, 1956, *WP*, January 10, 1956; Sarah Brown, "Communism, Anti-Communism and Massive Resistance: The Civil Rights Congress in Southern Perspective," in Glenn Feldman, ed., *Before Brown: Civil Rights and White Backlash in the Modern South* (Tuscaloosa: University of Alabama Press, 2004), 180; Charles Martin, "The Civil Rights Congress and Southern Black Defendants," *Georgia Historical Quarterly* 71 (1987), 50–51. On the Martinsville case, see Eric Rise, *The Martinsville Seven* (Charlottesville: University Press of Virginia, 1995), quotes at 60, 61, 64.

73. John Sherman, *A Communist Front at Mid-Century: The American Committee for Protection of the Foreign Born, 1933–1959* (Westport, CT: Praeger, 2001), (quotes from 1, 63, 70); *EAL*, 19–20 (quote from 19); Caute, *Great Fear*, 243–44; Jeffrey Garcilazo, "McCarthyism, Mexican-Americans, and the Los Angeles Committee for the Protection of the Foreign Born," *Western Historical Quarterly* 132 (2001), 273–95. See also the ACPFB collection held at the University of Michigan at Ann Arbor.

74. On the Peace Information Center, see David Lewis, *W. E. B. Du Bois* (New York: Holt, 2000), 546–53 (quotes from 547, 549); Gerald Horne, *Black and Red: W. E. B. Du Bois and the Afro-American Response to the Cold War, 1944–1963* (Albany: State University of New York Press, 1986), 125–36. On the American Peace Congress, see Horne, *Black and Red*, 191–99; Robbie Lieberman, *The Strangest Dream: Communism, Anticommunism and the U.S. Peace Movement, 1945–1963* (Syracuse, NY: Syracuse University Press, 2000), 101–6 (quotes from 100, 102–3); *NYT*, July 30, 1956.

75. Robert Szymczak, "From Popular Front to Communist Front: The American Slav Congress in War and Cold War, 1941–1951" (Ph.D. diss., University of Lancaster, 2006); Jeffrey Ryan, "The Conspiracy That Never Was: U.S. Government Surveillance of Eastern European American Leftists, 1942–59" (Ph.D. diss., Boston College, 1990); Bontecou, *Federal Loyalty-Security Program*, 181–82; Philip Jenkins, *The Cold War at Home: The Red Scare in Pennsylvania, 1945–1960* (Chapel Hill: University of North Carolina Press, 1999), 156–63; *EAL*, 28–29.

76. *EAL*, 737–38; C. Alvin Hughes, "We Demand Our Rights: The Southern Negro Youth Congress," *Phylon* 48 (1987), 50; Johnetta Richards, "The Southern Negro Youth Congress: A History" (Ph.D. diss., University of Cincinnati, 1987).

77. Mindy Thompson, *The National Negro Labor Council* (New York: American Institute for Marxist Studies, 1978); *EAL*, 509–10; *WP*, June 25, 1978; NNLC news release, June 28, 1954, in PACLU.

78. *NYT*, June 1, August 9, September 11, 1951, April 7, 1952, April 23, December 1, 1953, February 17, 1954, February 28, 1957; *LAT*, January 5, 1950, June 9, 1951; *WP*, August 3, 1954, February 16, 1955.

79. Lili Bezner, *Photography and Politics in America: From the New Deal into the Cold War* (Baltimore: Johns Hopkins University Press, 1999), 16–72; Tucker, *This Was the Photo League* (quotes from forward, 18); Fiona Dejardin, "The Photo League: Aesthetics, Politics and the Cold War" (Ph.D. diss., University of Delaware, 1993, quotes from 372, 437); Fiona Dejardin, "The Photo League," *History of Photography* 18 (1994), 159; Dean Brierly, "The New York Photo League," *Camera & Darkroom* 14 (1992), 30.

80. *EAL*, 512; collection on "Camp Midvale/Friends of Nature" at TL, New York University.

81. Kate Weigand, *Red Feminism: American Communism and the Making of Women's Liberation* (Baltimore: Johns Hopkins University Press, 2001), 46–64 (quotes from 49, 63–64); Amy Swerdlow, "The Congress of American Women," in Linda Kerber, ed., *U.S. History as Women's History* (Chapel Hill: University of North Carolina Press, 1995), 296–321 (quotes from 299, 304–6).

82. Constance Myers, *The Prophet's Army: Trotskyists in America, 1928–1941* (Westport, CT: Greenwood, 1977) (quote at 185); A. Belden Fields, *Trotskyism and Maoism: Theory and Practice in the United States* (Brooklyn, NY: Autonomedia, 1988).

83. Fields, *Trotskyism and Maoism*, 139, 172.

84. *EAL*, 820; Albert Acena, "The Washington Commonwealth Federation" (Ph.D. diss., University of Washington, 1975); Margaret Miller, "Negotiating Cold War Politics: The Washington Pension Union and the Labor Left in the 1940s and 1950s," in Cherny, *American Labor*, 190–204; Countryman, *Un-American Activities in the State of Washington*, 41–65, 87–115.

85. *CSM*, November 15, December 5, 1947; *WP*, December 28, 29, 1947, January 5, 1948.

86. NA LRB, Minutes of November 14–15, 1947, meeting, 18, 21, 23–26, 83. For a listing and short biographies of LRB members, see *LAT*, November 9, 1947.

87. NA LRB, Minutes of November 14–15, 1947, meeting, 80–85.

88. NA LRB, Minutes of December 3–4, 1947, meeting, 3, 6–11, 13–14, 18–19, 21; NA DOJC, Richardson to Clark, December 3, 1947; Clark to Richardson, December 14, 1947.

89. NA LRB, Minutes of December 16–17, 1947, meeting, 131–33, 136.

90. FBI FOIA, Tamm to Ladd, December 17, 1947; NA DOJA, Richardson to Clark, December 18, 1947; Richardson to Clark, December 30, 1947; Clark to Richardson, January 7, 1948.

91. NA LRB, LRB Meeting, March 2, 1948, 2–3, 6–7, 22–23, 26, 33, 35, 59, 67, 71.

92. Ibid., 46, 61, 146–47, 149–52, 155–57, 165, 171.

93. Ibid., 3, 19–20, 26, 34, 179–80.

94. Ibid., 11, 19, 48, 56, 58.

95. EBP, Richardson to Executive Departments, March 9, 1948 (two separate memos); NA LRB, "Sample Handbooks furnished to new members of LRB," March 25, 1948, 1, 3, 8.

96. NA DOJC, Clark to Richardson, March 15, 1948; "Communist Activities among Aliens and National Groups," 321–22; NA LRB, "Sample Handbooks"; NA CSC, "Training Manual Prepared by the LRB Staff," Spring 1948, Box 14.

97. FBI FOIA, St. Louis FBI Office to Hoover, September 10, 1953; Belmont to Boardman, June 2, 1955; Chicago FBI Office to Hoover, December 18, 1958.

98. FBI FOIA, Ladd to Hoover, March 29, 1947.

99. FBI FOIA, Campbell to Hoover, September 10, 1948; Hoover to Campbell, September 29, 1948.

100. NA CSC, "Training Manual Prepared by the LRB Staff"; NA DOJC, "Idaho Pension Union" (undated).

101. NA DOJC, DOJ press release, April 22, 1953.

102. NA LRB, Memoranda, Box 15, "Reports of Investigations," Box 5.

103. NA DOJC, Quinn to Harris, April 21, 1949.

104. NA LRB, Minutes of May 4, 1948, meeting, 66–73.

105. Ibid., 80–82, 91–92, 96, 103–6; *WP*, May 5, 28, 1948; *NYT*, May 28, 1948; NA DOJC, Clark to Richardson, May 27, 1948.

106. *NYT*, *WP*, May 29, September 26, 1948; *FR*, July 9, 1948, 9368–69, December 31, 1948, 32068; NA LRB, Richardson to Clark, May 28, 1948; Clark to Richardson, September 17, 1948.

107. NA LRB, Clark to Richardson, September 17, 1948.

108. *FR*, December 31, 1948, 9366; NA LRB, Minutes of March 15–16, 1949, meeting, 182–83, Bingham address to American Bar Association, September 18, 1951.

109. NA DOJC, Hoover to Clark, February 4, 1948; Ford to Hoover, February 11, 1948, 534/1. FBI FOIA, Wall to Ladd, March 16, 1948; San Francisco FBI Office to Hoover, March 31, 1948; New York FBI Office to Hoover, April 6, 1948; St. Louis FBI Office to Hoover, April 7, 1948.

110. NA DOJA, Hoover to Ford, June 11, 1948; Ford to Hoover, July 16, 1948; Ford to Hoover, September 29, 1948.

111. NA LRB, Richardson to Executive Departments, June 23, 1948; Minutes of September 30, 1948, meeting, 43–45. ACLU microfilm reel 253; EBP, Richardson to Executive Departments, November 2, 1948.

112. NA DOJA, Hoover to Clark, November 30, 1948; Ford to Hoover, December 14, 1948; Hoover to Ford, December 21, 1948.

113. NA DOJA, Ford to Hoover, January 25, 1949; Hoover to Ford, February 3, 1949; Ford to Hoover, February 14, 1949.

114. NA LRB, Executive Committee, December 17, 1948; Memo from LRB to Executive Agencies, December 17, 1948; *FR*, December 31, 1948, 9370.

115. NA LRB, Executive Committee, January 27, 1949, October 6, 1952; LRB, "Report on the Federal Employees Loyalty Program," May 1950.

116. NA DOJC, Hoover to Clark, April 14, 1948; NA DOJA, Clark to Hoover, May 3, 1949; Clark to Hoover, May 19, 1949; Hoover to Clark, May 27, 1949.

117. NA LRB, Minutes of June 15, 1949 meeting, 7–9, 63.

118. Ibid., 15–16, 56, 89–90.

119. Francis Thompson, *The Frustration of Politics: Truman, Congress and the Loyalty Issue, 1945–1953* (Rutherford, NJ: Fairleigh Dickinson University Press, 1979), 57; NA LRB, Minutes of May 4, 1948, meeting, 66; NA DOJC, Bingham quoted in DOJ memo "for the Attorney General" by J. Lee Rankin (undated, but early 1953); Ralph Brown, *Loyalty and Security: Employment Tests in the United States* (New Haven, CT: Yale University Press, 1958), 494–96.

120. Bontecou, *Federal Loyalty-Security Program*, 174; "Report of the Commission on Government Security," 85th Cong., 1st Sess., Doc. 64 (1957), 653; *WP*, May 7, 1957.

121. NA DOJC, Hoover to Clark, April 14, 1948; Bingham quoted in DOJ memo "for the Attorney General" by J. Lee Rankin (undated, but early 1953); "Security and Constitutional Rights," 226–27. FBI FOIA, Ladd to Tamm, January 17, 1948; Executive Conference to Hoover, January 23, 1948; New Orleans FBI Office to Hoover, March 1, 1948. In general, on FBI break-ins and other legally dubious activities, see Athan Theoharis, *Spying on Americans: Political Surveillance from Hoover to the Huston Plan* (Philadelphia: Temple University Press, 1978).

122. NA CSC, "Training Manual Prepared by the LRB Staff"; ACLU microfilm reel 262, Clark to Americans for Democratic Action, May 10, 1949.

123. Brown, *Loyalty and Security*, 494–96; *CT*, June 3, 1948; *WP*, *WS*, November 28, 1949; Bontecou, *Federal Loyalty-Security Program*, 174–75.

124. Adam Yarmolinsky, compiler, *Case Studies in Personnel Security* (Washington, DC: Bureau of National Affairs, 1955), 10, 20, 109–10, 128, 133; *WP*, November 11, 1953.

125. Yarmolinsky, 1–3, 33, 45, 49, 104; *NYHT*, May 19, 1948, *WP*, September 24, 1948.

126. Stanley Kutler, *The American Inquisition: Justice and Injustice in the Cold War* (New York: Hill & Wang, 1982), 33–58; Susan Brinson, *The Red Scare, Politics and the Federal Communications Commission, 1941–1960* (Westport, CT: Praeger, 2004), 106–7.

127. *NYT*, March 12, April 6, 1950; *WP*, May 19, 1951

128. Brown, *Loyalty and Security*, 31, 385.

129. William Tanner, "The Passage of the Internal Security Act of 1950" (Ph.D. diss., University of Kansas, 1971).

130. *CR*, May 14, 1948, 5861; *Time*, June 18, 1951; Ellen Schrecker, introduction to Paul Kesaris, ed., *Records of the Subversive Activities Control Board* (Frederick, MD: University Publications of America, 1988), x–xv (microfilm).

Chapter 3. Challenges to AGLOSO, 1948–1955

1. For the JAFRC, I have relied upon newspaper articles and court rulings and the general information about Spanish loyalist relief organizations contained in Eric Smith, "Anti-Fascism, the United Front, and Spanish Republican Aid in the United States, 1936–40" (Ph.D. diss., University of Illinois at Chicago, 2007), and Peter Carroll and James Fernandez, eds., *Facing Fascism: New York and the Spanish Civil War* (New York: Museum of the City of New York, 2007). For the NCASF, I have used, in addition to press accounts and court rulings, Louis Nemzer, "The Soviet Friendship Societies," *Public Opinion Quarterly* 13 (Summer 1949), 265–84; Eleanor Bontecou, *The Federal Loyalty-Security Program* (Ithaca, NY: Cornell University Press, 1953), 189–91; *EAL*, 30–32; and, especially, the organization's archival materials in the TL at New York University. The IWO is thoroughly covered in Thomas Walker, *Pluralistic Fraternity: The History of the International Worker's Order* (New York: Garland, 1991), and Arthur Sabin, *Red Scare in Court: New York versus the International Workers Order* (Philadelphia: University of Pennsylvania Press, 1993).

2. The district court briefs are included in the organizations' petitions for *certiorari* before the Supreme Court: *NCASF v. McGrath*, petition filed January 23, 1950; *IWO v. McGrath*, filed May 11, 1950; *JAFRC v. McGrath*, filed January 25, 1950. Unless otherwise indicated, all legal materials pertaining to this case were examined in the U.S. Supreme Court library.

3. The district court rulings are included in the briefs referred to in the preceding footnote.

4. *JAFRC v. Clark*, 177 F. 2d 79 (1949), *IWO v. McGrath*, 182 F. 2d 368 (1950). Judge Edgerton dissented in the latter case. The NCASF case was decided without opinion on October 25, 1949, citing the *JAFRC* ruling (U.S. Court of Appeals for the District of Columbia, No. 10,165). The briefs are included in the petitions to the Supreme Court for certiorari, referenced in footnote 2, above.

5. See note 2 for this and the following two paragraphs.

6. Brief for Respondents in Opposition, *JAFRC v. McGrath*, March 1950.

7. Brief for Petitioner, *NCASF v. McGrath*, filed September 20, 1950; Brief for Petitioner, *IWO v. McGrath*, October 13, 1950; Brief for Petitioner, *JAFRC v. McGrath*, filed September 29, 1950; Brief for Respondents, *JAFRC v. McGrath*, October 1950.

8. *CT*, October 24, 1955.

9. The following paragraphs are based on the papers of Justices Tom Clark (Tarlton Law Library, University of Texas at Austin), Stanley Reed (University of Kentucky Library), Harold

Vinson (University of Kentucky), and, at the Library of Congress, the papers of Robert Jackson, Hugo Black, Felix Frankfurter, Harold Burton, and William Douglas.

10. The following paragraphs are all drawn from the Supreme Court ruling in *Joint Anti-Fascist Refugee Committee v. McGrath*, 71 S. Ct. 624 (April 30, 1951).

11. TL, NCASF collection, Morford to National Council, May 2, 1951. See also the IWO ad in the May 24, 1950, *NYT*.

12. *NYT*, May 30, June 8, November 7, 1950, May 2, 1951, February 13, 1973; *WP*, May 2, 1951, February 15, 1973; Sabin, 284–351.

13. NA DOJD, Baldridge to Palmer; Williams to Palmer, May 9, 1951.

14. NA DOJD, Palmer memo (undated, approximately May 1951).

15. NA DOJC, Rankin to Attorney General Herbert Brownell (undated, but written in early 1953 from internal evidence).

16. NA DOJB, Perlman to Whearty, June 13, 1951; Murray to Foley, August 21, 1952; Foley to Assistant Attorney General James McInerney, October 10, 1952.

17. NA LRB, Minutes of 15th meeting, May 17, 1951, 101–2; October 19, 1951; Staff Memorandum No. 17; Walter Dodd, Chairman, Regional Loyalty Board to Chairman Hiram Bingham, February 28, 1952; Executive Committee Minutes, October 27, 1952.

18. NA LRB, Minutes of December 13, 1951, meeting, 5, 75, 78–79; NA DOJB, Bingham to Attorney General Howard McGrath, March 12, 1952; Foley to McInerney, March 25, 1952.

19. PACLU, Levy to files, June 5, 1951; *NYT*, June 9, 1951.

20. DOJ FOIA, McInerney to Bingham. NA DOJB, Bingham to Brownell, March 12, 1952; Foley to McInerney, March 25, 1952.

21. FBI FOIA, Hoover to McGranery, March 10, 1952 (crossed out); Belmont to Ladd, March 18, 1952; Tolson to Hoover, March 18, 1952; Hennrich to Belmont, February 25, 1953.

22. NA DOJB, McInerney to Bingham, April 8, 1952; May 8, 1952. NA DOJA, Hoover to McGrath, September 19, 1952. NA LRB, Bingham to McGrath, September 18, 1952; Bingham to Hoover September 23, 1952.

23. "Nomination of James P. McGranery," Hearings before the SJC, 82d Cong., 2d Sess., May 5–8, 1952, 60–62, 102–3.

24. NA DOJB, McInerney to McGranery, July 11, 1952.

25. NA DOJB, Foley to Murray, August 21, 1952; NA DOJA, Murray to files, September 4, 1952.

26. NA DOJA, Murray to McGranery, October 10, 1952.

27. NA DOJA, Lyons to Murray, December 24, 1952.

28. NA DOJA, Olney to Rogers, February 13, 1953; FBI FOIA, Hennrich to Belmont, February 25, 1953.

29. NA DOJC, Rankin to Brownell (undated, but written in early 1953 from internal evidence).

30. SCL, *JAFRC v. McGranery*, 345 U.S. 911, appeals court briefs; *WP*, March 17, 1952.

31. *JAFRC v. McGrath*, 104 F. Supp. 567 (April 23, 1952); *WP*, April 24, 1952.

32. FBI FOIA, Baumgardner to Belmont, April 30, 1952; NA DOJB, Baldridge to McInerney, May 7, 1952. TL NCASF collection, Rein to Morford, May 6, 1952; Morford to Dr. John Kingsbury and others, May 19, 1952.

33. SCL, *JAFRC v. McGranery*, 345 U.S. 911, Petition for Writ of Certiorari.

34. SCL, *JAFRC v. McGranery*, 345 U.S. 911, Brief for Respondents in Opposition.

35. *JAFRC v. McGranery*, 345 U.S. 911 (1953); TL NCASF collection, Morford to Mrs. Marion Ulmer and others, June 23, 1952.

36. NA DOJD, "Agenda Relating to the Listing of Organizations," March 25, 1953; FBI FOIA, Baumgardner to Belmont, April 25, 1953.

37. *NYT*, April 23, 30, 1953, *WP*, April 23, 30, May 4, 1953; *CT*, *LAT*, April 30, 1952; NA DOJC, Attorney General to Heads of Departments, April 29, 1953; Attorney General to Heads of Departments, April 27, 1953 (marked "not used").

38. *FR*, May 12, 1953.

39. FBI FOIA, Baumgardner to Belmont (with Hoover handwriting), May 14, 1958; Hoover to Olney, May 22, 1953. NA DOJC, Olney to Hoover, July 1, 1953.

40. NA DOJC, Foley to Olney, September 11, 1953.

41. FBI FOIA, Ladd to Hoover, September 30, 1953.

42. *CT*, *NYT*, *LAT*, February 5, 1954; NA CGS, Olney to Wright, June 28, 1956; FBI FOIA, Stanley to Rosen, March 9, 1956.

43. NA DOJC, Olney to Mertig, April 2, 1954; Olney to Leonard, May 21, 1954; Michaloski to Alderman, July 24, 1956; Tompkins to Chuman, September 21, 1956.

44. NA DOJC, Brownell to Hoover, October 21, 1953; Brownell to Wilson, October 27, 1953. FBI FOIA, Hoover to Ladd and others, October 21, 1953.

45. NA DOJC, Nelson to Olney, November 20, 1953.

46. NA DOJC, Waterman to Irons, November 30, 1953 (two separate memos).

47. NA DOJC, Brownell to Young, December 30, 1953; Rankin to Olney, December 10, 1953.

48. NA DOJC, Olney to Higley, Olney to Young, January 6, 1954 (two separate memos); Bienvenu to Rogers, March 19, 1954; Rogers to Olney, May 17, 1954. NA DOJD, Rogers to Adams, July 23, 1954; CGS, "Government Personnel Loyalty Programs," March 22, 1955.

49. NA DOJC, Irons to Doherty, October 14, 1954.

50. NA DOJC, Doherty to Yeagley, November 12, 1954; Waterman to Irons, November 15, 1954; Tompkins to Adams, November 19, 1954; Tompkins to Rogers, December 15, 1954.

51. *WP*, *CSM*, *NYT*, December 31, 1954; *WP*, *NYT*, January 2, 1955; NA DOJD, DOJ Press Release, December 30, 1954; *NYT*, April 12, September 29, 1955; *LAT*, April 12, 1955; *WP*, January 2, April 12, 1955; NA DOJC, Tompkins to Hoover, January 19, 1955; DOJA, Young to Brownell, March 21, 1955.

52. *CSM*, December 31, 1954, May 15, 1955; *WP*, January 1, 1955; TL NCASF Collection, Wolf to Brownell, May 8, 1953.

53. PACLU, Levy to Board of Directors, May 13, 1953; Board of Directors' Minutes, May 18, 1953.

54. *Pacific Citizen*, May 8, 1953; NA DOJD, Masaoka to Brownell, May 18, 1953; Chuman to Brownell, May 25, 1953; Olney to Chuman, June 4, 1953.

55. PACLU, Baldwin to Monty, March 10, 1954; ACLU National Security Committee Minutes, May 10, 1954; Baldwin to Levy, May 10, 1954; Levy to Baldwin, June 4, 1954.

56. DDE, Ann Whitman Papers, Eisenhower to Brownell, November 4, 1953; *NYT*, *WP*, June 16, 1953, *CSM*, June 17, 1953.

57. NA DOJC, Rankin to Rogers, February 15, 1954; Rogers to Rankin, March 3, 1954.

58. DDE, Ann Whitman papers, Brownell to Eisenhower, March 22, 1954.

59. *NYT*, *WP*, June 3, December 8, 1954, *CSM*, June 2, 1954.

60. NA DOJC, Tompkins to Hoover, January 19, 1955; McNamara to Waterman, April 15, 1955; Tompkins to Alderman and others, February 1955 (date unclear).

61. NA DOJC, Waterman to Alderman, June 17, 1955; Alderman to Koffsky, September 1, 1955; Williamson to Alderman, January 27, 1956; Waterman to Alderman, March 6, 1956.

62. NA DOJC, "Statement of Assistant Attorney General William F. Tompkins before the Subcommittee on Reorganization of the Senate Committee on Government Operations, March 8, 1955"; Waterman to Alderman, March 6, 1956. DOJA, Brownell to Olney, January 10, 1956; FBI FOIA, Rosen to Stanley, March 9, 1956; DDE, Ann Whitman papers, Brownell to Eisenhower, October 6, 1956.

63. NA DOJC, Irons to Waterman and others, April 28, 1955; Waterman to Irons, April 14, 1955; Alderman to di Girolamo, August 31, 1955. NA CGS, Ladd to Tracy, June 21, 1956.

64. NA DOJC, Waterman to Irons, May 3, 1955; Waterman to Abell, June 2, 1955; Waterman to Alderman, August 3, 1955; Waterman to Designations Unit attorneys, November 10, 1955.

65. NA DOJC, unsigned, undated (but apparently second half of 1955) memo in DOJ files.

66. *WP*, May 4, 1953, April 30, August 6, 1954; TL NCASF papers, Morford to Mrs. Marian Ulmer and others, July 9, 1953; "Opposition to Motion to Dismiss as Moot," *JAFRC v. Brownell*, July 2, 1953, U.S. Court of Appeals for the District of Columbia Circuit; *JAFRC v. Brownell*, 215 F. 2d 870 (1954).

67. TL NCASF papers, Morford to Mrs. Ulmer and others, August 11, 1954; "Petition for Rehearing," *JAFRC v. Brownell*, U.S. Court of Appeals for the District of Columbia, August 16, 1954.

68. *WP*, September 25, 1955; *NYT*, February 16, 1955, June 1, 1955; *WS*, February 26, September 25, 1955; *NCASF v. Brownell*, 148 F. Supp. 94 (1955).

69. *WP*, *NYT*, February 9, 1956; *NCASF v. Brownell*, 243 F. 2d 222 (1957); TL NCASF papers, Morford to Dr. Corliss Lamont and others, December 3, 1956.

70. TL NCASF papers, Morford to Dr. Corliss Lamont and others, March 18, 1957, July 22, 1957; *NCASF v. SACB*, 322 F. 2d 375 (1963).

Chapter 4. AGLOSO under Attack and in Decline, 1955–1969

1. The material on Sen. Cain in this chapter is a condensed version of the author's article, "'Raising Cain': Senator Harry Cain and His Attack on the Attorney General's List of Subversive Organizations," *Pacific Northwest Quarterly* 98 (2007), 64–77. As this article is fully footnoted, readers are referred to it for documentation concerning Cain.

2. CGS, Hearings before SGOC on S. J. Res. 21, 84th Cong., 1st Sess., March, 1955 (quotations from 479–81, 607, 640); *CSM*, October 7, 1955.

3. "Administration of the Federal Employee Security Program," Hearings before SCSC Subcommittee, 84th Cong., 1st Sess., May–September 1955 (quotations from 523, 938).

4. "Security and Constitutional Rights," Hearings before SJC Subcommittee on Constitutional Rights, November 1955 (quotations from 218–19, 235–38, 299, 301, 314–15, 328, 330, 332, 340, 348); *WP*, *NYT*, November 13, 18, 1955; *NYT*, November 29, 1955; *CSM*, December 10, 1955.

5. "Subversive Activities Control Act of 1950," Report of the SISS to the SJC, 84th Cong., 1st Sess., 1955 (quotations from 4–9); *WP*, *NYT*, *CSM*, June 29, 1955.

6. NA DOJA, Irons to Pollack, May 3, 1955; Irons to Yeagley, May 9, 1955; undated (but apparently second half of 1955), unsigned memo in DOJ files.

7. NA DOJC, Malone to Foley, August 22, 1952; NA DOJD, Foley to McInerney, October 21, 1952. For the congressional history of the Gwinn Amendment, see *CR*, February 27, 1952, A1232–33, March 20, 1952, 2939–40, April 23, 1952, A2498, May 25, 1953, A2886; "Independent Offices Appropriations, 1953," Hearings before the Subcommittee of the SAC, U.S. Senate, 82d Congress, 2d Session, 1024–25, 1041–43, 1056, 1088–89, 1097, 1397–1401. For law review articles on the amendment, see Henry Williams, "Tenant's Loyalty Oaths," *Notre Dame Lawyer* 30 (1956), 193–94; "Constitutionality of Denying Federal Housing to Members of Subversive Organizations," *Columbia Law Review* 53 (1953), 1166–70; "Evictions under Gwinn Amendment for Refusal to Sign Loyalty Oaths Denied," *Columbia Law Review* 55 (1955), 1222–24; "Constitutional Law—Tenancy in Federal Housing Projects—Requirement of Oath of Non-Membership in Proscribed Organizations," *Howard Law Journal* 2 (1956), 136–40; "Constitutional Law—Action by the United States in Undertaking to Evict Tenants from a Federal House Project," *Georgetown Law Journal* 44 (1956), 330–33; "Denial of Federally Aided Housing to Members of Organizations on the Attorney General's List," *Harvard Law Review* 69 (1956), 551–59; "The Gwinn

Amendment: Practical and Constitutional Problems in Its Enforcement," *University of Pennsylvania Law Review* 104 (1956), 694–702.

8. *WP*, August 7, 1955; *NYT*, August 8, 1955.

9. Summaries of many of the legal challenges to the Gwinn Amendment are included in various issues of the *Journal of Housing*, including February 1953, 70; February 1955, 53ff.; May 1955, 166; August–September, 1955, 280–81; December 1955, 428; January 1956, 21; and August–September, 1956, 279.

10. *CT*, *NYT*, November 9, 1955; *WP*, November 9, 1955, August 3, 11, 1956; NA DOJA, Doub to Brownell, July 3, 1956.

11. Kutcher told his story in his 1953 book, *The Case of the Legless Veteran* (reprinted in 1973 by Pathfinder Press of New York). His story was also the subject of a 1981 documentary with the same title, directed by Howard Patrick (see *NYT*, July 11, 1981).

12. *NYT*, August 26, 1948, May 27, 1951.

13. *NYT*, June 21, 1956; *WP*, June 21, 1956, June 5, 1958; *Newsday*, February 12, 1989.

14. For this and the next few paragraphs see, generally, MSP; Peter Drucker, *Max Shachtman and His Left* (Atlantic Highlands, NJ: Humanities Press, 1994); Olive Golden, "Administration of the Attorney General's List of Subversive Organizations: The Case of the Workers Party—Independent Socialist League" (MA thesis, University of Chicago, 1962); *EAL*, 694–95, 852–53.

15. *NYT*, November 19, 1951; Golden, "Administration of the Attorney General's List," 18.

16. *NYT*, July 17, 1954; *WP*, July 20, 1954.

17. The next paragraphs draw on the extensive coverage of the ISD hearing in Golden, "Administration of the Attorney General's List," and in *Labor Action*. The hearing received sporadic mainstream press attention, for example *NYT*, July 1, 26, 27, 1955; *WP*, July 20, 26, 27, 1955.

18. FBI FOIA, Baumgardner to Belmont, July 11, 1958 (with Hoover's notation), Memo to Tolson and others July 16, 1958; DOJ FOIA, Yeagley to Rauh, July 16, 1958.

19. *WP*, July 17, 1958; *NYT*, March 17, 1972; *EAL*, 853.

20. *WP*, November 11, 1955.

21. *WP*, November 29, 1958, April 23, May 19, December 4, 1959; *NYT*, January 28, May 10, 1956, March 4, 1958; *CSM*, November 19, 1955. For a general study of military discharges and AGLOSO, see Rowland Watts, ed., *Undesirable Discharge from the Armed Forces of the United States of America* (New York: Workers Defense League, 1956).

22. "Security and Constitutional Rights," SJC Subcommittee on Constitutional Rights, 84th Cong., 2d Sess., 1956, 851–935.

23. NA CGS, "Subversive Organizations," "American Bar Association Report of the Special Committee on Communist Tactics, Strategy and Objectives," February 1956, 6–7; *NYT*, *WS*, *WP*, May 9, 1956.

24. *Report of the Special Committee of the Federal Loyalty-Security Program of the Association of the Bar of the City of New York* (New York: Dodd, Mead, 1956), 154–57. For examples of news coverage, see *CSM*, *NYT*, July 9, 1956.

25. "Administration of the Federal Employees' Security Program," Report of the SCSC, 84th Cong., 2d Sess., July 21, 1956, 221–29; Report of the CGS (Washington, DC: Government Printing Office, 1957, reprinted by Da Capo Press of New York, 1971), 96–101, 652–54. For examples of news coverage, see *LAT*, *WP*, *NYT*, July 22, 1956, July 23, 1957.

26. NA DOJA, Tompkins to Brownell, March 2, 1956; NA DOJC, Waterman to Alderman, March 5, 1956. FBI FOIA, Stanley to Rosen, March 9, 1956; Cleveland to Gale, March 30, 1965.

27. FBI FOIA, Stanley to Rosen, March 9, 1956; Belmont to Boardman, March 21, 1956; Cleveland to Gale, March 30, 1965.

28. NA DOJA, Waterman to Alderman, April 5, 23, 1956; Doherty to Tompkins, November 6, 1956. NA DOJD, Section 4, Devine to Alderman, November 15, 1956.

29. NA DOJD, Alderman to Tompkins, November 16, 1956; NA DOJA, Alderman to Tompkins, November 16, 1955 (two separate memos).

30. NA DOJA, Conner to Alderman and Waterman, March 13, 1956; Alderman to Waterman, April 13, 1956; Waterman to Conner, April 17, 30, 1956. FBI FOIA, Sizoo to Belmont, March 28, 1956.

31. NA DOJA, Tompkins to Young, March 16, 1956.

32. NA DOJA, Waterman to Alderman, November 30, 1956; Alderman to Tompkins, December 17, 1956.

33. NA DOJA, Waterman to Alderman, January 14, 1957.

34. NA CGS, Kennelly to Tracy, December 18, 1956; Tracy to Ladd, December 20, 1956; Edwards to Contor, January 24, 1957. "Recommendations of the CGS: The Attorney General's List," all in CGS, "Subversive Organizations"; DDE, Records of Louis Rothschild, Contor to Edwards, January 18, 1957; Brownell interview: www.gwu.edu/~nsarchiv/coldwar/interviews/episode-6/brownell1.html.

35. NA DOJA, Tompkins to White, May 9, 1957; Devine to Tompkins, Waterman to Devine, June 25, 1957; Devine to Tompkins, September 24, 1957.

36. FBI FOIA, Baumgardner to Belmont, September 10, 1957.

37. On Red Monday, see Arthur Sabin, *In Calmer Times: The Supreme Court and Red Monday* (Philadelphia: University of Pennsylvania Press, 1999); Walter Murphy, *Congress and the Court* (Chicago: University of Chicago Press, 1962), 97–183.

38. Unless otherwise indicated, the following material is drawn from the ALW collection at the TL, which includes a complete file of all court proceedings.

39. Unless otherwise indicated, the next few paragraphs are drawn from briefs and other materials in the U.S. Supreme Court library.

40. "Memorandum for the Respondent Suggesting that the Case Is Moot," *ALW v. Brownell*, U.S. Supreme Court, October Term, 1957, No. 295; October, 1957; *ALW v. Brownell*, 355 U.S. 23 (1957).

41. FBI FOIA, Belmont to Hoover, October 6, 1957; FBI DOJ, Healy to files, October 4, 1957.

42. DOJA, Yeagley to Healy, November 29, 1958; Williams to Yeagley, August 8, 1958; Yeagley to Williams, August 19, 1958; AGLOSO lists marked Form No. DJ-90, January 22, 1959. DOJC, Waterman to Irons, April 15, 1955; Waterman to Alderman, October 26, 1955; Alderman to Foley, October 26, 1955; Tompkins to Burger, March 2, 1956. DOJA, memo by White (date unclear but apparently late 1957).

43. See, generally, Ann Fagan Ginger and Eugene Tobin, eds., *The National Lawyers Guild* (Philadelphia: Temple University Press, 1988); and Percival Bailey, "Progressive Lawyers: A History of the National Lawyers Guild, 1936–1958" (Ph.D. diss., Rutgers University, 1979).

44. Bailey, "Progressive Lawyers," 209, 223.

45. Ibid., 337–38, 371–72.

46. Ibid., 380–93.

47. Ibid., 374–403.

48. Ibid., 436–37; Thomas Reeves, *The Life and Times of Joe McCarthy* (New York: Stein & Day, 1982), 628–32.

49. Ibid., 445–46.

50. Ibid., 461; FBI FOIA, Hoover to Tolan and others, July 16, 1958; Ginger and Tobin, *National Lawyers Guild*, 158–59.

51. Bailey, "Progressive Lawyers," 358, 397, 444, 452, 547; *American Bar Association Journal*, July 1995; *WP*, May 24, 25, 1987. Jeff Woods, *Black Struggle, Red Scare: Segregation and Anti-Communism in the South, 1948–1968* (Baton Rouge: Louisiana State University Press, 2004), twice mistakenly says the NLG was placed on AGLOSO (136, 205).

52. *National Law Journal*, October 23, 1989; *Newsday, New York Law Journal*, October 13, 1989; *NYT*, October 1, 1989, June 25, 1982.

53. NA DOJA, Tompkins to Rogers, February 18, 1958.

54. NA DOJA, Waterman to Maroney, February 26, 1959; Waterman to files, December 30, 1959.

55. *NYT*, June 21, 30, 1957, March 9, 1961.

56. *NYT*, April 1, May 22, November 18, 1963, April 14, 1966, January 27, February 5, 1967.

57. *WP*, April 3, 1955, June 15, 1957, May 6, 1961, September 1, 1967; *NYT*, April 3, 1955, July 30, 1957; Susan Brinson, *The Red Scare, Politics, and the Federal Communications Commission, 1941 to 1960* (Westport, CT: Praeger, 2004), 159–94.

58. *NYT*, September 26, 27, November 26, December 1, 1957, April 8, December 13, 1958; *WP*, April 8, 1958, February 25, 1960.

59. *WP*, May 2, 1958, March 11, 1966, *Detroit News*, October 12, 1961; *NYT*, July 20, 1966.

60. *LAT, WP, NYT*, February 8, 1961; *WP, NYT*, February 9, 1961; *LAT*, February 11, 1961; *WP*, February 12, 1961.

61. *NYT*, September 16, November 6, December 6, 1955, January 23, March 3, September 5, December 4, 1956, July 1, 1960, April 19, August 11, November 22, 1961; *WP*, March 3, July 22, 1956; *LAT*, May 4, 10, 22, 1962; *Times of London*, May 19, 1962; Woods, *Black Struggle, Red Scare*, 50, 52, 61, 66; George Lewis, *The White South and the Red Menace: Segregationists, Anticommunism and Massive Resistance, 1945–1965* (Gainesville: University Press of Florida, 2004), 55–56, 64; Sabin, *In Calmer Times*, 207. See generally Manfred Berg, "Black Civil Rights and Liberal Anticommunism: The NAACP in the Early Cold War," *Journal of American History* 94 (2007); and Eric Arneson, "No 'Graver Danger': Black Anticommunism, the Communist Party and the Race Question," *Labor Studies in Working Class History of the Americas* 3 (2006), 13–52.

62. NA DOJA, Tompkins to Hoover (two separate memos), December 8, 1955, February 12, 1956; Brownell to Hoover, April 24, 1956; Alderman to Foley, February 8, 1957; Siegel to Brownell, February 26, 1957; Olney to Hoover, March 21, 1957.

63. "Supplementary Detailed Staff Reports on Intelligence Activities and the Rights of Americans," Book 3, final report of Senate Select Committee to Study Governmental Operations with Respect to Intelligence Activities, 94th Cong., 2d Sess., 1976, 452–54, 477–79; *WP*, July 16, 1963; *NYT*, July 17, 1963. For examples of numerous DOJ memos considering, but ultimately rejecting NOI designation, see NA DOJA, O'Shea to Alderman (three separate memos), September 23, 1955, May 21, 1956, July 25, 1956; Knight to Waterman, August 28, 1956.

64. *LAT*, April 7, 1961; FBI FOIA, Yeagley to Kennedy, February 3, 1961. On the ANP, see William Schaltz, *Hate: George Lincoln Rockwell and the American Nazi Party* (Washington, DC: Brassey's, 1999).

65. FBI FOIA, Katzenbach to Yeagley, February 15, 1961.

66. Ibid., February 20, 1961.

67. DOJ FOIA, Katzenbach to White, June 26, 1961.

68. FBI FOIA, Yeagley to Hoover, August 4, 1961; Baumgardner to Sullivan, August 7, 1961; *WP, NYT*, August 10, 1961.

69. LBJ, "1961 Review of Loyalty and Security Programs and Report to the President," December 18, 1961, Central Files, PE6.

70. *WP*, February 8, 1962; LBJ, Moyers to Johnson, February 24, 1965, Johnson to Macy, February 24, 1965, Macy and others to Johnson, November 1, 1965, Central Files, PE6; *LAT*, May 18, 1965. For the Port Huron statement, see http://www.voiceoftheturtle.org/library/porthuron.php.

71. *LAT*, July 26, 1962; *NYT*, July 17, 1963; *WP*, July 16, 1963, August 13, 1964; *CSM*, July 20, 1965; http://mcadams.mu.edu/russ/jfkinfo3/exhibits/stuck3.htm; http:www.ratical.org/ratville/JFK/LHO.html (accessed November, 2007).

72. *NYT*, November 16, 1998. There is a massive literature on the Abraham Lincoln Brigade; by far the most useful source on post–World War II persecution of the group is Peter Carroll, *The Odyssey of the Abraham Lincoln Brigade* (Stanford, CA: Stanford University Press, 1994).

73. *WP*, February 24, 1967. Unless otherwise cited, information about the VALB and IWW suits is based on briefs and other documents in the U.S. Supreme Court library.

74. On the IWW generally, Melvin Dubofsky, *We Shall Be All: A History of the Industrial Workers of the World* (Chicago: Quadrangle, 1969), remains the standard. For post–World War II developments, see *WSJ*, May 20, 1970.

75. FBI FOIA, Hoover to New York FBI Office, March 11, 1971; *FR*, April 16, 1970; FMP, Kleindienst Notice, February 15,1973; *WP*, October 25, 1972.

76. *NYT*, February 12, 1975, September 29, 1977, April 7, 1986; June 14, 1987, October 16, 1998; *WP*, October 5, 1983. In general, see Peter Glazer, *Radical Nostalgia: Spanish Civil War Commemoration in America* (Rochester, NY: University of Rochester Press, 2005).

Chapter 5. The Nixon Administration's Abortive Attempt to Revive AGLOSO, 1969–1974

1. *WP*, January 5, 1967.

2. NA SACB, Mahan to Califano, August 29, 1968; Mahan to Ellsworth, February 11, 1969.

3. RMN: EKP, Ehrlichman to Krogh, March 25, 1969; Krogh to files, March 27, 1969.

4. NA SACB, Mahan to Krogh, April 30, 1969.

5. Ibid., Mahan to Flanigan, June 23, 1969.

6. RMN: JDP, Krogh to Mitchell, November 21, 1969; Alexander to Krogh, February 16, 1970; EKP, Mahan to Nixon, December 22, 1969.

7. DOJ FOIA, Rehnquist to Mitchell, February 18, 1970; Bruce Oudes, ed., *From the President: Richard Nixon's Secret Files* (New York: Harper & Row, 1989), 98.

8. RMN: EKP, Huston to Krogh, February 20, March 20, 1970.

9. NA SACB, Mahan to Krogh, February 20, 1970.

10. Ibid., Mahan to Flanigan, February 27, 1970; Oudes, *From the President*, 104.

11. "Departments of State, Justice and Commerce, the Judiciary and Related Agencies Appropriations for 1971. Part 4: Related Agencies," Hearings by the HAC, 91st Cong., 2d Sess., April 13, 1970, 738–46; *NYT*, April 21, 1970; RMN: EKP, Higby to Krogh, April 10, 1970; Yeagley to Krogh, April 16, 1970; JDP, Mahan to Krogh, April 16, 1970.

12. RMN: EKP, Krogh to Ehrlichman and Haldeman, April 16, 1970; Huston to Krogh, May 6, 1970.

13. RMN: EKP, Krogh to Brown, May 25, 1970; JDP, Schwartz to Krogh, March 28, 1970.

14. *CR*, June 2, 1970, H4985–88; RMN: EKP, Krogh to Ehrlichman, June 12, 1970; JDP, Mahan to Harlow, June 19, 1970.

15. "State, Justice, Commerce, the Judiciary, and Related Agencies Appropriations," SAC, 91st Cong., 2d Sess., June 24, 1970, 871–912.

16. RMN: JDP, Huston to Haldeman, July 29, 1970; Petersmeyer to Huston, August 13, 1970.

17. RMN: JDP, Huston to Haldeman, September 15, 1970.

18. "Hearings Regarding the Administration of the Subversive Activities Control Act," HISC, 91st Cong., 2d Sess., September 30, 1970, 5140–5264 (includes letter from Mardian to Committee, November 30, 1970).

19. RMN: JDP, Dean to Pauken, September 29, 1970, Huston to Dean, October 1, 1970, Pauken to Dean, Dean to Hoover, Dean to Mitchell, Dean to Staff Secretary, October 2, 1970 (four separate memos).

20. RMN: EKP, Mahan to Nixon, October 27,1970; Dean to Sloan, November 12, 1970; Sloan

to Mahan, November 12, 1970. DOJ FOIA, Goldklang to Rehnquist, November 25, 1970; November 27, 1970.

21. DOJ FOIA, Mardian to Mitchell, December 4, 1970.

22. RMN: JDP, Huston to Dean, January 29, 1971; Dean to Kehrli, February 8, 1971.

23. Ibid., Mardian to Mitchell, March 1, 1971.

24. Ibid.

25. RMN: JDP, Dean to Parker, March 5, 1970.

26. "Administration of the Subversive Activities Control Act of 1950," Hearing of the HISC, 92d Cong., 1st Sess., April, 1971, 524–33, 562—63, 600–1, 653–98, 774–77, 784–85, 845–47, 886–89, 1060–69, 1096–97; June–August, 1971, 2474–87, 2502–11, 2654–63, 2730–31, 2756–65, 2798–2810, 2882–87, 2906–15, 2986–89.

27. "Department of State, Justice, and Commerce, the Judiciary and Related Agencies Appropriations," HAC, 92d Cong., 1st Sess., May 5, 1971, 758–68; "State, Justice, Commerce, the Judiciary and Related Agencies Appropriations," SAC, 92d Cong., 1st Sess., July 6, 1971, 901–10, 975–80. For examples of news coverage, see *NYT, WP, LAT*, July 7, 1971.

28. RMN: WHCF, National Security, ND6-2, Mardian to Dean, May 6, 1971; Dean to Schultz and Ehrlichman, May 11, 1971.

29. Ibid., Dean to Nixon, June 21, 1971; DOJ FOIA, Kauper to Dean, May 28, 1971.

30. RMN: WHCF, National Security, ND6-2, Dean to Ziegler, July 6, 1971; JDP, DOJ press release, July 7, 1971; Executive Order 11605, released by White House July 8, 1971 (with order dated July 2), published in *FR*, 1971, 12831, dated July 2, with notation stating it was received in Archives on July 7. For examples of news coverage, see *NYT, WS*, July 8, 1981; *Philadelphia Inquirer*, July 9, 1971.

31. Mardian to McClellan, July 8, 1971, published in "State, Justice, Commerce, the Judiciary and Related Agencies Appropriations," 1971, 981–1000.

32. *WP*, July 15, 1971, *WS*, July 18, 1971; *CR*, July 19, 1971, 25889; FMP, Mahan to Rooney, May 24, 1971.

33. *CR*, July 19, 1971, 25874–25902; July 27, 1971, 27305–12; August 2, 1971, 18854–55; August 3, 1971, 29031–53.

34. Ibid., July 16, 1971, 25573–75; July 19, 1971, 25895; July 27, 1971, 27459; August 3, 1971, 29032–35.

35. Ibid., July 19, 1971, 25896, 25902; August 3, 1971, 29044–45.

36. Ibid., July 19, 1971, 25893–94, 25901–2; July 27, 1971, 27308–9; August 3, 1971, 29049.

37. RMN: JDP, Krogh to Dean, Dean to Krogh, both July 20, 1971.

38. *CR*, July 19, 1971, 25901; July 27, 1971, 27306–7, 27405–6; July 31, 1971, 28605. DOJ FOIA, Kauper to Dean, July 26, 1971.

39. "Hearings Regarding the Administration of the Subversive Activities Control Act," HISC, 92d Cong., 1st Sess., July 29, August 3, 1971, 3000, 3006, 3026, 3031–37, 3043–46, 3092, 3106–7.

40. RMN: JDP, Dean to Mardian, August 11, 1971; Mahan to Dean, August 12, 1971.

41. "President Nixon's Executive Order 11605," SJC Subcommittee on Separation of Powers, 92d Cong., 1st Sess., October 5, 7, 1971, 1–3, 8, 10, 11–13.

42. Ibid., 15–16, 21, 23, 25, 34, 36.

43. Ibid., 38–39, 43–47, 53.

44. Ibid., 55–63.

45. *FR*, September 10, 1971, 18280–81.

46. NA SACB records, FMP, various issues of *FR*, all for the period October 1971–October 1972; *Twenty-Second Annual Report of the SACB* (Washington, DC: GPO, 1973), 18.

47. Complete documentation concerning the ASU lawsuit can be found in NA, SACB, Case Files, Box 253.

48. The full text of Griesa's ruling and other documents concerning the SWP suit were published in Margaret Jayko, ed., *FBI on Trial* (New York: Pathfinder, 1988). For samples of news coverage, see *WP*, October 6, 1975, May 29, August 1, 8, September 5, 15, 1976, September 21, 1977, July 9, 1978, May 1, 1981, August 26, 1986; *NYT*, April 4, September 5, 15, 1976, December 31, 1978, March 20, 1979, April 23, July 3, 1980, April 3, 26, 1981, August 26, 1986; *LAT*, March 17, 1988.

49. "Hearings Regarding the Administration of the Subversive Activities Control Act," HISC, 92d Cong., 2d Sess., January 27, 1972, 5740–45, 5750, 5757–58, 5761, 5765–67, 5803, 5929–38.

50. Ibid., 5770, 5775, 5782, 5806.

51. "Departments of State, Justice and Commerce, the Judiciary and Related Agencies Appropriations for 1973," 92d Cong., 2d Sess., January 29, March 1, April 10, 1972, 636–37.

52. Ibid., 28–31, 40–45.

53. RMN: JDP, Mahan to Kinsey, February 22, 1972; FMP, McNamara to SACB, January 17, 1972.

54. "State, Justice, Commerce, the Judiciary, and Related Agencies Appropriations," SAC, 92d Cong., 2d Sess., April 26, 1972, 2045–47; *WP*, April 26, 1972.

55. "Additional Functions for SACB," Report of HISC, 92d Cong., 2d Sess., May 9, 1972, 1–15, 42–52; see also "The Federal Civilian Employee Loyalty Program," Report of HISC, 92d Cong., 2d Sess., 1972.

56. *CR*, May 18, 1972, 18044–48.

57. *CR*, May 30, 1972, 19077, 19080, 19086, 19089, 19097, 19101–2.

58. Ibid., 19083–84, 19091–92.

59. *CR*, June 15, 1972, 21053–54, 21057–64.

60. Ibid., 21055, 21065, 21069.

61. *CR*, June 8, 1972, 20376; FMP, American Legion to Senators, June 13, 1972.

62. "To Amend the Subversive Activities Control Act," Hearing by SJC, 92d Cong., 2d Sess., June 29, 1972, 3–9, 43; *WP*, October 11, 1972; *LAT,* October 14, 1972; *CR*, October 13, 1972, 35847–50, 35656–58.

63. RMN: JDP, Dean to Ehrlichman, December 7, 1972; NA SACB, Carlucci to Mahan, January 26, 1973.

64. *Budget of the U.S. Government, Fiscal Year 1974* (Washington, DC: GPO, 1973), 951; NA SACB, Garment to Mahan, February 1, 1973. FMP, Mahan to Mansfield, February 2, 1973, Ash to Mahan, June 27, 1973; *NYT*, March 22, 1973.

65. Aurora, IL, *Beacon-News*, March 17, 1973 (Copley News Service article); *CR*, March 28, 1973, 10038–44.

66. DOJ FOIA, Peterson to Richardson, June 5, 1973.

67. DOJ FOIA, Dixon to Richardson, August 6, 1973.

68. FBI FOIA, Kelley to Dixon, September 38, 1973; DOJ FOIA, Dixon to Lindebaum, October 12, 1973.

69. DOJ FOIA, Dixon to Saxbe (undated but mid-January, 1974); *LAT*, August 29, 1973, April 4, 1974; *WP* August 30, 1973, April 4, 6, 1974; *NYT*, April 4, 6, 1974.

70. RMN: WHCF, ND 13–14, Saxbe to Ash, April 18, 1974; Ebner to Linder, May 3, 1974.

71. *NYT, LAT, CT*, June 2, 1974; *FR*, June 6, 1974, 20053; *NYT, LAT, WP*, June 5, 1974.

72. RMN: WHCF, ND 6–2, Levey to Nixon, June 17, 1974.

73. *NYT*, November 13, 1974, October 27, 1980; Guenter Lewy, *The Federal-Loyalty Security Program: The Need for Reform* (Washington, DC: American Enterprise Institute, 1983); David Marin, *Screening Federal Employees: A Neglected Priority* (Washington, DC: Heritage Foundation, 1983; the latter two books argue that an increased scrutiny is required for federal loyalty screening in the wake of post-1973 developments).

Bibliographical Essay

The heart of this book is based on research in archival materials or materials obtained through the Freedom of Information Act (FOIA) that have rarely, if ever, been accessed by other researchers. Between 2002 and 2006 I obtained thousands of pages of FOIA materials from the Federal Bureau of Investigation (FBI) and the Department of Justice relevant to the Attorney General's List of Subversive Organizations (AGLOSO). In addition to documents relevant to AGLOSO generally, I obtained from the FBI papers related to some particular AGLOSO-designated organizations, including the Washington Bookshop Association, the Eleanor Progressive League, and others. Aside from FOIA materials, the most critical documents were accessed at the National Archives in College Park, Maryland, many of which were declassified for the first time in response to my requests. Especially important were AGLOSO-related archives from the Department of Justice (Record Group 60, especially files 146-200-2-012, 146-200-2, 146-06 and 146-200-2-04), the Subversive Activities Control Board (Record Group 220), the Commission on Government Security (Record Group 220), and the Civil Service Commission and the Loyalty Review Board (Record Group 146). During my research, I also examined a large volume of papers from the presidency of Richard Nixon, especially those of John Dean and Egil "Bud" Krogh; at the time these papers were maintained by what was formally known as the Richard M. Nixon Presidential Materials Project; by the time this book appears, they were scheduled for transfer to the Nixon Presidential Library in Yorba Linda, California. Critical materials were also examined at the Harry S. Truman Presidential Library in Independence, Missouri, notably the Eleanor Bontecou, A. Devitt Vanech, and Stephen Spingarn Papers, and at the Dwight D. Eisenhower Presidential Library in Abilene, Kansas, particularly the papers of Eisenhower's secretary Ann Whitman. I also used materials in the U.S. Supreme Court library in Washington, D.C., while researching several cases considered by the court (notably, but not only, *Joint Anti-Refugee Committee v. McGrath*) and the papers of a variety of Supreme Court justices in the Library of Congress, Washington, D.C. (and, in a few cases, held elsewhere). Although numerous congressional hearings and reports touch on AGLOSO, the most important of them are "Security and Constitutional Rights," Hearings before SJC Subcommittee on Constitutional Rights, 84th Cong., 1st Sess., November, 17, 1955 (entire session on AGLOSO); "President Nixon's Executive Order 11605," SJC Subcommittee on Separation of Powers, 92nd Cong., 1st Sess., October 5, 7, 1971; and "The Federal Civilian Employee Loyalty Program," Report by HISC Subcommittee on Loyalty-Security, 92nd Cong., 2nd Sess., 1972.

I also utilized the American Civil Liberties Union collection at the Princeton University Library in Princeton, New Jersey; the Francis McNamara papers at the George Mason University Library in Fairfax, Virginia (especially relevant to the Subversive Activities Control Board); and, at the Tamiment Library at New York University in New York City, papers from the National Council on American-Soviet Friendship, the National Lawyers Guild, the Abraham Lincoln Brigade, the Independent Socialist League (Max Shachtman Papers), and the Nature League of America. At the Special Collections Department of the University of Michigan at Ann Arbor, I used materials from their collections on the American Committee for the Protection of the Foreign Born and the California Labor School. I also obtained (via mail) key documents from the David Lasser papers at the library of the University of California, San Diego (especially, but not only, pertinent to the Workers Alliance) and from the Albert Glotzer papers at the Hoover Institution library in Stanford, California (which arrived too late to fully incorporate but are especially relevant to the Independent Socialist League).

As mentioned in the preface to this book, general studies of AGLOSO are extremely scarce. The only substantial general survey of the subject was published fifty-five years ago as a chapter in Eleanor Bontecou's *The Federal Loyalty-Security Program* (Ithaca, NY: Cornell University Press, 1953), 157–204. Specialized aspects of AGLOSO are the subjects of several articles by the present author: Robert Justin Goldstein, "Prelude to McCarthyism: The Making of a Blacklist," *Prologue* 28 (2006), 22–33; "'Raising Cain': Senator Harry Cain and His Attack on the Attorney General's List of Subversive Organizations," *Pacific Northwest Quarterly* 98 (2007), 64–77; "The Grapes of *McGrath*: The Supreme Court Case of *Joint Anti-Fascist Refugee Committee v. McGrath*," *Journal of Supreme Court History* 33 (2008), 68–88; and "Kicking the Commies out of Public Housing: The Gwinn Amendment," tentatively scheduled for 2009 publication in *American Communist History*. Otherwise, aside from some law review articles on the Gwinn Amendment banning AGLOSO members from public housing cited in chapter 4 note 7, the only substantial publications on AGLOSO are a handful of short law review articles published fifty to sixty years ago that are generally highly legal/technical in orientation: "Designation of Organization as Subversive by Attorney General," *Columbia Law Review* 48 (1948), 1050–67; Agnes Neill, "The Attorney General's List of Subversive Organizations: Due Process Aspects," *Georgetown Law Journal* 42 (1954), 401–19; Donald King, "The Legal Status of the Attorney General's 'List,'" *California Law Review* 44 (1956), 748–61; "The Bill of Attainder Clauses and Legislative and Administrative 'Suppression of Subversives,'" *Columbia Law Review* 67 (1967), 1490–1511; and Albert Phelan, "The Power of the Attorney General to Declare an Organization Subversive," *Temple Law Quarterly*, 29 (1955), 95–102. There are two collections of federal loyalty program case studies, many of which include charges related to AGLOSO affiliations: on civilian cases, Adam Yarmolinsky, comp., *Case Studies in Personnel Security* (Washington, DC: Bureau of National Affairs, 1955); on military cases, Rowland Watts, ed., *Undesirable Discharge from the Armed Forces of the United States of America* (New York: Workers Defense League, 1956).

All newspaper references to AGLOSO from the *New York Times*, the *Washington Post*, the *Los Angeles Times*, the *Christian Science Monitor*, the *Chicago Tribune*, and the *Wall Street Journal* were accessed via the ProQuest Historical Newspapers electronic database. The vast majority of the approximately 280 AGLOSO-designated organizations were extremely obscure and have left barely a trace of their existence anywhere, except perhaps in the FBI files. However, substantial secondary studies exist for about 30 of the most prominent of these groups. Many of them are briefly discussed in the *Encyclopedia of the American Left* (Urbana: University of Illinois Press, 1990), as well as in several other sources, such as Irving Howe and Louis Coser, *The American Communist Party* (New York: Praeger, 1962); Harvey Klehr, *The Heyday of American Communism: The Depression Decade* (New York: Basic Books, 1984); and David Caute, *The Great Fear: The Anti-Communist Purge under Truman and Eisenhower* (New York: Simon & Schuster, 1978).

Howe and Coser's book (see just above) and Harvey Klehr and John Earl Haynes, *The American Communist Movement: Storming Heaven Itself* (New York: Twayne, 1992), are the best surveys of the Communist Party, which is additionally the subject of a huge number of specialized studies. The same is true of the Industrial Workers of the World, but the best survey remains Melvyn Dubofsky, *We Shall Be All: A History of the IWW* (Chicago: Quadrangle, 1969). The International Workers Order has been the subject of two book-length studies: Arthur Sabin, *Red Scare in Court: New York Versus the International Workers Order* (Philadelphia: University of Pennsylvania Press, 1993), and Thomas Walker, *Pluralistic Fraternity: The History of the International Worker's Order* (New York: Garland, 1991); as has the Socialist Workers Party: Constance Myers, *The Prophet's Army: Trotskyists in America, 1928–1941* (Westport, CT: Greenwood, 1977), and A. Belden Fields, *Trotskyism and Maoism: Theory and Practice in the United States* (Brooklyn, NY: Autonomedia, 1988).

Dissertations, books, and articles have also focused on a variety of other designated groups, most of which were considerably less prominent than those just referenced. The following is intended to give a sampling of the most important such studies (additional consulted materials are cited in the footnotes in connection with the discussion of individual groups): Gerald Horne, *Communist Front? The Civil Rights Congress, 1946–1956* (Rutherford, NJ: Associated University Presses, 1988); on the American Youth Congress, Robert Cohen, *When the Old Left Was Young: Student Radicals and America's First Mass Student Movement, 1929–1941* (New York: Oxford University Press, 1993); Hollis Lynch, *Black American Radicals and the Liberation of Africa: The Council on African Affairs, 1937–1955* (Ithaca, NY: Cornell University Africana Studies and Research Center, 1978); Mindy Thompson, *The National Negro Labor Council* (New York: American Institute for Marxist Studies, 1978); William Cobb, *Radical Education in the Rural South: Commonwealth College, 1922–1940* (Detroit: Wayne State University Press, 2000); Marvin Gettleman, "'No Varsity Teams': New York's Jefferson School of Social Science, 1943–1956; *Science & Society* 66 (2002), 336–359; Jess Rigelhaupt, "'Education for Action': The California Labor School, Radical Unionism, Civil Rights and Progressive Coalition Building in the San Francisco Bay Area, 1934–1970" (Ph.D. diss., University of Michigan, 2005). On Spanish loyalist relief organizations, Eric Smith, "Anti-Fascism, the United Front, and Spanish Republican Aid in the United States, 1936–40" (Ph.D. diss., University of Illinois at Chicago, 2007); Peter Carroll and James Fernandez, eds., *Facing Fascism: New York and the Spanish Civil War* (New York: Museum of the City of New York, 2007); and Peter Carroll, *The Odyssey of the Abraham Lincoln Brigade* (Stanford, CA: Stanford University Press, 1994).

Other organizations are covered in John Sherman, *A Communist Front at Mid-Century: The American Committee for Protection of the Foreign Born, 1933–1959* (Westport, CT: Praeger, 2001); Robert Szymczak, "From Popular Front to Communist Front: The American Slav Congress in War and Cold War, 1941–1951" (Ph.D. diss., University of Lancaster, 2006); Johnetta Richards, "The Southern Negro Youth Congress: A History" (Ph.D. diss., University of Cincinnati, 1987). On the Photo League, Fiona Dejardin, "The Photo League: Aesthetics, Politics and the Cold War" (Ph.D. diss., University of Delaware, 1993), and Beverly Bethune, "The New York City Photo League" (Ph.D. diss., University of Minnesota, 1979). On the Congress of American Women, Kate Weigand, *Red Feminism: American Communism and the Making of Women's Liberation* (Baltimore: Johns Hopkins University Press, 2001), 46–64, and Amy Swerdlow, "The Congress of American Women," in Linda Kerber, ed., *U.S. History as Women's History* (Chapel Hill: University of North Carolina Press, 1995). On the Workers Alliance, Chad Goldberg, "Haunted by the Specter of Communism: Collective Identity and Resource Mobilization in the Demise of the Workers Alliance of America," *Theory and Society* 32 (2003), 725–773. On the International Labor Defense, see

Jennifer Uhlmann, "The Communist Civil Rights Movement: Legal Activism in the United States, 1919–1946" (Ph.D. diss., University of California at Los Angeles, 2007). On the National Lawyers Guild, Ann Fagan Ginger and Eugene Tobin, eds., *The National Lawyers Guild* (Philadelphia: Temple University Press, 1988); Percival Roberts, "Progressive Lawyers: A History of the National Lawyers Guild, 1936–1958" (Ph.D. diss., Rutgers University, 1979). On the Independent Socialist League and affiliated groups, Peter Drucker, *Max Shachtman and His Left* (Atlantic Highlands, NJ: Humanities Press, 1994).

For additional groups see, Albert Acena, "The Washington Commonwealth Federation" (Ph.D. diss., University of Washington, 1975); and Arthur Casciato, "Citizen Writers: A History of the League of American Writers" (Ph.D. diss., University of Virginia, 1986); Samuel Walker, "Communists and Isolationism: The American Peace Mobilization, 1940–1941," *Maryland Historian* 4 (1973), 1–12; and Doug Rossinow, "'The Model of a Model Fellow Traveller': Harry F. Ward, the American League for Peace and Democracy, and the 'Russian Question' in American Politics, 1933–1936," *Peace and Change* 29 (2004), 177–220. Quite extraordinarily, the National Negro Congress has been the subject of four Ph.D. dissertations: John Streater, "The National Negro Congress, 1936–1947" (University of Cincinnati, 1981); Erik Gellman, "'Death Blow to Jim Crow': The National Negro Congress, 1936–1947" (Northwestern University, 2006); Hilmar Jensen, "The Rise of an African-American Left: John P. Davis and the National Negro Congress" (Cornell University, 1997); and Cicero Hughes, "Toward a Black United Front: The National Negro Congress Movement" (Ohio University, 1982).

On the Silver Shirts, Scott Beekman, *William Dudley Pelley* (Syracuse, NY: Syracuse University Press, 2005). On the German-American Bund, Leland Bell, *In Hitler's Shadow* (Port Washington, NY: Kennikat, 1973), Sander Diamond, *The Nazi Movement in the United States* (Ithaca, NY: Cornell University Press, 1974). On pro-Italian fascist groups, Gaetano Salvemini, *Italian Fascist Activities in the United States* (New York: Center for Migration Studies, 1977). On pro-fascist German-, Italian-, and Japanese-American organizations, Morris Schonbach, "Native Fascism during the 1930s and 1940s: A Study of Its Roots, Its Growth and Its Decline" (Ph.D. diss., University of California at Los Angeles, 1958).

Index

Hatch Act, 2, 17, 18, 19, 25, 46, 48, 49, 123, 124, 129, 130, 131, 132, 164, 191, 214, 269

Hawaii, 79, 80, 90

Healey, Harold, 222, 240, 247

Hennings, Thomas, 63, 208, 232

Hoover, J. Edgar

and implementation of post–World War II AGLOSO, 64, 66, 71, 74–76, 94–96, 100, 118, 126, 133–37, 140–41, 168–69, 174, 182–85, 189, 191, 195, 219, 222, 228–29, 236, 239–40, 244–47, 255, 259, 265, 282, 304, 317, 318 (*see also* Federal Bureau of Investigation)

and inception of Post–World War II Red Scare and AGLOSO, 44, 47–49, 52–54, 56–58

1919–1920 Red Scare, 4, 5, 6

during 1930s, 14–15, 18

during World War II, 20, 24, 27, 28

Hotels, 84, 88

House Civil Service Committee (HCSC), 45, 47, 48

House Committee on Internal Security (HISC), 278, 280, 281, 286, 292, 295, 296, 305, 307–11, 314, 316

House Committee on Un-American Activities (HUAC), 13, 17, 23, 45, 48, 64, 69, 70, 72, 77, 80, 82, 85, 89, 90, 109, 112, 115, 127, 129, 134, 135, 139, 140, 148, 149, 192, 208, 244, 247, 248, 250, 251, 261, 278, 282

House of Representatives, 17, 19, 36–38, 40, 43, 45, 47, 54–55, 147, 206

committees, 4, 6, 27, 41, 47, 64, 198–99, 261, 276, 287, 297, 307–08 (*see also specific House committees*)

and Nixon administration's attempt to revive AGLOSO, 291, 292, 295–96, 297, 309–11, 313, 314, 316

Huston, Tom, 274, 277, 280–81, 282, 284

Ichord, Richard, 278, 281, 286, 295, 296, 308, 309, 310, 316

Ickes, Harold, 16, 37, 68, 105, 111, 149, 243

Idaho Pension Union, 102, 127

Illinois, 62, 80, 83, 84, 86, 211, 251

Immigration and Naturalization Service (INS), 28, 38–39, 72, 73–74, 78, 90, 164, 321

denaturalizations, 1, 2, 9, 20, 22, 28, 31, 33, 39, 72, 73, 74, 109, 197

deportations, 1–9, 16–17, 19, 23, 31, 33, 39, 46, 68, 70, 72–74, 87, 109, 110, 126, 144, 192, 197, 199

detentions, 25

exclusions, 1, 2, 70, 72, 74

immigration laws (1903) 1; (1906) 9; (1917) 2; (1918) 2, 6, 8, 16; (1920), 2, 8; (1940) 2, 23; (1950) 2; (1952) 2

naturalizations, 1, 9, 28, 39, 72, 73, 74

Independent Socialist League (ISL), 72, 79, 96, 116, 185, 198, 200, 216–27, 231, 236, 241, 242, 247, 249, 257

Indiana, 80, 81, 83, 250

Industrial Workers of the World (IWW), 2, 3, 5, 8, 9, 66, 99, 102, 261, 262–65, 302

Interdepartmental Committee on Employee Investigations (ICEI), 37, 40, 41

Interior Department, 29, 77, 101

Internal Revenue Service (IRS), 69, 71, 104, 106, 108

Internal Security Act (ISA), 96, 103, 127, 145–47, 154–55, 163, 170, 180, 193, 199, 201, 203, 231, 233, 257–59, 263, 267, 271, 273, 274, 280, 290, 302, 309, 315

International Labor Defense (ILD), 11, 35, 37, 99, 101, 106–07, 108, 109, 129

International Workers Order (IWO), 11, 12, 21, 37, 67–69, 72–73, 76, 82, 87, 93, 99, 101, 111, 114, 142, 143

and legal actions related to AGLOSO, 148–61, 163, 176, 177, 200, 216–27, 231, 236, 241, 242, 247, 249, 257

Irons, David, 65, 186, 187, 189, 199–200, 210, 241

Italy, Italian-Americans, and pro-Italian groups, 25, 28, 30, 31, 32, 33, 34, 98, 131, 214, 263

Jackson, Robert, 154, 155, 156–58, 160, 243

Japan, Japanese-Americans and pro-Japanese organizations, 21, 25, 28, 30–32, 46, 73, 96, 97, 131, 192, 193

Japanese-American Citizens League, 192

Jefferson School of Social Sciences, 22, 67, 82, 88, 101, 102, 103, 224, 252

Jenner, William, 83, 209

Johnson, Lyndon, 217, 249, 251, 261, 270, 273

		DATE DUE	